THE PAPERS OF

James Madison

SPONSORED BY
THE UNIVERSITY OF VIRGINIA

THE PAPERS OF

James Madison

SECRETARY OF STATE SERIES

VOLUME 3

I MARCH–6 OCTOBER 1802

EDITED BY

DAVID B. MATTERN

J. C. A. STAGG   JEANNE KERR CROSS

SUSAN HOLBROOK PERDUE

UNIVERSITY PRESS OF VIRGINIA

CHARLOTTESVILLE AND LONDON

Publication of this volume of *The Papers of James Madison* has been made possible by grants from the National Historical Publications and Records Commission, the National Endowment for the Humanities, an independent federal agency, and the Florence Gould Foundation, with support from the University of Virginia.

THE UNIVERSITY PRESS OF VIRGINIA

First published 1995

Library of Congress Cataloging-in-Publication Data
(Revised for vol. 3)

Madison, James, 1751–1836.
The papers of James Madison : secretary of state series.

Vol. 2 edited by Mary A. Hackett and others.
Vol. 3 edited by David B. Mattern and others.
Includes bibliographical references and indexes.
Contents: v. 1. 4 March–31 July 1801–v. 2 1 August 1801–28 February 1802—v. 3. 1 March–6 October 1802.
1. United States—Foreign relations—1801–1809—Sources. 2. United States—Politics and government—1801–1809—Sources. 3. United States—History—1801–1809—Sources. 4. Madison, James, 1751–1836—Correspondence. I. Brugger, Robert J.
E302.M19 1986   973.4'6   85-29516
ISBN 0-8139-1093-5 (v. 1)
ISBN 0-8139-1403-5 (v. 2)
ISBN 0-8139-1541-4 (v. 3)

Printed in the United States of America

To

MERRILL D. PETERSON

Contents

CONTENTS

CONTENTS

CONTENTS

CONTENTS

CONTENTS

CONTENTS

CONTENTS

CONTENTS

CONTENTS

Preface

The documents in this volume cover James Madison's tenure as secretary of state from 1 March through 6 October 1802, and, as in past volumes in this series, the bulk of correspondence herein relates to the affairs of that office. The crush of business during these months strained the resources of the State Department, especially given Madison's continued ill health and the absence of Jacob Wagner, the chief clerk. Wagner was forced to offer his resignation when he moved to Philadelphia to recuperate from a nagging illness, and although Madison refused to accept it, the chief clerk's services were lost to the department until November 1802. Daniel Brent served in Wagner's stead. Madison himself noted apologetically several times in his correspondence that his sickness had prevented him from making timely responses, and the state of his health was mentioned on the floor of the House of Representatives as a reason why the Federalists should refrain from making unnecessary inquiries at the State Department. It was even the subject of a toast at a Richmond Fourth of July celebration that Madison be "speedily restored to health." Thus it was with a reduced staff and less than full vigor that Madison conducted the affairs of the State Department in this period (*Annals of Congress*, 7th Cong., 1st sess., 1136; N.Y. *Citizen*, 15 July 1802).

For the most part Madison's concerns during this time clustered around ongoing problems in the conduct of foreign policy, but there was at least one domestic event of note beyond routine patronage requests and the handling of territorial affairs. That was the agreement by which Georgia relinquished its western lands to the United States in exchange for a cash payment, the extinguishment of Indian land claims in Georgia, and the satisfaction of land claims in the newly ceded area. Although it appears that Madison did not take a leading part in the negotiation, the heavy task of sorting through the Yazoo land claims fell to his department, and he began this process late in the summer of 1802. The business was complicated by the fact that settlers in the area held a variety of titles awarded by Great Britain, France, and Spain over the years and by the number of speculators who had invested in Georgia lands through the auspices of such corporations as the New England Mississippi Land Company. As he began to address the problems involved in the settlement, Madison could have had little idea of the political consequences of the compromise, which would dog his steps until a final compensation act was passed by Congress in 1814.

Of greater immediate importance, however, were United States relations with the European powers, chief among them being France. Looming over the occasional irritations that marked the Franco-American relationship were two great issues: the ongoing French attempt to subdue the black revolt on the island of Saint-Domingue, and the retrocession of Louisiana from Spain to France. The two were closely linked in Madison's eyes, because the future occupation and exploitation of Louisiana by the French were contingent on the success of the military operation in Saint-Domingue.

As Tobias Lear, the United States commercial agent in Cap Français, reported to Madison in March and April 1802, French efforts to crush the rebellion had met with initial success, but it was not long before the Leclerc expedition ran into trouble. Resistance on the island did not collapse when the French occupied the port cities, and as the insurgent blacks retreated into the mountains and began guerrilla operations, Leclerc's attempts to provision his troops by foraging on the countryside became impossible. American merchants who had blithely traded with Toussaint L'Ouverture in great numbers before the invasion came under suspicion of providing the rebels with arms and ammunition, and Leclerc's need for supplies of all kinds led him to compel the sale of American goods to the French army at arbitrarily low prices. To add insult to injury, Leclerc insisted that the bulk of these cargoes be paid for in bills on France. These actions, as well as further trade restrictions on American shipping and the imprisonment of two ship captains, John Rodgers and William Davidson, led to howls of anger from American merchants and pressure on Madison to intervene on their behalf. The situation was further aggravated by Leclerc's refusal to acknowledge Lear as commercial agent, a move that left the United States with no formal representation on the island.

Meanwhile the Jefferson administration was of two minds on the subject of Saint-Domingue. It feared the success of the black revolt, ever mindful of its example to the nearly one million slaves within United States borders, but it feared in greater measure the reestablishment of the French on the island, a development that would create a base for the recolonization of Louisiana. The administration's ambivalence toward the situation in Saint-Domingue is demonstrated by Madison's responses to two of Louis-André Pichon's initiatives in the spring of 1802. The French chargé d'affaires was trying desperately to amass enough cash and credit in the United States to supply the French army in Saint-Domingue. For this purpose he pressured Madison to fund the French claims for spoliations approved under the Convention of 1800, a move that Madison agreed to because he hoped it might induce the French to make a similar decision on a far greater number of American claims. On the administration's recommendation, Congress speedily provided the funds for those claims. But Madison rejected Pichon's request for a loan as being politically impossible. He was seconded in his refusal by Robert R. Livingston in Paris, who, while bombarding Talleyrand with diplomatic notes on a variety of topics and getting nothing but evasions in reply, feared that loans to France or bills drawn on the French treasury would only hinder his attempts to get the French to pay their American debts and would thus effectively end the possibility of achieving justice for American merchant claims.

Madison shared Livingston's frustration in dealing with the French, and nothing proved more infuriating to the Americans than the silence surrounding the retrocession of Louisiana. Despite the fact that the cession was common knowledge in Madrid and Paris, neither Livingston nor Charles Pinckney at Madrid could elicit a formal acknowledgment of the transfer or its terms. Thus Madison waited anxiously to learn whether the cession included the Floridas or whether it protected American treaty rights to navigate the Mississippi River and deposit goods at New Orleans. For the moment, Madison could do little more than repeat his instructions to Livingston to raise with the French the strong objections the United States had to their occupying New Orleans. And in the face of silence in Madrid, Madison directed Pinckney to propose once again the purchase of the Floridas from Spain.

In Madison's view, a French colony in Louisiana might lead to closer ties with Great Britain as a counterfoil, if not—as Jefferson put it in typical hyperbolic style—marriage with the British fleet and nation. Neither hoped it would come to that, but diplomatic relations with Great Britain had warmed somewhat with news of the signing of the definitive treaty. The end of the war in Europe meant that American seamen impressed by the Royal Navy were liberated, momentarily eliminating one area of friction, and Madison's consular correspondence was full of queries about the support and transport of these penniless sailors. Settlement of article 6 of the Jay treaty was agreed to, and a lump sum of £600,000 was provided to compensate British merchants holding pre–Revolutionary War debts. The commission under article 7 of the same treaty, covering British spoliations of American ships in the early 1790s, took up its work again. The Maryland bank stock claim also proceeded on its weary way to settlement. And negotiations over two boundary issues—fixing the border between Maine and New Brunswick and providing American access to the Atlantic Ocean from Passamaquoddy Bay—were initiated at this time.

Of greatest potential importance to Madison was the effort to reduce or eliminate British tonnage duties, a long-standing issue that promised to assume larger significance in the light of the impending expiration of the Jay treaty in 1803. These and other matters were handled to Madison's satisfaction by United States minister Rufus King, a Federalist, despite the sniping of Republicans working or visiting in London. For his part, King was tiring of his duties and resigned in August 1802. He left London in the spring of 1803, returning home, as was rumored and proved true, to run against Jefferson in the 1804 presidential election.

In Spain, Republican appointee Charles Pinckney failed in his attempts to carry out Madison's instructions, though more through the intransigence of the Spanish court than his own lack of effort. Two issues stood high on Madison's agenda with Spain—a mass of claims against the Spanish government from depredations on American shipping and the future of the Floridas.

Spanish spoliations feature prominently in Madison's 1802 correspondence. There were two important sets of claims. One encompassed colonial depredations, especially claims of merchants who had been lured by Spanish agents and the possibility of immense profits to trade with Buenos Aires and other South American ports. The other arose from the activities of French privateers who had preyed on American shipping while operating out of Spanish ports during the Quasi-War. Pinckney had been instructed to negotiate the appointment of a board of commissioners that would judge the merits of all the American claims and award damages. What he could not get the Spanish to agree to, however, was the inclusion of the latter class of claims, and this was a point on which Madison refused to retreat. According to Pinckney, the Spanish refusal was based on questions of equity and domestic politics. Spain claimed that it had been forced to allow France the use of its ports and had gained no financial advantage from the privateering. Madison maintained that it was a question of sovereignty and international law that left the Spanish liable to compensate American losses. In the end, though a convention to establish a claims commission was signed in August 1802, this class of claims was excluded from the agreement.

In the matter of West Florida, Madison continued the campaign to acquire the territory that would last for more than a decade. The goal of the administration in gaining possession of West Florida, as Madison saw it, was to ensure access to the Gulf of Mexico for American settlers in the Southwest. This included not only New Orleans but also lesser ports on the gulf that provided a deposit for goods brought along the river highways from Tennessee and the Mississippi Territory. Equally important, West Florida in American hands would create a natural boundary along the Mississippi River with Spain that would end the threat of disunion posed by the prospect of a strong French presence in Louisiana. Madison felt so strongly about this possibility that he authorized Pinckney to offer the Spanish a guarantee of their territory west of the Mississippi River. But Pinckney got nowhere when he proposed the Florida purchase, and the administration's assumption that the Floridas were included in the retrocession of Louisiana to France eventually led it to drop the purchase proposal for a time.

Perhaps none of Madison's activities in the State Department demonstrated the vagaries of early nineteenth-century diplomacy so much as did United States relations with the Barbary States. Time and distance made the setting of policy and its fulfillment more an act of faith than a decision to be monitored, weighed, and adjusted. The war with Tripoli continued, with the small American squadron cooperating with Swedish warships in a desultory blockade of that port and in convoying American merchant ships throughout the Mediterranean. Most of the reports sent to Madison from American consuls were filled with complaints that the navy lacked energy and force, but a more likely explanation was that the tiny force was simply spread too thin to be fully effective. On the basis of previous dispatches indicating the willingness of the pasha of Tripoli to begin peace negotiations, Madison instructed James Leander Cathcart on 18 April 1802 to open talks, but the disposition of the Tripolitans toward peace was disrupted by the capture of the American merchant brig *Franklin* on 17 June 1802 and the imprisonment of its crew. This momentary advantage gained by Tripoli suspended all talk of peace until full negotiations were opened in May 1805.

In the context of the Mediterranean war, Madison made two decisions that had little impact on policy at the time but are interesting in the light of subsequent American diplomacy. The first was his response to the plan proposed by William Eaton and Cathcart to replace the current pasha with his brother in an elaborate American-backed coup d'état. Without wishing to know the details, Madison gave his blessing to the scheme. In the second Madison departed from past practice by agreeing to informal cooperation with Sweden—in fixing the blockade, convoying merchant ships, and even negotiating peace with Tripoli—as long as the resulting peace treaty did not formally link the two countries in any way.

Other developments, besides the capture of the *Franklin*, also threatened to upset the prospects for peace in the region. In the middle of August news reached Washington of the declaration of war on the United States by the emperor of Morocco. The American consul at Tangier, James Simpson, had angered the emperor by withholding passports for Moroccan grain ships in order to enforce the embargo against Tripoli. No sooner had the war been declared, however, than a truce was agreed to, although not in time to prevent the Jefferson administration from reacting to the possibility of a wider Mediterranean war by ordering reinforcements for the naval squadron already there. This provoked some grumbling from Gallatin about the high cost of naval expeditions, a concern he was to voice repeatedly throughout his years in the Treasury Department. But by September, as news of the end of the crisis reached the Virginians at their piedmont retreats, the war had returned to its previous footing with Tripoli.

Thus, by the time of Madison's departure from Montpelier in the early days of October, little progress had been made on the major issues of the day. No formal announcement had yet been made by France or Spain on the status of Louisiana, although the former country was poised to launch an expedition to recover it. French troops were barely in control of the island of Saint-Domingue. The Spanish-American convention had been limited in scope by virtue of the failure to agree on the admission of the so-called French claims. And the war continued against Tripoli. Within the next six months, all but the last two situations would change.

Acknowledgments

The editors are grateful for the painstaking and cheerful assistance of Timothy D. W. Connelly and Donald L. Singer of the National Historical Publications and Records Commission in the preparation of this volume. We would also like to thank James Lewis, Peter Kastor, Hal Wells, and Taylor Fain, our graduate assistants, for their fine efforts, as well as the following individuals for their suggestions and assistance: Gary J. Arnold of the Ohio Historical Society; John Catanzariti of the Papers of Thomas Jefferson; Julia Clancy-Smith of the History Department, University of Virginia; Douglas E. Clanin of the Indiana Historical Society; Cynthia Farar of the Harry Ransom Humanities Research Center, University of Texas at Austin; Marie E. Lamoureux of the American Antiquarian Society; Lee Langston-Harrison of the James Monroe Museum and Memorial Library; Kurt Piehler of the Papers of Albert Gallatin; Daniel Preston of the Papers of James Monroe; John Rhodehamel of the Huntington Library; Lucia C. Stanton of the Thomas Jefferson Memorial Foundation; Janet Whitson of the Detroit Public Library; and our friends at the Papers of George Washington.

Editorial Method

The guidelines used in editing *The Papers of James Madison* were explained in volumes 1 and 8 of the first series (1:xxxiii-xxxix and 8:xxiii) and in the first volume of the secretary of state series (1:xxv-xxvii). Considerable effort has been made to render the printed texts as literal, faithful copies of the original manuscripts, but some exceptions must be noted. Missing or illegible characters and words in a damaged or torn manuscript are restored by conjecture within angle brackets. Words consistently spelled incorrectly, as well as variant or antiquated spellings, are left as written; however, misspelled words that may appear to be printer's errors are corrected through additions in brackets or followed by the device [*sic*]. Brackets used by Madison and other correspondents have been rendered as parentheses. Slips of the pen and minor errors in encoding and decoding letters have been silently corrected; substantial errors or discrepancies, however, have been noted.

The amount of material in the period covered by the secretary of state years has led the editors to adopt a policy of increased selectivity. The primary criterion in the editors' decision to print, abstract, or omit a document is a judgment on whether or not it illuminates James Madison's thoughts or his official and personal life. The degree of involvement he had with the document, either as recipient or sender, is of paramount concern. Other considerations, though not decisive in themselves, have been whether the document was of a routine nature (such as a letter of transmittal, application, or recommendation) or was of intrinsic interest in adding a new dimension to our understanding of the man or, in the case of a lengthy document, whether it had been previously published in an easily accessible source such as *American State Papers* or *The Territorial Papers of the United States*. A large number of bureaucratic documents were generated as a result of the broad responsibilities of Madison's office; those that produce little useful information and do not warrant abstracting are silently omitted (such as letters of appointment, ship's papers, and patents). Occasionally, omitted documents are referred to in the notes.

In preparing abstracts the editors have tried to summarize the contents of manuscripts, avoiding unnecessary detail while providing readers with a guide to the most important issues raised and the writer's approach. Editorial additions to these abstracts (except for the purposes of identification) appear in brackets or in footnotes. Place-name spellings in abstracts have been modernized and variant spellings of personal names standardized.

Because of the nature of the office, this series includes more letters in foreign languages than our other series; when printed in full, such letters are followed by a condensed translation. Where documents appear in languages with which Madison was relatively unfamiliar, the clerical translation he used is included when available.

Pertinent information related to the documents is set forth in the provenance notes. Routine endorsements are not noted except in the case of State Department clerks Jacob Wagner and Daniel Brent. Most of the information on the covers of documents (such as addresses) is ignored; postmarks are noted only when more than three days elapsed before posting. When the enclosures mentioned are newspapers or other ephemeral publications that would have been immediately separated from the document, the absence of such items is not noted in the provenance. The order of documents continues unchanged from the previous series.

Depository Symbols

In the provenance section following each document the first entry indicates the source of the text. If the document was in private hands when copied for this edition, the owner and date are normally indicated. If the document was in a private or public depository in the United States, the symbol listed in the Library of Congress's *Symbols of American Libraries* (13th ed.; Washington, 1985) is used. Where the symbol DLC stands alone, it indicates the Madison Papers in the Library of Congress. In the case of foreign depositories, explanations of the symbols are below. The location symbols for depositories used in this volume are:

AAE	Archives du Ministère des Affaires Etrangères, Paris
AHN	Archivo Histórico Nacional, Madrid
AR	Algemeen Rijksarchief, The Hague
CSmH	Henry E. Huntington Library, San Marino, California
DLC	Library of Congress, Washington, D.C.
DNA	National Archives, Washington, D.C.

	CD	Consular Despatches
	DD	Diplomatic Despatches
	DL	Domestic Letters
	IC	Instructions to Consuls
	IM	Instructions to Ministers
	LAR	Letters of Application and Recommendation
	LOAG	Letters from and Opinions of Attorneys General

LRD	Letters of Resignation and Declination
ML	Miscellaneous Letters
NFC	Notes from Foreign Consuls
NFL	Notes from Foreign Legations

G-Ar	Georgia Department of Archives and History, Atlanta
ICHi	Chicago Historical Society
In	Indiana State Library, Indianapolis
InU	Indiana University, Bloomington
M-Ar	Massachusetts State Archives, Boston
MB	Boston Public Library
MdAA	Hall of Records Commission, Annapolis
MHi	Massachusetts Historical Society, Boston
MiD	Detroit Public Library
MiU-C	William L. Clements Library, Ann Arbor, Michigan
Ms-Ar	Mississippi Department of Archives and History, Jackson
N	New York State Library, Albany
Nc-Ar	North Carolina State Department of Archives and History, Raleigh
NHi	New-York Historical Society, New York City
NjMoHP	Morristown National Historical Park, Morristown, New Jersey
NjP	Princeton University, Princeton, New Jersey
NjR	Rutgers University, New Brunswick, New Jersey
NN	New York Public Library, New York City
NNMus	Museum of the City of New York
NNPM	Pierpont Morgan Library, New York City
O	Ohio State Library, Columbus
OkTG	Thomas Gilcrease Foundation, Tulsa, Oklahoma
PHarH	Pennsylvania Historical and Museum Commission, Harrisburg
PHC	Haverford College, Haverford, Pennsylvania
PHi	Historical Society of Pennsylvania, Philadelphia
PP	Free Library of Philadelphia
PPGi	Girard College, Philadelphia
PRO	Public Record Office, London
RPB-JH	Brown University, John Hay Library, Providence
RPJCB	John Carter Brown Library, Providence
RS	Riksarkivet Biblioteket, Stockholm
SSSPL	M. E. Saltykov-Shchedrin State Public Library, St. Petersburg, Russia
Vi	Virginia State Library, Richmond
ViU	University of Virginia, Charlottesville

Abbreviations

FC   File copy. Any version of a letter or other document retained by the sender for his own files and differing little if at all from the completed version. A draft, on the other hand, is a preliminary sketch, often incomplete and varying frequently in expression from the finished version. Unless otherwise noted, both are in the sender's hand. A letterbook copy is a retained duplicate, often bound in a chronological file, and usually in a clerk's hand.

JM   James Madison.

Ms   Manuscript. A catchall term describing numerous reports and other papers written by JM, as well as items sent to him which were not letters.

RC   Recipient's copy. The copy of a letter intended to be read by the addressee. If the handwriting is not that of the sender, this fact is noted in the provenance.

Tr   Transcript. A copy of a manuscript, or a copy of a copy, customarily handwritten and ordinarily not by its author or by the person to whom the original was addressed.

Abstracts and Missing Letters. In most cases a document is presented only in abstract form because of its trivial nature, its great length, or a combination of both. Abstracted letters are noted by the symbol §.

The symbol ¶ indicates a "letter not found" entry, with the name of the writer or intended recipient, the date, and such other information as can be surmised from the surviving evidence. If nothing other than the date of the missing item is known, however, it is mentioned only in the notes to a related document.

Short Titles for Books and Other Frequently Cited Materials

In addition to these short titles, bibliographical entries are abbreviated if a work has been cited in a previous volume of the series.

Annals of Congress.   *Debates and Proceedings in the Congress of the United States . . .* (42 vols.; Washington, 1834–56).

ASP.   *American State Papers: Documents, Legislative and Executive, of the Congress of the United States . . .* (38 vols.; Washington, 1832–61).

Brant, *Madison.*   Irving Brant, *James Madison* (6 vols.; Indianapolis and New York, 1941–61).

Carter, *Territorial Papers.* Clarence Carter et al., eds., *The Territorial Papers of the United States* (28 vols.; Washington, 1934–75).

Evans. Charles Evans, ed., *American Bibliography . . . 1639 . . . 1820* (12 vols.; Chicago, 1903–34).

Ford, *Writings of Jefferson.* Paul Leicester Ford, ed., *The Writings of Thomas Jefferson* (10 vols.; New York, 1892–99).

Kline, *Papers of Burr.* Mary-Jo Kline, ed., *Political Correspondence and Public Papers of Aaron Burr* (2 vols.; Princeton, N.J., 1983).

Knox, *Naval Documents, Barbary Wars.* Dudley W. Knox, ed., *Naval Documents Related to the United States Wars with the Barbary Powers* (6 vols.; Washington, 1939–44).

Malone, *Jefferson and His Time.* Dumas Malone, *Jefferson and His Time* (6 vols.; Boston, 1948–81).

Mayo, *Instructions to British Ministers.* Bernard Mayo, ed., *Instructions to the British Ministers to the United States, 1791–1812*, Annual Report of the American Historical Association for the Year 1936, vol. 3 (Washington, 1941).

Miller, *Treaties.* Hunter Miller, ed., *Treaties and Other International Acts of the United States of America* (8 vols.; Washington, 1930–48).

OED. Oxford English Dictionary.

PJM. William T. Hutchinson et al., eds., *The Papers of James Madison* (1st ser., vols. 1–10, Chicago, 1962–77, vols. 11–17, Charlottesville, Va., 1977–91).

PJM-PS. Robert A. Rutland et al., eds., *The Papers of James Madison: Presidential Series* (2 vols. to date; Charlottesville, Va., 1984—).

PJM-SS. Robert J. Brugger et al., eds., *The Papers of James Madison: Secretary of State Series* (3 vols. to date; Charlottesville, Va., 1986—).

Rowland, *Claiborne Letter Books.* Dunbar Rowland, ed., *Official Letter Books of W. C. C. Claiborne, 1801–1816* (6 vols.; Jackson, Miss., 1917).

Senate Exec. Proceedings. Journal of the Executive Proceedings of the Senate of the United States of America (3 vols.; Washington, 1828).

Shaw and Shoemaker. R. R. Shaw and R. H. Shoemaker, comps., *American Bibliography: A Preliminary Checklist for 1801–1819* (22 vols. to date; New York, 1958—).

Syrett and Cooke, *Papers of Hamilton.* Harold C. Syrett and Jacob E. Cooke, eds., *The Papers of Alexander Hamilton* (26 vols.; New York, 1961–79).

U.S. Statutes at Large. The Public Statutes at Large of the United States of America . . . (17 vols.; Boston, 1848–73).

WMQ. William and Mary Quarterly.

Madison Chronology

3 May	First session of Seventh Congress ends.
14 May	JM and family leave Washington for Montpelier.
ca. 27 May	Jefferson visits JM at Montpelier.
31 May	JM and family arrive in Washington from Montpelier.
ca. 1 August	Leave Washington to visit Harewood.
11 August	Arrive at Montpelier from Harewood.
ca. 21 August	Jefferson visits JM at Montpelier.
18 September	JM and family visit Jefferson at Monticello.
7 October	Arrive in Washington from Montpelier.

THE PAPERS OF

James Madison

§ From Elias Vander Horst. *2 March 1802, Bristol.* Transmits copies of his letters of 12 and 13 Feb.,[1] since which nothing worth communicating has occurred. Forwards four letters from Rufus King and encloses newspapers and the latest London price current.

RC (DNA: RG 59, CD, Bristol, vol. 2). 1 p. Written at the bottom of Vander Horst to JM, 12 and 13 Feb. 1802. Copy (ibid.) dated 3 Mar. 1802. Enclosures not found.

1. *PJM-SS*, 2:464 and n.

§ From William Marshall. *3 March 1802, Charleston.* Introduces Mr. Read[1] of Charleston, whose "object in Visiting The Federal City, will be particularly explained to You."

RC (DLC). 1 p.

1. Robert Read was a South Carolina merchant with business dealings in Cuba (see JM to John Morton, 7 Apr. 1802).

§ From James Leander Cathcart. *4 March 1802, Leghorn.* No. 2. Has learned that the U.S. ship *George Washington*, which arrived 31 Jan. from Tunis and Naples and sailed a few days later with merchant vessels under convoy, reached Marseilles safely. The *President* was repaired at Toulon and has sailed for Gibraltar. Eaton arrived in Leghorn on the *George Washington* and remained until 28 Feb. He will stop at Naples "to determine a point of some importance full details of which is forwarded by him to the department of State by this conveyance"[1] and then proceed directly to Tunis. Before his departure from Leghorn, Eaton received reports from Turner at Tunis that "no alteration had taken place" there. Encloses copies of latest reports from Tripoli and observes that "the very elements seem to have declared in our favor, & if government thinks proper to decree the destruction of Tripoli for the iniquity of their Bashaw, never did, & probably never will so favorable an opportunity present itself." Swedish admiral Cederström arrived in Leghorn "some days since" after consultation with Commodore Dale; "the result I am not inform'd, but from the circumstance of his taking onboard here a large quantity of cash I presume he will act similar to the Danes." Is anxious to receive instructions from the president.

RC and enclosures (DNA: RG 59, CD, Tripoli, vol. 2). RC 2 pp.; docketed by Wagner; printed in Knox, *Naval Documents, Barbary Wars*, 2:78. Enclosures include a copy of a 20 Dec. 1801 letter to Cathcart from Nicolai C. Nissen at Tripoli discussing the formal protest he made against the Tripolitan Jews for not paying an obligation of $1,929 when it became due, relaying rumors of a reconciliation between the pasha of Tripoli and his brother, reporting a defeat sustained by the pasha's troops, and describing the "deplorable situation" in Tripoli owing to two years of drought (4 pp.; docketed by Cathcart as received 19 Feb. 1802 "& forwarded to Dept. of State March 4th. 1802"; on the last page Cathcart addressed a note to JM, dated 4 Mar. 1802, in which he commended Nissen's conduct relative to the Jews and criticized Richard O'Brien's "system of dependance & implicit faith in the Sanhedrim [*sic*]"). Cathcart apparently also enclosed an extract from another letter to him from Nissen, 25 Dec. 1801, reporting that a "most violent gale of wind" had destroyed several ships, including the pasha's thirteen-gun corvette, and inquiring whether an action for debt should be brought against the Jews in Europe (1 p.; Cathcart appended the note, "I am of opinion that no action ought to be brought against the Tripoline Jews at Leghorn, the debt ought undoubtedly to be paid by those who contracted it"); and a copy of a note from Nissen headed, "Departure & arrival of Cruisers at Tripoli Decr. 25. 1801," describing the movements and appearance of Tripolitan cruisers (1 p.; filed with Cathcart to JM, 28 Dec. 1801; printed ibid., 1:645–46). Cathcart may also have enclosed a copy of a letter to him from Capt. Samuel Barron at Malta, 9 Jan. 1802, commenting on the violent winds he had encountered on his voyage from Leghorn and conveying news from Tripoli received through Joseph Pulis, the consul at Malta (2 pp.; printed ibid., 2:15–16), to which Cathcart appended a "Memorandum" stating that he felt "highly sensible of the honor confer'd on him by the President & Senate in their appointment of Mr. Pulis merely from his recommendation" and that although Pulis did not speak English, "to counterballance that inconveniency he corresponds with all the Barbary States & has it in his power more than any other person to procure us accurate intelligence."

    1. See Eaton to JM, 22 Feb. 1802 (*PJM-SS*, 2:483).

§ From Obed and Aaron Mitchell. *4 March 1802, Nantucket.* "We the Subscribers being owners of the ship Minerva Sailed from this place on a whaling voyage to the Brazils & Woolwick [Walvis] Bay in 7th Mo 1799, upon her return with a full load of oil . . . the 5th of 10th Mo 1800 was captured by a French Privateer of 12 Guns." The vessel was ordered to Guadeloupe, but on 14 Oct. it was retaken by the British ship *Gaite* and "ordered for the Port Saint Johns [St. John, Antigua] arrived there the 17th. of the same." On 1 Nov. a British vice-admiralty court condemned the *Minerva.* "And seeing she was taken by the French after the Treaty was signed in France we think it not improbable that our demand may be good upon the French." Requests JM's advice on how to proceed.[1]

    Tr (N). 1 p.; marked "Copy." A marginal note in an unidentified hand reads, "NB. I cannot find at the Dept: that any answer was written to the above letter. I. A. C."

    1. The Mitchells owned a large whaling firm in Nantucket that produced illuminating oil and spermaceti candles. In 1846 the Mitchells' claim was described: "Ship Minerva, Fitch, 1,500 barrels of oil on board; value $30,000; one of the original owners living, sixty-eight years old, *poor*; master still alive, seventy-eight years old, with small means and many dependants; one of the crew alive, *poor; claims never sold*" (Robert A. Davison, *Isaac Hicks: New York Merchant and Quaker, 1767–1820* [Cambridge, Mass., 1964], pp. 86–87; Alexander Starbuck, *History of the American Whale Fishery* [2 vols.; 1878; New York, 1964 reprint], 1:91 n.). The U.S. was still pursuing this claim as late as 1886 (see *House Documents*, 49th Cong., 1st sess., 1:18).

From Rufus King

No. 55.

Sir   London Feb. [March] 5. 1802

    Commodore Dale while at Toulon having informed me that he might have occasion to draw upon Messrs. Mackenzie and Glennie for more than the amount of the Funds in their hands subject to his Draughts,[1] I communicated the same to these Gentlemen, who have assured me that the Commodore's Bills shall be duly honoured.

The arms which have been making by Mortimer for the Bey of Tunis are completed; and I shall desire Bird Savage & Bird to have them sent by the earliest opportunity to our Consul at Gibraltar with Instructions to him to deliver them to the first American Frigate which touches there on her way up the Mediterranean.

On account of the double execution of the order for Cloths, the mounting of a Tagan,[2] and I believe an excess in the Costs of the arms and Jewels above the Estimate, the Funds remitted to Bird Savage and Bird for this Service will prove deficient between two and Three Thousand Pounds: the money on hand will be wholly applied, and I shall desire Bird savage & Bird to give their acceptances at two months for the Balance. As they will advise the Secretary of the Treasury of the particulars of this Business, it is unnecessary that I should trouble you farther with it.

Lord Pelham a few days ago shewed me a Letter from Mr. MacDonough the British Agent at Tripoli, exculpating himself from the charge of having excited the Bashaw of that Regency to make war upon the United States.[3] He explicitly denies the charge, and encloses a Certificate to the same effect, signed by the Bashaw himself. Mr. MacDonough having thought it necessary to solicit this Certificate from the Bashaw will serve to shew him that his hostility to the United States may not be agreeable to Great Britain.

The Bill authorising the Crown to suspend the Tonnage and Countervailing Duties upon American Ships and Cargoes is still before Parliament, but will without doubt pass in a few days. The Debate to which it has given rise, so far as regards General Gascoigne, one of the Members from Liverpool, appears to have been for mere electioneering purposes; and with respect to Doctor Laurence and Mr. Wyndham the occasion, however unconnected, was made use of as an opportunity to talk about the Negotiation at Amiens, and the dangerous Dominion of France.[4]

I have seen a Letter dated Paris Feb. 26. which says "it is definitively settled to send a Colony to Louisiana and Florida. General Bernadotte is to have the direction and command of it: preparations are making for the first Expedition whose departure will perhaps depend upon the accounts expected from St. Domingo. It is asserted that the Indian Nations adjoining to Florida have Agents now here for the purpose of making Treaties with this Country to unite themselves with the Troops and Settlers that may be sent from hence. The establishment of this Colony is a darling object and will be pursued with ardour and upon a great scale, unless the affairs of St. Domingo shall for the moment derange the plan. Louisiana, Guiana and the desert Island of Tristan de Cunha are each spoken of as places to which the rebellious and untractable Negroes and people of Colour may be sent from St. Domingo and the other french Colonies." With perfect respect and Esteem, I have the honour to be, Sir, Your obedt. & faithful Servt.

RUFUS KING

RC (DNA: RG 59, DD, Great Britain, vol. 10); letterbook copy (NHi: Rufus King Papers, vol. 55). RC in a clerk's hand, signed by King; docketed by Brent. Letterbook copy dated 5 Mar. 1802—the correct date according to internal evidence.

1. For Richard Dale's letter to King of 5 Jan. 1802, see Knox, *Naval Documents, Barbary Wars*, 2:13–14.
2. This was probably an approximation of yataghan (or ataghan), a long dagger sheathed in a silver or gold scabbard, worn by men in the Ottoman Empire.
3. On the charges against Bryan McDonogh, see King to JM, 14 Dec. 1801 (*PJM-SS*, 2:316–17 and n. 2).
4. In his 5 Mar. remarks before the House of Commons, Isaac Gascoyne complained that the bill "would infringe upon the Navigation act, which, next to the great charter of our liberties, ought to be kept inviolate." French Laurence countered that "whatever might be the expediency or inexpediency of the measure, we must adopt it, if we were bound to do so by good faith." He repeated the rumor that the French planned to "carry on a war of Custom-house duties with us, and, if possible, to ruin our trade." William Windham stated that although he had no doubt the countervailing duties should be removed, he was uncertain "whether it was proper to pass an act to take them off before it was known that the duties in America had been abolished." As to the French, he said, Great Britain now had to contend with a power "which had not been seen since the time of Charlemagne" (*Parliamentary History of England*, 36:351, 354–55, 357–58).

§ From James Leander Cathcart. *5 March 1802, Leghorn.* No. 3. States that "during Mr. Eaton's delay at Leghorn he inform'd me that no consideration on earth could have sufficient weight to induce him to remain in Barbary a moment after our affairs were terminated with Tripoli. . . . I therefore request that I may be removed from Tripoli to Tunis as I presume I have a prior right to that appointment to any person in the United States in consequence of having already negotiated the alteration in our Treaty with that Regency in 1799." Promises to remain in Tripoli "after our affairs are permanently settled until the will of the President is known relative to the change." Requests JM's recommendation for the post, "for altho the Salary is the same at Tunis that it is at Tripoli the society of the former is much better & more extensive which renders the change very desirable to a Man who has a young family to educate." Should his request be granted, pledges that "no degrading concession shall ever be made" by him.

RC and enclosures (DNA: RG 59, CD, Tripoli, vol. 2). RC 2 pp.; marked "duplicate." Filed with the RC are several documents, some dated later than 5 Mar., which are docketed as received with Cathcart's 5 Mar. dispatch. These include duplicate copies of two letters from Nissen to Cathcart. In the first, dated 29 Nov. 1801, Nissen reported the absence of U.S. ships off Tripoli since September and recent events there, including the default of the Jews on their bond (3 pp.; docketed by Cathcart as received 19 Feb. 1802 and "Forwarded to the seat of govt. by the Philadelphia Captn. Razor March 5th. 1802"); in the second letter, 5 Jan. 1802, Nissen stated that the Jews had paid $1,300 toward the sum they owed and had asked him to intercede with Cathcart on their behalf (3 pp.; on the verso of the last page Cathcart wrote a note addressed to JM and dated 17 Apr. 1802, "Mr. Nissen has recoverd 1300 dols. from the Jews of Tripoli in part payment of the cloth plunder'd from me by the Bashaw in 1799. & is in hopes to recover the remainder consequently when I receive that sum I shall give the United States credit for it in my next acct. curt having charged the United States with the value in my acct. curt. dated 31st. Decr. 1800"). Cathcart also sent extracts from two of his letters to Nissen (4 pp.). In his 15 Mar. 1802 letter Cathcart reported that according to a letter from Rufus King to Eaton, British consul Bryan McDonogh was to be removed from Tripoli and that Joseph Ingraham was in Leghorn and had signed a certificate on 22 Feb. retracting all "defamatory insinuations" against Cathcart; he discussed prospects for peace with Tripoli and the "advantages resulting from a vigorous coercion" of the pasha. In his 14 Apr. 1802 letter, Cathcart requested information about the Tripolitan navy, Tripoli's preparations for defense, and popular opinion there relating to Hamet Pasha's accepting the governorship of Derna; he sent his private family cipher (not found) to ensure secrecy. Also enclosed with the RC were a copy of a letter to Cathcart from Eaton, 28 Mar. 1802, stating that he had "found means to secure Siddi Mohammed by engaging the Sahibtappa" (1 p.; docketed by Cathcart as received 8 Apr.; printed in Knox, *Naval Documents, Barbary Wars*, 2:97), and an extract of Cathcart's reply, 10 Apr. 1802, approving Eaton's efforts and warning that "if one of the males [in the reigning pasha's family] escape it will occasion perpetual disturbance & rebellion at Tripoli this you had better inculcate in the mind of Hamed Bashaw, inform him that the five fingers of the immortal Allah! is directed against his brother; . . . in short my dear Sir work upon their passions, make use of their absurdities & superstitions" (3 pp.; printed ibid., 2:111–12), to which Cathcart appended the note, "For the particulars during the reign of Hamed Bashaw I beg a reference to the History of the Revolution in Tripoli forwarded to the Department of State in the french tongue, & for my opinion relative to opposing him to his brother the usurper I refer to my letter of the 2nd. July 1801."

§ From Bartholomew Dandridge. *5 March 1802, Aux Cayes.* Received news of the arrival of twenty-five to thirty thousand French troops at Cap Français and Port Républicain about 10 Feb.[1] First reports indicated the French troops met a friendly reception. Subsequent reports—that "at both places the Troops arriving from France were opposed & fired upon at their landing by the troops of Toussaint & Dessalines" and that both towns were "burnt & all the white & mulatto inhabitants without exception were butchered by the negroes"—caused the "greatest anxiety among the whites for the safety of their lives & properties." The most accurate information available indicates Toussaint's troops destroyed Cap Français on the French approach. Has heard nothing from Lear. States that French troops were fired at during their landing at Port Républicain. General Dessalines, in his retreat from that town, "carry'd off much treasure," destroyed all plantations in his path, and burned the town of Léogane. At Jacmel he "showed evident intention of burning the town & murdering the white & mulatto inhabitants," but the black commandant of the place and "the soldiers, shewing no disposition to execute his bloody & inhumane orders," he retreated to the mountains. Dessalines had ordered General Laplume, commander of the southern department, to defend Aux Cayes as long as he could but if overpowered to destroy the town and its white inhabitants. "It is impossible for me to express the gratitude that is due by me & all the americans residing in this Department, to our benevolent & humane Generl. Laplume," who was prepared to oppose the "savagely cruel mandate" of Dessalines. "A few days since Genl. Darbois arrived here with 700 or 800 men from Port republican & every thing is now perfectly tranquil in the south Department." Leclerc has ordered an embargo on all American vessels, reportedly occasioned by the discovery of an American ship at St. Marc bearing gunpowder and arms for Toussaint. The embargo "will be attended with much delay & expence to several of our vessels now laden with produce & ready to depart for the Ud. States." This letter is sent by a schooner bound for Baltimore, which has liberty to depart because it has been engaged to transport one hundred soldiers to Jérémie. Lear's last letter informed him of his appointment as U.S. commercial agent at Port Républicain in place of Ritchie; has not received any communication from JM on the subject.

RC (DNA: RG 59, CD, Cap Haitien, vol. 4). 6 pp.; docketed by Brent. Extract printed in the *National Intelligencer*, 5 Apr. 1802.

1. On 29 Jan. 1802 a French invasion force of twelve thousand men under the command of Gen. Charles-Victor-Emmanuel Leclerc arrived off the east coast of the island of Hispaniola. The attempt by the French to retake and pacify the island's black population through two years' bitter fighting ultimately failed (Ott, *Haitian Revolution*, pp. 139–62; see also Tobias Lear to JM, 28 Feb. 1802, *PJM-SS*, 2:499–522).

§ From William C. C. Claiborne. *6 March 1802, "Near Natchez."* Refers to his letter of 5 Feb.[1] advising JM of his request to Wilkinson to construct a blockhouse at a central location to store spare arms from Fort Adams; hopes the president will approve it.[2] Is currently occupied with the difficult task of organizing the militia. The election of members of the territorial legislature, to be held the fourth Monday in July, has caused "party divisions, infinitely more rancourous than any I have ever witnessed in our Mother States." Will forward a copy of the territorial laws passed at the last session as soon as they are printed. Reports that Steele has recovered his health.

Letterbook copy (Ms-Ar: Claiborne Executive Journal). 2 pp. Printed in Rowland, *Claiborne Letter Books*, 1:53–54.

1. *PJM-SS*, 2:447.
2. In a letter of 8 Apr. 1802, Secretary of War Henry Dearborn gave Claiborne permission to build a blockhouse and quarters for a company of troops on a site near Natchez. Claiborne constructed the installation near the territory's new capital, Washington, and named it Fort Dearborn (Dearborn to Claiborne, 8 Apr. 1802, Claiborne to Dearborn, 24 May 1802 and 2 Mar. 1803, Rowland, *Claiborne Letter Books*, 1:110–12, 112–13, 276).

§ From George W. Erving. *6 March 1802, London.* No. 6. Reports the proceedings of the Board of Commissioners under article 7 of the British treaty "respecting one of the appointments in connection with that Board with which the President has been pleased to honor me." Encloses six related letters and extracts so that "the business may be now fully before you." Was authorized by JM's letters of 27 July 1801[1] to take up Cabot's duties, particularly in the "ascertainment of losses upon references made by the commissioners." Gave letters to King and assumed that the president's instructions would be carried out when the board reassembled. On 16 Feb. the board directed letters to be written to Cabot and Glennie "requiring them to attend their duty"; on 23 Feb. Erving received a letter from King with a postscript to which he replied on 24 Feb., when he also "gave formal notice to the Board of my appointments." Wrote again to the board on 27 Feb. enclosing an extract of his letter of appointment, which was read to the board on 2 Mar. On the same day a letter in his favor from King was read, and Erving presented himself to the board, which "recognized me as agent for claims . . . as well as for conducting the cases in the Courts." However, the board observed that the office of assessor was their own appointment, not that of the U.S. government—a fact which they "imagined . . . had not been understood by the secretary of state"—and that in their opinion the offices of agent and assessor were incompatible. The agent's objective was to "Swell the claimants account of loss," while that of assessor was "fixing the Estimate of loss on an Equitable footing." In addition, the board was "perfectly satisfied" with Cabot's "conduct & ability." Erving responded that he could not say what JM's understanding of the appointment was but JM's instructions were clear; that Cabot had been informed "there was no necessity for his attendance" in London and "*all* his duties . . . were assigned to me"; and that it was reasonable to conclude "that the individual designated by the President woud as a matter of course be the person chosen by the Board." As to the incompatibility of the appointments, Erving argued that Cabot had been appointed commercial agent and served as assessor. Gore and Pinkney replied that Cabot's agency soon ceased—"that it did in fact merge in that of Mr Williams." Erving found the board's "objection of incompatibility [was] so strongly urged" that further opposition "woud not promote the interest of the Claimants or facilitate my duties," and on 4 Mar. he wrote to the commissioners to that effect.

Points out that Gore must have known that Cabot acted as private agent for American claimants, rendering him "objectionable on the Score of incompatibility." The same can be said for Glennie. The position of assessor is a "place of great profit," with a payment of ten guineas for each case reported on. "The commissioners now leaving with me the care of bringing the cases from the Courts collecting the documents, & stating the claimants Account of loss, assign the assessorship to Mr Cabot, the duties of which office are certainly not so great & the Emoluments of which are so profuse."

RC and enclosures (DNA: RG 59, CD, London, vol. 8). RC 8 pp. Another copy of the RC (ibid.), marked triplicate and docketed by Brent, bears a postscript dated 17 Mar. in which Erving reported that in Williams's accounts duly forwarded to JM there were two entries in which cash was paid to Samuel Cabot in the capacity of commercial agent. Another copy of the 17 Mar. postscript (ibid.), in Erving's hand, includes an 18 Mar. postscript: "The French have received Accts of the Landing effected by their Troops in St Domingo, & Buonoparte has been congratulated by the two Emperors on the *settlement* of the Italian Republic." The enclosures (5 pp.), numbered by Erving, are copies of (1) a postscript of a letter from Rufus King to Erving, 22 Feb. 1802, inquiring whether Erving had informed the board of his appointment; (2) an extract from Erving's 24 Feb. 1802 reply, stating that he had assumed King would have done so but at King's suggestion he had that day written to the board; (3) a notation of a letter from Erving to the board, 24 Feb. 1802; (4) Erving to the board, 27 Feb. 1802, enclosing an extract from JM's 27 July 1801 letter of appointment; (5) King to Erving, 28 Feb. 1802, stating that he would write to the commissioners to preclude any doubt of the appointment; and (6) Erving's 4 Mar. letter to the commissioners withdrawing from the office in question.

1. *PJM-SS*, 1:482 and n.

§ From George W. Erving. *6 March 1802, London.* Private No. 8. Has reported in an accompanying letter "all that has passed upon the subject of my appointment." Is "perfectly satisfied" with the situation; has full schedule of responsibilities without assessorship. But "upon the score of Emolument—here is certainly a very great deduction without any proportionable deduction of business." Notes Pinkney's assertion that Cabot was not overpaid at a salary of $2,500 a year plus payment for his reports; suggests that Cabot was "most profusely overpaid" for his reports and "the arrangement had very much the appearance of a job." In response to Gore's statement that Cabot's office "sunk into that of Mr Williams," suggests that Williams should receive a pay increase or perhaps Cabot should refund a portion. Truth is Cabot and Williams "made what the Law calls 'Hodge-podge' of their Offices & salaries"; Cabot "was as much agent for claims after his appointment to the assessorship as before." Suggests that there have been irregularities in the commission's use of contingency funds and excessive clerical staff. King's secretary is also a secretary to the commission at a salary of £160 a year. Erving had expected to be nominated to the assessorship by the American commissioners and accepted by the British commissioners "without difficulty." However, King declined to introduce him to the commission, expressing "his unwillingness to '*interfere*,'" and wrote to them with reluctance only after "I wrote to him pretty urgently in the letter which inclosed the Extract of yours." Pinkney "denied all responsibility in his situation to the American government, he sat there as an independant judge"; Gore agreed. If this impartiality, rather than support of American claims, had been shared by the commissioners under article 6 of the Jay treaty that met at Philadelphia, it would have cost the U.S. "some millions of dollars." Given this attitude, the commission might as well be "composed altogether of Englishmen."[1] States that even King admits the motives of Pinkney and Gore in shutting him out of the assessorship are based on partisan politics. "In fine tho' English federalism is defeated in America, amongst our public officers here it yet triumphs."

State of negotiations at Amiens remains a "profound Mystery." The ministry "has been obliged to pluck up Courage Enough to send something like a spirited Remonstrance" to complain of the delay; it is said, though "scarcely to be beleived," that Addington "demanded an immediate conclusion of the treaty." Napoleon is "improving Every moment, & shoud the war recommence will be found in a much more formidable attitude." Erving anticipates categorical demands upon the British by Napoleon in the near future. Hopes, however, that "both parties will see their interest in terminating this contest," for peace "must be productive of great political advantages to us." Mercantile losses will be more than offset by "improvements of the interior." French mercantile policy in the West Indies is more "liberal & rational . . . than under their old Government"; the British are sure to "follow their Example." Speeches in Parliament "begin to hold a proper language with respect to the United States," even though "the real disposition is not changed." Observes that King has "great apprehensions" about Louisiana. It appears that France has "so many objects of immediate & pressing interest to attend to, that no apprehensions of mischeif can be Entertained from that quarter for some time." Hopes differences may be negotiated; France can have no interest in pursuing a plan "so odious & offensive" and one leading to such a "misunderstanding." "These ghosts however which we conjure up are very agreeable to people here, who will help us to get or guarantee to us any thing,[2] providing that we will connect ourselves with their desperate fortunes."

RC and triplicate (MHi: Erving Papers); duplicate (CSmH). 8 pp.

1. Duplicate copy has an additional sentence here: "In Mr Pinckneys situation a man may perhaps be so upright as to bend backwards."

2. In the duplicate copy this sentence begins: "These phantoms however which we conjure up are very agreeable to the people here, who woud help us to get, or guarantee to us territories in the moon . . ."

§ From Louis-André Pichon. 7 March 1802. Sends a report of the secretary of the treasury on the claim of [Paul] Coulon, a French merchant.[1] Asks JM to interest himself in the case to see that Coulon receives justice.

RC (DNA: RG 59, NFL, France, vol. 1). 3 pp.; in French. Enclosure not found, but see n. 1.

1. Gallatin's report, dated 22 Jan. 1802, which looked unfavorably on Coulon's demand for payment, is printed in *ASP, Claims*, pp. 251–55. The House passed a bill for Coulon's relief on 12 Apr. 1802, but the Senate failed to concur (*Annals of Congress*, 7th Cong., 1st sess., 266–67, 1163). For Coulon's petition to Congress asking for compensation for his loss as owner of the prize ship *Betty Cathcart*, detained in Wilmington, North Carolina, see Pichon to JM, 29 Sept. 1802.

To Andrew Ellicott

DEAR SIR   WASHINGTON Mar. 8. 1802
    Having been lately a good deal out of health, & the Chief Clerk confined by the same cause for some days past, several letters have been unavoidably unanswerd, & among them yours asking the aid of the Dept. of State in exchanging scientific information with a Correspondent in Europe.[1] You will now please to accept the information that whatever facility can be properly afforded for the purpose will readily be so, and particularly that of transmitting your letters in the manner you suggest. With great respect & esteem I am Dear Sir Your obedt. servt.

                                    JAMES MADISON

RC (DLC: Ellicott Papers).

1. On Ellicott's correspondence with Jean-Baptiste-Joseph Delambre, see Ellicott to JM, 20 Feb. 1802 (*PJM-SS*, 2:480).

From John Dawson

DEAR SIR.   HOUSE OF REPRES. March 8. 1802

I am very sorry for the information which you came on the last Evening relative to Skipwith's claim. I fear it will prove very injurious to him, as he has drawn bills, counting on this fund, which will be protested. I have written to Mr. Purviance to come to this place, under an expectation that he can give some usefull information.

On conversing with the Secy of the treasury I find, that some directions relative to myself must be given by you to that department. I inclose you a statement of the time of my absence, & the amt. of money paid for my passage—there are other expences which I was forcd to incur—which are not mentiond, but which, it appears to me, ought to be paid by the goverment—the thing is however submitted. Yrs with much Esteem

J DAWSON

RC and enclosure (DLC). Dawson's enclosed 8 Mar. 1802 statement (1 p.) reported his March 1801 meeting with Jefferson, who asked him to carry the ratified treaty to France, his subsequent movements prior to his return to Washington on 13 Jan. 1802, and the amounts he paid for his passage.

From James Monroe

DEAR SIR   RICHMOND March 8. 1802.

Since my last respecting mr. Skipwith's claim[1] to reimbursement of the money advanc'd by him to replace what was robbed from him in Paris, of the sum entrusted to him to be remitted to our bankers in Holland, I have been in Albemarle & brought down with me many documents, most of which are original, relative to that affair, which are forwarded you by the mail. In these you will receive the original letters of the bankers to me, of the ministers of foreign affrs. & finance in answer to my application for leave to export the money, statments of their agencies in the business by Mr. Van Staphorst & Mr. Purviance, a decln. of Mr. Skipwith relative to the deposit, & his report of the amt. & circumstances attending the robbery, as also some letters of the Secry. of the Treasury.[2] All these documents being original belong to me. Some of them such as Mr. Van Staphorsts & Purviance's statments, & Skipwiths decln., are of a private nature, intended for use only in case they became necessary to expose the authors of certain calumnies which you intimated were circulated, to my prejudice, in a certain stage of that affair.[3] I communicate them to you that you may see the precise ground on which every thing appertaining to it stands. A view of the other original documents is only necessary that they may be compard with the copies heretofore furnished, that a possibility of error may be guarded against. After you have made what use of them you think fit I shall be glad to receive them back, tho' that may not be till we meet in the summer in Albemarle. You will observe that till the payment of the money wh. took place between the 27th. or 8th. of Octr. & 5th or 6th. of Novr. 1795. the business was entirely in the hands of Mr. D'allarde,[4] managed on my part by Mr. Van Staphorst & Mr. Purviance. At the moment the payment was made the convention was giving ground to the directorial govt., wh. was not organised for several days: I recd. from Mr. de la Croix a notification of his appointment to the office of foreign affrs. on the 9th. bearing date on the 7th which I answer'd on the 10th. as you will see in my publication pa: 295.[5] My letter asking permission to export the money was on the 12th. In addition to the formal official applications by me, others were daily made by Mr. Skipwith & Mr. Van Staphorst or some of my family for leave to export the money. These gentln. were in daily communication, I mean the two first, with the Treasury department, and incessantly pressed for the permission which I had formally asked. You will readily conceive I had other objects to attend to at the time, and that I had a motive for prefering informal applications for such an accomodation as that wh. was sought: tho' I am persuaded I cod. not have been more attentive to the object, than I was, under any circumstances. It is still matter of surprise to me that the Secry. of the Treasury shod. send me a bill to Lubbert & Dumas at Hamburg, wh. they were to pay, in a letter addressed to them, sealed, which of course I cod. not see, for which funds were at the time provided, and let me know nothing abt. it: it is more surprising that he shod. let that bill rest in that state for a year, without giving any order respecting it. D'allarde I recollect suspected foul play as to the fund deposited in London with Cazenove & Co:. I think Harrison & Sterret were connected with it: it occurs that D'allarde informed me that when he applied to Cazenove for the money he evaded payment, tho' he was to have had the benefit of it, on payment of the bill on him. However I know nothing as to the real merits of that part of the transaction. Among the papers sent you is an answer of mine to a letter of D'allarde on that subject, which I wish preserved. I expect I have his letter in Albemarle. Mr. Skipwith's claim rests on its own merit. I presume all the necessary documents are now before you respecting it. He undertook the business without a view of profit, as you will see by many documents, to save expence to the U States, and in the hope of rendering an useful & acceptable service to his country. I do not think that he used one farthing of the money while it was in his possession. Indeed it was impossible for him to do it, being boxed up immediately for transportation & permission to transport it daily expected. The subterfuge on which his claim to reimbursement was evaded, was worthy the character who practic'd it, and peculiarly becomes the epoch in our history to which it belongs. I say this on the idea that the documents presented were satisfactory to prove that the loss was actually sustained, and that no neglect or misconduct was attributable to him on that head. I do not know how far it may be proper to confine the report to the case of the loss simply & the claim of reimbursement, or to take into view a summary of the whole transaction. Of this you will judge and act accordingly. To me it is a matter of perfect indifference. If the affr. is entered into generally you will also judge how far it will be proper to present the whole or any part of the papers sent you. We desire our best regards to Mrs. Madison & the family. Sincerely I am yours.

JAS. MONROE

RC (NN: Monroe Papers).

1. Monroe to JM, 5 Feb. 1802 (*PJM-SS*, 2:445–46).
2. Among the documents Monroe forwarded were probably Charles Delacroix to Monroe, 15 Nov. 1795; Willink, Van Staphorst, and Hubbard to Monroe, 24 Dec. 1795; John Henry Purviance to Monroe, 31 Dec. 1796; Jacob Van Staphorst to Monroe, 25 Dec. 1797; statements of Fulwar Skipwith, 28 July 1796 and 8 Mar. 1797; Skipwith to Monroe, 27 Mar. 1796, with a note by Monroe dated 8 Mar. 1802; Oliver Wolcott to Monroe, 23 June 1795 and 16 Sept. 1796; and Monroe to d'Allarde, 11 Mar. 1797 (NN: Monroe Papers).
3. Monroe here refers to accusations made against him in 1796 while he was U.S. minister to France that he speculated in French property and had been criminally neglectful in the theft of U.S. bullion destined for the payment of American loans in Holland (*PJM*, 16:302–3, 304 n. 4).
4. Pierre-Gilbert Leroy, baron d'Allarde (1749–1809), was a political economist who contributed to the debates over monetary policy and public credit in Revolutionary France. For a time he was the partner of James Swan in the firm d'Allarde, Swan et Cie (*Biographie universelle* [1843–65 ed.], 1:493–94; Howard C. Rice, "James Swan: Agent of the French Republic, 1794–1796," *New England Quarterly*, 10 [1937]: 464–86).
5. Monroe, *A View of the Conduct of the Executive* . . . (Philadelphia, 1797; Evans 32491).

From "A Plain Man"

SIR,   [8 March 1802]
    The system of the administration generally, but especially that part of it which respects the courts, is believed to be so hostile to the Union, and so

opposed to your former opinions on the subject, that I cannot resist the inclination I feel, to ask your attention to a few observations, on a point so universally interesting.

The friends of the constitution, who consider that instrument as a law limiting the powers of the legislature, have maintained, with unanswered and unanswerable force of argument, that the general clause which says, 'the judges both of the supreme and inferior courts shall hold their offices during good behavior';[1] is obligatory on the legislature. That being descriptive of the tenure of office, and not restrictive of the power of a particular department; being intended to preserve purity in the administration of justice, by securing the independence of those who administer it, and not merely to prevent a particular department, from the exercise of a particular power it would otherwise possess; the clause forms a barrier round the judiciary, which neither the legislature nor the executive can rightfully overleap.

In opposition (I will not say in answer) to this reasoning, the ministerial band contend.

1st. That if the legislature violate the constitution, yet the act is obligatory, not only on individuals, but on the courts likewise, and that judges sworn to support the constitution, must give to such acts the effect of laws legitimately enacted, and be governed by them in opposition to the instrument which its friends consider as the sacred source from whence all the powers of every department are derived.

2d. That the words 'the judges both of the supreme and inferior courts shall hold their offices during good behavior,' are *intended* to restrain the executive and not the legislative power.

With respect to the first argument, I shall not stop to demonstrate its direct tendency to prostrate the constitution at the feet of the legislature, and to introduce, in all its force, the principle of Parliamentary omnipotence, a principle heretofore so much reprobated, and which it is the great object of a written constitution to resist. Nor shall I employ myself in marking to these gentlemen, the palpable contradiction of maintaining, that the judges are bound by a law violating the constitution, and yet that the juries are at liberty to deny its force. It would be unnecessary to dwell on these contradictions, because inconsistency must be habitual with men who believe all means may be used to effect the end desired, and because the motive for this inconsistency is too apparent to escape the slightest observer—They have already adopted means to select their jurors, they are only adopting means to *pick* their judges! But I will ask you, sir, can this be your opinion? Have you so entirely surrendered your judgment? Have you put yourself so completely in the hands of your party, or its chief; have you so totally effaced from your mind all its former correct course of reasoning; as to embrace this new doctrine?[2]

If this be possible, it would be in vain to urge you to reflection; it would be time misspent to press you to summon up your powers, and to make one manly, one patriotic effort, to relieve your country from a principle, which, in a state of independence you would believe to be more fruitful of evil, than any which, if I may refer to ancient allegory, ever escaped from the box of Pandora.

Unwilling to take up this opinion of you, I shall pass to the second proposition.

It maintains that the clause of the constitution which ordains that 'the judges both of the supreme and inferior courts shall hold their offices during good behavior,' is intended to secure their continuance in office against an executive, and not against a legislative act.

In vain has it been urged that the terms are used without limitation, without being applied to any particular department, and consequently that they must be so understood. That there is not a syllable in the constitution restraining their operation merely to the executive, nor a syllable which gives to the legislature the power of removal. That to contend for this application, is, capriciously, to set up a mere arbitrary distinction, which prostrates every principle of sound construction, and destroys the use of language, by taking from words their plain signification. The ministerialists insist on so understanding the constitution because they will so understand it, and they, unfortunately for America, constitute a majority.

Let me then ask you sir, who must possess some influence with your party, to check for a moment the mad career you are running, for one instant to resume your former self, and think systematically and virtuously.

The words of the constitution, if obligatory on the legislature as well as the executive, must be admitted to protect the judges as well against a legislative, as executive removal from office. There being in the constitution no words to counteract them, it can only be by mere implication, that a power over the continuance of judges in office is to be attributed to the legislature.

Will you sir, admit, that express words of the constitution are to be overruled by implication? Implication not founded on any words whatever—not on any specific grant of power which can by any possibility be construed to comprehend a control over the existence of the judicial department, but on the broad undefinable nature of legislative powers? Will you admit this construction to be made by the legislature itself, which, in making it, enlarges its own power? If the legislature may imply powers in itself, against the express words of the constitution, what are its limits and where are we to search for them? Is not the constitution itself a mockery, and are not the oaths, taken to support it, worse than a mockery.

But let us examine what the ministerialists term a reason in support of this till now unheard of construction.

They say that but for this restriction, the general power of removal from office given by the constitution, in all cases, to the executive, would have enabled that department to remove the judges, to prevent which this clause was inserted, declaring that they shall hold their offices during good behavior.

The truth of this proposition has been very properly denied—but let us for the sake of the argument admit and examine it. To a mind capable as yours has been of correct reasoning, this may not be time entirely thrown away.

What, let me ask you, is, in truth, the sum of this argument?

It amounts, if I understand it, to this. The words though general, could only be designed to check and limit a power given by the constitution, and therefore apply only to the executive, to whom alone the power of removal is given.

Reflect, sir, turn the subject in your own mind, and if it amounts to any thing more, say what that any thing is.

If this be its amount, is it possible for any man possessing a distinguishing mind, to hesitate one moment in pronouncing the argument conclusive against those who urge it?

If it be intended as a restraint on the power of removal given by the constitution, then the restriction being expressed without limitation, must apply to any or all the departments, to which the power designed to be restrained, is given. I ask you sir, if this be not the plain and inevitable conclusion from the words used and from the argument.

'The judges shall hold their offices during good behavior.' This say gentlemen is only to restrain the implied power of removal given in the constitution. Then, does it not restrain that power in any department implied to possess it? And can it be exercised by a department, to which the constitution neither gives it expressly nor by implication?

Let us suppose the implied powers of removing officers generally, to have been expressed, and then apply to them the restrictive clause of the constitution, as it is actually expressed.

They would stand thus. The legislative or executive may remove at pleasure all officers who shall be appointed, except the judges; but 'the judges both of the supreme and inferior courts, shall hold their offices during good behavior.'

Or thus:

The executive alone shall possess the power of removing at pleasure all officers except the judges who 'shall hold their offices during good behaviour.'

If the implication be conformable to the first statement; if under the constitution the power of removal may be exercised by either the legislative or executive, then the man would be thought insane himself, or to suppose those he addresses to be so; who, in any other times than these, would pronounce the restraining, not to be co-extensive with the empowering clause.

If the second statement be supposed to express what the constitution implies, then let me ask with what propriety can the legislature exercise in any form, the power of removal? If the power of removing from, like that of nominating to office, be exclusively in the executive, is it not usurpation in the legislature to claim it?

The restraining clause, accompanying and limiting the power of removal wherever it is to be found, restrains the exercise of that power wherever it may be placed, so far as respects the judges. If it be in the legislature then the legislature is forbidden to use it as to the judges; if it be not in the legislature, then to usurp it is tyranny.

Can the legislature exercise a power not given by the constitution? You, I am inclined to think, will admit that it cannot. The ministerial party, however disposed to sophisticate away the plain meaning of words, will not yet, in direct terms, aver that it can. If so, the power of removal from office must be given by the constitution, or it cannot exist. I call that given which is fairly to be implied from the nature, of powers expressly granted. If it be given either in express terms or by implication, then it is restrained so far as respects the judges, by the clause declaring that they shall hold their offices during good behavior. If it be not given to the legislature, but is exclusively bestowed on another department, so that the restriction on the power applies to that other department, then it is not less a violation of the constitution to usurp it.

Than this my mind is incapable of conceiving a clearer proposition.

If it be a power incidental to legislation, I answer that an incidental power cannot be stronger, or less subject to limitation, than one granted by express words; an express grant to the legislature of the general power of removal from office, would, it has been shown, be restrained by the clause declaring that power not to extend to the judges, who are to hold their offices during good behavior. Then an incidental power of removal must be restrained by the same clause.

The delusion of the moment must pass away. The Genius of America only sleeps. It cannot be dead. It will arouse itself, and shake off the thick veil of prejudice now cast over the public mind. When that shall happen, what sir, will be the opinion entertained of you, if it shall be believed that you were the advocate of the present system?

A PLAIN MAN.

Printed copy (*Washington Federalist*, 8 Mar. 1802).

1. Article 3, section 1, of the U.S. Constitution.

2. The writer was probably referring to JM's support of the Judiciary Act of 1789, in which JM advocated a federal judiciary "co-extensive" with the executive and legislative branches of

government, where judicial power was "made effective for its objects" and where judges would "hold their tenures during good behavior, by virtue of the constitution" (*PJM*, 12:367–68). The constitutional debate over the repeal of the Judiciary Act of 1801 is discussed in Ellis, *The Jeffersonian Crisis*, pp. 36–52.

§ From Rufus King. *8 March 1802, London*. No. 56. Reports that Austria is "highly dissatisfied, as justly she may be, with the issue of the meeting at Lyons."[1] Obstacles delaying conclusion of definitive peace treaty and the "unexampled stagnation of the Trade of this Country" have abated ardor for peace in Great Britain as well. This change in the "temper of the public mind" is attributed to Napoleon, whose views are "inconsistent with the Repose and independence of every part of Europe." Adds that "Instructions have been sent to all the Naval Arsenals to prepare the Ships of War for actual Service; the channel fleet will immediately sail, and . . . these demonstrations are accompanied by an explicit Demand on the part of England that the definitive Treaty . . . be signed without any farther Delay." Still believes that peace will be concluded; England will not "depart from the Preliminaries"; France will sign because it is extremely advantageous to do so.

RC (DNA: RG 59, DD, Great Britain, vol. 10); letterbook copy (NHi: Rufus King Papers, vol. 55). RC 2 pp.; in a clerk's hand, signed by King; docketed by Brent. Printed in King, *Life and Correspondence of Rufus King*, 4:78–79.

1. For the result of the Lyons council, see King to JM, 27 Feb. 1802, *PJM-SS*, 2:496 and n. 1.

From Rufus King

No. 57.

SIR,   LONDON Mar. 9. 1802.

As your Letters to me concerning Mr. Ervings appointments do not explicitly state the Presidents intentions in respect to his being employed as an Assessor to the Commission under the seventh article of our Treaty with this Country,[1] I desired him to send to the Board an Extract of his Instructions which define his Duties and which would be Sufficient to shew the Presidents expectation on this point. I at the same time wrote a Letter to the Board Copies of which, and of their Answer, you will find annexed.[2]

I likewise subjoin the Copy of a Note from the Prussian Charge d'affaires, to which I have answered, that I would lose no time in apprizing you of its Contents.[3] With perfect Respect and Esteem, I have the honour to be, Sir, Your ob. & faithful servt.

RUFUS KING

RC and enclosures (DNA: RG 59, DD, Great Britain, vol. 10); letterbook copy (NHi: Rufus King Papers, vol. 55). RC in a clerk's hand, signed by King; docketed by Brent as received 31 May. For enclosures, see nn. 2 and 3.

1. JM wrote to King on 27 July 1801 regarding Erving's appointment (see *PJM-SS*, 1:482 n.; printed in King, *Life and Correspondence of Rufus King*, 4:80 n.).

2. King enclosed a copy of an 8 Mar. 1802 letter to him from the Board of Commissioners (3 pp.), signed by John Trumbull, Maurice Swabey, John Anstey, Christopher Gore, and William Pinkney, stating that they could not receive Erving as assessor on the grounds explained in the enclosed extract (5 pp.) from the minutes of their proceedings of 2 Mar. The minutes included transcripts of JM's 27 July 1801 letter to Erving and King's letter to the Board of Commissioners, 27 Feb. 1802, stating that Erving was appointed to replace both Samuel Williams as agent for claims and appeals and Samuel Cabot as assessor. The board concluded that the two appointments were incompatible, and they forwarded a 4 Mar. letter Erving wrote to them after being informed of their decision (1 p.), offering to withdraw from the office of assessor (see also Erving to JM, 6 Mar. 1802 [two letters], and Pinkney and Gore to JM, 9 Mar. 1802).

3. King enclosed an 8 Mar. 1802 letter to him (1 p.; in French) from Louis Balan, informing him that Jacob Eberhard August Steinmetz had been appointed Prussian consul at Charleston.

§ From Christopher Gore and William Pinkney. *9 March 1802, London.* Informs JM that Rufus King "has addressed to the Board an official Notification" of the president's appointment of George W. Erving to succeed Williams and Cabot. "The general Terms of this Notification . . . have been explained by an Extract of a Letter of the Secretary of State to Mr. Erving of the 27th. of July last. . . . Altho' it will be manifest upon a bare perusal of our Letter of the 17th. ulto.[1] that it was written under less precise notions of the actual views of the Government on this Subject than are furnished by this Extract, we think it proper expressly to state that we were at that Time ignorant of the Intentions of the President that Mr Erving should supersede Mr. Cabot in the Employment of assessor to our Board. The only knowledge we had then procured of Mr. Ervings appointments . . . did not lead us to suppose that any other Character was meant than such as Mr. Cabot had filled under the appointment of the Government of the United States. As Mr. Erving has never made any Communication whatsoever to the American Commissioners on the subject of his appointments . . . we were consequently more exposed to a misconception of the true extent of the wishes of the President in his favor." Explains that Cabot was sent to London by President Washington in 1796 "to assist the Sufferers by Spoliation in making out their Statements of Loss and Damage, in Collecting and arranging their Proof, and in obviating its defects; for which services he was to receive a fixed Salary payable by the United States." Shortly after his arrival the board recognized the need for two experienced merchants to assess damages in the cases referred to them; on 1 Feb. 1797 they passed an order to that effect, and Glennie and Cabot were formally appointed. The board stipulated their duties and paid them out of the common fund established for the board's expenses. "It was in form and substance the act of the Board in all its Stages. . . . It is with our Duties that they are charged." States that to entrust this work "to any but Persons approved by ourselves would be to trifle with our Oaths and to equivocate with our Duty." The enclosed copy of the proceedings of the board on 2 Mar. shows that upon formal objections by one of the British commissioners, the board was compelled, though with great reluctance, "to decline Mr. Ervings assistance as one of their

Assessors." They are persuaded that Erving's nomination "has arisen entirely from some accidental misapprehension in the United States, as to the origin, nature, and Duties of this employment." Even so, "it is our Duty to say that our own opinions have not been declared to be in favor of Mr. Erving." The objection to the employment of the advocate for claimants as assessor of damages to be awarded to those claimants is "too strong to be resisted." Encloses Erving's letter of 4 Mar. showing "the Result of his Reflections" on the subject. Points out that "it does not seem to be probable that his opportunities of mercantile Experience have been equal to the diversified and complicated Purposes of our Assessorship—or that his Leisure is likely to be such as to put it in his power to discharge its Duties." Cabot by contrast has given his "diligent and undivided attention to the Business." Expresses the hope that the president will "see fit to grant to the original choice of the Board (still approved by every member of it) the aid we have already had the Honor to ask for it."

RC and enclosures (DNA: RG 76, Great Britain, Treaty of 1794 [Art. 7], Papers Relative to the Commissioners, vol. 4); draft (owned by William Reese Company, New Haven, 1988). RC 10 pp.; in a clerk's hand, signed by Gore and Pinkney; docketed by Brent as received 26 May. Draft in Pinkney's hand. Enclosures (9 pp.) are a copy of the Board of Commissioners' 8 Mar. 1802 letter to Rufus King and its enclosures (for another copy, see King to JM, 9 Mar. 1802, n. 2).

1. *PJM-SS*, 2:473–74.

To Horatio Gates

MY DEAR SIR   WASHINGTON Mar. 10. 1802

I duly recd. your two kind letters of the 11 & 16. Ult:[1] the former by the mail, the latter by Genl Stephens. I need not assure you that the requests of both have been attended to, but I ought to account for the delay in acknowledging them, by pleading the frailty & fluctuations incident to my health. I learn with much pleasure that you enjoy so comfortable a share of this blessing, and that it is doubled to you by the full measure of it enjoyed by Mrs. Gates.

The politics of the present day present so wide a field, that both for your sake & my own, I will no farther glance at the subject than to congratulate you that Europe once more sees the sword in the scabbard, and that notwithstanding the menacing tone within the doors of Congress, there appears little danger that our internal tranquility will be disturbed. The Newspapers will give you Lear's information from St. Domingo which is again becoming a Theatre of blood & devastation.[2]

I thank you most cordially for the invitation to your hospitable mansion, but I can not promise myself the benefit of it. In my relaxation, from this place, I am obliged to keep in mind that I am a farmer, and am willing to flatter myself, that my farm will be the better for my presence.

I return you the letter from Genl. Armstrong,[3] whose great talents are acknowledged I find by all parties, & consequently whose resignation could not fail to excite regret in the one which claimed them. It is fortunate that he has found so respectable a successor.

Mrs. Madison offers her affectionate regards to Mrs. Gates & yourself, to which you will both permit me to add mine. Yrs. very sincerely & respectfully

JAMES MADISON

RC (NN: Emmet Collection).

1. *PJM-SS*, 2:457, 470.
2. The *National Intelligencer* of 10 Mar. 1802 published extracts of Tobias Lear's 12 Feb. letter to JM describing the arrival of the Leclerc expedition and its efforts to reassert French sovereignty in Saint-Domingue (see *PJM-SS*, 2:462–64).
3. For John Armstrong's letter to Gates on the former's resignation, see Gates to JM, 16 Feb. 1802 (*PJM-SS*, 2:470, 471 n. 2).

§ To Edward Jones. *10 March 1802, Department of State, Washington.* "Your Letters of the 13th. January and 8th. february have been received.[1] Tho' the Consular Act allows but 12 Cents a day to shipwrecked, sick, or captive seamen, other Laws have been since passed from year to year allowing a reimbursement to the Consuls who may *necessarily* exceed that sum. No appropriation for the purpose has been passed this year, but it is hardly to be doubted that it will be done before the session closes."

Letterbook copy (DNA: RG 59, IC, vol. 1). 1 p.

1. *PJM-SS*, 2:393, 450.

§ From David Lenox. *10 March 1802, London.* Acknowledges receipt of JM's 1 Jan. letter in answer to his of 12 Oct. 1801[1] requesting the president's permission to return to the U.S. "I had with you anticipated the discharge of all Seamen claiming protection as American Citizens on Peace taking place, . . . under the idea that as Men would not be wanted for the Navy, this Government would prefer discharging those who might be supposed most dissatisfied with the Service, but in this I have been disappointed." Encloses copies of his correspondence with the Admiralty on the subject. Although impressments have ceased, applications continue to be made from seamen on ships arriving from foreign nations, "& since my last return, to the 1st. Insta⟨nt⟩ they Amount to ninety five." Also encloses a list of "the cases of Seamen where proof's have been transmitted from the Department of State, unanswered at the date of my last Return, as well as . . . those cases where proof has since been received." Definitive treaty has not yet been signed. Plans to embark for the U.S. in May; will "on my arrival repair to the seat of Government."

RC and enclosures (DNA: RG 59, CD, London, vol. 8). RC 3 pp.; docketed by Brent as received 19 May. Enclosures are Lenox to Evan Nepean, 17 Oct. 1801 (2 pp.), stating his wish to terminate his official agency as soon as possible, offering to provide a list of all seamen who claimed to be Americans but were detained because they lacked documents to prove their citizenship, and requesting that when these men were discharged they be furnished with proof of the wages due them; Nepean to Lenox, 20 Oct. 1801 (2 pp.), stating that the commissioners of Admiralty had no objection to his proposal; Lenox to Nepean, 23 Oct. 1801 (3 pp.), enclosing a list of 558 seamen who had been refused discharge by the Admiralty because they had no citizenship documents and asking for their release on the grounds that they would not be needed during peacetime; William Marsden to Lenox, 26 Oct. 1801 (3 pp.), informing him that the commissioners of Admiralty had denied his request, both because the cases in question had already been considered and because "the admission of the principle that a Man declaring himself to belong to a foreign State should upon that assertion merely . . . be suffered to leave the service would be productive of the most dangerous consequences"; and a list (2 pp.) of 26 impressed seamen with the action taken by the Admiralty on their cases. JM transmitted extracts from the RC and enclosed correspondence to the House of Representatives on 22 Dec. 1802 (printed in *ASP, Foreign Relations*, 2:472–73).

    1. *PJM-SS*, 2:172–73, 362.

§ From Stephen Sayre. *10 March 1802, Philadelphia*. "Knowing, that I have not only deserved well of my country, but that my sufferings intitle me to high expectations, I cannot yet persuade myself to believe, that you will much longer leave me to lament the sacrifises I have made.[1] . . . *I ask to be replaced, in some degree, to that independence, which has been taken away, by the enemies of my country*. . . . There are some situations which, I am confident, I can fill with honor to your choise—you must forgive me therefore, if I see others, who have less experience, & slender pretensions, when compared to mine, repeatedly prefer'd, in filling the list of preferment, & patronage. . . . Be pleased to look back . . . & conscientiously say, that all the appointments, even in your own department, have been decided, by the weight of superior talents, & fitness for office?—in other departments, the world knows they were not. Are you resolved, seriously, & rigidly, to pursue your maxim, well express'd in your letter, you did me the honor to write, on my return from Washington[2]—if you are, I am more than confident, that I cannot be long neglected. . . . I beseech you to believe, that your best friends, who know me, in this city, are astonish'd, & deeply lament, the apathy of an administration, who may be said, to be of their own election, in the long neglect of men, who ought to be remember'd, & that those who deserve execration are still continued in the most honorable, & profitable employments—the friends of the President excuse him by presuming he is govern'd by the disposition of his Ministers. . . . I do not pretend to know, how far, or in what cases Mr Jefferson leaves the choise of public servants to the heads of departments—I recollect however, that he refer'd me to yourself, when I had the favor of a conversation in your office. No arrangements having then been made—I return'd without complaining; resolved to wait, till you had fair opportunity of gratifying my hopes. . . . As to any immoral action, tending to dishonor—I never have committed one. . . . Must I then suppose myself wanting in talents? I had not this character in England—men of the first capacity, & highest reputation did not think it degrading to call me their friend—most men there, thought it an honor. . . . I cannot conclude this letter without saying, I think it hard, indeed, that you will not inform me, whether I may, or may not expect, some employment. Presuming you must, 'er this know your own intention, as well as that of the President—there can be no state of the mind so unpleasant as that of uncertainty & suspence. You will therefore do me a favor, to inform me what I ought to expect."

RC (DLC). 4 pp.

1. For Sayre's claims for compensation and patronage from the government for his Revolutionary War services, see his letters to JM of 16 May, 9 June, and 21 and 30 Oct. 1801 (*PJM-SS*, 1:186–87 and n. 1, 284–87, 2:190–91, 213).
2. JM to Sayre, 23 May 1801 (not found, but calendared in *PJM-SS*, 1:226).

From Stephen Girard

Sir   Philadelphia 11 March 1802

The Inclosed is copy of a Memorial which I have delivred to the Secretary of State in the year 1795[1] although I have ever Since that period been very industrious in requesting my friends in Europe to take every Steps to recover my just claim against the french Republic I am Still unpaid being desirous to Settle that business I am induced to Send to Paris the bearer of this letter Mr Jos: Curwen[2] for the purpose of Soliciting payment.

Persuaded of your good disposition towards rendring justice to the Citizens of the U States I take the liberty to beg as a particular favour that you will give Mr Joseph Curwen a letter for the Minister Plenipotentiary of the U States at Paris requesting that Gentleman to make Such application to the french Government as you will judge proper. I am with Respect Sir your mo: obt Servt

STEPHN. GIRARD

RC (DLC); letterbook copy (PPGi: Girard Papers). Enclosure not found.

1. Girard's claims included reimbursement for supplies provided to the French government at Saint-Domingue in 1792 and 1793 as well as indemnification for the capture and condemnation of his vessels *Kitty* in 1794 and *Nancy* in 1795 (Albert J. Gares, "Stephen Girard's West Indian Trade," *Pa. Magazine of History and Biography*, 72 [1948]: 333–34).
2. Joseph Curwen was a Philadelphia merchant and Girard's business associate. Despite nearly a year in France, he failed to settle the claims (L. H. Butterfield, ed., *Letters of Benjamin Rush* [2 vols.; Princeton, N.J., 1951], 2:1082 n. 3; John Bach McMaster, *The Life and Times of Stephen Girard: Mariner and Merchant* [Philadelphia, 1918], p. 439).

§ From Levi Lincoln. *11 March 1802, Washington.* Relates circumstances of the case of the vessel *Mercator*,[1] "alledged to be Danish property, and for the capture of which a claim is now made on the United States." The *Mercator* was seized off

Saint-Domingue by the American schooner *Experiment* on 14 May 1800; six hours later, while sailing under the American flag, it was seized by the British armed ship *General Simcoe* and taken into Jamaica, where the vessel and cargo were condemned in vice-admiralty court as lawful prize of the British captors. "There is no circumstance seperate from the decision of the admiralty court, by which it can be determined, that either of the seizures were justifiable. The legal presumptions are, however, in favor of them." States his opinion that "if the Danish subject has sustained an injury, or has cause of complaint it is against the british. The first captors are not liable for the conduct of the second. . . . On general principles, the Danish subject ought to resort to the british captors for his compensation. . . . But admitting the American Captor liable, on a lengthy and critical research, I can find no principle of the law of nations, or adjudication, by which the Government is bound to answer in the first instance, for the unlawfull captures of its subjects, or become so, from their insolvency, or avoidance." Concludes that the U.S. ought not to interfere in the case "unless it be to aid the sufferer by their weight, in his application to the british Government."

RC (DNA: RG 59, LOAG). 3 pp.; docketed by Brent. Printed in Hall, *Official Opinions of the Attorneys General*, 1:106–8.

1. For Jared Shattuck's *Mercator* claim, see Richard Söderström to JM, 10 June 1801, and Peder Blicherolsen to JM, 16 Jan. 1802 (*PJM-SS*, 1:290–92, 295 n. 1, 2:401).

From the American Whig Society

(Circular)

Dr Sir.   Princeton March 12th. 1802.

The American Whig Society, in the college of N. Jersey, having, by the late unfortunate conflagration which consumed the College edifice, lost almost the whole of their valuable library,[1] together with all their furniture, have resolved to apply to their ancient members who are now established in different quarters of the United States, to solicit their generous, and brotherly aid in repa[i]ring their important losses. The library at the time it was consumed, consisted of about 800 volumes, estimated at the value of 3,000 Dolls. The other effects amounted to about 800 Dollars.

As the College is likely to be replaced in its former state, or even in better condition than it was, we are ambitious to restore our institution to its former respectability. Animated with this desire, we take the liberty, which we hope will be approved, of addressing individually all our absent members who still feel for the honour, and utility of a Society in which they have formerly reaped so much pleasure, and improvement. A small aid from each in books, or in money addressed to John Middleton Clk of the Committee,

to the care of the Revd. Saml. Stanhope Smith, will be received as the gift
of a brother.

J. MIDDLETON Clk.
of the Committee

Wm. A. Neill, Jno. Boggs, A. Johnston &
Thos. H Ellis committee in behalf of
the American Whig Society.

RC (NjP).

1. The Nassau Hall fire of 6 Mar. 1802 destroyed nearly the entire libraries of the two
literary societies and all except one hundred of the college library's three thousand books. The
college president, Samuel Stanhope Smith, blamed the fire on a group of Jacobin-inspired
students (Mark A. Noll, *Princeton and the Republic, 1768–1822: The Search for a Christian En-
lightenment in the Era of Samuel Stanhope Smith* [Princeton, N.J., 1989], pp. 157–59). Smith
indicated in a letter to Aaron Burr that he had written to JM asking him to cooperate with
Burr in fund-raising efforts, but that letter has not been found (Smith to Burr, 12 Mar. 1802,
Kline, *Papers of Burr*, 2:690).

§ From Richard Cooper. *13 March 1802, Cooperstown.* "I have to inform you that I
have sold the greatest part of the articles in my possession belonging to the United
States, and I hope to be able in a few weeks to make a final settlement with
Government."[1]

Tr (DNA: RG 233, President's Messages, 7A-D1). 1 p. Marked "Copy." Enclosed in JM
to Jefferson, 29 Mar. 1802, and transmitted to the House of Representatives, 31 Mar. 1802
(*Annals of Congress*, 7th Cong., 1st sess., 1119).

1. For Cooper's aborted expedition to Lake Superior and JM's demand that he sell the
property purchased for the trip, see JM to Cooper, 13 May and 6 Nov. 1801 (*PJM-SS*, 1:170,
171 nn., 2:226).

§ From Rufus King. *13 March 1802, London.* No. 58. Reports there is no further
information on the negotiations at Amiens since his last letter. In a "*free conversation*," Addington "*yesterday told me that* during the last Fortnight *his mind had* bal-
anced whether *to wish the conclusion or rupture of the negotiation*" but that the British
were ready to sign a definitive treaty "provided it be done without any farther
Delay." Fleets are preparing for sea; if negotiations fail, war will resume "with encreased activity and zeal." Suggests Napoleon may believe that war would promote
his own views and authority more than peace. Great Britain may also see war as
preferable to "*the only peace* now to be obtained." Apprehends a "most serious interruption" of U.S. trade in the West Indies if war is renewed. Will attempt to secure
just treatment from Great Britain for American navigation should negotiations fail.

RC (DNA: RG 59, DD, Great Britain, vol. 10); letterbook copy (NHi: Rufus King Papers,
vol. 55). RC 2 pp.; in a clerk's hand, signed by King; docketed by Brent as received 10 June.
Italicized words were written in code; key not found. RC decoded interlinearly by Wagner.
Printed in King, *Life and Correspondence of Rufus King*, 4:81.

To Robert R. Livingston

DEAR SIR   DEPARTMENT OF STATE March 14. 1802

This will be handed to you by Mr. Curwan who is charged with sundry claims by Mr. Stephan Gerard of Philada. against the French Republic.[1] Mr. Gerard is a very respectable Merchant & Citizen of the U. States, and feels so strongly both the justice & importance of his claims, as to depute Mr. Curwan to Paris for the purpose of supporting them. He has expressed an anxiety also that they should be particularly recommended to your patronage, which you will permit me to do in consideration both of his personal character, and of the extensive wrongs he has suffered. The same anxiety has been expressed by Capt Jones the representative of the City of Philada. in Congress who takes a warm interest in behalf of his friend Mr. Gerard. Mr. Curwan will give you all the explanations due to the case, and will I am persuaded, experience from you all the aid in it, which it is proper for you to bestow. With the sincerest esteem & regard I remain Dear Sir Your Obedt. hbl sert.

JAMES MADISON

RC (NHi: Livingston Papers). Cover marked by JM, "Mr. Curwan." Docketed by Livingston.

1. See Stephen Girard to JM, 11 Mar. 1802, and nn.

From Robert R. Livingston

(No. 7 Copy)

DEAR SIR,   PARIS 24th. [14] March 1802

I yesterday recieved the duplicate and triplicate of your letter of the 19th. december last the original not having come to hand.[1] This is the first and only letter I have been honored with from you since my arrival. I immediately sent one of the copies of the Presidents proclamation to the Minister of Foreign Relations with the enclosed note no. 1.[2]

I had before anticipated the inconveniences that peace might occasion to our commerce and as I found that the subject was but little understood here and that it was the favorite idea that France had nothing to do to make herself a great naval power but to imitate the British restrictions upon the commerce of other nations—I threw together some hasty thoughts upon the subject which I put into the hands of Marbois, Consul le Brun (who reads english) Mr. Volney &c. and at the same time prepared a translation that I got other members of the court to read. I enclose a copy of it.[3] Most of the persons to whom I gave a perusal of it were struck with many circumstances in it which they had not adverted to—but it is a rule here that no person intrudes an idea on the first Consul unless he asks their opinion or the conversation naturally leads to it.

The favorite idea at present is a navigation law and restrictive duties to confine the carrying trade to themselves. In conversation with Taleyrand I proposed to him some such commercial arrangements as present circumstances appeared to exact and hinted at the disadvantage that might result from a number of our seamen going into the British service. But he declined doing any thing in the business and defered it till Mr. Otto should go to America.[4] The fact is that *Taleyrand is decidedly unfriendly to the United States.*

On recieving your letter I yesterday sent him the Note No. 2.[5] I had before mentioned to you the duty on tobacco and what I thought the best means of counteracting it. I shall send you a tariff of the duties as soon as I can get it made out, which is a matter of much more difficulty here than in other countries. On the business of Louisiana they have as yet not thought it proper to give me any explanations tho I have omitted no opportunity to press the subject in conversation and ultimately by the note sent you on the 25th. February (a duplicate of which was forwarded on the 28) with the copy of another note enforcing the above, to which I have as yet recieved no answer.[6]

The fact is they believe us to be certainly hostile to this measure and they mean to take possession of it as early as possible and with as little notice to us as they can.

They are made to believe this is one of the most fertile and important countries in the World, that they have a much greater interest with the indians than any other people, that New Orleans must command the trade of our whole Western country And of course that they will have a leading interest in its politics. It is a darling object with the First Consul who sees in it a mean to gratify his friends and to dispose of his Armies. There is a man here who calls himself a frenchman by the name of Francis Tatergeny[7] and pretends to have great interest with the Creek Nations. He has been advanced to the rank of a General of division. He persuades them that the indians are extremely attached to France and hate the Americans, that they can raise 20,000 warriors, that the country is a Paradise &c. &c. I believe him to be a mere adventurer but he is listened to & was first taken up by the old Directors.

I cannot help thinking that it would be adviseable for the present Congress to take Measures for establishing the Natchez or some other port and giving it such advantages as would bring our vessels to it without touching at Orleans—on this subject however you will form a better judgement than I can. I have but one hope left as to defeating this cession it consists in *alarming Spain and England.* The *Spanish minister* is now *absent but* I have not *failed to shew* in the *strongest light* to the *minister of Britain the dangers that will resul*t to them from the *extension of the French possessions into Mexico* and the probable *loss of Canada* if they are *suffered to possess it.*

I have requested Mr. King to press this subject also as opportunity offers. I enclose a copy of my last letter to him.[8] If the treaty does not close soon I think it would be adviseable for us to meet at Amiens & have accordingly proposed it to him.

I believe that such is the state of things here and such the desire for peace that *Britain may force them to relinquish Louisiana* particularly as the people here are far from desiring *the establishment of any foreign colonies which they consider as weak points & drains* for the *population & wealth.* Prussia and the Emperor have acquiesed in the business of the Italian Republic. Britain still keeps possession of Alexandria.

On the business of payments I can add nothing new. My notes are still unanswered, tho I am promised that they shall be within a few days as well as those that relate to the conduct of the council of Prizes of which we have some cause of complaint tho in fact much less than the clamors of some ship owners would make us believe. My notes enumerate all the cases I have been able to collect—and upon two the Ann and the commerce it is very problematical whether the decisions are not conformable to the treaty. The discharge however in *the state they now are*[9] and the enormous bills of charges in many cases render the acquittal illusory. I have remonstrated on the subject—as have the Ministers of Denmark and Sweden but no answer has been recieved by either of us.

I have also ventured to make the enclosed proposition on the subject of the debt[10] prompted by the desire of satisfying the numerous American creditors and believing that the guarantee of a loan would not be very dangerous on our part as the amount would not be considerable & I mean If the thing should be acceeded to to take such Measures of security as I think will render us safe. At all events the whole amount will remain among us—and perhaps it would be better to facilitate a credit in this way than to suffer them to go on ruining individuals from whom they will obtain them. My last note suggests what I think the duty of our government relative to this object. I very much fear that the necessities of the Armament will induce them to embroil us anew by seizing our property in the islands & even at sea.

I only hint at this that measures of precaution may be taken. I should however mention that nothing I believe will be done on the subject of the note as I fear they have already sold the greater part of the dutch debt. For the fact is that nothing which could be converted into money has escaped the rapacity of Government or individuals.

I have with great difficulty procured an order for the payment of Archambals bills for the Trumbul and Olive after the owners had waited here 6 months and then without interest or damages. The demand of the Pegou is I hope also in the way of payment.[11]

As to the Contract demands the Minister of Marine told me I might as well ask him to cut off his fathers head as to ask payment.

However on this subject I shall be better informed when they reply to my note. I believe that they may possibly put the debt upon their 5 pr Ct. loan which is now at 57. but will in that case fall considerably—so that at most the creditor after waiting many years will sink half his debt—but as they hint necessity has no Law. Their expenses exceed their income and the government is at this moment maintained by anticipations at an interest of from 12 to 18 pr Ct. Notwithstanding this apparent scarcity of money extravagance of every kind is at the highest pitch and every article of life double its former price. I must again mention that I recieve no Newspapers from America till after they are too old to be interesting except what I get from my private friends.[12] The œconomy that forbids them to come from the seaports by post has rendered the sending them at all useless and they may as well remain in the Printers shops as at Bourdeaux or Nantes. The postage of news papers is very trifling if only put in wrappers. 7 papers will cost less than 6d. I have had one letter from Mr. Pinckney but it contains no information on the subject of Louisiana. The enclosed letter from Mr. Obrien[13] having been sent open to me I availed myself of the information it contained by a communication of it to the Neapolitan Embassador who stands very well here urging the policy of availing himself of this moment of discontent with France England & Algiers to get the subject taken up at Amiens—where nothing has yet been concluded. You will remark a passage in General LeClercs communication to this government of which I am afraid I shall hear more.[14] I am Dear Sir, with much consideration & respect your Mt. Obt. Hle. St

Robt R Livingston

RC and enclosures (DNA: RG 59, DD, France, vol. 8); draft (NHi: Livingston Papers); letterbook copy and copies of enclosures (NHi: Livingston Papers, vol. 1). RC in a clerk's hand, signed by Livingston. RC misdated; correct date supplied from letterbook copy (see also n. 1). Unless otherwise noted, italicized words and letters are those encoded by Livingston's secretary and decoded here by the editors (for the code, see *PJM-SS*, 2:304–5 n.). RC decoded interlinearly by JM. For surviving enclosures, see nn. 2, 5, and 8.

1. The duplicate of JM's letter to Livingston, 19 Dec. 1801, is docketed as received 13 Mar. 1802 (*PJM-SS*, 2:322–24 and n.).

2. Livingston's enclosure no. 1 is a copy of his letter to Talleyrand, 13 Mar. 1802 (2 pp.), which covered a copy of Jefferson's proclamation promulgating the Convention of 1800 and noted, "By this it will appear that the government of the United States did not consider the explanation annexed by that of the French Republic as occasioning any change in the treaty

or requiring a new ratification." Livingston added that a law making appropriations for executing the American obligations had been under consideration by Congress and "has undoubtedly passed before this."

3. According to Livingston's "Journal of correspondence with the Secretary of State" (NHi: Livingston Papers, vol. 7) this enclosure was a copy of an essay by Livingston "on the relative situation of France B[ritai]n & Amer[i]ca as commercial & Maritime nations." Its receipt was acknowledged by François Barbé-Marbois, 20 Pluviôse an X (9 Feb. 1802), and by Charles-François Lebrun, 21 Pluviôse an X (10 Feb. 1802) (NHi: Livingston Papers). The essay is printed in *ASP, Foreign Relations,* 2:578–81.

4. Louis-Guillaume Otto, the French minister to Great Britain, refused the appointment as minister to the U.S. and in 1803 was sent as minister to Bavaria (Jean Tulard et al., *Dictionnaire Napoléon* [Paris, 1987], p. 1276).

5. Enclosure no. 2 is a copy of another letter to Talleyrand dated 13 Mar. (3 pp.), in which Livingston announced that Congress was considering a law repealing duties which discriminated between imports in foreign vessels and those in U.S. vessels and that the British legislature was considering a similar law. He urged Talleyrand to examine "the alterations that will be made between the relative situation of Great Britain, the United States and France by the reciprocal repeal of discriminating duties by the two former, while they continue to burthen and impede the activity of commerce between the two latter."

6. Livingston referred to the notes enclosed in his letter to JM of 26 Feb. 1802 (*PJM-SS,* 2:493, 494 nn. 1 and 2).

7. Louis Le Clerc Milfort (Milford) (ca. 1750–1817), also known as François Tastenegy, was a French adventurer who, by his own account, arrived in North America in 1775, traveled throughout the continent, and settled among the Creek Indians. He became friendly with Alexander McGillivray, whose sister he married, and fought alongside the Creek in various campaigns, gaining the title *tastanégy,* or warrior. Upon McGillivray's death in 1793, Milfort made a strong bid to replace him as head chief of the Creek but was disappointed and returned to France in 1795. There he mounted a campaign to have himself appointed ambassador to the Creek nation. His repeated attempts were unsuccessful. News of the retrocession revived his project, and believing the sale of Louisiana would be a dreadful mistake for France, he published his memoirs in 1802 under the title *Mémoire ou Coup-d'œil rapide sur mes différens voyages et mon séjour dans la nation Crëck* (Paris, 1802) (Milfort, *Memoirs; or, A Quick Glance at My Various Travels and My Sojourn in the Creek Nation,* trans. Ben C. McCary [1959; Savannah, 1972 reprint], pp. 7–12).

8. Livingston enclosed a copy of his letter to Rufus King, 10 Mar. 1802 (4 pp.; extract printed in *ASP, Foreign Relations,* 2:515), declaring that France had been placed at the mercy of Great Britain "by stripping herself of her fleet and a large army." On the other hand, he warned, should France take over Louisiana, "it is impossible to see the extent of the power she will have in and over America." He observed that since Louisiana had no precise boundary, the fate of Mexico was easy to predict. The boundary between Canada and Louisiana was also unsettled, and the native Canadians and the Indian tribes had always been friendly to France, so that "it is impossible to say what [the French] influence may be upon our western country in case of a controversy with Great Britain." Livingston concluded by offering to meet King at Amiens "if any opening is given for pressing the business of Louisiana."

9. Underlined in RC.

10. The document sent to JM has not been found, but it was probably a copy of Livingston's three-page memorandum, "American debt the means and Manner of discharging it with the smallest inconvenience to France" (AAE: Political Correspondence, U.S., 54:206–7, filed after Livingston to Talleyrand, 13 Mar. 1802). In it, Livingston proposed that the Batavian Republic, which was indebted to France for over 20 million florins, open a loan in Paris to which the American debt, once liquidated, would be subscribed. The loan would be guaran-

teed by France and repaid in installments, with interest of 6 percent per year payable quarterly. The U.S. government would at the same time allow France to open a loan for 5 million livres in the U.S. on much the same terms. The plan, according to Livingston, would give France immediate access to the Dutch debt and—from the U.S. loan—more than enough cash to cover purchases in the U.S.; the Dutch would be allowed to repay their debt in an orderly fashion; and the U.S. would gain "the reimbursement of an active Capital to her Citizens."

11. For the *Pégou*, see *PJM-SS*, 2:359, 360 n. 4, 467.

12. In response to complaints like this from Livingston and Charles Pinckney, JM directed Daniel Brent to write David Gelston in New York and George Latimer in Philadelphia on the subject. Brent relayed JM's instructions "that you avail yourself of all opportunities to forward to the Ministers entitled to them the papers in your Hands—and that you hereafter cause to be endorsed on the packages they form 'Newspapers, to be put in the Post Office'" (Brent to Gelston, 9 June 1802 [DNA: RG 59, DL, vol. 14]).

13. Livingston probably enclosed O'Brien's 1 Feb. 1802 dispatch to JM, in which the consul reported the British reaction to claims made by Algiers on property condemned by the British during the war. The dey insisted that no settlement would be made on thirty-five Neapolitan and Maltese ships Algiers had seized until the British made good on the Algerine claims (*PJM-SS*, 2:432–33).

14. For the passage referred to by Livingston, see his letter to JM of 15 Mar. 1802.

From Charles Pinckney

(Private)

DEAR SIR   March 14: 1802 IN MADRID

My last Dispatch[1] will have fully informed you of the state of things here my removal from the Escurial to Madrid & that Mr: Graham arrived here about the 20th: January. By him I recieved for the first time the Wish of our Government to endeavour to obtain the cession by sale from this Court of the Floridas[2] & as I know it would be difficult if not impossible to do so without the concurrence & perhaps aid of the influence of France I immediately wrote to Mr Livingston in cypher on the subject[3] & am now waiting his answer to commence the negotiation. I am hopeful it will arrive in time for this opportunity. If it does I shall without delay transmit the letter I have prepared to the secretary of state & will send you a copy of it. As the influence of the Prince of Peace at this court is all powerful & nothing of importance can be effected without his consent & indeed patronage I have prepared a copy of this application for his Use & am to be favoured with an interview in a particular & private manner with him on the subject & if any thing can be done, it is alone in this Way. My last letters will have informed you of the politeness & attention of the Ministers to Me since my arrival & of their apparent Wish to attend to my numerous applications for the release of Ships & cargoes & of their having directed the Quarantine to be discontinued in all cases of Vessels coming from Ports in which their Consuls certify there is no contagious Disorder. I have as yet expended no Money, or paid any for contingencies that come properly within the last Quarter, I shall close my accounts up to the last of this month & transmit them. I wrote to you that as it would be uncertain whether there would be Strength enough in the Senate to carry my confirmation that I would be obliged to you to give me the earliest information But that should it be otherwise & the confirmation carried that I wish the Presidents permission in the summer to visit Rome which can be accomplished in a few Weeks during the time the Court is absent on its Excursion to visit the Mediterranean Parts of Spain & meet the Naples Family on the occasion of the double marriage.[4] During this time nothing can be done & Before this the Florida Question will be decided to which I will pay unremitted attention. I wish much to go to Rome for a few Weeks & to walk on the same ground where Brutus & Cato once walked & I trust the President will have no objection. I have instructed all the Consuls as you directed respecting the Expenditure of monies & am incessantly engaged in endeavouring to obtain Releases of our Vessels & confirmation of some of the favourable decisions which have been given in their inferior tribunals. But the number of cases which are now before the Counsel of War is so great & some of them so intricate, & as their modes of proceeding are so extremely tedious, I have proposed to the Secretary To agree to the proposition sometime ago made by Colonel Humphreys for the appointment of Commissioners to decide the questions of Capture & Compensation by arbitration[5] in the former mode of one being appointed by each & those two to draw for the third—to be appointed of men highly distinguished for their knowledge & integrity & in situations of life to place them beyond the reach of an improper influence. My next to you will contain the whole of this & the Florida application—but as to the result it is impossible to say. You were right to conjecture in your private letter to me by Mr: Graham[6] that you did not hope much. More depends upon France in the Business a great deal than Spain. The Treaty which you have recieved between Lucien Bounaparte & the Prince of Peace expressly recognizes the Cession of Louisiana[7] & leaves no doubt on the subject. It is necessary for me to say here that *not having recieved your Letters* or any Direction respecting the attempt to obtain the two Floridas before 20 January it was impossible for me to move earlier in the Business than I have done. I have seen the Prince of Peace & am all ready & have been so for sometime waiting to hear from Mr Livingston respecting what he concieves to be the Wish or View of France in the Business. I have Written to him twice in Cypher & I mention these things to you to shew that I shall always endeavour to manifest the same zeal & activity in Business here that I trust I have invariably & in every instance done at home.

I had much doubt what I ought to do as to fixing myself with a house in Madrid. Because I feared our strength, until the Vermont & Mary Land Elections. When I heard of them I immediately took Colonel Humphreys[']s house & purchased all his furniture little doubting that from these recent Elections, if the republican interest is as true & honest as I believe it is & as I know they ought to be to one another that the nomination will be ultimately confirmed. If it is not, this purchase of furniture & my coming here will be a considerable inconvenience, But I will endeavour to make the best of it & will then on my own account but for the Benefit of my countrymen, set out to View the remainder of the most important parts of Europe which I have not yet seen & if nothing prevents, I am hopeful to return with the Languages & as intimate a knowledge of Europe, as any of our countrymen have done who have not staid longer than myself, & this additional knowledge which could only be acquired by a personal examination & attentive View of things at this very important period of the Peace, will enable me I trust when I return, to take my stand again in the field of politics with increased Weight. I confess as I mentioned to the President in one of my Letters, I should like much to remain two years more in a public character in Europe to compleat my Examinations & if this can be done, if not in Spain, in any proper situation elsewhere I hope he will do it & I will thank you to consider it. My Commission expires at the End of the Session of the Present Senate,[8] & as this is the long Session & much to do I shall consider that the last of April or the Beginning of May if I do not hear Before. Please direct to me to the care of Patrick Joyes & Hijos & present me in the most affectionate & respectful terms to the President & Believe me my dear Sir with great regard & affectionate respect & attachment Yours Truly

CHARLES PINCKNEY

RC (DLC).

1. Letter not found.

2. For JM's instructions for obtaining the cession of the Floridas, see his letter to Pinckney, 25 Sept. 1801 (*PJM-SS*, 2:131–32).

3. See Pinckney to Livingston, 4 Feb. 1802 (NHi: Livingston Papers).

4. Pinckney referred to the marriages of Francisco Gennaro, prince of Naples, to the infanta María Isabel of Spain and Fernando, prince of Asturias, to Princess María Antonia of Naples. The double marriage between first cousins took place on 4 Oct. 1802 (Douglas Hilt, *The Troubled Trinity: Godoy and the Spanish Monarchs* [Tuscaloosa, Ala., 1987], pp. 134–36).

5. David Humphreys's proposal for a bilateral claims commission was renewed as late as June 1801 (see Humphreys to JM, 29 June 1801, *PJM-SS*, 1:361).

6. Letter not found.

7. For the Treaty of Aranjuez, see Rufus King to JM, 20 Nov. 1801 (*PJM-SS*, 2:254, 255 n. 1).

8. Pinckney's new commission as minister to Spain was enclosed in JM's letter of 5 Feb. 1802 (*PJM-SS*, 2:442 and n. 4).

§ From Fulwar Skipwith. *14 March 1802, Paris.* Has not written to JM since Livingston's arrival, having had nothing to report on American claims. "Respecting those Claims, I here submit two separate Statements,[1] the first comprehending, under different heads, such as were committed to my charge, whilst in the Office of Consul General, and those . . . that have been intrusted to me, since my coming to the place of Commercial Agent. The second Statement exhibits, with remarks on the Papers wanting those that cannot be prosecuted untill the necessary Documents shall be sent forward.[2] All of the first Class are now before the Commission of *Comptabilité,* for the Purpose of being revised and liquidated, . . . but [the commission's] powers only extend to giving Certificates of liquidation, which are afterwards subject to the Inspection and Controul of the Government." Doubts that Livingston's efforts to obtain relief for claimants will be successful; "I am but too well satisfied that he will not find in the Governt. either the intention or disposition of rendering Justice on the score of my Countrymen's Claims." Under this impression and having little else to do, plans to embark in early summer on a visit to Virginia, leaving Thomas Melville, Jr., in charge of agency business. Seeks president's approval.

RC (DNA: RG 59, CD, Paris, vol. 1); enclosures (DLC: Causten-Pickett Papers, French Spoliation Claims, A-C, box 9). RC 3 pp.; in a clerk's hand, signed by Skipwith; docketed by Brent as received 6 Sept., but a copy reached the State Department by 20 May 1802 (see n. 2). For enclosures, see n. 1.

1. Skipwith enclosed "A Statement of American Claims lately re-submitted to the Commission of Comptabilité" (8 pp.), which was comprised of a chart that included the claim, its origin, items of the accounts presented, and the sum claimed; and "American Claims not submitted to the *Comptabilité* for want of sufficient Vouchers" (5 pp.), which included the name of the claimant, nature of the claim, and observations. Both documents were docketed by Brent as enclosed in Skipwith to JM, 14 Mar. 1802; the second bears Brent's penciled note, "May 20th, Extracts went to the Parties concerned, except to Mr Minor, whose residence is not known" (see n. 2).

2. On 20 May 1802 Daniel Brent sent a circular letter to those identified in Skipwith's second statement, stating that "a letter has just been received at this office from Fulwar Skipwith . . . of the 14th March last, enclosing a list of American claims which had not been submitted by him to the Commission of 'Comptabilite' . . . for the want of sufficient vouchers" and annexing extracts from the list (DNA: RG 59, DL, vol. 14).

From Andrew Ellicott

DEAR SIR   LANCASTER March 15th. 1802

Your favour of the 8th. came to hand yesterday, and I have taken the earliest opportunity of forwarding the packet for Mr. de Lambre, and thanking you for your willingness to take charg⟨e⟩ of it.

Your health is a matter of great importance to your Country at this time, and I fear that too close an attention to the duties of your office has occasioned your present indisposition: If my suspicions are well founded, I am convinced that we shall lose more by your bad state of health, than we shall gain by your extreme attention to business.

With sincere wishes for your speedy, and perfect recovery I am with great esteem your friend and Hbe. Servt.

ANDW; ELLICOTT.

FC (DLC: Ellicott Papers).

From Robert R. Livingston

DEAR SIR   PARIS 15th. March 1802

After closing my packet I recd the note of which the within is a copy.[1] It amounts to nothing, but it must serve to keep me quiet a few days longer—till they see what turn the business takes at Amiens which becomes more & more doubtful. The bad news from St Domingo also renders it necessary to keep us in suspence. I have already expressed my fear that American property in the Islands will not be very safe & the passage in le Clerks Letter relative to the powder & Arms may serve as an apology.[2] I am dear Sir with the most respectful consideration Your Most Obt hum: Servt

ROBT. R LIVINGSTON

RC and enclosure (DNA: RG 59, DD, France, vol. 8). For enclosure, see n. 1.

1. The enclosed copy of a letter from Talleyrand to Livingston, 23 Ventôse an X (14 Mar. 1802) (1 p.; in French; docketed by Brent), acknowledged receipt of various notes from the American minister about debts and American prize cases, which had made the basis of a report to Napoleon. All such questions, the foreign minister assured Livingston, would be studied with interest and attention (printed in *ASP, Foreign Relations,* 2:514).

2. Leclerc's letter of 20 Pluviôse an X (9 Feb. 1802) to the minister of marine, Denis Decrès, was published in the Paris *Moniteur universel,* 24 Ventôse an X (15 Mar. 1802). The general reported that he had "found at the cape a certain quantity of supplies, a great quantity of cannon, and munitions of war of every kind. The guns, cannon, and powder had been furnished by the United States" (editors' translation).

From Joseph H. Nicholson

SIR   March 15. 1802

It appears from a Letter which I have just received from the Secretary of the Treasury,[1] that the sum of $35,319⁸/₁₀₀ has been advanced by the Government of the United States to the Marquis La Fayette, by several of our Foreign Ministers, then residing at the respective Courts of London, Paris and the Hague

By Mr. Thos. Pinckney	21,933 $^{48}/_{100}$
By Mr. King and Mr. Adams Junr.	7,876 $^{3}/_{100}$
By Mr. Monroe[2]	5,509 $^{57}/_{100}$
	35,319 $^{8}/_{100}$

It likewise appears that no more than \$24,424 have been appropriated by Law and I wish to know by what Authority a sum has been applied to this Object beyond that appropriated.[3] This Information I presume can be furnished from your Office, and I will thank you for as early a Communication on the Subject, as may be convenient. I have the Honor to be Sir with very high Respect Yr. Ob. Servt.

JOSEPH H. NICHOLSON

RC (DNA: RG 59, ML). Docketed by Brent.

1. Gallatin wrote to Nicholson on 11 Mar. 1802 in response to Nicholson's 6 Mar. request as chairman of the House committee of investigation for information and accounts on the advances to Lafayette (Nicholson to Gallatin, 6 Mar. 1802, and Gallatin to Nicholson, 11 Mar. 1802, *Papers of Gallatin* [microfilm ed.], reel 6).

2. Someone, possibly JM, added an asterisk here and wrote in pencil in the lower margin, "*Advanced M de Lafayette in 1795 & 1796."

3. The act allowing Lafayette \$24,424 for his active service as a major general in the Continental army had been approved on 27 Mar. 1794 (*Annals of Congress*, 3d Cong., 1st sess., 1428). JM's reply has not been found, but for Congress's further attempts to compensate Lafayette and JM's involvement therein, see Madison and Lafayette's Louisiana Lands, 26 Oct. 1809 (*PJM-PS*, 2:35–38).

§ To Louis-André Pichon. *15 March 1802, Department of State.* Acknowledges Pichon's note of 18 Feb.[1] The president received the news of the peace concluded between France and Great Britain not only with the lively interest that humanity should take at the end of such a long and bloody war but also with the sympathy owed to a friendly nation with which the U.S., under the auspices of peace, desires to expand its relations.

Has informed Pichon previously that the U.S. regards it as outside its accustomed rule to enter into a general interpretation of a treaty, preferring to make decisions only in particular cases. The president, nevertheless, acknowledges the importance that the French government attaches to the explicit adherence of the U.S. to the sense of article 6 of the recent convention and, as a consequence of the frankness and cordiality that the U.S. tries to show on all occasions to the French government, has authorized JM to declare that it is understood that the terms of that article ensure French ships and corsairs, as well as their prizes, a perfect equality in U.S. ports with the ships, corsairs, and prizes of any other nation whatsoever and that it is in this sense the article has been understood uniformly by the U.S. and in this sense it will be executed on its part.

Greatly regrets the possibility that there exists a difference of opinion between the two governments in the affair of the *Insurgente.*[2] The president agrees with Pichon that a distinction must be made between a national ship and a private ship.

The restitution of the latter is commonly stipulated in adjustments of national differences. The object of the stipulation in that case is to indemnify the individuals for the goods they have lost. As for national ships, they are rarely given a place in restitution clauses. The indemnity in this case is not financial but consists instead of national dignity. In consequence, when this restitution is rendered impossible by a chain of accidental causes, satisfaction cannot, as it can in a question of private property, be found in financial equivalents; it is to be found entirely in the respect shown publicly for the underlying principles. That the U.S. considers this important is reflected in its handling of the *Berceau.*

Has learned with pleasure of the progress of American reclamations now before the Council of Prizes and believes that, in spite of some discouraging judgments, the claims will finally be adjusted according to their true principles. Makes no other observations on this part of Pichon's note except to say that the delays of which Pichon complains, although unfortunate, are not cause for any genuine concern. They arise from the political structure of the U.S. government, and the outcome will convince Pichon that they should not be attributed to unwillingness on the part of the U.S. to execute faithfully all the parts of the treaty.

Tr (AAE: Political Correspondence, U.S., 54:219–20). 4 pp.; in French. Docketed as enclosed in Pichon's dispatch no. 41 (1 Germinal an X) to Talleyrand.

1. *PJM-SS*, 2:476–78.
2. For the *Insurgente*, see *PJM-SS*, 1:400 n. 5.

§ From Richard Söderström. *15 March 1802, Washington.* "I fear very much that I by this my letter will too much intrud upon your usual goodness. But circumstanced as I am at present in consequence of a multiplicity of business which Calls for me to Philadelphia for Accots. of a number of people in Europe, Obliges me to Solicit your kind determination in the Case of which I have had the Honor of laying the Records before you, not doubting In the least but that you will Judge the Claims to be a proper one and that payment for same will and can't be refused. The Attorney General have informed me that his intention was to report today to you on the Subject. If you after receiving same should be of opinion that the owner should and ought to petition Congress for the payment, I will immediately Submit to your directions & endeavour to obtain apropriation made for same Claims. I trust you will be so obliging and pardon this my forwardness in asking your assistance in this business."

RC (DNA: RG 59, NFC, vol. 1). 2 pp.

To Robert R. Livingston

SIR,   DEPARTMENT OF STATE, March 16th. 1802.

Your two favours of the 10, continued on the 12th Decr., and of the 31 of the same Month, have been duly received, as were the two of preceding dates written on your arrival at Nantz and L'Orient.[1]

We are anxious to know the result of your communications with the French Government on the subject of restitutions, both as to the rules by which they are to be settled, and the prospect of their being satisfied. From the information of Mr Pichon, it seems that the nett proceeds only will be allowed where the property has been sold; which will operate against the United States in the proportion in which the claims of their citizens exceed those on the side of France. As the object of the stipulation is rather to restore what has been lost, than what has been gained, there appears to be good ground for contending that the gross and not the nett proceeds should be the measure of indemnification. Mr. Pichon gives us to understand also that the non-existence of the Insurgente at the date of the Treaty, will be no bar to the demand of her value. On a former occasion he had admitted the contrary, and his private opinion is no doubt still the same; but it is overruled by instructions from his government.[2] It is still hoped that the claim will not finally be pressed. A copy of my answer to a late note of Mr Pichon, which I send you[3] chiefly on account of the other subjects contained in it, will shew you what has been added to the former reasoning addressed to him on the case of the Insurgente.

The uncertainties supposed to attend a fulfilment of the Convention by the French Government, have excited a lively sensation in our Citizens having claims under it; and have produced applications both to the Legislature and the Executive, urging a retention of the monies due to French claimants, as an eventual fund for the justice stipulated to themselves. A proceeding of this kind, however, is liable under existing circumstances at least, to the strongest objections. It would be grounding a breach of faith, on the presumption only of a breach of faith on the other side, and would be considered as mingling insult with injury. It would furnish a motive and a pretext for disregarding a compact; the complete and favourable execution of which it is our interest to require and to excite by our example. And it ought the less to be wished by our citizens, as the sum to be paid by the United States, if distributed among them, would bear so small a proportion to their claims, that it could not, according to any just calculation, balance the danger to which these would be subjected by such a precaution. A different course therefore has been pursued. The requisitions of Mr Pichon have been answered by promises of good faith, and of payment as soon as legal provision for it shall be made. He will even be permitted to receive, under the instructions, from his government the sums due to individuals who do not themselves put in their claims. This is an arrangement not entirely agreeable, but it is pressed with much anxiety; and probably has relations to the armament at St Domingo which give it a critical value. A refusal of it therefore, would not only be taken unkindly, but might, by suspicion, be connected with an unfriendly policy charged on the preceding administration, towards the French interests in that Island.

For the state of things there I refer you to the letter of Mr. Lear in the News-papers herewith forwarded.[4] No information of later date has been received from that quarter. I refer you to the news-papers also for the late proceedings of Congress, and the subjects at present before them.

Your suggestions with respect to Mr. Patterson did not come to hand till he had left the United States. When last heard of, he was at Gibraltar. A commission for him is herewith enclosed; but if he should be indifferent to a Consular appointment, or should be willing to accept one for the Seven Islands as you presume, the Commission need not be delivered, and the person acting as Consul at L'Orient may continue in his functions.[5] The situation of this gentleman was unknown to the President, and it is left with you to arrange, as you may find best, the matter between him and your friend Mr Patterson; keeping in mind that the President does not wish the inclinations of the latter to be violated.

The subject of your letter to Mr. *King* of the 30th of Decr. is regarded by the President as not *less delicate* than you have *supposed*[6] considering the particular views which *Great Britain may mingle with ours* and the danger that a confidential *resort to her* may be *abused for* the purpose of *sowing jealousies* in *France* and thereby *thwart our object* you *and Mr. King* will *both be* sensible that *too much circumspection cannot be employed.*

This letter might have been made fuller, but the short notice of the opportunity, required the abridgment. With sentiments of the truest respect & consideration I remain Dear Sir Your most Obedient servt

JAMES MADISON

RC (NHi: Livingston Papers); letterbook copy (DNA: RG 59, IM, vol. 6). RC in a clerk's hand, except for JM's complimentary close and signature. Docketed by Livingston as received 15 May. Italicized words are those encoded by JM's clerk and decoded here by the editors. RC decoded interlinearly by Livingston. Enclosures not found.

1. Livingston to JM, 12 and 22 Nov. and 10, 12, and 31 Dec. 1801 (*PJM-SS*, 2:237–38, 265–66, 302–4, 309–10, 359–60).

2. For Pichon's opinions on the *Insurgente* case, see his letters to JM of 9 Dec. 1801 and 18 Feb. 1802 (*PJM-SS*, 2:298, 476–77, 479 n. 2).

3. JM no doubt enclosed a copy of his 15 Mar. 1802 letter to Pichon.

4. Most of the text of Lear's 12 Feb. letter to JM (*PJM-SS*, 2:462–64) appeared in the *National Intelligencer* on 10 Mar. 1802.

5. For Livingston's recommendation of William Patterson, see his letter to JM, 1 July 1801 (*PJM-SS*, 1:368, 369 n. 2). For his subsequent reflections on the post at Lorient and its then-current occupant, Aaron Vail, see Livingston to JM, 13 and 22 Nov. 1801 (*PJM-SS*, 2:238 and n. 1, 265–66). Patterson's nomination as commercial agent at Lorient had been confirmed by the Senate on 26 Jan. 1802 (*Senate Exec. Proceedings*, 1:402, 405).

6. In his 30 Dec. 1801 letter to Rufus King, Livingston described his inquiries at the French foreign ministry about the status of Louisiana and his conviction that the retrocession had taken place. He then asked King "in what light" these developments were seen in Great Britain. After remarking that "it will certainly, in its consequences, be extremely dangerous to

her," Livingston went on to give King some "hints" that "may be made use of with the British ministry, to induce them to throw all the obstacles in their power in the way of a final settlement of this business, if it is not already too late," warning King of the "importance of not appearing yourself, or permitting me to appear much opposed to it, if you find the thing concluded" (*ASP, Foreign Relations*, 2:512). See also Livingston to JM, 31 Dec. 1801 (*PJM-SS*, 2:359, 360 n. 2).

§ From Stephen Cathalan, Jr. *16 March 1802, Marseilles.* Informed JM in his last dispatch on 29 Sept.[1] that the bond required of him as U.S. commercial agent had been sent to Felix Imbert of Philadelphia; assumes Imbert will have forwarded it to JM. Has received JM's circular of 1 Aug. 1801[2] and will "follow your directions accordingly." Has given the local health office a certified copy "of the paragraph of your Said Letter, as well as of the Circular from the treasury department to the Collectors of the Customs, on what is relative to the bills of health to be delivered by them to the Masters of Vessels, before they Sail out from the ports of the United States." Has also given them a copy of the form of such bills of health. Encloses a copy of their reply.[3] Notes that U.S. vessels are subjected to quarantine only "when they have touched to some ports in the Mediterranean, from whence a quarantine is ordered here, or when they have been visited at Sea." Encloses a list of American vessels entering Marseilles between January and December 1801 and a list of American vessels departing from his district during the same period [not found]. Has been delayed in sending reports because he was unable to get two manifests from the captains; "in future you may rely on my Exactitude in sending them to you, in the first days of July and January." Reports that the *President*, which was "repairing in toulon," departed 10 Feb. The *George Washington* arrived via Toulon at Marseilles on 14 Feb. and on 26 Feb. convoyed four American vessels through the Straits of Gibraltar. "The dispatching of these Ships, employed so much my time, that I could not embrace their opportunity to write you a line." Two Swedish frigates have arrived; one is ready to sail for Tripoli, and the other will be under repair for at least three weeks before leaving for the same destination. The U.S. frigate *Philadelphia*, which had been ordered by Commodore Dale to be at Leghorn 10 Mar. to convoy vessels to Marseilles, was reported to have been at Malta three weeks earlier, "obliged to heave down for a leak to repair it." The *Boston* was also at Malta, "and the American Vessels here which could not be ready to Sail with the Washington have Sailed Since and will now Sail without convoy." Reports that two Tripolitan cruisers sailed from Tripoli "but in a violent Storm one was lost and the other reintered in the port of Tripoly in a poor State." Suggests Toulon as port of call and repair for U.S. naval squadron as it is "best situated in the Center of the Mediterranean." When the new squadron expected in the Mediterranean arrives, "the American Consuls or Agents Should receive positive orders to forbid Any American Vessels to sail out from their respective ports without Convoy; but Such Convoy ought to be regulated in a manner, that each 30 days or thereabout Such convoy Should offer in our ports." Notes that it is fortunate the Tripolitans have not captured any American ships.

"Tho' I have not yet received my Exequatur which has been lately refused by the minister of Foreign Relations in a conversation the Minister Plenipy. of the Un. St:

at Paris had with him on that Subject, I have not yet lost all hopes of obtaining it by my relations who are also relations to the first Consul. . . . In the meantime I continue in the full Exercise of this office." Asks JM to "entreat the President of the United States to be so good as to wait till all hopes of Success Should be lost" before appointing someone to replace him. In a postscript of 24 Mar., transcribes a letter from the commander of a British brig recently arrived at Marseilles from Malta, reporting that as of 17 Feb. there were two American frigates at Malta, neither "wanting any repairs."

RC and enclosure (DNA: RG 59, CD, Marseilles, vol. 1). RC 6 pp.; docketed by Brent as received 20 May. A duplicate copy (ibid.) is dated 10 Mar. 1802 and is incomplete. Extracts from RC printed in Knox, *Naval Documents, Barbary Wars*, 2:87. For surviving enclosure, see n. 3.

    1. *PJM-SS*, 2:151.
    2. *PJM-SS*, 2:1–4.
    3. Cathalan enclosed a copy of a letter from the guardians of public health of Marseilles, 16 Dec. 1801 (5 pp.; in French). After commending the U.S. for joining the "Sainte Coalition" of European states endeavoring to control contagious diseases by issuing certificates of health and employing quarantines and other public health measures, the French health officials pointed to alarming reports from New York newspapers, and from a European consul in Charleston, South Carolina, that a yellow fever epidemic had struck Charleston and Savannah. Quarantine decisions, they wrote, could not be made on the basis of ships' health certificates alone.

§ From John M. Forbes. *16 March 1802, New York*. "I have now the honor to enclose, duly executed, one of the Bonds forwarded from your Department, having retained the other agreeably to your instructions."

RC (DNA: RG 59, CD, Hamburg, vol. 1). 1 p. Enclosure not found.

§ From Wade Hampton. *16 March 1802, Charleston*. "I take the liberty of introducing to your notice, a friend of mine, Mr. Read. He has some business at the seat of Government which I have had no opportunity of judging of, but if you should find it convenient & proper to render him any services, I can only say I shall be very grateful for them."

RC (DLC). 1 p.

§ From Josef Yznardy. *16 March 1802, Philadelphia*. Having left Baltimore because of the precarious state of his health, has received at Philadelphia JM's letter [not found] returning his consular bond because it was not signed in the presence of witnesses; regrets the omission and will send his son to take care of it. The enclosed letter exposes the fraud perpetrated by Captain Nelson in Cadiz. Notes that Juan Antonio Butler is a wealthy and respectable person. Asks JM's advice on whether to publish this information in the newspapers or be silent; asks to be informed if JM takes steps to seize the ship.

RC (DNA: RG 59, CD, Cadiz, vol. 1). 2 pp.; in Spanish. Enclosure not found.

§ From Josef Yznardy. *16 March 1802, Philadelphia.* States that he was ready to embark but finds himself detained because his bailsman in the Israel case, Mr. Price, wants to be relieved of the commitment.[1] Asks JM to protect him from his persecutors; believes he cannot stay in the U.S. without risk to his life. Has seen Dallas, who said that his opinion would have been different if he had seen the new documents Yznardy recently submitted to him. Expresses his gratitude for the $3,000 paid on the balance of his account with the U.S. on condition of surety bond, which will be easily provided. Pledges his possessions in Spain to fulfill his obligations.

RC (DNA: RG 59, CD, Cadiz, vol. 1). 3 pp.; in Spanish.

1. For Yznardy's brief imprisonment in Philadelphia, see Jacob Wagner to JM, 17 Aug. 1801 (*PJM-SS*, 2:50, 53 n. 8).

From Louis-André Pichon

GEORGETOWN le 26. Ventose an 10. (17. Mars 1802.)

Le Soussigné, par Suite de la confiance entiere qu'il n'a cessé de mettre dans Ses rapports avec le Gouvernement des Etats Unis, S'est empressé hier de donner, à Monsieur le Secrétaire d'Etat, communication des dépêches qui lui ont été adressées conjointement par les commandans des forces de terre et de mer de la République Française récemment arrivées dans la colonie de St. Domingue. Ces dépêches imposent au Soussigné le devoir de faire, auprès du Gouvernement Fédéral, des démarches Sur lesquelles il a déjà anticipé dans une note antérieure à l'occasion de la Guadeloupe,[1] prévoyant l'issue que les affaires de St. Domingue prendraient à l'arrivée des autorités et des forces Françaises.

Les événemens derniers de la colonie en question Sont malheureusement trop connus. Ils ne laissent plus de doute Sur le projet des chefs Noirs de rejetter toute Soumission à la France et, il faut le dire, à la couleur Blanche et aux Nations civilisées, et d'exiger une domination Séparée dont l'expérience a Suffisamment demontré le caractère et la tendance future: Il n'y a aucun doute que toutes les nations policées, et particulierement celles qui ont dans leur Sein, ou dans leurs possessions, un Etat de Société analogue à celui qui existait dans cette colonie, ne Soient interessées au rétablissement de l'ordre interverti Si longtems. Le concert qui parait S'être operé entre toutes les nations Européenes pour atteindre ce but, prouve à quel point la conviction est portée parmi elles à cet egard. Les Etats Unis doivent l'éprouver au même degré: En Conséquence le Gouvernement Français, aujourd'hui à même de travailler efficacement à cet ouvrage, à le droit d'attendre d'eux qu'ils ne permettront pas à leurs citoyens d'entraver et de violer les droits de la République Française, aussi bien que le droit des gens, en Suivant, avec les negres révoltés, aucun commerce Soit pour leur porter des Munitions Soit pour verser des approvisionnemens.

Le Général en chef de l'armée de la République et L'Amiral commandant les forces navales ont pris des dispositions pour empêcher ce commerce; les bâtimens qui tenteraient de le faire Seront confisqués, Sans préjudice de la punition des commandans. Il est à craindre que ces mesures rigoureuses n'entrainent des incidens propres à compromettre la bonne harmonie et il Semble que les Etats Unis pourraient, de leur coté, en adopter de propres, à la fois, à éviter ces incidens et à dissiper les impressions désagréables qui paraissent Subsister relativement aux communications qui ont eu, Jusqu'à ce moment, lieu entre St. Domingue et les Etats Unis. De telles mesures Seraient certainement faites pour convaincre le Gouvernement de la République de la Sincerité des dispositions et des assurances qui ont été manifestées au Soussigné, relativement aux colonies et notamment à celle de St. Domingue.

Le Soussigné doit aussi faire connaitre à Monsieur Madison qu'afin de Surveiller plus éfficacement les relations du commerce étranger avec la colonie, le Général en chef a déterminé qu'il ne Serait admis que dans les deux ports du Cap et du Port Républicain: Tous les autres ports lui Sont fermés; il Sera éssentiel au commerce des Etats Unis d'être instruit de cette disposition ainsi que de celles qui ont été notifiées plus haut,[2] et le Soussigné Se propose de converser ultérieurement avec Mr. Madison à ce Sujet.

Le Soussigné prie Mr. Le Secrétaire d'Etat de vouloir bien porter à la connaissance de Monsieur Le Président des Etats Unis l'objet de la présente note et en même tems il a l'honneur de l'assurer de Son respect et de Sa parfaite consideration.

L. A. PICHON

CONDENSED TRANSLATION

Notes that on 16 Mar. he informed JM of dispatches that had been addressed to him jointly by the commanders of the French military and naval forces recently arrived at Saint-Domingue. These dispatches oblige him to take the steps he had anticipated in a previous note about Guadeloupe. Recent events in Saint-Domingue no longer leave any doubt about the plans of black leaders there to reject submission to France and, in effect, to all whites and to all civilized nations. There is no doubt that all nations under the rule of law, especially those which harbor slaves within their society, are interested in reestablishing the previous state of things. The cooperation among European nations proves their conviction in this regard, which must be shared by the U.S. Consequently the French government expects that the U.S. will not allow its citizens to impede or violate international law by trading in munitions or provisions with the rebellious blacks.

The military and naval commanders have taken measures to prevent this trade. Vessels that attempt such commerce will be confiscated. Fearing that these severe measures will result in incidents detrimental to good relations, suggests that the

U.S. adopt its own measures to avoid incidents. Such actions will convince France of the sincerity of American assurances relative to the colonies. Foreign trade with Saint-Domingue will be permitted only at Cap Français and Port Républicain. It is essential that these policies be made public. Proposes to converse with JM later on this subject. Requests that JM bring this note to the president's attention.

RC (DNA: RG 59, NFL, France, vol. 1); Tr (AAE: Political Correspondence, U.S., 54: 229–30). RC in a clerk's hand, signed by Pichon.

1. In his letter of 1 Feb. 1802, Pichon had informed JM of trade restrictions enforced by France on the occasion of the rebellion against French authorities on Guadeloupe (*PJM-SS*, 2:433–34).

2. The *National Intelligencer* reported on 19 Mar. the suspension of trade between the U.S. and Saint-Domingue except at Cap Français and Port Républicain. It also published the text of an 18 Mar. announcement to that effect from Pichon, which also prohibited the transportation of ammunition and provisions to the insurgent blacks. On 24 Mar. the paper printed a translation of General Leclerc's 16 Feb. order proclaiming Toussaint and Christophe outlaws and the establishment of other provisions tantamount to declaring martial law.

From Edward Thornton

Private

DEAR SIR,   PHILADELPHIA 17th March 1802.

With your passion for chess, I think I shall very easily stand excused for taking the liberty of informing you that on my arrival at this place I found the proposed publication of Phillidor's games was entirely suspended on account of the want of subscribers, the requisite number being calculated at 150 or 200, while in this city there are not more than forty or fifty names yet put down. My own little knowlege of Washington enables me to say that there are many persons who would wish to procure this work; and if you are of this opinion, I should flatter myself that you would give some celebrity to this publication by procuring the name of the President and your own, as well as that of many other amateurs. If you should be able to make out any small addition to the list of subscribers, and will do me the honour of forwarding it to me, I will give it to the publisher, who only wants encouragement to commence the impression.[1]

I shall not stay here above ten or twelve days, particularly if the Packet should arrive: and if I can be of any service to Mrs Madison or yourself in bringing anything from this place, I beg you will lay your commands upon me. I have the honour to be Your very faithful Sert

EDWD THORNTON

RC (DLC).

1. The French composer François-André Danican (1727–1795), known as Philidor, was famous for his book *L'analyze des échecs*, first published in London in 1749. The Philadelphia *Aurora General Advertiser* of 12 Jan. 1802 advertised a subscription for a Philadelphia edition of the English translation to be published by James Humphreys and Joseph Groff (price, $2.50), but an American edition did not appear until 1826. Humphreys did publish a chess book in 1802 that included some of Philidor's games under the title of *Chess Made Easy*. JM later owned a copy of *The Elements of Chess: A Treatise Combining Theory with Practice* (Boston, 1805), which included "the whole of Philidor's Games," while his friend Jefferson owned, among other chess books, a first edition of Philidor (*Biographie universelle* [1843–65 ed.], 12: 935–37; Ralph K. Hagedorn, *Benjamin Franklin and Chess in Early America* [Philadelphia, 1958], pp. 48, 51; "Books from the Library of James and Dolley P. Madison," Stan. V. Henkels Catalogue No. 821, pt. 6 [9 May 1899], item 285; Sowerby, *Catalogue of Jefferson's Library*, 1:530).

§ From John Morton. *17 March 1802, Havana*. Refers to his letter of 20 Jan.[1] informing JM that the admission of U.S. vessels to Cuba "had become reduced to a System of tedious & expensive negotiation." Since then, two groups of nearly fifty American ships each have been admitted on payment of 6 percent on the amount of the invoices of their cargoes. Losses to the ships have resulted not only from this charge but also from ordinary port expenses, interest on employed capital, and damage to cargoes from the delays. "And the further Effect of this Kind of Embargo upon our Vessels was, that by creating a great Influx of Merchandize & provisions at once into the market, & the necessity many were under of disposing of them immediately, the Spaniards supplied themselves almost on their own terms: and I will venture to pronounce them the most ruinous Voyages ever made to this island." However, even these terms for admittance have been closed, and no entry into the harbor has been permitted for about ten days. Observes that the governor's disposition to be fair is counterbalanced by his caution and timidity. "The Circumstance which finally produced an absolute refusal of Admission to our Vessels was . . . the representations of a respectable class of Merchants here (the most so as to property) principally connected in the Trade between the Mother-Country & the Colonies; which stated the Consequence of admitting the Americans to supply the Market to be an obstacle, if not an exclusion, of their own citizens." Has conferred with the governor about how existing accounts with U.S. citizens will be settled if communications are cut off; the governor insists that "as the Trade had never been *open*, but only *suffered*, [the Americans] could not, or should not, have extended any Concerns beyond the reach of a very short period to adjust." The governor did repeat his promise to delay enforcement of his January order for the departure of foreigners. Concludes that because of a shortage of provisions and the inability of Spain to provide for the colony, "a very short time must . . . show in still stronger light, their precarious situation; & inevitably lead, I think, to a further admission of our provisions, Lumber, & other articles of the first necessity."

RC (DNA: RG 59, CD, Havana, vol. 1). 7 pp.; docketed by Brent.

1. *PJM-SS*, 2:414–15.

§ To Charles D. Coxe. *18 March 1802, Department of State.* "I have the pleasure to inclose you a Commission as Commercial Agent of the United States for the port of Dunkirk in France, issued in consequence of the Senate's confirmation of your appointment, and request the renewal of your Official bond, for which purpose a blank is also inclosed."

RC (SSSPL). 1 p.; in a clerk's hand, signed by JM. Enclosures not found. The Senate had confirmed Coxe's nomination on 26 Jan. 1802 (*Senate Exec. Proceedings*, 1:405).

§ From Sylvanus Bourne. *18 March 1802, Amsterdam.* Transmits the latest issues of the Leiden *Gazette.* Although many months have passed since the signing of peace preliminaries between France and Great Britain, no final arrangement has been made and the state of suspense is prejudicial to commerce. British government has ordered a "respectable fleet" to sea; this has created alarm as to the prospects for the deliberations at Amiens. The visit of the former stadtholder's son to Paris has given rise to various speculations; "the most reasonable presump⟨tion⟩ is that it is for the purpose of arrang⟨ing⟩ the species & quantum of indemnity wh⟨ich⟩ his father is to receive for the loss of ⟨his⟩ possessions in this Country." Expresses his pleasure at finding by the recent treasury report on U.S. finances that the country is enjoying prosperity. "The misfortunes of Europe afford us a lesson which if wise we shall not fail to profit of."

RC (DNA: RG 59, CD, Amsterdam, vol. 1). 3 pp.; docketed by Brent as received 31 May.

§ From William Eaton. *18 March 1802, Tunis.* Adds to what he wrote in the enclosed letter to Rufus King that on arriving in Tunis, he found Hamet Pasha "yielding to his brother's instances and on the point of departing for Derne a Province of Tripoli, the Government of which is promised him." Has refused Hamet's request for a passport and "told him very candidly that if he departed we must consider him in the light of an enemy," even to the extent of carrying him and his retinue as prisoners of war to America. Has assured him "if he would adhere to his former arrangements I did not doubt but that before the expiration of four months he might be offered to his people by an American Squadron. I tell him the sole object of his brother is to cut his throat." The bey has refused Hamet further provisions, so he proposes awaiting the outcome in Malta. Eaton has consented only to his going to Leghorn or Sardinia. "If he departs on other terms I shall send an armed Ship after him, & if possible carry him and retinue to some Italian Port." Adds that Captain McNeill stopped at Tunis on 29 Jan. since when there has been no news of him. In a 26 Mar. postscript, states that Hamet Pasha "has manifested an unequivocal disposition to come into my plans heretofore detailed; he is assured of a revolution in his favor if he can be offered to his people with Sufficient show of force: but he is surrounded by Turks and Arabs Subjects of his brother sent him as protectors, in so much that he cannot act." Encloses copies of his plans. "If they succeed it will be productive of incalculable advantages if they fail I am conscious of having exposed myself to the imputation of at least too much Zeal."

45

RC (DNA: RG 59, CD, Tunis, vol. 2, pt. 1); letterbook copy (CSmH). RC 3 pp.; in a clerk's hand, signed by Eaton; marked "Copy. A." and enclosed with Eaton's 4 Apr. dispatch. Printed in Knox, *Naval Documents, Barbary Wars,* 2 : 90–91. Postscript not on letterbook copy. Enclosures not found, but enclosures B through E in Eaton's 4 Apr. dispatch are apparently duplicates of those sent with the original of this letter (see Eaton to JM, 4 Apr. 1802, and n. 1).

§ From John Lamson. *18 March 1802, Trieste.* Notes that his last letter of 29 Dec. 1801[1] was sent shortly after his arrival in Trieste; since then he has received JM's circular letter[2] and will pay careful attention to its instructions. Observes that the information he can obtain on commerce "will seldom be accurate especially in a port like this, no duties being payable little attention is paid to entries." Discusses the commercial importance of Trieste, "being a free port in a central situation," and suggests his commission be altered "to make it general for all the ports of the Emperor in the Adriatic, including Venice," until the commerce becomes important enough to attract U.S. citizens as consuls. "By this means a Uniform system may be adopted in all the ports and thus prevent the int[e]rests of our Merchants from suffering by the rivalship which might be created should these offices pass into the hands of foriegners. . . . Indeed the Goverment here have put this construction on my commission and have given me their Exequator accordingly & in consequence I shall venture to name agents in the different ports Untill I receive your instructions to the contrary." Requests that he be considered for the post of naval agent in the Adriatic if such a post is to be created. Quotes a notice from a Frankfurt newspaper, dated 9 Feb. at Stockholm, which says that Tripoli has acquired a three-masted vessel in Smyrna to be used against American and Swedish ships. Will wait until June to send "a return of all the American Vessells that have ever visited this port" so that it will be more complete.

RC (DNA: RG 59, CD, Trieste, vol. 1). 2 pp.

1. *PJM-SS,* 2 : 353.
2. Circular Letter to American Consuls and Commercial Agents, 1 Aug. 1801 (*PJM-SS,* 2 : 1–4).

§ From Richard Söderström. *18 March 1802, Washington.* "As I am fully convinced that acting only as agent agreeable to power of Attorney for an Individual, and not in any publick Capacity I have no Claim to any determination from, or right to make any direct application to the Executive, and less in consequence of the obliging informations you have both in writing and Verbell given me; which is, that when the Court of the United States have given their final Decree in any Case, the Claimer must petition Congress for the money, when no appropriation is made.[1] In consequence of this, and of what you told me yesterday, which confirmed the above, that application for such payments must be made to Congress, I have therefore prepared a petition which I intend to have presented to Congress to day, and of which I have the Honor to inclose you a Copy."[2]

RC and enclosure (DNA: RG 59, NFC, vol. 1). RC 2 pp.

1. See JM to Söderström, 23 July 1801 (*PJM-SS*, 1:461).

2. Söderström enclosed a petition to Congress (4 pp.) on behalf of Paolo Paoly, master of the Danish merchant schooner *Amphitheater*, which sailed from St. Thomas in January 1800, was taken at Saint-Domingue as a prize by Capt. William Maley of the U.S. armed schooner *Experiment*, and was subsequently condemned in the district court at Philadelphia as a French armed vessel; in May 1801 the sentence was reversed on appeal in the Pennsylvania circuit court. A bill for Paoly's relief was passed by both houses of Congress in April 1802 (*Annals of Congress*, 7th Cong., 1st sess., 259, 1141).

From Albert Gallatin

DEAR SIR   March 19th 1802

Mr Steele is anxious to have Mr Marshal's accounts so far stated as to be enabled to judge whether any further appropriation will be necessary. A statement somewhat similar to that furnished by Mr Kimbal in relation to Mr Pickering's account would be necessary.

The enclosed[1] shows the sums advanced and to whom; but for what purpose &, therefore, under what head of appropriation to be arranged? is the question. It is presumable that the letters transmitting the money or the letters applying for the money must show for what object it was asked & remitted.

Will you be good enough to cause at least the attempt to be made by an investigation of those letters? I make the application at the express request of Mr Steele. Your's respectfully

ALBERT GALLATIN

RC and enclosure (DNA: RG 59, ML). Docketed by Wagner.

1. Gallatin enclosed an "Accompt of monies for which John Marshall Esqr. late Secretary of State will be credited by the following named persons to whom they were paid over and concerning which the Comptroller of the Treasury wishes information as to the objects of expenditure originally designated by the said Secretary" (1 p.). The persons listed included Rufus King, several American consuls and agents, and Lisbon bankers John Bulkeley & Son, and the amounts advanced totaled $146,131.51. For Marshall's comments on the ensuing treasury report, see his letter to James A. Bayard, 12 Apr. 1802 (Herbert A. Johnson et al., eds., *The Papers of John Marshall* [6 vols. to date; Chapel Hill, N.C., 1974—], 6:106–7).

From Jacob Wagner

DR. SIR   WASHINGTON, 19 March 1802

The Physician who attends me having advised me to ride to Baltimore, in the hope of finding an alleviation of my lingering disorder, I propose to commence the journey to morrow afternoon or the next morning.[1] If any thing pressing should require my assistance in the mean while, a letter addressed to me at Baltimore will be certain to find me: and if Mr. Brent or Mr. Pleasonton will do me the favor to call upon me to morrow morning I will explain to him, a few arrearages of business which demand immediate attention.

I am certain you will do me the justice to believe that it is not among the smallest of my sufferings to be obliged to reflect upon the abrupt seperation I am under the necessity of making from the office at a period of peculiar pressure. Should my health revive I shall as soon as possible return to my duty: but if otherwise, I shall be consoled by the recollection of the favors which you have never ceased to extend to Dr. Sir Your faithful & obed. servt.

JACOB WAGNER

RC (owned by Charles M. Storey, Boston, Mass., 1961).

1. Wagner's illness prevented him from returning to his duties until November 1802 (Wagner to JM, 1 Nov. 1802 [DLC]).

From James Yard

DEAR SIR   PHILADA. March 19. 1802.

I take the liberty of introducing to your acquaintance the Bearer Mr. perkins of Boston,[1] who goes to your City in order to represent to Government the Treatment which he & Some of his friends have received from the Spaniards in so. America. His Situation & my own are so exactly alike that the Same Measures will be adopted by us jointly for the Recovery of our property. When you have heard from him the Detail of the Case of the Ship Diana, you will know nearly every Circumstance relative to my Ship Asia & Brig Dolly. I dispatched those Vessels in the Fall of 1800 under a Contract with the Spaniard, with whom Mr perkins contracted, making all the Advances in Consideration of an Engagement on his part to allow me one half the Profits & to secure me free Admission into the Spanish ports in the South seas. My Vessels arrived at Lima; the Cargoes were forcibly taken from them, appraised at very low prices & sold at those prices. The proceeds are lodged in the Treasury until the Kings pleasure is known. Under all the Disadvantages of restricted prices the proceeds of the two Cargoes have yielded more than half a Million of Dollars. Mr. perkins's sold for $157.000. From the Amount of these sums you will see the Importance of these Transactions & I doubt not will afford every Relief in your power.

After mature Deliberation I have determined to proceed myself to Madrid & there endeavour to procure Satisfaction. But as it is a Business of a very delicate Nature & such as may excite the Jealousy of the Government, I have concluded to begin my operations without applying to our Minister. I have powerful friends there who can take their Measures without Eclat & of Course with more security. Yet in the Event of my making no progress thro' their means & other *powerful Agents* which I shall carry with me I must beg the Interference of our own Government. With this View I shall be thankful if you would oblige me with your Reccommendation of my Case to Mr. Pinckney in a Letter written especially for the purpose, to be delivered or not as I may think proper; also with a Line of Reccommendation to be delivered in all Events. I conceive that this Arrangement will be the most proper for the Occasion & I hope therefore may meet your approbation. As it is probable that I shall also go to France England & Holland I hope you will excuse me if I trespass so far as to beg a Line to our Ministers in those Regions. You have doubtless heard of my Misfortunes & have taken a friendly part on the occasion. The Efforts which I am now about to make if Successful will amply provide for past Engagements & future Wants.

Mr. Perkins and I have agreed in opinion that it would not be proper to Say any thing on the subject to the Spanish Minister at Washington. I am very respectfully Dear sir Your obliged servt

JAMES YARD

RC (DLC).

1. This was Samuel G. Perkins, who also carried a letter of introduction to JM from Edward Stevens of Philadelphia, 19 Mar. 1802 (DLC; 1 p.). Perkins, partner in the Boston firm Stephen Higginson and Company, was the brother of Boston merchants James and Thomas Handasyd Perkins, who along with Higginson and Company were owners of the ship *Diana* (Freeman Hunt, "Thomas Handasyd Perkins," in *Lives of American Merchants* [1856; 2 vols.; New York, 1969 reprint], 1:50, 51; Memorial of James Perkins et al., 23 May 1822 [DNA: RG 76, Spain, Treaty of 1819, Allowed Claims, vol. 23]). For the case of the *Diana*, see Stephen Higginson to Alexander Hamilton, 10 Oct. 1803 (Syrett and Cooke, *Papers of Hamilton*, 26:157–58 and n. 1).

§ From James Simpson. *19 March 1802, Tangier.* No. 38. Forwards a copy of his dispatch of 20 Feb.[1] Reports that the *Essex* arrived on 24 Feb. and sailed again on 26 Feb. On 13 Mar. the Batavian sloop of war *Daphne* arrived "with dispatches from that Government, containing assurances that an Embassy would be sent to Muley Soliman without delay"; the ship went on to Tunis and Algiers "with similar intelligence." Relates the general belief that when the Dutch negotiate to renew their treaty a subsidy will be required of them; "but as Admiral de Winter[2] comes to the Mediterranean with a respectable Fleet, they may probably obtain a ratification of their Antient Treaty, under its influence." Swedish stipulations of munitions for

Morocco have arrived, and [Peter] Wyk, the Swedish agent at Tangier, has gone to present other articles to the emperor. Dale has written from Gibraltar that he could not grant a passport for the Tripolitan vessel there without first obtaining permission from the president.[3] "I am highly sensible of the very great impropriety of Muley Soliman making such a request, but with him it is not proper to speak all we think; for this reason, rather than impart Commodore Dales determination, . . . I have thought better to intimate to this Government . . . that [Dale] left the decision of the matter to his Successor and the Swedish Admiral. . . . This has satisfied them in the moment." Should an absolute refusal be necessary, hopes that Sweden will join the U.S. in it. Confirms that the emperor has agreed to allow wheat to be sent to Tripoli but believes it will be almost impossible to charter vessels while Tripoli is blockaded. Dale urged him to see the emperor "in order to do away the favourable sentiments he seems to entertain towards the Tripolines"; knows JM will understand he cannot do so without presidential authorization. "At this moment in particular, such a measure is by no means necessary," for Wyk will use his efforts on behalf of Sweden and the U.S. to convince the emperor that supporting the Tripolitans is inappropriate. Expresses doubt that the two frigates being built at Rabat will be finished by summer owing to lack of stores and amount of work remaining. Has heard that orders have been received recently at Tetuán to hasten the completion of two rowing galleys and that the emperor intends to buy some small vessels to be used as cruisers.

"His Majesty has been pleased to express himself in very gracious terms, on subject of the House mentioned in No. 37,[4] he has directed it shall be sold for his benefit. . . . I have visited the House and find it very extensive, but by no means offering those principal accommodations required, such as a dancing Room & drawing Room, of that size indispensably necessary to a Consular House here. That part of the House not finished may be converted into these and some Bed rooms, this and other necessary alterations . . . may cost about three thousand dollars." Has offered 4,000 ducats for the house.

Has heard repeated reports of the outbreak of the plague along the coast of Er Rif four to six days' journey east of Tetuán. Requests instructions as solicited in his dispatches nos. 20 and 23[5] on the subject of U.S. vessels loading in Morocco "whilst the Plague rages"; "as the Vessels tradeing from this Country to the United States carry Goat Skins, Cow hides, Wool & Feathers, all which are very dangerous Articles, I beg with all due submission to recommend Government establishing a regulation for Trade, when the Plague or any Contagious disorder shall actualy exist."

RC (DNA: RG 59, CD, Tangier, vol. 1). 4 pp.; marked duplicate; docketed by Brent as received with Simpson's 13 May dispatch (no. 39). Extract printed in Knox, *Naval Documents, Barbary Wars*, 2:91–92. Jefferson communicated a brief extract to Congress with his annual message on 15 Dec. 1802 (printed in *ASP, Foreign Relations*, 2:465).

1. *PJM-SS*, 2:481.
2. Jan Willem de Winter (1761–1812), who as vice admiral of the Batavian fleet was defeated and taken prisoner by the British in the Battle of Camperdown in 1797, negotiated treaties with the Barbary states of Tripoli, Tunis, and Algiers in 1802. De Winter would later become a marshal of the French Empire (Tulard, *Dictionnaire Napoléon*, p. 1752).

3. Dale wrote two letters in response to Simpson's letter referring to him Mawlay Sulai-man's request for a passport for the Tripolitan ship *Meshouda* blockaded at Gibraltar. In the first, Dale stated that while "it will always give me pleasure to comply with the wishes of his highness . . . in this instance it is not in my power, nor can it be done without the orders of the President." In the second letter Dale repeated this and advised Simpson to see the emperor himself (Dale to Simpson, 4 and 8 Mar. 1802, Knox, *Naval Documents, Barbary Wars,* 2:77, 80–81).

4. Simpson to JM, 20 Feb. 1802 (*PJM-SS,* 2:481).

5. Simpson to the secretary of state, 17 Aug. 1799 and 14 May 1800 (DNA: RG 59, CD, Tangier, vol. 1).

§ From Richard Söderström. *19 March 1802, Washington.* "For fear I should dis-please you and do wrong in presenting the Petition to Congress which I had the Honor of sending you Copy of Yesterday—I have stopt same, till you will be pleased to inform me that I do right, and that same is pleasing to you."

RC (DNA: RG 59, NFC, vol. 1). 1 p.; docketed by Brent.

To James Monroe

Dear Sir   Washington March 20. 1802

I now return the letters to you from Mr. Purviance[1] & Cambaceres,[2] with an acknowledgment of those in which they were inclosed. The papers last recd. from you in relation to Mr. Skipwith will be of use in establishing one or two material points. His case has been a hard one, but it may be questioned whether he be well founded in the extent of his claims for in-terest & Agency for Claims. The Report ⟨o⟩n it should have been required from the Treasy. not from this Dept. It involves considerable research & some difficulties & has been further delayed by the pressure of business & the sickness of the Chief Clerck of this Dept. Congs. have not yet passed the appropriation for the French Treaty, which with certain delicacies touchg St. Domingo, have added to my occupations. Our latest acct⟨s.⟩ from Europe are indecisive on points important to us. [. . .] for Mrs. Mon-roe & yourself our sincerest regards

James Madison

RC (DLC). Damaged by removal of seal.

1. See *PJM-SS,* 2:395–96.

2. This was probably Jean-Jacques-Régis de Cambacérès to Monroe, 12 Dec. 1801 (NN: Monroe Papers), in which the second consul assured Monroe "that the spirit of our present Government is entirely bent on maintaining those tyes that should for ever subsist betwixt the two Nations."

From Gabriel Christie

Dear sir   London March 20th 1802

I arrived hear about the 7th inst. and deliverd the letters which you in-trusted to my charge the day after my arrival,[1] your letter of introduction to Mr King[2] secured me a very polite reception, and I have had frequent conversations with him respecting the Political situation of our Country and this. He as well as the rest of our Public agents the Consul excepted speak highly of the disposition which this Country entertains towards America and seem desirous that I should be impressed with the same opin-ion, but that will be no very easy task for them to execute, perhaps the rooted aversion that I have had to this Country for a long time past may be the cause of my unbeleafe, but whin I hear the Speaches of some of their Public men in Parliment, and am often obliged to listen to the contemp-teous observations of private individuals respecting my Country I am en-clined to think that their disposition towards us is not so very favourable as some persons hear would wish me to beleave and I am further enclined to think that the arrangement which was made by Mr Jefferson whin Secty of State that no Public Agent should be longer out of his Country than seven years at one time will be found to be a very judicious one.

Whin I saw you last I made application for my son Charles Christie to be appointed Consul at Canton which I would now wish to decline, I am informd from good authority hear that Mr Pintard our Consul at Madeira has left that Country and owing to some pecuniary embarrassments will not be able to return to it soon, and that the buisness is carried on by a person as his agent who is not an American Citizen, but an Irish man of the name of Charles Alder, this being the case and Knowing that the President has no desire to appoint any person to office who is not an American Citi-zen; I am enduced to solicit the appointment for my Son as Consul at Ma-deira, and I will be answerable for his being found fully competent to the undertaking. It would greately oblige me if you wd be so kind as to solicit the President on his behalf and endeavour to procure the appointment for him as soon as Possible I shall consider my self under great obligations to the President for this favour, and as it's the first of the Kind I ever re-quested, and very probabely will be the last I shall ever request if it can be done with propriety I have reason to hope the President will gratify me, should that be the case I will thank you to transmitt the appointment to-gether with instructions under cover to Captn Charles Christie at the East India Coffee House in Corn hill London, my son is now in India but will be hear early in June next. And if the President should be of opinion that he must go to America before he can receive the appointment he will do so but it would be more convenent for him to receive it hear. Should this application be inadmissable you wd greately oblige me by giving me the earliest information of it directed as above. As the future prospects of my son depends in a certain degree on the receipt of this appointment your intrest in procuring it for him will confer an obligation on Dear sir your Friend & Obt Sert

G Christie

RC (DNA: RG 59, LAR, 1801–9, filed under "Christie"). Docketed by Jefferson.

1. Christie carried dispatches from JM to Rufus King and David Lenox (see David Gelston to JM, 13 Jan. 1802, *PJM-SS*, 2:393). He also carried a letter of introduction from JM to George W. Erving (*PJM-SS*, 2:355).
2. Letter not found.

From Charles Pinckney

Dear Sir   March 20: 1802 In Madrid

I have yesterday recieved your favour by Mr: Rose Campbell[1] & immediately sit down to answer it. You say that only three Letters have been recieved from me. This is astonishing. I wrote four from the Helder & Amsterdam—one from the Hague: one from Brussells & Two to the President from Paris—one by Way of Havre & the other of London. The latter I gave to Mr Grant to forward. From Bourdeaux two & this is the fourth from Madrid & one from the Escurial.[2] Until however very lately the Post from Madrid is extremely uncertain & from the Length of time that occurs & the uncertainty even from Paris for some months past I am not much surprised at some of my Letters miscarrying. I am hopeful however that all from the Escurial & Madrid will get safe—& these will give you some statement of our affairs here. They will inform you of the number of our Vessels that have been detained & condemned of those that are still in suspence, & the remedy I have proposed to the Spanish Government as the only probable one of ever soon deciding these things. It is that of the nomination of Commissioners in the mode formerly adopted. I am still waiting the answer to my different Letters to Mr: Livingston written since the 2d. Febry. on the subject of Louisiana & the Floridas as much more must depend upon the influence of France & her opinion, than any thing else. It is said that Spain is discontented with the cession she has made & that it is one of the reasons of Mr Urquijos disgrace,[3] but situated as We are We must not only move with deliberation but with great caution & delicacy. I mean to go to Aranjuez in about a Week & I trust when you recieve my propositions to the Minister that you will not only approve them but particularly the manner in which they have been offered. You may be assured that every thing shall be done by me to smooth over things that are unpleasant & obtain by mild & moderate language & conduct, the Justice that is due to our citizens. I have already found this efficacious in many instances & the release of more ships than had occurred for some time & the removal of the Quarantine, where the Spanish consuls certificate is produced, are joined to their speedy answer of my letters a proof of the Wish of their Government to oblige us. How far they may do so in the case of the Floridas remains to be proved. If the Object of France has been to obtain Louisiana in order to bridle the conduct of the Western Country & hold a check over their commerce, they will oppose the cession to us as it will defeat their intentions in a great degree to put us in posession of Florida.

I fear too that the Spaniards will consider it dangerous to give us such ports in the gulf of Mexico & so near to Cuba & their continental posessions. If the French have made them believe it is necessary to have their nation as a Barrier between us, they will consider this attempt to obtain Florida as verifying the predictions of the French & be of course disinclined to it. I foresee all these Objections but am nevertheless determined to make the attempt in consequence of your Instructions. The only hope I have is from their Want of Money here & as I have held out the idea to them of a purchase I am hopeful they will treat. I am to have an interview with the Prince of Peace on the subject & as soon as I can collect or discover his opinion I shall be able to know if it is possible to succeed. If he patronises the attempt we shall do very well but if he is opposed to it nothing can be done. I have been & am so much employed in the Business of reclamations & in the numerous suits now depending in their Tribunals that I scarcely have a moment to myself. You can have no idea of the immense labour of this Mission & the accumulated Business of it. I am now recieving every day answers & representations on Business that has occurred in many instances 2, & 3 Years Since & numerous ones in 12, 10 & 6 months & been that time before either their Departments or Tribunals. My representations on the subject of the Supposed Blockade of Gibraltar & on the Floridas have been made in the Spirit & terms of your instructions.[4] I am also collecting all the information I can with respect to their discriminating Duties in Italy Spain & Portugal & have written to all our Consuls in these three countries a circular Letter on the subject. I have likewise purchased a small mercantile Book on the same which I mean To send you when I can find an Opportunity. I send you at present no Opinion on the affairs of Europe generally because until the arrangements at Amiens are finished it is impossible to say what will be their future fate—if Bonaparte is honest it is in his power to give rational liberty not only to France but to all the newly formed republics of Batavia Italy & Switzerland: I still hope he will do this at a proper time. If he does not after all the lost Blood & Treasure of the last 12 Years our own will be the only truly free country in the World—the only one which in the *general Deluge* of the rights of Man has been suffered by a benignant providence whose designs are unsearchable *to float* like the Ark of Noah untouched to preserve those Seeds which are yet one Day to repeople a World of Liberty.

I am sorry to inform you that I have been very sick for some Weeks. The cold keen air of these high Castilian hills higher it is said from the Sea than the Top of the Alps gave me some thing bordering on a Pleurisy. I am however now able to go out again & will Write You in future fully & constantly by Bourdeaux & Cadiz. Present me in the Most affectionate & respectful terms to the President. His Speech is exceedingly praised here & all Europe turns an astonished & I fear some of them a suspicious Eye to our rising & happy country. With a wish that heaven may continue to bless it with Liberty peace & Content I conclude myself with affectionate regard & sincere friendship Dear Sir Yours Truly

CHARLES PINCKNEY

This is the only paper of the Size you mention I can get. They all Write on Quarto Paper.

The Court goes to Barcelona to meet the Naples Family in September on the double Marriage. As no Business can be done here during that time the Minister going with the Court & as Barcelona is half way to Rome I wish you very much to obtain the Presidents permission for me to Visit the antient residence of Brutus & Cato. I can do it at the same time & shall be absent but a few Weeks.

RC (DNA: RG 59, DD, Spain, vol. 6). Second postscript written on verso of cover. Postmarked New York, 19 May; docketed by Brent as received 22 May.

1. JM to Pinckney, 19 Dec. 1801 (*PJM-SS*, 2:325). Rose Campbell was a Baltimore ship captain who came to Madrid to pursue the case of the ship *Clothier*, which had been seized at Lima, Peru, in May 1800 for violating the Spanish law forbidding trade with Spanish colonies (David Humphreys to Cevallos, 6 Mar. 1801 [DNA: RG 59, DD, Spain, vol. 6]).

2. Of Pinckney's letters to JM here mentioned, only those of 14 Sept. 1801 (from Amsterdam), 22 Sept. 1801 (from The Hague), and 14 Mar. 1802 (from Madrid) have been found (see *PJM-SS*, 2:112–13, 126).

3. Chevalier Mariano Luis de Urquijo, the former first minister of state, had been supplanted by Pedro Cevallos Guerra in 1800 (*PJM-SS*, 1:53 n. 2). For Urquijo's dismissal, see Hilt, *The Troubled Trinity*, pp. 116–18.

4. In a 24 Mar. 1802 letter to Cevallos (extract printed in *ASP, Foreign Relations*, 2:479–80) that treated a number of topics at length, Pinckney challenged the legality of the Gibraltar blockade, following closely the seven points outlined in JM's instructions of 25 Oct. 1801 (*PJM-SS*, 2:199–202; see also Pinckney to JM, 6 Apr. 1802, n. 3).

From Charles Pinckney

(Private)

DEAR SIR   March 20 1802 IN MADRID

The present opportunity I avail myself of to send you another copy of the same Book on the Duties & commercial regulations of Spain[1] which I am hopeful you will recieve safe. This will go so slow by Mules to Bayonne & from thence to Bourdeaux that all my other letters written at the same time & I expect others written after will very probably reach you before this as I am obliged to send the Book by a private opportunity to Bourdeaux & not by Post. I therefore only say to you by this that from an Express just arrived they are every moment expecting the news of the conclusion & signing of the Definitive Treaty.

If you could conveniently send me by some good Opportunity either to Mr Terry or Iznardi at Cadiz or Kirkpatrick at Malaga or Mr Montgomery at Alicant: a very good likeness of the President at full Length you will much oblige me. I have one—but it is small & not very like & it is my wish to have one at full Length to place with General Washingtons & Columbus[']s in my large Salle. I began housekeeping a few Weeks agoe & I trust in polite & decorous attentions the "Casa de America" as they call it here will be at least equal to any of them. I have two public nights in the Week & shall endeavour by every means in my power to make our Nation & myself as agreeable as possible to Spain. With my affectionate respects to the President & compliments to your good Lady I am my dear friend Yours Truly

CHARLES PINCKNEY

RC (DLC).

1. This book—which Pinckney also referred to in his public dispatch of 20 Mar. and his dispatches of 24 and 28 Mar.—was probably the *Almanak mercantil* (see Pinckney to JM, 14 Aug. 1802, and n. 3).

§ From Rufus King. *20 March 1802, London.* No. 59. Reports that Bird, Savage, and Bird will send to the Treasury Department the accounts for the Tunisian present and encloses copies of his letters on shipment of the articles. Has had no word from Hargreaves since he left Algiers;[1] in early February Eaton was temporarily in Leghorn for his health. Nothing decisive has occurred in the negotiations at Amiens, but public opinion indicates the treaty will be "speedily concluded" in light of "Accounts of Toussaints opposition in St. Domingo." Bill on countervailing duties has passed the House of Commons as it was introduced and should be completed in a few days.

RC and enclosures (DNA: RG 59, DD, Great Britain, vol. 10); letterbook copy (NHi: Rufus King Papers, vol. 55). RC 1 p.; in a clerk's hand, signed by King; docketed by Brent as received 31 May. Printed in King, *Life and Correspondence of Rufus King*, 4:83. Enclosures are copies of a 16 Mar. 1802 letter from King to Gavino (1 p.) reporting shipment on the British frigate *Medusa* of a case containing guns and pistols, which comprised the remainder of the "Peace Presents" to the bey of Tunis, and forwarding a 16 Mar. letter to the commander of the first American frigate to land at Gibraltar on its way to the Mediterranean (1 p.), directing him to forward the case to Eaton at Tunis, and a 16 Mar. letter to Eaton (3 pp.) reporting on the arrangements for delivery of the case and other articles sent earlier. A 15 Mar. account listing the arms sent to Tunis is printed in Knox, *Naval Documents, Barbary Wars*, 2:86.

1. For Lewis Hargreaves's role in delivering part of the U.S. tribute to the bey of Tunis, see King to JM, 14 Dec. 1801, and John Gavino to JM, 11 Jan. 1802 (*PJM-SS*, 2:316–17, 387).

§ **From George Washington McElroy.** *20 March 1802, Philadelphia.* Has been informed of his appointment as U.S. consul for the Canary Islands. Wishes to receive his commission as soon as possible, "being now on the point of Sailing for Teneriffe." Reports the existence of an illegal trade "between some English houses in Teneriffe and their correspondents in Great Britain," which employs captains "who have been in America, tho . . . not entitled to Citizenship." Discovery of this trade will result in suspicion of legal American trade by neutral nations.

RC (DNA: RG 59, CD, Tenerife, vol. 1). 2 pp.

§ **From Elias Vander Horst.** *20 March 1802, Bristol.* Transmits a copy of his letter of 3 Mar.[1] and four letters from Rufus King; encloses newspapers and a London price current. "The Season here for Agricultural pursuits was never more favorable than at present, nor do I recollect the fields at any former period so early in the year, wearing a more promising appearance."

RC (DNA: RG 59, CD, Bristol, vol. 2). 1 p. Written at the bottom of Vander Horst to JM, 3 Mar. 1802. Enclosures not found.

1. See Vander Horst to JM, 2 Mar. 1802, and n.

To Thomas Bulkeley

SIR WASHINGTON, DEPARTMENT OF STATE. March 22d. 1802.

The President having appointed William Jarvis Esqr. by whom this will be handed to you, consul of the United States at Lisbon, you will be pleased to receive him as your successor, and to deliver to him the several documents, letters, &c. which may belong to the consulate; to which you will be Kind enough to add any other information by which you may be able to assist the commencement of his functions. I am Sir &c.

JAMES MADISON.

Letterbook copy (DNA: RG 59, IC, vol. 1).

From Daniel Clark

Sir   Philadelphia 22 March 1802

Since I had the pleasure of seeing you in Washington I have heard a variety of reports concerning Luisiana on the subject of which I did not think it proper to trouble you, but having been assured by Mr Duane two days since that the Province was unquestionably ceded to the U. S. and that he had received his information from a Source on which he could place the utmost reliance, and the Aurora of this morning mentioning an arrangement having taken place respecting it,[1] I am induced to apply to you & request you will favor me with such particulars as may be communicated respecting it. Independent of the pleasure I shall receive in learning so important a piece of news, I think I shall have it in my power to render a Service to the Merchants trading to New Orleans if the matter is so far advanced as to suffer it to be made public—there are now from 80 to 100 sail of American shipping in New Orleans waiting for Cargoes & many are on the way to that Place—the Intendant in consequence of the old spanish systems of Colonial Trade is about to shut the Port,[2] and will reduce our Commerce in that Quarter to the importation of articles necessary for the supply of our own territory on the River & exportation of its Produce—by this step we will lose an important Branch of our Trade—if however the Cession of the Province is a measure likely to take place on being advised of it from hence, he will not put the measure in execution. Should it be deemed improper in the present state of the Business to make a Communication to me with respect to it, I take the Liberty of suggesting that thro' the Chevalier Yrujo to whom no doubt the negociation must be known, a hint might be given to the Intendant of Luisiana from which our Citizens would derive great Benefits. As you know how particularly I am interested in this great Event I hope you will excuse on that account the Liberty I have taken in requesting information from you respecting it. I remain Sir Your most obedient servant

DANIEL CLARK[3]

RC (DNA: RG 59, CD, New Orleans, vol. 1).

1. The Philadelphia *Aurora General Advertiser* of 22 Mar. 1802 stated that the efforts of Robert R. Livingston and Charles Pinckney had been successful in thwarting French plans to colonize Louisiana and hinted that Spain would soon cede the territory to the U.S. The next day's paper was more specific, reporting that "it was publicly said in the Coffee House of this city last week that the island of New-Orleans was ceded to the United States, and we suppose the tract of about 40 miles between that island and our boundary line along with it."

2. It was not until 18 Oct. 1802 that Juan Ventura Morales, Spanish intendant in Louisiana, revoked the American right of deposit at New Orleans (DeConde, *This Affair of Louisiana*, p. 119).

3. Daniel Clark (ca. 1766–1813) was born in Ireland and moved to New Orleans in 1786,

where he joined his uncle and namesake and quickly established himself as a merchant of prominence. He became an American citizen in 1798 and was appointed consul at New Orleans by Jefferson in 1801. In the ensuing years, Clark played a major role in Louisiana politics through his relationships with James Wilkinson, William C. C. Claiborne, and Aaron Burr. He served one term in Congress as a delegate from Orleans Territory (1806–8).

From Tobias Lear

No. 22

SIR,   CAPE FRANÇOIS March 22d: 1802.

I yesterday received the duplicate of the letter which you did me the honor of writing on the 26th of feby.[1]

I hope my conduct, which you will find detailed under date of the 21t of feby,[2] will meet the approbation of the President. Keeping in view the interest of our Citizens here, as well as the relation in which our nation stands with the Fr. Republic, I have endeavoured to conciliate the esteem of the Governmt. here, and, at the same time, ma[i]ntain the rights of our Citizens. The intemperate conduct and expressions of many Am. Captains and others, have not seconded my views; and many delays and vexations have been experienced by our Vessels. Upon the whole, however, I have ma[i]ntained my ground, altho' I meet with bitter censures from those, whose imprudence, if not check'd, wd. have created serious difficulties. I have reason to think I stand well with the Genl. in Chief, the Prefect, and other principal officers: And, difficult and delicate as my situation is, I shall persevere in the conduct I have hitherto pursued.

The General in Chief has been absent since the 17th of feby, which is one reason of the inconveniencies we have experienced; as the Island is under military law, he is the only person to whom we can look for effectual relief in difficult cases.

An Embargo has been laid on all Vessels in Port, by order of Genl. Boyer, who commands here, since the 8th inst. He yesterday informed me he wd. permit ten Am. Vessels to sail; and I hope others will be permitted to depart as they may be ready.

Admiral Guanteaume[3] sailed about ten days ago, with six ships of the line, it is said for France. Admiral La Touch[4] commands at Port au Prince: And the Admiral in Chief, Villaret,[5] left this place two days ago, in a frigate, for Port au Prince, to see the Genl. in Chief. He is about to sail for the U. States, as soon as he returns, with 5 or 6 ships of the line, it is said, for provisions &c. and that he will return again on this Station.

The Blacks have been in great force in the neighbourhood of the City, for some time past. They have completely devastated the Country about the Cape: And the force here is so small, that we have been in a state of seige: And many who were not acquainted with the strength of the place, have been in constant expectation of an Attack.

Three of the black Generals, vizt. Clerveau, Maurepas, and Paul Louverture, brother of the Genl. and who has commanded at Santo Domingo, have surrendered, with part of their troops:[6] but there appears no immediate prospect of reducing the Island to complete subjection. The principal part of the Fr. force is in the South.

It is true that a force is destined to take possession of Louisiana. It is *reported that General Barnadotte with 10 ships* [of] *the line is daily expected here on his way to take possession of that country.* That this *will be done* I *have no doubt* but in *the present state of the island* all the *force which* [may] *arrive here* will be *kept* for the present.

I enclose an order for releiving provisions & Lumber from duties for 3 months—also a recital of facts made by the Municipality respecting the burning the Cape &c.[7]

The number of Am. Vessels now in port are about 75, and they are daily arriving. I expect the adventurers hither will sacrifice much property. For if the Govermt. shd. decline to take the provisions, they wd. not sell for their first cost. Dry Goods are a perfect drug. With sentiments of the highest respect and purest attachment, I have the honor to be Sir, Your most obedt sert

TOBIAS LEAR.

P. S. It is probable I shall make a visit to the U. States after the Genl. in Chief shall have returned hither, and the Am. Affairs are put in a regular train.

RC and enclosures (DNA: RG 59, CD, Cap Haitien, vol. 4); FC (ibid.). RC marked "*Duplicate*"; docketed by Brent. Italicized words are those encoded by Lear and decoded here by the editors using a key from the Lear family papers (owned by Stephen Decatur, Garden City, N.Y., 1958). Words in square brackets were omitted in coding in the RC and are supplied from the FC. RC decoded interlinearly by JM. For enclosures, see n. 7.

1. *PJM-SS*, 2:489–90.
2. Lear was probably referring to his dispatch no. 21, which was dated 28 Feb. 1802 (*PJM-SS*, 2:499–522).
3. Honoré-Joseph Ganteaume (1755–1818) went to sea at fourteen, served in the French navy under the comte d'Estaing during the American Revolution, and rose to the rank of admiral during the Napoleonic Wars. In January 1802 he left France as commander of a squadron of ships carrying arms to Saint-Domingue (Tulard, *Dictionnaire Napoléon*, p. 773).
4. Louis-René-Madelène Le Vassor de La Touch-Tréville (1745–1804) saw combat in the naval battles of the American Revolution. He commanded a squadron in the Saint-Domingue expeditionary force (*Biographie universelle* [1843–65 ed.], 42:10–12).
5. Louis-Thomas Villaret-Joyeuse (1748–1812) was a veteran of the French naval wars with Great Britain in the Indian Ocean and the Far East as well as numerous naval battles of

the revolutionary wars. Tapped to head the naval forces for the Saint-Domingue expedition, Villaret later served as captain general of Martinique (1802–9) and governor general of Venice (1811–12) (Tulard, *Dictionnaire Napoléon*, p. 1725).

6. Generals Clairveaux and Jacques Maurepas—who had fought with Toussaint since 1793—and Paul L'Ouverture, Toussaint's brother, surrendered to the French authorities and took rank in Leclerc's army, where they led troops against their former comrades (Robert Debs Heinl, Jr., and Nancy Gordon Heinl, *Written in Blood: The Story of the Haitian People, 1492–1971* [Boston, 1978], pp. 67, 105; James, *Black Jacobins*, pp. 310–12, 346).

7. Lear enclosed letters to him from the chief of naval administration at Cap Français, 18 Ventôse an X (9 Mar. 1802) (1 p.; in French), and Charles-Cézar Télémaque, 14 Ventôse an X (5 Mar. 1802) (1 p.; in French) (both filed after Lear's dispatch no. 23 to JM, 29 Mar. 1802).

From Robert R. Livingston

No. 8

DEAR SIR,   PARIS 22d. March 1802.

I have nothing to add to the letters just sent you by the way of Baltimore but the enclosed note just recieved[1]—from this you will find that the construction given to the second article of the convention differs materially from ours & will if supported greatly narrow the ground of our claims. You will also see in it rather an evasion of the points I have pressed them upon than an answer to them. But even this is more than they have done for the ministers of Denmark & Sweden who have got no sort of answer to their notes: and it will be of use as it enables me to go more fully into the discussion. It will be well to retain all they may have to claim from us & to make no payment till matters are arranged here.

I could wish to know how much (if any thing) we are indebted to this government, as I may in that case satisfy some claims by obtaining setoffs. The injury that our country has recieved by the precipitancy of the last administration. The revocation of the treaty & the abrogation of the second article in the convention are incalculable. God knows what would be the effect of garrisoning Louisiana with black troops which is by no means an improbable measure as they will not incline to keep them in their islands. I have the satisfaction of thinking that I at present stand very well with the court as I am assured thro' channels I can depend upon, tho I was seen on my first arrival as too much attached to democratic principles, but I have carefully avoided the smallest interference in the politics of the country or any association that might give umbrage. The definitive treaty is not yet signed tho it is generally understood here that the principal difficulties are removed.

The Emperor of Germany & King of Prussia have acquiesced in the business of the Italian Republic.[2] The Ministers of other powers have hither to been silent on the subject—may it not be well in us to compliment upon it? It is said here that Tripotian [*sic*] corsairs have sailed under British Colors & with British passes[3]—should not this fact be enquired into & noticed?

I would send duplicates of the last dispatches but I fear we shall not have time by this conveyance. I must give Mr. Sumter a little leisure since he has been only married two days. I am Dr. sir with the most respectful attachment your Most Hle. St.

ROBT R LIVINGSTON

RC and enclosure (DNA: RG 59, DD, France, vol. 8); draft (NHi: Livingston Papers); letterbook copy and copy of enclosure (NHi: Livingston Papers, vol. 1). RC in a clerk's hand, signed by Livingston. Docketed by Brent, with his note: "enclosed in Mr Livingston's No 9—of March 27th 1802." For enclosure, see n. 1.

    1. Livingston enclosed a copy of Talleyrand's letter to him of 29 Ventôse an X (20 Mar. 1802) (9 pp.; in French), in which Talleyrand addressed the points made in Livingston's various notes on American claims. To Livingston's argument for including in those claims the ships and cargoes detained in French ports during the embargo declared in July 1798, Talleyrand responded that the mutual renunciation of article 2 of the Convention of 1800, as agreed to in the convention's ratification, implied a renunciation of indemnities for losses effected by the embargo (see *PJM-SS*, 1:206 n. 3; Bonnel, *La France, Les Etats-Unis, et la guerre de course*, p. 64). To Livingston's criticism that France was delaying compensation to those Americans whose ships had been taken as prizes, Talleyrand responded by pleading the complexity of the cases in point.

    2. Napoleon's elevation to the presidency of the Italian Republic was received in European courts with muted disapproval (Deutsch, *Genesis of Napoleonic Imperialism*, pp. 83–84).

    3. Livingston probably was referring to the rumor current in the fall of 1801 that three Tripolitan cruisers had been outfitted at Mahón and had sailed for Tripoli under British colors with Minorcan crews to avoid American searches (David Humphreys to JM, 9 Nov. 1801, and William Kirkpatrick to JM, 27 Nov. 1801, *PJM-SS*, 2:233, 278 and n.).

From Louis-André Pichon

March 22d. 1802.

Mr. Pichon offers his respects to Mr Madison and begs leave to give him the trouble of perusing and forwarding to the Secretary of the Treasury the inclosed paper which relates to the already mentioned subject of drafts on france.[1] Mr P. after a conversation on that topic with the Secretary of the treasury has thought it might conduce to a compliance of Mr P.['s] wishes to State his proposals in writing. Indeed the more Mr P. reflects on the subject, the more he persuades himself that the mode proposed would subject the Executive Govent. of the United States to no not the smallest grounded reproach, for an undue facility to a foreign government it being a matter in the mere course of the negociations which the Treasury must make every day to remit to Europe, and turning altogether on the ideas which the treasury may entertain of the solvability or insolvability of the French Treasury; and the negon. proposed if the same is believed to exist, being expedient as well to the American as to the French Treasury: it is indeed to Mr Pichon and to the army at St Domingo of great importance and is so far a circumstance where it is in the power of the U. S., merely by pursuing their own concern, to show france an amicable and well wishing disposition.

Mr. Pichon sets off to morrow for Philadelphia where he requests Mr Madison to forward him within four days if convenient his answer to the last note of Mr P. on St Domingo; Mr P. going to Phila. on purpose to dispatch the Cutter arrived from france back to Brest. Mr. Pichon will repair to the State office to take Mr Madison's command: this is a memorandum in case he does not meet him there. Mr Pichon will make but a stay of a few days at Phila. If Mr Madison will also forward his dispatches for Mr Livingston & Mr Skipwith they will be delivered to the captain with Mr Pichon's packets.

RC and enclosure (NHi: Gallatin Papers).

1. The "inclosed paper" was a letter from Pichon to Gallatin, 22 Mar. 1802 (4 pp.), requesting the secretary of the treasury to buy French government bills of exchange totaling $400,000 issued to purchase supplies for the Leclerc expedition at Saint-Domingue. Pichon attempted to convince Gallatin the purchase would benefit both sides: the French would not have to sell large numbers of bills in the public market, and the U.S. would have an easy way of remitting funds to Europe. JM forwarded Pichon's letter to Gallatin on the same day (JM to Gallatin, 22 Mar. 1802 [ibid.; 1 p.; docketed by Gallatin, "Pichon wanting to sell his bills to Govt. for relief of San Domingo. Rejected by me"]).

§ From Carlos Martínez de Yrujo. 22 *March 1802, Washington.* Refers to his demand made a long time ago of the U.S. government to execute the stipulations of article 5 of the treaty between Spain and the U.S. in the pursuit of the bandit Bowles,[1] long resident among the Indians in U.S. territory. Does not know what steps the U.S. has taken to comply with the stipulations of the article. If anything has been done, it has not been efficacious; Bowles has continued his forays against the Floridas and, according to reports, has also stirred up the Creek Indians and other tribes against those Spanish territories. The interest the U.S. has in protecting its frontiers and in restraining the Indians under its jurisdiction, coupled with his good opinion of the president, would be sufficient to reassure Yrujo that the U.S. will take steps to stop the abuses and irregularities committed by the Indians within its borders. But besides these motives of policy and humanity a formal obligation exists. Copies an extract from article 5 of the treaty: "'*And the better to obtain this effect*' (vizt, to maintain peace and harmony among the several Indian nations who inhabit the country adjacent to their Boundaries) '*both parties oblige themselves expressly to restrain by force all hostilities in the part of the Indian nations living within their boundaries* &ca.'" [2]

Flatters himself the U.S. will fulfill the stipulations of this article and rid Spanish territory of this adventurer, who causes and has caused so much damage to its frontiers. Requests to be informed of the measures the U.S. has adopted to obtain an end as necessary as it is important.

RC (DNA: RG 59, NFL, Spain, vol. 2). 3 pp.; in Spanish; in a clerk's hand, except for Yrujo's complimentary close and signature. Docketed by Brent.

1. William Augustus Bowles (1763–1805), a Maryland-born adventurer and director general of the Creek nation, sought to expel the Spanish from the Floridas and create a Muskogee state under British protection. His three filibustering expeditions—1788, 1791, and 1799–1800—were unsuccessful, and he died in a Havana prison (J. Leitch Wright, Jr., *William Augustus Bowles: Director General of the Creek Nation* [Athens, Ga., 1967], pp. 1, 19–35, 55–86, 119–41, 169–71). For an earlier letter from Yrujo to JM on this matter, see *PJM-SS*, 1:261.

2. For article 5 of the Pinckney treaty of 1795, see Miller, *Treaties*, 2:322–23.

¶ From James Ross. Letter not found. *22 March 1802.* Mentioned in Daniel Brent to Ross, 14 May 1802 (DNA: RG 59, DL, vol. 14), as a letter enclosing the deposition of John and Joseph Dunlap in support of their claim against Spain. Brent informed Ross that JM "thought it best to address a complaint to the Spanish Government" through Charles Pinckney at Madrid and had written to Pinckney accordingly; "he charged me also to signify to you, that some additional testimony will perhaps be useful, to give force to this deposition, . . . and that agreeable to a suggestion in your letter, he has informed Mr. Pinckney this testimony could be procured, and would be sent to him if necessary."

§ From Albert Gallatin. *23 March 1802, Treasury Department.* "Enclos'd I have the Honor to transmit for your Information, the duplicate of a Letter from Messrs. Bird, Savage & Bird, Bankers of the United States, at London, dated January 13th. 1802—as also duplicates of the Accounts therein referr'd to."

RC (DLC: Gallatin Papers). 1 p.; in a clerk's hand, signed by Gallatin. Enclosures not found, but for a letter to JM from Bird, Savage, and Bird of 13 Jan. 1802, see *PJM-SS*, 2: 392–93.

From Elias Boudinot

Dr Sir   PHILADELPHIA March 24t 1802

Altho' I am much averse from intermeddling with the appointments of Government, well knowing the great difficulties attending them, yet from the peculiar Situation and adverse Circumstances of Mr. Isaac C. Barnet of Bourdeaux, a Son of an old Acquaintance who died in the Army during our late Struggle with Great Brittain,[1] I am constrained to trouble you with this Letter.

I have been privy to the encouragement and even assurances of Government made to him, if he would continue at his Post, until peace should take place with France. I have been informed from the best authority, that his Conduct has been correct & useful. General Washington in his life time considered him as a very promising Officer of Government and among the best in France.

Suffer me then Sir, to save you time, to enclose an original Letter, I have just recieved from Mr. Barnet, which will better communicate his real Situation, than any language of mine; and I shall be much obliged by your returning it, when you have done with it.

I do not mean, by this Communication, to urge any thing on Government they have reasons for disapproving, but barely to possess you with his Statement of Facts, and to beg such an Answer as you may think expedient, and which may decide his expectations and ascertain his future prospects. He seems to have his Eye, on the Consulate either of Antwerp or Lisbon. Government only can determine the propriety of th⟨e⟩ Application. I have the honor to be with great respect D Sir Your very Obedt Servt

Elias Boudinot

RC (DNA: RG 59, LAR, 1801–9, filed under "Barnet"). Enclosure not found.

1. Dr. William M. Barnet (or Burnet) (d. 1783) came from a politically prominent New Jersey family and served as a Continental army surgeon in the American Revolution (Isaac Cox Barnet to Jefferson, 10 Sept. 1801 [ibid.]; Heitman, *Historical Register Continental*, p. 88). For more on Isaac Cox Barnet, see Kline, *Papers of Burr*, 2:617–18 n. 1.

From Charles Pinckney

Dear Sir   Madrid March 24: 1802

I Will thank you to excuse the paper I write on as it is the only paper of this Size I can find the Spaniards using altogether for their Writings the Quarto post & this Size only for covers & common purposes.

This is the third Letter I have written you this fortnight & the reason is to mention to you that from the account just recieved We have every reason to fear that the Vessel which I gave you the account of & which carried my original & second Dispatch to you With the statement of my arrival & reception here & of the number of our claims & their situation has been lost. I therefore take the earliest opportunity to send you a copy of the claims under their different heads, by which you will be enabled to judge of the extent & arduousness of the Business of this Mission. I have unremittingly attended to it & shall continue to do so & it is with pleasure I have seen some Vessels released since I have been here & I am hopeful a disposition to do more. I am moving with great caution—& preparing the best & most probable means of obtaining, if possible the Floridas. The whole of these papers will soon be forwarded to you—that is as soon as I can get a more safe & certain conveyance than the Post commonly is either to Bourdeaux or Cadiz or indeed any port in Spain—the roads being at this time so infested *with robbers* that I am afraid many of our Letters may have miscarried in that way. Indeed from the interior & remote situation of Madrid I fear this frequently happens. I have heard but once from my children since I left America & but twice or three times from you. I can send you nothing from hence about Amiens to which place all Europe now anxiously looks, as we have different reports every day & none of them true. I have purchased a Book for you which will give you the most recent account of the Mercantile regulations & Duties of Spain & mean to send it by the first good conveyance I can meet as it can not go by Post. I have also Written to all our Consuls for their accounts of the regulations in their different ports & hope to posess you fully of them. When we know what they will do at Amiens I will then endeavour to give you my Opinion of the State of Europe & it's probabilities. Until then it is impossible even to conjecture for Bounopartes conduc⟨t⟩ in the affair of the Cisalpine makes it extremely difficult to penetrate his further Views. I still hope for the best from him, or at any rate that whatever may happen here, *our ark* will be suffered to float untouched. I shall be happy to hear from You & with my affectionate respects & best Wishes to the President for his health & honour I remain With the same to you my dear sir Yours Truly

CHARLES PINCKNEY

I mentioned to you in my former Letters that the King of Spain goes in the latter End of August or September to Barcelona to meet the Naples Family on account of the double marriage. His Ministers go with him & during this time no Business can be done here of course. Now as Barcelona is very nearly half way to Rome, & I can easily go there from Barcelona, going by Water to Genoa or Naples, & as I shall be able, if no accidents happen, to return to Madrid nearly as soon as the King does, I am hopeful the President will give me leave to go to Rome for a few Weeks, while the King is absent, whom I will accompany as far as Barcelona, & if convenient go from thence, with the Naples Family to Italy. If I obtain the Presidents permission for this Short absence, & I should notwithstanding find any unforeseen occurrences arise⟨n⟩ which Would make my presence necessary with the Spanish court, I will then be governed by circumstances & not go. As I am to stay sometime longer at this court I wish much to see Italy, & as the indulgence of these *short absences* has been generally granted to other ministers I am sure it will be also very chearfully given to me, for the very little time I expect it will take me to compleat it or occasion me to be absent from my Post In Madrid.

My best to Mr Gallatin, Mr Lincoln Mr: Dearborn & Mr Smith. I am happy to find the New administration move with so much advantage to their Country & Honour *to Themselves.*

RC (DNA: RG 59, DD, Spain, vol. 6). Docketed by Brent. Enclosure not found.

§ Resolution of the House of Representatives. *24 March 1802.* Discharges the committee to whom was referred on 15 Feb. the petition of Timothy Williams and others and refers the petition to the secretary of state, "with instruction to examine the same, and report his opinion thereupon, to the House."[1]

Ms and enclosure (DNA: RG 59, ML). Ms 1 p.; marked "Extract from the Journal"; signed by William Lambert, acting for John Beckley; docketed by Brent. For enclosure, see n. 1.

1. The undated petition of Timothy Williams, John Williams, and Joseph Lee, Jr. (1 p.), requested the Senate and House of Representatives to retain the sums they "were about to provide for Compensation to France for Captures *before* the Treaty [Convention of 1800]," so that the subscribers might receive redress for the brig *Traveller,* captured and condemned by the French at Ile de France after "the Treaty was known there." No report by JM on this petition has been found.

To Tobias Lear

SIR   DEPARTMENT OF STATE. March 25th. 1802.

I have duly received your Letters of Feby 12th. and 28th. the latter of which includes your Journal from Febry 1st. to that date.[1] The latter having but just come to hand, has been but barely perused.

We are fully sensible of the difficulties and anxieties into which you have been thrown by the late occurrences. It is with pleasure that I can console you with an Assurance, that your exertions have appeared to the President to justify his confidence in your zeal and judgment. To these you must still be referred in a great degree, for the conduct best adapted to the fluctuations and contingencies in which you are placed. A thorough recognition of the authority of the French Republic; a cultivation of good understanding with the chiefs deputed by it to St. Domingo, and a patronage of our rights and interests, both national and individual, form the outline by which you must be guided. As it may be satisfactory to you, to see the ground taken in our communications with Mr. Pichon and Admiral Villaret, in relation to the present state of things, I enclose herewith copies of the Answers to a note of the former to the Secretary of State, and to a letter from the latter to the President.[2] You will also receive a sett of Newspapers, in which you will find the late proceedings of Congress, and other ocurrences at home, as well as accounts from abroad.

The frequency and particularity of your communications are justified, by the importance of the scene in which your trust is to be executed, and will continue to be acceptable. With great respect &c. &c.

J. M.

Letterbook copy (DNA: RG 59, IC, vol. 1).

1. *PJM-SS*, 2:462–64, 499–522.
2. JM to Pichon, 25 Mar. 1802, and JM to Villaret, 25 Mar. 1802.

To Louis-André Pichon

DEPARTMENT OF STATE March 25th. 1802.
The Secretary of State has laid before the President the note of Mr. Pichon of the 17th. inst. and has the honor to assure him that his communications on the subject of St. Domingo, and the arrival there of an armament from France, have been received with all the interest which the ties of sincere friendship between the United States and the French Republic ought to inspire.

The note of the Secretary of State of Feby. 16.[1] has already explained to Mr. Pichon the principles by which the conduct of the United States would be guided on such an occasion and he is now charged by the President to repeat that those principles will be observed with the most faithful and friendly attention: Mr Pichon will not doubt therefore that the declaration that a revolt exists in St. Domingo against the French Republic, and that all foreign trade with that Island is limited to the two ports of Cape Francois & Port Republicain, will receive from the United States the respect which is due the authority under which it is made, and is understood as subjecting individual citizens to the penalties legally attached to prohibited commerce. This assurance is given with the greater cordiality because it is attended with a confidence that whilst the just expectations of the French Republic will be thus fulfilled on the part of the United States, the rights of their lawful commerce will be no less respected by the authorities & officers of the French Republic; and it is with particular satisfaction that the Secretary is able to acknowledge the force given to this confidence by the friendly sentiments and assurances which have been expressed to the President by the admiral commanding the fleets of the French Republic in the West Indies.

Tr (NHi: Livingston Papers); Tr (AAE: Political Correspondence, U.S., 54:264). First Tr sent as enclosure in JM to Livingston, 26 Mar. 1802; docketed, "Recd. 2d. June 1802. in letter No. 3. from Sy. of State." Second Tr in French; enclosed in Pichon to Talleyrand, 11 Germinal an X (1 Apr. 1802).

1. JM undoubtedly meant his letter to Pichon dated 15 Feb. 1802 (*PJM-SS*, 2:469).

To Louis-Thomas Villaret-Joyeuse

SIR   DEPARTMENT OF STATE, March 25th. 1802.

I have the honor to inform you that the President of the United States has recd. your letter of the 17th. Instant.[1] He takes that just interest in its communications, which ought to flow from the friendly dispositions of the United States towards the French Republic, and from the importance which the future condition of St. Domingo may bear to other countries, as well as to that of which it makes a part. The United States will not fail to manifest on this occasion, the full respect which is due to the authority of the French Republic, and to the regulations adopted by it as necessary to give tranquility and happiness to a portion of its dominions so much distinguished by past calamities. Should any American Citizens therefore be allured into illicit commerce of any kind with that Island, they will contravene the purposes of their own government, at the same time that they will make themselves responsible to the jurisdiction of that against which the offence is committed. In giving to you these assurances, I am charged by the President to acknowledge his satisfaction in those which you have expressed of a solicitude to cause the lawful commerce of our Citizens to be respected; and to add, that the fleets and wants of the French republic, will find in the Ports of the United States, every proof of hospitality which is due to a nation with which the ties of former friendship have been so happily renewed. Accept the perfect respect and consideration, with which I have the honor to be &c.

JAMES MADISON.

Letterbook copy (DNA: RG 59, IC, vol. 1); Tr (NHi: Livingston Papers); Tr (AAE: Political Correspondence, U.S., 54:265). First Tr sent as enclosure in JM to Livingston, 26 Mar. 1802. Second Tr in French; enclosed in Pichon to Talleyrand, 11 Germinal an X (1 Apr. 1802).

1. Villaret to Jefferson, 27 Pluviôse an X (16 Feb. 1802) (DNA: RG 59, NFL, France, vol. 1).

From Wilson Cary Nicholas

DEAR SIR   [ca. 25 March 1802]

The enclosed letter was sent to me by Genl. Marshal, who begs that you will send it under cover to Mr. Livingston with a request that he will give it a conveyance. I have obtained a list of all the French Vessels that were captured by the vessels of the U. S. upon comparing that list with your report I find it contains upwards of twenty vessels not included in your report,[1] I have marked all the vessels in this list that are in the report. Will you be so good as to inform me how it happens that those vessels not noticed by you are not to be paid for, the right of appeal (if it exists) I presume applies to them as well as to others, it has been attempted to induce a belief that if we admit the principle that one vessel is to be paid for because a right of appeal existed, that it will involve us for millions. It is important therefore to be able to say what the utmost sum will be that we may be bound for. Be pleased to let me have the enclosed list and any information that you may think proper to give by 12 O'Clock. I am Dear Sir your affectionate hum. Serv.

                                                         W. C. NICHOLAS

my note will be paid when due[2]

RC (PHC). Undated. Conjectural date here supplied on the basis of internal evidence (see n. 1). Enclosure not found.

1. On 25 Mar. Nicholas was appointed chairman of a Senate committee considering a bill to make appropriations for defraying expenses that might arise from carrying into effect the Franco-American Convention of 1800 (*Annals of Congress*, 7th Cong., 1st sess., 204). The report that Nicholas refers to is probably the estimate prepared by JM of expenses necessary for carrying the convention into effect, which was submitted to Jefferson on 11 Jan. 1802 (printed in *ASP, Foreign Relations*, 2:365); the report as printed, however, does not include a list of captured French vessels. There is such a list of fifteen ships under the heading "Statement of French armed vessels captured by the public armed vessels of the United States on or before the 30th of September 1800 & not condemned on that day, and of those captured since that day," dated 3 Mar. 1802 (DNA: RG 59, ML; 2 pp.; docketed by Wagner).

2. For the sum Nicholas borrowed from JM, see his letter to JM, 4 Feb. 1802 (*PJM-SS*, 2: 439–40).

§ From James Anderson. *25 March 1802, Paris.* Requests JM to confirm his appointment, made by Fulwar Skipwith,[1] as vice-agent of the U.S. at the port of Cette. Recalls his service as commercial agent for fourteen months at Brest in the years 1794–95.

RC (DNA: RG 59, CD, Cette, vol. 1). 2 pp.; marked "Duplicate"; docketed by Brent. Anderson was confirmed as commercial agent at Cette (now Sète) in January 1803 (*Senate Exec. Proceedings*, 1:433, 440).

1. See Skipwith to JM, 30 Mar. 1802.

§ From William Savage. *25 March 1802, Kingston, Jamaica*. Encloses a list of American seamen discharged from [British] ships of war at Kingston since his last list. Also sends a list of "Americans still on board the navy here" and suggests that many can be liberated if documents are sent in a timely manner. There are more than forty warships at Kingston; Great Britain intends to keep a strong force "during the attempts of the French to subjugate the Colony of Hispaniola." Has found it necessary since January to assist great numbers of American sailors in finding passage to the U.S. and provisioning them while at Kingston.

RC and enclosures (DNA: RG 59, CD, Kingston, Jamaica, vol. 1). RC 2 pp. First page written at the bottom of a copy of Savage's 12 Feb. 1802 dispatch (*PJM-SS*, 2:464). Docketed by Brent as received 30 June. Enclosures are a list of "American Seamen discharged from British Ships of War since 19 December 1801" (2 pp.) and a "list of persons on board the several ships of war on the Jamaica Station represented to be Americans," dated 25 Mar. 1802 (2 pp.).

To Robert R. Livingston

Sir,   Department of State March 26th. 1802.

My last was of the 16th. instant to which I have nothing new to add on American claims, but to repeat our anxiety to learn the result of your proceedings on that subject. I have received yours of Jany 13th. with the papers to which it refers.[1] The copy of the Treaty between France and Spain has been republished as you will find in the National Intelligencer of this City, from a Paris Gazette.[2] The date of this instrument with some verbal accounts from Spain, leave it possible yet, that the Cession of Louisiana may have been suspended, if not revoked, by some subsequent transaction between the parties; to say nothing of the language held to you on that subject by the French Minister of Foreign relations. The appearance in the Paris Papers of the Treaty above referred to, will lead, no doubt, to further conversations in which it will be difficult to avoid a disclosure of the real State of the matter.

The House of Representatives have passed unanimously the appropriation for the French Convention, and the Senate will no doubt pass it with as little delay as their forms will permit; & probably with unanimity also.[3]

I have just received a letter from Mr. Lear of February 28th.[4] No decisive operations in the army had taken place against Toussaint, who is said to have taken positions, with his scattered troops, in the Mountains. The devastations of the Country have been considerable, and some Massacres have also taken place; but there has been less of both than were at one time apprehended. Some disagreeable clashing appears to have happened between the Supercargoes of American Vessels, laden with provisions at Cape François and the French Commanders, which has terminated in prices and payments not satisfactory to the former, and probably not politic for the latter. Three fourths of the payment is to be made in Bills on the French Government at sixty days sight.[5] It will be perceived that the punctual and ready payment of those bills is of great importance, not only to the creditors, but to the French Government whose future supplies in this Quarter may depend on it: in both views you will no doubt press the subject.

I enclose for your information copies of answers to a late note of Mr. Pichon to the Secretary of State, and a letter from the French Admiral at St. Domingo to the President.[6] In these you will see the sentiments which it has been thought proper to express in relation to the State of things in St. Domingo. Considering the discordant opinions entertained by different descriptions of our Citizens on points involved in it, as well as questions of public law which may grow out of it, the circumspection which has been used is not misapplied. It was of much importance at the same time to manifest a just respect for the authority of the French Republic, and a friendly regard to its interests, in both of which respects I trust we have succeeded, because I am sure we have been sincere.

For the proceedings of Congress and other domestic occurrences, I refer to a file of Newspapers sent herewith. The inattention in the printers of which you complain, in forwarding to you regularly this source of information will be corrected by a fresh instruction to them. With sentiments of the truest esteem & consideration I am Dr Sir Your obedt hbe servt

JAMES MADISON

RC and enclosures (NHi: Livingston Papers); letterbook copy (DNA: RG 59, IM, vol. 6). RC in a clerk's hand, except for JM's complimentary close and signature. For enclosures, see n. 6.

1. *PJM-SS*, 2:389–91.
2. The Treaty of Aranjuez between Spain and France, dated 21 Mar. 1801, was published in the *National Intelligencer* on 24 Mar. 1802. It was taken from the Paris *Journal des Debats* of 17 Jan. 1802.
3. The bill, which had been introduced in the House on 12 Mar. and passed twelve days later, was approved by the Senate on 1 Apr. (*Annals of Congress*, 7th Cong., 1st sess., 250, 998, 1075–76). For its text, see *U.S. Statutes at Large*, 2:148.
4. *PJM-SS*, 2:499–522.
5. On the RC a sentence follows here that has been erased but is faintly legible: "A part of the French fleet it is understood will ere long ⟨be in our Ports?⟩ on ⟨its?⟩ return to France."
6. JM enclosed copies of his 25 Mar. letters to Pichon and to Villaret.

§ To Jacob Clement. *26 March 1802, Department of State, Washington.* Acknowledges receipt of Clement's letter of 2 Feb. [not found] concerning the capture of the brigantine *Experience*. Since the claim appears to fall under the terms of the convention with France, suggests Clement make a representation of his case to Robert R. Livingston and returns his papers for that purpose.

Printed copy (Paul F. Hoag Catalogue [New Canaan, Conn., 1964], item 90). Also offered for sale in *The Collector*, No. 866 (1979), item M-695.

§ From Andrew Ellicott. *26 March 1802, Lancaster.* "The bearer Moses Cotes has communicated to me his plan of an improved Saw-Mill, for which I presume he will be asking for a Patent.[1] I think the improvement merits attention, as it combines simplicity with usefulness. I hope by this time you have recovered your health."

RC (DLC). 1 p.

1. On 1 Apr. 1802 Moses Coates was granted a patent for his "Improvement in a saw mill, which returns the log after each cut" (*ASP, Misc.*, 1:427). An advertisement for the invention was printed in the *National Intelligencer*, 21 July 1802.

§ From Levi Lincoln. *26 March 1802, Washington.* "In answer to your communications, as contained in the letter of the attorney Genl. of the Mississippi territory, enclosed by Governor Claiborne respecting claims to vacant lands in that territory,[1] I can state little more than general principles, and a loose opinion on the described cases. . . . Nothing can be clearer, than that all grants, made by the Spanish Government after the ratification of the treaty, by which the land was ceded to the United States, are void. A claimant who had, in fact, obtained a patent or a title before that time, under the spanish, or since, under the American Government, can alone hold by his grant." Thus, "the only question is, when was the patent granted?" A deed takes effect from the time of its delivery, and every deed is presumed to be delivered on the day of its date. But if a deed is challenged, then its execution must be proved, in which case "the greatest latitude should be given for the admission of evidence, & especially in suppression of fraud." If evidence in the possession of the Spanish government is needed, "a line from the Spanish minister, at this place, on the subject, may be useful."

"Mention is made of an action's being brought by one Green against the United States for the recovery of public lands and buildings, and in which, after a verdict for the demandant, a new trial has been granted. It is not perceived, how an action could be brought against the United States.[2] . . . As no case is stated, I do not see how Government can be bound by any verdict which may be given in the case, nor can I give any opinion on the subject."

RC (DNA: RG 59, LOAG); Tr (Ms-Ar: Claiborne Executive Journal). RC 3 pp.; docketed by Brent. Printed in Hall, *Official Opinions of the Attorneys General*, 1:108–10.

1. Mississippi Territory attorney general Lyman Harding's letter (not found) was enclosed in Governor Claiborne's 20 Jan. 1802 letter to JM. Claiborne asked JM to submit Harding's letter to Lincoln and request his opinion on the validity of antedated Spanish land grants and on the best method for investigating them (*PJM-SS*, 2:413). If JM wrote to Lincoln when he communicated these letters, his letter has not been found.

2. The public land in question was the Villa Gayoso, the summer residence of former Spanish governor Manuel Gayoso de Lemos in Jefferson County, Mississippi Territory, which comprised some six "framed Buildings ill finished" on about two hundred acres of land. It was claimed by Everard Green, son of Col. Thomas Green, a former Virginian and Continental army veteran. The Green family had contested Gayoso's use of the land, and when the Spanish

turned the property over to the U.S. Army they transferred their dispute to the U.S. (Winthrop Sargent to Timothy Pickering, 29 Sept. 1798 and 1 Nov. 1799, and Sargent to John Marshall, 1 June and 10 Aug. 1800, Rowland, *Mississippi Archives*, 1:57, 184, 236, 265; Claiborne, *Mississippi, as a Province, Territory, and State*, 1:228–29 nn.).

§ From Hans Rudolph Saabye. *26 March 1802, Copenhagen.* Transmits a duplicate of his last letter of 16 Jan.[1] Has since received JM's letter of 28 Nov. 1801 regarding Henry Harrison of New Jersey,[2] who "has been found here in the capacity of a Private in one of the Regiments, quartered in this city, where he was listed for the space of eight years." Has gained Harrison's discharge by reimbursing the regiment for its outlay and has paid "for fitting him out with Clothes &c. for the voyage"—a total expenditure of about 63 piasters, "which no doubt will be reimbursed me by his family." Harrison will work for his passage on the ship *Mary* bound for New York. Reports that American ships are subject to "an additional duty of one half more" than that paid by ships of countries with commercial treaties with Denmark. "As long as the War lasted, the paying of this additional duty, was not insisted on, of those who requested to be exempted from it. But now, on peace taking place, it is again put in force. This has induced me to draw a Petition, explaining this matter in it's full light." Encloses a copy and relates unofficial information that sugar, "the principal article, on which the additional duty could be imposed," will only be charged 1 percent more duty when imported in American bottoms than when carried in Danish bottoms. Encloses also a translation of his request to the Danish government in the case of the ship *Hercules*, Capt. William Story, lost on the Elbe River. "Agreable to ancient Laws, the Government lays claim on one third of what is saved from the Vessels lost on the Coast of Holstein." Hopes to obtain not only an exception in this case but also a change in the general rule. Informs JM that an American sailor, John Brown, arrived in Norway "in a most pityful Situation," claiming to have been on the *Samuel Elling* bound from New York to Hamburg when the ship, with the captain and eleven crewmen, was "totally lost" off the Norwegian coast.

RC (DNA: RG 59, Misc. Duplicate Despatches); enclosures (DNA: RG 59, CD, Copenhagen, vol. 1). RC 3 pp.; docketed by Brent; with a note in Wagner's hand, "Extract about Harrison for Mr. English of Geo. Town." Duplicate of RC (ibid.) docketed by Brent as received 8 July. Enclosures are a petition to the Danish government, n.d. (2 pp.), requesting a relaxation of the extra duty imposed on American ships; and Saabye to Count von Bernstorff, 22 Feb. 1802 (3 pp.), on the American claim to the cargo of the *Hercules*.

1. *PJM-SS*, 2:401–2.
2. *PJM-SS*, 2:284 and n. 1.

To Samuel G. Perkins

WASHINGTON Saturday Mar. 27. 1802

Mr. Madison presents his compliments to Mr. Perkins, & incloses the letters of which he wished to be the bearer to Mr. Yard. The one which concerns Mr. Higginson & Mr. Perkins as well as Mr. Yard, is left open for Mr. P's perusal.[1]

RC (DNA: RG 76, Spain, Treaty of 1819, Allowed Claims, vol. 23). Addressed by JM to Perkins at "Stelles Hotel / East of the Capitol."

1. The letter was probably JM to Pinckney, 27 Mar. 1802.

To Charles Pinckney

SIR   WASHINGTON DEPARTMENT OF STATE March 27. 1802

Mr. Higginson & Mr. Perkins of Boston have represented to this department that they have a claim of great importance which they propose to address to the Spanish Government for injuries in South America, to a commercial undertaking for which the necessary sanctions had been given by the competent authorities.[1] Mr. James Yard of Philadelphia will address to that Government a claim of still greater amount, founded on similar injuries, in a parallel case. Mr. Yard means to pursue his redress in person at Madrid, and will charge himself at the same time with the claim of his friends Mr. Higginson & Mr. Perkins. To his explanations therefore, in both cases, I refer you, with a request that you will give to the claimants the advice & support to which they are entitled by the wrongs which they appear to have suffered, by the magnitude of the interest they have at stake, and by the respectability of their characters; and to which I am persuaded you will be induced by a sentiment of benevolence, as well as by a principle of public duty. With highest respect & esteem I remain Dear Sir Your Most Obedt. servt

JAMES MADISON

RC (DNA: RG 76, Spain, Treaty of 1819, Allowed Claims, vol. 6); letterbook copy (DNA: RG 59, IM, vol. 6).

1. See James Yard to JM, 19 Mar. 1802, and n. 1.

From Richard Bland Lee

DEAR SIR,   SULLY March 27. 1802

Mrs. Lee requests me to send under cover to you the inclosed.[1] Permit me to add an hope that you will visit us again on your way to Orange for two reasons, one on account of the pleasure it will always afford us to see you here, & the other that you may judge of my farming operations, and aid me with your advice as to future projèts.

Such is the increasing acrimony of Party spirits if I am to judge from the Newspapers, that I have laid myself almost under the prohibition of saying nothing, & scarce permit my mind to think on Politics. Social intercourse has been too much imbittered—and God grant, that the divisions of opinion may not end in the severest national calamity. But under all circumstances, the esteem formed of your character in my early years having the strongest possession of my mind permits me to subscribe myself most sincerely Your's

                                        RICHARD BLAND LEE

RC (DLC: Lee Papers). Docketed by JM.

1. Enclosure not found, but it probably was a letter from Elizabeth Collins Lee to her childhood friend Dolley Madison (see *PJM-SS*, 1:384 n. 1).

From Robert R. Livingston

No 9
DEAR SIR   PARIS 27h. March 1802

The vessel not going so soon as was expected gives me an opportunity of informing you that the definitive treaty was signed the day before yesterday differing very little from the preliminary Articles. You will find it in the enclosed papers. It is however understood that Martinique is to remain with the british till the debts are ⟨paid for French prisoners.⟩ I send you a note (No 1) from the minister of the marine[1] on the subject of some seamen carried of[f] by Capt Mc.Neil[2] whose conduct as I learn from Commo. dale has been upon this & other occasions such as merits a strict enquiry. At Gibralter he left 4 of his own officers on shore—who have been put to great difficulty & distress to find their way to his ship. At Touloun he reported himself direct from L'Orient (tho he had stoped at Gibralter) in order to avoid the quarantine & thereby committed the honour of the country had the deception been discovered. I am very fearful

76

that the violence of his passions unfits him for the command of a ship of war—tho I have no compt to make of his treatment to me & my family which was perfectly proper so far as regarded myself or them. I also enclose my answer (No 2) to this note which I hope will meet the presidents approbation.[3]

I send enclosed (No 3) my answer to so much of the Ministers note as relates to his observations on the debt[4]—Not having yet had leasure to reply to what relates to prizes.

What I apprehended & predicted in one of my former letters relative to the conduct the French would pursue in the west Indies has I am informed already come to pass. I thought it proper to let the minister know that I was not ignorant of it in hopes that it may aid to ⟨ex⟩pedite the justice they owe us here & shall expect your orders with the official advises you may think proper to give me on this subject (No. 4) is a copy of my note.[5] I easily forsee the flame that this measure will occasion in America & the handle it will give to the opposers of the Administration but I do not so easily see the means you have of redress shd France continue as I much fear she will this system of tyranny which she will endeavour to cover by her necessities. I have both in my public & private letters from my first view of the state of things here endeavoured to discourage our people from giving new credits. But even this will not be an adequate remy. against acts of violence. An *embargo is the only one I see short of actual hostil⟨ities⟩ but before this reaches you Congress will have taken its own measures I trust they will be alike firm & prudent.*

I long since informed you of the heavy duty upon tobacco & suggested the propriety of a similar duty upon the export in foreign ships. Since this subject has engaged you⟨r⟩ Attention I have collected the best information I can on th⟨e⟩ partial inconveniences to which our ships are lyable h⟨ere.⟩ On Leaf tobacco the duties are pr. hund: in foreign Ships 33 franks—in French ships 22—difference 11—this am⟨ounts⟩ to a prohibition—£4 Stg pr. Hogd. is now given for freight i⟨n⟩ French bottoms no Americans can be Chartered ⟨at⟩ any rate to bring tobacco. Fish imported in American or foreign bottoms—10 franks duty—in french 25 sous—difference 9 fr. 75 ctms besides this by a late law 17 Ventose an 1⟨0⟩ a bounty is given to the owners of fishing vessels of 50 fra⟨nks⟩ pr. Man employed in the Newfoundland fishery 15 franks or on the little banks—12 franks pr. myriagrame to french fishermen for fis⟨h⟩ exported from france or from the banks to their colonies 6 franks for the same quantity exported from French ports to Spain Portugal Italy or the Levant—5 franks if exported directly to those places from the banks—a small bounty is also given upon the oil drawn from this fishery—the port duties on foreigners importing fish are also advanced to 6 franks for 5 myriagrames.

Port duties on french Ships.		On foreign coming into a french port
Bound to the channel, north sea Bay of Biscay &c.	3 Sols pr Ton	50 Sols—average difference 45½ Sols in favor of french Ships.
to a mediteranian french port	4 do.	
from Assia Africa or America to a french port	6 Do.	

This is exacted from our ships even if driven in by stress of weather & they go out without unloading.

There are also several advantages in Storages of goods designed for reexportation. It is certainly worthy the consideration of Congress to consider how these disadvantages are to be contravailed. ⟨I⟩ have endeavoured to impress France in the essay I sent you[6]—with the folly of attempting to raise a marine by a commercial warfare. I was this day at the palace to congratulate on the peace when the first Consul took occasion to mention that he hoped the President would forbid the blacks being supplied. I told him I would communicate his wishes on that subject to the President who I did not doubt would treat them with attention. I much wish that no pretence may be offered on our part to cover their violences as I fear they will readily catch at very slight ones. And the rather as the Minister of the Marine complained to me of the supplies of arms found at the Cape which Genl Le Clerk wrote had been furnished by us—*perhaps if an embargo is laid it would be well to* urge this as a reason for it, since it can not be doubted that if the trade is free *our vessels will go to the blacks who pay rather than to the w[h]ites who give bills.* I have yet been honoured with only one set of dispaches from you. Reports laws—financial & statistical information lai⟨d⟩ before congress would be of daily use to me as would any ob⟨ser⟩vations of your own or of our writers on the commerce of our country. I have the honor to be Dear Sir With the most respectful consideration Your Most Obt hum: Sert

ROBT R LIVINGSTON

Draft (NHi: Livingston Papers); enclosures nos. 1–3 (DNA: RG 59, DD, France, vol. 8); letterbook copy and copies of enclosures nos. 3 and 4 (NHi: Livingston Papers, vol. 1). Italicized passages are underlined in the draft; Livingston apparently intended them to be encoded. Words and parts of words in angle brackets are illegible in the draft or missing from torn margins and have been supplied from the letterbook copy. For enclosures, see nn. 1 and 3–5.

1. Enclosure no. 1 is a copy of Denis Decrès to Livingston, 3 Germinal an X (24 Mar. 1802) (2 pp.; in French; docketed by Brent), in which the minister of marine com-

plained of Captain McNeill's behavior in ordering the U.S. frigate *Boston* to sail while three French officers were dining on board. McNeill refused to allow the gentlemen to leave the ship anywhere on the French coast. They finally disembarked at Tunis.

2. Daniel McNeill (1748–1833), who captained privateers during the Revolutionary War and slave ships afterward, was commissioned a captain in the U.S. Navy in 1798. The incidents referred to here, as well as others, earned him the disapproval of Commodore Richard Dale and the Navy Department, and McNeill was dismissed from the service in October 1802 (Christopher McKee, *A Gentlemanly and Honorable Profession: The Creation of the U.S. Naval Officer Corps, 1794–1815* [Annapolis, 1991], pp. 191–93).

3. Enclosure no. 2 is a copy of Livingston's response to Decrès of 5 Germinal an X (26 Mar. 1802) (2 pp.; docketed by Brent), promising that if the allegations against McNeill were substantiated, the president would "treat with the utmost severity an act so repugnant to his own feelings of propriety, & to his wishes to promote harmony between the two nations." Livingston also offered to pay "any reasonable expense" for the return of the French officers.

4. Enclosure no. 3 (11 pp.; docketed by Brent) is a copy of Livingston's 5 Germinal an X (26 Mar. 1802) answer to Talleyrand's note of 20 Mar. 1802, in which Livingston took exception to the French foreign minister's interpretation of the second article of the Franco-American Convention of 1800 and of the reference to it in the ratification (see Livingston to JM, 22 Mar. 1802, and n. 1). Talleyrand had held that American losses owing to the embargo were not to be included in the American debt. Livingston maintained that in the negotiations for the convention there was not "the smallest reference to vessels that France retained in her ports at great expense to the proprietors" and furthermore that article 5 expressly stipulated the payment of "every debt contracted by the public." Livingston went on to press Talleyrand for details on the time and method of compensation to be made to American creditors under article 5 of the convention.

5. Livingston's enclosure no. 4 is a copy of his letter of 27 Mar. 1802 to Talleyrand (1 p.), in which he objected to Leclerc's intention to requisition American cargoes in Saint-Domingue at low prices "& to pay for them ⅕ in money & the remainder in bills upon Paris . . . while so many of those bills are dishonored by non-payment."

6. See Livingston to JM, 14 Mar. 1802, and n. 3.

From Charles Pinckney

(Private)

DEAR SIR   March 28: 1802 IN MADRID

Hearing of an opportunity by an American Gentleman to Bourdeaux I avail myself of it to send you a Book containing a general list of what are here called the reales derechos of the Customhouses & a pretty good view of their commercial regulations. It is in spanish & I could get no translation of it either in French or English but as it appears to be complete on the subjects it treats of you can easily make it out, for the Spanish is very easy. I am hopeful it will be more fortunate than my other Letters & that it will arrive safe. In addition I have Written to all the Consuls in the different ports (& included Portugal & Italy) for their information as you have requested on commercial subjects & particularly on the discriminations of Spain & Portugal & Italy to the Disadvantage of our commerce in favour of their own. I am hopeful by this means to send you complete information on the subject. I have transmitted to the Secretary of State & the Prince of Peace my Letter on the subject of our claims & the purchase of Florida[1] & am now waiting for another interview with the Prince of Peace & Mr. Cevallos to be able to see what will be the probability of our Success. For my own part I apprehend the Spaniards think We are near enough to them already & will very much fear giving us Ports in the Gulf so much nearer—besides We have here to day a report that the cession of Louisiana to the French has become a difficult Question at Amiens, as the British feel themselves much interested. If so our difficulties in the acquisition of Florida will be increased also. However I should suppose you will have no objection to things remaining as they are for a time—that is that Spain be allowed to retain both Louisiana & Florida. If Louisiana is really to be held by France, We certainly ought to Wish to have Florida & the only chance I think is in the Spaniards Want of Money & desire to get it—this may tempt them to sell. By the next conveyance You will recieve copies of my official communications on this subject. I am still however unwell & am waiting with anxiety the opening of the Spring. The cold & uncommonly rough Winter in all the south of Europe & the inundations in the southern & indeed in almost every part of France will make provisions very high next Year in France & Spain. They are now indeed very high here & in France. You Wrote to me sometime since, which I did not recieve for a great while, about my secretary who appears to be a well informed sensible Young man.[2] I took the first floor & it's appurtenances inhabited by Colonel Humphreys & in it are only three Rooms & a kitchen. One a large saloon for large companies—a dining parlour & a chamber—very handsome, but alone sufficient for a single person, or married one, having no children as there is but one chamber. I found Colonel Humphreys had always kept his Office & the Papers & archives of the Mission at Major Youngs house who was also his secretary & Consul General. As Major Young is single & one of the best men I ever knew—as the Books & archives have always been there—the house an excellent & pleasant one & as Major Youngs knowledge & indeed intimate acquaintance with the train of the Whole Business of Captures & reclamations is essential to our proceeding with accuracy, & as I had not a room in my own I proposed to them to live together at the Office & I would pay the additional rent & take care that it should be no Expence to Mr: Graham who would at the same time dine with me when he pleased—by this means too he would be more his own Master & should any thing occur to alter hereafter this arrangement I will take care to make it agreeable to him.

I mentioned to you that as the King of Spain goes to Barcelona in September, *which is half way to Rome*, & as it is now fixed, if I live, that I am to stay here sometime as Minister near this court, that I wished the Presidents

Leave of absence for a few Weeks to see Rome, & I promise if no accident prevents to return to Madrid nearly as soon as the King can. His secretaries of state go with him. Of course no Business can be done during his absence & this is such a time for a few weeks absence that I am sure the President will have the goodness to consent to it. All the powers of Europe nearly have sent to *congratulate the* new King of Etruria on his accession to the Throne; as we have much trade with one part of his Dominions & have no Minister nor mean to have any in Italy—if You do not think it anterepublican & wish it done, I can & will do it with pleasure as I pass through Florence on my way to Rome, if permitted this short leave of absence by the President.

I request you to send me any intelligence you please under cover to Mr: Bulkely to Lisbon respecting the request I made you of a Letter of Credit on him or an authority to draw by way of Lisbon when the Exchange is greatly here in favour of Lisbon as it is now, & against Amsterdam nearly 8 per centum which is a serious difference. I have therefore hitherto drawn nothing either on one account or the other since my arrival which is the reason of your recieving no accounts from me as yet.

I only mentioned the Congratulation of the King of Etruria because all the European states have done it—& as we have no Minister in Italy nor is it worth our while, to have one there, or to send one *on purpose*—& as, if, I obtain permission of absence for a few Weeks to go to Rome, my road will be through Florence, I thought I would mention it to You, & if the President wishes, it can be done without the least inconvenience.

Please present me affectionately to the President & our friends at Washington & Believe me With great regard Dear Sir Yours Truly

CHARLES PINCKNEY

I must again apologize for the Paper none else of this Size was to be had in Madrid. I have just heard of the arrival of some English Paper & hope my next will be a better.

As it was too bulky to send by the french post I have this morning delivered the Letter & the Book of commercial regulations for you to Mr Peter Kuhn of Philadelphia[3] to be fowarded by him to Mr Lee our Consul at Bourdeaux & I trust it will arrive safe. Please write to me By Duplicates & either By Bourdeaux, Cadiz, Corunna Bilboa or Malaga or Lisbon.

RC (DLC). Marked "Duplicate."

1. See Pinckney to JM, 6 Apr. 1802, and n. 3.

2. Letter not found. It was probably JM's private letter to Pinckney carried by John Graham and mentioned in Pinckney's letter to JM of 14 Mar. 1802. Graham arrived in Madrid on 20 Jan. 1802 and probably carried JM's dispatches to Pinckney of 11 and 25 Sept. 1801 (*PJM-SS*, 2:100–101, 131–32).

3. Peter Kuhn, Jr., was the son of Philadelphia merchant Peter Kuhn (1751–1826) and the

nephew of Dr. Adam Kuhn, a prominent Philadelphia physician. He was appointed U.S. consul to Genoa in 1804 (John W. Jordan, *Colonial and Revolutionary Families of Pennsylvania*
[1911; 3 vols.; Baltimore, 1978 reprint], 1:528–29; *Senate Exec. Proceedings*, 1:476, 477).

§ From James Blake. *28 March 1802, Baltimore.* In answer to JM's letter of 21 Mar.
[not found], received 27 Mar., reports his inability to "proceed to my department
in France" because of claims "amounting to eleven or twelve thousand dollars"
against his wife's estate that remain to be settled; "it will not, probably, be in my
power to leave the United States until about the middle of next summer." Has been
unable to learn if any vessels are cleared for Antwerp. If that happens "before the
time I mentioned," asks that the president allow him to appoint an agent to officiate
for him in the meantime.

RC (DNA: RG 59, CD, Antwerp, vol. 1). 1 p.

§ From Daniel C. Brent. *Ca. 28 March 1802.* Points out that the congressional
session is ending and nothing has been done regarding the District of Columbia.
"So defective & oppressive is the present system, as it relates to Jails & Warrant-
Executions, that I feel it a duty to state them. . . . The Laws of Congress assumeing
the Jurisdiction over the District of Columbia have mad[e] no provision for erect-
ing Jail's, the Laws of Maryland authorise the Levy Court's to raise the sum only, of
$400 pr Annum, for the repairing of Jails; this sum is not Sufficient to Build one,
and if it was, it cannot be apply'd that way. . . . Under the p[r]esent laws of this
District no Jail can be Built without the enterposition of Congress. When I came
into office[1] there was no Jail in the County of Washington, A House, the only one
I could get, was rented, it is so insecure that Guards are necessary, it is too small, &
altho a small house adjoining has been Rented, in which the Jailor lives and to which
the Debtors are permitted to resort, Yet their situation is wretched indeed—so
many are the Criminals kept in close Confinement that as the warm weather ap-
proaches disease of the most Malignant kind must ensue. This consideration renders it absolutely necessary that immediate measure's should be adopted respecting
a Jail. . . . The Jail in Alexandria is little better, has been presented by the Grand
Jury as a publick nuisance." Notes that in Washington County there are fourteen
criminals and runaways in confinement and twenty-three debtors. Encloses "an exact list of the persons confined and the Cause of Confinement together with the
dimensions of the rooms of the prison."[2] Fears many prisoners will be added within
a few days on a number of criminal and civil actions, one of which is warrant executions—"that is Executions Issued by a single Majestrate for sums less than $20."
States that the warrant system in Washington County is "a fruitfull and Melancholy
source of Commitment; It is a System extreemly oppressive on the lower Class of
Citizens. . . . I think the better system would be not to put a debtor in Jail for a less
sum than $20." Asks JM to lay his letter before the president "if you think Sir, the
subjects I have mentioned worthy of notice."

RC and enclosure (DNA: RG 46, President's Messages, 7A-E2); Tr and Tr of enclosure
(DNA: RG 233, President's Messages, 7A-D1). RC 4 pp.; in a clerk's hand, signed by Brent.
Undated. Enclosure 3 pp.; see n. 2. Jefferson transmitted Brent's letter and enclosure to Con-

gress on 29 Mar. 1802. The Senate committee reported a bill but postponed further action until November 1802 (*Annals of Congress*, 7th Cong., 1st sess., 207, 293, 298, 304).

1. Daniel C. Brent was appointed U.S. marshal for the District of Columbia in March 1801.

2. Brent listed the names and "Cause of Commitment" of twenty-one debtors and fourteen criminals. The statement of "Dimensions of Jail in Washington County" indicated that the debtors occupied two rooms measuring 10 by 14 feet and 8 by 9 feet, and the two rooms for the criminals measured 9 by 12 feet and 5 by 7 feet.

§ From George Washington McElroy. *28 March 1802, Philadelphia.* Requests JM "to deliver the bearer hereof Mr. Yznardy my commission; directing me to whom I must deliver the required bonds."

RC (DNA: RG 59, CD, Tenerife, vol. 1). 1 p.; docketed by Brent, with the note "Commission sent."

To Thomas Jefferson

DEPARTMENT OF STATE March 29th. 1802.

The Secretary of State, to whom has been referred by the President of the United States a Resolution of the House of Representatives of the 23d Inst.,[1] requesting the President to communicate to that House such information as he may have received relative to the Copper mines on the South side of Lake Superior, in pursuance of a Resolution of the 16th. April 1800, authorising the appointment of an Agent for that purpose,[2] begs leave to lay before him the Copy of a letter of the 24th. September 1800, from the late Secretary of State to Richard Cooper Esqr., of Cooper's Town in the State of New York, appointing him an Agent, in pursuance of the last mentioned Resolution—and the Copy of one from the Attorney General of the United States, of the 30th. March 1801, at that time acting as Secretary of State, to the said Richard Cooper, signifying to him that as the Resolution in question contemplated an execution of the work and a report thereof, in time for the consideration of Congress at its next Session, and this had not been done, it was thought necessary to suspend the further prosecution of it, and that he was accordingly to do so.[3] The Secretary also begs leave to lay before the President copies of sundry other letters on this subject,[4] which, together with those mentioned above, serve to give a view—of the whole transaction, so far as this Department has had an agency in it, tho' they do not afford the particular information required by the Resolution referred to the Secretary of State, by the President. All which is respectfully submitted.

JAMES MADISON

RC and enclosures (DNA: RG 233, President's Messages, 7A-D1). RC in a clerk's hand, signed by JM. Jefferson transmitted the RC and enclosures to the House on 31 Mar. 1802 (*Annals of Congress*, 7th Cong., 1st sess., 1119). For enclosures, see nn. 3 and 4.

1. The resolution is printed in *Annals of Congress*, 7th Cong., 1st sess., 1074.

2. For the resolution under which Richard Cooper was employed, see JM to Cooper, 13 May 1801 (*PJM-SS*, 1:170, 171 n. 1).

3. JM enclosed copies of John Marshall to Cooper, 24 Sept. 1800 (1 p.), and Levi Lincoln to Cooper, 30 Mar. 1801 (1 p.).

4. Cooper to Lincoln, 25 Apr. 1801 (1 p.); JM to Cooper, 13 May and 6 Nov. 1801, Cooper to JM, 31 May and 30 Nov. 1801 (*PJM-SS*, 1:170, 241, 2:226, 288), and Cooper to JM, 13 Mar. 1802.

§ From Abraham R. Ellery. *29 March 1802, New York.* Solicits the consulship at Naples. Refers JM to Aaron Burr for a recommendation.

RC (DNA: RG 59, LAR, 1801–9, filed under "Ellery"). 1 p. Ellery's application was unsuccessful; he moved to Natchez, Mississippi Territory, in 1803 (Kline, *Papers of Burr*, 2:824 n.).

§ From John Elmslie, Jr. *29 March 1802, Cape Town, Cape of Good Hope.* Has supplied the American merchant ship *Equator* with a mast, which he procured in lieu of a spare foreyard left behind by Captain Preble of the *Essex*. Encloses a promissory note [not found] from the master of the *Equator* to pay the secretary of the navy "what ever sum may be assessed for the value of the same." Also encloses a copy of a protest left by the chief officer of the Philadelphia ship *Asia*, "who was forcibly detained with two Boys belonging to said ship, with the boat, logbook & other papers by Capt. Nicols commander of the English whaler Walker of London."[1] On the *Walker*'s arrival in Table Bay, Elmslie represented the matter to acting governor Dundas and requested the release of the chief officer, Peter Sutter, and the two boys. They were released, but the boat and papers were detained.

"As the Cape of Good Hope is likely by the preliminaries of Peace to change masters; It may not be improper just to hint, the advantage which the Citizens of America trading to the east of the Cape would derive from being permitted to touch at the Cape in order to refresh and in case of distress to refit, with liberty to dispose of so much of their cargoes as is necessary to defray their expences."

RC (DNA: RG 59, CD, Cape Town, vol. 1); enclosure (DNA: RG 76, British Spoliations, 1794–1824, Ship "Asia"). RC 4 pp.; docketed by Brent as received 9 June. For surviving enclosure, see n. 1.

1. The enclosed copy of Peter Sutter's affidavit of 5 Mar. 1802 (18 pp.) is accompanied by a statement signed by Elmslie, 8 Mar. 1802, that Sutter "was sworn to the truth of the aforegoing Declaration Before me." The affidavit gives a lengthier version of the events described in Jacob Peterson to JM, 13 Apr. 1802. JM forwarded both documents to Rufus King, 23 July 1802 (second letter).

§ From Rufus King. *29 March 1802, London.* No. 60. Annexes a copy of Lord Hawkesbury's note announcing the signing of the definitive treaty.

RC and enclosure (DNA: RG 59, DD, Great Britain, vol. 10); letterbook copy and copy of enclosure (NHi: Rufus King Papers, vol. 55). RC 1 p.; in a clerk's hand, signed by King; docketed by Brent. Cover postmarked New York, 22 May. Hawkesbury's 29 Mar. note, copied on the same page as King's dispatch, reported the arrival of the definitive treaty of peace signed at Amiens on 27 Mar. by representatives of Great Britain, France, Spain, and the Batavian Republic. RC and enclosure printed in King, *Life and Correspondence of Rufus King*, 4:93.

§ From Tobias Lear. *29 March 1802, Cap Français*. No. 23. Transmits copies of his dispatches of 28 Feb. and 22 Mar., since which one warship and two frigates have arrived from France with troops. "*Nothing more* has *occurred respecting Louisiana. That it is ceded to France is true and that part* of the *forces sent out* are *intended* [for] *that country* there is *no doubt but I* are¹ still *of opinion* that *if they* touch *here there* will be *employment* for the *troops* in the *island* for *some time* to *come.*" Neither the general in chief nor Villaret has returned. "I am very desirous of seeing the General in Chief [Leclerc] on many accounts; but I cannot venture to go to Port au Prince . . . lest he should arrive here in my absence. As he made no Arrangements for issuing the Bills on France, which were to be in part payment for the Cargoes bought, . . . the Vessels which have delivered their Cargoes return home, and have left this business to be settled by their Agents. This is a serious inconvenience." Although an embargo formally exists, "every Vessel obtains permission to depart." On 28 Mar. the prefect [Bénézech] issued orders to the customhouse to admit no American vessel without Lear's certification that it is American property nor to allow departure without his passport. Has received the original of JM's 26 Feb. letter with commissions for himself, Caldwell, and Dandridge; "to these Gentln. I have written, and communicated the instructions in your letter respecting the conduct to be observed by our Consuls &c.—but I retain the Commissions until I can have an interview with the Genl. in Chief." In all their communications, the prefect and General Boyer express "the most friendly sentiments towards the Am. Commerce." A British frigate arrived 28 Mar., and the captain and officers received "every possible mark of attention and respect"; a French frigate sent from Cap Français to Jamaica some weeks ago received similar treatment. "I have invited the Prefect, Genl. Boyer, and the principal Officers in the land and sea service to dine with me tomorrow; and I hope all differences & irritations which have taken place here, between the Citizens of the two nations, will subside." In a postscript of 30 Mar. reports "a pretty severe engagement yesterday about ten miles from hence" between blacks reportedly led by Christophe and newly arrived French troops, in which the former are supposed to have lost more than four hundred men. "Accounts from the South say that Genl. Desselin (the blk. Genl.) has been obliged to abandon a strong hold, which he had near St. Marc's, after losing 800 men. We do not know exactly where Toussaint is."

RC (DNA: RG 59, CD, Cap Haitien, vol. 4); FC (ibid.). RC 4 pp.; in a clerk's hand, except for Lear's signature and postscript; docketed by Brent. Italicized words are those encoded by Lear and decoded here by the editors using a key from the Lear family papers (owned by Stephen Decatur, Garden City, N.Y., 1958). RC decoded interlinearly by JM. Duplicate copy (ibid.) bears an additional postscript, dated 2 Apr., reporting Admiral Villaret's return from

Port-au-Prince and adding: "as I find that the Genl. in Chief will remain for some time in that quarter, I have determined to sail tomorrow morning for that place. . . . In consequence of the meeting between the Genl. in Chief and the Admiral, it seems the Ships, which I mentioned in my letters wd. go to the U. States, will go to France." Extract from RC printed in *National Intelligencer*, 18 [19] Apr. 1802.

    1. "Am" in FC.

§ From Carlos Martínez de Yrujo. *29 March 1802, Washington*. In order to preserve the friendliest relations with the U.S. government and avoid occasions for differences between the U.S. and Spain, notifies JM that the Spanish policy prohibiting neutrals from trading with Spanish colonies will be energetically enforced, even to the point of confiscating contraband vessels. Hopes the U.S. will take steps to ensure that this resolution will be generally known and assures JM that the king of Spain has no other object than to promote the trade and profit of his subjects.

    Tr (AHN: State Archives, vol. 5630). 2 pp.; in Spanish; in a clerk's hand, except for Yrujo's complimentary close and signature. Enclosed in Yrujo to Cevallos, 31 Mar. 1802.

To Charles Pinckney

SIR,   DEPARTMENT OF STATE, March 30th 1802

My last was of the 5th of February,[1] and 27th of March. I have as yet received no letter from you since your arrival at Madrid. By one from Colo Humphreys, written a few days after it took place, we learn that you were then confined by indisposition, and had not presented your credentials.[2] We are anxious to hear from you on the several subjects with which you have been charged; particularly on that of Louisiana. By a Treaty entered into between Spain and France in March 1801, and lately published in the Paris newspapers,[3] it appears that in an antecedent treaty, the cession of that Country had been stipulated by Spain. Still it is possible that the cession may have been since annulled; and that such was, or was to be the case, has been stated in verbal accounts from Madrid. At Paris, Mr Livingston has been given to understand by the French Government, that the Cession had never been more than a subject of conversation between the two governments. No information however, has been received from him subsequent to the publication of the Treaty of March 1801, which must have led to some more decisive explanations.

The copies herewith inclosed, of a memorial of sundry inhabitants living on Waters running from the United States thro' Florida into the Gulph of Mexico,[4] and of a letter from the late Mr. Hunter representative in Congress of the Mississippi Territory, will present to your attention a subject of some importance at this time, and of very great importance in a future view. The Treaty with Spain having as these documents observe, omitted to provide for the use of the Mobille, Catahoochee and other rivers running from our territory through that of Spain, by the citizens of the United States in like manner with the use of the Mississippi, it will be proper to make early efforts to supply the defect. Should a Cession, indeed, including the Spanish Territory Eastward of the Mississippi have finally taken place, it can answer no purpose to seek from the Spanish Government, this supplemental arrangement. On a contrary supposition, you will avail yourself of the most favourable moment and manner of calling its attention to the object. In support of our claim you will be able to use the arguments which inforced that to the navigation of the Mississippi. If it should be observed, that a greater proportion of these rivers, than of the Mississippi, run thro' the exclusive territory of Spain, it may be a set off, that the upper parts of the rivers run exclusively thro' the territory of the United States, and do not merely divide it, like the Mississippi from that of Spain. But neither the one nor the other circumstance can essentially affect our natural rights. Should the Spanish Government be favourably disposed, it will be proper for you to pave the way for a formal convention on the subject, endeavouring to obtain in the mean time, such regulations from its authority, and such instructions to its officers as will answer the purposes of our citizens. Among other hardships of which they now complain, and for which a regulation is particularly wanted, one I understand is, that the article cotton, which is acquiring rapid importance in that quarter, must, after it has been conveyed to Mobille, be shipped to New Orleans and pay a duty of about 12½ ⅌ Cent before it can be exported.

The copies of a letter from E. J. Berry and of another from E. Jones herewith also inclosed, present another subject which will claim your attention.[5] This is not the only complaint that has been received, of abuses relating to the effects of Americans deceased within the Spanish jurisdiction on the Mississippi. It seems so reasonable and necessary that the Consul residing there, or persons deriving authority from the deceased owner, should be allowed to take charge of such effects, that it is hoped a regulation for that purpose may be obtained from the justice and liberality of the Spanish Government.

Stephen Higginson Esqr. of Boston, has asked anew the attention of this department to two claims on the Spanish Government, one on his own account for the ship Pattern and cargo, the other on account of himself and Mr. William Perkins for the ship General Washington. As the papers and proceedings in both cases will have passed into your hands from those of Colo. Humphreys,[6] and as your general instructions embrace all such cases, it is sufficient to refer to these, and to apprize you of the anxiety of the party interested that his claims may receive your early attention and best exertions. He estimates the amount of their losses at not less than $150,000. A like anxiety has been expressed to this Department by Messrs. Stoker, Amory & Hays, of Boston, who have, as they say, forwarded to you their complaints and documents. You will be pleased to forward to Malaga the inclosed letter which is connected with their pursuit of redress.

We have just received from Mr. King a Convention signed by him with the British Government,[7] commuting the British claims on the U. States under the sixth Article of the Treaty of 1794 into a nett sum of £600,000 sterling payable in three anual instalments; and fixing the same periods and proportions for paying the awards to be made under the 7th Article. The Convention has just been laid by the President, before the Senate.

For the proceedings of Congress and other domestic occurrences, I refer to the collection of newspapers herewith sent. To them also I refer you for the latest accounts from St Domingo. I have the honor to be &c. &c. &c.

JAMES MADISON

Letterbook copy (DNA: RG 59, IM, vol. 6). Enclosures not found.

1. *PJM-SS*, 2:441–42.
2. David Humphreys to JM, 18 Dec. 1801 (*PJM-SS*, 2:321).
3. See JM to Robert R. Livingston, 26 Mar. 1802, n. 2.
4. This petition, from "sundry inhabitants" of Washington County, Mississippi Territory, was presented to the House of Representatives on 15 Feb. 1802. It requested that a "port of entry and delivery may be established at such a convenient point on the Tombigby river, as may command the navigation of the said river, as also, that of the Allibama river in the said territory" (*Journal of the U.S. House of Representatives*, 7th Cong., 1st sess., p. 237).
5. "E. J. Berry" may be a clerk's misrendering of E. H. Bay. An extract from Bay's letter to JM of 4 Nov. 1801 was transmitted by Jefferson to Congress on 24 Feb. 1802, along with an extract from a 10 Aug. 1801 letter from Evan Jones, as part of a request for a marine hospital in New Orleans (*PJM-SS*, 2:28–29, 221–22). An earlier letter from Jones referred to the problem of American citizens who died intestate in Louisiana (Jones to JM, 15 May 1801, *PJM-SS*, 1:184).
6. Stephen Higginson had broached the subject of his claims against Spain to David Humphreys in early 1801 (Humphreys to JM, 27 Mar. 1801, *PJM-SS*, 1:52).
7. For King's negotiations and the signing of the convention, see King to JM, 9 and 11 Jan. 1802 (*PJM-SS*, 2:380–81, 383–85).

To the Speaker of the House of Representatives

SIR,   DEPARTMENT OF STATE, March 30th 1802.

In obedience to an order of the House of Representatives, of the 25th Instant,[1] I have the Honor to send you the enclosed statement,[2] shewing the application of the appropriations for Clerk-hire in the Department of State for the years 1799, 1800 & 1801. I am, Sir, with very high respect, Your Mo: Obedt Servant,

JAMES MADISON

RC and enclosure (DNA: RG 233, Reports and Communications from the Secretary of State, 7A-E1.1); Tr and Tr of enclosure (DNA: RG 233, Transcribed Reports and Communications from the Secretary of State, 5C-B1). RC in a clerk's hand, signed by JM; addressed to Nathaniel Macon as Speaker of the House. On 30 Mar. JM's report was read and tabled in the House (*Annals of Congress*, 7th Cong., 1st sess., 1097). For enclosure, see n. 2.

1. The resolution, dated 25 Mar. 1802, requested the secretaries of state, treasury, war, and navy to submit "a statement of the application of the appropriations made by Congress for clerk-hire in their respective departments, specifying the persons, and the salaries allowed to each, for the last three years" (DNA: RG 59, ML).

2. The enclosed statement (2 pp.) listed the State Department clerks and their compensation for the years 1799, 1800, and 1801. Those listed for 1801 were Chief Clerk Jacob Wagner, $1,750; Christopher S. Thom, Stephen Pleasonton, and Daniel Brent, $800 each; John C. Miller, $750; William Crawford, $700; Hazen Kimball ("from 1st. Jany. to 15th. Novr. 1801"), $889.94; and William Johnston ("for occasional Clerk Hire"), $20.

From Chauncy Bulkley

HONORD SIR   CHATHAM IN CONNECTICUT March 30th 1802
   I Take the Liberty of Calling on your Honer For Some Asistance in Gitting My Partner alfred Isham Recommend to the French Genral and Agants at the Iland of Hispanolia I Expected to Have ben at Washington My Self to Laid a Claim For a French Capture that I Sufferd in July 1797 but I Concluded to See What Congress Did on Account of French Spiolations if you Will Please to Write Me a Letter to the French Genral Recomending Me and My Partner Alfred Isham I Shall Ever Acnolige it as a Particular Favour From your Humble Servant
                                                CHAUNCY BULKLEY

If you Please to See Mr Granger the Genral Post Master and Mr Dana thay Can Inform you about Our Credit and abileties.

RC (DNA: RG 76, France, French Spoliation Claims, folder B). For Pierpont Edwards's introduction of Bulkley, see his letter to JM of 30 Oct. 1801 (*PJM-SS*, 2:212).

From Jacob Wagner

DR. SIR   BALTIMORE 30 March 1802
   I beg your excuse for the liberty I take in covering the two enclosed letters to your address.
   Since I have been here I have had the injudicious medical treatment I sustained at Washington corrected; and by the change of air and use of

exercise there is a flattering expectation of my being restored to even better health than I formerly had. It is at present faulty only in the appetite, which has been excessively weakened.

If I can at this distance contribute towards the labours of the office, it will afford me satisfaction to receive your commands. I have the honor to remain With respectful attachment Your most obed. servt.

JACOB WAGNER

RC (DLC).

§ From Leopold Nottnagel. *30 March 1802, Philadelphia.* States that he is about to depart for Europe and requests a passport for himself and his wife and children; returns one granted by Pickering in 1800. Edward Jones at the treasury will receive the passport on his behalf.

RC (DNA: RG 59, ML). 1 p.; docketed by Brent.

§ From Joseph Pitcairn. *30 March 1802, Hamburg.* Has received laws of last session of Congress from the U.S. consul at London. Observes that the number of U.S. ships coming to Hamburg will decrease with the peace but Holland will be a readier market for ships trading north of France and England. "Some Connection it appears to me may yet be maintained, for the Sale of Maryland Tobaccos, Rice and New England Rum—the Returns linens, either for Wear, or the West Indies, Russia goods, which are generally plenty, Window Glass, and Sheathing Copper." A definitive peace is imminent; it is delayed by Spain and the election of Bonaparte as president of the Italian Republic. It is said Great Britain will keep Malta and Switzerland will be made truly independent. Indemnities remain a troublesome issue. Wrote to Livingston at Paris on 27 Jan. explaining his mode of accounting for money used in support of sick or distressed sailors pursuant to JM's letter of 1 Aug. 1801 but has had no reply. Reports that in the case of the ship *Hercules*, Captain Story, of New York, he has had the "ready and able assistance of our Consul Saabye at Copenhagen . . . and we have the most sanguine hopes of not only getting the 100000 Dolls for the owners of the Hercules, but of obtaining a recall of that ordinance entirely."

RC (DNA: RG 59, CD, Hamburg, vol. 1). 3 pp. Postmarked Philadelphia, 13 June. Docketed by Brent as received 15 June.

§ From Fulwar Skipwith. *30 March 1802, Paris.* "With the approbation of Mr. Livingston I have taken on myself to appoint Mr. James Anderson of Charlestown, So: Carolina sub commercial Agent for the port of Cette in the Mediterenean, and I take the liberty of adding my own request to his, that the President may be pleased to confer on him the appointment of Agent or vice-commercial for the aforesaid port and its dependences. The interests and conveniency of our trade to that port, have for some time past required the aid of such an Agent, and I beg leave through you, Sir, to assure the President that Mr. Anderson in that character is in every respect intitled to his confidence."

RC (DNA: RG 59, CD, Paris, vol. 1). 1 p.; docketed by Brent as received 6 Sept.

§ From Elias Vander Horst. *30 March 1802, Bristol.* "As the Vessel is now on the point of Sailing I have only a moment left to enclose you the London Gazette Extraordinary, of yesterday's date, containing an Acct. of the Signing of the Definitive Treaty of Peace, at Amiens, on the 27h. Instt." Also encloses a few more newspapers and the last London price current.

RC (DNA: RG 59, CD, Bristol, vol. 2). 1 p. Enclosures not found.

To J. C. Amory and Others

GENTLEMEN   WASHINGTON, DEPARTMENT OF STATE, March 31st 1802.

I have just written to Mr Pinckney, the Minister of the United States at Spain,[1] and have called his attention to the case represented by your letter of the 22d January last,[2] some time since received at this Office: and it will be well for you also to write to him on the same subject. I am, Gentlemen, very respectfully, Your Obedt Servant,

JAMES MADISON

RC (DNA: RG 76, Spain, Treaty of 1819, Allowed Claims, vol. 59). In a clerk's hand, signed by JM. Addressee not indicated. Docketed: "James Madison's letter to J. C. A & other Owners of Ship Mercury recd April 10. 1802."

1. See JM to Pinckney, 30 Mar. 1802.
2. Letter not found.

To Richard Harrison

DEPARTMENT OF STATE March 31. 1802

From the tenor of the within extract, the commencement of Mr. Dawson's allowance seems to be fixed by the date of his leaving the seat of Goverment on his mission to France, and the termination of it by the arrival of the ratification of the Convention at the seat of Government on the 9th. of October 1801, it being presumed that if it had been brought by himself, as the instructions anticipated, the time would have been nearly the same. No better rule for an estimate offers itself. If the actual expence of his passage home had been ascertained by his direct return, that expence would have been the rule. As his return was not direct, it must remain with the Treasury Department to substitute a reasonable estimate. The instructions do not seem to warrant any allowance for expences beyond the daily compensation, and those of passage.

JAMES MADISON

RC and enclosure (owned by Philip D. and Elsie O. Sang, River Forest, Ill., 1961). The enclosure (1 p.), in Brent's hand and dated 29 Mar. 1802, is an extract from Dawson's instructions, followed by the notation: "The Secretary of State, in answer to the Auditor's note, sends him the foregoing extract from Mr Dawson's instructions, and informs him that the Ratification of the Convention between this Country & France was received on the 9th of October 1801, at the Seat of Government." For Dawson's instructions, see *PJM-SS*, 2:352 n. 1. Harrison's note to JM has not been found.

Memorandum from Albert Gallatin

[ca. 1 April 1802]

The original vouchers to J. Swan's account (my office being so weak at this moment that I cannot have them immediately transcribed) are sent herewith. Mr Wagner will be pleased to give a receipt to the Register for the papers.

It appears thereby that Van Staphorst & Cie. credited the United States for the sale of the bullion on the 5th May 1796—that it was only 30th Septer 1796 that Mr Swan produced the receipt on which he claimed payment; but it is probable that between June & August of the same year the Treasury had received information at least of the bullion being paid in Paris, which induced them to make what is called in the Secy.'s letter *advances*. But the time when Van Staphorst's account of sale was received may possibly be discovered by reference to the files of their letters which will be searched as soon as Mr Jones can attend the office.

The second letter of Mr Swan contains charges against Mr Skipwith, said to be supported by extracts of Dallarde's letters. These extracts, nor Mr Monroe's receipt of 25th Decer. are not in the file of papers lodged in the Register's office. They may perhaps be amongst the files of this office & will be sought for as soon as Mr Jones returns.

The letter of Mr Skipwith dated 23 March 1796 has not been found. The copy of the answer will be forwarded. The date when Mr Monroe's letter of 30 March 1796 was received does not appear.

A. G.

RC (DNA: RG 233, Reports and Communications from the Secretary of State, 7A-E1.1). Undated. Docketed by a clerk, "Note from the Secretary of the Treasury to the Secretary of

State, accompanying a letter and report from the Secretary of State on the memorial of Fulwar Skipwith received the 7th. of April, 1802" (see JM to the Speaker of the House of Representatives, 6 Apr. 1802). Enclosures not found, but the copies of Treasury Department correspondence enclosed in JM's 6 Apr. report were doubtless made from the documents supplied by Gallatin. See also Monroe to JM, 8 Mar. 1802.

To Ebenezer Stevens

SIR,   DEPARTMENT OF STATE, April 2d 1802.
You will be pleased to draw on the Purveyor, at ten days sight, in favor of Mr Stephen Kingston, for the remainder of the freight on the Peace and Plenty which may be still due to him. A Policy of Insurance in this case is herewith sent to you. I shall cause six thousand Dollars to be remitted to Mr Whelen to answer your Dft.[1] I am, respectfully, Sir, Your very Obedt Servant,

JAMES MADISON

RC (InU). In a clerk's hand, signed by JM. Addressed to Stevens "or his Agent" at New York. Docketed as received 7 Apr. and answered 8 Apr. 1802 (letter not found).

1. For the financial arrangements for the shipping of U.S. treaty stipulations to Tunis on the *Peace and Plenty*, see Stevens to JM, 4 Feb. 1802 (*PJM-SS*, 2:440).

Memorandum from Tench Coxe

(Private)   [ca. 2 April 1802]
The extinction of the modern republics.

The result of the Consulta at Lyons merits the attention of the American Government.[1] When the Peace of Oct. 1801 was known here, it was observed[2] that there were no provisions in favor of the republican form of government, no Securities for its existence. The first consul of France was its *arbitrary Chief, de facto*. The English obtained their end, "*of some form of monarchy in France.*"
The Consulta of Lyons has placed Buonaparte at the head of another Government. It *was* a republic. Its new name "*Italian*" applies to an extensive region. It may well give rise to a suspicion that all Italy is to be brought under one Government, and that it is not to be republican. The moment of time is singular & impressive.
If this matter does not interrupt the proceedings at Amiens, if it does

not produce *genuine* agitations & difficulties there, if it be persevered in & peace is not interrupted, it will appear a reasonable suspicion, that it is the result of a secret coalition of the heads of the European nations to extinguish the Republics of Europe without opposition. If such an understanding exists among them, this is a master stroke in policy & execution. Holland & Switzerland sharing the same fate, Europe will be as little or even less republican than in 1788. If 100.000 consular troops are to come to our quarter of the world under the plea of reordering the West Indies, if England, Spain, & Denmark are to have troops & navies there as well as France, it will be easy to abandon the negroes and give those troops other destinations. These suggestions of prudence may appear like refinements upon the state of things. But it is conceived, that the circumstances which have taken place in Italy, the new name of things there & the circumstances which may soon follow will enable us to judge whether they are great irregular and extraordinary stretches of power in the middle of critical & important negociations, which shall appear to excite in Austria, Great Britain, Russia, Prussia & Turkey the *due* & *natural* dissatisfaction & opposition; *or* whether they are part of a plan secretly understood among the principal Sovereigns. If the latter, the worst omens to the liberty & tranquility of mankind appear on the face of this unexpected & extraordinary transaction. It may be the prelude to the extinction of the modern *European* republics, and it can only be by a wonderful favor of divine providence, if the evil should cease to be inflicted there.

RC (DLC). Unsigned; in Coxe's hand. Docketed by JM, "Coxe Tench / 1801." Dated ca. 1801 in the *Index to the James Madison Papers*. Conjectural date here assigned on the basis of the announcement in the Philadelphia *Aurora General Advertiser*, 2 Apr. 1802, of Napoleon's election to the presidency of the Italian Republic.

1. For Napoleon's election at Lyons, see Rufus King to JM, 27 Feb. 1802, *PJM-SS*, 2:496 and n. 1.

2. For Coxe's previous essays addressed to JM on European affairs, see *PJM-SS*, 2: 258–59.

From Thomas Moore

RETREAT 4th. Month 2nd. 1802

Agreeably to Law I lately deposited in thy Office a small pamphlet on agricultural subjects.[1] Thy character as a person of general information, & more especially as a successful practical farmer, induces me to believe that thou art very competent to judge of the merits of the work, my present object is therefore to request that if on reading thou should be of opinion that it contains any useful information, thou will please to mention it occasionally to any of the members of Congress (particularly from the southern States,) in order to promote its circulation. If my first views in publishing were *patriotic*, I have now in my wish to disseminate the additional *sinister* one of being refunded the *expense* of publication. I expect there are some copies in the book Stores in the City, & I believe a considerable number yet with the printers. With much respect I am thy friend

THOS. MOORE[2]

P. S. If thou should incline to write me a line on the subject, (Brookeville) is our post-Office.

RC (DLC).

1. Thomas Moore, *The Great Error of American Agriculture Exposed* . . . (Baltimore, 1801; Shaw and Shoemaker 951).
2. Thomas Moore (1760–1822), a resident of Montgomery County, Maryland, was an inventor and agriculturalist whose model farm attracted widespread notice. He worked as chief engineer on a number of public works projects, including the James River and the Chesapeake and Ohio canals, and he managed several industrial enterprises. In 1806 Jefferson chose Moore as one of three commissioners for the construction of the National Road from Baltimore to Ohio (Van Horne, *Papers of Benjamin Henry Latrobe*, 3:19 n. 1; T. H. S. Boyd, *The History of Montgomery County, Maryland* . . . [1879; Baltimore, 1968 reprint], pp. 90–92; JM to Moore, 29 Apr. 1806 [NNPM] and 25 July 1806 [DNA: RG 59, DL, vol. 15]).

From Louis-André Pichon

SIR   PHILADELPHIA 2d. April 1802.

I have received with your polite letter of the 26th. your answer to my St. Domingo note[1] with your packets for france and for this latter Colony. I will forward them with due care. I have been very much mortified at receiving no Sort of answer to my overtures relative to bills and am extremely concerned if it is not in the power of the United States to aid france in So unexpected a Situation. We, I believe guaranteed the Dutch loan for them after peace, when of course we were not under obligation to do it.[2] This good office appears not to be of the description of those which were rendered under common and reciprocal engagements and for common purposes. The credit of France must be very low indeed if the U. S. will not take bills on her treasury to make necessary remittances. If something had been done I would have taken up all the bills So impolitically and So unjustly forced on your merchants at St Domingo, and have agreed to take from the Stores of the U. S. Such articles as they might have wished to part with. I beg you will excuse the last mention which I will make in this confidential way on this Subject. My present difficulties have nearly broke my heart both as a french man and as the agent of my country.

If it could be by any means obtained could not, Sir, the Government put in my hands the whole amount of the claims. I will pay Mr ⟨Cheriot?⟩ immediately ⟨on⟩ my bill.[3] I beg, sir you will accept of the assurance of my sincere regard and respect

L A Pichon

RC (NN).

1. JM's reply to Pichon on the subject of Saint-Domingue is dated 25 Mar. 1802; if there was a covering letter of 26 Mar., that letter has not been found.

2. In November 1781 France borrowed ten million livres from the Dutch government on behalf of the U.S. and guaranteed the repayment of the loan (Samuel Flagg Bemis, *The Diplomacy of the American Revolution* [Bloomington, Ind., 1967], pp. 168–69).

3. This is a reference to French claims under the Convention of 1800, for which Congress was in the process of making provision. JM's report of 11 Jan. 1802 had estimated the cost of carrying the convention into effect (JM to Jefferson, 11 Jan. 1802, *PJM-SS*, 2:386).

§ From Jacob Lewis. *2 April 1802, London*. Reports that he decided to visit Great Britain on his way to Calcutta to take up his post as U.S. consul "as well for obtaining an Exequatur which might render me independant of the Colonial Goverment of Bengal as for making some arrangements in my private & Mercantile affairs." Applied for his exequatur through the agency of Rufus King on 9 Feb. "On the 30th. of March being the day on which the News of the Conclusion of the peace between Great Britain & France was announced I recd. the Inclosed Communication. . . . In Consequence of this disapointment I purpose to return without delay to the United States, & Encourage myself to hope that you will extend your kind patronage towards me in some simular situation."

RC and enclosures (DNA: RG 59, CD, Cape Town, vol. 1). RC 1 p. Enclosures are copies of King to Lewis, 27 Mar. 1802 (1 p.), enclosing King to Hawkesbury, 6 Feb. 1802 (1 p.); and Hawkesbury to King, 23 Mar. 1802 (1 p.). Hawkesbury refused to issue the exequatur because "as no Foreign Nation has a Consul at Calcutta, his Majesty's Government Cannot sanction Mr Lewis's appointment." For Lewis, see *PJM-SS*, 2:40 n. 5.

§ From Edward Stevens. *2 April 1802, Philadelphia*. Encloses Timothy Pickering's observations on Stevens's claim for reimbursement of expenses incurred during his mission to Saint-Domingue. Encloses as well a statement of his account with the U.S. and a certificate from James Yard. Has no doubt their testimony will show his claim to be well founded. Notes that he presented the grounds of his claim "when I had the pleasure of seeing you"; adds a few remarks on the various charges, including expenses for stores and passage money, the hire of vessels to carry dispatches, journeys on public business, advances to American seamen, house rent and personal expenses at Cap Français, and a secretary's salary. Asks JM to point out the best mode of settling his account.

Tr and Tr of enclosures (DLC: Jefferson Papers). Tr 5 pp. Enclosed in Gallatin to Jefferson, 31 Mar. 1804. Enclosures include copies of Stevens's account with the U.S. (4 pp.), showing a balance of $27,325 in his favor; Timothy Pickering's statement, dated 23 Mar. 1802 (4 pp.), of Stevens's service as consul general at Saint-Domingue, supporting the "propriety and justice of his claim"; and the deposition of James Yard, dated 2 Apr. 1802 (2 pp.), attesting to Pickering's promise to reimburse Stevens's expenses for the mission to Saint-Domingue.

§ From William C. C. Claiborne. *3 April 1802, "Near Natchez."* "It is confidently reported at New Orleans that East & West Florida's are Ceded to France; I have understood, that no official information of the Cession, had reached the Governor General of Louisiana, and that he denies the truth of the *report; it* is nevertheless generally believed and has occasioned much anxiety & uneasiness among the Inhabitants of Orleans." The territorial militia "continue in an unorganized state, & the general want of Arms presents an insuperable barrier to their organization." Requests "a loan of about one thousand stand of Arms" for the militia, which would add to the "security of this exposed Settlement."[1] The acts of the legislature remain unpublished. There is only one printer in the territory, "a scarcity of Types, & I may add too of Industry." "I continue to be much harassed with Visits from my Choctaw Brethren; these poor, Idle & humble People are really great pests to this Territory." No less than two or three hundred of them are "Encamped within six Miles around Natchez, & for a support, they almost *entirely* depend upon begging & Stealing." Finds it "difficult to *shield* the *Indians from much violence.*" Requests permission to employ an interpreter. "Under the Spanish government, the Indians were accustomed to receive Presents & provisions at Natchez.... I have no Presents to make, ... but they notwithstanding, will not, & cannot, be persuaded to remain in their own Lands." Party spirit seems to be subsiding, and "a decided majority of the Citizens are pleased with the Second Grade of Government, & *the manner* in which, it has been administered."

Letterbook copy (Ms-Ar: Claiborne Executive Journal). 2 pp. Printed in Rowland, *Claiborne Letter Books*, 1:69–70.

1. Henry Dearborn had already addressed Claiborne's request for arms by sending five hundred rifles and three hundred muskets to New Orleans to be sold to members of the territorial militia (Dearborn to Claiborne, 10 Mar. 1802, Rowland, *Claiborne Letter Books*, 1:104).

§ From Peter Stirling. *3 April 1802, Barcelona.* Notes that his last letter of 19 Dec. 1801,[1] sent by way of Lisbon, enclosed an abstract of the arrivals of American ships at Barcelona from 2 Apr. 1800 to 7 Dec. 1801. Encloses an abstract of the arrivals from 10 Jan. 1802 to 26 Mar. 1802. "The American merchantmen that come this way ... come to bad markett. Wheat and Flower is an article that is not plentifull here, but we are now near the Crop."

RC (DNA: RG 59, CD, Barcelona, vol. 1). 1 p.; docketed by Brent. Enclosure not found.

1. *PJM-SS*, 2:327.

From Louis-André Pichon

PHILA. 4th. April 1802

Mr. Pichon presents his respects to Mr. Madison & incloses to him extracts of dispatches from St. D/ge.[1] The two last in date are those which he received by the Necessity Victualling frigate lately arrived here to take a load of provisions. Mr. Benesech's letter attempts to make Some apology for what was done at the Cape in relation to the american merchants. The vessell which Mr. P. thought of expediting to france goes to St. Domingo. The last arrived frigate will Sail for that country within 19 or 20 days. In the mean while Mr Pichon dispatches an officer to france who Sails from hence on wednesday or thursday & who carries Mr. Madison's letters to Mr. Livingston with Mr. P. dispatches. Mr. P. expects to be at washingn. next thursday.

RC and enclosures (DNA: RG 59, NFL, France, vol. 1). RC docketed by Brent.

1. Pichon enclosed extracts from three letters (7 pp.; in French). Leclerc's letter of 26 Pluviôse an X (15 Feb. 1802) requested Pichon to send the 6,000 quintals of flour ordered by the minister of marine, as well as other supplies. He also directed Pichon to tell American merchants that "their conduct toward me will determine my conduct toward them" (editors' translation). Pierre Bénézech's letter of 7 Ventôse an X (26 Feb. 1802) informed Pichon that Admiral Villaret was sending a ship to the U.S. for supplies and reported that Leclerc had found it necessary to sequester American ships at Cap Français and force the sale of their cargoes. Bénézech went on to explain the rationale and details of the transaction so that Pichon might respond accurately to complaints of the U.S. government. The third extract is Villaret to Pichon, 11 Ventôse an X (2 Mar. 1802), in which he asked Pichon to send flour, biscuit, and salt provisions for the land and naval forces, both of which were in need of provisions.

§ From William Eaton. *4 April 1802, Tunis.* Refers JM to enclosures marked A, B, C, D, and E giving information of his actions from 12 to 24 Mar.[1] *Gloria* made safe journey to Malta, having left Tunis 26 Mar. and arrived back 3 Apr. Off Malta, the *Gloria* "happily fell in with Captain McNeill," who gave its mission "his approbation and concurrence"; calls JM's attention to McNeill's letter to him and instructions to Captain Bounds (enclosures H and I).[2] "By engaging the Sapatapa in the project,"[3] Eaton persuaded Hamet Pasha to go to Malta and remain there under American protection. Encloses letter of recommendation given to pasha.[4] "I now dispatch the Gloria to Gibraltar[5] in hopes of her falling in with our Squadron . . . and to pass through the Commodore's hands these Dispatches in order that he might conform his arrangements to them if they correspond with his orders from the President."[6] The bey has refused to provision American warships "under pretext of its being a Violation of the laws of the Profet to provision an enemy of a Mahometan," but Eaton believes the real reason is his refusal to grant the bey's merchantmen passports for Tripoli.

98

RC and enclosures (DNA: RG 59, CD, Tunis, vol. 2, pt. 1); letterbook copy (CSmH); Tr (DLC: Cathcart Papers). RC 2 pp.; in a clerk's hand, signed by Eaton. Printed in Knox, *Naval Documents, Barbary Wars*, 2:104–5. Enclosures were designated A through I by Eaton and enclosures B through I marked duplicate (see nn. 1–4). Also filed with the RC are copies of Eaton's 4 Apr. letters to Capt. Joseph Bounds and to the commander of the U.S. squadron (see n. 6).

1. Eaton's enclosure A is a copy of his 18 Mar. 1802 dispatch to JM. In enclosure B, a copy of Eaton to Rufus King, 18 Mar. 1802 (1 p.), Eaton informed King that the presents had arrived from Great Britain and were "highly acceptable" to the bey but that Eaton had decided to retain the "large Sabre" as "a good Article for the Sublime Porte in Case of a negocation." In enclosure C, a copy of Eaton to James L. Cathcart, 18 Mar. 1802 (3 pp.), Eaton discussed his plans regarding Hamet Pasha, added in a 26 Mar. postscript that "the inclosed to the Department of State will show you my measures" and that Dr. Turner would provide further details, and appended a copy of the 26 Mar. postscript to his 18 Mar. letter to JM. Enclosure D, Eaton's instructions to Capt. Joseph Bounds of the ship *Gloria*, 24 Mar. 1802 (2 pp.; printed in Knox, *Naval Documents, Barbary Wars*, 2:94–95), ordered Bounds to deliver the enclosed letter to Captain McNeill of the *Boston* or, if he should not find McNeill but should find the ship carrying Hamet Pasha and his subjects, to take the Tripolitans from the ship and deliver them to the first American warship met or to Cathcart at Leghorn. The 24 Mar. letter from Eaton to McNeill, enclosure E (2 pp.; printed ibid., 2:95), explained Eaton's reasons for placing the *Gloria* in public service and his plan to use Hamet Pasha as an "instrument of pacification" at Tripoli; "if this object can be effected no doubt it would bring about a revolution in Tripoli and the assassination of the usurper, and save to the United States the loss of many lives and much expense—An object well worth extraordinary exertions."

2. In enclosure H, McNeill to Eaton, 31 Mar. 1802 (1 p.; printed ibid., 2:98), McNeill agreed to cruise off Derna to intercept the vessel carrying Hamet Pasha and to authorize Captain Bounds so that the *Gloria* might "act under [Eaton's] directions" until the American naval squadron arrived from the U.S. Enclosure I is a copy of McNeill's orders to Bounds, 31 Mar. 1802 (1 p.; printed ibid., 2:98–99).

3. Yusuf Sahib-at-Taba was the Tunisian prime minister. Enclosure G is a copy of Eaton's 28 Mar. 1802 letter to Cathcart describing arrangements made with Sahib-at-Taba to get Hamet Pasha's cooperation, for which the former was to be paid $10,000 (1 p.; for another copy, see ibid., 2:97).

4. Eaton's letter of recommendation for Hamet Pasha of 29 Mar. 1802, enclosure F, was addressed "To Any American Commander or Agent in the Mediterranean." It requested that "every possible assistance" be given to the pasha, who was to go to Malta and wait for the American fleet which would then take him to Tripoli "to demand the restitution of his Throne and rights" (1 p.; printed ibid., 2:97).

5. In the letterbook copy, Eaton placed an asterisk here and wrote at the end of the letter, "*The Gloria sailed for Gibraltar Apl. 11. 3 oclock P.M."

6. In his 4 Apr. 1802 letter to Captain Bounds (3 pp.; printed ibid., 2:105), Eaton ordered him to "immediately shape your Course for Gibraltar" to deliver the dispatches to either the U.S. commodore or John Gavino; in a postscript dated 7 Apr., Eaton added that he was enclosing a duplicate set of dispatches for Gavino. In his letter addressed "To the Commander of the U. States Squadron in the Mediterranean," 4 Apr. 1802 (1 p.), Eaton noted that the dispatches to the secretary of state carried by Captain Bounds were "passed open through your hands for your perusal." He expressed his conviction that "these measures will obtain your Concurrence and Support as they promise incalculable advantages to the honor and interest of the United States."

§ From George Washington McElroy. *5 April 1802, Philadelphia*. Acknowledges receipt of JM's letter "enclosing my commission with instructions &ca." [not found] and returns one of the bonds as instructed.

RC (DNA: RG 59, CD, Tenerife, vol. 1). 1 p.

To the Speaker of the House of Representatives

Sir,   DEPARTMENT OF STATE, April 6th 1802
 I have the Honor to send herewith a Report on the Memorial of Fulwar Skipwith, agreeably to a Resolution of the House of Representatives, of the 19th Januy last, and to be, with very high respect, Your Obedt Servant,
                                             JAMES MADISON

[Enclosure]

DEPARTMENT OF STATE, 6th. April 1802.
 The Secretary of State to whom was referred by the House of Representatives the Memorial of Fulwar Skipwith, stating certain claims against the United States, respectfully submits the following report.
 The memorialist represents that in the year 1795, while he acted as Consul General for the United States at Paris, his House was robbed of three Ingots, amounting in value to 4550 Dollars which had been deposited under his care by direction of the Minister Plenipotentiary of the United States to the French Republic; that at the request of the said Minister he advanced that sum for the purpose of making up in Holland the fund to which the said Ingots belonged, drawing at the same time for his reimbursement by the direction of the said Minister, bills on the United States to the amount of his advance: and that the said bills were protested, and the advance never repaid.
 This representation appears to be established in every essential point, by satisfactory documents. It also appears that no recompence was ever made to, or charge made by, the memorialist for his trouble in receiving and taking charge of the Ingots committed to him; and that no fault or negligence in the means used by him for keeping or recovering the lost Ingots, can be reasonably imputed to him.
 The refusal of the Secretary of the Treasury to repay the Memorialist the sum advanced by him is explained in a letter from Mr. Wolcott to Mr. Monroe, Dated Septr. 16th. 1796, of which a copy is herewith reported No. 1. and from which the following is an extract, "I deem it unnecessary at this time to express any opinion as to the precautions taken by

Mr. Skipwith to secure the bullion, whilst in his possession, because, by my contract with Mr. Swan, the proceeds of the bill were to be at his risk until lodged in the hands of our bankers at Amsterdam. It is for this reason that I did not conceive myself at liberty to pay the draft drawn on me by Mr. Skipwith for the money which he states to have expended in the purchase of bullion to replace an equal quantity missing out of his Store of the parcel received from Dallarde and Swan."

On recurring to the said contract, a copy of which No. 2. is herewith reported, it appears that in pursuance thereof the said James Swan was bound to furnish bills on his House at Paris payable to the Minister Plenipotentiary of the United States (of which bills the ingots in question were part of the proceeds) that on the payment thereof, amounting to 120.000 Dollars in value and on the obtaining the necessary passports from the French Government, the said sum was to be forthwith transported to Amsterdam at the risk and expense of the said James Swan & delivered to Messrs. Wilhem & Jan Willink, Nicholas & Jacob Van Staphorst & Hubbard on account of the United States: and that within thirty days after due evidence should be produced at the Treasury of such delivery, the price of the bills were to be then paid.

It may be proper to add that from a report of the then Attorney General, a copy of which No. 3. is herewith reported, it appears that he concurred with the Secretary of the Treasury in opinion that the United States were not liable to the Memorialist for the advance made by him to supply the loss occasioned by the robbery of his House.

With this view of the subject however, it is necessary to combine the following considerations.

The first is that admitting the deposit in the hands of the memorialist to have been at the risk of James Swan, the memorialist received it as the property of the United States, and made his consequent advance for their use, under directions of the Minister Plenipotentiary which he was at least justifiable in respecting and pursuing.

But it appears in the next place that the Minister Plenipotentiary himself was equally justifiable in the part which he had in the transaction. Not only were the bills made payable to him, by which means the proceeds necessarily passed under his care; but according to information from the Treasury Department, it appears that no copy of the contract between the Secretary of the Treasury and James Swan was transmitted to the said Minister Plenipotentiary. The information which appears to have been given him with respect to the tenor of it is contained in a letter of June 23d. 1795 to him from the Secretary of the Treasury, of which a copy is reported No. 4. In this letter it is said to Mr. Monroe that "if the bill [from which the Ingots proceeded][1] is accepted and the transportation of the money assured [by passports from the French Government] you will be pleased to notify the

House of Wilhem & Jan Willink Nicholas & Jacob Van Staphorst & Hubbard of Amsterdam of what shall have been done; and you will expedite the delivery of the funds through the House of Dallarde, Swan & Company; who are to co-operate to place the same in Amsterdam." In another paragraph it is said "I will attempt no apology for troubling you with a business which is foreign to your Diplomatic duties, because I know that your Zeal for the interest of the United States will readily induce you to comply with my request, and because you will percieve that your co-operation is really necessary to the success of an interesting object."

Altho the intention of the writer in this case, with the contract in his Mind, might annex to his expressions the same ideas as are expressed in that instrument, it appears both from the conduct & correspondence of Mr. Monroe, that he considered, and as the Secretary conceives justly considered, his zeal for the interest of his Country, and the preservation of its public faith abroad, as made responsible for effectuating with as little delay as possible the remittance to the Bankers of the United States in Holland. And as this construction of his duty was favorable in every view to the conveniency of the House of Mr. Swan in Paris, it may be presumed that they would not be forward in suggesting a different one.

With respect to the Official opinion given by the Attorney General it is to be remarked, that as it was founded on the contract or on the contract and the letter above cited taken together, it is not applicable to the question which now presents itself.

To turn the memorialist over to a claim of reimbursement from Mr. Swan who, as may be inferred from a letter from him of Septr. 30th. 1796, to the Secy. of the Treasury (an extract of which No. 5 is reported herewith) would contest its legality, would appear the less justifiable on the part of the United States, and the more hard against the memorialist; inasmuch as it appears by an extract of a letter from Mr. Monroe to the Secretary of the Treasury of Jany. 14th 1796, N. 6. herewith also reported, and a letter from the latter of the 14th April 1796, that the loss and replacement of the Ingots was known at the Treasury a considerable time prior to the payment of James Swan under the contract; so that it was in the power of the United States to have included the advance made by the Memorialist in the settlement with Mr. Swan; if he and not the United States were to bear the loss; or if it were doubtful on which of the parties the loss ought to fall, it would seem no unreasonable expectation, in behalf of the Memorialist, considering the circumstances and authority under which he acted, that his speedy repayment should be either satisfied by the United States, or secured to him by their precautions.

From this view of the whole subject the Secretary concludes that the United States are in justice bound to admit against themselves, in the first instance at least the claim of the Memorialist to be reimbursed the sum advanced by him to replace the value of the Ingots of which he was robbed, with interest from the date of the advance according to the legal rate at Paris where the advance was made, and where the Memorialist then resided and has since continued.

The memorialist further represents that on the 1st. of November 1796, he forwarded a resignation of his Commission of Consul General; that the notification of its acceptance by the President, was not received until the 1st. of May 1799, that during this interval, from respect to the public good, he continued to exercise the functions of his Office, rendered the more necessary and the more laborious by the absence of a public Minister and by the circumstances of the crisis; but without receiving any of the emoluments of Office, notwithstanding a considerable expenditure incurred by him in the hire of an Office, Clerks, postages, Stationery &c.: and that he considers himself entitled to compensation for these services and expences.

On this part of the Memorial the Secretary of State is of opinion, that as the Memorialist might have so expounded or modified his resignation as to have legally claimed the emoluments of Office until it should be accepted, and as the Official emoluments were to be derived from individuals not from the public, the United States are not in rigor bound to make the compensation prayed for. Nevertheless considering the extraordinary lapse of time during which he was in suspense, and probably led by daily expectation of being relieved from it, to prolong his services and expences, it is conceived that liberal justice would not be exceeded by a compensation as nearly equal as can be estimated to the emoluments which would have accrued: and still more reasonable that at least his actual expenditures should be reimbursed.[2] All which is respectfully submitted

JAMES MADISON

RC and enclosures (DNA: RG 233, Reports and Communications from the Secretary of State, 7A-E1.1); Tr (DNA: RG 233, Transcribed Reports and Communications from the Secretary of State, 5C-B1). RC and enclosed report in a clerk's hand, signed by JM. In addition to JM's report, twelve supporting documents are filed with the RC and docketed as accompanying JM's letter and report. The enclosures described in JM's report (nos. 1–6) are printed in *ASP, Claims,* pp. 270–72. The other documents are Gallatin's memorandum to JM, ca. 1 Apr. 1802, and copies of James Swan to Oliver Wolcott, 6 May 1795 (2 pp.), offering to contract to pay the interest owed by the U.S. to the Dutch bankers; Monroe to Wolcott, 10 Sept. 1795 (2 pp.), agreeing to arrange for the transfer of specie to Holland if necessary; Joseph de Broeta at Antwerp to J. B. Prevost at Paris, 21 Mar. 1796 (1 p.), announcing the safe arrival of the specie at Antwerp; Monroe to Wolcott, 30 Mar. 1796 (3 pp.), announcing the same and discussing the theft from Skipwith's office; and the full text of Swan to Wolcott, 30 Sept. 1796 (4 pp.; mistakenly docketed as a letter to Skipwith).

1. JM's brackets, here and below.
2. The bill for Skipwith's relief was composed of two parts. The first was the reimbursement for his advance to the U.S. to cover the theft of the silver ingots; the second was compensation for his consular services. This latter was defeated in the House in a vote in the

Committee of the Whole. The bill, thus amended, passed the House on 16 Apr.; the Senate followed suit on 3 May (*Annals of Congress*, 7th Cong., 1st sess., 304, 1162, 1191–92, 1194).

From Thomas Doughty

SIR,   CHARLESTON So. CAROLINA April 6th. 1802

As in the letter You did me the honor to address me last fall,[1] You mentioned that You would, in conformity to my request, take the necessary Steps, to have the monies, received in Holland for the Wilmington Packett claim,[2] drawn to this Country—

You will oblige me by informing me, if You have been enabled to do so, and if it has been effected, what amount in dollars, the same has render'd. I am Sir Very respectfully Your most obt.

THOS DOUGHTY.

RC (DNA: RG 76, Netherlands, Misc. Claims, ca. 1793–1847). Docketed by Brent.

1. Letter not found. Doughty probably referred to Jacob Wagner's letter to him, 22 Sept. 1801, mentioned in Doughty to JM, 5 Oct. 1801 (*PJM-SS*, 2:161).
2. For Doughty's claim to the *Wilmington Packet*, see his letter to JM, 11 Sept. 1801 (*PJM-SS*, 2:103 and n. 1), and Hill, *William Vans Murray*, pp. 49–50 and n. 12.

From Charles Pinckney

SIR   April 6: 1802 IN MADRID

I have the honour to inclose you several letters for your inspection—the first respecting Captain Mullowney of the United States Ship Ganges.[1] I replied to it by saying that agreeably to the request of his Majesty I would transmit it to our Government—that I knew nothing of the circumstances & had no doubt our Government would do What was proper. To the second respecting Commodore Dale I made the inclosed reply, & as I now send it to you at the request of the King I have considered it but as due to Commodore Dale to transmit at the same time his & our Consul at Gibraltar's details of this affair.[2] As We have very important objects in View with this court you will percieve in all my correspondence with them a moderation of Language & expression of affection, which I believe the honour of the King & his friendship for us always to deserve. I am convinced too, that it is infinitely at present the best mode to proceed with them & the most probable to obtain our own just & honourable Ends. I do not send you the Definitive treaty from hence because it has not been published here & you will get it so much sooner from France & England. Being here more than Four hundred miles from the Ocean it is impossible to transmit intelligence except sometimes from the Mediterranean. But even that is extremely uncertain as letters are sometimes Months coming from Algiers to this place. The proposition respecting Florida & the appointment of Commissioners is still before the Court here & under consideration.[3] It would seem as if they wished first to hear from France. As soon as I can give you a definitive opinion of our prospects in this business you shall hear fully from me. With the Most respectful Esteem & regard I am dear sir Yours Truly

CHARLES PINCKNEY

Please to present me respectfully & affectionately to the President.

RC and enclosures (DNA: RG 59, DD, Spain, vol. 6). RC docketed by Brent. For enclosures, see nn.

1. Pinckney enclosed a copy of Cevallos's letter to him, 6 Mar. 1802 (2 pp.; in Spanish), which relayed a complaint from the governor of Cuba about the conduct of John Mullowny, commander of the U.S. ship *Ganges*, in seizing a French corsair off the coast of Cuba near Matanzas and taking his prize into Havana harbor, where he refused to verify his claim to the vessel. Although Pinckney disclaimed any knowledge of the situation, JM had referred the case to him in a letter of 9 June 1801 (*PJM-SS*, 1:276; see also Yrujo to JM, 4 June 1801, *PJM-SS*, 1:262 and n. 1).

2. These enclosures (7 pp.; docketed by Brent as enclosed in Pinckney's 6 Apr. dispatch) include copies of Cevallos's letter to Pinckney, 10 Mar. 1802 (in Spanish), complaining that Commodore Richard Dale had insulted Spain by calling that country a nation of savages, and Pinckney's reply (undated, but apparently written 2 Apr.), explaining that Dale's words on that "*extraordinary occasion*" were meant to apply only to the personnel of the forts—who "so wantonly sported with the properties & Lives" of Americans—and not the entire Spanish nation. Also included are copies of two letters Pinckney enclosed to Cevallos: Dale's heated letter to the governor of San Roque, 27 Oct. 1801 (see Knox, *Naval Documents, Barbary Wars*, 1:608–9), condemning attacks on two American ships from Spanish forts, which had resulted in the death of an American seaman and damage to the vessels, and observing that "such conduct resembles more the Savages than a civilized Nation"; and John Gavino to David Humphreys, 30 Oct. 1801, corroborating Dale's description of the attacks. For Humphreys's response to this incident, see his letter to JM, 23 Nov. 1801 (*PJM-SS*, 2:266–67).

3. In his long letter to Cevallos of 24 Mar. 1802 (15 pp.; docketed by Brent as enclosed in Pinckney's 6 Apr. dispatch), Pinckney formally broached the subject of a U.S. purchase of the Floridas. Pinckney disclaimed any desire on the part of the U.S. to increase its power by accession of territory, explaining that the U.S. merely wanted to secure the free navigation of the Mississippi River and fix "so valuable & great a natural Boundary" between itself and its Spanish neighbors. He reminded Cevallos of the extraordinary eighteen-year increase in the U.S. of "Inhabitants, commerce, strength and Revinue," making it the "second or third commercial Nation in the world." He pointed out that since over half the nation's territory was "situated on the Mississippi, and the Rivers & Waters running into it," free navigation of the river was "essential & indispensable" to the "Happiness & Tranquillity" of the American people. In order to safeguard the rights of Americans and also to ensure good relations with Spain, Pinckney wrote, he was charged "to open a Negotiation with His Majesty for the pur-

chase & cession of East & West Florida, and should the cession have finally taken place, as is reported, of that part of Louisiana lying on the east bank of the Mississipi, The Undersigned in the name of his Government most earnestly intreats to be informed of it officially, in order that his Government may be enabled to . . . make the same sincere & affectionate proposals to their good Friends the French Republic for the small part of Louisiana on the East bank of the River, as they now do to their good Friend His Catholic Majesty for the Floridas." In the same letter, Pinckney renewed David Humphreys's proposal for the appointment of commissioners to adjudicate spoliation claims, presented the U.S. government's position on the blockade of Gibraltar (see Pinckney to JM, 20 Mar. 1802 [first letter], and n. 4), and requested permission for a U S consul or commercial agent to reside in New Orleans.

From John Strode

DR. SIR   CULPEPER 6 April 1802

Should You, Your Lady and family make a Visit this Spring to Your Seat in Orange; pray confer on me the honor of taking my House in Your route, for One Night at least; Capt. Winston I must grant has the highest Claim to the favour of both You and Your Lady; but it cannot be consistant with the principles of equity & Justice that He Should engross Your whole time, while in the County; pray then, Spare a few hours on me; I am well aware that if my poor Cot were ten Steps further off the road I could not presume to merit the Attention; but its so convenient, that there is few, if any, perhaps indeed not One individual republican in the Union, who would not like me be paind to See You *almost* always Pass. We have had a favourable Winter, Spring is Opening upon us most delightfully, human Subsistance flows in abundance, nothing appears to be now wanting but Money, how far an excess of that Specific Article wd. lend to encrease our happiness I am not philosopher enough to determine; Yet I am sure a few thousands wd. be very usefull to a poor man in my Situation. Pray Sir be pleased to favourable [*sic*] commend me to Your Amiable Lady & family. With all possible respect and esteem, I am Worthy Sir Yr. most Obedt

JOHN STRODE

RC (DLC).

§ From John Langdon. *6 April 1802, Portsmouth.* Recommends Gen. Michael McClary[1] to be marshal of the district of New Hampshire in place of [Bradbury] Cilley, whose term has expired and who "has been and still is a high Federalist." Believes it important that the marshal be a Republican.

RC (DNA: RG 59, LAR, 1801–9, filed under "McClary"). 1 p.; docketed by Jefferson.

1. Michael McClary (1753–1824), of Epsom, New Hampshire, fought with the militia at Bunker Hill and served in the Continental army until his resignation in 1778. He was adjutant

general of New Hampshire, 1792–1813, and a state senator, 1796–1802. Jefferson nominated him as marshal on 27 Apr. 1802, the Senate confirmed his appointment two days later, and he served in the post until the year of his death (Isaac W. Hammond, ed., *New Hampshire: Provincial and State Papers* [13 vols.; Concord, N.H., 1882], 11:630–31; *Senate Exec. Proceedings*, 1:422, 423, 3:312, 314; Boston *Columbian Centinel*, 28 Apr. 1824).

To Rufus King

Sir,   Department of State, April 7th 1802

My last was of the 25th of February,[1] since which yours to No 53[2] inclusive have been received.

That of January 9[3] was accompanied by the Convention entered into with the British Minister on the subject of the VIth article of the Treaty of 1794. It was laid before the Senate as soon as the documents proper to be communicated along with it could be prepared; and was taken up there as soon as some particular subjects before the House were disposed of.[4] I have delayed this letter to the last moment allowed by the Packet in the hope of being able to let you know the result. No vote however having yet been taken, I can only say in general that the delay is not to be regarded as any omen unfavourable to the transaction, and that the best informed conjectures seem to be that it will be agreed to without dissent. In the mean time it will be a satisfaction to you to know that your judgment and success in managing the negotiation has received the entire approbation of the President.

The readiness with which the British Government has undertaken a revision of the countervailing regulation, has a favourable aspect on the friendly relations between the two countries, and it is hoped will be followed by other proofs of respect for our just and reasonable expectations. The zeal with which you have espoused this object, and the cogent representations used in support of it, have also merited and received the approbation of the President. By republications here from London papers of later date than your letters, I find that a Bill had actually been introduced into the House of Commons on the plan desired.[5] It is to be wished that it may pass into a law and arrive here in time to give a shape to the Act of Congress, precisely coinciding with it; otherwise there may be danger of some variance in the mutual conditions which will suspend the effect of both till one or both of the Legislatures shall be reassembled. For a considerable time past the proposition on this subject made in Congress by General Smith,[6] has slept on the table. He did not wish to press it against a mercantile current that appeared to set against it. There is reason to believe that owing to ignorance and jealousy, this current has not even yet entirely ceased. The case is too plain however to be long misunderstood, and appeals to too strong an interest to be long unfelt. The acknowledgement on the part of Great Britain of the inequality of the measure complained of, and her consent to rectify it, will co-operate strongly in placing the subject in its true light. I understand that the attention of Congress will be immediately recalled to it; and if it should still be opposed, the very singular phenomenon will be exhibited of a perseverance in error at the expense of interest on one side, after the interest of the other has yielded to the force of truth and justice.

The just claim of the United States to reciprocity in the intercourse with the British West India and other Colonies, has not been lost sight of by the President. But it was not foreseen that the British Government would so soon be disposed to hearken to it; and it was not thought prudent to mingle demands which might embarrass each other. We learn with much satisfaction that you have found the crisis so favourable for bringing this subject before the British Government, and I am authorized to assure you, that instead of crossing the views of the President in the steps you have taken in relation to it, you could not have more satisfactorily have [sic] promoted them. The manner and degree in which the object is to be pursued he leaves to your discretion informed as it will be by indications on the spot; and guided by the general policy of the United States, which having no objects not warranted by reason and right will rely as long as possible for the attainment of them on seasonable appeals to the interest, the justice and the friendship of others. In this policy the President most sincerely concurs, and sees therefore with particular pleasure every successful result of it. The late conduct of the British Government towards this Country seems to authorize some confidence that it begins to understand better both its own interest, and the American character. And you may on all proper occasions give assurances that it will find in the President a disposition to meet its friendly advances in a manner that will strengthen the good will, and extend the useful intercourse between the two countries.

I observe that the Lord Chancellor has assured you that the Maryland claim to the Bank Stock shall be speedily decided. This is a subject which was particularly pressed in my last letter: and I am led by the sensibility to it in the State of Maryland to repeat my wish that the exertions which you are making may be completely successful. I have the honor to be &c. &c. &c.

JAMES MADISON

Letterbook copy (DNA: RG 59, IM, vol. 6). RC offered for sale in American Art Association Catalogue, 8–9 Apr. 1926, item 413. A typescript of the RC supplied in 1959 by James G. King of New York, N.Y., indicates that it is docketed as received 31 May, with the note: "Approbation by Pr. of the Convention concerning the Debts, &c."

1. *PJM-SS*, 2:489.
2. King's dispatch no. 53 is dated 13 Feb. 1802 (*PJM-SS*, 2:465).
3. *PJM-SS*, 2:380–81.

4. The convention was introduced into the Senate on 29 Mar. 1802 under cover of a message from President Jefferson explaining the negotiations undertaken by King with the British government and requesting the Senate's advice and consent. The Senate began consideration of the agreement on 3 Apr. and several days later requested information on the size of claims under the articles 6 and 7 of the Jay treaty. The executive complied, and after debate the convention was ratified on 26 Apr. by a vote of 19 to 2 (*Senate Exec. Proceedings*, 1:415, 417, 418, 419–20, 421).

5. The report, under a London dateline of 17 Feb., was published in the *National Intelligencer*, 7 Apr. 1802.

6. For Samuel Smith's resolution, see *PJM-SS*, 2:323, 324 n. 3.

From William Croghan

Sir JEFFERSON COUNTY KENTUCKY April 7th. 1802
In Consequence of the Death of Your Brother Ambrose, Colonel Richard Taylor & myself were under the Necessity of bringing Suits in Chancary against You & Nelly Madison for Lands we bought from Your Brother belonging to you & he, when he was in this Country in March 1792 he Sold us those lands.[1] I gave him my Bond for the payment of 104½ Acres of the land I bought from him, which Bond he lost on his Journey from this Country, which he Informed me of By letter Shortly After his Arrival in Virginia, and requested I would not pay it except, I think to Hubbard Taylor, Major John Lee or their Orders. Some time After about the time the bond was due Colonel Richard Taylor, & James Taylor Junr. then of Orange Applyd to me for & received the payment £94.—a Copy of the receipt is Inclosed.[2] Should my Bond have come to hand be so Obliging as to return it to me, or tear my Name out. The bearer Mr. Denis Fitzhugh will wait on You with the Decrees and take Charge of the Deeds both for Colonel Taylor & Myself. I am with great respect, Your Most Humble servant

W CROGHAN

RC and enclosure (DLC). For enclosure, see n. 2.

1. For William Croghan's previous attempts to obtain clear title to land he had purchased from JM and his brother Ambrose, see Richard Terrell to JM, 24 Sept. 1799, and Affidavit on Kentucky Lands, 25 Sept. 1799 (*PJM*, 17:270–71, 271–72 and n. 1).

2. Croghan enclosed a copy of Richard Taylor's receipt for £94 "in full payment for one hundred four and one half acres of land lying on the Ohio River, . . . which land Ambrose & James Madison sold sd. Croghan March 12th. 1792 when said Croghan passed his bond for the payment £94 which bond is lost or mislaid in consequence of which the money is now paid me for said Madison and I do hereby at the request of said Madison hereby indemnify said Croghan from ever paying said Bond or any part thereof" (1 p.; filed among the undated Madison papers [vol. 91]).

§ To Rufus King. *7 April 1802, Washington.* "I have to acknowledge several of your late private letters, which I cannot at this moment refer to by dates. It is probable that all written by you have been received; duplicates and triplicates being so, of all the originals that have come to hand. I write this particularly to acknowledge that of Jany. 12th[1] in which you incline towards a trip into France and the neighbouring countries, during the season least requiring your presence in England. I have communicated to the President your wish on this point, and have the pleasure to inform you that he readily acquiesces in it."

RC (NjP: Crane Collection). 1 p.; marked private; in a clerk's hand, signed by JM.

1. *PJM-SS*, 2:388.

§ To John Morton. *7 April 1802, Department of State.* "The bearer Robert Reed Esqr. of Charleston South Carolina, has business of importance which calls him to the Havanna. Your successor Mr. Young,[1] not being likely to be there so soon as Mr. Reed, I recommend him to your patronage. He is represented to me as a very respectable citizen, and as such, I wish him to be placed in the view of those in authority, to whom he may have occasion to apply."

Letterbook copy (DNA: RG 59, IC, vol. 1). 1 p.

1. Robert Young, of the District of Columbia, was nominated by Jefferson to be commercial agent at Havana on 2 Feb. 1802. The Senate confirmed the appointment the next day (*Senate Exec. Proceedings*, 1:406, 407).

§ From Rufus King. *7 April 1802, London.* No. 61. Text of definitive treaty was published in the *Moniteur* of 26 Mar. In general it "seems to adhere pretty closely to the Preliminaries: in such Articles as have undergone a modification, it is not obvious that the alteration is favourable to the views of this Country. Malta . . . will be liable to the influence of France." Unless there is a separate article explaining how the Prince of Orange will be indemnified, the treaty "seems more likely to prove prejudicial than advantageous to this family"; it is said that the French and Dutch signed a convention exempting the Batavian Republic from contributions to such an indemnification.[1] Lord Grenville's principal objection will be the omission of an acknowledgment of ancient treaties upon which Europe's public law is based. "*He* and others are likewise much dissatisfied with the cession of Louisiana to France." In a conversation with King, Grenville said that "Ceylon, Trinidad, and the Cape, were as nothing in comparison to Louisiana and the Floridas" and added that "*Mr. Pitt* viewed the cession in the Same light" but knew nothing of it until after the preliminaries were signed. Loan of £25 million has been opened "at the moderate Interest of £3.18.2 per Centum." Income tax is to be repealed. New taxes to the amount of £4 million are to be levied on malt, hops, and beer, "assessed Taxes," and imports and exports. "The funds have risen considerably, and there seems to be very little opposition to the new Taxes." Law respecting countervailing duties was assented to by the king on 24 Mar.; "as it passed in the form of the Bill of which I sent you a copy, it is not necessary that I should send you a copy of the Law."[2]

RC (DNA: RG 59, DD, Great Britain, vol. 10); letterbook copy (NHi: Rufus King Papers, vol. 55). RC 5 pp.; in a clerk's hand, signed by King; docketed by Brent as received 12 June. Italicized words were written in code; key not found. RC decoded interlinearly by Wagner. The paragraph containing King's report of his conversation with Grenville about Louisiana is marked "Confidential" in the left margin. Printed in King, *Life and Correspondence of Rufus King*, 4:97–99.

    1. For the diplomatic wrangling over the Orange indemnity, see Schama, *Patriots and Liberators*, pp. 451–54.

    2. See King to JM, 18 Feb. 1802 (*PJM-SS*, 2:479). JM also received a printed copy of the act empowering the king to suspend countervailing duties, dated 24 Mar. 1802 (2 pp.; with a faintly legible notation written by JM in pencil, the first line of which is obscured: "[. . .] kept to be laid before Congress" [DNA: RG 59, ML]).

§ From Philippe-André-Joseph de Létombe. *7 April 1802, Paris*. Notes that the letter JM wrote him from Virginia on 25 Aug. 1801[1] could not have been more favorable to him. His passage from New York to Lorient and his arrival in Paris made him aware of his good fortune in having merited JM's commendation. The Americans and the French are very pleased with these evidences of JM's kindness and esteem; moreover, they value the one who is thus honored. JM's reputation is equally great in the two hemispheres. Hopes JM will long enjoy it and long continue in his post under a president born for the happiness of mankind. In a postscript, conveys his respects to Mrs. Madison and her sisters.

RC (DLC). 2 pp.; in French; docketed by JM.

    1. *PJM-SS*, 2:66.

To Charles Pinckney

Sir,   Department of State, April 8th. 1802

The inclosed memorial presents and explains a case resting on the same grounds with some already committed to you. The interest of the memorialists John Townsend and James Shuter of New York, as well as that of the United States require that your own discretion assisted by indications on the spot should regulate the degree as well as form of your interposition with the Spanish Government. We all know the extreme jealousy which pervades the Colonial policy of Spain; and it is probable that this jealousy may be in a higher excitement towards the enterprizes of our Commercial Citizens, than towards those of any other country. Much care ought to be used therefore in seeking reparation for past injuries issuing from this source, to avoid appearances and pretensions which may unnecessarily give greater force to it in future.

The claim of the memorialists will probably be resisted on the principle that those who voluntarily go within a foreign jurisdiction, are bound to observe and consequently to know the laws and regulations in force. This principle as a general is a just principle. There are nevertheless mitigations of its rigor, of which the case before us may fairly claim the benefit. The frequent and sudden changes which the Commercial regulations in the Spanish Colonies are known to undergo in times of War; the authority which is understood to be delegated to Governors or other Colonial Officers, to relax, by special permissions, the ordinary restrictions; the occasions frequently occurring for the exercise of this authority; the strong presumption derived from respect towards every government, that its officers understand and observe the laws; these are the considerations by which the memorialists appear to have been led into their Commercial project; and which are most likely to be of avail in rescuing them from the losses in which it terminated. It will deserve enquiry also whether the Governors who granted the licences in the present case, might not in fact have possessed a legal authority for the purpose. And if it be true, as is represented in the Memorial that the vessel and cargo were sold without the ordinary forms of trial and proof, this is another topic for just complaint.

You will observe that the treatment of the crew of the ship is represented as having been very inhuman and unwarrantable, and will please to attend to that circumstance in any communications you may have on the subject with the Spanish Government. If it should be found that they are still detained in their cruel situation you will take the proper steps for their relief.

The seizure of the vessel at so great a distance from the Spanish Coast, may seem to be a violation of our maritime rights; but as the uninhabited island at which the seizure took place, is not denied to be within the Spanish dominions, the proceeding could neither of right nor in prudence be protested against on that ground. I am with great respect & consideration &c.

JAMES MADISON

Letterbook copy (DNA: RG 59, IM, vol. 6). Enclosure not found.

§ From William Jarvis. *8 April 1802, Boston.* Encloses his bond [as U.S. consul at Lisbon]; his sureties are two respectable Boston merchants. Has seen letters that arrived on a vessel from Lisbon 6 Apr. reporting that the prince regent of Portugal had ordered a quarantine of up to forty days on vessels from the U.S. "A measure so distressing to our Mariners, so injurious to our Merchants & so unnecessary at such a season of the year (ie in February) surprises me very very much. . . . Had it taken place in some of the more enlightened Countries of Europe I should have supposed it savoured very strongly of a disposition unfavourable toward us; but to you I may be allowed to say Sir, that in this Kingdom it might have been occasioned by the Fears of the good old primate, or some timid Lady near the Princess's person. . . . I must beg the favour of instructions . . . on this or any other subject that may have come to your knowledge since I had the pleasure to see you. . . . No

passage at present offering from this, I fear that I shall be under the necessity of
going on to New York to obtain one, to which place I must beg the favour of your
addr⟨ess⟩ing me to the care of the Collector." Notes in a postscript that he has
learned that another vessel recently arrived from Lisbon was admitted to that port
after only a ten-day quarantine, "in consequence of haveing got the Span⟨ish⟩ Consul's Certificate to [its] Bill of Health." Adds that P. C. Brooks will forward a packet
of papers to JM regarding a vessel seized in the Brazils.[1]

RC (DNA: RG 59, CD, Lisbon, vol. 1). 3 pp.; docketed by Wagner. Enclosure not found.

1. See Thomas Bulkeley to JM, 16 July 1802, n. 3.

§ From Tobias Lear. *8 April 1802, Cap Français.* No. 24. Quotes the 2 Apr. post-
script he added to the duplicate of his dispatch no. 23;[1] reports that a severe indisposition kept him from going to Port-au-Prince as he intended then but he has
since learned that General Leclerc will arrive at the cape in ten or twelve days.
Notes that he had informed the prefect and General Boyer of his intention. "As the
Admiral was not on shore, I wrote to him on the same subject, informing him, as
I had done the others, and likewise that it was my determination to go to the
U. States, after my return from Port au Prince. I also asked him if any arrangement
had been made to furnish his fleet with provisions &c. if he shd. touch at the
U. States. This I did with a view of knowing if he was going thither." Encloses a
copy of Villaret's reply. "The Admiral will sail tomorrow or the day after, with a
squadron of eight or ten ships of the line for France, as it is universally said and
beleived; and that the object is to return immediately with more troops." Observes
that although American vessels meet with fewer difficulties "in the offices," the delays are still very great. "I am perfectly convinced that a great proportion of the
difficulties have arisen from the imprudence, not to say outrage, of our own Countrymen; not only the Captns. but others residing here." Is sending his son home
"before the hot weather comes on, which, I am apprehensive, will produce many
disorders in the City, which is still filled with the rubbish and ruins of the late fire,
and crouded with Soldiers, Sailors &c." Proposes to take his departure after he
meets with the general in chief unless his continuance becomes necessary; "I shall
leave Mr. Unite Dodge, a respectable American Merchant here, charged with the
consular duties for this place, until my return; or until other arrangements shall be
made."

RC (DNA: RG 59, CD, Cap Haitien, vol. 4). 3 pp.; docketed by Brent. Enclosure not
found.

1. See Lear to JM, 29 Mar. 1802, and n.

§ From Tobias Lear. *8 April 1802, Cap Français.* Has drawn on JM in favor of Clement Biddle of Philadelphia for $100, to be charged to his account with the U.S. for
money advanced for distressed seamen.[1] "My advances on this account exceeds this
sum; but I should not have drawn had it been permitted to send money out of the
Colony; or could a bill be had on Philada. . . . Till lately the expenses on this account

have been very small; but the great number of Vessels in port, the impossibility of preventing some from leaving their Vessels, who afterwards become sick or distressed, and several cases of ship wrecks which have happened, will increase the expense; but while I releive all real distresses, I shall endeavour to do so with as much œconomy as possible."

RC (DNA: RG 59, CD, Cap Haitien, vol. 4). 1 p.

1. Lear's letter to JM was enclosed in Lear to Clement Biddle, 9 Apr. 1802, which also enclosed Lear's bill of exchange, 8 Apr. 1802 (ibid.).

To Robert R. Livingston

DEAR SIR   WASHINGTON Apl. 9. 1802

Mr. Latil[1] a Frenchman by birth, but a Citizen of the U. States for near 20 years past, being about making a visit to his native Country, is desirous of being known to you. I have reason to believe that he possesses sufficient respectability and merit to entitle him to your civilities, and I therefore readily ask the favor of them in his behalf. I do it the more so as he has generally resided in Virginia, and consequently considers himself as doubly a fellow Citizen with me, and as I understand that he has no object in his visit, that can make my introduction or your countenance a departure from the general rules respectively laid down for ourselves. With highest respect & regard I am Dr. Sir your most obed set.

JAMES MADISON

RC (NHi: Livingston Papers). Docketed by Livingston, "recd Mr Lattle."

1. Joseph Latil acted as the agent of Pierre Augustin Caron de Beaumarchais in his claim against the state of Virginia in the 1780s. Latil married Lucy Randolph, a second cousin of Edmund Randolph, in 1787 (Edmund Randolph to JM, 27 Mar. 1787, *PJM*, 9:335 and n. 3).

From Samuel Cabot

SIR   BOSTON 9 Apl 1802.

I have this day reced from the Board of Commrs. acting in London under the 7th article of the British treaty an order, dated 15 Feb: 1802, directing me to hold myself in readiness as soon as possible to resume the duty of Estimating losses & assessing damages, as heretofore. This notice was accompanied by a letter from the american Commrs. expressing their desire that I shou'd speedily return to England. It is understood that a statement of these proceedings is already transmitted to our government, & that the

President of the United States has been requested to authorise my departure. Considering the length of time & degree of close application, which may be involved in a final adjustment of our claims pending under the Treaty, & the unavoidable expense of a Voyage & residence in London, it is believed that the remuneration to be expected from the Board is, in itself, inadequate. Shou'd the President (in consequence of any representation that shall be laid before him) deem it expedient to honor me with this appointment, it is respectfully submitted that in addition to the fees payable by the Board an adequate Stipend might be allowed & paid by the United States. If the Salary heretofore annexed to this office shoud be considerd a reasonable & just one the period of its commencement may be so far retrospective as to include the account renderd which still remains in your Department & with the Secretary of the Treasury, unadjusted.[1] It wou'd be useful to me early to learn what the president shall please to determine on the subject of this application. In the Event of my services being required I shall be able to embark for England, immediately after receiving your instructions. The peculiar situation in which I now find myself is my apology for addressing you on the present occasion. Most respectfully I have the honor to be sir, yr mo: ob: hb servt.

SAM CABOT

RC (DNA: RG 76, British Spoliations, 1794–1824, Unsorted Papers). Docketed by Brent.

1. Cabot had sent his account to JM on 3 Aug. 1801 and to Gallatin on 7 Sept. 1801 (*PJM-SS*, 2:7, 8 n. 2, 354–55 and n. 1).

From Edward Thornton

SIR,   WASHINGTON 9th April 1802.
    In obedience to instructions which I have received from His Majesty's Principal Secretary of State for foreign affairs,[1] I take the liberty of bringing back to your recollection the case of the British Transport Ship Windsor (the subject of my letter of the 23rd of July of last year)[2] which was taken forcible possession of by the French prisoners on board, and carried into the harbour of Boston.
    As these people possessed no sort of legal authority to make prize on His Majesty's Subjects, and as in a neutral and friendly port they could not derive from a decree of an Admiralty Court or an act of condemnation any right with which they were not before vested, the property of this vessel must still be regarded as never having been legally transferred from the original possessors.
    I learn from the correspondence of His Majesty's Consul at Boston, that

the Ship continued in that harbour on the 5th of December last, notwith-standing the orders (which you were so good as to announce to me) for her departure from the ports of the United States: and the signature of the preliminaries of peace, the intelligence of which arrived at that time, extin-guished all hopes of recovering the vessel by recapture on the high Seas. I therefore beg leave to express my hope, that under these circumstances, the President will be pleased to order the restitution of the Ship Windsor to her proper owners, if she be still within reach of the American Govern-ment, or otherwise to make them a due compensation for her loss. I have the honour to be with perfect truth and respect, Sir, Your most obedient humble servant,

EDWD THORNTON

RC (DNA: RG 59, NFL, Great Britain, vol. 2).

1. See Hawkesbury to Thornton, 13 Feb. 1802 (Mayo, *Instructions to British Ministers*, p. 191.
2. *PJM-SS*, 1:463.

From Noah Webster

SIR,   NEW HAVEN April 9th. 1802
I have directed a Copy of a work I have just published on Miscellaneous subjects,[1] to be sent from New York to your Care, to be deposited in the Office of State, in pursuance of the Act for securing to authors the right to their productions;[2] and I shall be much obliged to you for a certificate of the deposit.

You will see by that work how much I differ in opinion, from the leading men of the two parties. I wish for more harmony of Councils; but I have little hope of seeing that event.

I was an advocate for the British Treaty; but I am not satisfied with some of the provisions of it, & the more I consider the subject, the more I am convinced that some articles of it have laid the foundation for much future trouble. I refer to the subjects discussed in the work just mentioned. I have a great desire to know the Contents of a little [*sic*] written by the Secretaries of State & Treasury to Genl Washington, at Mount Vernon, just before he gave his assent to the treaty—a letter written in consequence of an urgent application of the British minister for a decision on the ratification of the Treaty.[3] I presume it must be in your office—at the same time I have no right to ask even for a sight of the contents. But I never reflect on the fact without a degree of regret, that any extraneous influence should have been exerted in such an important national question. But it is idle to indulge regret, or anticipate evil. A more temperate policy on the part of the present administration would have reconciled all sober, impartial federalists to the change, & this without any considerable sacrifice of principles on the part of the present ruling men. Accept my respects, with my best wishes for your personal welfare, & believe me Your Obedt Servt

N WEBSTER JUN.

RC (DLC: Rives Collection, Madison Papers). Docketed by JM.

1. For Webster's book, see *PJM-SS*, 2 : 288 n. 1.

2. Section 4 of the "Act for the encouragement of learning, by securing the copies of maps, charts, and books, to the authors and proprietors of such copies, during the times therein mentioned," dated 31 May 1790, required authors to send a copy of their work to the secretary of state within six months of the date of publication (*U.S. Statutes at Large*, 1 : 125).

3. Webster probably referred to the letter written to Washington by Timothy Pickering on behalf of himself, Oliver Wolcott, and Attorney General William Bradford on 31 July 1795, requesting the president's return to Philadelphia, ostensibly for discussions on the as-yet-unratified Jay treaty but in reality to expose to Washington the allegedly traitorous behavior of the secretary of state, Edmund Randolph, which led to the latter's resignation and disgrace (Reardon, *Edmund Randolph*, pp. 306–13).

§ To William C. C. Claiborne. *9 April 1802, Department of State*. Encloses Claiborne's commission as governor of the Mississippi Territory.[1]

Tr and Tr of enclosure (Ms-Ar: Claiborne Executive Journal). 2 pp. Printed in Rowland, *Claiborne Letter Books*, 1 : 115–16. Enclosure is a copy of a 26 Jan. 1802 commission by Jefferson appointing Claiborne to a three-year term.

1. Claiborne's earlier commission was an interim appointment, authorizing him to hold office until the end of the next Senate session (*PJM-SS*, 1 : 321 n. 1). Claiborne's nomination was confirmed by the Senate on 26 Jan. 1802 (*Senate Exec. Proceedings*, 1 : 401, 405).

§ From Daniel Clark. *9 April 1802, Philadelphia*. "Business of a private Nature requiring my presence in New Orleans I am induced to freight a small Vessel for the sake of dispatch and will leave this City on Sunday the Seventeenth inst. to proceed there direct. I think it incumbent on me to give you information of my resolution as soon as taken, that you may have an opportunity of forwarding any instructions you may think necessary or point out any thing in which I may be of service. On arrival in Luisiana I will advise you of the state of affairs there generally."

RC (DNA: RG 59, CD, New Orleans, vol. 1). 2 pp.

§ From Israel Whelen. *9 April 1802, Philadelphia*. Acknowledges JM's letter of 2 Apr. [not found] "and the remittance you directed to be made to me, and agreeably to your directions I have paid Mr. Kingston $5775. on a draft from Genl. Stevens's Agent for that sum, previously taking sufficient security that the charter party on Mr. Kingston's part had or would be completely & entirely fulfilled." Reports that "there are letters in town" from Captain Wood of the *Peace and Plenty*, telling of his arrival at his destination in December 1801.

RC (DNA: RG 59, ML); letterbook copy (DNA: RG 45, Purveyor's Office, Philadelphia). RC 1 p.; docketed by Brent.

From Rufus King

No. 62.

SIR,   LONDON Ap. 10. 1802.

Some months ago I informed you that *Mr. Jackson* would probably be sent *to the U. States as Mr. Liston's successor*. *Mr. Merry* had been previously thought of and indeed named *for this mission*. As I have had the opportunity of knowing *both these gentlemen* during *my residence here* it was not without some regret that I heard of the intention to appoint *Mr. Jackson in lieu of Mr. Merry*. From this information I have been led to make further Enquiry concerning their Reputations, and the result has proved rather to encrease than lessen my solicitude. *Mr. Jackson* is said to be positive, vain, and intolerant: he is moreover filled *with English prejudices* in respect to all other Countries, and as far as his opinions concerning *the U. States* are known, seems more likely to disserve than benefit a liberal intercourse between them and his own Country.[1]

On the other hand *Mr. Merry* appears to be a plain, unassuming and amiable man, who having *lived* for many years *in Spain* is in almost every point of Character the reverse *of Mr. Jackson* who were he to go *to America* would go for the sake of present employment, and with the hope of leaving it as soon as he could receive a similar appointment *in Europe* while *Mr. Merry* wishes for *the mission* with the view of obtaining what he believes will prove to be an agreeable and permanent residence.[2]

With these sentiments, I have believed it to be proper, to endeavour in every unexceptional way in my power to discourage and throw impediments in the way of *the mission of Mr. Jackson* and in a late conversation *with Lord Hawkesbury* he offered me what I thought a fair occasion of expressing my sentiments upon this subject. *His Lordship* received my Observations in good part, and promised to consider what I had said to him before any definitive step should be taken in the Business. I have followed up the opposition in other quarters which I thought likely to have an influence in the decision, and am not without Expectation *that Mr. Jackson* will be relinquished.

As the explicit designation of a particular character who would be agreeable, is matter of greater delicacy than to object to an Individual who might have been spoken of, I have rather confined myself to the latter course, in doing which, however, I was enabled indirectly, and by way of Contrast to *Mr. Jackson's* disqualifications, to describe qualifications which seem to be almost peculiar *to Mr. Merry.*

Annexed I send you copies of my Letter to Lord Hawkesbury and of his Answer declining to recognize Mr. Lewis as Consul of the United States at Calcutta:[3] a like Answer has, in a similar case, been lately given to the Envoy of Portugal. Conversing with one of the Directors of the East India Company concerning Mr. Lewis' appointment, he told me that before the late war, France had been solicitous to place a Consul at Calcutta: that from a persuasion that a Consul would be employed as a political instead of a Commercial Agent they had declined his admission; that the request would however probably be renewed, and in case An American Consul should be admitted, a French one could not be refused. With perfect Respect and Esteem, I have the honour to be, Sir, Your ob. & faithful servant

(Signed)   R<small>UFUS</small> K<small>ING</small>

RC and enclosures (DNA: RG 59, DD, Great Britain, vol. 10); letterbook copy (NHi: Rufus King Papers, vol. 55). RC marked duplicate; in a clerk's hand, signed by King; docketed by Brent as received 13 June. Italicized words were written in code; key not found. RC decoded interlinearly by Brent. Printed in King, *Life and Correspondence of Rufus King*, 4: 100–101. For enclosures, see n. 3.

1. King's predictions proved true when Francis James Jackson became Great Britain's minister to the U.S. in October 1809 (*PJM-PS*, 2:xxvii).

2. The choice of Anthony Merry to be British minister to the U.S. is discussed in Malcolm Lester, *Anthony Merry Redivivus: A Reappraisal of the British Minister to the United States, 1803–1806* (Charlottesville, Va., 1978), pp. 13–14.

3. King enclosed copies of his letter to Lord Hawkesbury, 6 Feb. 1802, announcing Jacob Lewis's appointment and requesting the "usual Exequatur to enable him to discharge the Duties of his office," and Hawkesbury's refusal, dated 23 Mar. 1802 (1 p.). JM also received copies of these letters from Lewis (see Lewis to JM, 2 Apr. 1802, and n.).

§ From Robert W. Fox. *10 April 1802, Falmouth.* Reports the arrival of several American ships with cargoes of flour and wheat. "Some of their Cargoes have been sold @ 45/ or 46/ ℔ Barrel and the Vessels have gone forward with the Cargoes, on being paid an additional freight by the buyers; others I beleive will take their Cargoes forward to Barcelona for account of the concerned." Flour and wheat are in demand at Barcelona, Leghorn, and Genoa, but sales are "very dull" at Falmouth; "indeed Trade is much at a Stand in most parts of this Nation." The *Surprize*, Captain Strong, of Philadelphia was abandoned at sea with a full cargo of cotton. The crew was picked up and landed at Falmouth 9 Apr.; "being destitute and no Vessels at this port bound to the United States, their expences will be considerable." Will recommend that they go to London on the first available vessel. Allowance of ten cents a day "will go but a little way in their Support." "West India produce is of very slow sale. Hemp has fallen considerably in Russia, but Tobacco supports its price. Several American Ships are about to go to that Country to load for the United

States. Copper in Cakes are now ⟨ab⟩out £120 ⅋ Ton at the Works; the manufac-
tor⟨ing co⟩sts about £12 to £14 ⅋ Ton." In a postscript, requests permission "to act
at this Port as Agent for the Dutch, to be employed by their Government to assist
the Masters of their Ships if shipwrecked on this Coast or in want of Supplies, provided I cou'd accept such an appointment consistently with being Consul of the
United States."

RC (DNA: RG 59, CD, Falmouth, vol. 1). 3 pp.; in a clerk's hand, except for Fox's signature
and postscript; docketed by Brent.

§ From Benjamin Fry. *10 April 1802, Newport.* Refers to his letter to JM of 2 Feb.[1]
enclosing accounts and papers relating to his claim against France for the capture
of the brig *Favorite* by a French privateer after the Convention of 1800 was signed.
Has not received a reply from JM "but was informd. by a line from my good friend
Christr. Ellery Esqr. that he Conversd. with you Sir on the Subject, and that you
informd. him my papers woud. be Returnd to me with a letter of directions &C and
that the Papers must be transmited to France, The expectation of payment at Gau-
deloupe being given up in consequence of the State of things there." Intends to take
passage in a vessel he is fitting out for Amsterdam "& from thence proceed to
France in Order to obtain payment for my Captured Property." Asks JM to forward
his papers soon, as his ship "will be ready for Sea before this Month is ended." Also
requests a letter of introduction to Robert R. Livingston and "any information or
directions you may please to afford me."

RC (DLC: Causten-Pickett Papers, box 47); draft (RPB-JH). RC 1 p.

1. *PJM-SS*, 2:437–38.

§ From James Maury. *10 April 1802, Liverpool.* States that he has never been reimbursed for sums he paid in support of American seamen before the arrival of David
Lenox and asks JM to direct Lenox's successor or the American minister to pay him
£101 2s. 5d. or "such part thereof as shall appear reasonable." Observes that little
or no change in the market for imports from the U.S. has resulted from the signing
of the definitive treaty. The king was empowered by Parliament on 24 Mar. to
suspend for one year the countervailing duties on American ships and the goods
imported in them, "but as that power has not yet been used, I cannot at present say
how it is likely to Affect our Shipping."

RC (DNA: RG 59, CD, Liverpool, vol. 2). 2 pp.; in a clerk's hand, signed by Maury.

§ From Tobias Lear. *11 April 1802, Cap Français.* No. 25. "On the ninth the Genl.
in Chief arrived here from Port au Prince, in a Frigate. In the forenoon of the tenth
I waited upon him, when he informed me, in the first moment of our meeting, that
he could not receive me as a public Character from the U. States, and desired I
would no longer exercise the functions of Commercial Agent in the Island. I demanded the reason of this Change. He observed that as he was an Officer subordinate to the Govt. of France, he had not the power to receive and acknowledge a

Consul from a foreign nation . . . and that on his arrival, he was so much engaged in a variety of important concerns, that he had received and acknowledged me without reflection. I told him I should have been relieved from much trouble and anxiety had this event taken place at our first meeting; but as it was, I should comply with his request, and no longer exercise the functions of Commercial Agent. . . . He then observed, that he was sorry to tell me he had been informed by letters and otherways, that I had written to the U. States, to caution the Citizens agt. sending their vessels or receivg bills on France in payment for their Cargoes, as these bills wd. not be paid; and also that I had done everything in my power to excite differences between the Citizens of the two Nations. I was astonished at this, and assured him in the strongest manner, that it was a base calumny and a scandelous falsehood. . . . I demanded the names of those who had given this information. He told me I should have them; and observed that he hoped I could remove the imputation. . . . On coming home I took the Arms of the U. S. from my door, and immediately wrote to the Genl. in Chief, informing him that I was fully satisfied with the reasons which he had assigned for not receiving and acknowledging me in my public Character, and requested he wd. be so good as to give them to me in writing . . . and again requested he wd. give me the names of those who had given him the information of which he had spoken. . . . To this letter I received no answer.

"I have written to Mr. Caldwell & Mr. Dandridge, informg them of this determination of the Genl. in Chief. . . . I shall embark in the course of ten days on board some vessel for the U. States.

"Admiral Villaret Joyeuse sailed yesterday for France. . . . The Batavian fleet of 6 or 8 ships will sail in a week or ten days for the Chesapeak.

"*Pecchion has written things which have caused disgust with the United States and the citizens thereof. Their conduct towards me is on that ground.*"

RC (DNA: RG 59, CD, Cap Haitien, vol. 4); FC (ibid.). RC 3 pp.; docketed by Brent. Italicized words are those encoded by Lear and decoded here by the editors using a key from the Lear family papers (owned by Stephen Decatur, Garden City, N.Y., 1958). RC decoded interlinearly by JM.

From Peder Blicherolsen

SIR   PHILADELPHIA 12th. of April 1802.

In a letter I had the honor to write You on the 16th. of January last,[1] I took the liberty to lay before You an official note, stating the particulars concerning the claims of one of the Kings my masters subjects against Capt: Maley, commander of the United States armed schooner *Experiment*, for having unlawfully captured, and afterwards allowed to be recaptured by an armed British Vessel from under his protection the Danish schooner *Mercator*: and further, as the said Capt: Maley was found to have left the United States, requesting that this Government would point out some mode, by which the owner of the captured property might obtain justice and reparation for the loss and injury he has sustained.

Though deeply lamenting the necessity of preying on the precious moments of Your time, devoted to so vaste a number of other pressing occupations and dutys, I feel it nevertheless indispensably incumbent upon me to torment You once more on this subject, and to repeat my demand to be favoured with an answer, acquainting me with the means to be employed in order to secure to an injuried country-man of mine such indemnification as the impartial laws of this country may deem him entitled to.

Being Yourself Sir placed in a station, which gives You a right to prescribe and to exspect similar exertions in similar cases from agents appointed under Your direction, so far from apprehending any displeasure on Your part by this my repeated zeal, I rather flatter myself to meet Your generous approbation, and I beg leave to assure You, that a true sentiment of personal esteem for Your generaly acknowledged principles has been on this occassion and shall henceforth constantly be an additional and powerfull inducement to me for the most vigilant performance of my dutys.

On the 16th. of February last the Danish colours were hoisted in our islands, and these again restored to their mother-country. The same friendly intercourse between this continent and the Danish colonies; which used to be so mutualy beneficial on both sides, will, I am confident, immediately resume its former activity, and the liberal principles constantly adhered to by my government, even with respect to those remote objects of its care, so contrary to those adopted by several others, will I hope for a long time continue to deserve from the United States an equally liberal exertion on Their part in averting whatever might in the least be obnoxious to this happy and truely natural reciprocity. I am with great respect Sir Your most obedient and humble servant

BLICHEROLSEN.

RC (DNA: RG 59, NFL, Denmark, vol. 1). Docketed by Brent.

1. *PJM-SS*, 2:400–401.

From James Monroe

DEAR SIR   RICHMOND april 12. 1802.

I took the liberty lately to forward to yr. care by Major Coleman who went to Alexa. a box containing the three pieces of tapestry, which are intended for Mr. Fenwick, he having promised to take charge of and sell them for me. Can you possibly convey them to his possession. He is I believe some where ⟨in th⟩e neighbourhood of the federal city. Will you also be so good as put the enclosed letter or such memo: ⟨fro⟩m it as the case warrants relative to the author,[1] in the hands of the Secretary of Treasury or navy or both. Dr. Eustace & (I presume) Genl. Dearbourne know him, who will vouch for what his pretentions are. I considered him an honest deserving man by his conduct in France & as such spoke of him to our govt. at the time. I wish it to be known to Dr. Eustace that I have made this gentn. known to you, as he has repeatedly requested me to do. Being acquainted with him in France, he thinks he has a claim on me here for similar good offices with those he experienc'd there, which I render without reluctance, on the opinion I formed of his integrity. Mrs. M. who has lately added a daughter to our family, unites in best regards to Mrs. Madison. Yr. friend & servt

JAS. MONROE

RC (James Monroe Museum and Memorial Library, Fredericksburg, Va.). RC torn. The editors are grateful to Lee Langston-Harrison of the Monroe Museum for her assistance in reading the damaged portion. Enclosure not found.

1. Monroe referred to John Leach, a sea captain and merchant from Boston who had resided in Paris when Monroe was minister to France. Monroe had previously recommended Leach for the post of U.S. consul at Dunkirk; this time Leach requested a position as commissioner of bankruptcy at Boston (Monroe to Edmund Randolph, 1 Aug. 1795, and Monroe to Jefferson, 7 July 1802, Hamilton, *Writings of Monroe*, 2:338–39, 3:355–56; Leach to Monroe, 7 June 1802 [DNA: RG 59, LAR, 1801–9]).

§ From David Gelston. *12 April 1802, Collector's Office, New York.* "Your letter for Mr. King, was this morning recd., and handed to the Post-Master, half an hour before closing the mail by the British Packet."

RC (DLC). 1 p.

From James Monroe

DEAR SIR   RICHMOND april 13. 1802.

The enclosed presents a case properly within the sphere of yr. own department. Mr. Barnet late consul at Bordeaux was appointed while I was in France to Brest, to wh. he was recommended by me, tho I am persuaded he owed his appointment to his friends in Jersey, for my recommendation was at a time, when it was more likely to injure than to benefit him. You will find him mention'd in my book page 355.[1] He is a nephew of Mr. Boudinot the director of the mint. What I then said of him I still think. I was then under an impression that he was a republican, but confess that I was inclined to doubt it after my return to America, not from any thing I ever heard of him, but the consideration that all the active & known republicans were dismissd by the then admn., & the character of his connections in this country. It is probable he owed his continuance in office to the influence of his connections and not to his political principles. I am persuaded that was the case for I really think him an honest respectable young man, and particularly meritorious for his attention to his aged mother. You will be so kind as shew his letter to the President.[2] I ought to add that I recd. sometime last autumn a letter from a Mr. Osman, or some such name, a nephew of Saml. Adams, written from Bordeaux in favor of this young man. It was my intention to communicate to you in person the contents of that letter in Albemarle, but forgot to do it. It was written in a masterly stile and the strongest glow of republican sentiment, & assured me that he Mr. Barnett was a republican. It spoke of his private as well as publick virtues in a manner to excite an interest in his behalf. Mr. Fenwick told me the above of Mr. Osman, & that he was very deserving of confidence. I communicate these things to you on the idea it is interesting to you to know them.

I have just recd. a letter from Mr. Gauvain at Baltimore informing me that he will sit out in a day or two with his lady for this place on a visit to my family. This gentn. was sometime in my office at Paris on the appointment of Mr. Skipwith to the consulate. He is a worthy sensible young man. His two sisters are married to Americans, Taney & Vans.[3] Being under the necessity of going to Albemarle to meet any persons who may be disposed to purchase my Land above charlottesville, which is advertised for sale on tuesday next, it will be a circumstance of peculiar embarrassment for him to arrive in my absence in the present situation of my family. I have written mr. Pichon to request, if in his power, that he will detain him there untill the latter end of next week, at which time I will be back. If you see Mr. Pichon it may possibly be in yr. power to hint something of the above. He will doubtless call on Mr. Pichon in passing thro Georgetown. He was to leave Baltimore tomorrow or next day. His views are mercantile. His intention is to settle in St. domingo; the object of his visit to this country to make acquaintance and form connections. Sincerely I am yr. friend & servt

JAS. MONROE

RC (NN: Monroe Papers). Enclosure not found, but see n. 2.

1. Monroe's book, *A View of the Conduct of the Executive*, included much of his correspondence as U.S. minister to France. The reference to Barnet is in a letter from Monroe to Secretary of State Timothy Pickering, 24 July 1796: "Permit me to make known to you the wish of Isaac Cox Barnet, a citizen of the United States, from Elizabeth town (Jersey) to be appointed consul at Brest. This young man is well recommended to me in point of morality; appears to possess adequate talents, and from what I hear, is industrious" (pp. 354–55).

2. Monroe probably enclosed Barnet's letter to him of 23 Jan. 1802, in which Barnet complained of his removal and requested Monroe's intercession (offered for sale in Robert K. Black Catalogue No. 123 [1969], item 137). According to the catalogue entry, the letter was docketed by JM.

3. Francis L. Taney of Baltimore and William Vans of Salem were American merchants living in Paris during Monroe's residence there (William Stinchcombe, *The XYZ Affair* [Westport, Conn., 1980], pp. 138–39).

From Jacob Peterson

SIR,   CADIZ April 13th. 1801. [1802]

I do myself the honor, and as Incumbent with my duty as a Citizen of the United States of America, Armed, And Commissioned under the Authority of his Excellency John Adams The *late* President of the United States to Set forth the following diabolical treatment, not only personal, but *National* Insult I recieved from the Ship Walker of London Commanded by John Nichols, and owned by Messrs. Wigram & Co.

It was on the 20th. day of January present year then off Cape Horn, I fell in and Spoke with Said Walker. He informed me that he was very much in want of Canvass & Sundry Chandelary Stores, to which I replied that if he would Send his Boat the next day that I would Spare him a Topsail, which was Complied with the next day and the walker recieved the Topsail with other Stores.

On the 22d. at 10 A.M. the Ship Walker bore down on my Larboard Quarter and at ¼ past 10 Sheared along Side, Hailed me and requested that I would send my Log book on board, That he would examine my Ship To which I replied, If you have any Authority to Examine my Ship, you will Send your boat on board And you Shall recieve every Satisfaction—upon which he fired a Shot over the Poop Deck, which Carried away the Quarter Rail & Some of the Rigging. Says he This is to bring you too. I then gave orders for my Steering Sails Top Gallant Sails and Courses to be taken in to bring the Ship too. But notwithstanding, Said Ship fired 2 Broad Sides into my Ship in the very Act of Compliance which almost left me a wreck in my Running rigging. When this was done I Said to him in the Very act of Compliance you have Acted So base & Cowardly As to fire 2 Broad Sides into my Ship—ho! ho says he I'll abide by the Consequences. At 45 mt. past 10. AM I Sent my first officer Mr. Peter Suter[1] on Board with the Log Book, to prevent if it was Still possible a Contest, which at last proved Inevitable. At 11 my boat returned with his note no 3 requesting me to Send my Clearance from Philadelphia Bills of Lading, and my Clearance from the last Port, and repair on board. The former I Granted but the latter I thought proper to decline.

Shortly after I recieved his note no. 4 full of Threats & Consequences if I did [not] repair on board, To which I Gave a possitive refusal. Lastly he Sent his note no. 5 wherein he says. I see *you* are determined not to Come on board. I request that you will Send the Gentleman Passenger, And after a few Questions we may likely proceed on our Voyage. To this Gentleman I Shewed his note. Says he—I Can have no objections to go on board his ship As I have my regular Pasport and have nothing to fear from him I may probably prevent any further Contest. With this Sentiment of Reconciliation the Gentleman went on board the walker. At 40 mt. past 5 P.M the Walker Sheared again along Side, and within a Short Pistol Shot. Capt Nicols requested me to Come on board his Ship and if I did not Comply with his request he would Sink the Ship under me and 5 minutes time he would only Grant me to Consider of it.

"I Answered that I would not Comply with his request while I Could Display the Colors of the United States of America, And if you have any thing to Communicate to me you must Come on board of my Ship. I request of you to Send my boat with my papers, officer, Passenger and the two lads on board. You have already informed me that you have found my papers Satisfactory. You have offered a national Insult, And have Insulted *me* Grossly. Therefore Consider well what you have done or what your base intention may be to do."

"Says he I will have your Cargo & more than your Cargo."

"You have brought me to the last extremity. Therefore be Cautious what you do. I will lose no more time by you, and if you fire again it will be on your Peril."

Says he I will do what I Can, & will fight my Waist Guns.

"I layed my Ship upon his Starboard Quarter Close along Side, and Gave orders for my men that in Case the Walker fired upon us, To fire upon her with a well directed Fire."

At this time it was nearly Six OClock. The walker fired upon me which was immediatly returned from the Asia and So effectually that every Shot Raking her. Smoke was Seen issuing from her Main Top, her Colors Shot Away, & the Second broad Side being fired I ordered to [stop] fireing—when I observed the Walker in Great Consternation, and making all Sail. They hoisted a Color again. I made all Sail After her and ordered the Bow Guns to play upon her, which Carried away her Mizen Topsail, but notwithstandg She Got away from me being very much superior in point of Sailing.

My only object was now, if Possible to bring my Ship again along Side of the walker, to extricate my officer, Passenger, and my two lads.

I pursued her under all Sail, but the wind being very light, She drew very fast from me insomuch That at ½ past seven OClock She was 4 miles a head of me. Through the night it Continued Calm, during which time I repaired Some of my wounded rigging and at day light Saw the walker about 4 miles to windward of me. I hove my Ship too, & repaired my main

Yard & wounded rigging to Give the Walker an Opportunity to Come down to me which he very prudently declined, as the former reception was too warm. And at Noon of the 23d I made all Sail to turn to windward & the Night following it became very thick and Squally lost the Walker. The Walker Mounted 14 Guns, Twelves, nines & sixes.

I am happy to add that I Came off without the loss of any Men, having only one wounded by the Topsail Tye being Shot Away. I am Sir with Great Respect Your Mo Obedient hum. Servt.

JACOB PETERSON
Commander

RC (DNA: RG 76, British Spoliations, 1794–1824, Ship "Asia"). Sent as enclosure in JM to Rufus King, 23 July 1802 (second letter).

1. For Peter Sutter's affidavit describing these events, see John Elmslie, Jr., to JM, 29 Mar. 1802, and n. 1.

§ To Sylvanus Bourne. *13 April 1802, Department of State, Washington.* "The President of the United States, to whom I have communicated the request contained in your Letter of the first february last,[1] just received at this office, yielding to the weight of circumstances which produced it, authorizes me to inform you, that you have his permission to come to this Country at the time you mention: But I have it in charge from him to add, that he expects your visit will be but a short one, and that you will accelerate your return to Amsterdam as much as possible. The United States having no longer a public minister in Holland, the great commercial intercourse which our Citizens have with that Town, must render your presence there on that account the more necessary: and you will for this reason appreciate the motive of the President for coupling a condition with the permission he gives you to visit this Country during the next autumn."

Letterbook copy (DNA: RG 59, IC, vol. 1). 1 p.

1. *PJM-SS,* 2:432.

§ From Henry Brockholst Livingston. *13 April 1802, New York.* Has learned from a bill for the reorganization of the judiciary now before the Senate "that the President is in future to appoint commissioners of Bankrupts in the several Districts." Recommends William Cutting[1] of New York City, a lawyer and former partner of his, for the post.

RC (DNA: RG 59, LAR, 1801–9, filed under "Cutting"). 1 p.; in a clerk's hand, signed by Livingston. Docketed by Jefferson.

1. William Cutting (1773–1820) was married to Livingston's second cousin Gertrude Livingston Cutting (Florence Van Rensselaer, comp., *The Livingston Family and Its Scottish Origins* [New York, 1949], pp. 84, 86, 93, 98, 114).

From Gabriel Christie

DEAR SIR   LONDON April 14th 1802

I wrote you on the 20th of last mounth by way of New York. But least some axcident should happen to my letter I am enduced to send this by way of Alexandria. In my last I informd you that I wished to decline the appointment of Consul at Canton for my Son and would wish him appointed Consul at Madera. Mr Pintard has left that place and I am told the duties are performd by a Mr Charles Alder an Irishman. This being the case and Knowing that the President has no wish to appoint any but American Citizens to office I am enduced to Solicit that appointment for my Son Charles Christie who I will answer for it will be found fully competent to the Task, it would greately oblige me if you would be so Kind as to Solicit the President on his behalf and endeavour to procure the appointment for him as soon as Possible. I shall consider my self under obligations for the favour, and have no doubt but I shall be gratify'd if it can be done with propriety. If it can be done, I will thank you to transmitt the appointment to me under cover to Captn Charles Christie at the East India Coffee House Cornhill London. And permitt me to request that should the application not be granted you will be so obliging as to advise me of it as early as Possible directed as above.

I mean to return to America in the fall. I wish I could sooner, I am mortify'd in the extreem at being obliged to remain amongst a People who hold my Country and Countrymen in so small estimation. If an american wishes to be respected in England he must deny his Country, and as I have always been one of those who take a pride in the acknowledgement I am some times treated in a manner not very greatefull to my feelings, the Government of this Country nay more the People of this Country hate America, their hatered proceeds from their fears that we shall er'e long become their rivals in every thing. We have nothing to expect from their Generosity altho some of our Public men would endeavour to pursuade me that they have every disposition to oblige us. I fear that there is more disposition in some of our People hear to oblige them than there is in them to oblige us, I feel pursuaded of this fact and cannot help expressing it, this is the conclusion I have drawn from my own observations and altho it's possible I may err yet I am enclined to beleave them just.

I find amongst our Commissioners hear that Mr Pinkny is the most prominent Character, and that the buisness of the Board is chiefly transacted by him. I find also that he is the only man amongst them whoes wishes are not hostile to our Executive, the Minister and them affect to be satisfyd but I can see Vexsation and Chagreen abundantly depicted in their countenances and sometimes in their conversation, great pains has been taken by some of Mr Pinknys friend⟨s⟩ in Maryland to make him declare Hostilities also against our Executive but they have failed, he is determined to judge for himself. He has told me that he has the utmost confidence in Mr Jeffersons Wisdom and entegrity. He is confident that the result of his administration will be found beneficial to our Country and unless he has just grounds to alter his opinion he holds himself bound to support his administration, therefore he has in a letter which I have seen a part of declined enlisting under the banners of the Maryland Anti Republican Juncto I am glad of it for he is an honest man, and we want the support of no others, he wishes much to return to america and tells me that if the British Commissioners can be made to attend to their duty that they will be able to close their Commission in twelve mounths from this time. Present my respectfull Compliments to our Worthy Chief Magistrate and beleave me Dear sir Your Obt sert

G Christie

RC (DLC).

From Louis-André Pichon

Georgetown le 24. Germinal an 10.

Monsieur,   (14. avril 1802.)

Le Congrès ayant fait l'appropriation nécéssaire pour mettre à exécution la convention Signée entre la République française et les Etats Unis, le 9. vendemiaire an 9,[1] J'ai l'honneur de vous adresser ci Joints deux tableaux[2] comprenant, le premier, la liste des bâtimens appartenant à la République française qui doivent être restitués par les Etats Unis d'après l'article 3. de la ditte Convention, et le Second celle des propriétés particulières dont Je réclame la restitution en mes mains, attendu l'absence des propriétaires et conformément à ce qui a été antérieurement convenu de la part du Gouvernement des Etats Unis. Je Joins à ces pieces, Monsieur, Extrait des instructions que Je recus, à mon départ, du Ministre de la Marine[3] lesquelles Sont une autorisation qui paraitra Sans doute Suffisante, indépendamment de ma responsabilité officielle, pour Justifier le versement de ces propriétés en mes mains auquel Monsieur Le Président des Etats Unis a bien voulu consentir.

J'ai divisé, Monsieur, Sous deux chapitres les propriétés privées: Le premier comprend les bâtimens amenés dans les ports des Etats Unis et condamnés en premiere instance par leurs cours de Justice. Le Second les prises conduites à l'Etranger et vendues Sans formes Légales. Pour cette espece de propriétés, J'ai pris le montant net des ventes tel qu'il est porté dans les renseignemens reçus par le département de la marine aux Etats Unis, quoiqu'il ne paraisse pas douteux qu'il y ait eu dans la Manutention, comme dans la distribution de ces propriétés, beaucoup de confusion et de désordre. J'ai Pensé que Sur ces procédés irréguliers, commis au loin et hors du contrôle des Gouvernemens Respectifs, il fallait couper court à toute discussion et user d'une conciliation dont, de part et d'autre, considerant le passé, on a également besoin.

J'ai porté, Monsieur, comme vous le verrez, dans ce tableau une prise Portugaise faite par un de nos corsaires, recapturée par un bâtiment Américain liberée par l'amirauté de St. christophe le 5. 7bre. 1800. et par conséquent rentrant dans la convention du 9. vendemiaire an 9. J'ai reçu du Ministre des Relations Extérieures un ordre Spécial de réclamer cette propriété, et vous trouverez ci Jointes deux pieces[4] qui constatent les circonstances de Sa libération et de Sa vente par l'agent des Etats Unis dans la colonie Susmentionée.

Quant aux prises conduites dans les Etats Unis, J'ai hésité, Monsieur à porter les montans nets; attendû le tort notable qui en résulte pour les propriétaires. Ces condamnations ayant eu lieu Sous les yeux des Etats Unis, partie du produit ayant été reçu dans leur trésor, il m'a paru, Monsieur, qu'il pourrait Sembler Juste d'allouer le montant brut des ventes. Si vous comparez les deux resultats vous verrez qu'en certains cas il y a une déduction réellement ruineuse Sur la propriété. Je citerai Seulement le cas des Deux Anges[5] qui de 75,000. Dollars est réduit à $53,000. et cette prise, vous le Savez, a été un acte réellement injuste et contraire à toutes les regles. Je laisse, Monsieur, à la Justice de Mr. Le Président à déterminer Sur cette question: Je dirai Seulement, pour l'examiner Sous le point de vue de la réciprocité, que les propriétés Américaines qui ont été vendues en France Subiront de bien moindres défalcations par la différence du marché: Les bâtimens Américains étaient généralement chargés de denrées qui Se vendaient cher en Europe et c'était le contraire pour nos bâtimens amenés aux Etats Unis: Une autre considération, qui ne me parait pas Sans quelque poids, c'est la différence des droits, aux Etats Unis et en france, Sur les denrées: laquelle est, de beaucoup, au désavantage de la france.

Quelque Soit le parti adopté, Je desire, Monsieur, qu'il le Soit de maniere à entrainer le moins de délais possible; La facilité qui m'est donnée par les Etats Unis perdant tous les Jours de Sa valeur par les retards qu'elle éprouve.

J'aurai l'honneur, Monsieur, de vous rappeler ultérieurement les indemnités qui Sont réclamées pour quelques prises. En attendant, Monsieur, Je vous prie d'agréer l'assurance de mon profond respect et de ma parfaite considération.

L. A. PICHON

CONDENSED TRANSLATION

The appropriation for executing the Convention of 1800 having been made by Congress, Pichon encloses two tables. The first lists ships belonging to the French government that must be restored under article 3; the second lists the private properties that Pichon claims on behalf of the absent owners. Also enclosed is an extract of his instructions from the minister of marine, which will serve as his authorization to receive these payments from the U.S. government. Has divided the private property into two parts: those ships brought to American ports and condemned by U.S. courts; and prizes taken to foreign ports and sold without legal proceedings. For ships sold outside the U.S., Pichon calculated the total amount due French nationals from information provided by the U.S. government. Included in this list is a Portuguese prize taken by France and then recaptured by an American ship. Has received a special order from the minister of foreign relations to reclaim this property; encloses two documents explaining the circumstances of the case. As for the prizes taken to the U.S., wishes to calculate the restitution due to French nationals according to the gross amount of the sales rather than the net amount. Cites the case of the *Deux Anges*, in which $75,000 has been reduced to $53,000. Asks that these questions be resolved with as little delay as possible.

RC and enclosures (DNA: RG 59, NFL, France, vol. 1). RC in a clerk's hand, signed by Pichon; docketed by Brent. For surviving enclosures, see nn. 2 and 3.

1. The "Act making an appropriation for defraying the expenses which may arise from carrying into effect" the Convention of 1800 provided a sum not to exceed $318,000 and was signed into law on 3 Apr. 1802 (*U.S. Statutes at Large*, 2:148).

2. The enclosed lists (5 pp.) are filed after Pichon to JM, 3 Dec. 1801.

3. Pichon enclosed two extracts from the minister of marine. The first, dated 12 Dec. 1800 (2 pp.), authorized Pichon to sell the ships in the U.S. claimed by French merchants for restitution and laid out the procedures for reimbursing the owners. The second extract, of the same date (2 pp.), instructed Pichon to sell, in certain cases, the ships claimed by France.

4. The enclosures relating to the case of the *Gloria dal Mar* have not been found.

5. For the case of the *Deux Anges*, see Pichon to JM, 4 Jan. 1802 (*PJM-SS*, 2:368 and n. 1).

§ From Thomas Bulkeley. *14 April 1802, Lisbon.* "I embrace this conveyance the Ship Perseverance . . . bound to New York (on board which goes Col Humphreys his wife my sister passengers taking with him a valuable acquisition to our Country of 100 Sheep of the famous Spanish breed as to quantity & quality of wool they produce)—To hand you the list of the trade to Porto to compleat the whole up to the 31 december last. . . . The quarantine laid on our vessels has been taken off a month since. It was not inflicted for more than ten days. . . . Yesterday I laid in a claim with this Government for seizure & condemnation at Pernambuco of the Schooner Samuel of Boston . . . on suspicion *only* of an intention of Illicit trade. The supercargo is here. . . . Whatever may be the result you shall be immediately informed to be enabled to lay the whole before His Excellency The President."

RC (DNA: RG 59, CD, Lisbon, vol. 1). 2 pp. Cover postmarked New York, 29 May. Docketed by Brent as received 3 June. Enclosure not found.

§ From Samuel Snow. *14 April 1802, Providence.* "I have the honour to enclose to you a semi-annual Report of Vessels entered at Canton between the last day of December 1800 and the first day of July 1801, received from my Agent there by a late arrival. No special communications accompanied this report."

RC (DNA: RG 59, CD, Canton, vol. 1). 1 p. Enclosure not found.

To Thomas Jefferson

DEPARTMENT OF STATE 16th April 1802

The Secretary of State, to whom has been referred by the President of the United States a Resolution of the Senate passed on the 12th. day of this Month,[1] requesting the President to cause to be laid before the Senate the Amount of claims preferred under the seventh Article of the Treaty of Amity, Commerce & Navigation with Great Britain, and of the sums awarded by the Commissioners and paid by the British Government, and a statement of the principles adopted by the said Commissioners in their proceedings under the said Article;

thereupon respectfully submits the following Report to the President: That agreeably to an estimate made on the 9th. of May 1798 by Samuel Cabot Esqr. at that time an Agent of the United States under the 7th. Article of the said Treaty, the claims preferred under that Article amounted to the sum of One Million two hundred and fifty thousand pounds sterling. The Document herewith submitted to the President, containing a general statement of monies received on Awards of the Commissioners will shew the sums awarded by them, and paid by the British Government under the Article in question of the said Treaty.[2]

It does not appear from any researches which the Secretary has been able to make, that the precise principles on which the Commissioners have proceeded, can be otherwise deduced than from the awards made in the several cases which have been decided. Any statement of them in detail is presumed not to be within the intention of the Resolution. All which is respectfully submitted

JAMES MADISON

RC and enclosure (DNA: RG 46, President's Messages, 7B-C3). RC in a clerk's hand, signed by JM. Jefferson transmitted the RC and enclosure to the Senate on 17 Apr. 1802 (*Annals of Congress*, 7th Cong., 2d sess., 876–78). For enclosure, see n. 2.

1. For the text of this resolution, see *Senate Exec. Proceedings*, 1:420.
2. The enclosure is a "Statement of Monies received by Awards of the Commissioners acting under the 7th. Article of the British Treaty" (3 pp.), which indicated that a total of

£93,755 1s. 7¾d. was received by claimants in forty cases through the hands of Samuel Bayard, Samuel Williams, and private agents. Two notes dated 1 Dec. 1801 were appended by George W. Erving, the first of which stated that public advances had been made in only nine cases and that the amount of expenses paid by the claimants was impossible to ascertain; the second note, in Erving's hand, stated that contrary to the "Statement of my predecessor that only 17 Cases were dismissed by the Board, . . . I find that there were in fact 31 Cases dismissed."

§ From William Bartlet and Others. *16 April 1802, Newburyport.* "Having certain information that the Board of Commissioners in London for adjusting our Claims upon the British Government for the Capture of our Property by British Cruizers, is again authorised to resume its operations, we are very desirous that Mr Samuel Cabot, who before acted as an Assessor of the damages to be awarded, should be again employed in that Office. Mr Cabot is intimately acquainted with the nature of our Claims & with the principles upon which damages are estimated by the Board; he enjoys fully the confidence of the Commissioners, & of the Assessor employed on the part of the British; and can therefore promote much more certainly, the interest of the Claimants & of the Country in that business than any other man. We believe that the Board, not less than ourselves, are impressed with a conviction, that they can appoint no one capable of facilitating their operation, and expediting the distribution of Justice to the Claimants in an equal degree with him. We therefore request that the President would be pleased to recommend to our Commissioners, to have Mr Cabot again appointed an assessor . . . & that he will allot to him an adequate compensation for his services, out of the Public Treasury." If a public salary is considered improper, "we shall readily acquiesce in having an amount deducted from the sums which may be awarded upon our several Claims sufficient to defray the expence of his Mission." The signatories would "voluntarily compensate Mr Cabot by allowing him a Commission upon the sums recovered; but this would be deemed a disqualification by the Board & prevent their appointing him."

RC (DNA: RG 76, Great Britain, Treaty of 1794 [Art. 7], Papers Relative to the Commissioners, vol. 4). 2 pp.; signed by William Bartlet and twenty-four others.

§ From John Rathbone. *16 April 1802, New York.* Has recently received a letter from his son John Rathbone, Jr., who is in France, "requesting that I would make application to our Government in his behalf for a Consular appointment to some Port in Europe." Encloses a recommendation that "may induce you to suppose that my Son is younger than he really is." He was born in 1777. Lists eleven cities in order of their "respective value to him if appointed." Requests JM to submit the application and enclosed recommendation to the president.

RC (DNA: RG 59, LAR, 1801–9, filed under "Rathbone"). 2 pp. The enclosure may have been a letter from Joseph Fay to Jefferson, 20 Apr. 1802, recommending the younger Rathbone (ibid.; docketed by Jefferson as received 23 Apr.). John Rathbone (1751–1843) and his son John, Jr., were prosperous New York merchants (Walter Barrett, *The Old Merchants of New York City* [5 vols.; 1870; New York, 1968 reprint], 1:353–54).

To Edward Stevens

Dear Sir,   Washington Aprl. 17th. 1802.

I duly received your Letter of the 2d. Instant with the several papers to which it refers. The delay in acknowledging it, has proceeded partly from an unusual accumulation of Business the pressure of which has been much encreased by the sickness & absence of the chief Clerk in the Department, & partly also from the real difficulty involved in the nature of the case. On one hand the positive testimony of Mr. Yard & the admissions of Mr. Pickering have great weight in every view as in an appeal to personal conviction they have decisive weight. On the other hand as the Commission and Title under which you went to St. Domingo do not cover the items in your Acct. and as no trace of the contract is found in either the Instructions or the Correspondence relating to your mission, the case is perhaps without a precedent and cannot be formed into one without much responsibility for its Character and consequences.[1] In this conflict of considerations I ought the less to anticipate the result as I may find it my duty to avail myself of the councile of others with whom I have official relations. I may say without Impropriety however that the result will gratify my personal disposition and confidence in proportion as it may be acceptable to yourself.

The mode of having your demand settled is by presenting it to the Treasury department where such Items will be admitted as are directly legal & such as depend on the sanction of the Dept. of State will be referred to it. The proofs of the Items are of course of Treasury cognizance. You are no doubt aware that the door is open for a direct application to Congress as well as for an appeal to that Authority from unsatisfactory decisions else where. You are probably also aware that an appropriation of funds by Congress will be needed to discharge the allowance whe⟨n⟩ever made under most of the items. With sincere respect & esteem I remain Dear Sir, Your most obdt. Servt.

                                   Sign'd   James Madison

Tr (MHi: Pickering Papers). Marked "(Copy)."

1. At this time, U.S. consuls, except for those resident in the Barbary States, did not receive salaries from the government, nor could they spend public money, other than for the relief of American seamen, without authorization from the government. Stevens had been appointed U.S. consul general to Saint-Domingue in 1799 and wished to be reimbursed for "expences incurred in this Mission," as JM put it in a subsequent report to the president, "on the ground of a promise from the Executive, on the faith of which he undertook the Mission" (JM to Jefferson, 20 Apr. 1804 [DLC: Jefferson Papers]).

To James Leander Cathcart

SIR, DEPARTMENT OF STATE, April 18th. 1802

In a letter with which Capt. Sterrett was lately charged for you[1] and of which a duplicate has been since forwarded, it was intimated that your services might be called for, and that it would be advisable for you to be prepared to embark at a short notice. I hope that this letter will have reached you, and have had its effect. The disposition to peace expressed by the Bashaw of Tripoli, on the appearance of Commodore Dale before that place,[2] with the impression which it is hoped has been made on him by the course and circumstances of the War, have led the President to conclude that the time is come when negotiations may advantageously take place. In order to make them more efficacious it is intended that the whole of our naval force destined for the mediterranean under the command of Capt. Morris, should rendezvous before Tripoli; and the Adams frigate being the last that is to sail for that purpose, Capt. Campbell will be the bearer of this dispatch.

The President confiding in your capacity, experience, and faithful regard to the interests of the United States, has thought proper that you should accompany this expedition, and be charged with the negotiation, which is to be combined with it.[3] You are accordingly instructed to embark and attend under such arrangements as Capt. Morris shall provide; and to proceed, as circumstances may invite, to the execution of the trust. As it is evidently desirable that the first overtures should come from the Bashaw, you will wait a reasonable time for the effect of his disposition on this subject, or of the awe inspired by a display of our force before his eyes and his Capital. Should no advances be made on his part, you may open a communication by referring to the wish heretofore expressed by the Bashaw, that an accommodation of differences might be brought about; and by observing that the President on being informed of it, had instructed you to let him know that notwithstanding the causeless and provoking declaration of war; and the force which is prepared and preparing by the United States to carry it on with full effect; yet from a love of peace in the United States, they are willing to receive him into friendship on the proper terms, which he may be told will include some indemnification for the expense which he has occasioned to the United States. This is a condition, however, which if not likely to be yielded, need not be pressed farther than will shew the high ground taken in the negotiation, and than will consist with a dignified release of the demand. But you are in the most peremtory manner to stifle every pretension or expectation that the United States will on their side make the smallest contribution to him as the price of peace. To buy peace of Tripoli, is to bid for war with Tunis, which having now received all the

135

tributes due to her, would immediately look to war, as the expedient for renewing them.

In case a satisfactory disposition for peace should be manifested, you may proceed to arrange a Treaty, subject to the approbation of the President, and to the constitutional sanction. The Treaty of the 4th Novr. 1796 of which a copy is herewith sent, and may also be found in the laws of the U States Vol. 4 p. 44,[4] may be taken for the basis and the body of it. You will omit however so much of the first Article as makes Algiers the guaranty, and of the last as makes the Dey the Arbiter and expositor of the Treaty; it being understood that a stipulation of this sort gives to that Regency an embarrassing connection with our affairs at Tripoli, and by wounding the pride of the Bashaw of the latter, adds the force of another passion to that of cupidity, in slighting his engagements. At the same time umbrage to Algiers ought to be avoided, by letting this change in the Treaty with Tripoli, be the act of the Bashaw, rather than of the United States, and be made so to appear to the Dey. No other part of the Treaty seems to be objectionable. But if there be any other which has been found inconvenient you are at liberty to omit it. As your residence and experience may have suggested also regulations which did not occur when the late Treaty was formed, but which may be useful in preventing impositions or disputes, the defects may be supplied. It seems particularly proper that the forceable use of american vessels by the Bashaw or his subjects,[5] and the liability of the United States for the property of Tripoli, taken out of American vessels by the enemies of Tripoli, sh⟨ould⟩ be guarded against.

The good disposition which Sweden has shewn to unite her measures with those of the U States, for controuling the predatory habits of the Barbary powers, and particularly for bringing Tripoli to proper terms of peace, requires that in the negotiations for the latter purpose, there should be some understanding with her officers and Agents, if they are so disposed; and that the negotiations should even go on hand in hand, if their objects and arrangements be favourable to the plan; keeping however the Treaties which may result, as absolutely unconnected and independent, both ⟨in⟩ the view of the Bashaw and of Sweden, as if formed without the least understanding between the U. S. & Sweden.[6] A joint appeal to the fears and interests of the Bashaw, by extinguishing the hope of dividing his enemies, will drive him to better terms with both. In any course of things it is desirable that you should avoid the appearance of turning the War of Sweden to any unfair advantage of the United States in making peace for themselves; a policy of such evil tendency in every respect, that nothing could advise it, but a discovery that Sweden was playing such a game against us.

It is expected by the President that you will cultiva⟨te⟩ the best understanding with Capt. Morris the commander of the Squadron; and that you will communicate with him with confidence and frankness in the conduct of your negotiations.

Should peace be established you will make with the Bashaw the arrangements for his receiving an American Consul as soon as one shall be provided. But you will have it understood that as the Consulate was interrupted so unjustifiably by himself, the reestablishment of it will give no title, even in point of usage, to presents of any sort. Should it be deemed expedient to send any little gratification along with a Consul, it will in that case have the advantage of being unexpected by the Bashaw, and the merit of proceeding from generosity and good will. Until a Consul shall be provided, you cannot do better than engage a continuance of the good offices of Mr Nissen, if he retains the confidence hitherto put in him. The President is sensible of his past services to this Country, and wishing him to have some recompence for them, will be glad of any explanations you can give as to the form and amount of a proper one.[7] It will be best that no particular expectation on this head should be raised in Mr Nissen; but you may let him know generally, that his friendly care of the affairs of the U. States has attracted the favourable attention of the President.

The Commission herewith transmitted will inform you that the future destination given you, is to the Consulate at Algiers, which will be opened for you by the resignation of Mr OBrian, and the permission given him to retire on your arrival.[8] The President having thought proper to discontinue the superintendance of that Consulate over others, your duties will be reduced accordingly, and therewith the salary to the standard of $2000 per annum. It being the Wish of the President to discourage on all occasions the venal and expensive customs with which Barbary now taxes the intercourse with civilized nations, it will be an agreeable circumstance if you can make yourself the Successor of Mr. OBrian, without the presents exacted from new Consuls. The attempt however must not risk the good understanding with that Regency. And if you deem the chance of success so slender as to require that you should go prepared to meet the demand, it may be most convenient for you to return from Tripoli to Leghorn, in order to provide the articles to be presente⟨d.⟩ For this purpose it is meant to lodge a fund there in due time. Were the Dey willing to accept in cash the value of the customary presents, the change would coincide with the general wish to simplify all our engagements in Barbary into a pecunia⟨ry⟩ form. I am with consideration Sir, your most Obt Sert.

JAMES MADISON

RC (MB); letterbook copy (DNA: RG 59, IC, vol. 1). RC in a clerk's hand, signed by JM. Enclosures not found.

1. JM to Cathcart, 6 Feb. 1802 (*PJM-SS*, 2:448).

2. JM probably referred to events described in Commodore Dale's letter to Robert Smith of 4 Oct. 1801, which told of the efforts of the pasha of Tripoli to negotiate a truce with the commander of the U.S. Mediterranean squadron (Knox, *Naval Documents, Barbary Wars*, 1: 593).

3. For the course of these unsuccessful negotiations, which did not take place until early summer of 1803 and from which Cathcart was excluded by Commodore Richard Morris, see Irwin, *Diplomatic Relations with the Barbary Powers*, pp. 126–27.

4. The "Treaty of Peace and Friendship between the United States of America and the Bey and Subjects of Tripoli, of Barbary" is printed in *The Laws of the United States in Four Volumes* (Philadelphia, 1799; Evans 36523), 4:44–48 (also printed in Miller, *Treaties*, 2:349–68).

5. JM referred to an incident in 1800 when the dey of Algiers commandeered the U.S. ship *George Washington* for his private business. In response, JM wrote that "the indignity is of so serious a nature" that it "deeply affected the sensibility not only of the President, but of the people of the United States." His subsequent instructions to Richard O'Brien sought to preclude a repeat of the offense (William Eaton to JM, 10 Apr. 1801, and JM to O'Brien, 21 May 1801, *PJM-SS*, 1:80, 82 n. 4, 214).

6. Cooperation with Sweden—and other northern European powers—in the Mediterranean had first been formally suggested by that country during the Adams administration but had been rejected. With Tripoli's declaration of war against the U.S., informal arrangements among U.S. and European consuls in the Mediterranean had been made for convoying neutral shipping and for shows of strength in the Barbary ports. JM's instructions were, therefore, the next logical step toward alliance, but his caution in keeping negotiations formally separate was justified when the Swedes made peace with Tripoli in the fall of 1802 (John Quincy Adams to JM, 25 June 1801, *PJM-SS*, 1:348–49; William Eaton to JM, 19 Oct. 1801, David Humphreys to JM, 9 Nov. 1801, and William Kirkpatrick to JM, 7 Jan. 1802, *PJM-SS*, 2:184, 233, 372; Eaton to JM, 22 Oct. 1802, Knox, *Naval Documents, Barbary Wars*, 2:305).

7. Nicolai C. Nissen, the Danish consul at Tripoli, had agreed to represent U.S. interests there in Cathcart's absence during the hostilities between the U.S. and Tripoli (Cathcart to JM, 16 May 1801, *PJM-SS*, 1:188). Cathcart suggested the "Presidents approbation" of Nissen's conduct might be shown by a letter of thanks and the gift of a "snuff box adorn'd with the arms of the United States set in brilliants of the value of five or six hundred dollars." JM ordered a gold snuffbox to be prepared and presented to Nissen (Cathcart to JM, 30 Aug. 1803, Tobias Lear to Nissen, 4 June 1804, and Cathcart to Nissen, 27 Aug. 1804, Knox, *Naval Documents, Barbary Wars*, 2:525, 4:148, 467).

8. The appointment of Cathcart as U.S. consul at Algiers was not acceptable to the dey, who, according to Richard O'Brien, "wanted here an american with a clean face." "His Character," the dey wrote President Jefferson, "does not Suit us as we know wherever he has remained that he has created difficulties and brought on a war." Jefferson later appointed Cathcart to the consulate at Tunis (O'Brien to JM, 11 Oct. 1802, dey of Algiers to Jefferson, 17 Oct. 1802, and JM to Cathcart, 16 July 1803, Knox, *Naval Documents, Barbary Wars*, 2:289, 301, 487–88).

To Thomas Jefferson

DEPARTMENT OF STATE, April 18th 1802

The Secretary of State respectfully reports to the President the information requested by the Resolution of the House of Representatives, of the

8th of January last relative to Spoliations committed on the Commerce of the United States, under Spanish authority; and also, relative to the imprisonment of the American Consul at Saint Jago de Cuba.[1]

This Report has been delayed longer than was wished: but the delay has been made unavoidable by the sickness and absence of the Chief Clerk in this Department, who had partially gone through the necessary researches, and could most readily have compleated them.

JAMES MADISON

RC and enclosures (DNA: RG 233, President's Messages, 7A-D1). RC in Brent's hand, signed by JM. The enclosed copies of correspondence and tables of captured vessels, which made up JM's report, were transmitted to the House of Representatives by the president on 20 Apr. and are printed in *ASP, Foreign Relations*, 2:440–58.

1. For the text of this resolution, see *Annals of Congress*, 7th Cong., 1st sess., 415.

From Delia Tudor

My Dear Sir   Boston April 18th: 1802.

Mr Tudor has had the honor to address a few lines to you[1] in favour of our son William now in Europe to whom the agency at Marseilles is a desirable Object. In behalf of an interest so dear I encroach perhaps on the limits of propriety in adding my request to his fathers to induce you to espouse his cause with the President of the U. S. You sir knew him a few hours only, but if the testimony of a Mother is admitted you will beleive his character formed on Principles of undeviating integrity & that he will evince by his conduct if a trust is confided to him that he respects himself too much to dishonor the appointment & by his assiduity & correctness, that he knows how to appreciate the distinction. You will be soon retiring from the fatigue of bussiness to the sequestered spot we once travers'd.[2] I offer my wishes that the ensuing summer may be propitious in every domestic occurrence. I hope Mrs Madison & Miss Paine will accept of my most affectionate attachment.

DELIA TUDOR

RC (DNA: RG 59, LAR, 1801–9, filed under "Tudor").

1. Letter not found.

2. Delia Jarvis Tudor and her son, William Tudor, Jr., had visited Montpelier in August 1801 (see JM to Jefferson, 16 Aug. 1801, *PJM-SS*, 2:47).

§ From John Appleton. *18 April 1802, Philadelphia.* Acknowledges JM's letter of 8 Apr. [not found] enclosing his commission as U.S. commercial agent at Calais.[1] Transmits his bond. "When at Washington I was led to expect by the President, that in case of vacancy at Dunkerque, it woud be annexed to my Department; if such an event shoud take place, will you allow me Sir to solicit your influence. . . . The two Ports of Dunkerque & Calais being so contiguous I coud attend to both, and the Commercial advantages of the former, woud remunerate for the unprofitable services I shall be called upon to perform at the latter." Proposes to embark at the first opportunity for France.

RC (DNA: RG 59, CD, Leghorn, vol. 1). 2 pp.

1. John Appleton (1758–1829) was the son of Boston merchant Nathaniel Appleton and the brother of U.S. consul at Leghorn Thomas Appleton. He was confirmed as commercial agent at Calais by the Senate on 9 Feb. 1802 (L. H. Butterfield et al., eds., *Adams Family Correspondence* [4 vols. to date; Cambridge, Mass., 1963—], 3:390 n. 1; Boyd, *Papers of Jefferson*, 14:60; *Senate Exec. Proceedings*, 1:406, 407).

§ From Carlos Martínez de Yrujo. *18 April 1802, Washington.* Complains of the indecorous invective aimed at the Spanish government by American newspapers for several months. Spain is only exercising its indisputable right to regulate trade with its colonial possessions. Criticism is unjust since the Spanish government, after deciding not to admit neutrals to Spanish ports in this part of the world, communicated this resolution to the U.S. government both in Washington and Madrid.[1] In order to check these complaints and to warn American merchants against clandestine trade with Spanish possessions in the Americas, declares that the king is determined not to admit foreign ships in his American ports and that any contravention of his royal order will be punished by seizure of the ship in question and its confiscation without remission, a policy followed by almost all nations with colonies in the Americas.

RC (DNA: RG 59, NFL, Spain, vol. 2). 2 pp.; in Spanish.

1. For Yrujo's announcement that Spain would strictly enforce its prohibition of neutrals trading with its colonies, see his letter to JM, 29 Mar. 1802.

§ From Louis-André Pichon. *19 April 1802, Georgetown.* In his letter of 4 Jan. 1802,[1] Pichon reported on the affair of the French ship *Cassius*, sequestered by the U.S. at Philadelphia in 1795, abandoned by the French minister, Adet, and subsequently sold. Requests restitution.

RC (DNA: RG 59, NFL, France, vol. 1). 1 p.; in French; dated 29 Germinal an X. In a clerk's hand, signed by Pichon.

1. *PJM-SS*, 2:368 and n. 2.

To James Simpson

SIR.   DEPARTMENT OF STATE. April 20th. 1802.
The two last letters from you were of the 8th. and 25th. of January.[1]

The inquietude indicated by the Emperor of Morocco, is a circumstance unexpected, and particularly unpleasant at the present juncture. Altho' his naval force is so feeble, the position of his harbours, the use that might be made of them, by enemies on the Coast of Barbary, and the influence of his example on Algiers and Tunis, give great value to his neutrality. The President expects therefore, that your most skilful management will be used for defeating the attempts to seduce him from it. To assist you in so doing, you are authorized, not only to assure him on all suitable occasions, of the respect which the President entertains for his character, and for the good faith which he has fulfilled the Treaty with the United States, but to let him know that as a particular mark of confidence in his friendship, the President, on learning the anxiety of the Emperor, on the subject of the Gun carriages, and the difficulties in obtaining them, has determined to make him a compliment of One hundred, which will be sent from the United States as soon as they can be compleated, and an opportunity can be provided. You will be careful in communicating this intention, to give it its full value, as a gratuitous proof of the esteem and friendship entertained for him, and as a means of conciliating him as much as possible for the present, without countenancing expectations in future. With the Gun carriages, it is probable that the President will address a friendly letter to the Emperor, but on this point it may not be necessary to say any thing to him.

An Original Treaty with Morocco, is lodged as you suppose in the office of State here;[2] and if its existence, or the fidelity of the translation should be called in question, it may become necessary to transfer it as you suggest, to the consular office at Tangier.

The President chuses that you should not go into the plan of building a consular house at the expence of the United States.

Your two Bills of 1200 & 800 Dollars, drawn in favor of John Gavino have been accepted. The acceptance however is not to be understood as having reference to a compensation of any sort beyond that heretofore established, which I am not authorized to hold out to you. At the same time, it is equally to be understood, that in precluding such a claim, no opinion is meant to be conveyed, unfavorable to the manner in which your public trust has been discharged. I am Sir, very respectfully &c.

JAMES MADISON.

Letterbook copy (DNA: RG 59, IC, vol. 1).

1. *PJM-SS*, 2:378–80, 421.

2. The Treaty of Peace and Friendship of 1786 between Morocco and the U.S. is printed in Miller, *Treaties*, 2:185–223.

From Charles Pinckney

DEAR SIR   MADRID April 20: 1802

I wrote you this morning[1] since which I have received the inclosed from Mr Cevallos the first Secretary of State.[2] I have already informed you that altho *this is nominally the post of prime minister, yet that in fact the Prince of Peace who is generalissimo of the army and navy and the great favorite of the king, is at present the principal mover. His marriage with one of the king's cousins* seems to have secured *his power* and there are said to be *secret reasons* independent of *this marriage* which make it probable that *during the king's life* at least *this influence will* continue.[3] I was pleased to find him extremely polite & attentive and apparently much disposed to be our Friend. At the same time I found here as in Holland & France a great want of knowledge, not only of the Nature of our Government & its tendencies; but also of the actual state of things and the consequence is[4] was of to Spain, to be always upon the most friendly terms with us. For these reasons, and to make them better acquainted with us & to impress upon them the importance not only of Amicably & Honorably arranging our claims for Spoliations; but also of doing all that now is in their power to secure to us the means of freely navigating the Mississipi, in a manner to prevent disputes in future, I transmitted to the Secretary of State the inclosed Representation,[5] and at the same time I sent a copy of it to the Prince of Peace requesting his attentive examination & support.

In the part of it which relates to the claims of our Merchants I have incorporated I beleive, all your opinions upon this Subject, and in renewing the proposition sometime since made by my Predecessor (Colo Humphreys) for the nomination of commissioners to be chosen by each party, I beleive we have done the only thing possible to give our Citizens a chance of ever being relieved from the delays, & expences, & frequently   [6] of these Tribunals. *If we get the third or fifth commissioner (as the number may be) the thing is settled; but even if we lose the odd one,* It is infinitely better for our claimants to have their causes brought before this Board than the ordinary Tribunals—because they will not only have their own countrymen present to explain & reason for them; but the spaniards whom I expect to be appointed will probably be men not only of knowledge; but of that high character & standing, which will place them above the reach of improper influence. You will observe in my Letter to Mr Cevallos I have strongly impressed the necessity of this sort of appointment. By his Letter inclosed you will find in reply to me he says "the King has no objection to the nomination of Commissioners." I shall now proceed to state to him the detail of the authorities of these Commissioners, which I wish to be exactly the same as their powers under the Treaty in 1795, except that they are not to be confined merely to the cases of vessels & cargoes captured.[7]

I shall also contend for their sitting in Washington or Philadelphia; but as the last commission sat there, it is probable they will say it is but fair, this should be in Madrid. I shall however use all my exertions to have it in America & upon such principles as are equal & honorable, and such as I trust will meet the Presidents approbation. I may be mistaken, but I confess I have much confidence in the Justice & Honor of the King & his Cabinet. I believe too I have made them better acquainted with us than they were formerly and in a way agreeable to them—in the release and dismissal of Vessels detained, in the acquittal of others, in the affair of the Quarantine & in their present apparent willingness to come into the appointment of Commissioners, I have at present no reason to complain of their inattention to me. *As they pride themselves very much upon the extent of their empire I did not know how they would take a proposal to dismember it. I know they have been extremely sore upon the affair of Trinidad*[8] *and* viewing the *extent of the seacoast of the Floridas* & its *admission of us into the gulf I was fearful they would* answer *at once that it was a possession so necessary to his majesty that he could not part with it. Much more* however *depends in this business on France than Spain* for which reason *I have wrote three letters to our minister in France* urging *him to use his* influence *at Paris* as much as possible.

In the affair of the Floridas you have charged me with a difficult Business. I have however brought it before them in the manner most likely to effect it, if it is possible. I suppose the affectionate terms in which the proposal has been made & the Nature of the reasonings induced them to give it consideration, and altho: not probable I think it possible that the thing may be carried into effect.

In case of their agreeing to treat on this Subject I will then go into detail with them on our Discounts & on the Terms, the Sum, mode & times of payment of the balance, on all of which I wish you to instruct me—particularly as to the Sum to be given for both or for either, or for West Florida alone. Another thing has struck me which it is my Duty to state to you—it is that as Florida never was a part of the American Union or of the Territory claimed by them, if the Spaniards should be disposed to sell it, what is the particular mode to be adopted to sanction the receipt of the Cession, & the admission of the new Territory into the Union?[9] We shall however have full time to consider these questions for this Court moves extremely slow in important Negotiations & the Prince of Peace yesterday speaking of this affair said "upon these points it was necessary to *have in view the event of those now depending with the French Government.*"[10] The Definitive

Treaty being signed & published in France, I cannot conceive what he alluded to unless there were difficulties still existing in the cession of Louisiana to France, if this is the case they then will postpone any opinion to me
until they hear from France. In the interim as I beleive I know the true &
indeed the only mode to be well with this Court, I shall endeavour by every
act of Attention Moderation, and Friendship which is in my power to render them as much our Friends as possible. On this Subject you will soon
hear from me again. I am collecting all the mercantile information respect[ing] discriminations & regulations of Commerce in my District &
hope you will receive safe such as is already transmitted.

I repeat to you there is every prospect of Grain being high this year in
every part of Europe—in France & all the south of Europe the rough cold
Winter has destroyed nearly all their Crops & I suppose that England has
not done much better.[11] Bread is rising in this Capital & occasioned some
days ago some tumult here in which six Boxes or Stalls in one of their corn
Markets were burnt by the Populace—it has since subsided. In my next I
am hopeful to send you my Propositions to the Secretary of State on the
Subject of the appointment of Commissioners. I have been very unwell;
but you may always expect from me when well the most regular communications & zealous & active attention to the Business of the Mission,
which I can assure you employs us from morning to night from the numerous applications I have to make on the subject of Captures, Detentions &
other vexatious interferences with our Commerce during the War.[12]

I am collecting still further information for you on the subject of mercantile regulations & discriminations & shall regularly transmit you every
other species of information in my power, & be glad to hear from you in
return as I have yet recieved but three Letters from you since my arrival in
Europe. Please present Me respectfully & affectionately to the President,
& believe me always Dear Sir with the highest Esteem & most sincere regard Yours Truly

CHARLES PINCKNEY

I am also preparing another Letter on the subject of endeavouring to obtain
the residence of a Consul or agent at New Orleans which you find they
object to as incompatible with their general colonial regulations.

[Since writing the above I have found that the 21st Article of the Treaty
will not embrace all our Claims, and have therefore varied it so as to use in
my proposition, *general terms*,[13] and should they agree to this, the Commissioners will be authorized to consider every Claim. I have submitted the
proposition (a Copy of which is inclosed)[14] on Tuesday & yesterday, I received the answer inclosed,[15] in which as I apprehended, they think in point
of fairness & convenience, the Commissioners should sit here, the last having met in America. The great object being with us to obtain the Commis-

sion on general principles—I shall not object to their sitting in Madrid, if I find they make a point of it, as I think you will be able to find some americans content to accept, of such Talents, Integrity, & Experience in this Business, as will qualify them to be Commissioners, and if I am so fortunate as to bring the Business to the close I wish, I recommend Mr Moses Young our Consul at Madrid, who ought certainly to be one, as he has a knowledge more extensive, intimate, and correct, of all these claims than any other Man can acquire in many Months. As to his Principles & Integrity they are universally known & acknowledged. The other ought unquestionably to be a sound & able Lawyer.

I have only to add that as I expected they insist upon the Junta sitting in Madrid. In answer to this I have sent the inclosed Letter Number 5 [16] & prepared the Convention leaving the Name of the Place blank. To this in their usual manner & with great deliberation, I suppose they will answer in the course of this Month. I sent you in the inclosures of my last Dispatch Via Cadiz, their answer respecting the sale of Florida which was that "in an affair of such great importance His Majesty would require time to consider & answer the proposition," & as I have reason to suppose they are still negotiating with France of course I must wait with patience their own time. I write the President next Week on some particular subjects in Cypher & shall send & inclose the Letter open to you to have decyphered. I am to request that all Gazettes, & large Bundles which are *not very* important may have Written on them "not to be put into the Post office but sent by *the Carriers*" [17] & may be sent to the Consuls of the different Seaports to whom I have Written to prevent as much as possible the immense Expences of the Post office here which is for these Bundles sometimes 20 & 25 Dollars. I request my affectionate & sincere respects to the President & accept them my dear sir for Yourself & Mr Gallatin & our friends at Washington. With regard & Esteem I am dear sir Yours Truly

CHARLES PINCKNEY
May 12: 1802
IN MADRID]

RC, duplicate, and enclosures (DNA: RG 59, DD, Spain, vol. 6). RC in a clerk's hand, with Pinckney's corrections and additions (see n. 12); docketed by Brent. Second and third postscripts are not on the RC but are supplied within brackets from the duplicate copy; the second postscript is in a clerk's hand; the third is in Pinckney's hand and signed and dated by him. Unless otherwise noted, italicized words are those encoded by Pinckney's secretary; key not found. RC decoded interlinearly by JM. For enclosures, see nn. 2 and 14–16.

1. Letter not found.
2. Pinckney enclosed copies of three letters to him from Cevallos, all dated 7 Apr. 1802 (2 pp.; in Spanish). The first acknowledged a 2 Apr. letter from Pinckney (see Pinckney to JM, 6 Apr. 1802, n. 2) and stated that in response the king had repeated his orders to Spanish

colonial officials to treat the American squadron in the Mediterranean with respect. In the second (translated interlinearly by Wagner), Cevallos wrote that the king had no objection to the suggestion in Pinckney's 24 Mar. 1802 letter that commissioners be named to adjudicate U.S. maritime claims against Spain (see Pinckney to JM, 6 Apr. 1802, n. 3). Cevallos's third letter was in response to the proposal in Pinckney's 24 Mar. letter regarding purchase by the U.S. of the Floridas and observed that a subject of so much consequence deserved great attention; Cevallos also relayed the king's refusal of Pinckney's request to permit the residence of a U.S. consul at New Orleans.

3. Manuel Godoy, the Prince of the Peace, had risen from royal bodyguard to the highest reaches of the Spanish state through his influence on Queen María Luisa and her husband, King Charles IV. Whether, as was common currency in European courts at the time, this influence extended to sexual favors with the queen or not, Godoy exercised a near total ascendancy over the royal couple from 1788 until the expulsion of the Bourbons from the throne by Napoleon in 1808 (Hilt, *Troubled Trinity*, pp. 25–34).

4. "It" in duplicate copy.

5. Pinckney probably enclosed another copy of his 24 Mar. 1802 letter to Cevallos (see Pinckney to JM, 6 Apr. 1802, and n. 3).

6. Left blank in RC and duplicate.

7. Article 21 of the treaty of 1795 between the U.S. and Spain provided for a three-man commission to "terminate all differences on account of the losses sustained by the Citizens of the United States in consequence of their vessels and cargoes having been taken by" Spanish subjects. The commission sat at Philadelphia in 1798–99, awarding $325,550.07 on a total of forty cases (Miller, *Treaties*, 2:335–37; Samuel Flagg Bemis, *Pinckney's Treaty: A Study of America's Advantage from Europe's Distress, 1783–1800* [Baltimore, 1926], pp. 389–90).

8. By article 4 of the Treaty of Amiens, Trinidad was ceded to Great Britain, whose forces had captured the island from Spain in 1797 (Gertrude Carmichael, *The History of the West Indian Islands of Trinidad and Tobago, 1498–1900* [London, 1961], pp. 40–42, 52).

9. Here Pinckney anticipated the constitutional conundrum posed to the Jefferson administration by the purchase of Louisiana and its integration into the U.S. For the constitutional questions surrounding the purchase, see Malone, *Jefferson and His Time*, 4:311–32.

10. Underlined in RC.

11. This section is marked in pencil, and "to be published" is written in the left margin.

12. The remainder of the RC and the first postscript are in Pinckney's hand and are not included in the duplicate copy.

13. Underlined in duplicate.

14. Pinckney probably enclosed an undated document (2 pp.; filed between Pinckney's letters to JM of 14 and 15 Aug. 1802) proposing terms for a board of commissioners to be appointed "in order to terminate all differences on account of the losses sustained by the Citizens of the United States in consequence of the Acts committed by the Subjects of his Catholic Majesty, and others, within his Dominions, contrary to the Laws of Nations, or in violation of the Stipulations of the existing Treaty."

15. Cevallos's 21 Apr. response (1 p.; in Spanish; translated interlinearly by Wagner) rejected Pinckney's stipulation that the board of commissioners meet in the U.S., stating that the board should meet at the same place as the tribunal that would judge on the demands presented.

16. Pinckney enclosed a copy of an undated letter to Cevallos (3 pp.; marked "Number 5"; docketed by Brent) arguing that having the board of commissioners sit in the U.S. would be more "convenient and equitable" because all the claimants resided in the U.S. and "all the proofs, witnesses and papers" were there also.

17. Underlined in duplicate.

§ To Benjamin Fry. *20 April 1802, Department of State.* "Agreeably to your letter of the 10th Inst, I have written the enclosed letter to Mr Livingston [not found], who is charged with the patronage of such claims as yours upon the French Government, and your papers are herewith returned to you."

RC (DLC: Causten-Pickett Papers, box 47). In a clerk's hand, signed by JM.

§ From Sylvanus Bourne. *20 April 1802, Amsterdam.* Acknowledges JM's letter of 25 Jan.,[1] to which he would have replied before this had not the "distressing situation" of his family rendered him almost incapable of attending to business. "It is, About three weeks that Mrs Bourne (in consequence of child bearing) has been entirely deprived of her reason & suffered under the most violent fits of delirium. She still remains in the same afflicting situation—which I hope by the blessing of Heaven may soon take a favorable change when I shall specifically attend to the Object of yr requests, & transmit you the Reply."

RC (DNA: RG 59, CD, Amsterdam, vol. 1). 1 p.

1. *PJM-SS*, 2:417–18.

§ From Daniel Clark. *20 April 1802, Philadelphia.* "I have received your Letter of the 18th. ulto. [not found] with the Commission inclosed in it, and in consequence of your directions transmit you the Bond required for the performance of my duty as Consul. Immediately after my arrival at New Orleans I shall have the Honor of addressing you on the Subjects recommended to me and will exert myself to the utmost to be of service in that Quarter."

RC (DNA: RG 59, CD, New Orleans, vol. 1). 1 p.

§ From Unite Dodge. *20 April 1802, Cap Français.* Informs JM that Lear left 17 Apr. for Baltimore on the ship *Ardent*, Captain Groom. "Previous to Colol. Lear's departure he favoured me with a promotion to perform the duties of the office, in his absence—as far as relates to Certificates, Protests &ca for American citizens, which I shall perform to the best of my abilities." Captains Rodgers and Davidson are still imprisoned "without any prospect of relief by Trial or otherwise"; only Lear can provide complete and accurate details. "The same unfriendly disposition manifested from the arrival of the Fleet, still continues. . . . The port of St. Domingo is open to our Vessels from this date—the same as this & port republican." In a postscript dated 30 Apr., adds with "inexpressible pleasure" that "Capt. Rogers is the Bearer of this—he was released together with Capt. Davidson on the 28th. Inst."

RC (DNA: RG 59, CD, Cap Haitien, vol. 4). 3 pp.; marked "Duplicate." Docketed by Brent as received 24 May.

To Caleb Strong

SIR,   DEPARTMENT OF STATE April 21. 1802.

I have been honored with you[r] letter of March 10.[1] inclosing a Resolution of the Legislature of Massachusetts relating first to a survey of the boundary between that commonwealth, and the British Provinces of New Brunswick & lower Canada; & secondly to a definition of the jurisdiction of certain Islands in or near the Bay of Passa-maquody.[2]

The latter subject had been so far anticipated by instructions of the 28th. of July last, to the Minister Plenipotentiary of the United States at London,[3] as to be brought to the attention of the British Government. And Mr. King will be authorised & instructed to take the further steps necessary for accomplishing the object in view.

The other object of the Resolution will receive from the President all the attention which is due to it & to the wishes of the Legislature of Massachusetts thereon. With perfect respect and consideration, I have the honor to be Your most Obedient servant.

RC (M-Ar). In a clerk's hand. Signature clipped.

1. Letter not found.
2. Resolution 132 of the Massachusetts General Court, dated 10 Mar. 1802, requested the governor to apply to the U.S. government for the appointment of commissioners to fix the boundary between Maine and New Brunswick "by actual survey," using "fixed monuments," and to ascertain the jurisdiction of the islands in and near Passamaquoddy Bay (*Resolves, &c., of the General Court of Massachusetts* [Boston, 1802; Shaw and Shoemaker 2626], pp. 72–73).
3. *PJM-SS*, 1:484.

From Peder Blicherolsen

SIR   PHILADELPHIA April 21st. 1802.

Without allowing myself to make reflexions upon any one law of the United States, howsoever prejudicial and hurtfull its effects might appear to me, with respect to generally acknowledged principles—and far from any intention of even troubling this government with complaints in cases where Danish subjects are found guilty of having acted in opposition to such laws, I think it my duty in the present case of Mr. Robert Cuming, who is innocently and cruelly suffering under a malicious et vexatious misapplication of the law, that prohibits the equipment of Vessels for the Slavetrade in the ports of the United States,[1] to call for justice and protection.

A mere perusal of the documents which Mr. Cuming will have the honour to lay before You, Sir, stating the strange usage, he has labored under for several months at New-York,[2] will, I am sure, cause You as much indignation and compassion as it has me. He is a worthy Danish subject, and he is unlawfully prosecuted in this country in a manner equally ruinous to his health and fortune: both these circumstances entitle him to the particular protection of a government, the justice of which is generally acknowledged, and who cannot but be acquainted with the liberal and friendly treatment, which all Americains and american concerns constantly meet with even in a perspicuous manner in His Danish Majesty's Dominions. I allways understood from the private conversations You have honoured me with, that a strict reciprocity was and would be the general regulator of the measures and dealings of this Government towards foreign nations.

I repeat Sir, that I shall never allow myself to make observations on any existing law of the country: I shall as much as it lies in my power take care, that my country-men shall be properly informed and warned at their arrival, in order to prevent involontary contraventions. However, as the aforementioned law, from the vexations Mr Cuming has of late so undeservedly sustained, seems apt to prove in the hands of either ill-intentioned or t[h]rough their fanatical errors mislead people, a very easy and dangerous instrument of persecution, I hope You will not look upon it as being altogether inconsistant with the competence of my office, if I take the liberty to represent to You Sir, how desirable it would be to devise on some means to check this pernicious tendency of that law, in as far as the consequences of a similar attempt might be experienced by some other Dane, to whom it would perhaps be as difficult afterwards to secure a reparation adequate to the injury sustained, as it may be now to indemnify Mr. Cuming, whose very considerable losses in more than one respect cannot easily be calculated. I have the honor to be with very great respect Sir Your most obedient and humble servant

BLICHEROLSEN

RC (DNA: RG 59, NFL, Denmark, vol. 1). Docketed by Brent.

1. "An Act to prohibit the carrying on the Slave Trade from the United States to any foreign place or country," 22 Mar. 1794 (*U.S. Statutes at Large*, 1:347–49).

2. On 7 Jan. 1802 the New York surveyor of customs seized the *Young Ralph*, owned by Robert Cummings, filing suit for the ship's condemnation because it had allegedly been fitted out for the slave trade in violation of section 1 of the 1794 Slave Trade Act. Cummings claimed that the ship was outfitted for the slave trade when he bought it and that he was sailing for Senegal for a cargo of gum and not slaves. Edward Livingston prosecuted the case for the U.S.; Alexander Hamilton acted for the defense. On 19 Mar. the court found for the defendant and the case was dismissed. Livingston immediately appealed, and the appeal worked its way through the courts until it was dismissed on 18 July 1805 (Julius Goebel, Jr., et al., eds., *The Law Practice of Alexander Hamilton: Documents and Commentary* [5 vols.; New York, 1964–81], 2:847–49).

From James Lyon and Richard Dinmore

Washington 21 April 1802

The editors of the American Literary Advertiser, James Lyon and Richard Dinmore,[1] present their respects to Mr. Madison; and request of him, to take into consideration, the propriety of making their paper, an organ through which to convey to the public, the laws of Congress. They beleive it has been customary, to publish the laws, in two papers at the seat of Government, and therefore hope, that when the Secretary of State considers, 1st that the plan of the paper is such, that a copy of it, will be delivered, to every printer and book-seller in the United States; and that 2ndly. it is expressly designed to disseminate correct information, and to refute the calumnies against the government, which they have been compelled to bear, unnoticed in this district for more than a year, he will be convinced, that the merit of the institution, entitles it, to the patronage requested. It may be objected that the number of Copies issued as yet, is but inconsiderable, and that the paper is issued but once a Week—but they expect the allowance for the insertion of the laws, will be proportionate, to the numbers printed, and they pledge themselves immediately upon the granting their request, to issue their paper twice a Week.

RC (DLC).

1. Lyon and Dinmore's *American Literary Advertiser* was published weekly from 27 Mar. 1802 until 20 Mar. 1804. There is no evidence that JM arranged for them to publish the laws of the U.S. (Brigham, *History and Bibliography of American Newspapers*, 1:98).

§ From Charles D. Coxe. *21 April 1802, Philadelphia.* "I am extremely sorry that in consequence of several untoward and unforeseen accidents which have interven'd since the acceptance of my commission, I am at this late period under the disagreable necessity of returning it. . . . The total loss of a considerable sum at Cap François, in consequence of the recent burning of that place, and the privation (by Congress) of a considerable amount of Drawbacks, which I conceived myself as justly entitled to; has so entirely deprived me of the means of supporting myself at so unprofitable a post as Dunkirk, that I am induced to hope you will do me the justice to believe this step of mine is taken in consequence of imperious necessity as Mr. Appleton who will deliver you this, can more particularly inform you."

RC (DNA: RG 59, ML). 1 p.

§ From Edward Stevens. *21 April 1802, Philadelphia.* Has received JM's letter of 17 Apr. and is obliged for JM's attention to his claim. Is well aware of the difficulties arising from the lack of official documentation, but "the several Sums I have charged were actually expended in the public Service, from a Firm Persuasion that they would be reimbursed, and I thought myself authorised by my verbal Instructions to incur these Expences." Trusts they will be accepted on the "Principle of Equity." Has authorized his friend Dr. Thornton to present the claim to the Treasury Department on his behalf. Requests JM to assist Thornton with "any other Formalities that it may be necessary to comply with." Introduces the bearer, Robert Cummings, "a respectable Merchant of the Island of St: Croix, who goes to Washington on Business with the Government of the U. States."

RC (DLC). 2 pp.

¶ From James Yard. Letter not found. *21 April 1802*. Calendared as a one-page letter in the lists probably made by Peter Force (DLC, series 7, container 2).

§ From William Jones. *22 April 1802, Philadelphia*. Writes on behalf of some of his mercantile friends of Philadelphia who wish to recommend Isaac Cushing,[1] "a citizen of the United States and resident merchant and partner in a very respectable House in Marseilles," for the office of commercial agent at that city. Notes that because Cathalan is a French citizen, his "holding of the office of a foreign Consulate . . . is incompatible with the regulations of french Government."

RC (DNA: RG 59, LAR, 1801–9, filed under "Cushing"). 2 pp.; docketed by Jefferson.

1. JM also received a letter recommending Cushing from Lucas Elmendorf, 28 Apr. 1802 (ibid.; 1 p.). Cushing was "a Native of Massachusets related to Judge Cushing's family at S[c]ituate," who was a partner in the firm Samadet & Cushing located at Marseilles (John Codman to William Eustis, 15 Apr. 1802 [ibid.]).

§ From William Kirkpatrick. *22 April 1802, Málaga*. Transmits duplicate of his letter of 9 Feb.[1] Reports arrival of *Enterprize* and its departure for Malta. *Essex* continues to blockade Tripolitan cruiser at Gibraltar. Has received information that *Philadelphia* had arrived at Leghorn to convoy ships to Marseilles, Barcelona, Alicante, and Málaga. Plague has broken out at Oran, Arzew, and Er Rif; ships arriving from those places are turned away without communication. Good health prevails "in this City, and the Adjacent Country." Quarantine law continues unchanged "since the regulation mentioned in my last": those ships with a bill of health signed by the Spanish consul in the originating port are allowed entry; others are "kept in Observation" ten to twenty days.

RC (DNA: RG 59, CD, Málaga, vol. 1). 2 pp. An extract regarding the status of the quarantine law appeared in the *National Intelligencer* on 16 July 1802.

1. *PJM-SS*, 2:452.

To Peder Blicherolsen

Sir   Department of State April 23d. 1802

Your letter of the 12th inst. preceded by that of January 16th[1] has been duly received. The case of the Mercator, which is the subject of both, having been referred with many other subjects to the Attorney General,[2] some time elapsed before I could avail myself of the benefit of his observations, and as an apology for the subsequent delay, I must ask you to accept the pressure of business incident to the present Season, with some adventitious circumstances [*sic*], which have contributed to the same effect.

According to the usual course, injuries committed on aliens as well as citizens, ought to be carried in the first instance at least, before the tribunals to which the aggressors are responsible; in these the facts can be best investigated, and the points on which the question depends, be most fully brought into view. In the case of the Mercator, it is the more proper, that this course should be pursued, as the circumstances stated in the documents give so imperfect a view of it. Notwithstanding the absence of Captain Maley a resort of this kind can be effected by proper instructions to an Attorney of the United States, which will be given as soon as you shall be pleased to signify the district in which you wish the judicial proceeding to be instituted.

In the mean time, as it may be made an eventual question, distinct from the conduct of Captain Maley, how far the capture of the Mercator, whilst in the custody of the American prize-master and flag, by a British armed ship the General Simcoe, ought to make the United States rather than Great Britain, liable to the Danish claimants, the most candid consideration will be given to whatever observations you may please to make, with a view to shew that under such circumstances, the law and usage of nations justify the pursuit of redress against the United States, instead of the positive authors of the injury. By that law and the usage authorized by it, the decisions of the President will be scrupulously guided. &c. &c. Accept, Sir, the sincere esteem and consideration With which I have the honor to be &c

(signed)   James Madison

Tr (DNA: RG 46, Transcribed Reports and Communications from the Executive, vol. 4). Marked "(Extract)." Enclosed in JM to the Senate, 30 Mar. 1810 (*PJM-PS*, 2:292).

1. *PJM-SS*, 2:400–401.
2. For Levi Lincoln's opinion in the case of the *Mercator*, see his letter to JM of 11 Mar. 1802.

§ From William Jarvis. *23 April 1802, Boston.* Notes that he last wrote to JM on 8 Apr., with a postscript on 9 Apr., and states that a few days later "a Gentleman acquainted me that he thought it probable he should send a Vessel to Bordeaux, in which case I could have a passage, this he has finally concluded to do & I expect she will sail in ten days." Has given up his plan to go to New York to get passage there; "this way the quarantine will be avoided." Has heard that the Portuguese quarantine is enforced unevenly, "some Vessels being admitted to an entry in 12 or 15 days others are obliged to lay 20, 30 & even 40 days, but those with the Spanish Consul's Certificate to the Bill of Health, or comeing from ports where the Yellow Fever has seldom prevail'd are the most favoured."

RC (DNA: RG 59, CD, Lisbon, vol. 1). 2 pp.; incomplete.

To Samuel Cabot

SIR,   DEPARTMENT OF STATE April 24. 1802.
    I have received your letter of the 9th. of this Month, and also a communication from the American Commissioners appointed under the 7th. Article of the British Treaty to which it alludes.[1]
    It is not observed that any substantial difference existed between the appointment of Commercial Agent and that of Assessor to the Board under that article. The former seems to have been created and a Salary annexed to it by this Government, before the Board was organized, and consequently before the system of practice for its proceedings was fixed by itself. The appointment of Assessors, and yourself as one of them coinciding with the purpose of your appointment in the former character they became blended in you. Thus therefore you received the annual Salary from the American Government, whilst the efficient Office which you executed was derived from the Board. By this statement (which is not so strictly confided in as to exclude correction) it is not intended to disavow the services you rendered occasionally, which strictly considered and as generally practised, fell within the line of duties ascribed to the other Agency in London, relative to spoliations. But it did not appear to admit of doubt, that if any separate functions are connected with the Commercial Agency as distinguished from the Office of Assessor to the Board, they might be conveniently united with the other Agency, and in fact they were, if they existed, committed to Mr. Erving.
    The representation by the American Commissioners of the utility of your past services as Assessor, and of your capacity to render them in future in a manner not to [be] expected from others has been duly considered by the President. In forming his determination two reflections have arisen upon it. 1st. that there may be an infraction of principle involved in the grant of a Salary by one party to a person assigned to act as an Assessor

which is synonimous with an Arbitrator between litigant parties, unless the grant be known and assented to by the other party. 2d. that half of Mr. Ervings compensation of two thousand Dollars having been intended as a remuneration for his services in connection with the Board, and therefore suspended till its recommencement, it would be necessary in order that the former expense of the Board might in this respect not be exceeded, to deduct $1000 from the Salary of $2,500 formerly allowed to you.

Upon the whole therefore the President has agreed that you may receive the annual compensation of $1500 as an inducement to continue to execute the Office of Assessor under the Board, to commence from your embarkation for London; provided that if on communicating the circumstance of the Salary to the Board of Commissioners, the British Commissioners should disapprove of it, you shall receive from the United States no more than the expenses of your passage to and from London, estimating each passage at a Quarters Salary.

Your accounts have passed from this Department to the Treasury, where they are or will be finally settled. I am very respectfully Sir, Your most obt. servant,

JAMES MADISON

RC (MHi); letterbook copy (DNA: RG 59, IC, vol. 1). RC in a clerk's hand, signed by JM.

1. Christopher Gore and William Pinkney to JM, 17 Feb. 1802 (*PJM-SS*, 2:473–74).

From Christopher Gore and William Pinkney

SIR   LONDON April 24. 1802.

We have the Honor to transmit herewith enclosed a Copy of a List lately prepared by us of the American Claims depending before our Board, in which the actual State of each Claim in reference to the judicial Remedy, and of course to the extraordinary Title to Redress under the Treaty is explained.

To render this List perfectly intelligible it may be proper, after so long a suspension of our operations, to mention that the American Commissioners upon the Expiration of the Term limited by the Treaty for the Exhibition of Complaints were of opinion, and so decided in June 1798, in the Case of the Sally—Hayes, that it was no longer required of a Claimant to proceed in the ordinary Course of Justice for Compensation, but that having regularly and without Laches persevered in the Judicial Experiment until the Lapse of that Term the Treaty was satisfied and our Jurisdiction complete.

In this Opinion the 5th. Commissioner, on a formal Question being taken, concurred; but the British Commissioners (who held that the Judicial Remedy must be indefinitely prosecuted until it should be absolutely exhausted, even to the last Process of Execution against Captors, Owners and Sureties) considered it as so important in its consequences, and exceptionable in its principle that they made a Declaration in writing, which they caused to be entered on the Journals of the Board, "that they did not think themselves competent under the words of the Treaty, or the Commission by which they acted *to take any share* (without the special Instructions of the Kings Ministers) in the Decision of any Cases in which the Judicial Proceedings were still depending in the ordinary course of Justice." To this Declaration was subjoined an avowal of their "Readiness to proceed in any Cases not subject to this Question." From this Declaration as well as from the repeated assurances of the British Commissioners there was no room to doubt that if at any Time we should endeavour to give Effect to the above mentioned Opinion, by acting upon it, they would defeat such an attempt by Seceding; and as it was understood that this might perhaps be avoided by the Instructions which it was hoped the British Government would ultimately think proper to give to its Commissioners upon this subject, it appeared to us to be adviseable to wait a reasonable Time for such Instructions.

The Result was that early in August 1798. the British Commissioners[1]

RC (DNA: RG 76, Great Britain, Treaty of 1794 [Art. 7], Papers Relative to the Commissioners, vol. 4). Incomplete. In a clerk's hand. Enclosure not found.

1. RC ends here. The remaining page or pages have not been found.

From Robert R. Livingston

No. 10.

DEAR SIR   PARIS 24th. Apl 1802

I send with this duplicates of my two last letters & the notes that have since passed between me & the minister on the subject of prizes[1] tho I found much clamor on my arrival I confess I have found less reason for it than I expected there are not more than four or five cases on which we have any just cause of complaint. The Winyaw mentioned in my note was evidently british property covered by one Thompson a scots merchant at New York & I was very doubtful w[h]ether I shd have noticed the case but for the danger of the precedent.[2] The Ann & the Commerce were taken carried into a spanish port & there condemned by the french consul who *de-*

clined recg any appeal none therefore was brought.[3] After the treaty the question was whether they were *finally condemned* the owners insisting that tho no actual appeal existed yet it would have existed had the consul permitted one to be lodged. The court here determined that no appeal being actualy lodged & the decree carried into effect before the convention whether the decission of the consul was right or wrong the business was ended by the convention. The Rodolph Frederick was condemned for having fought after the flag was struck.[4] The Hope was taken in the West indies after the convention [was] signed the Council of prizes have orderd the proceeds to be placed in the public treasury till the owners of the privateers can be notified of the appeal.[5] These are all the cases in which I have had cause to complain & except the case of the Rodolph Frederick I think it at least very doubtful if the decissions are such as we have reason to be dissatisfied with. The notes I send you shew you however that I have neglected nothing that it lays with me to do. I find myself extreamly at a loss from having not one of the papers of our different coms. & diplomatic members here they having been all carried away by Mr. Elsworth (as Mr. Montflorence informs) so that I know not the points of difference at the time of the negotiations which would throw much light upon doubtful parts of the treaty or at least furnish arguments. I have ventured to guess at them but you will find that the strict words of the 2d article are certainly against my construction of it & the 5th Article by having united two different subjects is not so clear as I would wish. It is singular too that the word condemnation shd. be translated *confiscations*—which certainly does not carry its true meaning.[6] I had yet had the pleasure of but one dispatch from you & duplicates of the same being that of the 18th. decr.[7] Papers come to me from no port but New York tho arrivals from the eastern ports are very frequent particularly from Salem & Boston.

The business most interesting to us that of Luissania still remains in the state it was the minister will give no answer to any enquiries I make on that subject. He will not say what their boundaries are what are their intentions & when they will take possession. And what appears very extraordinary to me is that by a letter I have just red from Mr. Pinkney I find that he still supposes that the floridas are not included in the cession & he writes me that he has made a proposition to purchase them which lays before the minister with whom he is to have a conferance on the subject.[8] You may however be fully assured that the floridas are given to France that they are at this moment fiting out an armament from here to take possession this will be commanded by genl Bernadotte the number of troops designed for this object are between 5 & 7000 they will shortly sail for New Orleans unless the state of affairs in St Domingo shd. change their destination you may act upon this information with absolute certainty since I have no doubt of the channel thro' which I have red And if I had they would have been removed by *the Spanish minister to whom a few days ago at Tallerands table I expressed my surprize in a jesting manner at their finding the Americans such bad neighbourgs as to have exchanged their lodgings he shruged up his shoulders and told me he was sorrey for it.* We were too near to the Minister & in too large a circle to continue the conversation. I wish our government had been explicit in their instructions to me on this subject I forsee so much mischief in the measures that *france will or may adopt if they once take possession that I could have wished to have been empowered to employ some millions in warding it off whether I could have effected it by those means is doubtful but they are the only ones that present the smallest prospect of success. It would be wise immedeatly to take measures to enable the Natches to rival New Orleans I have suggested the means &* I hope they will not be neglected by the Congress that is now siting. That you may Judge of the light in which this country is viewed by some here *I send you the extract of a paper that now lays before the minister.*[9] If Congress make the Natches a free port & if the state of affairs in St Domingo shd. employ the troops designed for Luissania *time will still be left for gold to operate here but it must be plentifully & liberally bestowed not barely in the assumption of debts but in active capital afforded* in supplies to aid their armaments in the islands. Give me your instructions *as to the utmost amount if* as you will be better able to judge than I can *the affrs of St Domingo are like to be protracted.*

You will find by the enclosed papers that the concordat has been adopted with very great ceremony & stile [10] the whole corps. diplomatic assisted & we were specialy requested to put four horses to our carriages. Sunday is again observed at the public offices instead of decadi [11] *every thing here is going back fast to the old order of things. The greatest expence is expected at Court in dress &c.* In so much that the Northern courts have very wisely diminished that of their Ambassadors &c. by giving them a uniform dress. You may live here as you please but to have any influence or consideration in the present state of things you must live as they do & for this purpose you must expence three times your appointment—every thing being in Paris at the most extravagant rate more so by much as I am informed than in London.

I find that I was misinformed relative to Martinique there is no reserve of it in the Treaty.

Some measures should be taken relative to the expences incurred for seamen by our commercial agents. Caps. shd not be alowed to discharge them & ship new crews at a foreign port or to leave them sick in Hospitals without making provission for them. The accounts of Mr Lee amount to upwards of 8000₶. It would I believe be much better to have their accounts audited in America where some enquiries can be had from the Caps & seamen than here where the minister must receive every voucher without the possibility of examination. I have the honor to be D sir with the most respectful essteem & the highest consideration Your Most Obt hum: Servt.

RRL

Draft (NHi: Livingston Papers); letterbook copy and copies of four enclosures (NHi: Livingston Papers, vol. 1). Italicized passages are underlined in the draft and numbered 1–7; Livingston apparently intended them to be encoded. Extracts from the missing RC are printed in *ASP, Foreign Relations*, 2:515–16. The enclosures, according to a list in Sumter's hand headed "sent to Sey. of State with letter No. 10" (DNA: RG 59, DD, France, vol. 8), included duplicates of Livingston's 27 Mar. dispatch and his earlier correspondence with Talleyrand and Decrès; copies of his correspondence with Talleyrand since his 27 Mar. dispatch; "Copy of extract alluded to in letter No. 10"; and "Moniteurs from 28th. Ventose to 5 floreal inclusive—a few exceptions." Of these, only the duplicate copy of Talleyrand's 20 Mar. 1802 note survives (see Livingston to JM, 22 Mar. 1802, and n. 1), but for Livingston's letterbook copies of his correspondence with Talleyrand, see n. 1.

1. Two of the notes concerned the settlement of claims under the Convention of 1800. Talleyrand to Livingston, 17 Germinal an X (7 Apr. 1802) (2 pp.; in French), reiterated the French government's understanding of the suppression of article 2 of the convention; he also noted that he had written a report to the first consul on Livingston's proposal for the liquidation of the debt France owed U.S. creditors and would inform Livingston of the result of Napoleon's decision. Livingston to Talleyrand, 17 Apr. 1802 (7 pp.), argued that article 5 of the convention "amounts to an express stipulation to pay every debt due to individuals except such as they might claim for indemnities for captures and condemnations" and with the absence of article 2, "the 5th. Article stands alone as a promise to pay." Livingston went on to object that "while you limit the treaty to the narrowest possible construction on one part you allow to the Council of Prizes a latitude which renders it nugatory on the other" (see n. 2). Also enclosed were copies of two more letters from Talleyrand to Livingston. In a second letter dated 17 Germinal an X (7 Apr. 1802) (1 p.; in French), Talleyrand acknowledged Livingston's letter of 27 Mar. 1802 on the subject of actions taken by Leclerc against U.S. merchant captains in Saint-Domingue and reported that he had passed the note on to the minister of marine; and in a letter dated 26 Germinal an X (16 Apr. 1802) (1 p.; in French), Talleyrand invited Livingston to attend the Easter service at Notre Dame with Napoleon and his ministers.

2. It was argued by Talleyrand that in judging prize cases the rules of the Convention of 1800 should be supplemented by maritime regulations mutually agreed on by the nations of the world. The example he gave was the case of the *Winyaw*, in which the Council of Prizes was forced to examine not only whether the ship's papers were in order, according to article 4 of the convention, but also if the ship carried papers that proved it was not American. Livingston took issue with the wide latitude given to the courts by Talleyrand's construction, calling for a strict adherence to "the rules prescribed by the treaty" and arguing that if fraud had taken place in the case of the *Winyaw*, it was for U.S. courts to decide (Talleyrand to Livingston, 29 Ventôse an X (20 Mar. 1802), and Livingston to Talleyrand, 17 Apr. 1802 [letterbook copies, NHi: Livingston Papers, vol. 1]).

3. The ship *Ann*, William Robinson master, of Baltimore was owned by R. Oliver & Brothers and carried a cargo of wine and $40,000 in specie. The ship *Commerce*, Gideon Gardner master, also of Baltimore, carried $50,000 in specie. The two ships were captured by the French privateer *Fly*—the *Ann* on 25 June and the *Commerce* on 4 July 1799—and taken to Cadiz (*ASP, Foreign Relations*, 2:450, 451).

4. For the case of the *Rodolph Frederic*, see Fulwar Skipwith to JM, 29 Oct. 1801 (*PJM-SS*, 2:211 and nn.).

5. For the case of the ship *Hope*, which had not been decided, see Livingston to JM, 15 Feb. 1802 (*PJM-SS*, 2:468 n. 1).

6. The conflict over the interpretation of article 2 of the Convention of 1800 is discussed in Livingston to JM, 27 Mar. 1802, n. 4. Article 5 required the payment of "debts contracted by one of the two nations, with individuals of the other, or by the individuals of one, with the individuals of the other," but it excluded "indemnities claimed on account of captures, or confiscations [*condemnations* in the French text]" (Miller, *Treaties*, 2:462).

7. Livingston referred to JM's letter of 19 Dec. 1801, a duplicate of which was dated 18 Dec. (see *PJM-SS*, 2:322–24 and n.).

8. See Pinckney to Livingston, 4 Feb. 1802 (NHi: Livingston Papers). For Pinckney's efforts to purchase the Floridas, see his letter to JM, 20 Apr. 1802.

9. This extract has not been identified.

10. The text of the Concordat between Napoleon and Pope Pius VII was published in the Paris *Moniteur universel*, 17 Germinal an X (7 Apr. 1802). The agreement was celebrated on Easter Sunday, 18 Apr. 1802, with a mass in the cathedral of Notre Dame in Paris (see the program for the day's solemnities printed in the *Moniteur*, 27 Germinal an X [17 Apr. 1802]).

11. *Décadi*: the tenth day of a *décade*, or group of ten days, in the French revolutionary calendar was a day of rest.

§ From William C. C. Claiborne. *24 April 1802, Natchez*. On 18 Apr. received JM's letter of 22 Feb.[1] enclosing Dr. David Lattimore's commission as a member of the legislative council of the Mississippi Territory; Lattimore, who has accepted the appointment, "unites to pure Republicanism, handsome Talents & an Honest Heart." The "utmost harmony" exists between Americans and Spaniards at New Orleans. Supports the president's proposal for a hospital at New Orleans, as Americans "often descend the Mississippi, at an unhealthy Season of the year, and many lives are lost at Orleans, for the want of attendance & comfortable Lodgings."[2] Believes the "difficulty & expence of procuring" deckhands for the voyage down the Mississippi River to New Orleans would "in a great measure, be remedied by the establishment of a convenient Hospital at Orleans, for the reception of Sick and disabled Americans."

Letterbook copy (Ms-Ar: Claiborne Executive Journal). 2 pp. Printed in Rowland, *Claiborne Letter Books*, 1:89–90.

1. *PJM-SS*, 2:482.

2. On 24 Feb. 1802 President Jefferson sent to Congress "information respecting the situation of our seamen and boatmen frequenting the port of New Orleans, and suffering there from sickness and the want of accommodation." He suggested Congress might want to make "hospital provisions" at that port for U.S. seamen (*Annals of Congress*, 7th Cong., 1st sess., 191).

§ From James Leander Cathcart. *25 April 1802, Leghorn*. No. 4. "The enclosed extracts from my correspondence & Mr. Eatons dispatches will inform you of our actual position, every thing seems to be in a train to promise apparently a satisfactory conclusion to this war which I assure you envolves serious consequences 'tho visibly it is of little moment. I have before observed that Tunis and Algiers have their eyes fix'd on Tripoli to know how far their depredations will be tollerated; & you may depend Sir the manner we conclude with that Regency will be the criterion from which the other Regencys will take precedent & example."

RC and enclosure (DNA: RG 59, CD, Tripoli, vol. 2). RC 1 p. Cathcart enclosed extracts (3 pp.) from two letters to him from Nissen, 15 Jan. and 3 Feb. 1802, the first reporting the intention of the Spanish consul at Tripoli to purchase "a swift sailing brig of ten guns" from the pasha to serve as a packet between Spain and Tripoli, "which will facilitate our communications." In his 3 Feb. letter Nissen added that the pasha "has made the Spanish Consul a present of the Brig"; he also wrote that "Spain means to make a *brilliant* figure in Tripoli or at least their Consul at the expence of his Government," that Tripoli was "nearly destitute of every sort of provisions," and that the pasha's brother had accepted the governorship of Derna. On the verso of the last page Cathcart wrote a note to JM, warning that if any of Nissen's letters were published his name should be omitted to avoid "doing him an injury" and adding: "DeSouza the present Spanish Consul . . . is notorious for being a creature of the Bashaws, he is an old man & has went to Tripoli to lay his bones in peace with his ancestors the moors. I cant say I should like to rise at the sound of the great trump encircled by Turks moors Arabs Renegades Jews & base perfidious christians who had sacrificed the honor & interest of their Nation to their own ease and emolument lest I might be over look'd in the crowd & risque being condemn'd to keep their company to all eternity which would be a hell indeed."

To Thomas Jefferson

Sir!   City of Washington April 26th. 1802.

We have the Honor to enclose a copy of an Agreement enter'd into between the Commissioners of the United States and those of Georgia,[1] in pursuance of the Act entitled "An Act supplemental to the Act entitled 'An Act for an amicable settlement of Limits, with the State of Georgia; and authorizing The Establishment of a Government in the Mississippi Territory.['"][2]

The nature & Importance of the Transaction have induced the insertion of a clause, which renders it necessary that the Subject shou'd be communicated to Congress, during their present Session.[3] We have the Honor ⟨to⟩ be very respectfully, Sir! Yr. Obt Servants

                                        James Madison
                    (signd.)   Albert Gallatin
                                        Levi Lincoln

Tr and Tr of enclosure, two copies (DNA: RG 46, President's Messages, 7A-E2; and DNA: RG 233, President's Messages, 7A-D1). Another copy of the enclosure (OkTG), which was sent by the Georgia commissioners to Governor Tattnall, 24 Apr. 1802, is certified by JM as a "True Copy of the Original, remaining in the Office of the Department of State."

1. The enclosed agreement between the U.S. and Georgia, signed on 24 Apr. 1802 (4 pp.; printed in *ASP, Public Lands*, 1:125–26), ended a year of serious negotiations between the

three U.S. commissioners (JM, Gallatin, and Lincoln) and the three Georgia commissioners (James Jackson, Abraham Baldwin, and John Milledge). By its terms, Georgia ceded all claim to land west of the Chattahoochie River (the so-called Yazoo lands) upon the following conditions: that the U.S. pay Georgia $1,250,000 to cover expenses incurred by the latter; that persons settled within the ceded territory on 27 Oct. 1795 be confirmed in their land grants; that the ceded lands be considered a common fund for the benefit of the U.S. but that Congress might appropriate within one year up to five million acres or the proceeds thereof to satisfy other claims; that the U.S. extinguish all Indian claims to land within the state of Georgia; and that the ceded territory be admitted as a state whenever it fulfilled the conditions of U.S. law. The U.S. accepted the conditions of the cession and agreed to relinquish any claim or title to lands within the state of Georgia. Georgia ratified the agreement on 16 June 1802 (Josiah Tattnall, Jr., to JM, 18 June 1802). Evidence indicates that Gallatin took the leading role among the U.S. commissioners in drawing up the agreement, although the political fallout from it dogged JM throughout his subsequent career (see Gallatin's notes on agreement with Georgia commissioners, April 1802, and James Jackson to Gallatin, 22, 23 [four letters], and 24 Apr. 1802, in *Papers of Gallatin* [microfilm ed.], reel 7).

2. This act was signed into law 10 May 1800 (*U.S. Statutes at Large*, 2:69–70).

3. Jefferson submitted this letter and the articles of agreement to Congress on 26 Apr. 1802 (*ASP, Public Lands*, 1:125).

Memorandum from Theodorus Bailey

Tuesday Morng. 27. April 1802.

Enquiries at the Office of Secretary of State.

How much did it cost under the late Administration to pay Algiers for the years 1796–97 & –98?

How much was paid by the present Administn. to the same, for the years 1799–1800 & 1801?

Mr: Bailey will be under obligations to the Honorable Mr. Madison if he will favor him with answers to the queries above stated.

RC (DLC).

From Joseph Fenwick

Sɪʀ   Philadelphia 28 April 1802.

Seeing from the public prints that there was a probability of Mr. Lear's return from St. Domingo[1]—if my services there could be usefull to the U. S. as principal Agent I can offer them in the course of four or five months from this.

An interest in several important plantations in that Island held by the family of my wife leads me to look forward to a visit there for the preservation of her fortune, my own having been much delapidated by the belligerant powers during my residence in France. I shall embark in the May packet for London to attend a claim for captured property pending under the 7th. article of the treaty with England: two weeks will enable me to put it in such a train as to require no longer my personal attendance—from thence I shall go to France where it will require a month or two to regulate my concerns in a manner to be left with an Attorney in fact—and from there I coud proceed direct or via America as it might be deemed advisable, to St. Domingo, so as to reach it in Augst. or Septemr. and I trust under such advantages as few Americans coud obtain.

From an acquaintance with several leading characters in the government of France, and a family connection with some high in office, their impressions of my friendly wishes to that Country, I could obtain such instructions for the Commanders in the West Indias as to ensure a favorable reception, & carry into the exercise of any public function that consideration & confidence necessary to do for the trade of my Country what justice & its true interests required. While at Paris, if you thought it advisable, I could confer with Mr. Livingston on the most eligable measures to obtain such Commercial regulations relating to the West Indias as the interest of the United States might point out—the present situation of things will certainly render some temporary arrangements expedient, which well conducted might tend to more permanent ones. If you think well of this proposal Sir & there should be an opening for it, do me the favor to communicate it to the President. In making this tender of services I trust Sir the time is at hand when the unfavorable reports circulated against me have been found by the unprejudiced to have originated in defamation.[2] The persecution I have experienced for my attachment to those principles which led the present patriotic men into office, and the little good, if any, I may have done while employed could not be more gratefully compensated than by a mark of their regard, even a honorary one only; it would effectually restore that consideration my opponents (perhaps more for their own purposes than to injure me) have strenuously labored to rob me of, and which the small portion of abilities Nature has alotted me, has not the force alone to do without other aid.

I had no intention of importuning you or Mr. Jefferson on this topic had it not have grown out of the first part of this letter which the recent events in the West Indias gave rise to. With the greatest respect I have the honor to be Sir your most obedient Servant

JOSEPH FENWICK

RC (NN).

1. On 27 Apr. 1802 the Philadelphia *Gazette of the U.S.* published a report that Tobias Lear intended to leave Saint-Domingue for the U.S. in a few days. The next day the newspaper reported that Lear's consular "functions were suspended, and he was on the eve of his departure."

2. For the "unfavorable reports" and Fenwick's answer to them, see Fenwick to JM, 16 Apr. 1801 (*PJM-SS*, 1:94–95 and nn.).

From Albert Gallatin

SIR,   TREASURY DEPARTMENT April 28th. 1802.

Amongst the claims laid by Mr. Pichon, under the convention with France, there are three which have been suspended, and on which your opinion is requested.

1st. He claims the "Magicienne," formerly "Retaliation," Francis Lagaux, Commander, taken by the Merrimack, condemned at Philadelphia, on 29th. November 1799. This vessel is not in the list furnished by the Navy Department, and certified by you, in as much as she was condemned before the treaty, and probably no appeal entered. But he claims her as a public vessel. The best proof of that fact must be derived from the papers of the vessel, & these it is presumable may be obtained by application to the court.[1]

2d. He also claims one half of a sum of money, about 5,000 dollars taken on board the Berceau;[2] the other half, which was the share of Government having been already paid to him by your order. The date of the condemnation of the Berceau, is necessary, as, although she was restored under the convention, as a public vessel, the money is not embraced by that clause of the Treaty relating to the restoration of public vessels; but comes under the article of vessels and property not condemned when the convention was signed: and I have stated to Mr Pichon, that, at all events, the money advanced to the prisoners, beyond the usual allowance, and which Mr. Letombe had engaged to repay, ought to be deducted from the money now claimed.[3]

3d. He claims 7,213 dollars and 24 cents, proceeds of sales of the cargo of "L'Heureux," which money was libelled in the District Court of Massachusets, and remains uncondemned for want of proof. In that case it does not seem necessary that the money should be paid from the Treasury; and I would beg leave to suggest the propriety of writing to the district attorney of that State, in order that he may obtain an order from the court for the disposal of the money. The convention being now law, and the money not being condemned, it is to be expected that the court will direct its repayment to the claimants whenever they shall appear.[4]

The Navy Department may probably give further information on those three points if it shall be wanted, in order to enable you to form your opinion. I have the honor to be very respectfully Sir, Your Obedt. Servt.

ALBERT GALLATIN

RC (DLC: Gallatin Papers). In a clerk's hand, signed by Gallatin; docketed by Brent. Filed with the RC is a page containing additional information on the three cases discussed by Gallatin; the page is written in two unidentified hands, the second of which is indicated below by italics (see nn. 1, 3, and 4).

1. The accompanying page notes: "In the case of the Magicien—She was condemned in the District Court of Pennsa in Novr 1799—sold by the Marshall of that District for 3500 Dollars—the nett proceeds 3285.20 were paid into the Treasury & the whole sum has been vested in stock of the funded debt of the U: S: on account of the fund for Navy Pensions &c. under the Acts of 2 March 1799 & 23rd Apl. 1800—*This was a National Vessel.*"

2. For Pichon's demand and JM's response, see Pichon to JM, 17 May 1801, and JM to Pichon, 12 June 1801 (*PJM-SS*, 1:192, 305–7).

3. The accompanying page notes: "In the case of the Berceau. Money taken on board 5172-92—one half of which has been paid to Mr. Giraud by Mr. Brown—*condemned December 8th 1800.*"

4. The accompanying page notes: "In the case of the Heureux Captur'd April 2nd 1800. A small vessel with Coffee—sold at Cape Francois for 7213-25—deposited in Court in specie—This case is still in Court undecided for want of Proof—Capt. Little having put all the people belonging to the sloop on shore at Cape Francois & no Claimant has appeared. *The vessel sank, being old & leaky.*"

To William Savage

SIR.   DEPARTMENT OF STATE. April 29th. 1802.

Your two Letters of the 20th. and 25th. January last[1] have been received, and the two Bills which you draw upon me on those days, the first in favor of James Martin for fifteen hundred and Eighty Eight Dollars and thirty Cents, and the other for fifteen hundred Dollars in favor of Elliston and John Perott, have been accepted. But the acceptance is not to be understood as having reference to a compensation of any sort, for I am not authorized to hold it out to you, over and above the ordinary Commissions of your agency in the West Indies. I am respectfully &c.

JAMES MADISON.

Letterbook copy (DNA: RG 59, IC, vol. 1).

1. *PJM-SS*, 2:415, 464.

From Bird, Savage, and Bird

Sir,   London 29th. April 1802.

Inclos'd we send you dupe. of our last respects of 22d. Ulto.[1] The Arms having been shipp'd on board the Medusa frigate, by order of His Excellency Rufus King we made the following insurance on them, vizt. £5⟨810⟩. valued at the amount of the cost of the Arms by the Medusa frigate to Gibraltar & at and from thence by ⟨any⟩ American Ship of War to Tunis ⟨at 2½⟩ ℔ Ct., duty £10. making £137.⟨0.2⟩ to the debit of the Barbary fund. We have already appriz'd you of the various advances we had been induced to make at the request of Mr. King beyond the funds in hand, in doing which we have deviated from the Secretary of the Treasury's positive instructions.[2] Mr. King lately call'd on us to make a payment to Mr. Lenox of £800. to be charg'd to the fund for the relief of Seamen. As this wou'd have been a further deviation from our instructions, there being only £260.1.9 remaining on this accot, we propos'd to pay that Amount, but stated that circumstanced as we were as agents bound to act by positive instructions we cou'd not see how we could further deviate from till we should receive answers from you & the Secretary of the Treasury to our letters requiring special instructions on this point.

As the former instructions were so positive, we felt ourselves plac'd in a situation of peculiar delicacy & responsibility for having deviated from them, & as we ⟨knew⟩ that our letters of 13th. Jany. to you[3] & the Secretary of the Treasury had got out, we deem'd it most proper to suspend any further deviation till we shou'd receive your answers, & have paid Mr. Lenox only £250. which he preferr'd to receiving the precise balance.

We are the more anxious for your answer to our letters & for such remittances owing to the state of all the accts. which is as follows.

Diplomatic fund, balance		£ ⟨19⟩.19.9
Payments to be made in May for		
Mr. King's and Mr. Munro's salaries	£ ⟨376.5.4⟩	
British treaty fund balance due from us		£ ⟨593⟩. 5.1
Payments to be made in May for		
Mr. Pinckney's & Mr. Trumbull's		
salaries	£ 7⟨30⟩.—.—	
Prize cause fund———balanc'd		
Barbary treaty fund balance due to us		
(including an engagement to pay		
Mawhood & Co. £766.15.4)		£⟨3149. 1.2⟩
Suspence acct. due to us for payments		
to Arrowsmith Fader & Butterworth		
for Maps & Books		£ ⟨200⟩. 6.6

By this statement it appears that the balance due to us on all the accounts in the Month of May will amount to £4102.7.5 without any provision for the large demands of the Proctors for prosecuting prize ⟨Offers⟩.

We request your early attention to this statemnt & to a ⟨plan⟩ for the further payments which will be falling due in the subsequent Months & we are with great respect Sir Your most obedient Servan⟨ts⟩

BIRD SAVAGE & BIRD

RC (DNA: RG 59, Letters Received from London Bankers, Illegible Press Copies). RC is a letterpress copy, marked "Origl. ℔ William; via New York / (Copy)." Angle brackets enclose words and numbers blurred in RC and supplied by conjecture. Docketed by Brent.

1. Letter not found.
2. Albert Gallatin to Bird, Savage, and Bird, 13 Aug. 1801 (*Papers of Gallatin* [microfilm ed.], reel 5).
3. *PJM-SS*, 2:392–93.

Circular Letter from Thomas Jefferson

April 29. 1802.

Th: Jefferson asks the favor of the heads of the departments to examine and consider the charges of Colo. Worthington against Govr. St. Clair[1] with the answer of the latter and the documents in support or invalidation of the charges; & to favor him with their opinion in writing on each charge distinctly, whether 'established' or 'not established,' and whether those 'established' are sufficiently weighty to render the removal of the Governor proper?

TH: JEFFERSON

FC (DLC: Jefferson Papers).

1. The charges against Arthur St. Clair made by Thomas Worthington (on behalf of a number of Ohio Republicans including Nathaniel Massie and Edward Tiffin) were enclosed in a 30 Jan. 1802 letter from Worthington to Jefferson. The ten charges included usurping and misusing power, the levying of arbitrary fees, the appointment of his son as attorney general, and the avowing of "his hostility to the form and substance of republican government." Having learned of the charges against him, St. Clair hastened to defend himself in a letter to the president, 13 Feb. 1802. A more detailed defense followed, with a number of supporting documents, and this evidence was what Jefferson requested JM and the other cabinet members to consider in detail on 29 Apr. In the meantime St. Clair had asked Ohioan George Tod to write JM his recollection of a conversation in which St. Clair was said to have spoken "disrespectfully of the President" and "declared hostility against all republican government." Tod obliged, writing JM that on the occasion he "did not hear him speak one

disrespectful word of the President." JM submitted his opinion to Jefferson in a memorandum dated 19 June 1802 (Thomas Worthington to Jefferson, 30 Jan. 1802, with the enclosure, "Charges Exhibited to the President of the United States," St. Clair to Jefferson, 13 Feb. 1802, St. Clair to Tod, 21 Apr. 1802, "Certificate as to an Alleged Private Conversation of Governor St. Clair," 26 Dec. 1801, Smith, *St. Clair Papers*, 2:565–70, 566–67 n., 573–74, 581–83, 585–86 n.; George Tod to JM, 29 May 1802; JM to [Levi Lincoln?], 14 May 1802; Daniel Brent to JM, 25 May 1802; JM to St. Clair, 23 June 1802). For the political background to the accusations against St. Clair, see Massie to JM, 12 Feb. 1802, *PJM-SS*, 2:460–61 and nn. For a fuller picture of the decision to censure St. Clair, see Cunningham, *Process of Government under Jefferson*, pp. 50–56.

§ From Sylvanus Bourne. *29 April 1802, Amsterdam.* Regrets that the situation of his family, an account of which was given in his last letter, still prevents him from attending to JM's request. Apologizes for apparent neglect of his duties.

RC (DNA: RG 59, CD, Amsterdam, vol. 1). 1 p.

§ From Peter Stirling. *29 April 1802, Barcelona.* "It is Publickly Said here, and I observe the Board of Health begin to take measures, for avoyding an introduction in this Country, of a Pestilential, Epidemical, Disorder, that has of late broke out, and rages in *Oran*, on the Barbary Shore. Said Board of Health is officially informed, of that reigning malady there, that it dayly Sweeps, great numbers of People off. The Summer Season coming on is much to be dreaded. In this Country Health is enjoyed as fully as ever."

RC (DNA: RG 59, CD, Barcelona, vol. 1). 1 p.; marked "Copy." In a brief note to JM also dated 29 Apr. 1802 (ibid.; filed at the end of 1802), Stirling enclosed a copy (misdated 1802) of his 19 Dec. 1801 dispatch.

To Rufus King

SIR,   DEPARTMENT OF STATE April 30th. 1802
I enclose a protest by Capt. Newell[1] of the American Schooner Sea Flower, which shews that the habits of the British Commanders in impressing our Seamen have not ended even with the State of War which was made a pretext for the outrage. The spirit lately manifested by the British Government, and which the Government here is sincerely desirous to meet and to cultivate justifies our confidence, that your representation on the subject will have its due effect. That Government cannot be made too sensible of the tendency of such flagrant abuses of power to exasperate the feelings of this Country; nor be too much prepared for the reformation on this subject which will doubtless be insisted on by this Country, in case of a renewal of

the war, or whenever another war shall take place. With sentiments of great respect & esteem, I remain, Sir, Your most obt. servt.

JAMES MADISON

RC (NjP); letterbook copy (DNA: RG 59, IM, vol. 6). RC in a clerk's hand, signed by JM; docketed as received 1 July. King noted on the cover: "Wm. Munro & Lindsay Addison seamen on board the Sch. Sea Flower of Phil. Nichs Newell Master, impressed off antigua Mar 23d. 1802 by the Frigate Emerald—see Letter to L Hawkesbury, July 12. 1802." Enclosure not found. King's letter to Hawkesbury is printed in King, *Life and Correspondence of Rufus King*, 4:145–46.

1. This was possibly the Nicholas Newell (d. 1809) who applied for the post of captain of the revenue cutter in Savannah, Georgia, and who later served in that capacity in Charleston, South Carolina (Newell to JM, 18 July 1806, and John Brickell to JM, 21 July 1806 [DNA: RG 59, LAR, 1801–9]; Boston *Columbian Centinel*, 24 June 1809).

From Jacob Wagner

DEAR SIR   WASHINGTON 30 April 1802

The heavy oppression and gloom under which I am labouring and which I have no prospect of recovering from but by an entire exemption from business, accompanied with a change of scene, render it necessary, that I shou'd take my leave of your office.[1] It is impossible for me to express to you the sensations with which this determination is made: they cannot be conceived but by those who have felt.

Permit me to tender my gratitude & thanks for your uniform kindness to me, and at the same time to request you to excuse any errors I may have committed in my official career. With perfect esteem & respect, I have the honor to be, Dr Sir, Your most obed. servt.

JACOB WAGNER

RC (ViU). In an unidentified hand, except for Wagner's complimentary close and signature.

1. JM refused to accept Wagner's offer to resign. The *Washington Federalist* of 12 May 1802 reported that JM "with equal honor to himself and Mr. Wagner, declined accepting the resignation at this time; saying that as Mr. Wagner had brought on this ill health from his close attention to the duties of his office, he ought not to retire until his health was perfectly restored." The editor went on to say, "We are happy to have it in our power to record this instance of liberality and politeness, as the present administration, has given so few examples of such conduct."

§ From Rufus King. *30 April 1802, London.* No. 63. Reports ratification of definitive treaty and the proclamation of peace "with the accustomed formalities." British begin to reduce army and navy, and the "warrants and orders to impress Seamen have been recalled." Lenox has closed his agency and delivered his papers to Erving, as a special office for the relief of American seamen is now unnecessary.[1] Sweden has acceded to the June 1801 convention between Great Britain and Russia;[2] the latter considers the system of armed neutrality to be "completely annulled and abandoned; not only as a general code of maritime Law, but even in its more limited meaning of a specific Engagement between Russia and the other Confederates." Merry rather than Jackson will be Liston's successor as minister to the U.S.

RC (DNA: RG 59, DD, Great Britain, vol. 10); letterbook copy (NHi: Rufus King Papers, vol. 55). RC 3 pp.; marked duplicate; in a clerk's hand, signed by King; docketed by Brent as received 30 June. Printed in King, *Life and Correspondence of Rufus King*, 4:112–13.

1. David Lenox reported closing his office in his letter to JM, 20 May 1802.
2. For the convention signed between Russia and Great Britain on 17 June 1801 to which Denmark and Sweden became signatories, see King to JM, 14 July 1801 (*PJM-SS*, 1:410–11, 412 n. 1).

§ From William Marshall and Others. *30 April 1802, Charleston, South Carolina.* Recommends Simon McIntosh,[1] a Charleston lawyer, for the post of commissioner of bankruptcy.

RC (DNA: RG 59, LAR, 1801–9, filed under "McIntosh"). 1 p. Signed by Marshall, Theodore Gaillard, O'Brien Smith, Paul Hamilton, and James D'Oyley. Docketed by Jefferson.

1. This was probably the Simon McIntosh who was the son of Lachlan McIntosh (d. ca. 1789) of South Carolina. The father served in the General Assembly of that state (1776) and styled himself a "gentleman" of Charleston (Edgar et al., *Biographical Directory of the South Carolina House of Representatives*, 3:459).

§ From John Webb.[1] *30 April 1802, Charleston.* Sends JM a copy of his letter to Colhoun[2] and a duplicate of the certificate enclosed in it, "as there is a probability Mr. Calhoun may not be in the City, on the Arrival of the Mail at Washington." Asks JM to present these to the president if Colhoun is absent and if the proposed alteration in the appointment of commissioners of bankruptcy has taken place.

RC and enclosures (DNA: RG 59, LAR, 1801–9, filed under "Webb"). RC 1 p.; docketed by Jefferson. Webb enclosed a certificate of recommendation signed by Thomas Bee and six others, 28 Apr. 1802 (1 p.), and a copy of his letter to Colhoun, 28 Apr. 1802 (2 pp.), explaining that he held an appointment as commissioner of bankruptcy under Judge Bee and asking to be continued in that office by Jefferson.

1. This was probably the John Webb (1744–1807) who was a wealthy Charleston merchant (Edgar et al., *Biographical Directory of the South Carolina House of Representatives*, 3:756–57).
2. John Ewing Colhoun (or Calhoun) (1750–1802), a cousin of John C. Calhoun, was a Princeton graduate and lawyer who fought under Gen. Andrew Pickens during the Revolutionary War. He served repeatedly in the South Carolina House of Representatives and in the state's Privy Council. Colhoun was elected to the U.S. Senate in 1800 as a Republican but

voted with the Federalists against the repeal of the Judiciary Act of 1801. He died in office (Harrison, *Princetonians, 1769–1775,* pp. 368–70).

To Albert Gallatin

SIR, DEPARTMENT OF STATE, WASHINGTON May 1. 1802.
You will be pleased to cause a warrant to be issued in favor of John Davidson for four hundred and fifty three dollars and nine cents, to be paid out of the fund for defraying the expenses incident to the intercourse with the Mediterranean powers, he being the holder of a bill of Exchange for that sum, drawn upon me by James Leander Cathcart, the drawer to be charged with the same on the books of the Treasury. I have the honor &ca.
JAMES MADISON.

Letterbook copy (DNA: RG 59, DL, vol. 14). JM similarly requested Gallatin to issue warrants for expenses incurred for Barbary affairs, State Department contingencies, the relief of U.S. seamen, and carrying out the provisions of the Jay treaty, the amounts of which ranged from $100 to $30,000. Those requests omitted from this volume—available on National Archives microfilm M-40—are dated 5, 8, 11, and 13 (three letters) May, 3, 4, 15, 22, and 23 June, 7, 13, 24, 29 (two letters), and 31 July, 9, 22, and 30 Aug., and 2 Sept. 1802.

To Richard Harrison

SIR DEPARTMENT OF STATE WASHINGTON May 1: 1802.
The enclosed account is sent to you, that it may be settled at the Treasury.[1] A reasonable compensation, to be ascertained by the Accounting Officers of that Department, is to be allowed to Capt. Wood, for the passages of the American seamen to this Country. Their sea stores were furnished at the public expense, by the Commercial Agent of the United States at Bordeaux before their departure from France—but the Captain is entitled to reimbursement for any additional supplies furnished, or extraordinary expenses incurred by him on their account. I am, Sir, respectfully &ca.
JAMES MADISON.

Letterbook copy (DNA: RG 59, DL, vol. 14).

1. The account of Capt. John Wood for transport on the *Thames* of American seamen stranded in European ports amounted to $533.07 (DNA: RG 217, First Auditor's Accounts, no. 13,394). See also William Lee to JM, 18 Feb. 1802 (*PJM-SS,* 2:479).

To William Hull and Others

GENTN.   CITY OF WASHINGTON May 1st. 1802

We are ready according to the terms of our Commission to enquire into the claims which may be made to any part of the lands containd within the conditional cession of Georgia[1] & for that purpose we invite you to communicate to us with precision the nature & extent of the claims made by yourselves & other persons whose agents you are.[2] Transcripts of the several deeds company Articles & other papers shewing the chain of Title & your authority to make a proper release will be particularly desirable.

Beyond that enquiry our powers do not extend further than receiving your propositions for compromise & reporting our opinion thereon to Congress. We can make no propositions to you which should be binding on the United States nor can we state at present an opinion which we have not yet conclusively formd & which must be the result of an investigation of the title which may be vested in the claimants of the circumstances under which they acquird it and of the Consideration actually paid by the persons in whom the claim is now vested. You must be sensible that on the ground of compromise those several considerations must have their weight and that we have not yet received all the information necessary to justify in us the expression of a final opinion.

We are at the same time sincerely desirous that a compromise should take place & that such terms may ultimately be offerd by Congress to the claimants as considering their actual disbursements and the situation of their claim they shall find it their interest to accept. Under our present imperfect view of the subject we consider it as desirable if it shall be found practicable that the present claimants may be fully reimbursd for the monies actually paid by them & although a general rule cannot be adopted which shall on that principle apply to each individual case yet after the necessary information shall have been received & compared some average price per Acre or some gross sum for the whole may be agreed on which will in a general view of the subject reach the object.

From this as well as from the agreement with Georgia you will perceive that it is not our intention to report in favour of a compromise grounded on a purchase or on a confirmation by the United States of your title to any considerable portion of the lands you claim & that the several proposals you have heretofore made cannot be considerd by Us as admissable. We do not intend to recommend any thing farther than an indemnity to be paid out of the proceeds of a certain portion of the lands & which shall not bear Interest. It results from thence that in calculating what that indemnity should be not only the nature of the title but also the manner in which & time when the purchase money was paid by the present claimants as well as the time when the fund intended to satisfy them will probably become productive must be taken into consideration. We have the honor to be very respectfully Gentlemen your Obedt servts

> JAMES MADISON
> ALBERT GALLATIN
> LEVI LINCOLN

RC (PHi). In a clerk's hand, signed by JM, Gallatin, and Lincoln. Addressed to Hull, Samuel Dexter, Benjamin Hitchborn, and Samuel Ward.

1. Section 10 of the "Act supplemental to the act intituled 'An act for an amicable settlement of limits with the State of Georgia; and authorizing the establishment of a Government in the Mississippi territory'" authorized the commissioners appointed to negotiate the Georgia cession "to inquire into the claims which are or shall be made by settlers or any other persons whatsoever, to any part of the aforesaid lands," and to report this information "together with their opinion thereon" to Congress (*U.S. Statutes at Large*, 2:69–70).

2. William Hull and the other addressees of this letter were agents for the New England Mississippi Land Company, shareholders of which had invested in the Yazoo lands. The state of Georgia had subsequently held these purchases to be fraudulent and had conditionally ceded the lands to the U.S. a few days before this letter was written (see JM and others to Jefferson, 26 Apr. 1802, and nn.).

To Rufus King

SIR,   DEPARTMENT OF STATE, May 1st. 1802

Your several letters to No 56[1] have been duly received. The Convention relating to the 6th and 7th articles of the Treaty of 1794 has at length received the sanction of the Senate, two members only dissenting, and is herewith forwarded to you under the necessary forms of ratification, to be exchanged for the British ratification. The delay in the Senate pretty certainly proceeded from circumstances little connected with the merits of the Convention. Altho' provision might be made at the ensuing session of Congress in time for the first instalment due from the United States, the President has recommended an immediate appropriation for the object as a proper evidence of the disposition of our public Councils. The controversies incident to those articles being thus amicably and finally adjusted, it is hoped and expected that the Board under the 7th will now go on with alacrity in dispatching their business, as well for the satisfaction of the claimants, as for abridging expence to the public; and the President wishes you to quicken the progress in whatever way a spur can be properly applied.

Notwithstanding the obvious and important interest which this country has, in freeing its navigation from the ruinous disadvantage thrown on it by the countervailing regulations of Great Britain, such impressions have been made by perverted views of the subject, even on the classes of people more particularly interested in the carrying trade, that the patrons of the measure introduced into Congress, have concluded not to push it further at the present Session. The consequences will be that whatever conditional measures of justice may be taken by Great Britain will be without effect until another session of Congress; that in the mean time, if the war be not renewed, British ships will monopolize the exportation of our produce to British ports; and that besides the temporary loss, a lasting wound will be given to our navigation by throwing our ships for such a period out of employment. Should indeed your endeavours be successful in obtaining an immediate and unconditional removal of the discriminating duty on ships carrying Tobacco, the evil may be sensibly alleviated, both to those who cultivate that bulky article of freight, and to those who carry it to Great Britain.

We are fully aware of the tendency of the reported Cession of Louisiana, to plant in our neighbourhood troubles of different kinds, and to prepare the way for very serious events. It has accordingly been a primary object with the President to obviate such an arrangement.

Our intelligence of late date from St Domingo is that altho' advantages have been gained by the French troops, the war is likely to be spun out beyond the first calculation. The conduct of the French commanders or of some of them, as well as of some of the American traders has been unfortunate for both. Mutual irritations and perplexities have been the fruit of it. And to increase the evil Le Clerc has just recalled in the most abrupt manner, from Mr. Lear, the permission granted him to exercise the functions of a Commercial Agent. He grounds the measure on a want of power, which he says he did not reflect on in the hurry of his arrival. But it is probable that certain calumnies and intrigues against Mr Lear, were at least mingled with the unadvised proceeding. As Mr. Lear's conduct has unquestionably been the reverse of what Le Clerc supposed, it is possible that enquiry may lessen the mischief, but an impression will be an immediate effect, which cannot be at once removed. It was for a considerable time the purpose of Admiral Villaret to call at some of our ports: but he has sailed with 8 or 10 ships for France, and it is now said that the Batavian Fleet of 6 or 8 ships will come into the Chesepeake. There has been no report here, that a British fleet from the West Indies would make a like visit.

I have received thro' Mr Chase a few days ago the copy of a law lately passed by Maryland,[2] which he requests might be got to your hands as soon as possible. You are sufficiently apprized of the anxiety which is felt in relation to the Bank stock which is the subject of it. It is a matter of considerable importance to the State, and I hope from your last information, it will soon be terminated to its satisfaction.

In consequence of a representation lately made by Mr. Pinckney and

Mr Gore on the subject of an assessor to the Board, and of the advantage expected from the experience of Mr Cabot in that Station, the President has agreed to allow him as an inducement to return to it, the annual sum of $1500; on condition that such an allowance be not objected to by the British members of the Board. The information has been transmitted to Mr Cabot but his answer is not yet received. Congress will adjourn on Monday. With sentiments of great respect & Esteem, I remain, Sir your most Obt Sert.

JAMES MADISON

I am this moment informed of the passage of the Bill making provision for paying the instalments stipulated in the late Convention.[3]

RC (NjMoHP); letterbook copy (DNA: RG 59, IM, vol. 6). RC in a clerk's hand, except for JM's signature and postscript; docketed as received 1 July. Enclosures not found.

1. King to JM, 8 Mar. 1802.
2. JM referred to a law passed by the Maryland legislature on 31 Dec. 1801 that authorized King to accept the Maryland bank stock in his own name, allowed Samuel Chase 4 percent of the amount retrieved for the state and 4 percent of any uninvested dividends, and instructed Chase on the method of disposition of the stock should it in fact be awarded to the state (Radoff, *The Bank Stock Papers*, no. 5 of *Calendar of Maryland State Papers* [Annapolis, 1947], p. 24).
3. The bill "making an appropriation for carrying into effect the Convention" between the U.S. and Great Britain passed the House of Representatives on 29 Apr. It passed the Senate on 3 May and was signed into law the same day (*Annals of Congress*, 7th Cong., 1st sess., 303, 1253; *U.S. Statutes at Large*, 2:192).

To Robert R. Livingston

SIR,   DEPARTMENT OF STATE WASHINGTON, May 1st. 1802

My last of which a duplicate is now sent, was of the twenty sixth day of March. I have since received yours not then acknowledged including the Dispatch of Feby 26[1] which came to hand two days ago.

The conduct of the French Government in paying so little attention to its obligations under the Treaty, in neglecting its debts to our citizens, in giving no answers to your complaints and expostulations, which you say is the case with those of other foreign Ministers also, and particularly in its reserve as to Louisiana, which tacitly contradicts the language first held to you by the Minister of Foreign Relations, gives tokens as little auspicious to the true interests of France herself, as to the Rights and the just objects of the United States. We have the better ground to complain of this conduct, as it is so much at variance with the example given by the Government here. The appropriation was no sooner carried thro' the Legislative forms,

than the settlement of French claims under the Treaty commenced; and
with the advantage of every facility that could be afforded on our part in
ascertaining them; And as Mr Pichon was authorized to receive those due
to individuals not applying, the whole amount has been already discharged,
excepting in a very few cases which may require further examination. The
claims were liquidated according to the nett proceeds of the sales, as heretofore intimated to you, altho' it is still believed that restitution according to the gross amount or value at the time of capture, not only would
be more favourable to the United States but more just in itself. The payment to Mr Pichon without a special Power from the claimants was by no
means the choice of the President, but was so much pressed, as a test of the
disposition of this Country towards the French Republic at a critical moment, that it could not be properly refused. The sum received by him is
$140,841-25 Cents. That paid to individuals is $74,667-41.[2]

It is proper to observe to you that in all cases where sales were made by
the American Captors prior to the date of the Convention, without the trial
and condemnation requisite, we have admitted the title to restitution without regarding the lapse of time between the capture and the Convention,
or making a question how far cases of that description were within the contemplation of the instrument. You will of course avail yourself of this proceeding on the part of the United States to inforce a correspondent rule in
their favour, in case a different one should be contended for by the French
Government. You will not fail to insist also, if occasion should require, that
in cases where the time allowed for appeals, had not run out at the date of
the Convention, it could not be necessary for the claimants afterwards to
enter appeals. The Convention by recognizing all claims not barred by final
condemnation at its date, evidently rescued them from all further subjection to judicial investigation.[3]

The Cession of Louisiana to France becomes daily more and more a
source of painful apprehensions. Notwithstanding the Treaty of March
1801, and notwithstanding the general belief in France on the subject, and
the accounts from St Domingo that part of the armament sent to that island
were eventually destined for Louisiana, a hope was still drawn from your
early conversations with Mr Talleyrand that the French Government did
not mean to pursue the object. Since the receipt of your last communications, no hope remains but from the accumulating difficulties of going thro'
with the undertaking, and from the conviction you may be able to impress,
that it must have an instant and powerful effect in changing the relations
between France and the United States. The change is obvious, and the
more it can be developed in candid and friendly appeals to the reflections
of the French Government, the more it will urge it to revise and abandon
the project. A mere neighbourhood could not be friendly to the harmony
which both countries have so much an interest in cherishing: but if a pos-

session of the mouth of the Mississippi is to be added to other causes of discord, the worst events are to be apprehended. You will consequently spare no efforts that will consist with prudence and dignity, to lead the Councils of France to proper views of this subject, and to an abandonment of her present purpose. You will also pursue by prudent means the enquiry into the extent of the Cession, particularly whether it includes the Floridas as well as New Orleans; and endeavour to ascertain the price at which these, if included in the Cession, would be yielded to the United States. I cannot in the present state of things be more particular on this head, than to observe that in every view it would be a most precious acquisition, and that as far as the terms could be satisfied by charging on the acquisition itself, the restitutions, and other debts to american Citizens, great liberality would doubtless be indulged by this Government. The President wishes you to devote every attention to this object, and to be frequent and particular in your communications relating to it.

According to the latest accounts from St Domingo the French troops had been considerably successful in dispersing the Blacks, but it is uncertain how long the War there may be protracted by the irregular enterprizes of the latter, and by the advantages they derive from the climate. You will have found from the Newspapers, that much irritation and perplexity were the consequence of ill conduct on the part of the French Commander, on his arrival, met as we learn from Mr Lear, by a conduct not less blameable on the part of the Americans trading there. To the other errors of General Le Clerc he has lately revoked the permission given to Mr Lear to exercise the functions of Commercial Agent, alleging for a reason that he had no authority for granting the permission, and had inconsiderately taken the step in the hurry of his arrival. He acknowledged at the same time, that he had been led to consider Mr Lear as rendered justly obnoxious to him by throwing discredit on his Bills, and promoting irritations between the French and the Americans. In this view of Mr Lears conduct Le Clerc must have been grossly misled by calumnies and intrigues, for the conduct of Mr Lear has been in every respect highly meritorious, for the prudence, the moderation, the candor and conciliatory tone of it. Of this Le Clerc may be expected to be by degrees satisfied, as Mr Pichon already is; and so far the evil may be mitigated; but with various other circumstances connected with the transactions at St Domingo, it has been unfavourable to the kind sensations which it has been our endeavour to cherish. You will remark also in the Newspapers that the idea of a visit from the French fleet, and of pecuniary succours from the Government of the United States, has excited not a little sensibility in some quarters of the Union.[4] It was at one time the purpose of Admiral Villaret to come to this Country with part of his fleet, and as it was feared that he would come without money or credit to obtain supplies for even the first wants, it was anticipated that applications would be made for a Loan in some form or other from the Government of the United States. The fleet however has not arrived and is understood not to be coming, and no application has in fact been made for pecuniary facilities, other than that of purchasing for purposes of the United States in Europe, bills drawn on the French Government; which application was rejected for reasons sufficiently obvious. It is now said that the Batavian part of the fleet is destined to the Chesepeake and will probably arrive in a few days.

Congress will probably adjourn on Monday. For an account of their proceedings and other domestic occurences, I refer you to the printed papers herewith sent. With sentiments of great respect &c &c.

JAMES MADISON

P S. I have communicated to the President your wish to make a visit to England, and have the pleasure to inform you of his consent. He leaves the time and the duration of your absence to your own judgment, assuring himself that both will be in due subordination to the important duties of your station.

Letterbook copy (DNA: RG 59, IM, vol. 6).

1. *PJM-SS*, 2:492–94.
2. For the law authorizing this appropriation, see Pichon to JM, 14 Apr. 1802, and n. 1.
3. Article 4 of the Convention of 1800 states, "Property captured, and not yet definitively condemned, or which may be captured before the exchange of ratifications . . . shall be mutually restored" on the showing of valid proof of ownership (Miller, *Treaties*, 2:459).
4. See, for example, the criticism of the Jefferson administration in the *Washington Federalist*, 23 Apr. 1802, and the *Gazette of the U.S.*, 20 Apr. 1802.

To Robert R. Livingston

private

DEAR SIR   WASHINGTON May 1. 1802

You will receive by Mr. Dupont herewith a public letter on th⟨ose⟩ subjects most important in your hands. You will receive at the same time a private letter from the President[1] in which he refers for fuller communications than he gives on the subject of Louisiana & the Floridas. I have thought it best however not to go as far into certain views of the subject as he has done, because they are in fact more proper for a private than public letter & because also it is impossible to strengthen what he has said. I might add, if these reasons were less satisfactory, that my short notice of the time of Mr. Dupont's departure, and the necessity of writing some important letters to others in the same hurry, would have obliged me to be somewhat concise. I drop this line merely to explain the variance between the

Presidt's. private & my public letter, availing myself also of the occasion to assure you of the great regard & esteem with which I am Dear Sir Yours

JAMES MADISON

RC (NNMus). Docketed by Livingston.

1. In this famous and much quoted letter, Jefferson spelled out in detail the course he wished Livingston to pursue in his negotiations with France over Louisiana. The retrocession of Louisiana and the Floridas to France, the president wrote, "compleatly reverses all the political relations of the U.S. and will form a new epoch in our political course." Because of its strategic economic value, New Orleans was the "one single spot, the possessor of which is our natural and habitual enemy." Spain might have held it without trouble for years, but the "day that France takes possession of N. Orleans . . . we must marry ourselves to the British fleet and nation." Conflict, though much to be deplored, was inevitable, and this should be pointed out to the French government. Should France consider Louisiana indispensable for supplying its West Indies possessions, Jefferson told his minister, then he must work for the cession of New Orleans and the Floridas to the U.S. "Every eye in the U.S. is now fixed on this affair of Louisiana. Perhaps nothing since the revolutionary war has produced more uneasy sensations through the body of the nation." Jefferson concluded by noting that his private letter was written as a supplement to JM's "to impress you with the importance we affix to this transaction" (Jefferson to Livingston, 18 Apr. 1802, Ford, *Writings of Jefferson*, 8:143–47; the significance of this letter is further explained in Malone, *Jefferson and His Time*, 4:254–58).

From Samuel Cabot

SIR   BOSTON 1 May 1802.

I have the honor to acknowledge the recet of your letter dated the 24th ulto. authorising my return to London for the purpose of executing the duty of an assessor, under the 7th art: of the British treaty. In obedience to your instructions I shall immediately repair to England, for which place I have already engaged my passage in a Vessel that is intended to sail from hence by the 15th instant. Altho' the proposed yearly salary of 1500 dollars is barely sufficient to defray the current expences incident to a residence in London, yet desirous of rendering myself useful & being influenc'd by the personal solicitations of our Commrs. & many of the claimants who have urged my return, I have concluded to re-engage in this business; not however without the hope that my Stipend may (by the liberality of the President of the United States) be eventually augmented to the sum formerly granted me; & which it is conceived was but an adequate one. In making my pecuniary arrangements for the support of my family during my absence, I have calculated on the early payment of my accot. now with the Secretary of the Treasury. The recet. of this money here, prior to my embarkation, together with any advances which the government may deem it expedient to make me towards my present undertaking, will be peculiarly acceptable at the present juncture. It is presum'd that my Salary, as it falls due will be, as heretofore, discharged by our minister resident in England. Any farther instructions or commands from your Department that may be seasonably transmitted me, will be duly attended to, by sir, your most obedient & very hum. servant

SAM CABOT

RC (DNA: RG 76, British Spoliations, 1794–1824, Unsorted Papers). Docketed by Brent.

§ To George Deneale. *1 May 1802, Department of State, Washington.* "I send herewith a Commission of the Peace for the County of Alexandria, in the District of Columbia, to be deposited, and to remain in your office."

Letterbook copy (DNA: RG 59, DL, vol. 14). 1 p. George Deneale (1766–1818) was a colonel of militia and clerk of the U.S. Circuit Court in Alexandria County (Franklin L. Brockett, *The Lodge of Washington* [Alexandria, Va., 1876], p. 116). A nearly identical letter of the same date was sent by JM to Uriah Forrest for the county of Washington, District of Columbia (ibid.; 1 p.).

To Pierre Samuel DuPont de Nemours

WASHINGTON May 2. 1802

Mr. Madison presents his best respects to Mr. Dupont de Nemours, and requests that he will be so obliging as to take charge of some despatches for the American Minister at Paris,[1] which are forwarded by the present mail to the post-master at Philada. They are to be handed by him to Mr. Dupont. Should a failure happen, Mr. M. will take it as a favor, if Mr. Dupont will please, before he embarks, to have application made at the post office. Mr. Madison intreats Mr. Dupont to accept his friendly wishes for an agreeable voyage, and the most happy prospects on his arrival.

RC (Hagley Museum and Library, Wilmington, Del.).

1. DuPont was intended to be more than a messenger. Jefferson hoped that the well-connected Frenchman might "be able to impress on the government of France the inevitable consequences of their taking possession of Louisiana" through talks with French government officials. DuPont noted after he received JM's dispatches and Jefferson's private letter to Livingston of 18 Apr. that he would "support their contents with all my feeble might" (Jefferson to DuPont, 25 Apr. 1802, DuPont to Jefferson, 30 Apr. 1802, Dumas Malone, ed., *Correspondence between Thomas Jefferson and Pierre Samuel du Pont de Nemours, 1798–1817* [Boston, 1930], pp. 46–49, 52–61).

From Edmund Randolph

D<small>EAR SIR</small>   R<small>ICHMOND</small> May 3. 1802.

The inclosed papers have been in my hands for several weeks; having been sent, as you will perceive, to me by Mr. Brooke, for the purpose of being submitted to the chancellor.[1] Mr. Wm. Madison having spoken to me several times at Fredericksburg on this subject, and made appointments for coming hither to bring it to a conclusion, And failing in all, I was too much at a loss, to be justified in offering those documents to the judge, until I should hear from you. Knowing, that being absent from home, and immersed in the pressing business of office, you could not attend to the case at Washington, I have reserved it for your return to Orange; which, Mr Macon tells me, is expected to be immediate. I wish you to instruct me; as the mode, in which Mr. Wm. Madison has proceeded, embarrasses me not a little. I am dear sir yr. affte friend

E<small>DM</small>: R<small>ANDOLPH</small>.

RC (DLC). Docketed by JM. Enclosures not found.

1. These papers were most probably documents in support of the friendly suit in chancery instituted among members of JM's family to settle the complicated estate of James Madison, Sr. (see William Madison to JM, 22 Sept. 1801, *PJM-SS*, 2:124–25 and n. 1).

From Carlos Martínez de Yrujo

W<small>ASHINGTON</small> 3 of May 1802

The Undersign'd Envoy Extraordinary, & Minister Plenipotentiary of H. Cathc. Majesty, takes the liberty of calling the attention of the Secretary of State to a desagreable event, which took place in Philadelphia on the 7 of April last, in which H. M. Flag & some of his subjects receiv'd from a furious multitude the most scandalous insult, for which, he appeals to this Governement in the most serious manner for obtaining a proper satisfaction.[1]

At the demand of the Crew of the Spanish Brig *Cabo de Hornos* the Marshall at Philadelphia got possesion of her in order to bring her to a public sale, & pay with the monies arising therefrom the arrears due for wages to the Spanish Sailors; & during the sale was to take place, the Marshall left the Brig in custody of the Saylors. On the 7 of April last as the crew were at dinner on a neigbouring house, the Brig was surpris'd by a croud of Carpanters, & Blacksmiths, who had along with them a chain to fasten her, for some demand on their part; but the Spanish saylors being appris'd of this intrusion & under the impression, given them, that *nobody* could touch the Vessel without their consent, resisted the attempt; in consequence a quarell ensued in which the Crew of the Spanish Brig depriv'd the carpanters & Blacksmiths of their chain, & hoisted the Spanish Flagg on the Brig, as a signal of the protection they were entitled to, by the existing treaty between the King & the United States, the rights of hospitality, & the self-persuasion of a just & honest conduct, as they could not consider themselves as aggresors in the last contest.

A great number of people were by this time assembled near the Brig: sometime afterwards the Sheriff appear'd with his Constables, & his apparition operated as a signal for a general discharge of Stones from the Mob against the Spanish Vessel. In the beginning the Spaniards confin'd their endeavours to shelter themselves from the cloud of Stones falling on them, untill two of them prov'd wounded; when getting hold of the same Stones thrown against them, flung them back to the Crowd, & wounded in their turn one, who afterwards has been found to be a Constable. As soon as the Sheriff approach'd the Brig & the Crew were informed of his being a officer of Justice, they gave up all defence, & far from opposing his entrance they receiv'd him with respect. In this interval of calm which ensued, the furious multitude attack'd the Brig on all sides, beated, wounded & tighted with ropes the saylors, & not contented to have exercis'd their rage on every thing they mett with upon Deck, struck down the Spanish Colours which were flying on the mainmast, & one or two Ruffians getting hold of them, & after waving the Flag in the air as a mark of triumph, they tore it to pieces, & threw them into the air to the repeated huzzas of the populace. Those incredible transactions took place under the eye of the Sheriff, sorrounded by his constables, & there is strong reason to believe, that had he been as active in preserving order as in overpowering a handful of unprotected strangers, all those excesses could have been prevented.

The Undersigned truly attached to justice & truth, declin'd to act as soon as he was inform'd of those extraordinary transactions, well aware how, in buiseness of this nature, the first impressions are generally incorrect by the influence occasion'd by resentment on one hand, & the confusion & the rapidity of events on the other. He has in consequence not neglected in this interval any step which could tend to clear up the circumstances of this unfortunate accident, with the view to appear before this Governement not as a blind & indiscriminating Supporter of H Catc. Majesty's Subjects but as a Moderate & firm defender, as well of their rights, as of the honor of the Nation, so shamefully compromis'd in the present case. The results of his investigations have produc'd the preceding account, & all its parts are founded on *sworn evidences* of some of the Spanish Crew, before the Consul General of Spain, in whose office shatter'd remains of the destroy'd Flag are equally to be found.

The Spanish Saylors beaten, & insulted, even when secur'd by the Sheriff, have been since sett at liberty; strong indication of their innocence, or that if in any way coulpable their error arose from some mistake, or want of Knowledge of the lenguage, manners, & laws of the Country.

The Undersign'd Envoy Extraordinary, without entering on the observations it would be on his power to make on the partial conduct of the Sheriff on this occasion, calls again the attention of the Secretary of State to the agravating circumstance of the Striking down the Spanish Colours tearing of the National Flag, & throwing into the air its remains with the utmost ignominy. This insult is too glaring & of too much magnitude to be lett pass in silence; in consequence of which the undersign'd address himself to the Secretary of State in the most serious manner to obtain from the American Governement the satisfaction due to the King his Master for the said insult, satisfaction which will not prove difficult, if the Governement of the United States desirous of Showing a disposition to give it, offer in the News Papers the reward of 500 or 1000 Dollars to the person who will discover the perpetrator or perpetrators of such a criminal Act, & that once found out they may be prosecuted & punish'd as the Law requires.

The Undersign'd prevails of this opportunity to renew to the Secretary of State the sentiment of his high consideration.

                                                      CARLOS MRTNZ DE YRUJO

RC, two copies (DNA: RG 59, NFL, Spain, vol. 2); Tr (AHN: State Archives, vol. 5630). Yrujo sent JM one copy of the RC in English (marked "Copie") and one in Spanish (dated 9 May 1802); both copies are docketed by Brent. Tr in Spanish; undated.

1. The incident was noted in the *Gazette of the U.S.*, 8 Apr. 1802, as an "affray" in which sixteen Spanish sailors were arrested for the beating of a sheriff's deputy who was trying to chain the ship to a wharf. JM's response was to request that the state of Pennsylvania investigate and prosecute the matter if necessary. After writing to Jefferson and Attorney General Lincoln, JM asked Gov. Thomas McKean and the attorney for the district of Pennsylvania, A. J. Dallas, to carry out a thorough investigation. The matter was concluded in August 1802 when the attorney general of Pennsylvania issued a *nolle prosequi* after the sailors had made restitution to the injured man (JM to Jefferson, 11 May 1802; JM to McKean, 11 May 1802; JM to Dallas, 12 May 1802; JM to Yrujo, 12 May 1802; Lincoln to JM, 12 May 1802; Jefferson to JM, 14 May 1802; McKean to JM, 16 Aug. 1802).

§ From Rufus King. *3 May 1802, London*. No. 64. Reviews arrangement made with Bird, Savage, and Bird for the disbursement of public money in Great Britain and describes measures he adopted for securing money recovered in prize cases. All money recovered from captors or British government is deposited in the Bank of England, credited to him in his official capacity, and paid out to claimants after deducting costs incurred by the U.S. The latter amounts are deposited with Bird, Savage, and Bird and used for the prosecution of appeals. The two accounts will show the disposition of these funds. Explains all this by way of introducing the refusal of Bird, Savage, and Bird to reimburse David Lenox for advances he made for seamen's relief. The firm indicates that direct instructions from the secretary of the treasury forbid them to make advances on the public credit. Since these instructions in effect "transfer the superintendence and control of the public Expenditures in this Country from the Minister, to the Agents of the Treasury," he will no longer regard U.S. financial matters in Great Britain as under his "control or direction."

RC (DNA: RG 59, DD, Great Britain, vol. 10); letterbook copy (NHi: Rufus King Papers, vol. 55). RC 6 pp.; in a clerk's hand, signed by King, docketed by Brent. Printed in King, *Life and Correspondence of Rufus King*, 4:114–16.

§ From Elias Vander Horst. *3 May 1802, Bristol.* Forwards copies of his last letters,[1] which were sent by the Bristol packet via Boston, a letter from Rufus King, and newspapers. "The Season here continues remarkably fine for Vegetation, . . . in consequence of which, and the late favorable Harvest, the prices of all kinds of Provisions have fallen considerably."

RC (DNA: RG 59, CD, Bristol, vol. 2). 1 p.

1. Vander Horst to JM, 20 and 30 Mar. 1802.

From John McWhorter

SIR.   ST. GEORGES, STATE OF DELAWARE. May 4th. 1802.

   In a Letter of recommendation that I handed into the States department dated March 18th. 1801.[1] I made application for One of the Surveyors Offices in the Western Ohio, or Mississippi Territories, if such appointments were to be made by the President of the United States. General Lincoln[2] then Officiateing in the States department was of opinion there was no such appointments to make. I have not yet received any other answer.

   I now take the Liberty to make application for one of the appointments to be made Under an Act of Congress Signed and Approved March 30th. 1802. Viz. An Act to regulate Trade and intercourse with the Indian tribes and to preserve peace on the frontiers.[3]

   There is a part of the boundary line Specified in Said Act that I have formerly Surveyed in the year 1790. Viz. That part of the Mianders of Ohio River from the mouth of Kentucke River down to General Clarks Grant, the field notes of this Survey I have now in possession, And have a desire to compleat this part and to run ascertain and mark such other part of the Said Boundary line as the President of the United States may think proper to direct or appoint to me. If this is not to be obtained I rest for any thing further at the will of the President. I expect my character as an honest man and friend to Liberty and Republickanism are sufficiently recommended in my first application from the respectability of the Gentlemen who Signed it to need no other Recommendatory Letter.

I now in a short time expect to remove to the Northwestern Territory, And if the President of the United States, do consider me worthy of one of these appointments the favour will be gratefully acknowledged and I will engage on my part to perform the duties of my office faithfully to the best of my Judgment from instructions I may receive, & I hope to the gratification of the publick.

An answer to this previous to the twentieth Inst. would be confering an Obligation on your Sincere friend and Huml. Servt.

JOHN M.WHORTER

RC (NHi).

1. Letter not found.
2. Attorney General Levi Lincoln.
3. Section 1 of the act called for the boundary line, "established by treaty between the United States and various Indian tribes," to be "clearly ascertained, and distinctly marked" and specified the lines to be surveyed (*U.S. Statutes at Large*, 2:139–41).

§ From William Eaton. *4 May 1802, Tunis.* Reports that on 2 May "it was announced to the Bey that an American frigate had captured four Coasting Vessels belonging to his Subjects, bound to Tripoli. . . . Immediate restitution of Vessels and cargoes were demanded by the Bey. Yesterday and to day have been consumed in discussion on the subject." To the bey's argument of "the principle *of free bottoms free goods*," Eaton replied that this "was never construed to extend to a blockaded port." The bey inferred from the president's letter of 9 Sept. 1801[1] "an implied order to respect his flag, Vessels and Subjects in all Situations," but Eaton insisted that "a fair construction could only imply that respect so long as he or his Subjects respected the laws of neutrality." The bey threatened reprisals; Eaton offered retaliation. "Thus we stand here." While convinced that "this Regency dare not attempt a System of reprisals," Eaton believes "indemnity will be hereafter reclaimed." Still, "this is not the moment to yield in the smallest matter. . . . It will be Seasonable enough to be generous when they shall be taught to appreciate duly our generosity." Has heard nothing from the pasha of Tripoli's brother since 31 Mar. when he sailed for Malta.

RC (DNA: RG 59, CD, Tunis, vol. 2, pt. 1); letterbook copy (CSmH); Tr (DLC: Cathcart Papers). RC 2 pp.; in a clerk's hand; docketed by Brent as received 16 Sept. Printed in Knox, *Naval Documents, Barbary Wars*, 2:142–43.

1. In describing his orders to the commander of the U.S. Mediterranean squadron, Jefferson wrote: "We gave, illustrious friend, in strict charge to our officer, chief in command, to respect and treat with particular friendship your flags, your vessels, and your subjects, . . . and we trusted you would yield him that hospitable reception, and those accommodations in the ports of your dominions which his necessities require" (Jefferson to the bey of Tunis, 9 Sept. 1801, *ASP, Foreign Relations*, 2:358).

§ From John Halsted. *4 May 1802, Perth Amboy*. States that due to the death of Daniel Marsh, the office of collector of Perth Amboy is vacant. Solicits the appointment and encloses testimonials of his fitness for the position.

RC and enclosures (DNA: RG 59, LAR, 1801–9, filed under "Halsted"). RC 1 p.; docketed by Jefferson. Of the two recommendations enclosed (3 pp.), one was signed by two persons, the other by thirty-four. John Halsted (ca. 1732–1813) had been appointed collector of Perth Amboy, New Jersey, in 1789 and served until his removal by John Adams in 1800 (*Senate Exec. Proceedings*, 1:10, 12, 341; Halsted to George Washington, 29 May 1789, W. W. Abbot et al., eds., *The Papers of George Washington: Presidential Series* [3 vols. to date; Charlottesville, Va., 1987—], 2:407–9 and nn.).

§ From William Willis. *4 May 1802, Washington*. "From some of the remarks you made, in the Conversation I had the honor to have with you this day; I have reason to beleive that some misinformation has been given you, of my leaving Barcelona. . . . When I left Barcelona, I had hopes of finding some property in Europe, belonging to James Muirhead & Co of Charleston, for whom I had made very large advances. . . . Even with all my exertions, I was not in time; for all the funds which had been in Europe belonging to that house, had been drawn out of the hands of their agents before I could reach them. This being the case I conce[i]v'd it to be very necessary for me to pursue it to the United States, . . . and as soon as I had determind on this I gave information of my intentions to Mr Pinckney the Minister of the United States at Madrid. . . . The business of the Consulate, will be conducted in my absence, by Mr Peter Stirling. . . . All mercantile men are expos'd to such as I have met with, and I conceive it would be extremely hard, if the business which I have follow'd to establish and support the Consulate, should be the cause of the loss of that property and consulate too. . . . I request the favor of you Sir, that if any charge is given against me, to take the trouble of causing notice to be given to me of it, and time for me to collect proofs to confute them. . . . I shall set out tomorrow for New Bedford Massachussetts to embrace once more my aged Parents and shall then avail myself of the first opportunity of a Passage to Barcelona."

RC (DNA: RG 59, CD, Barcelona, vol. 1). 3 pp.; docketed by Brent.

¶ To William Stewart. Letter not found. *4 May 1802, Department of State*. Offered for sale in Stan. V. Henkels Catalogue No. 1454 (15 May 1931), item 45, which notes that it is a one-page letter "regarding the enclosure of William Stewart's commission as Consul of the U.S. at Smyrna."

From Thomas Jefferson

Tʜ: J. ᴛᴏ J. Mᴀᴅɪsᴏɴ   May 5. 1802.

I think it is dean Swift who says that a present should consist of something of little value, & which yet cannot be bought for money.[1] I send you one strictly under both conditions. The drawing was made by Kosciusko for his own use, and the engraving also I believe.[2] He sent me four copies, the only ones which have come to America. The others I give to my family, and ask yourself & mrs. Madison to accept of the one now sent.

FC (DLC: Jefferson Papers).

1. Jonathan Swift wrote, in "On the Death of Stella": "She used to define a present, That it was a gift to a friend of something he wanted or was fond of, and which could not be easily gotten for money" (Swift, *Miscellaneous and Autobiographical Pieces, Fragments, and Marginalia,* vol. 5 of *The Prose Writings of Jonathan Swift,* ed. Herbert Davis [14 vols.; Oxford, 1951–68], p. 233).
2. For the portrait of Jefferson executed by Thaddeus Kosciuszko, see Alfred L. Bush, *The Life Portraits of Thomas Jefferson* (Charlottesville, Va., 1962), pp. 41–42.

From Beriah Norton

HONORD. SIR   EDGARTOWN May 5th. 1802.

I beg Leave one More to trouble you with a line on the Distressing Business of which I had the Honor of waiting on you when I was Last at the Seat of Government. I recd. a few days Since, a Letter from Mr. Williams our Member in Congress in which he informs Me that thrue the Goodness of the President, with your good advice, he Mr. Williams, Expected, that the President would in the Corse of this Spring Pardon & Discharge Elihu Marchant from that Part of his Sentence that relates to his Emprisonment,[1] as to the fine of one hundred Dollars he had his Doubts whether that would be taken of. Pray Sir Give Me Leave to Obsearve, that I beleave, that it is Emposable for Marchant to Procure the Money, as to his Particular frinds in this Place he has But three Men here of his Near Connections & I am Extreemly Sorry to Say that by reason of very hard fortune we are Not able to rase the Money, it is Needless for Me to inlarg. I am Confident Sir that from your Natureal tender & human fealings you will Make Such representations to our Good President as togather with his frindly Disposition, the Said fine of 100 Dollars will be Given up to the Poor & unfortunate, if it is by Any Means Consestent. I remane Sir your Most obed. Huml. Sert.

BERIAH NORTON

RC (DNA: RG 59, Petitions for Pardon, no. 50).

1. For the case of Elihu Marchant, see Joseph Jones to JM, 16 June 1801 (*PJM-SS,* 1: 321–22 and n. 1).

§ To George Blake. *5 May 1802, Department of State, Washington.* "It becomes necessary, under the late Convention with France, that an order of the District Court of Massachusetts should be obtained without delay, for the disposal of the money arising from the sales of the cargo of 'L'Hereux,'[1] a french vessel captured by Captain Little on the 2d. April 1800 which money was libelled in that Court and remains uncondemned for want of proof. I request you therefore to take upon yourself the trouble of doing this."

Letterbook copy (DNA: RG 59, DL, vol. 14). 1 p.

   1. See Gallatin to JM, 28 Apr. 1802, and n. 4.

§ To Alexander J. Dallas. *5 May 1802, Department of State, Washington.* "To satisfy some enquiries of the Secretary of the Treasury respecting a claim of Mr. Pichon under the Convention with France it becomes necessary that authenticated transcripts of the proceedings of the District Court of Pennsylvania in the case of the 'Magicienne,' formerly 'Retaliation,' should be procured, so far as they may go to prove this vessel to have been a National one.[1] I must therefore ask the favor of you to take upon yourself this trouble, and that of sending the papers to me. The Magicienne was condemned by a decree of the Court in November 1799."

Letterbook copy (DNA: RG 59, DL, vol. 14). 1 p.

   1. See Gallatin to JM, 28 Apr. 1802, and n. 1.

§ From John Gavino. *5 May 1802, Gibraltar.* No. 86. Refers JM to his dispatch no. 85 [not found]. Reports arrival on 25 Apr. from Tunis of "the American Ship Gloria Commanded by Jo: Bounds taken in the service by Consul Eaton, who brought me the Inclosed dispatches, to which & the Copy of said Gentlemans Letter to me anexd, beg leave to referr." The commander of the Tripolitan ship laid up at Gibraltar has returned from Tangier "but has caused no movement." Sir James Saumarez is charged with the evacuation of Minorca.[1] The U.S. frigate *Constellation*, Captain Murray, "this day Anchord in this Bay," as did the *Essex* and *Philadelphia*, "and as the latter goes Home, Capn: Barron will be the bearer of this and to whom referr for the Occurrencies on this side of the Globb."

RC and one enclosure (DNA: RG 59, CD, Gibraltar, vol. 2). RC 2 pp. Printed in Knox, *Naval Documents, Barbary Wars*, 2:144. Enclosure (1 p.) is a copy of Eaton to Gavino, 4 Apr. 1802, with instructions for the disposition of Eaton's dispatches sent by the *Gloria* under Joseph Bounds. For other enclosures, see Eaton to JM, 4 Apr. 1802, and nn. 1 and 6.

   1. Pursuant to the terms of the Treaty of Amiens, Great Britain returned the island of Minorca to Spain on 16 June 1802. British admiral James Saumarez, a naval veteran of the American and French revolutionary wars, evacuated the British troops from the island (Desmond Gregory, *Minorca, the Illusory Prize: A History of the British Occupations of Minorca between 1708 and 1802* [Rutherford, N.J., 1990], pp. 214–15; Gavino to JM, 28 June 1802).

§ From Rufus King. *5 May 1802, London.* No. 65. Reports that bill imposing duties on imports, exports, and ship tonnage passed House of Commons and will undoubtedly become law.[1] Bill revives most provisions of the Convoy Act[2] but raises duties on imports by one-fifth and reduces duties on goods exported to America by one-half. Because of increased quantity and superior quality of American cotton, it was proposed to place a higher duty on it than on Turkish cotton, but after conferring with King the officials reduced the duty to the lowest rate, equal to that imposed on Turkish cotton. Since the proposed tonnage duty on U.S. vessels is as low as on those of any other country, "so far as respects discrimination there is nothing to complain of." Encloses copy of a letter to Vansittart on "the abolition of all discrimination between the Purchasers of British Manufactures."

RC and enclosure (DNA: RG 59, DD, Great Britain, vol. 10); letterbook copy (NHi: Rufus King Papers, vol. 55). RC 3 pp.; marked duplicate; in a clerk's hand; docketed by Brent as received 5 July. Printed in King, *Life and Correspondence of Rufus King*, 4:119–20. Enclosure (4 pp.) is King to Nicholas Vansittart, 29 Apr. 1802 (printed ibid., 4:111–12).

1. The parliamentary debate on the import and export duties bill took place on 27 Apr. (*Parliamentary History of England*, 36:548–57).
2. The 1798 Convoy Act imposed duties on exports from and imports to Great Britain carried in foreign ships. The revenue from these imposts went ostensibly to defray the costs of protecting neutral shipping from French depredations. For King's efforts to modify the contents of the bill before passage, see Perkins, *First Rapprochement*, pp. 77–78.

§ From James Maury. *5 May 1802, Liverpool.* Encloses prices of imported American articles. "The immensely unprecedented Imports of Cotton, and particularly from Georgia, Carolina & the Mississippi, have already reduced the prices of the less valuable sorts. . . . Grain & flour seem daily on the decline."

RC and enclosure (DNA: RG 59, CD, Liverpool, vol. 2). RC 1 p.; marked "(duplicate)"; in a clerk's hand, signed by Maury. Enclosure is a one-page list of "Prices Current of American Produce at Liverpool 5th. May 1802."

§ From Joseph Pulis. *5 May 1802, Malta.* Reports that the dethroned pasha of Tripoli, who had long taken refuge in Tunis, has reached a settlement with his usurping brother to govern Bengasi. He is now in Malta. The British are beginning to evacuate Malta while waiting for the Order of St. John of Jerusalem to replace them according to the terms of the definitive treaty. Previously informed JM that the frigate *Philadelphia* left sixty barrels of damp gunpowder to be put in a state of service;[1] has had the powder restored to its original condition and placed in the powder magazine where it awaits orders. Discusses a circular sent by the U.S. consul at Algiers in regard to the signals used by Algerine corsairs at sea.

RC (DNA: RG 59, CD, Malta, vol. 1). 3 pp.; in French. In a clerk's hand, signed by Pulis. Docketed by Brent as received 6 Oct.

1. See Pulis to JM, 21 Feb. 1802 (*PJM-SS*, 2:482).

To Albert Gallatin

SIR   DEPARTMENT OF STATE 6th. May 1802

I request that under Warrants on the appropriations mentioned in the enclosed estimate the sums therein stated may be placed in the hands of Bird Savage & Bird in London—they to be charged with the same in the Books of the Treasury. I am very respectfully &ca.

JAMES MADISON.

[Enclosure]

Estimate for Six Months

Diplomatic	Salary of the Minister @ 9000.	4.500
	Do. of his Secretary " 1350	675
	Contingent say	900
British Treaty	Salary of 2 Commissioners under the 7th. Article of the Treaty @ £1500 stg.	6.666.67
	half the Salary of the 5th Commissioner	1.666.66
	Their Contingencies say	2.666.67
	Compensation to 2. Agents @ 2.500.	2.500.—
Relief of seamen	Salary of the Agent for the relief of seamen	1.500.—
	Expences of Do. say	1.800.—
Prosecution of claims in prize causes	Payment to Proctors say	25.000
		$47.875

Letterbook copy and copy of enclosure (DNA: RG 59, DL, vol. 14).

To William Jarvis

SIR.   DEPARTMENT OF STATE. May 6th. 1802.

Your two Letters of the 8th. and 23d. of April have been received. In consequence of the first, a copy of the regulations for guarding our vessels against unnecessary quarantine in Foreign ports,[1] was sent to the collector of Boston, thro' whom I hope, you will have received it.

With respect to claims of our Citizens on the Portuguese Government, the general rule to be followed is, that you aid them by your consular interposition in the spirit recommended in your printed instructions,[2] and in the manner most likely to obtain the redress, to which the cases may be respectively entitled.

Besides the case of the Samuel, with whose papers you are already charged, that of the Aurora, John B. church supercargo,[3] and another under like circumstances will be put into your hands. Mr. church proposes to go to Lisbon himself, the better to pursue his object. He is recommended to me as a young Gentleman of worth and in that respect, as well as in his character of an American Citizen, will doubtless receive the proper attentions from you. His papers will explain the ground of his claims. As far as it can be shewn, that the vessels were taken by force, on the high Seas, and not within the Portuguese jurisdiction, that the condemnation took place without giving to the claimants the opportunities usually allowed by the laws of the country, to defend their cause, or that their persons were treated with unwarrantable and unusual severity, you will have particular topics to urge in their behalf, in addition to an appeal to the friendly disposition of the United States towards Portugal, and the mutual interest they have, in doing liberal and conciliatory justice to the citizens and subjects of the other. I am &c.

J. M

Letterbook copy (DNA: RG 59, IC, vol. 1). RC offered for sale in Goodspeed's Catalogue, "The Flying Quill," Spring 1980, item 41.

1. For the regulations, see Circular Letter to American Consuls and Commercial Agents, 1 Aug. 1801 (*PJM-SS*, 2:2–3, 4 n. 1).

2. Standing Instructions to American Consuls and Vice-Consuls, 10 June 1801 (*PJM-SS*, 1:288–89).

3. John B. Church, Jr. (b. 1779), was the son of the New York merchant John B. Church, a business associate and brother-in-law of Alexander Hamilton's (Syrett and Cooke, *Papers of Hamilton*, 3:658 n. 10).

To Louis-André Pichon

SIR,   DEPARTMENT OF STATE 6th. May 1802.

I am just informed that two Citizens of the United States, John Rogers late a Captain in the Navy and Wm. Davidson have been arrested at Cape Francois by orders of the General in Chief, put into the most rigorous confinement, and otherwise treated as the vilest of Malefactors.[1] Notwithstanding the presumption arising from the characters of those Citizens against the justice of the proceeding, there might have been room for suppositions which ought to suspend a definitive opinion, if the grounds of it had not been explained in a letter from General le Clerc to Mr. Lear of the   of   [2] from which the enclosed is an extract of what relates to the subject.[3]

I forbear Sir to make a single comment on the nature of those allegations or the use which has been made of them. You cannot fail to view both in their true colours and mischevous tendencies; and I assure myself that anticipating the sentiments of your Government, you will employ the weight of your interposition in accelerating the release of Capt. Rogers and Mr. Davidson and repairing the wrongs they have suffered. Accept Sir the assurances of my respect and consideration

JAMES MADISON

Letterpress copy of RC (DLC: Jefferson Papers); letterbook copy (DNA: RG 59, DL, vol. 14); Tr (NHi: Livingston Papers). Letterpress copy of RC in a clerk's hand, signed by JM; sent as enclosure in JM to Jefferson, 7 May 1802. Tr in Brent's hand; sent as enclosure in JM to Livingston, 7 May 1802. Enclosure not found, but see n. 3.

1. The details of the imprisonment of U.S. naval captain John Rodgers and merchant captain William Davidson of Philadelphia are given in Rodgers to JM, June 1802.
2. Left blank in all copies.
3. JM undoubtedly enclosed the extract from Leclerc to Lear, 25 [27] Germinal an X, of which he sent a letterpress copy to Jefferson (see JM to Jefferson, 7 May 1802, and enclosure).

To John Read, Jr.

SIR,   DEPARTMENT OF STATE, WASHINGTON May 6: 1802.

The President having ratified the late Convention with England it is necessary that the expenses incident to the Sixth Article of the Treaty between the two Countries should immediately cease.[1] You will be pleased to give instructions to the Special Agents employed under that Article conformably with this Intimation, and to consider the establishment of your own Office, including all the appointments in it, as likewise at an end. Mr. Evans will deliver to you the books and papers in his possession, belonging to the United States,[2] and you will place them, with the others under your care, in some safe depositary at Philadelphia, where they may remain 'till they can be conveniently removed to this place. I am, very respectfully &ca.

JAMES MADISON.

Letterbook copy (DNA: RG 59, DL, vol. 14).

1. The work of the commission appointed under article 6 of the Jay treaty to negotiate a settlement of pre–Revolutionary War debts owed to British nationals was annulled by the convention of 8 Jan. 1802, which provided that the U.S. pay the sum of £600,000 sterling to Great Britain to discharge all claims made upon U.S. citizens under the article (Moore, *International Adjudications*, 3:356; see also Rufus King to JM, 9 and 11 Jan. 1802, *PJM-SS*, 2: 380–81, 383–85).

2. Griffith Evans, secretary of the commission, handed the papers to U.S. agent Read and to William Moore Smith, the British agent (Moore, *International Adjudications*, 3:22, 346–47; JM to Evans, 7 May 1802).

From Unite Dodge

SIR   CAP FRANÇAIS May 6. 1802.

The famous Genl. Toussaint Louvre: arrived in Town this afternoon accompanied by several french Officers, his own aides des camps, horse Guards &cie. Soon after a General Salute was fired by all the Fleet; it might have been in honour of the General in Chief who happened to be on board the Admirals Ship when Tousstt: alighted at his House.

I received a Letter a few days past directed to the 'Ex-Consul,' from the commandt. of the place, inviting me to reclaim several Imprisoned american Seamen; as I knew that if they had been guilty of any particular crime my reclamation wou'd not release them, I answered, that I was not the 'Ex-consul' & cou'd not officially require the seamens release, but hop'd if they had not been guilty of any crime or misconduct, that he would discharge them without delay. Two days after I sent to the Goal to enquire if they were still there & found they had been dismissed the day before.

I shall endeavour to transmit, by the month of June, a correct statemt. of american Vessels, their Cargoes &ce, altho' none of the Captains think proper to present themselves at the office except for Protests & Certificates & particularly when embarrassed in Business with which I have no authority to interfere.

I have only time to add that the Gouvt. begin to give proofs of a desire to do away some of the vexatious & unnecessary delays of office in the entry & clearance of american vessels. But that will not prevent the most ruinous Voyages for a long time to come. It may not be improper to inform you, Sir, that I have heard several of the principal officers of Gouvmt. speak as if they were very dissatisfied with the americans generally, in consequence of reading several pieces against them, printed in the public news Papers of the United States as if they contained the sentiments of the Gouvmt; and it is not so easy a matter, as any person acquainted with the constitution & Gouvt. of the US woud suppose, to convince them of the contrary. I am, with great Respect, Sir, Your very Obedt. Servt

U DODGE

RC (DNA: RG 59, CD, Cap Haitien, vol. 4). Docketed by Brent as received 30 May.

From Stephen Sayre

S<small>IR</small>   P<small>HILAA</small>. 6th May 1802

I have requested it as a favor, to know, whether I may, or may not expect, some appointment from Administration.

If you conceive the refusal of an answer ought to be conclusive, you are not perfectly acquainted with my character—for—since I am compel'd to pass the line of delicacy, you must pardon me, if I draw some just & natural conclusions, and presume, that others have been provided for, more on account of their situation—or those who recommend them, than positive fitness for office, or claims on the nation.

My services are at an end—they must be unpleasant to the recollection—but it is one of the inconveniencies attending your situation—you must be told of them.

I do not deny you may possess the great & leading principles of patriotism & love for your country, but you must permit me to suppose it possible, that in the pressure of applications you may forget the man who has the clearest claims to protection. Let me beseech you to save me the expence of attending on you in person—if you do so, rely upon it, you will find me full of thanks & gratitude—if I must dance attendance at your door, it will be most unpleasant to myself and distressing to you.

I cannot point out employment—but I will ask—do you know any other person who would better accomplish the business of settling the line to be drawn in upper Canada, between the United States & the British Government?

Is it too great a favor to make some short reply to this note? I am with due respect yours &c &c

S<small>TEPHEN</small> S<small>AYRE</small>

RC (DNA: RG 59, LAR, 1801–9, filed under "Sayre"). Docketed by Jefferson.

§ To Richard Söderström. *6 May 1802, Department of State.* "Messrs Warner and Leit of Saybrook have expressed an anxiety to this Department to know the fate of the representation which you were so good as to make some time ago to the Swedish Government, concerning their Brigantine Matilda, captured by the French near the Island of St Bartholonews [*sic*]. I ask the favor of you therefore to enable me to satisfy their enquiries."

RC (RS); letterbook copy (DNA: RG 59, DL, vol. 14). RC 1 p.; in a clerk's hand, signed by JM. The case of the *Matilda* had not been resolved as late as 1807 (Jonathan Warner to JM, 27 Nov. 1807 [DNA: RG 59, NFC, vol. 1]).

§ From Nicholas Low. *6 May 1802, New York.* States that the United Insurance

Company, of which he is president, has several suits pending in the New York Supreme Court, "in one of which it has become necessary to send a commission for the examination of a witness at Lisbon; and in the others to send commissions for the examination of witnesses at Madrid." The nature of the suits and the proposed witnesses are given in the enclosed letters to Don Thomas Stoughton, the Spanish consul, and Joaquim Monteiro, the Portuguese consul, at New York. Owing to the "very considerable amount" of property involved and the uncertainty as to "whether the witnesses, and particularly whether the Portugese Secretary for Foreign Affairs, will consent to be examined," Low solicits JM's "recommendation to our Consul at Lisbon and to our Minister at Madrid to give the commissions which shall be addressed to them all the attention and facility in their power."

RC (DLC: Causten-Pickett Papers, box 26). 1 p.; unsigned. Enclosures not found.

§ From Willink and Van Staphorst. *6 May 1802, Amsterdam.* "We had the honor to address you on the 10 February[1] acknowledging receipt of your esteemed favor 11. September Ulto.[2] and have Since been deprived of any of your letters. The purport of the present is that Ch: Pinckney Esqe. Minister of the U. S. at the Court of Madrid has sent us copy of your letter 11. September Ulto. directing us to hold subject to his disposal any Sums of money requisite for the payment of the Consuls whose Accounts Mr. Ch. Pinckney is authorised to Settle: in consequence thereof we have forwarded unto him the necessary letters of credit for Lisbon and Italy."

RC (DNA: RG 59, Letters Received from Bankers). 1 p.

1. Letter not found.
2. *PJM-SS*, 2:103.

¶ From Rowland Hazard. Letter not found. *6 May 1802, South Kingston, Rhode Island.* Acknowledged in Daniel Brent to Hazard, 17 May 1802 (DNA: RG 59, DL, vol. 14). Asks about the prosecution of his claims against Great Britain and France. Brent replied that George W. Erving had replaced Samuel Williams in Great Britain and suggested that Hazard write to Robert R. Livingston regarding his claims against France.

To Thomas Jefferson

private

DEAR SIR   WASHINGTON May 7. 1802

Mr. Lear arrived here the day before yesterday a few minutes after your departure. He confirms the information as to the imprisonment of Capt: Rodgers & Davidson. Inclosed is a copy of le Clerc's explanation on the subject, of my letter to Pichon with his answer, and of a letter to Mr. Livingston which I shall forward to Philada. this evening, that it may overtake the despatches already in the hands of Mr. Dupont. The other information given by Mr. Lear is that the state of things in St. Domingo augurs a protracted if not a doubtful warfare, that the ports abound, and superabound with every necessary, that money has lately arrived both from France & from the Havanna, that the irritations between the French & the Americans are occasioned by faults on both sides, and that there probably is a mixture of antirepublican venom in those of the French. From a confidential communication made to him, it appears that the idea in the Army is that Republicanism is exploded, that Monarchy must be forced, and that Buonaparte is the proper successor to the cashiered dynasty; but that it is the ⟨party⟩ &c. and not the nation that wishes this revolution.

Mr. Smith is not yet returned from Baltimore. Mr. Gallatin left us this morning. Genl Dearbourn will go for a few days to Philada. on monday or tuesday.

I inclose a recommendation of A Collector for Amboy,[1] that in case you decide in your absence, all the candidates for that vacancy may be before you. With the most respectful attachment I remain Yours

JAMES MADISON

[Enclosure]

"Extract of a letter from the Genl. in chief of St. Domingo to Mr. Lear dated Cap. 25 Grl. an. 10.[2]

"Vous avez paru, avoir des inquietudes sur l'arrestation des MMrs Rodgers et Davidson. Vous ne devez pas ignorer les propos et les bruits allarmants, que le premier s'est permis de repandre sur l'armèe francaise, a son arrivèe aux Etats Unis. Il n'est pas permit a un negociant pour favorizer ses speculations, d'inquieter le commerce de sa nation; et de calomnier une armèe. Quant au second: le nom qu'il avait donnè a son bâtiment, lors de son depart des Etats Unis, m'avait d'abord donnè des inquietudes sur son compte, qui n'ont fait qu'accroitre par des rapports que J'ai obtenu."[3]

TRANSLATION

"You seem anxious about the arrests of Messrs. Rodgers and Davidson. You cannot be ignorant of the angry remarks and alarming reports made about the French army by the first on his arrival in the U.S. A merchant is not permitted to disturb his nation's commerce and to malign an army in order to promote his own speculations. As for the second, the name he gave his ship when he sailed from the U.S. first aroused my suspicions about him, which were only increased by the reports I obtained."

RC and enclosures (DLC: Jefferson Papers). RC docketed by Jefferson as received 13 May. The enclosed extract of Leclerc's letter to Lear is a letterpress copy in JM's hand. JM also enclosed letterpress copies of his 6 May letter to Pichon, his 7 May letter to Livingston, and Pichon's 7 May reply.

1. Probably John Halsted to JM, 4 May 1802.

2. A copy of this letter that Lear subsequently forwarded to JM is dated 27 Germinal an X (17 Apr. 1802) (see Lear to JM, 22 June 1802, and n.).

3. William Davidson's ship was the *St. Domingo Packet* (Philadelphia *Aurora General Advertiser*, 1 Jan. 1802). According to a letter from Saint-Domingue published in the *Aurora* on 11 May 1802, Davidson was suspected of participating in a mercantile venture with Toussaint L'Ouverture. The ship, the letter noted, "is now in the harbour of Cape-Francois, with Toussaint's figure for a head."

To Robert R. Livingston

SIR,   DEPARTMENT OF STATE, May 7. 1802.

The inclosed extract of a letter from Mr. Lear to Le Clerc the General in Chief at St. Domingo and of another from the latter to him,[1] will explain an outrage against two respectable American Citizens, one of them lately an Officer in our Navy, which excites no less astonishment as a wanton departure from just principles than indignation as an insult to the United States. I inclose also the copy of a letter which I have written to Mr Pichon on the subject.[2] He views the proceeding in its true light, and I presume will interpose with all the weight he may possess. There ought to be as little doubt that the French Government will manifest on the occasion its respect for the character and friendship of this Country, as well as its regard to the character and commerce of its own, by affording instantly every reparation of which the case is susceptible. You will accordingly adapt your representations to that object, whilst you give to them the tone recommended by the friendly relations which subsist between the two Countries and which it is as much the Wish of the United States, as it is the interest of both, to cherish and perpetuate.

My last informed you of the abrupt revocation by Genl. le Clerc of the permission he had given to Mr. Lear to exercise the functions of Commercial Agent at Cape Francois. Mr. Lear is ⟨just⟩ returned from that place. He describes the state of things as auguring a protracted warfare; and even a doubtful issue to it, if the waste of French troops be not repaired by ample reinforcements. The administration is perfectly military; and not more characterized by that circumstance, than by an ignorance or disregard of the external interests of the island. More indiscretion cannot be well imagined than has taken place, in relation to the commerce with this country. Unfortunately the misconduct of some of the Americans engaged in it has contributed to wound the confidence on which all commercial intercourse is founded. It appears notwithstanding that the ports there at the present moment, abound with every species of necessary supplies.

Having learnt that Mr. Dupont is delayed in his departure, I shall send this to Philadelphia in expectation that it will go with the dispatches with which he is already charged for you. With sentiments of great respect & consideration I am, Sir, your Ob⟨t.⟩

JAMES MADISON

Letterpress copy of RC (DLC: Jefferson Papers); letterbook copy (DNA: RG 59, IM, vol. 6); enclosures (NHi: Livingston Papers). Letterpress copy of RC in a clerk's hand, signed by JM; sent as enclosure in JM to Jefferson, 7 May 1802. Last paragraph not in letterbook copy. For enclosures, see nn. 1 and 2.

1. JM enclosed copies of Tobias Lear's letter to Leclerc, 14 Apr. 1802 (3 pp.; in Brent's hand), protesting the "unprecedented imprisonment of Captains Rodgers and Davidson," demanding to know "the cause of their confinement and harsh treatment," and informing Leclerc that the U.S. government would "not see with indifference its Citizens treated with undeserved indignity, or unjustifiable cruelty"; and Leclerc's reply of 27 Germinal an X (17 Apr. 1802) (2 pp.; in French) officially notifying Lear that he would no longer be recognized as an accredited agent of the U.S. and explaining the arrests of the two Americans (for JM's extract from Leclerc's letter, see the enclosure in JM to Jefferson, 7 May 1802).

2. JM to Pichon, 6 May 1802. JM apparently also enclosed a copy of Pichon's 7 May reply (see Livingston's letterbook copies of JM's 7 May dispatch and enclosures [NHi: Livingston Papers, vol. 2]).

From William E. Hūlings

SIR   NEW ORLEANS 7th. May 1802.

You are, no doubt, acquainted with the suspension of the American Consular functions in this place, which took place by Order of his Catholic Majesty on the 9th. October 1799.[1] And of my continuing, as Vice Consul of the U. S., to give such papers to the Citizens of said States, as were *Necessary* to their safety and benefit, under a well founded belief that the Governt. of this Port wou'd take no umbrage at my doing so. Since which I have uninterruptedly exercised the duties of my employ (with respect to American Citizens only) until the day before Yesterday, when I recd. from his Exclly. Don Manuel de Salcedo a letter, of which the inclosed is a true Copy.[2]

I am persuaded that my well informed friend Daniel Clark Esqr. has given you a perfect knowledge of every Circumstance relative to the Interests of the United States, and their Citizens in this Port, and of the great necessity there is for the Public residence of a Consul, or Agent of their Nation, as long as it shall continue to be the place of their deposit.

We have a vast number of Boats in our harbour from the American

Settlements, ladened with flour, tobacco, bacon, Salt Pork, Beef, Cordage; some Hemp; and Cotton of Natchez and Tenessee.

The Markets are exceedingly dull & Cash very scarce; And although there are upwards of thirty five American Vessels in Port, freight cannot be had to St. Domingo, the Windwd. Islands, or Jamaica under three to four dollars pr. barrel of flour.

We are in much uncertainty respectg. the cession of this country to France; every day brings us contradictory reports. We have been alarmed by some information recd by a Providence Gazette, stating that an Account had been brot. from London to that port, under date of the 8th March, that a rupture had taken place between England and Spain. No Vessel has arrived since to confirm or destroy the News. I am Sir With the greatest respect Your Most Obedt. humble Servt.

WM. E HŪLINGS

RC and enclosure (DNA: RG 59, CD, New Orleans, vol. 1). Docketed by Brent.

1. See Hūlings to JM, 2 May 1801 (*PJM-SS*, 1:139 and n. 1).
2. In his letter to Hūlings, 5 May 1802 (2 pp.; in Spanish), Manuel de Salcedo quoted a letter from the intendant of Louisiana indicating that Hūlings was continuing to perform the duties of vice-consul of the U.S., and he reiterated the order to Hūlings to abstain from all public functions.

§ To Griffith Evans. *7 May 1802, Department of State.* "The late Convention with England having received its full Ratification, your appointment under the Seventh Article[1] of the Treaty of 1794 has of course ceased. You will probably learn from Mr. Thornton the disposition of the Books and papers belonging to the British side in your office—Mr. Read will receive whatever share of them ought to remain with the United States."

Letterbook copy (DNA: RG 59, DL, vol. 14). 1 p. RC offered for sale in the Carnegie Book Shop Catalogue No. 132 (3 Mar. 1948), item 237.

1. This is apparently a clerk's error; an extract printed in the Carnegie Book Shop Catalogue reads, "VIth Article."

§ From Rufus King. *7 May 1802, London.* No. 66. Asserts that a great principle of U.S. policy is "to maintain and perpetuate the union of our Country." Expresses concern over the cession of Louisiana and the Floridas to France, because it is a measure calculated "to weaken and divide us." Has reinforced verbal communications between British ministers and himself on this subject through a confidential letter to Lord Hawkesbury, which is enclosed with the minister's answer.[1] The subject is considered by all men of consequence in Great Britain "as a measure of the greatest consequence," with "an unavoidable influence upon the duration of Peace."

RC and enclosures (DNA: RG 59, DD, Great Britain, vol. 10); letterbook copy (NHi:

Rufus King Papers, vol. 55). RC 2 pp.; in a clerk's hand, signed by King; docketed by Brent. Printed in King, *Life and Correspondence of Rufus King*, 4:122. For enclosures, see n. 1.

1. King's letter to Hawkesbury, dated 21 Apr. 1802 (3 pp.), requested "in confidence" an explanation of the British position on the rumored cession of Louisiana and the Floridas to France (printed ibid., 4:108–9). Hawkesbury's 7 May 1802 letter to King (3 pp.), marked "*Confidential*," underlined the importance of the retrocession question to the British government and noted that the event "should render it more necessary than ever" that a "spirit of Confidence" should exist between Great Britain and the U.S. As for the free navigation of the Mississippi River, Hawkesbury went on to say, "it is perfectly clear, according to the Law of Nations, that in the event of the District of Louisiana being ceded to France, that Country would come into the Possession of it, subject to all the Engagements which appertained to it at the Time of Cession." He concluded by assuring King that the British had received no indication from France or Spain that the cession had taken place (printed ibid., 4:123).

§ From Louis-André Pichon. *7 May 1802, Georgetown.* Acknowledges JM's letter of 6 May; will write to Leclerc on the subject of it at the first opportunity. Assures JM that the general in chief, when he sees the impressions his actions have produced, will speedily make the reparations due to the U.S.

RC (DNA: RG 59, NFL, France, vol. 1); letterpress copy of RC (DLC: Jefferson Papers); Tr (NHi: Livingston Papers). RC 1 p.; in French. Tr in Brent's hand; in French.

To Arthur St. Clair

SIR   DEPARTMENT OF STATE May 8. 1802.
Among the papers delivered to this Department along with your defence against the charges of Col. Worthington &ca.[1] we do not find the documents produced in support of them. As your defence was sent to the President after a hasty perusal, without particularly looking into the papers inclosed with it; and which I presumed I had seen before, the documents in question may have been returned & been mislaid, on this supposition time has been taken to search for them. The second however being unsuccessful, and it occurring that the missing papers may have got among others, and remain with them, I ask the favor of you to see whether this be the case, & if it be to forward them. You may recollect that they were furnished at a different time from the copy of the charges, and may thence be the less unlikely to remain apart from them. Very respectfully I have the Honor to be &⟨ca.⟩

JAMES MADISON.

Letterbook copy (DNA: RG 59, DL, vol. 14).

1. For the charges against St. Clair and the administration's response, see Circular Letter from Thomas Jefferson, 29 Apr. 1802, and n. 1.

§ To Messrs. Warner and Leit. *8 May 1802, Department of State.* "I have just written to Mr. Soderstrom for such information as may enable me to satisfy your enquiries concerning the fate of your claim upon Sweeden[1]—this Gentleman having long since made a representation of it to his Government, by the request of that of the United States. When his answer is received I shall lose no time in communicating its contents to you."

Letterbook copy (DNA: RG 59, DL, vol. 14). 1 p.

1. No letter from Warner and Leit to JM has been found.

§ From Stevens Thomson Mason. *8 May 1802.* Recommends the bearer, Lund Washington,[1] "as a person desirous and capable of filling the office of a Clerke in your Department should any vacancy occur."

RC (DLC). 1 p.

1. This was probably the Lund Washington (b. 1767) who was the son of Robert Washington and Alice Strother Washington of Green Hill, Virginia (Abbot, *Papers of Washington: Presidential Series,* 1 : 369 n. 1).

From Samuel Hanson of Samuel

Sir,   WASHINGTON, 9th. May, 1802

I came hither this morning to wait on you, in order to Solicit the appointment lately become vacant by the resignation of Mr. Wagner. Not finding you at home, I take the liberty of leaving a few lines, presuming that they may answer the purpose of a personal interview. In forming an estimate of my character, I would beg you, Sir, to take it, not from the representations of persons prejudiced against me on account of my rupture with the Directors of the Bank of Columbia; but from Some of the best men in existence, residing in and near the district, who have known me, and been my real and Steady friends, for near 30 Years. To the Same authority I would refer you for a knowledge of my pretensions, on the score of competency to the discharge of the duties of the office. Of those pretensions, such as they are, it would not become myself to Speak. It may not be improper, however, to State that I translate the French Language with great facility; and that, if the knowledge of the Spanish be also necessary to the due discharge of the office, I would engage to acquire it, to a sufficient degree, in the course of a few weeks. This engagement my previous acquaintance with the Latin & French would, if I do not greatly deceive myself, enable me to perform. With great respect I am, Sir, Your most obedt

                                                         S HANSON OF SAML[1]

RC (DLC).

1. For Samuel Hanson of Samuel, see *PJM-SS*, 2:93 n. 2. Hanson was hired as a clerk in JM's office in October 1802 (Hanson's oath of office, 14 Oct. 1802 [DNA: RG 59, ML]). For his subsequent career, see *PJM-PS*, 2:277 n. 1.

From Thomas Jefferson

TH: J. TO J. MADISON.   MONTICELLO May 9. 1802.

The road through Ravensworth is renderd absolutely impassable for a four wheeled carriage by a single change made lately by one of the mr. Fitzhughs in his plantation. You must not therefore attempt it, but go on to Fairfax C. H. & there turn off to Songster's. Bull run is now passed at an excellent ford, and the hills by a great deal of work have been made quite good. The road between Elkrun church & Norman's ford is bad, as it generally is, but it will be better by the time you come on. All the rest is fine.

I think mr. Wagner should be instructed to take decisive measures for having a sheet of the laws printed daily till done.[1] A person direct from Kentucky, tells me a person of known credit had reached there from New Orleans which he left March 6. and affirms a French governor had arrived there, without troops, and had taken possession of the government. He was so positive that if we have nothing later from thence, I should think it possible. Adieu affectionately.

RC (DLC); FC (DLC: Jefferson Papers). FC dated 6 May 1802.

1. JM passed along Jefferson's suggestion to Daniel Brent, who was acting as chief clerk in Wagner's absence. Brent reported the near completion of the publication task in a letter to Jefferson dated 21 May 1802 (DLC: Jefferson Papers).

§ From James Leander Cathcart. *9 May 1802, Leghorn.* No. 5. Has not heard from "Barbary" but supposes Eaton persuaded Hamet to remain at Malta until the U.S. naval squadron arrives with instructions from the president. Has been informed that the *Enterprize* arrived "with dispatches at Gibraltar" and immediately went in search of the *Boston*, "who I presume is off Tripoli, but this is only conjecture as I have not been favor'd with a line from Captn. McNiel since his arrival." Encloses "all the information I am at prest. master of."

RC and enclosures (DNA: RG 59, CD, Tripoli, vol. 2). RC 1 p. Enclosures, docketed by Brent as received in Cathcart's 9 May dispatch, are a translated extract from Joseph Pulis's letter to Cathcart, 13 Apr. 1802 (1 p.), reporting the arrival at Malta of a Russian ship carrying Hamet Pasha, "who it seems is reconciled to his brother & is going to take upon him the government of Derna or Bengasi provinces of that Regency," noting that the Russian ship captain had apparently "suspended their departure" in consequence of Pulis's warning that Tripoli was under blockade by U.S. ships, and describing his efforts to forward this information to Captain McNeill so that Hamet would be intercepted if he proceeded on his voyage; and a copy of Cathcart's reply, 9 May 1802 (2 pp.), commending Pulis's "zeal for the publick service" while warning him to "strenuously avoid commiting the honor of the United States or involving us in paltry bickerings with other nations" and requesting the "earliest intelligence" of the *Enterprize*'s arrival in Malta and Hamet's departure, should he leave the island.

To James Leander Cathcart

SIR,   DEPARTMENT OF STATE May 10th. 1802.

The Adams frigate, by which you will receive my last, containing instructions on the subject of peace with Tripoli, and of your appointment as successor to Mr. obrien at algiers, meeting with unexpected delay; I make use of it to inform you that I have drawn on the Secretary of the Treasury for $24,000, which he will place in Leghorn subject to your orders as soon as he can make the arrangement. This sum as you have been already apprized, is meant for your admission as Consul to the Dey of algiers. I need not repeat, that it will be an agreeable circumstance, if your admission can be effected without it; or with as small a portion of it as possible; or that if a present be unavoidable, it will be less disagreeable in the simple form of Cash, than in the troublesome one of jewelry &c.

The accounts which we continue to receive strengthen our expectation, that you will find the Bashaw of Tripoli in a proper disposition to peace, and be able to conclude it on terms admissible by the United States. However able this Country may be to carry on the war with effect, the expence and trouble of it, and the encreased risk whilst at war with one of the Barbary powers, of getting into war with the others, are with the President just motives of solicitude for the success of your negotiation. Very respectfully, I am &c.

JAMES MADISON.

Letterbook copy (DNA: RG 59, IC, vol. 1).

To William Eaton

SIR.   DEPARTMENT OF STATE. May 10th. 1802.

Your several letters not heretofore acknowledged have been received down to that of the 22d. day of february last.[1] Your Bills amounting to

Sixteen thousand Dollars in favor of Stephen Kingston and John Shaw, will be paid;[2] but it is regretted that the draughts were made, particularly that for future contingencies, without the statement of your accounts, which had been enjoined. I hope you will lose no time in supplying the omission, and that on a settlement with the Treasury Department, the result will justify me in accepting, as well as you in making the draughts.

The present intended for you by the Government of Denmark, cannot be accepted without the permission of Congress, who have manifested in other instances a determination against such a practice.[3] The door is nevertheless open to your application, if you should incline to make it, to that authority. The President can do nothing in the case.

In order to make a due impression on the Bashaw of Tripoli, the Frigates in the Mediterranean, are to rendezvous before that place, and Mr. Cathcart will attend in order to take advantage of that impression, to meet the Bashaw in negociation for putting an end to the war.[4] This information will, the President trusts, lead you to favor the object, as far as circumstances may enable you, and particularly to exert yourself, if necessary, in keeping the Bey of Tunis in proper temper towards the United States during the crisis. I learn from London, that Jewels and arms to the amount of £6573..15..4 sterling, have been forwarded for him, of which you will no doubt make the most for the public advantage. I am very respectfully. &c.

JAMES MADISON.

Letterbook copy (DNA: RG 59, IC, vol. 1).

1. Eaton to JM, 22 Feb. 1802 (*PJM-SS*, 2:483).
2. See Eaton to JM, 13 Dec. 1801 (*PJM-SS*, 2:313–14).
3. For the gift from Denmark, see Eaton to JM, 17 Nov. 1801 (*PJM-SS*, 2:249 and n.). For Congress's unwillingness to allow the acceptance of such gifts, see JM to William Vans Murray, 7 Jan. 1802 (*PJM-SS*, 2:370 and nn.).
4. For JM's instructions for conducting these negotiations, see his letter to James Leander Cathcart, 18 Apr. 1802.

To James Sullivan

SIR   DEPARTMENT OF STATE May 10. 1802.

The establishment with the British Government of a proper boundary in the jurisdiction of the Islands in Passamaquody Bay and of proper regulations in navigations in navigating the channels between the same, is an object which for some time has engaged the attention of the Executive, and which, it appears by a late Resolution of the Legislature of Massachusetts is much desired by that State.[1] The inquiries into which you have been led particularly, as an agent on the part of the United States Under the   [2] Article of the Treaty of 1794. induce me to ask of you the favor to communicate whatever information or observations you may think will be of use to Mr. King in vindicating our rights where they are covered by the Treaty, or in adjusting, advantageously, our interests, where the obscurity of the treaty may require a compromise. To give you full possession of the subject I take the liberty of enclosing you a copy of what was said to Mr King thereon in July last[3] and of requesting that you will be good enough to let me have your communications at as early a day as you can make convenient. I have the Honor &ca.

JAMES MADISON.

Letterbook copy (DNA: RG 59, DL, vol. 14); Tr (M-Ar); Tr (MHi).

1. For the resolution of the Massachusetts legislature, see JM to Caleb Strong, 21 Apr. 1802, n. 2.

2. Left blank in all copies. In 1796 James Sullivan (1744–1808), who had written a history of Maine and who was at that time attorney general of Massachusetts, was appointed as agent to represent the U.S. before the commission authorized under the provisions of article 5 of the Jay treaty to determine what river was intended as the St. Croix River, the boundary between the U.S. and Nova Scotia. Sullivan was a prominent Boston lawyer and a pillar of the Republican party in New England, who served, among other political posts, as governor of Massachusetts, 1807–8 (Miller, *Treaties*, 2:249; Moore, *International Adjudications*, 1:15).

3. See JM to Rufus King, 28 July 1801 (*PJM-SS*, 1:484).

From Robert R. Livingston

No. 11.

DEAR SIR   PARIS 10h May 1802

I am just informed by a letter from Mr. Curwen at Antwerp that he has brought despatches for me but that he can not come up with them in less than 10 days. This will necessarily suspend any farther application to the government on the subject of debts or Luissania having not been favoured wh. a line from you since last decr. I wish to receive your instructions on these interesting subjects. By a letter of the 5th. of March from Mr. Lear[1] I find that the merchants are satisfied with the measures persued at St Domingo so that my application to the government on that subject will of course be considered as premature.[2] I however am very much surprised that the business has been so easily acquiesced in, I had hoped that past experience would have kept our merchants from granting new credits and thereby rendering the payment of their old debts more remote & our demands less attended to. In daily expectation of the arrival of these bills I have procured a *promise* from the minister of marine that they shall be pun[c]tualy paid. *But 60 days makes a great change in the state of things here and had our merchants given no farther credits money would have been found for* no provissions can be sent from here And the necessity for esstablishing a future credit wd have had great effect on the measures that might be taken with respect to our past contracts.

I was much pleased to find in Mr. Lears letter the instructions you had given him relative to his conduct with respect to France[3] it was an unequivocal proof that their suspicions as to our wishes & views with respect to the Islands were unfounded & it had a tendency to exonerate the government when our merchants were suspected of favouring the blacks. For this reason I put it in the hands of the Minister & told the first consul that I had done so, at which he appeared to be pleased.

A few days ago another plot was discovered *against the life of the first Consul in which Genl Delmas[4] & a Coll. of Dragoons were concerned both* have escaped from the officers sent to arrest them some obscure people have been taken up & the thing is as little noticed as possible tho it has given serious uneasiness *as discontents prevail in the army particularly in that part of it which composed the army of the Rhine who are dissatisfied with the little notice that is taken of Moreau[5]*—as well as with the number *of new officers that have been made from among those that were opposed to the revolution.* This among other circumstances will lead this government *to pass over this plot without endeavouring to dive too deeply into it.** I pray that I may not be quoted for any matter of intelligence from this country as I find I have been in some of our newspapers. You will find in the papers a state of the finances of france[6] I have no doubt that if no accident happens to the first Consul that they will be able very soon to look all demands in the face & that they will ultimately pay them but for the present every claim meets with great difficulty. I am very sorry that I have had yet no official information of the sums voted by us for carrying the treaty into effect as I would have made it the basis of a new demand. Indeed I know nothing of what passes with you except from my private friends who are often inaccurate. Not a single paper has reachd me from any port but New York tho there are constant arrivals from the eastern ports. As I have but just heard of the conveyance by which this goes

---

*You will find a vote of the Tribunate to give to the first consul "un gage é[c]latant de la reconnaissance nationale."[7] *This has excited various conjectures & by many considered as leading to an immediate change of government it has recd. some check from the discovery of the discontents I have mentioned but is not yet laid asside.*

I can only send you this hasty letter. After receiving your despatches I shall take such measures as you may direct & send you the result. I pray you to believe that I am Dear Sir With the highest essteem Your Most Obt hum: Servt.

R R LIVINGSTON

Draft (NHi: Livingston Papers); letterbook copy (NHi: Livingston Papers, vol. 1). Italicized passages are underlined in the draft; Livingston apparently intended them to be encoded.

1. Tobias Lear described the invasion of Saint-Domingue by French forces and the destruction of Cap Français by General Christophe and his troops. He went on to inform Livingston of the arrangements made with General Leclerc for Americans to supply provisions to the French army, which included bills of exchange drawn on the French government. Lear expressed confidence that the bills would be paid on time, although, he wrote, "many doubt them from their past experience of French Paper." He told Livingston he had suggested to Leclerc that both parties would benefit if arrangements could be made to pay the bills in the U.S. or, failing that, to establish a fund in Holland where the U.S. "had large payments to make" (Lear to Livingston, 5 Mar. 1802 [AAE: Political Correspondence, U.S., 54:187–92]).

2. See Livingston to JM, 27 Mar. 1802, and n. 5.

3. For JM's instruction to Lear not to "controvert or offend the authority of the French," see his letter of 8 Jan. 1802 (*PJM-SS*, 2:373). It was, as Lear put it in his letter to Livingston, "peculiarly pleasing to me, as it entirely accorded with my own sentiments" (Lear to Livingston, 5 Mar. 1802 [AAE: Political Correspondence, U.S., 54:191]). Livingston gave the original of Lear's letter to Talleyrand.

4. Antoine-Guillaume Delmas (1766–1813) was a promising general of division who served in Italy (1799) and with the Army of the Rhine under Moreau (1800). He spent the years from 1802 to 1813 in disgrace, returning briefly to active duty only to be killed at the Battle of Leipzig. His early retirement was due to his "outrageously irreligious attitude" and not to any failed assassination attempt (Tulard, *Dictionnaire Napoléon*, p. 587). A notice from a Paris newspaper, dated 10 May, printed in the *National Intelligencer* of 16 July 1802, detailed the circumstances surrounding Delmas's comments to Napoleon on the celebration of the Concordat.

5. Jean-Victor Moreau (1763–1813), as commander of the Army of the Rhine, was the architect of the successful campaign against Austria that culminated in the decisive victory at Hohenlinden in December 1800 and led to the peace negotiations at Lunéville. For a time, Moreau was one of the few who rivaled Napoleon in the affections of the army and the French people (*Biographie universelle* [1843–65 ed.], 29:256–62).

6. The French national accounts for *an X* and the projected budget for *an XI* were published in a supplement to the 12 Floréal an X (2 May 1802) issue of the Paris *Moniteur universel*.

7. On 8 May, Chabot de l'Allier, presiding over a session of the tribunate, vowed that Napoleon would be given a brilliant token of national recognition (*Moniteur universel*, 20 Floréal an X [10 May 1802]). While Napoleon expected to be offered the consulship for life, the legislature offered no more than reelection as first consul for ten years. When Napoleon balked at this measure, a group of senators proposed a national plebiscite on the question of a life consulship, and the first consul's life tenure was approved by over three million Frenchmen (Tulard, *Dictionnaire Napoléon*, pp. 1338–39).

From Robert R. Livingston

No. 12.

Dear Sir,   Paris 10th. May 1802

Since my letter of this morning I have recieved farther information on the subjects there hinted at. In consequence of the resolution of the Tribunat mentioned in my letter a motion was brought forward in the Senate to invest the First Consul with the Consulate for life. This was violently opposed—one of the members in a most animated speech was so hurried on that He droped the following memorable expression *what this Corsican this man from an island* where the *Romans* declared they could not find *a man worthy of being a slave.* It terminated in a resolution to offer an extention of the term ten years beyond the constitutional period. This I am credibly informed will be refused. Whether the matter will rest here is very uncertain. *We are perhaps at the moment of a new revolution.* What I told you of the plot was correct. Delmas has been deported & several others are suspected. The fact is the *dissatisfaction* among the *heads of the army* is pretty extensive. The troops from Italy are to be embarked as is said for St. Domingo & to be victualed out by the Italian states. It is however suspected that their destination is for the east & not for the west. The ready acquiescence of the two Emperors & Prussia in the late change in Italy & the *close connection* that has of late *taken place between* Count Marcoff & the first Consul & Ministers & their numerous conferences leads to this conclusion—*that the Porte* is to be sacrificed as *Poland was.*[1] Bernadottes destination is not changed—at least it was not 10 days ago.[2] He is at present one of the *discontented tho brother in law* to *Joseph Bonaparte.* You will see the necessity of the utmost secrecy on the subject of this letter. I am Dear Sir with the highest consideration your Most obt. He. St.

Robt R Livingston

RC (DNA: RG 59, DD, France, vol. 8); draft (NHi: Livingston Papers); letterbook copy (NHi: Livingston Papers, vol. 1). RC in a clerk's hand, signed by Livingston; docketed by Brent. Italicized words are those encoded by Livingston's secretary and decoded here by the editors. RC decoded interlinearly by JM. Draft filed at 16 May 1802.

1. The negotiations then taking place between the Russian ambassador, Count Markov, and Talleyrand were on the subject of the German states, not the Sublime Porte (Turkey) (Deutsch, *Genesis of Napoleonic Imperialism,* pp. 51–55).

2. For the rumor that General Bernadotte was to command the French expedition destined for the occupation of Louisiana, see JM to Lear, 8 Jan. 1802, and Livingston to JM, 26 Feb. 1802 (*PJM-SS,* 2:373, 374 n. 4, 493).

§ To Samuel Cabot. *10 May 1802, Department of State.* Acknowledges Cabot's letter of 1 May "communicating your intention to return to London as an assessor to the

Board of Commissioners under the 7th. Article of the Treaty of 1794. on the terms explained in my letter of the 24th. ulto. beyond which I am not authorized to countenance any expectation." Informs Cabot his account has been settled at the Treasury Department and a warrant will be issued in his favor for $1,058.98. Authorizes him to draw on the State Department for $375 "as an advance of one quarters salary"; future payments will be made on request in London. Charges him with enclosed letter to Gore and Pinkney.[1]

Letterbook copy (DNA: RG 59, IC, vol. 1). 1 p.

1. JM to Gore and Pinkney, 10 May 1802.

§ To Christopher Gore and William Pinkney. *10 May 1802, Department of State.* "Your Letter of february 17th.[1] with the Documents annexed were duly received and laid before the President, who was pleased in consequence of your representation, to direct a Letter to be written to Mr. Cabot of which a Copy is enclosed.[2] By Mr. Cabots answer, I find that he proposes to comply with your summons to resume the functions of assessor to your board, and on the terms explained to him. He will embark without delay, and will probably be the bearer of this Letter."

Letterbook copy (DNA: RG 59, IC, vol. 1). 1 p.

1. *PJM-SS*, 2:473–74.
2. JM to Cabot, 24 Apr. 1802.

§ To Richard O'Brien. *10 May 1802, Department of State.* Has received O'Brien's letters "down to that of   .[1] Several statements of your accounts are included in the reception, which will go for settlement to the Treasury Department." O'Brien's bills in favor of John Shaw were paid, and a recent bill for $200 drawn by his mother will be paid,[2] but no other drafts should be made until the settlement is closed. Explains arrangements for negotiations with the pasha of Tripoli. Instructs him to keep the dey of Algiers in the "proper temper" during the crisis. "The President having appointed Mr. Cathcart to succeed you as consul at Algiers, you have permission to return to the United States . . . as soon as he shall be ready to take your place. You will be sensible of the obligation you will be under, to prepare the way for [Cathcart's] favorable admission and successful exertions." Any balances due from the U.S. at Algiers should be made known to Cathcart, "thro' whom provision will be made for them."

Letterbook copy (DNA: RG 59, IC, vol. 1). 2 pp.

1. Left blank in letterbook.
2. For the bills drawn in favor of Capt. John Shaw of the *George Washington*, see O'Brien to JM, 1 Feb. 1802 (*PJM-SS*, 2:432–33). For the "bill of Mrs. Arundel, for Two hundred dollars, the annuity to which she is entitled out of her son Captain OBrian's salary," see Daniel Brent to Mark Langdon Hill, 13 May 1802, and JM to Gallatin, 13 July 1802 (DNA: RG 59, DL, vol. 14).

§ To Charles Pinckney. *10 May 1802, Department of State.* "The documents herewith transmitted will explain the case of John Dunlop and others, american citizens, whose property has been taken from them, in addition to personal wrongs, under proceedings for which the Spanish Government is answerable.[1] You will include it with other claims which you are instructed to urge on that Government. It is presumed that the reports made by the subordinate authorities concerned in those proceedings with the notarial paper now sent, will supply all the information necessary to a just decision. Should further testimony be required, it is intimated that it can be had."

Letterbook copy (DNA: RG 59, IM, vol. 6). 1 p. Enclosures not found.

1. In the summer of 1801 John Dunlap arrived in New Orleans with a flatboat loaded with flour, which he subsequently shipped in the *Good Hope* of Boston, bound for Havana. The ship was captured by a Spanish brig and taken to Campeche, Mexico, where the crew was imprisoned and the ship and cargo sold. Dunlap protested the capture as illegal and claimed the value of the cargo and damages from Spain (case of the *Good Hope* [DNA: RG 76, Spain, Treaty of 1819, Allowed Claims, vol. 38]; James Ross to JM, 3 Mar. 1803, and enclosure [DNA: RG 76, Spain, Treaty of 1819, Misc. Records, ca. 1801–24]).

§ From John M. Forbes. *10 May 1802, New York.* Plans to embark for London on the ship *Iris* "on or before Sunday next." Offers to carry dispatches to U.S. ministers in England or France.

RC (DNA: RG 59, CD, Hamburg, vol. 1). 1 p.

§ From Thomas W. Fox. *10 May 1802, Falmouth.* Reports arrival of many American ships at Falmouth with cargoes of flour, most of which have been forwarded to Spain; a few have been forwarded to Le Havre. In England the markets are "abundantly supplied." "It is said that English Ships with Flour, are not permitted to land their Cargoes in France. Freights and Seamen's Wages are falling fast, and Trade is dull in England. The Wheat in the ground in this Neighbourhood looks very indifferent for want of rain."

RC (DNA: RG 59, CD, Falmouth, vol. 1). 1 p. Signed by Thomas W. Fox "for Rob: W. Fox." Thomas W. Fox regularly acted as deputy for his brother Robert during the latter's frequent trips to the country (Thomas W. Fox to Rufus King, 18 Jan. 1797, 2 July 1798, 18 July 1799 [ibid.]).

§ From John Gavino. *10 May 1802, Gibraltar.* No. 87. His last dispatch, no. 86, was prepared on 5 May "for this Conveyance of Capn. Baron who is detained by Contrary Wind." Encloses translation of 13 Apr. letter in Italian just received from Consul Pulis at Malta[1] and copy of paragraph from 7 May letter from Consul Simpson at Tangier.[2] The case of arms sent by Rufus King for Tunis will be shipped by the *Constellation*, which sails 11 May.

RC and enclosures (DNA: RG 59, CD, Gibraltar, vol. 2). RC 1 p.; docketed by Brent as received 30 June. Enclosures 2 pp.

1. Joseph Pulis informed Gavino that the frigate *Boston* had left Malta to blockade Tripoli and that the brother of the pasha of Tripoli had arrived in Malta on 11 Apr. on his way to Bengasi in Tripoli. The two brothers, Pulis believed, had settled their differences, but the deposed pasha seemed to have "suspended proceeding" after being told of the American blockade.

2. "I have learnt that the two frigates so long building at the Port of Larach have at last been Launchd which please acquaint Comedor Truxton, or the Capns. of any of our frigates [that] may be with you."

§ From Edward Jones. *10 May 1802, Pointe-à-Pitre.* "I take the earliest Opportunity to inform you of the arrival of the French Squadron at this Port on the 6th inst. with 4 or 5000 troops, and that peaceable possession was taken of this Town and the neighbouring Forts the Same Evening. Genl. Richpanse with most of the Squadron has gone down to Basseterre, where it is beleived Resistance will be made by the Blacks. An Embargo was laid immediately on the arrival of the Fleet but is now off." Encloses a copy of his letter to the prefect "on his refusing to receive me as Coml. Agent of the U. States." The prefect then sent for him, and "after reading the 10th. Article of the Treaty . . . he observed it was not intended to admit Agents in the Colonies, at the Same time he assured me of his friendly disposition towards our Commerce—tho' in a Short time it will be restricted as before the Revolution." Basseterre is to be the only port of entry for Guadeloupe. Will forward the regulations as soon as they are published along with other news.

RC and enclosure (DNA: RG 59, CD, Guadeloupe, vol. 1). RC 2 pp. Enclosure is a copy of Jones to Daniel Lescallier, prefect at Guadeloupe, dated 8 May 1802 (1 p.; docketed by Brent).

§ From William Kirkpatrick. *10 May 1802, Málaga.* Reports arrival of *Philadelphia*, *Essex*, and *Constellation* since his dispatch of 22 Apr.; "they all proceeded on the 3 Instant for Gibraltar, where I have already advice of their arrival." Encloses a royal order [not found] granting premiums on certain items exported from Spain to foreign ports in Spanish vessels. Another royal order has been issued which removes the duty on pitch and tar imported into Spain in Spanish vessels. Encloses a note, a copy of which he has forwarded to Charles Pinckney, describing "further discriminations made by this Government in favor of its own Navigation."[1]

RC and enclosure (DNA: RG 59, CD, Málaga, vol. 1). RC 2 pp.; docketed by Brent. Postmarked Boston, 9 July. For surviving enclosure, see n. 1.

1. Kirkpatrick enclosed a statement dated 2 Apr. 1802 (3 pp.) in which he argued that "the Spanish Government has . . . imposed such extravagant duties on the importation of all the Productions of the West Indies by foreign Vessels, as to amount to a total Prohibition."

§ From Richard Söderström. *10 May 1802, Philadelphia.* Acknowledges JM's letter of 6 May about the case of the *Matilda*, captured by the French near St. Bartholomew, and states that "the last answer I had from His Swedish Majesty's Minister for Foreign Affairs on this Subject, is, that in consequence of the War between Sweden & England last Year the examination which His Swedish Majesty directed to be made, had been delayed, and of course could not before the Island was restored to Sweden be properly done, and for these reasons the decision of His Majesty had been postponed." Will write again on the subject and communicate the answer to JM.[1]

RC (DNA: RG 59, NFC, vol. 1). 1 p. In a clerk's hand, signed by Söderström.

1. Daniel Brent wrote to Warner and Leit, 14 May 1802 (DNA: RG 59, DL, vol. 14), to inform them of the contents of Söderström's letter.

§ From Israel Whelen. *10 May 1802, Philadelphia*. Encloses invoice of articles refused at Algiers and brought back by Captain Shaw on the *George Washington*. "Captn. Shaw understood the reason assigned was, that it was a considerable time since they had been ordered and that they were not wanted at present: probably Mr. OBrien has written to you on the subject and explained it."[1] Has checked the orders he received to procure the cargo for the first voyage of the *George Washington* to Algiers in 1800 and found that the list of articles required is dated 2 Apr. 1799, before his appointment as purveyor; he received the list in late June or early July 1800. "In the list of Articles which I understood were for the Bacri's, there are references to samples No 1 @ 5 inclusive, to the amount of $10.000; I was refered to Messrs. Gillaspy and Strong for an explanation, they having been desired to procure them; all that could be obtained was only to amount of $1307:52, before the sailing of the Vessel; those now returned were procured by them afterwards, to go by the next vessel agreeably to directions from Mr. Marshall. . . . I am informed they are articles not easily injured, but that the demand for them is very small, and that they are greatly fallen in price, but it may be of no service to keep them on hand; will you be pleased to direct what shall be done with them."[2]

RC and enclosure (DNA: RG 59, ML); letterbook copy (DNA: RG 45, Purveyor's Office, Philadelphia). RC 1 p. Enclosure is an "Invoice of sundries shipp'd on Account of the United States on board the Ship George Washington," 14 July 1801 (1 p.), which composed part of the inventory shipped in 1801 (see Whelen to JM, 14 July 1802, *PJM-SS*, 1:412–13 and nn.). The articles listed were gum benzoin and other chemical products.

1. O'Brien informed JM he was returning goods the purveyor had sent by mistake (O'Brien to JM, 25 Nov. 1801, *PJM-SS*, 2:272).
2. In a letter of 14 May 1802 Daniel Brent replied that JM wished Whelen to sell the articles in question "on the best terms that can be obtained" (DNA: RG 45, Subject File).

¶ From Colin Auld. Letter not found. *10 May 1802*. Mentioned in Daniel Brent to Auld, 14 May 1802 (DNA: RG 59, DL, vol. 14). Expresses concern over the appointment of a successor to Henry Potter, a judge of the U.S. Circuit Court for the Fifth Circuit. Brent replied that a commission for Edward Harris of North Carolina had been made out and sent to the president in Virginia, making it probable that the new judge would receive the commission in time to "take his seat on the Bench by the first of June next."

To William C. C. Claiborne

Sir,   Department of State May 11th. 1802.

Your several letters from November 24. to the 6th. of March last have been successively received.

Such of them as fell within the purview of the War Department were communicated to Genl. Dearborn, who I have reason to beleive has bestowed on the subjects recommended a favorable attention.

I inclose the opinion of the Attorney General in the case where you wished it.[1] Altho' the phraseology used by him does not refer to the technical distinction between a chance[r]y and common law jurisdiction, the former having no distinct establishment in the Eastern states, yet you will find your idea justified that equity can always releive against fraud.

It is to be regretted that so much violence and vicisitude as you describe should afflict the inhabitants of a settlement, which both in its infant and frontier character more particularly needs the advantages of concord and stability. We rely much for a remedy on your patriotic dispositions and prudent counsels which as they develope themselves cannot fail to inspire the well meaning with confidence, and to repress the activity of others.

I can not yet give you any final information whether the spaniards are to remain your neighbours, or are to exchange that character with the french. It seems certain that a transfer of Louisiana was stipulated to the latter. Whether they will be diverted from the object, or abandon it of themselves as their true interest would advise, remains for time to explain.

Congress adjourned on monday the   [2] instant. As soon as the laws of the session shall be ready, a copy will be forwarded to you. The course of their proceedings will have come to your knowledge thro' the Newspapers, a file of the latest of which is herewith inclosed. I hope that in future you will receive them more regularly thro' the ordinary channel. With sentiments &ca

James Madison.

Letterbook copy (DNA: RG 59, DL, vol. 14); Tr and Tr of enclosure (Ms-Ar: Claiborne Executive Journal). For enclosure, see n. 1.

1. Levi Lincoln to JM, 26 Mar. 1802.
2. Left blank in letterbook copy; Tr reads "3d."

To Thomas Jefferson

private

DEAR SIR   WASHINGTON May 11. 1802

I have nothing new since my last either from Europe or the W. Indies. The elections in N. York are not yet finally known.[1] It is suggested that the efforts of the minority have prevailed beyond the apprehensions of the majority. Cabot accepts his mission on the terms proposed to him.[2] I have just recd. letters from Erving shewing the turn which the affair took in London, to be such as was conjectured.[3] The compatibility of his Agency with an Assessorship was denied by the Commissioners & made the ground of rejecting him. The Controversy ended in his relinquishing his pretensions, & of course he is prepared for the ground on which we have placed him. He is evidently soured with King & the Board, but professes a superiority to all personal considerations when in the way of his public duty. I inclose a solicitation for office according to the wish of the candidate.[4] I inclose also a letter from S. Sayre which will deserve no other attention than as it brings to view the necessity of thinking of proper persons for the service he recommends himself for.[5] I am at a loss for proper characters myself, & I do not find that any are particularly in the view of those more capable of pointing them out. My horses are not yet arrived. Yrs. always most respectfully & affectionately

JAMES MADISON

Yruyo has just delivered me a long narrative of a riot in Philada. which ended in an insulting destruction of a Spanish flag in the harbour, for which he claims due reparation to the honor of his Master.[6] He suggests that a reward be proclaimed for the apprehension of the offenders, which of itself will heal the wound, if the offenders cannot be traced. I shall consult Mr. Lincoln in the case. My first thought is that a letter be written to Govr. McKean, on the idea of its not being within federal cognizance.

RC (DLC: Jefferson Papers). Docketed by Jefferson as received 13 May.

1. The final report of the New York elections as printed in the *National Intelligencer* on 7 June 1802 (taken from the *Albany Register*) showed that of the seventeen representatives elected to the U.S. House of Representatives from that state, eleven were Republicans. All eight senators elected to the New York legislature were Republican, as were seventy-six out of ninety-nine assemblymen.

2. See Samuel Cabot to JM, 1 May 1802.

3. See George W. Erving to JM, 6 Mar. 1802 (two letters).

4. Enclosure not identified.

5. Stephen Sayre to JM, 6 May 1802.

6. Yrujo to JM, 3 May 1802.

To Thomas McKean

SIR   DEPARTMENT OF STATE May 11. 1802

The Minister of his Catholic Majesty, has complained to this Department of an indignity offered to his sovereign during a late riot in Philadelphia, in which besides certain violences committed on a number of Spanish sailors, the flag of a spanish ship was torn down and destroyed with the most aggravating insults. A copy of his representation on the subject, is herewith enclosed.[1] As the transaction is within the cognizance of the State authority, I have to request that you will cause the proper proceedings to be instituted for investigating its merits, and for doing what may be right in the case. I have the honor to be &ca.

JAMES MADISON.

Letterbook copy (DNA: RG 59, DL, vol. 14).

1. See Yrujo to JM, 3 May 1802.

To John Morton

SIR.   DEPARTMENT OF STATE. May 11th. 1802

A petition has been addressed to the President by Charles Drew,[1] representing that he sailed from Norfolk in Virginia in July last, for porto rico, where he purchased a Brig and proceeded to the Havanna; that he sailed thence for Philadelphia, but his vessel being upset, he and his crew were thrown back to the Havanna; That he again shipped himself at that place for Philadelphia, as master of the sloop Sally, one of whose owners having broken open the chest of a spaniard, the whole crew with himself, were thrown into a dungeon. He paints his situation as deplorable and prays that something may be done for his relief. You will please to enquire into the case, and to claim for him whatever may be due to him on the score of justice or humanity. I am Sir &c.

JAMES MADISON.

Letterbook copy (DNA: RG 59, IC, vol. 1).

1. Charles Drew's petition (not found) is listed in Jefferson's Epistolary Record (DLC: Jefferson Papers) as dated 24 Feb. 1802 and received by Jefferson 2 Apr. 1802. For Drew's case, see Vincent Gray to JM, 27 Sept. 1802.

To Charles Pinckney

Department of State, May 11th. 1802.

My last was of the 30th of March.[1] We are still without a line from you since your arrival at Madrid, and feel an increasing solicitude to hear from you on the subject of Louisiana. The latest information from Paris has confirmed the fact that it was ceded by a Treaty prior to that of March 1801; and notwithstanding the virtual denial of the Cession in the early conversations between Mr Livingston and the Minister of Foreign relations, a refusal of any explanations at present, seems to admit that the Cession has taken place. Still there are chances of obtaining a reversal of the transaction. The repugnance of the United States to it is and will be pressed in a manner that cannot be without some effect. It is known that most of the French statesmen best informed on the subject, disapprove of it. The pecuniary difficulties of the French Government must also be felt as a check; whilst the prospect of a protracted and expensive war in St. Domingo must form a very powerful obstacle to the execution of the project. The Counsels of England appear to have been torpid on this occasion. Whether it proceed from an unwillingness to risk a fresh altercation with France, or from a hope that such a neighbourhood between France and the United States would lead to collisions which might be turned to her advantage, is more than I can decide. The latter consideration might justly have great weight with her, but as her eyes may be more readily turned to the immediate and certain purposes to be answered to her rival, it is to be presumed, that the policy of England will contribute to thwart the acquisition. What the intentions of Spain may be, we wait to learn from you. Verbal information from inofficial sources has led us to infer that she disowns the instrument of Cession, and will vigorously oppose it. Should the Cession actually fail from this or any other cause, and Spain retain New Orleans and the Floridas, I repeat to you the wish of the President that every effort and address be employed to obtain the arrangement by which the Territory on the East side of the Mississippi including New Orleans may be ceded to the United States, and the Mississippi made a common boundary, with a common use of its navigation, for them and Spain. The inducements to be held out to Spain, were intimated in your original instructions on this point. I am charged by the President now to add, that you may not only receive and transmit a proposition of guaranty of her territory beyond the Mississippi, as a condition of her ceding to the United States the Territory including New Orleans on this side, but in case it be necessary may make the proposition yourself, in the forms required by our Constitution. You will infer from this enlargement of your authority, how much importance is attached to the object in question, as securing a precious acquisition to the United

States, as well as a natural and quiet boundary with Spain; and will derive from this consideration additional motives to discharge with a prudent zeal the task committed to you. With sentiments of Great respect &c. &c.

JAMES MADISON

Letterbook copy (DNA: RG 59, IM, vol. 6).

1. Since his letter of 30 Mar., JM had written to Pinckney twice about spoliation cases (JM to Pinckney, 8 Apr. and 10 May 1802).

§ To John Gavino. *11 May 1802, Department of State, Washington.* "Your several Letters up to No. 33,[1] of the 18. March, have been received. The accounts and vouchers which are enclosed in that, are sent to the Treasury Department to be adjusted. I request you to forward the enclosed Letters for Messrs OBrien and Eaton, by the first safe opportunities that offer from Gibraltar."

Letterbook copy (DNA: RG 59, IC, vol. 1). 1 p. Enclosures were probably JM to Eaton and to O'Brien, both dated 10 May 1802.

1. JM's clerk should have written "No. 83." Gavino's dispatches numbered 82 through 85 have not been found. His no. 81 is dated 30 Jan. 1802 (*PJM-SS*, 2:430), and his no. 86 is dated 5 May 1802.

§ From Griffith Evans. *11 May 1802, Office of the Board, Philadelphia.* Acknowledges JM's letter of 7 May informing him of the abolition of the Board of Commissioners under article 6 of the Jay treaty and of the consequent termination of his appointment. Has received a "similar intimation" from Thornton and will dispose of the papers as directed.

Letterbook copy (CSmH: Philadelphia Commission Letterbook 1). 1 p.

To Alexander J. Dallas

SIR   DEPARTMENT OF STATE May 12th. 1802.

The Minister of his Catholic Majesty has complained to this Department of certain outrages committed on Spanish subjects and a spanish flag in the harbor of Philadelphia. The copy of his representation inclosed will explain the particulars of the transaction.[1] As it is within the cognizance of the State authority, Governor McKean has been requested to cause the proper proceedings to be instituted for doing in it whatever the law may warrant. In order to give the more satisfaction to the spanish Government, by manifesting the interest which Government of the United States take in the result, it is thought proper that you should afford your aid in the prosecution, and I have accordingly to make that request of you. With great respect &ca.

JAMES MADISON.

Letterbook copy (DNA: RG 59, DL, vol. 14).

1. See Yrujo to JM, 3 May 1802.

To William Jarvis

SIR,   WASHINGTON, DEPARTMENT OF STATE, May 12th 1802.
   The President of the United Insurance Company, of New York, has represented to this Department,[1] that in an important suit to which they are Party, in the Supreme Court of the State, essential facts are in question which can not otherwise be established than by the Minister of foreign Affairs to her faithful Majesty;[2] for taking which a Commission will be forwarded. To this representation, which will be more fully communicated by themselves, a request is added, that it may be recommended to you to afford the Commission whatever facility may be in your power. As the object in this case is simply to educe truth, and promote Justice, it is hoped that the dignity of the Witness may not be an insuperable bar to the wishes of the party, and that your Countenance of the application, which You will of course manage with as much delicacy as possible, will not be construed into disrespect either to others or to yourself. I am, Sir, very respectfully, Your Mo: Obedt Servant,

JAMES MADISON

RC (MiD: Rare Books Collection). In Brent's hand, signed by JM.

1. Nicholas Low to JM, 6 May 1802.
2. JM sent a nearly identical letter to Charles Pinckney in which the preceding section reads: " . . . which cannot otherwise be established than by the testimony of several persons at Madrid, subjects of his Catholic Majesty" (JM to Pinckney, 12 May 1802 [DNA: RG 59, IM, vol. 6]).

To Carlos Martínez de Yrujo

DEPARTMENT OF STATE May 12. 1802.
   Mr. Madison has the Honor to inform the Chevalier d'Yrujo that no time has been lost in taking into Consideration the subject of his Note of

the 3d. instant; and that the Governor of Pennsylvania has been requested to cause to be instituted the proper proceedings for ascertaining legally the offences which have been committed against the subjects of his Catholic Majesty, and for bringing the offenders to justice. The Chevalier d'Yrujo will see in this instant interposition, on the part of the United States, a manifestation of their respect for his Catholic Majesty; and Mr. Madison equally flatters himself that the result will be as satisfactory, as the course taken will have been regular and fair.

JAMES MADISON.

Letterbook copy (DNA: RG 59, DL, vol. 14).

From Levi Lincoln

SIR   WASHINGTON May 12. 1802

I have the honor to enclose to you the communications which I recd., yesterday, from the Spanish minister,[1] together with my ideas on the Subject.

I can find no provision, in the Constitution, in any law of the United States, or in the treaty with Spain, which reaches the case—I have examined them particularly. The communication states a transaction, involving a highhanded breach of the peace, an outrageous riot, and an aggravated violation of the law of nations. The principles of this law, touching the present Subject, are stated generally & summarily in Vattel B. 2. Cap. 6.[2] The law of nations is considered as a part of the municipal law of each State. Their Courts, must be competent, to animadvert, on the above stated offences. I doubt the competency of the federal Courts, there being no statute recognizing the offence. Suppose a foreign minister should be grossly defamed, and he should choose to pursue the offender criminaliter, could it be, in the federal courts? I think not. The tearing of the national Flag, and other acts of insult, rendered the riot more attrocious. Probably the matter, in some of its circumstances has been misrepresented to Mr Yrujo. I presume the Sheriff had writs in favour of those mechanicks, who were about fastening the ship with chains, and that they were acting, in aid of him, in serving these processes.

I think the measures you proposed, of asking the Govr. of Pennsylvania, to cause an enquiry to be made, and the legal steps to be taken to bring the offenders to punishment are the proper ones. If the object of the peoples collecting, was an unlawful one, all & every one are liballe [sic] in law for what any one did. If so, or if the leaders are known, there can be no need for a proclamation offering a reward for the discovery of what is sufficiently notorious. Perhaps the Spanish minister may be particular, as it respects the proclamation—if so, and it should be thought expedient, & due the dignity of his nation to issue one, perhaps one, merely, warning of the danger, and cautioning against a repetition of such a daring outrage in future, would be the most useful. These are however only hasty ideas. I am Sir most respectfully your very Hum Sevt

LEVI LINCOLN

RC (DNA: RG 59, LOAG). Mistakenly docketed by Brent, "March 12th 1802."

1. See Yrujo to JM, 3 May 1802, about which JM consulted Lincoln (JM to Jefferson, 11 May 1802).

2. Book 2, chapter 6, of Vattel's *Law of Nations* deals with the "Concern a Nation may have in the Actions of its Citizens," that is, "what share a state may have in the actions of its citizens, and what are the rights and obligations of sovereigns in this respect" (Emmerich de Vattel, *The Law of Nations; or, Principles of the Law of Nature* [1st U.S. ed.; New York, 1796], p. 224).

From Robert R. Livingston

No. 13.

DEAR SIR   PARIS 12th. May 1802

I have only to add to my last that as I conjectured the Consul has rejected the continuance of his term for ten yrs Upon the ground of his having recd his office from the people they only can add to it. The Council of State have in consequence referred it to the people to determine not whether he shall be consul for *ten years* but for life. This business creates not the least sensation here Nor would it if by a decree of the Senate he was declared emperor of the Gauls. *The people are perfectly dead to political objects & alive only to pleasure & the means of procuring it.* The mode in which the sense of the people is to be taken (being similar to that by which the constitution was adopted) will insure its success even if any opposition—which is not probable—might otherwise have arisen.

The next step (& indeed I now think a necessary one) will be to fix the succession. *Here there is some difficulty. Joseph Bonaparte the elder brother is very unambitious—Lucian the 2d will hardly stick at any thing & it is said that his elder brother is fearful of being the only obstacle to his succession. The Consul wishes Louis who has married Madam Bonaparte['s] daughter who is now pregnant. Should she have a son reasons which I do not explain will if possible point the succession to him. Be however prepared to see a new dinasti esstablished in the present family & the old forms as much as possible restored. A house of lords or at least a pe[e]rage would be esstablished were it not for the difficulty of giving the wealth necessary to its support. I still however believe that Strings & Stars will eer long be found among the esstablishments of this Court.*[1] I have yet recd. no letters

219

from you but those of Decr last.[2] Mr. Sumter having determined to resign for reasons which I presume he will explain to the president[3] I trust that the system of appointing Secretaries to the Legation in which there are obvious inconveniences will be laid asside & that I may be permitted to name one who shall be subject to my particular regulations I shall make no appointment in my own family nor any which the president shd not fully approve. I have the honor to be dear Sir with the highest essteem Your Most Obt &c

Draft (NHi: Livingston Papers); partial Tr (DLC: Jefferson Papers); letterbook copy (NHi: Livingston Papers, vol. 1). RC not found but acknowledged in JM to Livingston, 15 Oct. 1802 (DNA: RG 59, IM, vol. 6). Italicized passages are underlined in the draft; Livingston apparently intended them to be encoded. For partial Tr, see n. 2.

1. In May 1802 Napoleon established the Legion of Honor, a new nobility based on loyalty to the first consul (Louis Madelin, *The Consulate and the Empire, 1789–1809* [London, 1934], pp. 146–48).

2. Partial Tr consists of the remainder of the letter, except for the complimentary close. It is docketed on the verso by Brent, who sent it to Jefferson (see Brent to JM, 7 Sept. 1802).

3. The resignation of Thomas Sumter, Jr., as secretary of legation in Paris resulted from a dispute with Livingston over the extent of the secretary's duties. Sumter insisted that his services would not be "dictated by the discretion of the Minister" and that Jefferson "could not have meant to offer me the situation of a drudge." Livingston complained that it was impossible to work with a man "who splits hairs about the extent of his duties, who weighs in the nicest balance, what is public & what a private correspondence, & who treats his principal with rudeness" (Sumter to Livingston, 27 Apr. 1802, Livingston to Sumter, 27 Apr. 1802, and Livingston to Jefferson, 4 May 1802 [DLC: Jefferson Papers]; Sumter to JM, 18 May 1802).

§ From William Savage. *12 May 1802, Kingston, Jamaica.* Reports that since his 25 Mar. dispatch, "three American Seamen was wantonly impressed & taken onboard a Transport—on my Application to the Admiral they was immediately liberated." Has found it necessary to assist several distressed seamen to return to the U.S. Encloses his last quarter's account amounting to $2,312.30. Has drawn on JM in favor of Mary Willis for $300.

RC (DNA: RG 59, CD, Kingston, Jamaica, vol. 1). 1 p. Docketed by Brent, with his note: "sent the account & vouchers referred to, to the Auditor's Office, June 6th 1802." Enclosed account not found. Filed with the RC is a list of American seamen "onboard Men of War on the Jamaica Station" and those discharged, as of 12 May 1802 (1 p.).

To Nicholas Low

SIR,   DEPARTMENT OF STATE May 13. 1802.

In consequence of yours to me, of the 6th. inst. I send you herewith a letter for Mr. Pinckney and one for Mr. Jarvis.[1] The last is nearly a copy of the first, which goes to you under a flying seal. You will see by that, that you are relied upon for a full Communication to these Gentlemen of the business recommended to their care by these Letters. I request you [to] forward the other letter for Mr. Pinckney, which is sent under this enclosure, by the first safe opportunity from New York. I am &ca.

JAMES MADISON.

Letterbook copy (DNA: RG 59, DL, vol. 14).

1. See JM to William Jarvis, 12 May 1802, and n. 2.

From James Monroe

DEAR SIR   RICHMOND May 13. 1802.

This will be presented you by Mr. Gauvain who with his Lady have made us a visit since I wrote you last. He is the Gentn. of whom I wrote you & whose trip I wished to delay a week on account of particular circumstances, of a domestic nature. He was in my family near a year, or indeed rather more, after the appointment of Mr. Skipwith to the consulate. He is amiable, well informed, perfectly upright, and attached to our country. His Lady is also very estimable for her connections in France & her own merit. Two of his sisters are married to Americans, one to Mr. Taney of Maryld., the other to Mr. Vans of Boston, the latter formerly appointed consul & I believe removed by Mr. Adams, tho of that I am not certain.[1] This gentn. passing thro' washington has express'd a wish to be personally[2] to you, to promote which object I have taken the liberty to give him this letter of introduction. Our best respects to Mrs. Madison, sincerely I am Dear Sir yours

JAS. MONROE

RC (DLC).

1. William Vans was appointed U.S. consul at Morlaix, France, in December 1794. His commission was revoked by John Adams in 1798 because of Vans's part ownership of a French privateer. Adams subsequently nominated William Foster, Jr., for the post (*Senate Exec. Proceedings*, 1:165; Timothy Pickering to Vans, 15 Dec. 1798, and William Vans Murray to Pickering, 15 July 1799, Frederick S. Allis, Jr., ed., *The Timothy Pickering Papers* [MHi microfilm ed.; 69 reels; Boston, 1966], reels 10, 25; *PJM-SS*, 2:397).

2. Monroe omitted a word here.

§ From James Simpson. *13 May 1802, Tangier.* No. 39. Forwards his dispatch no. 38 [19 Mar. 1802]. Reports that the emperor's plan to send wheat to Tripoli has been suspended but has not been entirely given up, despite his and the Swedish agent's efforts. Relays intelligence received 12 May that on 6 May the governor of Rabat had been ordered to send a schooner to Dar el Beida to load wheat for Tripoli and that a British brig had been chartered at Gibraltar for the same voyage. "Frequent representations on the distress of the people in Tripoly for Grain, I know have been made to Muley Soliman—whether his well known Charitable disposition towards all Mussulmen in want, may have induced him to endeavour at sending these supplys of Wheat (for he gives it gratis) or if it be done as an *aid* in their present Contest, it is impossible for me to say." His opinion is that "if Muley Soliman could give effectual aid to Tripoly in its present Contest for obtaining Subsidies from Sweden and the United States, he would do it." And should peace be settled with Tripoli on other terms than those of the former treaty, believes "this Government would be very ready to make a fresh attempt to get quit of that of 1786 with the United States." Has lodged "ample information on all these subjects" at Gibraltar for Commodore Truxtun and also advised the captains of the frigates "on this Station." The two frigates built at Rabat were launched on 2 May; "I am assured they are pierced for 26 Guns each on the Main deck; if so they must be much crowded, for no Ship of a suitable length, and draft of Water for that force, can enter any of the Ports of this Empire." Has heard nothing yet of the purchase of the small cruisers the emperor was said to have intended to station at Tangier. Has not yet closed on the purchase of the house but holds firm at his offered price of 4,000 ducats. The emperor, having had proof that a "very powerfull Tribe" living between Fès and the Atlas Mountains "had made offers of their assistance to two different Princes of the Royal Family towards dethroning him, . . . attacked their Villages with great Slaughter & very trifling loss to his Army." By all accounts, the plague has spread eastward and reached Oran.

RC (DNA: RG 59, CD, Tangier, vol. 1). 3 pp.; docketed by Brent as received 19 July. Extract printed in Knox, *Naval Documents, Barbary Wars*, 2:153. Jefferson communicated an extract to Congress with his annual message on 15 Dec. 1802 (printed in *ASP, Foreign Relations*, 2:465).

§ From Elias Vander Horst. *13 May 1802, Bristol*. Transmits a copy of his letter of 3 May. "In some of my former Letters I mentioned, that from the great extent of Sea-Coast within my Consular District, I had found it necessary to appoint five different Agents to act for me at the principal Ports." Lists them and requests that five sets of U.S. laws be sent "to guide them in the execution of the duties of their Office." Observes that the weather continues to be favorable for agriculture "though rather too dry at present." Encloses newspapers and a London price current.

RC (DNA: RG 59, CD, Bristol, vol. 2). 2 pp. First page written at the bottom of a copy of Vander Horst's 3 May dispatch. Enclosures not found.

To [Levi Lincoln?]

Dear Sir   May 14. 1802

Will you be so good as to forward me Govr. St. Clair's papers by the Mail as soon as the two Secretaries Dearborn & Smith with yourself shall have examined them. I make the request on the idea that they can be spared in time to be examined by me during my absence.[1] I expect to return to this place about the 1st. of June, and to be four days on my journey back. The mail leaves this every tuesday & friday evening before 7 OClock for Orange Court House, to which place I am to be addressed. Yrs sincerely

James Madison

RC (owned by Marshall B. Coyne, Washington, D.C., 1992). The addressee is not indicated but was probably Lincoln, since Albert Gallatin had already written a memorandum on the St. Clair case on 30 Apr. before leaving for New York. Lincoln wrote his report on the case on 25 May; he noted in his letter to Jefferson of 9 June that he had then delivered the papers to Robert Smith (Cunningham, *Process of Government under Jefferson*, pp. 51–54; Lincoln to Jefferson, 9 June 1802, Carter, *Territorial Papers, Northwest*, 3:227).

1. JM and his family left Washington for a two-week stay at Montpelier on 14 May (Daniel Brent to James Ross, 14 May 1802 [DNA: RG 59, DL, vol. 14]).

From Thomas Jefferson

Th: J. to J. Madison   Monticello May 14. 1802

I wrote you on the 9th. but whether the new post had got into motion at that time I know not. It related chiefly to the roads. Yesterday I recieved your's of the 7th. & 11th. It really seems doubtful whether the conduct of Le Clerc proceeds from the extravagance of his own character, or from a settled design in his government. So many things lately wear the latter appearance that one cannot be without suspicion. Your letter to Livingston will give them an opportunity of developing their views. The fact respecting the insult on the Spanish flag deserves enquiry. I believe the fray began by one of the crew knocking down a peace officer, where⟨upon⟩ the sheriff & posse took the whole crew, and had them committed, taking possession of the ship in the meanwhile for safe-keeping. This I have collected from the newspapers & some anonymous letters sent me on the occasion.[1] If the state government will take it up, it will be best to give it that direction. Sayre's letter is ⟨hi⟩ghly ⟨im⟩pudent. I recieved from your office some commissions to sign. Such as you had signed I now return to the office.

The others I have thought it would be sh⟨ortest⟩ to ⟨en⟩close to yourself to be left at Orange C. H. Affectionate [*illegible*] and respect.

FC (DLC: Jefferson Papers).

1. The Philadelphia *Gazette of the U.S.* of 8 Apr. 1802 carried a report of the incident. One anonymous letter was addressed to Jefferson on 14 Apr. by "Yankey Doodle" (DLC: Jefferson Papers).

§ From William C. C. Claiborne. *14 May 1802, "Near Natchez."* "The Legislature of this Territory met in Session on the 3rd. Instant and on the day following I made to the two Houses a Communication of which the enclosed is a Copy."[1] The legislature adjourned 13 May after making "several very wholesome Laws, amongst which is an Act to establish a College in the Mississippi Territory. . . . This College shall bear the name of 'Jefferson College.'" Washington, a town near Natchez that is "handsomely situated, well supplied with excellent Spring water, and said to be the healthiest Spot in the District," has been fixed by law as the site of future sessions of the legislature. During the last session, the legislature elected Thomas M. Green,[2] "a respectable and wealthy Farmer, warmly attached to the United States," to replace Narsworthy Hunter as the territory's delegate in Congress.

Letterbook copy and copy of enclosure (Ms-Ar: Claiborne Executive Journal). Letterbook copy 2 pp. Printed in Rowland, *Claiborne Letter Books*, 1:107–8. Enclosure 5 pp. (see n. 1).

1. In his address to the territorial legislature, Claiborne suggested amendments to the law requiring the publication of the laws and journals of the legislature and the act regulating the judiciary. He proposed a general health law "to prevent the introduction of the Small-pox, or other infectious Diseases," as well as a law establishing a "Seminary of Learning" (printed ibid., 1:97–101).

2. Thomas Marston Green (1758–1813), son of Col. Thomas Green and brother of Everard Green, served as the Mississippi Territory's delegate to Congress from December 1802 to March 1803 (William Buckner McGroarty, "Diary of Captain Philip Buckner," *WMQ*, 2d ser., 6 [1926]: 203–4 n. 55).

§ From Richard O'Brien. *14 May 1802, Algiers.* Reports sailing of twelve Algerine corsairs since 29 Mar.; so far they have "sent in" two Neapolitan ships, two Spanish vessels, and two French brigs. One American and two Swedish frigates were patrolling Tripoli on 31 Mar.; at that date no captures had been made by Tripolitan corsairs, all of which were then in port. "There Seems to be by the definitive treaty a prospect of a reform intended with the Barbary States. It would be our interest to facilitate the event. . . . The timber & Spikes on the Annuities with this place is anxiously Expected.[1] Allso Money to pay our debts to The Bacris &c." Adds in a postscript of 15 May that a forty-four-gun Algerine frigate has brought in a captured forty-four-gun Portuguese frigate. "The portugee has 312 men landed here & 42 killed & wounded, . . . a great affair to Algiers, & frigt. & Crew is a loss & dishonoure to portugal, which Cannot be retrived. . . . Further this day The dey declared That all Christian Corsairs which . . . had not Medittiranian passports shd. be Condemned & Considered as Enemies."

RC (DNA: RG 59, CD, Algiers, vol. 6). 1 p.; docketed by Brent. Postscript written on cover. Another copy (ibid.) is docketed by Wagner as received 31 Jan. and includes a more detailed postscript. An earlier version of the same dispatch (ibid.), dated 10 May with no postscript, mentions only three captures by Algerine corsairs.

1. JM was puzzled by O'Brien's reference to timber and spikes, and he directed Brent to write to Israel Whelen about the matter. Brent wrote Whelen that this was one of several letters where O'Brien had referred to the same expectation, "which the Secretary is at a loss to understand," and requested him "to explain it if you can." Whelen replied that O'Brien had sent him a copy of his letter to the secretary of state of 10 Mar. 1800 containing "a project for a ship" and an order for "timber, spikes &ca.," which Whelen had forwarded to the department on 27 Dec. 1800. Whelen wrote that he had received no orders to send the items and had "never supposed myself authorized to do any thing in the Algerine business, but what was particularly directed by the Secretary of State" (Brent to Whelen, 23 July 1802 [DNA: RG 59, DL, vol. 14]; Whelen to Brent, 24 July 1802 [DNA: RG 59, ML]; see also O'Brien to JM, 1 Feb. 1802, *PJM-SS*, 2:433).

From Alexander J. Dallas

The United States vs David Jackson	Circt. Ct. for the East Dist. of Penna.—May Session 1802 Larceny on the High seas. Trial and Conviction 14 May 1802

Sɪʀ   Pʜɪʟᴀ. 15 May 1802

David Jackson, a boy of fifteen years of age, was yesterday convicted of Larceny in the Circuit Court. The Jury have requested me to transmit his petition, and their recommendation, for a Pardon.[1]

He is a poor Lad, without family, or friends, in this part of the Continent. The Captain, with whom he sailed, and who prosecuted for the offence, does not give him a good character; but if the President shall deem it proper to grant a Pardon,[2] I will endeavour to prevail on the Inspectors of the Prison to exert themselves, in obtaining a Master, with whom there will be some chance of his reformation. I am, with the sincerest esteem, Sir, Yr. mo. obedt Servt.

A. J. Dᴀʟʟᴀs

RC and enclosures (DNA: RG 59, Petitions for Pardon, no. 48). RC docketed by Brent, with his note: "encloses a Petition of *David Jackson*, convicted of larceny, for a pardon—which was granted June 1st. 1802." For enclosures, see n. 1.

1. Dallas enclosed Jackson's petition to Jefferson (1 p.) for pardon from the conviction of

larceny for stealing two pairs of shoes valued at four dollars. On the verso is the jury's recommendation for mercy, 14 May 1802 (1 p.).

2. Daniel Brent sent this letter directly to Jefferson at Monticello (Brent to Jefferson, 21 May 1802 [DLC: Jefferson Papers]; Brent to Dallas, 21 May 1802 [DNA: RG 59, DL, vol. 14]); the president then sent it on to JM with his determination to pardon Jackson (Jefferson to JM, 24 May 1802).

§ From John J. Murray. *15 May 1802, New York.* Has made the arrangements described in his letter of 29 Jan. [not found] and has booked passage for himself and his family on the ship *Fanny* bound to Greenock; leaves about 1 June. As soon as possible after his arrival in Scotland, he will proceed to London for a few days. Offers to carry dispatches to Great Britain.

RC (DNA: RG 59, CD, Glasgow, vol. 1). 1 p.

§ From Elias Vander Horst. *15 May 1802, Bristol.* Reports the case of Mason Ryan, an American seaman discharged from the Bristol infirmary, for whom he booked passage on the ship *Alexander*, Capt. Ebenezer McIntosh. The captain refused to accept the infirm sailor, preferring to pay the $30 penalty once in the U.S. "Having no power to compel him either to receive the Man or to pay the penalty," reports the case to JM so that steps can be taken to deter such behavior in future. "If this benevolent & necessary Law is to be thus disregarded it must . . . leave our distressed Seamen often to perish in foreign Countries, as the allowance granted to them in case of sickness is by no means adequate to the expences." Trusts that a remedy for "this evil" will soon be found; otherwise, "it must in it's Tendency be highly injurious to our Navigation & Commerce." The mayor of Bristol would have assisted him in the case but lacked the power. Encloses local newspapers and a London price current.

RC (DNA: RG 59, CD, Bristol, vol. 2). 2 pp.; docketed by Brent as received 9 Aug. Enclosures not found.

§ From George Stacey. *16 May 1802, Chester.* Informs JM of his arrival at Chester from Ile de France. "Mr. Buchanan having been appointed Agent for the United States at that place, I conceived it a duty I owed to my family to quit the Colony by the earliest occasion, and accordingly advised that Government of my intention to resign my public functions, as you will see by the Copy of a Letter from the Administrators General of the Colony to me." Reports that news of European peace reached Ile de France from the government of the Cape of Good Hope several days before his departure, "which put a stop to the expedition of privateers." Offers to send JM "every intelligence I can, which may be useful to our Country," and notes that JM can address him "to care of Messrs. Davy Roberts & Co. Philadelphia."

RC and enclosure (DNA: RG 59, CD, Port Louis, vol. 1). RC 3 pp.; docketed by Brent. Misfiled at 1803. Enclosure is a copy of a letter from Governor-General Magallon and Intendant Chanvalon to Stacey, 4 Pluviôse an X (14 Jan. 1802) (3 pp.; in French), expressing satisfaction with the latter's conduct in office.

§ From James Blake. *17 May 1802, Baltimore.* "As it is probable, it will not be in my power to go to France, as soon as I expected, on account of the unsettled state of my affairs in this country—I beg leave to recommend my brother, D. T. Blake, Attorney at law, as a fit person to execute the duties of Vice-Commercial Agent in my department at Antwerp. He is a man of a fair reputation, and respectable talents, but of a sickly habit of body, which would induce him to change the climate for some time."

RC (DNA: RG 59, CD, Antwerp, vol. 1). 1 p.

§ From Rufus King. *17 May 1802, London.* No. 67. Reports strong support for the definitive treaty in Parliament despite Lord Grenville's speech against it. Will send a copy of the debates as soon as published.[1] Encloses a copy of the convention and additional articles between Great Britain and Russia,[2] together with the acts of accession of Denmark and Sweden. The article concerning trade with the colonies and Lord Grenville's speech on the Russian convention promote "as free a Trade between the Colonies and the North of Europe as may be carried on between them and the United States." This is a departure from the present system and may in time eliminate the "discrimination in favour of the direct Trade between the United States and Great Britain sanctioned by the last Treaty between Great Britain and Russia."[3] Also encloses a copy of the law imposing duties upon imports and exports and vessel tonnage. Eaton reports from Tunis that the gifts pleased the bey; Gavino has received the arms prepared by Mortimer and Company.

RC (DNA: RG 59, DD, Great Britain, vol. 10); letterbook copy (NHi: Rufus King Papers, vol. 55). RC 3 pp.; marked duplicate; in a clerk's hand, docketed by Brent as received 19 Aug. Printed in King, *Life and Correspondence of Rufus King,* 4:127. Enclosures not found.

1. Part of the House of Commons debate over the definitive treaty was published on 26 and 27 July 1802 in the *National Intelligencer.*
2. The additional articles to the convention between Russia and Great Britain were signed 20 Oct. 1801. Both the convention and articles were ratified by Great Britain on 5 May 1802 (Clive Parry and Charity Hopkins, eds., *An Index of British Treaties, 1101–1968* [3 vols.; London, 1970], 2:136, 137).
3. The previous convention between the two countries was agreed to in the summer of 1799 (ibid., 2:134).

From Daniel Brent

S<small>IR</small>,   W<small>ASHINGTON</small>, May 18th 1802.

I shall not trouble you with any of the letters that have been received for you since your departure, as they are generally unimportant, and not one of them requires your own attention. No private or foreign ones have been received. Mr Dallas has furnished the Copy of the proceedings of the District Court of Pennsylvania, in the case of the Magicienne, and I have sent it to the Secretary of the Treasury's Office, as you directed. The printing of the laws goes on very well; and no attention, on the part of your Office, will be wanting, to accelerate a completion of the work. Two Clerks, of other Offices, who write very good hands, are employed every after-noon on our Records, and I flatter myself that they will nearly bring them up by your Return, notwithstanding their being so much in arrear. Most of us, at the same time, are closely occupied, in arranging the papers &ca belonging to the Office. A duplicate Copy of the late Convention with England goes to the President to day, to be ratified by him. The public prints accompanying this contain all the news we have. I have the Honor to be, with true Attachment, Sir, Your Obedt. & faithful servt.

DANL BRENT.

RC (DLC). Docketed by JM.

From Thomas Sumter, Jr.

SIR,   PARIS 18th. May 1802

I must beg the favor of you to ask the Presidents leave for me to resign the commission he did me the honor to confer upon me.

It will, I hope, occasion no inconvenience to release me from an appointment which I find different from what I expected it to be—& you will add, Sir, to my personal obligations to you, by giving all possible dispatch to this request & to the Presidents consent. Be so kind, Sir, as to present my respectful compliments to Mrs. Madison & miss Paine—& believe me to be with the highest esteem your mo. obt. Hble St

THO. SUMTER JR.

RC (DLC); Tr (DLC: Jefferson Papers). RC marked "Duplicate"; docketed by JM. Tr docketed by Brent, who sent it to Jefferson (see Brent to JM, 7 Sept. 1802); filed with JM to Jefferson, 18 Aug. 1802.

§ From Griffith Evans. *18 May 1802, Philadelphia.* "In addition to the Books & papers of the late Board of Commissioners there remains in the office some Articles of furniture the joint property of the two Nations. . . . I conceive it to be most proper to solicit advice of the manner in which I ought to dispose of them. Probably sending them to Auction & crediting my Accot of disbursements with the proceeds may answer as well as any other."

Letterbook copy (CSmH: Philadelphia Commission Letterbook 1). 1 p.

§ From Henry Molier. *19 May 1802, Baltimore.* Acknowledges receipt of JM's letter of 26 Apr. [not found] enclosing his commission and instructions as U.S. consul at La Coruña. Encloses his bond, duly executed. "I am doing my best endeavour to close some concerns I have, yet, pending here and will not lose a moment to go out to the place of my destination."

RC (DNA: RG 59, CD, Cadiz, vol. 1). 1 p. Enclosure not found. For Molier, see *PJM-SS*, 2:389 and n.

§ From Israel Smith. *19 May 1802, New York.* Introduces the bearer, Albert Stevens, a lawyer who has lived in Benson, Vermont, for several years and wishes to resettle in Washington, D.C.

RC (DLC). 1 p.

From Robert R. Livingston

No. 14.

DEAR SIR   PARIS 20th May 1802

I have just been favoured with yours of the 16h of March the letters that I have heretofore sent together with copies of my different notes to the Minister on the subject of our claims have regularly apprized you of the state of our affairs here. I am sorry to say that the prospects of payment are yet very distant & that the construction given to the treaty on the subject of indemnities & which is at least rendered plausible by the terms will probably be insisted on—but I have had no answer to my last note on that subject. Believing that the *wants of France in the Islands & the impossibility of relieving them from here rendered this the critical moment for pushing our claims I have ventured to put in the enclosed note.*[1] You will probably find the expressions pretty strong but Sir I am satisfied that it *is upon our own energy & not upon the affections or the justice of this nation that we must rely, neither our form of government or our administration of it are such as are calculated to unite us with that of this country which differs from us as far as despotizm does from freedom — Œconomy from profusion simplicity from magnificence — &* strict morals from a general corruption of manners.

By shewing that we consider ourselves as the first people in our own hemisphere & that we fear no rival there we may command respect *& as far as our aid is needed justice if however a quarrel should be sought with us* (which however I think improbable) it is not upon demands founded in the strictest justice that they will seek the pretence. You are apprized that on learning of the treatment our vessels had recd. at Hispaniola I put in the note of which a copy had been sent you.[2] I afterwards recd. a letter from Mr. Lear of 5h. March[3] in which he was so obliging as to give me a very detailed account of what had passed there & took notice of their compeling the American shippers to part with their cargoes in the way I had heard—but as he did it without any terms of disapprobation & as your letter takes no notice of the transaction nor affords me any instructions on so interesting a subject I am some what at a loss how to act upon the occasion but my own feelings tell me that to pass it over without attention will be to invite a renual of violences upon our commerce & that if it is to be noticed *this is the moment to do it — because they at present stand most in need of our aid.* I have ventured to make it a part of the note sent in this day & the rather as I forsee that great clamours will be excited on this subject in America & that it may be useful to meet them by shewing that it has not been unattended to. Mr. Lears letter shewing in strong terms the good faith of our government wh. respect to St Domingo exemplifyed in the instructions you had given him & which he recites I thought it best to let the Minister see the letter which I did & at the same time informed the first consul verbealy of its contents.

I have stated to you in my last the only cases in which I had recd comps. of the decision of the council of prizes no answer to my last note on that subject has been recd. The rule here in acquiting is to give no damages to load the vessel with all the charges & to restore her in the state *she is.* You have a copy of my note on that subject to the Minister.[4] I submit it to you if this is the case whether you should not adopt the same rule & whether the expences employed on the Berceau shd. not make charges against the government.[5] I have heard nothing here relative to a claim *for the Insurgent & I am inclined to think it has been set up to afford a pretence to retain the money that will by your promise go into Pichons hands* & at the same time to leave open the claims of individuals under the treaty agt us. You will judge how far it would be proper if you give him the money to explify [*sic*] every particular claim & to take a discharge as to such claim. Tho I must own that I should have prefered retaining it as a kind of security for payments here at least till some specific plan had been chalked out for their discharge for in fact it wd have gone far to have satisfied our demands against this *government* for captures & condemnations because the greater part of these will be recoverable from the individual or satisfied by the mere restitution of the vessels & cargoes. As you have however determined otherwise I have tho't it best to derive the merrit you intended from it, & have accordingly so mentioned it in the enclosed note.

I yesterday called on the Minister & had a long conversation with him on the subject of our demands in which all I could get from him was an assurance that it was under consideration & I have therefore determined to bring him to something descisive by a note this he will be compelled to answer besides that it will fall under the consuls eye. The same conduct was held with respect to Luissania he would not acknowledge that the government had yet formed any specific plan with respect to it or that any troops were going out—but assured me in general terms that nothing would be done that should give us any just ground of complaint on the contrary their vicinity would promote our friendship. I will not trouble you with the answers that obviously presented to this reasoning it terminated however as all my conversations on this subject have done in nothing. I shall wait a few days in hopes of hearing from you after having recd a copy of my first note when I shall act agreeably to yr instructions or if you afford me none send in a second in which I shall press for a communication of the treaty with Spain which however I am in hopes you may receive thro Mr. Pinkney. I believe that for the present the armament designed for Luissiania will be sent to Hispaniola about which I find that much anxiety is entertained here. The Italian army as I informed you will embark (as is said) for America & in this case troops may be spared to send to Florida. It is not however clear that a project is not in agitation *for the divission of the turkish empire in* which case they will be destined to that object. The grounds of suspicion arise— First from the acquiessence of the two Emperors & Prusia in the transactions at Lyons & this even before the signature of the definitive treaty 2d From the long conferences which have latly taken place between the consul & the Russian Minister *who he personally dislikes & who* has hitherto been very little satisfied with any thing that passed at Court—& 3d from a proposed personal interview between the Emperor of Russia & the King of Prusia. These however are still mere conjectures since I can not find from the oldest & most vigilent of the foreign Ministers here that they place their suspicions upon any other grounds than those I have mentioned. In fact this court is at present the most impenetrable & the least accessible in the world, because there is in fact no council & no ministers. The first Consul acts entirely for himself no one about him has any personal consequence or consideration. Nothing is proposed but by himself, his will is never opposed & if any consultations are held they only extend to details relative to matters already resolved. He is a most astonishing man his conceptions are rapid a[s] lightening & the act almost accompanies the conception. I hear from America that great pains has been taken to represent me as not acceptable to this court—the contrarey is however the truth I have every reason to think that I share a portion of the Consuls essteem this I learn from several of my friends among his ministers & those of foreign nations. I find myself upon every occasion treated as the ministers of the highest rank & most in favor. But what I consider as the surest criterion is the attention of the courtiers which has for some time past been very particular with respect to me. And the facilities I find in the transaction of business while those of other powers who like us have much to demand with little power to enforce their demands are unable to get the slightest answers to their notes. I own however that on my first arrival & till I had formed some connections here & had time to do away impressions which arose from a belief that I was the agent of a violent democracy that would be dangerous to the views of the high⟨er⟩ powers here gave me some reason to think that I was not the minister they would have wished & if I remember right I informed you of this as I shall do if I find any change in their sentiments which is not improbable when they see my importunity on subjects that can not be pleasing to them. I shall be at no loss to discover the smallest change the little courtiers have eagle eyes & their treatment of you is an unerring thermometer.

I think it as important for a government to be well informed on this head as on any other because favors are sometimes granted or refused rather to the man than to his government—& as I have determined that my stay here shall not be long I can have no wish to deceive you or maintain an interest here by the smallest sacrafices of what I think my duty requires. It will be proper for you to know that this is no longer *a republic — That the people* & above all the philosophers have not the smallest influence in it—That it is the government of *one man whose will is the law*—Whose views are boundless & who has the means of carrying into effect in every part of Europe England excepted whatever he shall will—Who to a native dignity of soul adds a love of pomp splendour & personal consideration & who will be flattered by an attention to these circumstances. Count nothing *upon his affections.* And maintaing as you do our rights with dignity, avoid as far as possible offending his pride or that of a nation which has hitherto seen every thing yield to them. He has I believe generosity enough to be pleased with the first tho it may traverse his views—but not to forgive the last. Madame Le Clerk is his favorite sisster it is not improbable that she may be driven by circumstances & ill health from the I[s]lands to seek a temporary retreat in the United States anticipating this I have taken measures with my brother for her reception at New York & have offered her my country house.[6] The Consul has expressed great satisfaction in the offer & I pray you to send an order in case this shd happen to have her recd with military honors & furnished with a guard of honor this she will refuse but may accept a centinel. It will be best that this Order should be entrusted to the Mayor of New York to be communicated to the commanding officer only in case of necessity because the less a thing of this kind is mentioned the better in case she should not arrive, or if she should arrive *to prevent her geting into bad hands.* Connecting this with what I had told you of the state of things here it will not appear a matter of little moment triffling as it may seem in our eyes. The occurrences of the day are extreamly rapid. The reestablishment of religion—The Consulate for life, a new order of Nobility in the grand officers—The slavery of the blacks & the renual of the Slave trade have been the work of a few days. It was proposed in council of

State to settle the succession this was prevented by the first Consul. I have my own conjectures of the reason but they are of a nature not to be explained I go into no details because the papers I send will furnish them.

On the subject of Mr. Vail & Mr. Pate[r]son I shall conform to the presidents wish tho I sincerely think that Mr. Vails character & pretentions stand so high that some measure shd be taken to retain him Nantes is vacant & would be a better situation for Mr. Paterson & more agreeable.[7] The state of the republic of the 7 Islands is such a[t] present as not to admit of a consulate. Mr. Skipwith[’s] commission is only that of Commercial agent at Paris I think it would be convenient & proper to make him general commercial agent. The power of the Minister ought to extend to filling up vacancys & appointing to places where the commercial agents may be found necessary till the presidents pleasure is known. I have the honor to be Dear Sir With the highest essteem & respect Your Most Obt hum: Servt

RRL

Draft (NHi: Livingston Papers); letterbook copy and copy of enclosure (NHi: Livingston Papers, vol. 1). RC not found but acknowledged in JM to Livingston, 15 Oct. 1802 (DNA: RG 59, IM, vol. 6). Italicized passages are underlined in the draft; Livingston apparently intended them to be encoded. Draft filed at 10 May 1802. For enclosure, see n. 1.

1. Livingston enclosed a copy of his 18 May 1802 letter to Talleyrand (6 pp.). In it he complained that the French government was throwing "every possible obstruction" in the way of paying American claims, including the delay in liquidating debts, the failure to establish a fund for paying them or to allow interest on them once liquidated, and the creation of a new set of claims based on Leclerc's forcible purchase of cargoes at Saint-Domingue. Livingston went on to ask if the French government had made any arrangements to pay the American debts or the bills forced on American merchants in the West Indies, and he ended by reminding Talleyrand of U.S. measures to fulfill its obligations under the Convention of 1800, including the refurbishment of the *Berceau* and the passage of a bill in the House of Representatives appropriating $318,000 for the payment of French claims, "which sum I am informed by the Secretary of State . . . will be immediately placed in the hands of Mr. Pichon who will have the use of it till it is applied for by the proprietors under the treaty—and who will be thereby enabled to facilitate the operations of the french Commanders in the islands."

2. Livingston to Talleyrand, 27 Mar. 1802 (see Livingston to JM, 27 Mar. 1802, and n. 5).

3. For Tobias Lear's letter to Livingston, see Livingston to JM, 10 May 1802 (first letter), and nn. 1 and 3.

4. Livingston referred to his letter to Talleyrand of 24 Feb. 1802 (see *PJM-SS*, 2:494 n. 2). In this letter Livingston protested that even when a vessel was acquitted, "instead of awarding damages and costs or even restoring the capture in the situation that it *was when taken*, [the French courts] direct it to be restored in the state *it now is* & charge the whole costs of detention storage &c. to the captured." These charges, he declared, together with the pillage of the vessel, often exceeded the amount the cargo would sell for, and the result was a total loss for the owner.

5. On the *Berceau*, see JM to Jefferson, 11 Jan. 1802 (*PJM-SS*, 2:386–87 n.).

6. Pauline Leclerc, the first consul's sister, never took advantage of Livingston's offer of hospitality (Dangerfield, *Chancellor Robert R. Livingston*, p. 329).

7. For William Patterson and Aaron Vail, see JM to Livingston, 16 Mar. 1802, and n. 5.

From Charles Pinckney

(Private)

Dear Sir   May 20: 1802 In Madrid

Agreeably to your desire I now transmit the account of my Contingencies up to the last of May. There are some contingencies of Mr: Grahams for the Use of the Office which not being liquidated in time for this Opportunity will be included in the next account.

I have made no charge for the Expences of my Passage to Europe because I did not know whether I ought or not & before I did I thought it best to know from you what is your Opinion. Believing however that all our Envoys to France were & knowing that Mr Livingston was furnished with passages by the Government I did not know but that it would be allowed to me. On this subject however I will be governed by your Opinion & Directions. Every thing here is so monstrously dear that to us in America it appears incredible. I send you this as a private letter & therefore I take the Liberty to inclose you open a Letter written to my Daughter, *which please read* & then seal & forward it by Post. Remember when this Letter was written, it was not written with a View to be read by a secretary of state & a philosopher & statesman but to a little dear Girl of only Eleven Years old of whom I think perpetually & frequently with my Eyes full of tears. I wish now I had sent you those I wrote from Paris & Holland & other countries to shew you my Movements, But as I am hopeful one day to put them all, with my Opinions & reflections on paper, perhaps they will then be more worth your seeing. I did not describe them to the President, because he has seen them all & with more able & judicious Eyes than mine, although perhaps not with more industrious ones, for I have been extremely laborious & inquisitive & I only wish I had his method of digesting what I have seen.

In one of my last Letters I mentioned to you the enormous Expences & extravagant Charges for Letters brought here from foreign countries & particularly the United States. They mark them all as brought *in their own* Vessels across the Ocean *& sometimes I have had to pay thirty Dollars a day* postage. Every packet of Ships papers in Bundles of any kind pay the same & no Difference is made between Newspapers & others. I have therefore written to all the Consuls in the different ports not to send any large packets or Bundles except those marked "Department of State" by the Post, & I would be obliged to your Office to give the same Directions. I have stopped all Newspapers, except one from Paris & another from London which I concieve are necessary to the information of this Office & are with the American Papers sufficient.

The Post Office here never give receipts or Vouchers. I applied for, but was answered, it was not usual. I therefore wish this Expenditure to be as small as possible. I make one of my Domestics bring all the letters & keep a regular account which is always a long one from the letters I constantly receive on the subject of the numerous applications for Vessels captured. The expences of the Interpreter will be included in his annual account & I will send you his receipt. The other charges of my account are usual annual ones & fixed. Mr Graham has at my request opened a regular Book for Consuls & I have as yet paid but one small account for the Consul at Cadiz. I am hopeful to inclose you by this opportunity a Letter written part of it some time agoe & in cypher to the President which I will thank you to have decyphered & given to him. It is now some time since I heard from you & I will thank you when you write to note those Letters of mine you recieve.

The letter to my little Daughter which I wish you to read is in the letter to Mr Doyley & Mr Freneau. I have inclosed it there but left it open for you to read. When read please inclose it in the Letter to Mr Freneau & Mr Doyley again & seal that & send it by Post.

The ratification & consequent effects of the definitive treaty have created so much Business for this court which requires their immediate attention that I have not yet recieved an answer to my last proposal in which I reiterated the propriety of the Junta's sitting in our country. I expect to see Mr Cevallos again on Tuesday & shall write you what he says further. I am very anxious to hear from you as I have been indirectly informed that Congress have taken up the Business of Spanish Spoliations & I shall be exceedingly glad to know if they have recommended any particular mode to be pursued or what they have done.

The difficulty of my recieving advices here is great. I have lately recieved letters written nearly six months agoe. I am still collecting commercial intelligence for you & trust you will recieve it safe as I transmit it, as it goes by Duplicates.

I cannot persuade this Government to consent to a Consul or Agent from the United States residing at New Orleans. They seem to lament that they cannot but still steadily to pursue the line they have Adopted with respect to other Nations.

I have just recieved a Letter from Mr Isaac Cox Barnet our ex consul at Bourdeaux. His situation I wrote you before—it is really a hard one. Should any vacant consulship in France or Spain, or indeed any part of Europe, occur, I should be very glad, & so would all the Americans in Europe to see him have it. His knowledge, good character & filial piety have interested them al⟨l⟩ in his favour. Mr: Barnet was I am told one of the best Consuls We had in Europe.

As I choose to send my Letter and Opinions to the President about some things in Europe open to you in cypher to have decyphered, & to see likewise I find it cannot be finished for this post & I will send it the next &

conclude myself with my best respects to Mrs: Madison & my affectionate & sincere regard to the President & yourself & our friends at Washington dear sir Yours Truly

CHARLES PINCKNEY

Be so good as to tell the President if he can for a moment read my effusions to my little dear Daughter & remember that they *are written expressly for her to Understand, I beg him* to do so. But I dare say, he will not dislike the Costumes of the french & spanish Ladies.

[Enclosure]

Contingent Expences of the Mission of the United States to the Court of Spain for the following Expenditures—

1801
December 10:　To Expences of different Escorts on the
　　　　　　　roads to Madrid where dangerous　　　　26.—
　　　　　　　To Extra expence of Mules in consequence
　　　　　　　of my being obliged to go to the royal sitio　48.—

1802
January　　　To Expences of payments of fees for the
　　　　　　　last & present year to the Porters & offi-
　　　　　　　cers of the Department of State & others
　　　　　　　& for the attendance & care of Letters at
　　　　　　　the Post Office there the usual annual fee
　　　　　　　& Donations on my presentation to the
　　　　　　　King　　　　　　　　　　　　　　　　86.—
　　　　　　　To the Band of Music　　　　　　　　10
　　　10　　　To Expences of Books for the Office &
　　　　　　　Paper Wax & Quills & &　　　　　　　35.—
February 24　To so much paid in part for the Spanish
　　　　　　　translations for this Office to be included
　　　　　　　in the Translators General account for the
　　　　　　　year　　　　　　　　　　　　　　　　144 —
May　　　　　To the amount of Postage paid in Decem-
　　　　　　　ber for a few Letters & afterwards for the
　　　　　　　Office for January February March April
　　　　　　　& May　　　　　　　　　　　　　　366 ½
　　　　　　　To Extra Expences of mules going & re-
　　　　　　　turning to the royal Sitio on important
　　　　　　　Business & to a grand Gala　　　　　48.—
　　　　　　　　　　　　　　　　Dollars　　$763 ½

RC and enclosure (DLC). In the lower margin of the enclosure Daniel Brent noted: "No vouchers accompanied this account of Mr Pinckney / DB."

From James Sullivan

SIR   BOSTON 20th May 1802.

Having the honor of receiving your letter of the 10th. instant, I hasten to communicate to you my ideas of the subject matter of its contents.

When I was under a Commission as Agent of the United States, on the controversy with Great Britain, regarding the River St. Croix, I forwarded to the office of the Secretary of State, a map of the Bay of Passamaquady, of the Schoodiac, and of the lines of the whole dispute.[1] That map was accurately and elegantly composed from astronomical observations, and actual surveys. As that map is under your eye, there is no need of my sending a fac simile, but I refer you to that for an explanation of this letter.

The treaty of 1783 with Great Britain, evidently contemplates a river, as the St. Croix, which has its mouth in the Bay of Fundy.[2] Both rivers claimed by the parties, empty their waters in the bay of Passamaquady. The Agent of the United States urged the Commissioners to settle the boundary, through that bay to the sea; because the Treaty expressly recognized the mouth of the River, as in the bay of Fundy, which is [a] limb of the Ocean, and the other bay united with it, might be considered as the rivers mouth; but they declined it, on an idea that their Commission extended no further, than to an authority, to find the mouth and source of the river, and that, let which ever would be the river, it had its mouth three leagues from the sea, in Passamaquady bay: they therefore limited their decision, on its southerly line, to a point between St Andrews, and the shore of the United States.[3]

The whole of the waters of Passamaquady Eastward and Northward of Moose Island, and of the Island of Campo-Bello, are navigable for vessels of any burden. The Channel between Moose, and Deer Islands is the best. The Channel between Moose Island and the Continent of the United States, is shoal, narrow, & not navigable for vessels of consequence. That between Campo-Bello and the main, called the West passage, is rendered hazardous and dangerous by a bar of rocks, and is so narrow and shoal, that no vessel of considerable size will be risqued there, excepting on a fair wind, and at the top of high water. The tides there are exceedingly rapid, and rise near about fifty feet. Therefore any settlement which would deprive the United States, of a free navigation, as far to the Eastward & Northward as the channel you propose, that is to the one between Moose and Deer Islands; and North of Campo-bello, would ultimately destroy the important commerce, and valuable navigation of an extensive territory within the United States: for as you may observe on the maps, there is no river of consequence, between the Schoodiac, and the Penobscot; and that the waters which issue, from numerous and extensive lakes, in the interior parts of the country, running into the sea, as the Schoodiac, will give an advantageous, and invaluable transportation, to the articles of commerce.

Your construction of the Treaty of 1783, which renders the waters dividing the nations, common to both, (where they are navigable,) must be reasonable and just. The English people, have in many instances, practised upon the treaty, under such a construction. There has been no interruption to the American navigation, in any part of Passamaquady bay; but our vessels have proceeded through that bay to the shore of the United States, at and near Moose Island, and have gone into the Schoodiac, above St. Andrews point, & anchored on the Western side of the channel, where they have discharged their cargoes. There have been some seizures, where goods have been carried from those vessels, over the English side, but the goods have been condemned and the vessel discharged. These seizures being made within the jurisdiction of the United States, as to the vessels, were clearly infractions of the Law of Nations. There was a seizure lately made, of a vessel of one Goddard of Boston. She was taken from her anchor, on the American side of the channel, in the river established by the Commissioners as the St Croix, and carried over to new Brunswick, but she was acquitted by the court of Admiralty, with damages and cost. Campbell who made the seizure, appealed to England, merely to avoid the costs & damages, where the cause is now depending and under the attention of Robert Slade a Proctor, who is the advocate for Mr. Goddard.[4]

There is a clause in the Treaty, that the United States, shall comprehend the Islands, within twenty leagues of any of the shores of the United States, and lying between lines drawn due East from the aforesaid boundaries between Nova Scotia on the one part, and East Florida on the other, as they shall respectively touch the bay of Fundy and the Atlantic Ocean.[5] This circumstance that the mouth of the St. Croix, is settled to be, between St. Andrews point on the East and the American shore on the west, three leagues within the Island of Campo bello, draws this consequence to the treaty, that nearly all the Islands, in Passamaquady bay, are within the United States, by the above provision in the Treaty, unless they are taken out by an exception, which I shall presently notice. A line due East, (as you will see on the plan,) from the Schoodiac mouth at St. Andrews point, takes in nearly all the bay. A line South 67° East will go to the North of Campo bello and take two thirds of Deer Island on the West. A South East line, from the middle of the Schoodiac mouth, passes on the Channel—between Moose & Deer Islands, and thro' the centre of Campo bello.

The consequences attached to this provision, may be in some measure controuled by an exception annexed to it in these words "excepting such Islands, as now are, or heretofore have been, within the limits of the Province of Nova Scotia."[6]

The Island of Campo-bello is confessedly within the exception, and therefore it may be said, that the principle of common privilege, to navigable waters, will not give our nation, a right to a navigation northward of, and between that, & the other Islands in the bay, because that they, being all within the same exception, the right of a common navigation in both Nations, may not extend, to the waters between that and them.

But the answer to this, is, that the clause establishes the Jurisdiction of the United States, by lines which clearly include all the Islands in the Bay of Passamaquady, and all within the Bay of Fundy comprehended to the South of the East line drawn from St. Croix; while the exception can extend only to the Islands, formerly within the jurisdiction of Nova-Scotia, inclusive of the privileges necessary to the occupancy of them. The principle therefore of the common right to navigation on navigable waters, which divide two nations cannot apply here, because in that case, the line of national jurisdiction, seems to be settled on the channel, but here, in this case, the jurisdiction is definite, express, & ceded, according to the lines agreed on as above described.

The ancient charter of Nova Scotia, to Sir William Alexander in 1638, included all the country from the Kennebunk[7] to the bay of Chaleur.[8] The treaty cannot mean by the expression, "heretofore" within Nova Scotia, all the Islands in that Charter. If it means the Islands which were within a more recent description of it, where the boundary westward was the St. Croix, excluding the Territory of Acadia, which was placed under jurisdiction of Massachusetts, by the Charter of that Province in 1692, & bounded on that River.[9] The river Schoodiac being now the established St. Croix, there can be no question, in regard to Massachusetts, extending to the Channel where it joins that river. But Moose Island which I have described before, lies two leagues below, what the commissioners made the mouth of the St. Croix; and very near the American shore. This was never granted by the crown of England, or by the Government of Nova Scotia, before the Treaty of Peace: nor was there ever an occupancy of it, by subjects acknowledging the authority of Nova Scotia, nor did that Province ever attempt to exercise authority there. Long before the Revolutionary war, it was in the occupancy of people, of & from the late Province of Massachusetts bay. The soil has I believe, been granted by that Province, or by the state, since the Revolution to the People who had it in possession. I do not know the date of the grant. There have been, as I am informed, recent Grants, by the Province of New Brunswick, of that Island: but no formal claim on the part of the English nation has been made to it. The grantees of that Province, who have speculated on the pretended right of the English nation, have excited civil officers, under the authority of the Province [of] New Brunswick, to attempt to execute precepts there. These attempts were repelled, and I have not heard that they have been recently renewed. Should the jurisdiction of that Island be found within the English authority, there can be no doubt, how the right of property would be settled; this renders the dispute of consequence to the Commonwealth of Massachusetts, in a pecuniary point of view.

If the argument above stated does not prove that the Jurisdiction of the United States, is extended to all the waters of Passamaquady bay, but that the treaty leaves the navigable waters of the same, which form the natural boundaries common to both, it is of great consequence, that any claim made, under the crown of the English Empire, to Moose Island, should be subverted. But if their having the Island, under the reservatory exception, does not deprive the United States of the jurisdiction, on all the waters, Southward of the East line, drawn from the mouth of the Schoodiac, the consideration of the property alone, gives consequence to the question.

The channel where the waters more directly issue from the Schoodiac to the bay of Fundy, between Moose & Deer Islands; and between Deer Island & Campo bello, as described in your letter of Instructions to the Minister,[10] is, quite adequate to all navigation of our country.

You mention a resolve of the Legislature, wherein the subject of the Navigation in Passamaquady bay is mentioned: I have attended to a resolve of the tenth of March, which proposes, that the Governor should request the President of the United States to take measures for settling the disputed jurisdiction, to certain Islands in Passamaquady bay:[11] but I do not know of any dispute in that Bay, as to Islands, excepting what I have stated as to Moose Island.

The settlement, & plain establishment of a line from the head, or source of the Cheputnatecook, which is the source of the St. Croix; and empties its waters, through a long chain of Lakes into the Schoodiac, has become necessary, because that Massachusetts is making grants of the lands in that quarter: and the Province of New Brunswick is in the same practice, controversies may be created by interfering locations, in pursuance of, or under pretence of those grants. Such controversies can have no guide to their adjustment, excepting lines drawn thro' a vast extent of wilderness, where many known, & unknown causes, will affect the magnetic variations. These disputes on National or even Colonial, or State jurisdiction are not easily settled, where they are connected with private claims.

By the Treaty of peace it is provided, that the Boundaries shall be, "from the Northwest angle of Nova-Scotia, viz. that angle which is formed by a line drawn due North, from the source of the St. Croix, to the highlands, along the highlands which divide those Rivers that empty themselves into the river St. Lawrence, from those which fall into the Atlantic Ocean, to the Northwesternmost head of Connecticut river." [12]

You will see by the maps of that part of the country, that the line which runs North from the source of the St. Croix, crosses the river St. John, a great way south of any place, which could be supposed to be the highlands, but where that line will come, to the Northwest angle of Nova Scotia, and find its termination, is not easy to discover.

The boundary between Nova Scotia & Canada, was described by the Kings proclamation,[13] in the same mode of expression, as that used in the Treaty of Peace. Commissioners who were appointed to settle that line have traversed the country in vain, to find the highlands designated as a boundary. I have seen one of them, who agrees with the account, I have had from the natives, and others, that there are no mountains or highlands, on the Southerly side of the Saint Lawrence, and northeastward of the river Chaudiere. That from the mouth of the St Lawrence to that river, there is a vast extent of high flat country, thousands of feet above the level of the sea, in perpendicular height; being a morass of millions of acres, from whence issue numerous streams & rivers, and from which a great number of Lakes are filled by drains. That the rivers originating in this elevated swamp, pass each other wide asunder, many miles in opposite courses, some to the Saint Lawrence, and some to the Atlantic sea.

Should this description be founded in fact, nothing can be effectively done, as to a Canada line, without a Commission to ascertain and settle the place of the Northwest angle of Nova Scotia, wherever that may be agreed to be; if there is no mountain, or natural monument, an artificial one may be raised. From thence the line westward, to connecticut river, may be established, by artificial monuments, erected at certain distances from each other; the points of compass, from one to the other may be taken: and the ascertaining the degree of Latitude, which each one is placed on, from actual observation may be very useful. Though there is no such chain of mountains, as the plans or maps of the country represent, under the appellation of the Highlands, yet there are eminences from whence an horizon may be made to fix the latitude, from common quadrant observations.

In the description of the morass, which is said to crown the heights, between the United States & lower Canada, it ought to have been noticed, that though those swamps are vastly extensive, yet in the acclivity from the Atlantic, to their highest elevation, as well as in their declivity to the St. Lawrence, great tracts of valuable country are interspersed. On the banks of the river Chaudiere, and perhaps on the banks of other Rivers, running to the St Lawrence, the settlements are approaching fast towards those of the United States. This circumstance will soon render, an established line of national Jurisdiction, absolutely necessary.

Should there be any thing within my power which will give aid to the government on this occasion you will please to command me. I am &c. &ca

(signed)   JA SULLIVAN

Tr (NjMoHP); Tr (DNA: RG 76, Great Britain, Treaty of 1794 [Art. 7], Papers Relative to the Commissioners, vol. 4); Tr (MHi). First Tr sent as enclosure in JM to Rufus King, 8 June 1802.

1. The map to which Sullivan refers, "Plan of the Rivers Scoodic and Magaguadavic and of Passamaquoddy Bay, 1796–98," was drawn by George Sproule and Thomas Wright and was annexed to the 25 Oct. 1798 declaration of the commissioners under article 5 of the Jay treaty (Moore, *International Adjudications*, 2:372–74).

2. Article 2 of the 1783 Treaty of Paris between the U.S. and Great Britain states that one of the boundaries between the U.S. and Canada be drawn "East, by a Line to be drawn along the Middle of the River St Croix, from its Mouth in the Bay of Fundy to its Source" (Miller, *Treaties*, 2:153).

3. Sullivan reported the result of the St. Croix commission in a letter to Secretary of State Timothy Pickering on 25 Oct. 1798. In it he wrote that he had urged the commission to extend the boundary line and fix the mouth of the river "between Deer & Moose Islands or between Deer Island and State point in the Bay of Fundy." That proposal was rejected, and Sullivan expressed regret that because Passamaquoddy Bay was not to be considered "as sea," further negotiations might be necessary (Moore, *International Adjudications*, 2:374–75).

4. The question of jurisdiction over the islands in Passamaquoddy Bay, and thus over the navigable channels between them, was complicated by the heavy illegal American trade with New Brunswick, which was resented by such British customhouse officials as Colin Campbell of St. Andrews. For the local background of the boundary dispute between the U.S. and Great Britain, see W. S. MacNutt, *New Brunswick: A History, 1784–1867* (Toronto, 1963), pp. 123–41.

5. Article 2 of the 1783 Treaty of Paris (Miller, *Treaties*, 2:153).

6. Ibid.

7. "Kennebec" in other copies.

8. The text of the grant is printed in Moore, *International Adjudications*, 1:173–74.

9. For the charter of the province of Massachusetts Bay, dated 7 Oct. 1691, see ibid., 1:202–3.

10. JM to Rufus King, 28 July 1801 (*PJM-SS*, 1:484).

11. For the resolution of the Massachusetts legislature, see JM to Caleb Strong, 21 Apr. 1802, and n. 2.

12. Miller, *Treaties*, 2:153.

13. Sullivan probably refers to the original creation and grant of Nova Scotia to Sir William Alexander in 1621 (Moore, *International Adjudications*, 1:173–75).

From William Taylor, Sr.

DEAR SIR,   JEFFERSON COUNTY 20th. May 1802

I take the Liberty to ask your friendship impressed with an Idea that our acquaintance May excuse it. I have taken my Nephew J. Taylor into Partnership in conducting the Milling and Distilling business, and hearing of

Mr. Michael Kraffts New improvements, on Stills, of Trenton (N J) we had wrote him for his Pat. right,¹ which he hesitated to forward owing ⟨to⟩ the remote distance and the want of knowle⟨dge of⟩ our credibility as You are Generally known, we have mentioned to Mr Krafft that we expected you would be good enough to mention us to him, and if you would forwar- ward [*sic*] your oppinion to him in Trenton the favor will Confer a singular obligation on your friend.

I should not Sir have asked this favour but we are so anxious to get our Distilery imediately in motion, and we will not have it in our power to froward [*sic*] his fees untill the Fall remittances of our Merchants, and I knew of no acquaintan⟨ce⟩ in that Quarter to whom I could apply. Suf- fer me to Remain with my usial sentiments of respects and regard Your Obt H St.

WILLIAM TAYLOR SENR.²

RC (DLC). RC torn. Cover dated, "Louisville, Ky May 24th." Docketed by JM.

1. Michael Krafft (or Crafft) of Bristol, Pennsylvania, was granted a patent for the "con- struction of stills" on 28 Oct. 1801 (*House Documents*, 21st Cong., 2d sess., 2 : 378). He popu- larized his design in his book *The American Distiller* (Philadelphia, 1804; Shaw and Shoemaker 6606), and by 1804 he claimed that there were 217 distilleries "at work on his plan" (Harrison Hall, *The Distiller* [2d ed.; Philadelphia, 1818], p. 4).

2. William Taylor, Sr. (1759–ca. 1835), son of George Taylor of Orange County, Vir- ginia, and JM's second cousin, served in the Virginia Continental line during the Revolution- ary War (Hayden, *Virginia Genealogies*, p. 673; Vi: Francis Taylor Diary, 7 July and 22 Aug. 1794).

§ From David Lenox. *20 May 1802, London.* Reports that on 1 May he delivered to Erving "a List of 597 Seamen where answers have been returned to me, stating, that having no documents to prove their Citizenship, the Lord's Commissioners of the Admiralty could not consent to their discharge." Has little doubt, however, that most of those men have already been discharged. Encloses an abstract showing that only seven cases remain unanswered. In order to bring his official business to a close, he applied to Bird, Savage, and Bird for £800; "they informed me that no money had been remitted th⟨em⟩ this Year to the fund for the relief & protection of our Seamen; that about £250 was all they had . . . belonging to that fund, *& which was all they could pay*, alleging at the same time that this was conformable to instruc- tions which they had received from the Secretary of the Treasury." Rufus King intervened to no avail. Has accordingly settled the accounts with U.S. consuls from his own funds. The whole expense of his agency, exclusive of his salary, will not exceed £2,500. Expects to take passage for the U.S. on the *Maryland*, leaving about 1 June.

RC and enclosure (DNA: RG 59, CD, London, vol. 8). RC 4 pp. Enclosure (1 p.) is an abstract of applications made by Lenox for the discharge of seamen, 1 Oct. 1801 – 1 May 1802, showing 208 cases pending, of which 7 were unanswered. Filed with the RC is a list of "Cases of Seamen where proofs have been received from the Department of State," dated 20 May 1802 (1 p.). JM transmitted an extract from the RC and the enclosed abstract to the House of Representatives on 22 Dec. 1802 (printed in *ASP, Foreign Relations*, 2:471–72,473).

§ From Richard O'Brien. *20 May 1802, Algiers.* Notes the arrival on 15 May of an Algerine frigate with a Portuguese frigate captured on 8 May near Gibraltar. The Algerine frigate, flying American colors, had "ranged right along Side and Covered the Portugees's decks with about 250 turks and moors and in the run of ½ an hour became masters of The Portugee whom had made no preparation." The victory will "increase The pride and avarice" of Algiers. "At present there is 400 Portugee Captives at Algiers and to ransom them it will Cost portugal at the rate of 3000 dollars Each and if They Seek peace without first retriveing Their lost honour it will Cost them 2 millions of dollars. . . . This dishonourable event has happened for the want of that regular order and decorum requisite in all Govt. Vessels. This Circumstance will put The Corsairs of The other Christian powers on their gaurd [*sic*]—if at War with the Barbary States." The U.S. frigate *Constellation* arrived off Algiers 17 May; "I am sorrow to add I had no one letter from the departmt. of State by this Conveyance." Suggests reinforcing U.S. squadron in the Mediterranean with a "squadron of reserve" to prevent captures of U.S. vessels by Algerine corsairs that might "do us 2 Millions worth of damage before our frigates in This Sea Could Collect and be at Gibralter."

RC (DNA: RG 59, CD, Algiers, vol. 6). 1 p. Another copy of this dispatch was enclosed in Gavino to JM, 30 July 1802.

From Daniel Brent

SIR,   WASHINGTON, May 21st 1802.

You will receive herewith, under another cover, such letters belonging to the Office as may be interesting to you, and that I have opened since Tuesday last. And you will also receive, in the same package, several unopened ones, that have likewise reached the office since that day. I retain one of the papers referred to in Mr Skipwith's letter that I may send extracts of it to the persons interested.[1] General Dearborn has seen Governor Claiborne's.[2]

Mr Pintard,[3] of Hamburg, has drawn upon you in favor of Daniel McCormick, of New York, for 600 Dolls. & 73 Cents: and the latter has just sent the Bill hither, in a letter addressed to yourself, requesting payment.[4] Mr Pintard advised you some time ago that he should make this dft., and sent his accounts then, which are now at the Treasury. Under these circumstances, it may be well, perhaps, that the Bill should be honored: but in this case it will be necessary to send it back to N York, that Mr McCormick may authorise some one here to receive the money, which is not payable (the bill is at 30 days sight) 'till you will probably have returned. In the mean time, however, you will give such instructions in the case as you shall think proper. With the most respectful attachment, I am, Sir, Your very Obedt & faithful servt.

DANL BRENT.

RC (DLC). Docketed by JM.

1. The retained paper was a list of U.S. merchant claims against France, the prosecution of which had been stalled owing to a lack of supporting documentation (see Fulwar Skipwith to JM, 14 Mar. 1802, and nn.).

2. The letter was probably Claiborne to JM, 3 Apr. 1802, requesting arms for the territorial militia.

3. Brent meant Joseph Pitcairn, U.S. consul at Hamburg (see Pitcairn to JM, 26 Jan. 1802, *PJM-SS*, 2:424).

4. Daniel McCormick to JM, 17 May 1802 (not found). Brent acknowledged receipt of the letter and informed McCormick that JM had instructed him to reply that the bill would be paid on JM's return to Washington (Brent to McCormick, 26 May 1802 [DNA: RG 59, DL, vol. 14]).

§ From James Leander Cathcart. *21 May 1802, Leghorn.* No. 6. Acknowledges JM's letter enclosing the 6 Feb. act for the protection of the commerce and seamen of the U.S.[1] Encloses a copy of his dispatch no. 8 "& cannot imagine how it miscarried."[2] Has received no word from Barbary or about U.S. warships since his last dispatch. "I have kept myself in readiness to embark at a moments warning ever since the arrival of Comodore Dale in this sea, consequently will not detain Comodore Truxton four hours should he call or send for me before he proceeds before Tripoli which I most devoutly hope he may think necessary."

RC (DNA: RG 59, CD, Tripoli, vol. 2). 1 p.

1. See JM to Cathcart, 6 Feb. 1802 (*PJM-SS*, 2:448 and n. 3).

2. Cathcart's dispatch no. 8, dated 2 July 1801, had not reached JM by 6 Feb. 1802 (*PJM-SS*, 2:448 and n. 1). For the duplicate, see *PJM-SS*, 1:370–72.

From John Francis Mercer

MY DEAR SIR   ANNAPOLIS May 22d. 1802.

A Report has prevail'd here for some days past, which has created very uneasy sensations—it states a decree of the Chancellor of England in favr. of the Crown agt. the State of Maryland, for the Bank Stock claim'd by this State. From the terms of the communication made by our Minister Mr King, I am not without hopes, that if this shoud prove true it may have been in conformity with certain principles of arrangement before understood[1] & that finally it may not prove injurious to the State. But it is true that the subject itself is so important that all duties respecting it necessarily create anxiety—& ill success on the part of the State in this decree woud require farther & immediate Steps.

I therefore hope some communication (perhaps an unofficial one woud be best) respectig the foundation of these reports, as far as you may deem such warranted, & that you will not leave me without official advice whenever you may become possess'd of any decisive information on this subject. You will present my respectful Compls & those of Mrs. Mercer, to yr. lady, & believe me with the sincerest friendship & respect Yr Obt. Set.

JOHN FR: MERCER

RC (owned by Michael A. Jernakoff, San Francisco, Calif., 1982).

1. See Rufus King to JM, 9 Jan. 1802 (*PJM-SS*, 2:381).

§ From John Lamson. *22 May 1802, Trieste.* Has nothing of importance to report since his dispatch of 18 Mar. Encloses a list of all the American vessels that have ever visited the port. Observes that Trieste is "surrounded by an extensive and encreasing manufactoring country where the produce of the west Indies and many articles the growth of the United States are allways in great demand. . . . The principle articles of export are Hemp Iron & steell and articles manufactured from them, Coarse cloths, Linnens & Glass ware, and generally all articles from the Levant and Neighboring Islands."

RC (DNA: RG 59, CD, Trieste, vol. 1). 2 pp. Enclosure not found.

From Unite Dodge

SIR   CAP FRANCAIS May 23. 1802.
I have had this honour under dates of april 20, 30th.[1] & May 6 which being by Duplicates are doubtless at hand.

In obedience to the Consular Instructions, I must now acquaint you Sir, that the Yellow Fever or what is here termed La *Fievre Putride et Maligne* has lately made great ravages in the Town & harbour of the cape particularly amongst the Troops.

It is remarkable, however, that there has been very few or no instances of its attacking the old inhabitants or communicating to them, and I believe the disorder originates, not so much from the impurity of the air as from the imprudent & negligent manner which strangers are accustomed to treat themselves before & it after the first symtoms appear.

It nevertheless prevails onshore & onboard the american shipping, which I presume, is sufficient to justify this communication. I employed a person to assertain the number of deaths but he was obliged, *thro' fear*, to desist from making the necessary enquires.

I cannot refrain mentioning, altho' it may be improper & unnecessary, something that was told me the day before yesterday by a Mr. fulton An american by birth & now or lately in the service of France.[2] That he dined the day before onboard the Admls. Ship with the admiral & in compy with a Mr. Morin secrety to the Prefet who had just returned from the US on some important mission. That whilst in america he had been so prejudiced against the Gouvmt. & people as to talk in the most disrespectfull manner of both—wished for a War with the US. & intimated that they only waited to get possession of Louisanna to be revenged for all the injustice & ingratitude they are experiencg from us.

I am sorry it is in my power to add that every thing I hear or see that comes from the Gouvmt. or others whose observations merit any notice, tend, to confirm the belief, that this unfriendly disposition, instead of subsiding, as we have just reason to expect, appears to increase daily; and the best reason, that I can give for it, is because the americans will not consent to credit their property to any amt. & on any terms that may be proposed to them. I have the honour to be, With sentiments of high Respect Sir, Your Obedt. Servant

U DODGE

RC (DNA: RG 59, CD, Cap Haitien, vol. 3). Misfiled at 23 May 1801. Docketed by Brent.

1. Dodge's 20 Apr. 1802 dispatch bears a postscript of 30 Apr.
2. Samuel Fulton (b. ca. 1770) was an American-born military adventurer who entered French service in 1793 and was actively involved in intrigues aimed at Spanish territory in Florida and Louisiana. He met JM in Philadelphia in 1795 and the next year carried JM's private correspondence to Monroe in Paris, afterward serving in the French army in Europe and Saint-Domingue. Beginning in 1801, Fulton repeatedly and unsuccessfully applied to the administration for employment, preferably a position on the southwestern borderland. He settled at Baton Rouge by 1804 and was active in efforts to annex Spanish Florida to the U.S. (*PJM*, 16:304 n. 6; *PJM-PS*, 2:320–21 and n. 3; Fulton to Jefferson, 9 Floréal an IX [29 Apr. 1801] [DNA: RG 59, LAR, 1801–9]; Fulton to JM, 10 Aug. 1802).

From Thomas Jefferson

DEAR SIR   MONTICELLO May 24. 1802.

Our postrider having mistaken his day, brought us no mail on Thursday last. Yesterday I recieved a double one. In it were the inclosed letters. Those from Dupont[1] & Granger[2] are forwarded for your perusal, and I will recieve them again when I see you at your own house. The one from Dallas to yourself on Jackson's case I recieved from mr. Brent:[3] the recommendation of the Attorney of the district, & of the jury, & the circumstances of the case seem to be a good foundation of pardon, which I would wish to have issued therefore unless you disapprove it. They do not mention when the execution is to be; but probably it would be well to lose no time lest the pardon should get too late. If your clerks have it in readiness I will sign it on my arrival in Washington which will be in six days from this time. I will be with you on Thursday or Friday at farthest, unless rain prevents, and take your commissions for Washington. I have forbidden any mail to be forwarded to me later than the one recieved yesterday. Present my best respects to the ladies, and accept my affectionate salutations yourself.

TH: JEFFERSON

RC (DLC); FC (DLC: Jefferson Papers). FC misfiled at 20 May 1802.

1. Pierre Samuel DuPont de Nemours to Jefferson, 12 May 1802 (DLC: Jefferson Papers). DuPont was the bearer of letters from JM and Jefferson to Robert R. Livingston in Paris. In a letter of 25 Apr. 1802 covering those dispatches (ibid.), Jefferson had entreated DuPont to impress upon influential Frenchmen that France's possession of Louisiana would lead to war (see JM to DuPont, 2 May 1802, n. 1). DuPont's letter of 12 May proposed instead that the U.S. government offer to buy New Orleans and the Floridas and suggested that if Jefferson would offer generous terms it would be a simple matter to arrange. He also promised to try to smooth the points of irritation between the two countries over the French invasion of Saint-Domingue and the treatment of American merchants there.

2. Gideon Granger's letter of 14 May 1802 (DLC: Jefferson Papers) reported the latest news on the New York elections.

3. See Alexander J. Dallas to JM, 15 May 1802, and n. 2.

From Charles Pinckney

(Private)

DEAR SIR   May 24: 1802

As my letter to the President was not finished copying & putting into Cypher when my last was closed I now have the pleasure to inclose it to you & to request that you will have it decyphered & given to him. It will give you some idea of my Opinions of the people on this side the Globe & at the same time I can assure you I have more charitable & indulgent Opinions than any other of *our Americans* I have met with. I still hope—but they one & all despair & have no hope. When you see Paine Barlow & others from Paris & recieve *Mr Livingstons* letters you will find the Whole despairing. If the intelligence We have here is true that France is to declare Bonaparte 1st: Consul for Life, which I am told has been moved in the Tribu-

248

nate, that settles the matter & confirms all their Opinions. I have also heard that a new Squadron with troops under the command of General Berna-dotte is to sail soon for Louisiana to take possession of it. The french are notwithstandg. still negotiating some thing on that subject & I am privately informed that I can expect no answer (until this is decided) on the subject of Florida. I however mentioned to you in one of my former letters that if ultimately this Government should be inclined to treat for the Sale of the Floridas or either of them that I was at a Loss *What sum to fix* as the Value for either or both as you had *not mentioned,* any precise sum or fixed one in any of your Letters & that of course I should have to refer to you—if they answered favourably soon, still I must refer it to you unless in some of your Letters which I hourly expect You should speak of the sum.

I have drawn the Convention on the subject of Spoliations & our other claims as Broad & as general as possible & it is now before the Minister for his consideration. I have left the Place Where they are to sit Blank, but Madrid will be insisted upon by them as I find my predecessor Colonel Humphreys had by the order of Mr Adams said to this Court, that if Ma-drid was more convenient to them than the United States, that he had in-structions to consent to it, & as your instructions to me say nothing about the place, if I find We can get a board of Commissioners upon that condi-tion & no other, I shall consent to it. They know & have mentioned that We have a similar Board now sitting in London.

This Court has been & is so extremely occupied in consequence of the Definitive Treaty that they have not a moment to spare. Their posessions are so extensive that the arrangements for their Armies & navy & colonial Establishments & the alterations consequent on the Peace employ them continually it is for this reason added to their general habitudes that they are extremely slow in their Movements & I am now every day recieving answers to memorials & representations sent in by my Predecessor six months before my arrival. I however hope by giving them their own Time to keep them in their present good humour with me & to obtain the ap-pointment of Commissioners to decide our claims on fair & honourable Principles. As to the Floridas, as the Secretary of State has informed me it is of so much consequence & importance that his Majesty requires time to consider it, I shall wait to see, with patience, what will be the result & seize every opportunity & use every proper influence to obtain a favourable con-clusion to it. You will observe in my Letter to the President all I say about it.

I find I shall have some Difficulties about the Consuls in the settlement of their accounts at present I have settled but one small one & I have di-rected Mr Graham to open a Book to register their claims & to keep their Vouchers for the purpose of being forwarded to your Department. I have returned one or two accounts & am now making all the Enquiries about what are proper charges, in my power. On this subject I should wish to know your Opinions as nearly describing where Expenditures are proper, or on what occasions admissible, as may be in your power to give me—for of all the discretionary authorities I dislike, or rather fear, that of having the authority to say when the public money shall or shall not be expended appears to me the most delicate. The Consulship at Madrid is really a hard one at present on the Consul Mr Young, who in consequence of the numerous reclamations all centering here has an immensity of public Business without Emolument—for as Madrid is not a seaport he has no commercial advantages or fees like the other consuls, & has more Business than all the rest put together for he is indefatigable, & to him the American Claimants owe a great deal for his industry, in seeing their Business properly attended to before the different Tribunals. I recieve great assistance from him & should the Board of Commissioners be appointed to sit here I strongly recommend him as one, as he knows every case intimately & correctly & as his Judgment & integrity are sound & undoubted, & it will at the same time be giving him some kind of remuneration for his services. I mentioned to you the excessive Charges of the Post Office in Madrid on Bundles or packets coming from the United States, which are all charged & marked as if Brought in *Spanish packets* from their own Islands. I have remonstrated against this Excess without Effect. The only way to avoid the charge is to write on all not to be put into the Post Office & to direct that all of them should be sent to the Consuls to whom I have written on the subject to prevent sending them by the post. Another impropriety is that of their friends sending all the Letters & packets on private Business for all the Americans in Madrid & many other parts of Spain *Under seal to me.* I frequently open large packets & have not one Line for myself or on public Business. I mention these things to you as the regulations of the Post office are so extremely rigid here that if you refuse to take a Packet out of the Office they refuse you all your other Letters so that you are obliged to do it & to take them as they please.

I am hopeful you will hear no more about Captain Mullownys complaints[1] as I have said all that I could & which I supposed would be satisfactory to this court in exact compliance with your instruction. I am making also another Attempt to get a Consul allowed us at New Orleans & have used verbally & in writing all your arguments & such others as sugges⟨t⟩ themselves to me in favour of our claim; But if this country is so soon to be given up I suppose that will be a reason with them for declining to say any thing in favour of the request & leave us to ask it of the power which is to posess it & who will probably more readily grant it. Please Present my affectionate respects to the President—accept them Yourself & Believe me always dear sir Yours Truly

CHARLES PINCKNEY

I expect to return from the Sitio to Madrid about the 20 or 30th June.

I will thank you to note all the Letters you recieve from me as I apprehend some of my Letters must have miscarried—& some of yours to me as I have recieved very few. The Court will remain at Aranjuez until the End of June & in August goes to Barcelona. I do not trouble you with all the private anecdotes & conversations about matches & other things with which other Ministers fill their Letters who have nothing else to do, & which are totally uninteresting to us, because I know you neither wish or expect it. Whenever any alliance of consequence is to take place or any change in commercial regulations or relations occurs you shall hear of it immediately—& on the latter subject I have written you lately & am still preparing further details & communications.

[Enclosure]

[Charles Pinckney to Thomas Jefferson]

DEAR SIR   May 24: 1802 SITIO NEAR MADRID

I will now continue the confidential communication which I received, and which I hinted at in the last Letter I wrote you; but had not time to go into as the opportunity closed upon me before I expected it. It was in substance that *the court had been tricked by Mr. Urquijo into the cession of Louisiana* without being aware of *it — that it was a thing patched up between Berthier and Urquijo when he was here as envoy extra: to get Spain* to declare *war against Portugal and that a different paper had been given to the king to sign* from that *he had approved in the rough draught: that when the Prince of Peace was appointed to negociate with Lucien Bonaparte the treaty which was lately published at Paris the prince attempted to dispute the fairness and* validity *of the transfer; but that the French held them to it and added*[2] *them that nothing could save their mines and South American possessions⟨, but having the French as a⟩*[3] *barrier,* and that in consequence *of the cession they would guarantee them*—that notwithstanding *the thing had been* acquiesced *in with great reluctance, and to use the term of my informant, surliness on the part of Spain* that so many restorations were to be made *her and so many difficulties thrown in the way* that to please *her and smooth them over France at last agreed that Etruria should be considered* always *as a sort of dependency or* appendage *of Spain and held by a branch of her family*—that there can be no doubt *Spain has very great* uneasiness *on the subject: that she knows not which to dread most France or America; but that she* infinitely *prefers the neighbourhood of America,* that in that case in the worst of events *she would have only one to contend with; but* that the chance was *if the French possessed Louisiana and became powerful there, they and the Americans might one day* understand *each other and then she would have both. He further* said *that Spain looked upon her possessions in South America and the*

West Indies as hers but for a time and that if the United States went on to progress for the next twenty years as they had done in the last, *that not only Spain, but other powers would have to owe every thing to their moderation as far as respected American possessions—as their land* (and if they chose to make an exertion *in that way) their naval forces in that quarter of the* world *would be irresistible—that the European naval powers* always Jealous *of each other could never venture to share a sufficient number of ships or a sufficient force to resist with effect—that this added to the Americans* being *at home and with the* constant and immediate *use of every thing they wanted and the shelter* and *aid of their ports and their* unexampled and continued *progress in numbers commerce and revenue* made *them an object* very much to be attended to *by all the powers having and* valuing *their possessions in America.* That the constant conversation almost, *with the French minister and others* was on this subject. *That my proposition had been sent off* immediately *to the minister of Spain at Paris and that there in fact would the question of the Floridas be* decided: *that it was certain no* answer *would be given to me until the return of a courier, or some* answer *was received from Paris.* This is the substance of my first information, and from a channel I implicitly rely upon—*in consequence I wrote* immediately *to our minister at Paris and gave him notice that he might use his exertions to obtain the aid and* influence *of France, if he could* persuade *them as I think he might that their true interest* consisted in wishing *us the Floridas and the* undisturbed *possession of our share of the navigation of the Mississippi. If France* wants *them herself or if she* (to use their own words) *is preparing for* grand *events in our quarter of the world she will oppose the cession* and I think her conduct on this occasion may in some measure be consider'd as a test of *their intentions in America or at least in that neighbourhood.* I have no doubt *our minister in Paris will inform you fully with respect to the* disposition *of France and from me you will hear every thing that* the most unremitted, but discreet industry will permit. I was sorry to find, both in France and Spain a too general opinion entertained that our uncommon rise and unexampled increase of numbers, added to our particular local situation—called for the vigilant and perhaps Jealous attention of Europe or at least of the maritime part of it. There are certainly *other strong reasons to make most of them view us with attention: they may* perhaps *consider us as I expressed myself in one of my letters to* Mr Madison *as the only ark which has in the general* deluge *floated* untouched *and as* still *containing those seeds which may one day again burst into* Life and people *a world of liberty. It is an ark which they may not* wish the same safety & success to *as we suppose. Indeed in many* conversations *I have had with the ministers here who may be called, with respect to American questions neutral—those who are not from maritime countries or such as have possessions in our quarter of the world*—some of them seem to possess an anxiety to impart to me the unfriendly & jealous opinions they have heared expressed with respect to our Government & Country—for instance *the Prussian minister who* speaks *En-*

glish very well and who having been some time *in England*, appears to have caught a fondness for even that portion of Liberty which *the English* enjoy—he has frequently opened himself to me in praise of our Government & Laws and particularly the freedom of the Press there enjoyed. He has frequently too expressed his uneasiness for us about *the French holding Louisiana* and in almost every conversation he has with me, repeats this observation "Ah Sir your Excellent and Innocent Government knows not how many Enemies it has in Europe." *There has also been here* for nearly *fourteen years as their minister* a very able and learned *one from Saxony who in the time of Urquijo is* said *to have governed Spain by his* influence: *this man as* a true and liberal Philosopher is of course attached to the principles of our Government—he does not hesitate to avow it. *The king of Spain having* broken *off the match* intended *between the daughter of the elector of Saxony and the prince of Asturias in favor of the princess of Naples, the elector and his minister are both* displeased *so much so that this able and* ancient *minister is* desired *to withdraw.*

He has frequently expressed himself to me respecting the unexampled rise of our Country and the attention she attracts from the Maritime powers, and when I have endeavoured to say, certainly there can be no reason for this Jealousy, or even particular attention—that we are a harmless innocent nation of Planters & Merchants—without armies or navies—only anxious to send you our good things, and to take yours in return: that some of our Citizens are a little fond of Money, and that we only wish to be left at peace and quietness to obtain it by fair and honorable Commerce & Agriculture—that these are our great persuits: that if there is any ambition among us it is entirely of a literary nature, to excel as orators or writers: that there can or ought not to be the least Jealousy of us—because we have more Territory already than we know what to do with, and that as to Islands or distant Colonies, we would not accept them if they were presented to us. When I reason in this way, they answer it is very well to say so—the Government, like the Individual who is really ambitious and has great designs, always endeavours to conceal them until prepared to develope its plans. Do you think, says the *Saxon* to me one day, that we know nothing of United America here? Is it not easy to see the reason why your public men, who are doubtless instructed to do so, hold the language you do? Does not your President do the same—while he is obliged, in giving a state of the Nation to the Legislature to confess its unexampled rise, and the prospects it has: he endeavours at the same time to impress the Opinion that you are without Ambition and have no views, but to the settlement of your own Country and the increase of Men susceptible of Happiness and habituated to Economy & Industry. This is all very well and we will suppose that your President and present Rulers, and the opinions of your People are really such; yet who will answer that the same principles and opinions shall govern twenty or even ten years hence? Give a Nation strength and opulence and it will be impossible for her to be perfectly content and tranquil. *She will have some ambition*[4] *and restless* Statesmen *spring up to disturb the peace of others and* situated *as United America is she will be very apt to consider the neighboring possessions as a part of her own* Family, *that have been too long* separated *from her, and their present owners as* strangers *who have no right to interfere in her* Family *concerns — she will be very* likely to say *to them keep to your own quarter of the globe and leave us to ourselves. This say they the French see plainly and so does Spain and hence the cession of Louisiana, which will be peopled with troops black as well as white and is* intended *to be very strong.* Upon the whole his information went to convince me *that the French are extremely desirous of having the Floridas themselves and will of course oppose our getting them.* Wishing however to be convinced, if possible, of the true state of things I wrote to the Prince of Peace that if he had consider'd the nature of the application, (a copy of which I had inclosed him) and particularly the part of it that respected the Floridas, I would have the pleasure of an interview with him whenever he would fix—in his answer he requested me to postpone it until the decision or end of their Negotiations "now depending with France"—as nothing important could be done, until we knew their issue. From this I conjecture that France is still pursuing her negotiations with Spain respecting the Floridas & the Boundaries of Louisiana. *In consequence I wrote again to our minister at Paris not having received any* answer *to either of my former letters to him* until the 12th Ulto when *his communications which were in cypher went to confirm me of the truth of all I had heard respecting the Floridas and Louisiana.* As he has no doubt communicated to you fully the information & opinions, he has transmitted to me you will find from them that *there exists at present no probability of our either soon receiving an* answer *respecting the Floridas or when received of its being such a one as we could* wish—*he* seems *by his letter to me to fear that the Floridas are not now in the power of Spain and to confirm the opinion I* always *had — that if any thing is to be done on this subject it must be at Paris.* For my own part I shall do all I can, and in the way most pleasing to the Court here; and most likely to do the best that can be now done—having brought it before them in the way I have, I shall not endeavour by too pressing or repeated applications to precipitate a reply on a subject, which I fear is very embarrassing to them—on the contrary I will let them take their own time, and this I beleive will be the best way. I apprehend too that they are a little sore on the subject of Money.

The French who have been very much accustomed to *make the country of their enemy the theatre of war and the means of supplying their armies* cannot now do so *on the St. Domingo expedition — for this large sums of* efficient *money are necessary,* and it is said that *as Spain is now bringing home her long accu-*

mulating[5] *treasures from South America, that serious propositions have been made to her for the loan of such sums as are extremely* inconvenient *for her to furnish; but which she does not know how to refuse.* It is beyond a doubt that the current Expences of the French Government far exceed their present Revenues *and that Holland and Spain must furnish the means* for the greatest part of the West Indian Expedition, about the events of which you must be much better informed than we are here, as the *press is so much under the harrow both in France and Spain* that it is impossible ever to know the true state of things *from that.*

I could wish very much, to be able to give some opinions on the probability of Events in Europe; but this is a subject, now become so intricate, that the more I consider it, the more I am involved in doubt. *Bonaparte's conduct in* consolidating *the executive power of the Italian Republic with that of the French and in the Concordat with the pope,* and the consequent proceedings *in the French legislature on the subject of religion* makes it extremely difficult to *penetrate his further designs.*

Almost *all the real republics which* until lately *hoped he would have* relinquished *a part of his present enormous powers and given to France something like a free government, now begin to despair and to* suppose *that in fixing the principles and consolidating the power of the Italian Republic he has so clearly developed his own principles as to leave France little room to hope for an amelioration of her situation while he can retain his present power.* There are others also who think that supposing Bonaparte to be out of the question, the European Nations he controuls at present, are infinitely *too corrupt to receive a government like ours or indeed any other* kind of System, *than that military one which is at present imposed on them*—that from their Habits, Opinions and Manners *and their total want of knowledge of the nature of a free government and particularly from their corruption they are so accustomed to see every thing done by money or (if possible) other* still *worse means of favor or* influence—*that in fact they have lost their ignominy* in the peoples Eyes and it seems now to be a wonderful & almost incredible thing to them that any Governments or their Tribunals should be conducted *upon other principles or in an honorable or* uninfluenced *manner.* Many of them speaking of the *corruption and customs of Europe* and hearing *my accounts of the purity and honor of our government and tribunals* and how dreadfully *we should conceive the possibility of money* influencing *our measures or* decisions, have said they beleived *we were too honest for the rest of the world* and that *our government* must work Miracles, *if with all the intercourse we have with other nations it should* still *be able to keep our* Citizens and officers *honest. Such are the manners of this side of the* Globe, *and* such their opinions of us; but I trust that we shall be able to shew them, that as the Governments and Laws of Countries never fail to fashion the opinions & Manners of their Citizens our own will for ages, continue to receive their impressions from a System, which is as different from any thing I have yet seen, as Jove's, was represented to be from that of Pluto.

I am waiting with anxious impatience to know the result of the Negotiations pending between France and this Government on which, as the Prince of Peace told me, will depend a great deal and as soon as I know them, and the effect they will have here, I will inform you.

The Credit of this Government is rising fast in its pecuniary concerns— their Vales Reales (a Kings Debt), was more than 30 ⅌ Cent Discount when I arrived here, & is now, in Cadiz at 4, & here at 8 ⅌ Cent, & will soon be at par. They have received large quantities of Specie from America and will have more than Thirty Millions of Dollars in addition by December.

I have mentioned in my former Letters the great number of Claims I met here, and how much they have increased the Business of this Mission so much so, that I am kept constantly at work with Reclamations and the Business that flows from them. I beleive, except the French, that I have more Business than all the rest of the Foreign Ministers put together, for the Trade to Spain has been and now is much more extensive than I had expected.

Since writing the above I have been informed a courier is arrived with the intelligence that it is contemplated to declare Bonaparte Consul for Life—some say for 20 Years & that Bernadotte is immediately to go out with a Squadron & Troops to Louisiana to take posession of it. If this is true you will no doubt hear it much sooner from Mr Livingston than from hence & it will serve to confirm some of the information I have transmitted you.

I expect to return from Aranjuez in the latter End of June. The Court will go to Barcelona in September to meet the families of Naples & Etruria, & possibly Portugal on the subject of the intermarriages & to see & congratulate each other on the conclusion of their Dangers & difficulties. I am hopeful this Letter will find you & your friends all well & happy & with my best Wishes & most respectful & affectionate compliments I remain With the sincerest Regard Dear Sir Yours Truly

CHARLES PINCKNEY

RC (DLC); enclosure (DLC: Jefferson Papers). RC docketed by Brent as received 10 Aug.; also docketed by JM. Enclosure in a clerk's hand, except for the last two paragraphs, signature, and dateline in Pinckney's hand; docketed by Jefferson as received 19 Aug. Italicized words in enclosure are those encoded by Pinckney's secretary; key not found. Decoded interlinearly by JM.

1. On John Mullowny, see Pinckney to JM, 6 Apr. 1802, and n. 1.

2. This word was apparently miscoded.

3. JM's decoding of the section in angle brackets is obscured; the decoding here is supplied from a partial key compiled by the editors.

4. According to the key compiled by the editors, JM should have decoded "ambitious" here.

5. JM should have decoded "accumulated" here.

§ From John Morton. *24 May 1802, Havana.* Notes that he last wrote on 17 Mar. "Shortly after that date I repaired to the Baths of St. Diego, in the interior of this island, for the benefit of my health; leaving the business of the Department in the charge of Mr. Vincent Gray,[1] an American Gentleman who has been a considerable time employed therein." Nothing of moment occurred in his absence, except for the brief imprisonment of shipmasters who entered the port against regulations. Since then, however, several American vessels have been allowed to remain in port "in expectancy of a further permission to dispose of their Cargoes of provisions; but which notwithstanding the great scarcity of every Article both of foreign & domestic growth, has not yet been granted." Government has apparently relied on receiving supplies from Spain and Mexico. Transmits a local paper of 20 May containing a second order prohibiting the residence of strangers in Cuba; doubts that this will be enforced, although the edict "is couched in severe terms." At present there are few Americans remaining at Havana to be affected. Will soon be departing the island, leaving the department in Gray's charge. "The circumstance of my departure, and nomination of an Agent to remain, will probably bring the Question as to the residence of an Official character, in time of peace, to a decision. It has not yet, with regard to myself, been made the Subject of any explanation."

RC (DNA: RG 59, CD, Havana, vol. 1). 3 pp.; docketed by Brent as received 13 June.

1. Vincent Gray had been surveyor for the district of Alexandria, Virginia, and inspector of the revenue for the port of Alexandria from 1793 to 1798 before opening an office as a ship broker in that city. He acted informally as commercial agent of the U.S. in Havana from 1802 through the end of JM's tenure at the State Department (Gray to Alexander Hamilton, 26 Apr. 1803, Syrett and Cooke, *Papers of Hamilton*, 26:118–19 and n. 1; T. Michael Miller, comp., *Artisans and Merchants of Alexandria, Virginia, 1784–1820* [1 vol. to date; Bowie, Md., 1991–], 1:169–70; Roy F. Nichols, "Trade Relations and the Establishment of the United States Consulates in Spanish America, 1779–1809," *Hispanic American Historical Review*, 13 [1933]: 305, 312).

From Daniel Brent

SIR,   WASHINGTON, May 25th 1802.

The District Attorney at Boston, in a letter just received from him,[1] which is now likewise at the Secy of the Treasury's Office, gives notice, that the Circuit Court of Massachusetts, at its October Term last year, had passed a decree of Restitution in the case of the Cargo of the french sloop, L'Hereux—and that the money which had resulted from the sales of this Cargo was forthwith paid to the Atty of the Original Claimants and owners. Mr Griffith Evans has written to you for directions about the furniture of the Office of the late Board of Comms., to which he was Secy—what he shall do with it. It seems proper that he should be instructed to sell it at Auction, according to his own suggestion, and Credit his account of disbursements with the proceeds. Mr Barry, very much to my surprise, declines reimbursing the money advanced by the State of Virga, on account of the Ship-wrecked Portuguese, or paying Cap: Stone's demand for his advances and trouble on this score, tho' he told me some time ago that he would do both.[2] A dft. for 100 Dolls., payable at 10 day's sight, made by Colo: Lear on you before he left the Cape, has just been presented for acceptance, and I have told the holder of it that the money would be paid. Governor St Clair's defence and a number of documents connected with it accompany this letter, under another cover. I have the Honor to be, with the most respectful attachment, Sir, Your Very Obedt & faithful servt.

DANL BRENT.

RC (DLC). Docketed by JM.

1. George Blake's reply to JM's letter of 5 May 1802 has not been found.
2. James Barry was acting Portuguese consul general in the U.S. He refused to pay "the money in question" until he had received an answer to his letter to Lisbon "upon the Subject of the advances made in Norfolk by this Govt. for Some Portuguese Subjects" (Barry to Brent, 21 May 1802 [DNA: RG 59, ML]; JM to Barry, 4 Dec. 1801, and Monroe to JM, 15 Dec. 1801, *PJM-SS*, 2:294, 318, 319 n. 3).

From William Eaton

SIR,   TUNIS 25. May 1802.

Yesterday I recd. a note from the Beys prime minister demanding an interview with the Cap. of the schooner and myself this morning: but the schooner had already departed. I rendered myself at the palace to encounter, as I supposed, new perplexities; but on passing the usual ceremony with the Bey I discovered on his countenance an unusual air of complaisance. He signified to me that, after waiting a little, I should be informed of the object of calling me to the palace: accordingly, in about half an hour after, I accompanied the minister and commercial Agent of the regency into a private chamber—where, after a great deal of circumlocution, he came to the subject in view; which was nothing more nor less than a *Proposition of peace on the part of the Bashaw of Tripoli, through the mediation and under the guarantee of the Bey of Tunis.*

Here follows the substance of our conference.

"Have you done any thing" said the minister "on the subject of peace with Tripoli?"

Nothing.

"You are carrying on a war, at so great a distance, at very great expense, without a prospect of gaining any thing."

That we are very sensible of.

"Would you be willing to negociate a peace with Tripoli?"

Are you authorized to propose this question?

"I am."

Well, then I tell you very frankly we have no inducements whatever to *desire* a war with any nation on earth, much less with that which is now the subject of it. If Tripoli should make suitable retractions for the insult offered our flag, and reasonable indemnities for the expense resulting from it, she may think of peace; but, even then, we should think it hazardous to treat with the reigning Bashaw, after having seen such flagrant violations of his faith.

"If the Bey of Tunis would act as mediator between the parties, and take upon himself the guarantee of the peace on the part of Tripoli, would it remove this difficulty?"

We have great reliance on the good faith, equity and magnanimity of the Bey of Tunis; and should be very secure in his responsibility: but is it certain that this Bey would take on himself the guarantee of a peace in behalf of Tripoli?

"Yes! But if you talk of retraction and indemnities it would be idle to talk of peace: on the contrary, according to all custom, you must make the Bashaw a small present; though he would be willing to put up with something less than what he at first demanded."

We were not the first to violate the peace—we are not the first to demand it; if Tripoli be solicitous for it she must abandon the idea of imposing conditions: she will most certainly never receive a caroube* in consideration of her friendship—we do not set any value upon it.

"Nay; but, if you place no value on her friendship the security of your commerce in this sea, and the saving of the expense of armaments are objects of consideration in which you consult your own interest."

We never supposed our commerce in this sea more secure than at present, notwithstanding the war with Tripoli: and as to the expense of armaments, we accumulate nothing on that score from making the Mediterranean the manoeuvring ground of our seamen. We shall probably always have a squadron in this sea.

"But Tripoli is very poor—she cannot subsist without the generosity of her *friends*—give something then on the score of charity."

Tripoli has forfieted her title of *Friend*. Besides, there is a vast difference between the beggar who siezes my horse by the bit &, with a pistol at my

---

* ¹⁄₅₂ of a dollar.

breast, demands my purse; and him who, with one hand pressed to his heart the other hanging with his hat, asks charity for the love of God. The former merits chastisement; the latter excites commiseration. I leave you to apply the figure.

"I feel it: but the Barbary regencies never make peace without presents."

It is high time then that there should be a precedent.

"But you say you are disposed for peace!"

Yes! But you are not to understand me that we either wish or will accept it on dishonorable terms.

"There can be nothing dishonorable in making a small voluntary present to Tripoli."

Drop this subject, if you please: Tripoli is not in a right position to receive expressions of our hospitality. Nor am I vested with powers to negociate. I can only express to you the general, but fixed sentiment of my Government and Country, that *We prefer peace to war if we can have it on honorable terms*. And you are at liberty to express this sentiment to Tripoli—she may profit of it if she thinks proper: otherwise four or five years of warfare with that State, will be but a pastime to our young warriors.

"I shall send off a courier" said the minister "with the result of this interview."

At evening the commercial Agent was at my house; went over the same ground—Was sure that we should never have a peace without *paying something*; it would disgrace the regency. But he seemed extremely solicitous to have permission to write something promising to Tripoli on the subject of a negociation. He said, what the minister had asserted in the morning, that the only pretext the Bashaw of Tripoli had for breaking faith with US. was that the peace was not voluntary on his part; but forced on him by Algiers.

These overtures go to prove the embarrassed situation of our enemy; and promise, if suitable advantage is taken of it, a peace on our own terms. We have the high grounds of him at all points. I am partial to my original plan of restoring the rightful Bashaw, though nothing was said on the subject at the palace today. I think it highly probable that the reigning Bashaw has offered more *powerful arguments* to engage this minister in his interest than either his brother had the means or myself the discretion of offering. Besides, the Bey of Tunis is ignorant of that project. It will be seasonable enough to inform him of it after having ensured its success—in the mean time, let us amuse the usurper with his own propositions.

May 27. Advise comes officially, through the French house, today from Tripoli, that the Tripolitans have recaptured a prize vessel, bou⟨nd⟩ to Malta, with a sweedish officer and ten privates, and conducted them to Tripoli by the way of Bengazi. I fear that alliance will embarrass rather than assist US. The swede however has *kept his station* before Tripoli. No advise yet of the US. squadron.[1] I have the honor to remain with perfect respect, Sir, your Mt. Obed. servt

WILLIAM EATON

RC (DNA: RG 59, CD, Marseilles, vol. 1). Sent as enclosure in Cathalan to JM, 10 June 1802, and received in Washington by 31 Aug. (see Brent to JM, 31 Aug. 1802). Another copy of the RC (DNA: RG 59, CD, Tunis, vol. 2, pt. 1), marked "Duplicate," in a clerk's hand, signed by Eaton, and docketed by Brent as received 21 Sept., includes a 4 June postscript in Eaton's hand (see n. 1). Extracts from the duplicate copy are printed in Knox, *Naval Documents, Barbary Wars*, 2:159.

1. The paragraph dated 27 May is omitted in the duplicate copy, which includes instead a postscript: "June 4th. On the 28 ult. entered the US frige. Constellation Capn. Murray: took in fresh provisions and sailed for Tripoli yesterday. He brought the arms for this bey, which were delivered the 31. They were well accepted: and have produced permission to ship provisions. I have saved the sword. There are two small Tripolitan galliotts at sea. But by letters of 22d. ult. from our Charge of affairs at Tripi. we learn that the Bashaw is solicitous for peace. I fear the delay of our squadron will injure our affairs. W. Eaton."

¶ From Jonathan Dayton. Letter not found. *25 May 1802*. Acknowledged in Daniel Brent to Dayton, 29 May 1802 (DNA: RG 59, DL, vol. 14). Requests a copy of the acts of the second session of the Seventh Congress and a copy of the agreement between the U.S. and Georgia. Brent replied that "when the printing is compleated which is to form the first part of the 6th. Volume of the laws of the United States, and to comp[r]ise these acts, that part of the work will be forwarded to you"; he added that he would send either a printed or manuscript copy of the agreement "in a day or two." He sent the book on 12 July 1802 and apologized for neglecting to send the agreement (Brent to Dayton, 12 July 1802 [ibid.]).

From Andrew Ellicott

DEAR SIR   LANCASTER May 26th. 1802

There are a few papers in your office, which accompanied my despatches from Natchez to the former Secretary of State Mr. Pickering. They are the Proclamations issued by the Governor the Baron de Carondelet, and Gayoso during our discussions relative to carrying the Treaty into effect: of those papers I have no copies, and am now in want of them, for a work I am preparing for publication:[1] if therefore, it is not inconsistent with the regulations of your office, you will render me a particular favour, by furnishing me either with copies, or the originals—if the originals, they shall be safely returned to your office, immediately after I take copies of them. They accompanied my despatches of April 15th. June 4th. and 27th. in the year 1797.

This will be handed to you by Mr. William Barton,[2] a Gentleman, too well known to you, to need any recommendation from me.

Please to present my compliments to Mrs. Madison, and believe me to be with great sincerity your friend and Hbe. Servt.

ANDW; ELLICOTT

FC (DLC: Ellicott Papers).

1. JM's answer to this letter has not been found, but Ellicott published a number of proclamations, including those of Manuel Gayoso de Lemos, governor at Natchez, 29 Mar. 1797 and 22 June 1797, and those of Francisco Luis Hector, baron de Carondelet, governor of Louisiana, 24 May 1797 and 31 May 1797 (*Journal of Andrew Ellicott*, pp. 65–67, 94–95, 101–3, 116).

2. William Barton (1754–1817), brother of the naturalist Benjamin Smith Barton and father of the botanist William Paul Crillon Barton, was a judge in Lancaster, Pennsylvania (*PJM*, 12:286 n. 1).

From Levi Lincoln

SIR   WASHINGTON May 26th 1802

The authority given, by law to grant patents is unquestionably confined to the citizens of the U. S. The priviledge is a monopoly, in derogation of common right, and as it is not, ought not to be, extended, to foreigners. Was it to be, it would be subject to endless abuses, privations and embarrasments to our citizens. I have no doubt on the Question.[1] With sincere friendship your Humble Sevt.

L LINCOLN

RC (DNA: RG 59, LOAG). Addressed "To the Secretary of State U. S. / Washington / to be opened by Mr D. Brent." Docketed by Brent.

1. In JM's absence, Brent had sent a letter received at the State Department from William Sabation (not found) to Attorney General Lincoln for his opinion (Brent to Lincoln, 26 May 1802 [DNA: RG 59, DL, vol. 14]).

§ From Rufus King. *26 May 1802, London*. No. 68. Reports anxiety among British manufacturers and merchants "founded upon the Belief that France would exclude, either wholly or in a very great degree," British manufactures. "The prohibitory Laws of France passed during the War have been declared to be in force, and were it not for a recent and extraordinary Law which puts into the hands of the Chief Consul, provisionally, the whole Regulation of Commerce . . . no English Fabrics could be, as at present very few are, imported into France." That country has recently suggested that "certain understood and reciprocal Regulations . . . be established by Law, . . . according to which the Trade between the two Countries should be carried on for a limited time." Such a proposition is being considered by the British government, but it must be passed immediately or be referred to a new Parliament, "as it is believed that the present Parliament will be dissolved in the course of three weeks" so that elections may be held without interfering with the harvest. Suspects that financial condition of Bird, Savage, and Bird may "not be altogether free of embarrassment."[1] Communicates his apprehensions in confidence.

RC (DNA: RG 59, DD, Great Britain, vol. 10); letterbook copy (NHi: Rufus King Papers, vol. 55). RC 3 pp.; marked duplicate; in a clerk's hand; docketed by Brent as received 19 Aug. Printed in King, *Life and Correspondence of Rufus King*, 4:128–29.

1. The firm of Bird, Savage, and Bird was indeed in difficulty, and it failed in February 1803 (S. R. Cope, "Bird, Savage & Bird of London: Merchants and Bankers, 1782 to 1803," *Guildhall Studies in London History*, 4 [1981]: 213–15).

§ From Levi Lincoln. *26 May 1802, Washington.* Gives opinion on the case of a Portuguese brig "which you did me the honor of submitting to my consideration." On 28 July 1800 the brig was recaptured by Captain Rodgers of the ship *Maryland* after having been captured thirteen days earlier by a private armed schooner from Bordeaux. Rodgers arrived at St. Kitts on 20 Aug. with the brig. The admiralty court there refused to let the brig be taken to the U.S. for adjudication, assuming jurisdiction of the case "as one, respecting the ship of an ally captured from a common enemy, by an ally." The court ordered the brig to be "restored, on the payment of salvage." There was no appeal by the agent for the captors. "The minister for the french Govt. demand[s] this vessel,[1] or the salvage of the U. S. as being a vessel within the description of vessels, provided for in their treaty with France, & as not being finally condemned at signing of that treaty."

"In my view of the cause, it is not necessary to determine how far the Court of Admiralty is justified, by the laws of nations, in its proceedings, as they respect the U. S. or the Portuguise owners of the Brig.

"The words of the treaty are, '*property captured,* and not yet definitively *condemned,* or which may be *captured* before the exchange of ratifications, shall be mutually restored; on the following proofs of ownership': viz—with respect to merchandize, *passports;* with respect to cargo, *certificates;* and in case of the destruction of these documents, other proof.

"The property which is to be restored, is designated by the descriptive term '*captured*' and is such as was capable of being condemned as french property to the use of the Captors &c. and such as America could rightfully restore. . . . Besides—

"The word *captured,* as a technical & a descriptive term, does not include the meaning, and ought not to be construed, to have the effect, of the term *recaptured,* in the sense of the treaty. Also—

"The property of an ally recaptured, is incapable of being condemned, in the sense in which this term is used in the treaty; it of course, is acquitted, and the judgment of acquittal, is of itself an act of restoration. In no event could there be a judgment of condemnation. Further—

"The described Property is such, as a tittle to restoration, is capable of being proved, either by the passport of the ship, or a certificate of her Cargo. These documents, could have an operation as proof . . . only as applicable to original french ships. In the present case, these documents prove nothing more concerning a right of demand, in France than, in England, or, in Turkey. Again—

"The treaty was signed the 8th. of October 1800; previous to which, Judgement had been rendered & the property restored to the former owners, on the payment of salvage. The owners of the brig and cargo, are now repossessed of their property. The act is final as it respects all parties. Their rights are executed. There is nothing which, either the treaty, or further process, can operate upon.

"The French S[c]hooner took, or captured the Brig subject to the chances of a recapture, by its own crew, or another ship of the same nation, or by any other power, at war with France. The moment that a recapture took place, the first captors lost all claims on the recaptured property—and are, in the same situation, as tho' they had never made the capture. If it had been taken a third time, by another French ship, . . . these first captors would have not been considered as owners & would not have had any claims for salvage. . . . The portuguise, had a right, to get the repossession of their vessel, as against France, by any means in their power. . . . This right could not be abridged, in favor of France, by the American recapture. This event, extinguished the right of the first captors, in toto. . . .

"If they [sic] Brig had been in the possession of the American captors unproceeded against in law at the time the treaty was signed, still the case would have been the same. She would have been the property of Portuguise, and the United States, being bound to restore her to them on their payment of salvage, could not stipulate . . . to deliver her to France. Nor can they, be any more bound to pay the salvage over to France, than they would be, in case the Brig had been owned originally by Americans, and being captured by the French, had been recaptured by other Americans. Indeed the term, *salvage*, or a right to it, has no meaning, as applied to *first captors*—nor can the term *restore*, which implies a previous possession, which in the present case, the french in no sense of the word can be considered as having had.

"I am, upon the whole, decide[d]ly of the opinion, that the treaty does not authorize the French Govt. to make any demands on the United States for property recaptured from it, & which, they were obliged to restore to its original owners, on the payment of salvage."

RC (DNA: RG 59, LOAG). 5 pp.; docketed by Brent. Printed in Hall, *Official Opinions of the Attorneys General*, 1:111–13.

1. For Pichon's claim for the *Gloria dal Mar*, see his letter to JM, 14 Apr. 1802.

From Robert R. Livingston

No. 15
DEAR SIR,   PARIS 28h. May 1802
    Since my last I have acquired information which I can depend on relative to the intentions of this government with respect to Louissiania. Berna-

dotte is as I told you to command C[1] to be 2d in command Addet is to be prefet—but the expedition is delayed till about sepr. on account *(as Talle-rand expressed himself to Bernadotte) of some difficulty which he did not explain—* but which I have no doubt has arisen from the different apprehentions of France & Spain relative to the meaning of the term Louissiania which have been understood by France to include the florida's but probably by Spain to have been confined to the strict meaning of the term. This explains why I could never get an answer to my questions relative to the extent of the cessions—And upon which the french Government had probably no doubt till we started it.

Believing, if this conjecture as to the cause of the delay of the expedition was right, that no time shd be lost *in throwing obstructions in the way of its conclusion I wrote the note of which the enclosed is [a] copy*[2] *with the Double pur-pose of alarming Spain & furnishing her with arguments arising from* the good faith they owed us against giving their cessions the construction France would wish. I considered this as the more important because I believe that every negotiation for this object will be carryed on here. I shall however give the earliest & fullest information I can on this subject to Mr. Pinkney[3] who will enforce at Madrid the arguments I may use here *to excite the alarm of the court of Spain.*

I wait impatiently some farther instructions from you those I have in some sort prohibiting such measures as may shew any dissatisfaction on the subject of which however I doubt the policy the subject is so interesting as induce us to risk som[e]thing to defeat it. If I do not hear from you soon I shall present a pointed memorial to this government statg fairly & candidly our objection to their taking possession of the Floridas & demanding se-curity for the rights we had originaly & by treaty with Spain. I am Dear Sir with the most respectful attatchmt Your &c.

Draft and draft of enclosure (NHi: Livingston Papers); letterbook copy (NHi: Livingston Papers, vol. 1). RC not found but mentioned in JM to Jefferson, 11 Sept. 1802, and acknowl-edged in JM to Livingston, 15 Oct. 1802 (DNA: RG 59, IM, vol. 6). Italicized passages are underlined in the draft; Livingston apparently intended them to be encoded. For enclosure, see n. 2.

1. "Collot" in letterbook copy.

2. Livingston enclosed a copy of his letter of 28 May 1802 to José Nicolas de Azara, Span-ish ambassador to France (5 pp.; printed in *ASP, Foreign Relations*, 2:518), in which he broached the subject of the retrocession of Louisiana to France and inquired what provisions had been made to safeguard American rights under Pinckney's treaty. He observed that the treaty limited navigation of the Mississippi River to "the subjects of Spain & the citizens of the United [States] unless it shall be extended to others by special convention." Livingston said he presumed the Floridas were not included in the cession "because of the evident interest that [Spain] has in retaining them as a security for her territories in South America." He asked how—if the Floridas had been ceded—Spain intended to fulfill its obligation to control the

Indians resident in its territories and to ensure the right of U.S. citizens to deposit goods at New Orleans and to export them free of duty from that port.

3. Livingston informed Pinckney that his note to Talleyrand on Louisiana had gone unanswered and that the French minister's friendly assurances on that subject amounted to nothing. He reiterated the reasoning put forth in his letter to JM and communicated the contents of his letter to Azara (see n. 2). He noted that from Azara's reply "it appears first that the Floridas are not included & 2d. that the Spanish Ambassadour here is not entrusted with the negotiation," and he urged Pinckney to keep him informed of developments in Spain (Livingston to Charles Pinckney, 2 June 1802 [draft, NHi: Livingston Papers]).

From Ebenezer Stevens

SIR.   NEW YORK 28th. May 1802

I am favor'd with your respects of 24 Inst. respecting the proposition made by Mr. Kingston, of referring the business of Demurrage for the Ship Peace & Plenty, to Arbitrators of persons residing in Philadelphia.[1]

I think that it would be more proper, to have the business adjusted in this place, and that the public Interest, would be more benefited thereby, as I am knowing to the Circumstances, more than indifferent persons can be.

Should you coincide with me in opinion, I must request you will authorise me to settle the business. I will then make a settlement wth. him, on the best terms in my power.

Permit me to observe that the American Consul at Tunis deliverd to Capt Laughton of the Ship Grand Turk, a Cable, for the ship's use which belong'd to the United States, & I think that the Owners of the Ship, ought to account for it at the value of the same at the port of Tunis. As Mr. Stuart will shortly bring in a Claim, again⟨st⟩ the United states, on acct. of detention of the Shi⟨p,⟩ I take the liberty of requesting your advice, wheth⟨er⟩ I must charge him for the aforesaid Cable.[2] I have the Honor to be Sir with great respect Your Obdt Servt.

EBENR STEVENS.

RC (DNA: RG 59, ML).

1. Daniel Brent had written to Stevens on 24 May that "the Secretary of State before he left this place a few days past, directed me to write to you on the subject of a proposition which Mr. Kingston had made to him, to refer the question of demurrage for the detention of the Peace and Plenty to the Arbitration of persons living in Philadelphia, to be there settled. . . . His object is to learn of you, whether the public interest would be hazarded, in your opinion, by acceding to Mr. Kingstons' proposition." Brent added that JM "does not know, or recollect, the state of another claim on the Government for demurrage—that of the owners of the Grand Turk—whether arbitrators have been appointed, to settle the questions involved in the case, or not. He requests you therefore to favor him with any observations that you may think

will be useful" (Brent to Stevens, 24 May 1802 [DNA: RG 59, DL, vol. 14]). Brent also wrote to Stephen Kingston at JM's request, informing him that "the Secretary's determination on your proposition will probably conform with General Steven's answer, and that it will be made directly after this is received" (Brent to Kingston, 24 May 1802 [ibid.]).

2. For the claim of James Stewart & Co. for demurrage for the ship *Grand Turk*, see JM to Stevens, 18 Feb. 1802, and W. F. Gordon to JM, 27 Feb. 1802 (*PJM-SS*, 2:475 and n. 3, 495–96).

§ From William C. C. Claiborne. *28 May 1802, Washington, Mississippi Territory.* "I have the honor to enclose you, a Manuscript Copy of the Laws passed at the last Session of the Territorial Legislature; There being at present, no Secretary in the Territory, (Colo. Steele's time of service having expired) the original Laws, are deposited with me for safe keeping. The acts passed at the Session, previous to the last, are yet with the Printer; but I hope, the publication of them, will be completed in the course of next week, and if so, I will transmit you a Copy, by the next Mail."

Letterbook copy (Ms-Ar: Claiborne Executive Journal). 1 p. Printed in Rowland, *Claiborne Letter Books*, 1:114.

§ From Peter Stirling. *28 May 1802, Barcelona.* Transmits a copy of his last letter, dated 29 Apr., "being moved for general good and have to add that Scrupolous precautions are taken here to avoyd an introduction [of disease]. It is Said . . . that the infection is So pestiferous in *Oran* that great numbers are Swept off Dayly. . . . I likewise understand that the French Nation are going to be So Cautious as not to admitt into their Ports any Vessell from *oran* or its Neighbourhood. For the present perfect Health is enjoyed in Spain." Reports that he intervened with the superior court of Barcelona on behalf of the schooner *Polly* of Boston, Capt. H. H. May, and received the enclosed answer.[1]

RC and enclosure (DNA: RG 59, CD, Barcelona, vol. 1). RC 2 pp.

1. Stirling enclosed a document (1 p.; in Spanish, with English translation on verso) headed, "In assembly of the 11th. of may 1802." It ordered a thirty-day quarantine for Capt. Henry May's ship; "he could not be admitted with only 15. Days quarantine, as he was told on his first arrival, he Should perform; as during those, orders were received, to oblige Such Ships to a Strict quarantine that had Some touch, or Comunication with Some other, coming from the Coast of Africa."

§ Receipt from Nelly Conway Madison. *28 May 1802.* "Recd. of James Madison fifty dollars in part of what may be due to me out of the personal estate of my grandfather."

Ms (owned by W. Parsons Todd, Morristown, N.J., 1961). In JM's hand, signed by Nelly C. Madison.

From George Tod

Trumbull County May 29t. 1802

I am desired by Govr. St Clair to transmit to you whatever is within my recollection of an evenings conversation, at Chillicothe,[1] while the legislature of this Territory were in session, in which he was the principal supporter. In compliance Sir with his request, I will endeavor, as far as is within my recollection, to give you an accurate relation.

The evening of the day on which he recd. the President's Message, the Govr. spent with Genl. Paine, a member of the legislature from this County, and myself. The first subject conversed upon, was the Presidents Message.[2] Of this he spoke generally in terms of approbation; some parts of it however did not coincide with his political sentiments; particularly the suggestion of abolishing internal taxation. His reasons were it would be risking to much on a doubtful experiment. He then made the following remark & repeated it—that he liked experimental governments, but did not like *experiments* in governments; for that the consequences of experiments were doubtfull & much to be apprehended.

I have no recollection that the Govr. spoke a word in support of monarchy; or a syllable against the government of the United States. He on the contrary expressed himself as an admirer of our constitution and the principles of republicanism, as understood & practised by the late administration. He remarked, he had expended as much time & treasure in the establishment of our constitution & government, he believed as most men.

I did not hear him speak one disrespectful word of the President; nor did he treat the message, in the least degree contemptuously. Much he said about the Militia, & against it as being ineffectual, unless to withstand an invasion untill regular troops could be raised; but no expression fell from him like wishing for a standing army.

Considering the situation in which he was placed, surrounded by his enemies list'ning to catch every word which he used, much of his conversation might be deemed imprudent. Knowing the vigilence and disposition of his enemies, I whispered a word of caution to him. It however increased the spirit with which he supported the conversation. It is impossible Sir for me to relate the whole conversation which passed; much of it has escaped my recollection; as it was indifferent, did not treasure it up. Those who placed themselves with a veiw to catch what was spoken in a heedless moment, might remember many things, which most people, ever so inimical would have forgotten, or if remembered, Kept to themselves.[3] Had I thought any thing the Govr. uttered that evening could form a substantial objection to his being continued longer in the

office he now holds, the impression on my mind would have been deeper.
I am &c.

G. T.[4]

Tr (O).

1. See Arthur St. Clair to George Tod, 21 Apr. 1802 (Smith, *St. Clair Papers*, 2:581–83).
2. President Jefferson's message to Congress at the beginning of the session was read on 8 Dec. 1801. It suggested that Congress end internal taxation and cut government expenses, particularly by reducing the army and navy (Ford, *Writings of Jefferson*, 8:108–25).
3. Tod referred to a letter written to Jefferson by three Ohioans that related a conversation alleged to have taken place in Chillicothe, Ohio, on 19 Dec. 1801. The three asserted that they heard St. Clair "say and repeat many words and sentences in contempt and reproach of the Government of the United States; particularly that the said Government would finally settle down into an aristocracy, and from thence into a monarchy." According to the three, St. Clair made "several ludicrous and sarcastic observations on the militia," including the statement that "the militia were all damned nonsense," and said that the president's recommendations "were intended as experiments—a thing not to be admitted in government" (Francis Dunlavy and others to Jefferson, 26 Dec. 1801, Smith, *St. Clair Papers*, 2:585–86 n.).
4. George Tod (1773–1841) was a Connecticut-born, Yale-educated lawyer who settled in Ohio in 1800. He served in the Ohio state Senate (1804–5), as judge of the state supreme court (1806–9), and as presiding judge of the third judicial district (1815–34) (ibid., 2:584 n.).

§ From Louis-André Pichon. *29 May 1802, Philadelphia.* Encloses two commissions for commissaries of commercial relations: one for Lequinio de Kerblay at Newport, Rhode Island, and the other for Sotin at Savannah, Georgia. These two agents arrived several days ago and await the president's exequatur to enter upon their functions and leave for their posts.

RC (DNA: RG 59, NFL, France, vol. 1). 1 p.; in French. Enclosures not found. Joseph-Marie Lequinio de Kerblay and Pierre-Jean-Marie Sotin de la Condière received their exequaturs on 15 June 1802 (*National Intelligencer*, 21 June 1802).

§ From William Buchanan. *30 May 1802, Ile de France.* Acknowledges receipt of JM's standing instructions under date of 9 July 1801[1] as well as a copy of his commission as U.S. commercial agent for Ile de France and Bourbon; "the Vessel by which the Original was forwarded is unquestionably lost." Will follow JM's instructions "respecting returns of the American Vessels which may arrive within my district . . . tho' I am apprehensive it will be difficult to execute that part, which regards Cargoes, as most of our Countrymen are unwilling to give the necessary Information." Notes that the two blank forms mentioned in JM's instructions were omitted.

RC (DNA: RG 59, CD, Port Louis, vol. 1). 2 pp.; docketed by Brent as received 16 Aug. Duplicate (ibid.) dated 1 June; docketed by Brent as received 8 Sept.

1. See Standing Instructions to American Consuls and Vice-Consuls, 10 June 1801 (*PJM-SS*, 1:288–89).

§ From John Gavino. *31 May 1802, Gibraltar*. No. 88. Reports departure for Lisbon on 24 May of an English brig—converted from a captured Tripolitan ship—commanded by Capt. Anthony Lambertus. In a letter of 25 Apr. O'Brien reported that the Algerines had captured one Genoese and two Neapolitan vessels and that "Six other large Corsairs were ready for Sea." Has heard rumors in town of the Algerine capture of the Portuguese frigate *Cisne*; "if this account is verified the Algereens will be very haughty." The U.S. ship *Chesapeake* arrived on 25 May after a voyage of twenty-eight days and is undergoing repairs for a sprung mainmast. Has forwarded dispatch to U.S. minister at Madrid received from the State Department by the ship *Protector*. Encloses letter from Simpson at Tangier to JM. In a postscript notes that a recently arrived Danish frigate confirmed the capture of the *Cisne* by Algiers, reporting that the commander and twenty men were killed and that "the Moors on shore were so much Exulted, that no Christian could Speak."

RC (DNA: RG 59, CD, Gibraltar, vol. 2). 3 pp.; docketed by Brent. Printed in Knox, *Naval Documents, Barbary Wars*, 2:162–63. Enclosure was probably James Simpson to JM, 13 May 1802.

§ From John Rodgers. *June 1802, Baltimore*. Reports the "unjust, insulting, and Cruel Treatment" he received at the hands of French officials in Saint-Domingue. He arrived at Cap Français in late December 1801. "The Evening preceding the night the Cape was Burnt, I lost my passage on Board, in rescuing from the flames, a number of helpless Women, and Children. As soon as I found there was no possibility of getting on Board, . . . I soon resolved on taking an active part, in doing which, (by Strategem), saved a number of Houses, and a great quantity of valuable property: in fact, had the Fleet entered so soon as was Expected, I should have saved, or been the cause of saving near half the Town." He was treated "with every mark of Attention" by the French officers; "and, altho, an Embargo was Instantly laid; yet, on Application to General La Clerc, I was immediately granted permission to Depart. . . . The Civilities I received from Gen. La Clerc, added to the just claims I had to his friendship, induced me to return immediately to Baltimore, supposing I should have advantages in Trading to St. Domingo. . . . I prevailed on my friends . . . to load two Vessels, with Provisions; with which, on the 9th March last, I sailed for the Cape. . . . However, to my Astonishment, . . . shortly after my Arrival, the Cargoes of these Two Vessels, were taken from me, by the Government, at their own prices, without any Security for the payment, and myself, in a short time after, thrown into prison." He was arrested on 11 Apr., without being "afforded an opportunity of contradicting, and confuting (any) and (Every) unjust representation, which might have been circulated, to my prejudice." Orders were given to treat him like a criminal, and he was confined to a cell that "in Size, was very little more than double that of a large Oven; built entirely of Stone; the Door, with a small Iron Grate over its Top Excepted." There he remained about three hours and then was conducted to a place "still worse—A Dungeon, surrounded by a double Wall, and totaly Dark, except what light the Key Hole afforded. . . . Added to this, it was the Habitation of Lizards, Spiders, and many obnoxious Insects, peculiar to the Climate. In this situation, I was kept Four days, and Three nights, on Bread and

Water. . . . On the 4th day, the door of my Dungeon was opened; when I found a partner of the wrongs & Injustice I had suffered, standing in the yard—*A Mr. Wm Davidson of Philadelphia.* . . . On seeing Mr. Davidson, I could immediately discover the Effects of the Inhuman Treatment we had received. He was pale, and Languid, from breathing four days, and Three nights, in an Infectious Air, Intolerable Heat, Darkness, and every filth, and dirt, that can be imagined. . . . We began Devising a plan to get something to Eat, and with the aid of 25 Dollars, procured a Breakfast, and made an arrangement with a person . . . to furnish us with a little Meat, and Wine, during our Imprisonment." In order to send a message to the outside, "I was reduced to the necessity of Bleeding, myself, to procure Ink; with which, and the Assistance of Mr. Davidson's Toothpick, which I converted into a pen, made out to Write a few Lines to one of our Friends." On the ninth day of captivity, "we were removed to the most remote part of the Prison." On 25 Apr. they received an unsigned letter offering "service" for whatever "Sacrifis you can make." They later were visited by a person in disguise who offered them liberty for a fee. "To this unjust proposition, I felt so much Indignation, that I replyed, I would not buy my Liberty, even was I sure, I should Die in prison. . . . Mr. Davidson, choosing to sacrafice his own feelings, rather than those of a Wife, and Children, promised to give two, or four hundred Dollars. . . . However, it was never demanded. . . . The above Visitor, altho he was in disguise, I knew him to be Secretary to the Commandant." On 29 Apr. the two prisoners were conducted to the quarters of General Hardy, who ordered them to be placed aboard ship and sent off within four days "and not to Land again under pain of Death." In this interview Hardy "made use of such Scurrilous Abuse, as I feel almost Ashamed to repeat." "He said, He knew that I had been their inveterate Enemy, and that I ought to be Shot, or Hung. To which I only replied, that Sooner, or later, they would be made sensible of the unjust Treatment I had received. To this, He answered, with a mixture of insult, and contempt, you may now inform your Government, what kind of Treatment you have received from this Administration."

Mentions a circumstance that might have led to his imprisonment. On 2 Apr. 1801 he met with Clément, the commandant of the port, who "had sent for me, with an intention to Insult me—in which, He Shielded himself with the Functions of his Office." His insulting remarks were "pointed at the Officers of the American Navy." Rodgers informed General Hardy, commander of the northern department, of the incident, expecting him to "point out a mode of Redress," but "instead of doing so, He desired that I would inform him in writing, what had passed between us; Accordingly, I wrote him the following Letter."

Describes an interview with Clément held "on Sunday last," in which the commandant accused him of trading with Toussaint and insulting French naval officers. "I am sorry to be under the necessity of saying, that during the above Conversation, Mr. Clement's Language bespoke nothing but Insult, and contempt, to my Country, and my own person. . . . However, I have since learnt, (I conceive) the cause of Mr. Clement's Extraordinary Conduct; which it is *possible*, has been occasioned by some Mal representations, made by Mr. Pichon."[1]

Refers JM to Tobias Lear "for the Reasons why I have suspected Mr. Pichon's endeavouring to Injure me." Rather than justifying his own conduct, transcribes a 30 Apr. 1802 letter "Signed by every Respectable American Resident at the Cape," expressing "deep regret, and Indignation, for the Recent Treatment you have experienced here, . . . not from any misconduct of your own, but from Base misrepresentations, made to the Capt. General of this Colony."

RC (DNA: RG 76, France, Unbound Records Relating to Spoliation Claims, ca. 1885); FC (DLC: Rodgers Papers); partial FC (ibid.); Tr (DNA: RG 59, CD, Cap Haitien, vol. 4); letterpress copy of Tr (NHi: Livingston Papers). RC 21 pp.; in a clerk's hand, corrected and signed by Rodgers. FC in a clerk's hand, with corrections and additions in Rodgers's hand; these changes are incorporated in the partial FC but not in the RC or Tr.

1. According to James Barron, Rodgers "laid all the blame" for his imprisonment on Pichon, "a little man, with a little wife, and a little child, the three not weighing above 180 pounds; of this man he swore loudly, he would have revenge, threatning that where-ever he did meet him, he would kill or otherwise maim him to his satisfaction, so loud were those threats that Monsr Pygon thought it proper to complain to the State department, which brought forth a long letter from Mr. Madison [not found], to the aggrieved party, Captain Rodgers; in this letter, Mr. Madison refered Captain Rodgers to a letter written, or printed, by the queen of England, as an apology to the Empress of Russia, for the arrest of the Russian minister by an ignorant constable, and a tailor creditor, of the Minister, on a sunday morning; this letter was refered to, with a view to impress Captain Rodgers, of the sacredness of the character of a foreign functionary" (James Barron to George Blake, 14 Nov. 1848 [DNA: RG 45, Subject File, XP, Misc. Correspondence to and from Pursers]).

From Fontaine Maury

Dear Sir   New York June 1. 1802

Having a private Conveyance I take the Liberty to inclose you a Pamphlet just Published.[1]

If I can on any occassion Render my services acceptable to you at this place, where I have made an establishment in the Commission business, I shall have particular[2] therein, being with real esteem Dear Sir Your mo He

FONTAINE MAURY

RC (DLC). Docketed by JM.

1. The pamphlet was probably [James Cheetham], *A Narrative of the Suppression by Col. Burr, of the History of the Administration of John Adams* (New York, 1802; Shaw and Shoemaker 2021), publication of which on 29 May 1802 ignited a pamphlet war between followers of Aaron Burr and those of George and DeWitt Clinton that lasted well into 1803 ("The Pamphlet War," 15 July 1802, Kline, *Papers of Burr*, 2:724–28). JM's copy is in the Madison Collection, Rare Book Department, University of Virginia Library.

2. Maury omitted a word here.

§ From Thomas Appleton. *1 June 1802, Leghorn*. Has nothing of note to report except the "great embarkation of french troops in the different ports of Italy,"[1]

which required the impressment of "twenty or more vessels of various nations in-
discriminately." Among these was the *Syren*, Captain Reilly, of Philadelphia. "I remonstrated against the proceedure, and should, I am persuaded have obtained her
release from so unpleasant an employ, but . . . the conditions being found sufficiently advantageous, Captn. Noble of the Brigte. friend's Adventure of N York
accepted the hire," and the *Syren* was discharged.

"The freedom of Commerce of this port, joined to the circumstance that neither
our ships or their Cargoes pay any other duties than those imposed on Etrurian
subjects . . . have concurred to lessen the disadvantages that the peace with England
has generally occasioned to our Merchants trading in these Seas." Notes that only
twenty-two ships had arrived in Leghorn from the U.S. before his appointment;
since that period 154 cargoes have been sold. As the cargoes "Consisted principally
of East india goods, Havannah Sugars, coffee, Cocoa, cochineal &c.," the total
amount of the sales can be estimated at $17 million, half of which is "clear proffit
to the adventurers." "The return cargoes have consisted of florence and Lucca Oils,
Silks, marbled soap, anchovies, capers and drugs, these, except a small part consumed in the U States, have been sent from thence to the West-indies, and . . . have
uniformly found a quick, and advantagious market."

Traces the "principal outlines" of the political face of Italy. Has already forwarded the constitution of the Italian Republic as accepted at Lyons; "it has met
with as general an approbation, as could be expected, when one considers the numbers devoted to the interests of the disinherited Princes, in conjunction with the
power of the clergy."

"The abilities, firmness and integrity of Melzi the New President add dignity to
the government, while they silence the clamours of the nobles and the Priests."
Increased taxation is "borne with patience," and Italians "feel the happy effects of a
wise administration." Venice, which clung to "the principle of an unarmed neutrality, and whose fate has been lamented by every friend to republics of whatever
denomination, owes unquestionably her present subjection to the duplicity of her
politicks in the latter times of her existance as a sovereign State, and the conduct of
Buonaparte will ever find advocates with those who are informed, that the senate
had secretly determined to declare themselves should the arms of the Emperor become successful." This is known to the French. Venice's situation is "deplorable."
"Their provisionary government is composed of three nobles chosen by the Emperor, (who are as despotic as the former inquisition of State) and at the same time
obliged to endure all the military insolence of 25,000 Croates. Their navy was destroyed by the french, and their commerce with the republic." Cites as an example
of the "tyranny which is now exercised over them" the measures taken by Napoleon
to draw all gold and silver into the French treasury; this "immediately produced an
universal bankruptcy." "The Venetians are deprived of every means of redress: as
even remonstrance to the Emperor is interdicted except through the medium of the
very tyrants themselves—and to complain is the second order of crimes. On the
whole, I am persuaded there scarce exists a Procuratore of St. Marc who would not
consent to become a Citizen of a free government, and be reduced to the common
priviledges of the meanest plebian, in preference to the slavery they now alike
endure."

Ferrara, Bologna, and Ravenna "are now lopped from the dominions of the Pope, and form three departments of the italian republic." The pope is thus deprived of two million crowns annually, and the action endangers his temporal power. "The King of Etruria has long been Afflicted with epileptic complaints, which have in a great measure alienated the faculties of his mind; and these Attacks so frequently Seize him, that little hope remains that he can continue to govern his Kingdom with judgement.[2] The grand duke Leopold had effected with indiscribable pains and labour an absolute Submission of the clergy[3]—they were deprived of the right of Censure on the press, and the priests were alike amenable for their crimes in common with the rest of his subjects; together with a variety of other regulations which rendered the church much less intolerant in Tuscany than in the rest of Italy. The present King has re-established the clergy in their former prerogatives, . . . an act, which though it may forfeit him the esteem of one part of the community, has nevertheless Acquired him powerful advocates in another." French troops have left Rome and Naples "as stipulated by the treaty—10,000 embarked at Tarentio and 4000 at Ancona." Reports say "they are destined for the islands of the Archipelago." "That the forces of the northern powers are moving towards the possessions of the Grand Signior in Europe, I beleive also is equally certain.[4] The french general here a few days Since informed me, that . . . unless an accomodation ensued on the arrival at Paris of the Ottoman minister, events of the greatest magnitude would arise out of this combined Armament. The port of Venise would well suit the Italian republic, and the Emperor would find abundant compensation in the neighbourhood of Hungary, while the British would remain silent spectators of the spoils, should they be suffered to retain any part of Egypt. The Bashaw of Jannina has followed the example of Passan Oglû and invaded Albania. The destituted Beys have retired into upper Egypt, and joined to the Mamlucs oppose a powerful force to the Grand Signior. Never perhaps was the Ottoman empire so disturbed within by the revolts of its own subjects, nor from without by so potent a combination as now threatens it."

Requests JM's "attention to those parts of my late letters to the Department of State, relative to the Navy Agency within the jurisdiction of my consulate." Refers JM to Cathcart's dispatches for Barbary affairs.

RC (DNA: RG 59, CD, Leghorn, vol. 1). 7 pp.; docketed by Brent as received 16 Sept.

1. Article 11 of the Treaty of Amiens signed between Great Britain and France provided for the evacuation of French troops from the Kingdom of Naples and the Roman state (de Clercq, *Recueil des traités de la France*, 1:488).

2. Louis I, king of Etruria, died 27 May 1803 at the age of thirty (Edouard Driault, *La politique extérieure du Premier Consul, 1800–1803* [Paris, 1910], pp. 322–23).

3. Leopold, the grand duke of Parma, had, in the words of Gen. Henri Clarke, the French ambassador to the Kingdom of Etruria, snatched Tuscany from "sacerdotal slavery," only to see the king restore priestly authority and religious intolerance (ibid., p. 321).

4. France and the Ottoman Empire were in the final stages of peace negotiations at this time, and a treaty was signed on 25 June 1802. The Sublime Porte, however, continued to face internal revolts throughout the empire in Arabia, Iraq, and especially in the Balkans (Stanford J. Shaw, *Between Old and New: The Ottoman Empire under Sultan Selim III, 1789–1807* [Cambridge, Mass., 1971], pp. 280–82, 294–95, 298–311).

§ From William C. C. Claiborne. *1 June 1802, Washington, Mississippi Territory.* Acknowledges receipt of JM's letter of 9 Apr. enclosing his commission as governor of the Mississippi Territory.

Letterbook copy (Ms-Ar: Claiborne Executive Journal). 1 p. Printed in Rowland, *Claiborne Letter Books,* 1:116.

§ From William Willis. *1 June 1802, New York.* Has terminated his business and found a passage to France. Hopes to be in Barcelona in forty days. "I am inform'd (indirectly) that one of the Mr Montgomerys of Alicant were about to apply for the consulate of Barcelona, and from this I am led to conjecture the source of a great part of the Clamor rais'd against me, and such an opportunity no doubt will be very gratifying to them in order to be reveng'd of me for defending the interests of some american Citizens. . . . I can procure ten americans of respectable character, to give testimony in my favor, to one that will say any thing against my character."

RC (DNA: RG 59, CD, Barcelona, vol. 1). 2 pp.

From John E. Caldwell

SIR,   CITY OF SANTO DOMINGO 2d. June 1802.

A few days after I had received from Mr. Lear a commission of the President of the US. dated the 26th. January 1802—appointing me Commercial Agent of the US. for the city of Sto. Domingo &c.,[1] General Kerversau,[2] who commands the Spanish part of this Island, returned from an expedition against the blacks; he having been absent from here for several weeks past. I lost no time in waiting on him, in order to be informed whether the permission he had given me (when he first landed here with the European troops) to exercise, until further orders, the functions of my office at Sto. Domingo, would be withdrawn, or continued. He invited me to exhibit to him the commission I had lately received; which I did. Two days after I received from him a letter dated the 9th. Prairial, of which the inclos⟨ed⟩ (marked No. 1.) is a copy.[3] The substance & style of that letter appearing to me extraordinary & inconsistent with the dispositions that General had before manifes⟨ted⟩ I immediately waited on him for an explanation. I then told him that I had thitherto considered his first permission, & his tacit approbation since then a sufficient reason for me to continue the function⟨s⟩ of the office I held; that I had always been ready to cease exercising them, whenever I should apprehend that exercise to be obnoxious to the Government of that country. He answered me that he had received orders from the General in chief of the Island respecting all foreign agents, which orders he would shortly communicate to me: that he considered my mission to be to Toussaint, & that the manner in which my Commission was worded (not having mentioned the name of the Government of the country to which I was sent) was a *deep Jesuitical finesse* of the Secretary of State. To that & some other similar observations I was convinced a reply by me would be useless & improper. I therefore confined myself to saying to him that I should ask him for a passport to leave the country, & I retired. I shortly after wrote to him for that passport; the next day he sent me two; one for the Cape, & the other for the United States; both accompanying a letter of the 11th. Prairial (1st. June) of which the inclosed marked No. 2. is a true copy.[4] I sent him back the passport for the Cape, and kept the other, of which I send you also the inclosed copy.[5]

You will please to Observe that a vessel, just then arrived from the cape, had brought a confirmation of the account of Mr. Lear's departure, with a relation of many unpleasant circumstances that took place there previous to it.

I have taken passage on board an american vessel bound to St. Thomas, which sails tomorrow. From thence I shall shortly return to the United States. I have the honor to be with due respect, Sir, Your most obedient & humble servant

JOHN E. CALDWELL

P. S. On returning to Genl. Kerversau the passport for the cape—I wrote to him, that I would have it well understood that my accepting of the passport for the United States should not imply the inference drawn in his last letter to me, nor bear any consequence unfavorable to my appointment for this place, in any respect whatever.

JOHN E. CALDWELL

RC and enclosures (DNA: RG 59, CD, Cap Haitien, vol. 4). RC docketed by Brent as received 20 June. Duplicate (ibid.) docketed by Brent as received 12 July. For enclosures, see nn. 3–5.

1. For the delivery of Caldwell's commission, see JM to Lear, 26 Feb. 1802 (*PJM-SS*, 2: 490, 491 n. 4).

2. Gerard de Kerversau et Leborgne had been a French representative in Saint-Domingue and the French West Indies since 1796. Returning to France in 1801, he wrote an influential report urging the government to crush Toussaint L'Ouverture and the other black commanders rather than cooperate with them. As a part of the Leclerc expedition, Kerversau was assigned command of the Spanish part of the island (Paul Roussier, ed., *Lettres du Général Leclerc* [Paris, 1937], pp. 24–25, 78–79).

3. Kerversau's letter to Caldwell, 9 Prairial an X (29 May 1802) (2 pp.; in French) informed Caldwell that as the name of the French republic was not indicated on his commission, he considered the U.S. agent's mission to be absolutely foreign to France, and he gave Caldwell forty-eight hours to leave the cape.

4. Kerversau's letter of 11 Prairial an X (31 May 1802) (2 pp.; in French) described Leclerc's orders for the assembly at Cap Français of those foreigners who had been commis-

sioned to Toussaint as governor of the island for the French republic and the departure from the island within forty-eight hours of all those foreigners who had been commissioned to Toussaint himself. Kerversau demanded that Caldwell choose between these two categories.

5. Caldwell enclosed a copy of a passport dated 11 Prairial an X (31 May 1802) (1 p.; in French), which allowed him to return to the U.S. on a ship of his choice and stated that he would depart within forty-eight hours.

§ From James Leander Cathcart. *3 June 1802, Leghorn.* No. 7. "Yesterday" he enclosed dispatches from Eaton through 4 May.[1] Now encloses an extract of intelligence received from Tripoli "containing the most prominent transactions of that government from the 12th. of March to the 30th. of April," to which he adds the following extracts from Eaton's letter to him of 21 May.[2]

On the day before yesterday the Schooner Enterprize Lieut. Sterret arrived here, thirty six days [hours] from before Tripoli. He left there four Sweedish Frigates & . . . the Boston. The Swedish flagstaff is at len[g]th taken down & an end put to temporizing—some bickerings have since taken place between the Tripoline gunboats & the *allies* a few Moors have been kill'd & one Swede wounded. Mc.Niels grape & langrage were found an unwelcome *Regalia* to the boats; though he suffer'd nothing from their too elevated Shot.

. . . The captures of Tunisian merchantmen complain'd of have all been done by the Swedes, this circumstance relieves me from incalculable perpl⟨ex⟩ities with this government.

Lieutenant Sterret assures me that seven days ago, the Bash⟨aw⟩ Ciddi Mohamed, was at Malta waiting the arrival of our Squadron; Captn. Mc.Niel signifies to me by letter of the 17th. inst. that this is by arrangment between them, Thus things seem to be in a good train. . . .

An Express ship of War has lately arrived from England at Malta with orders for the immediate evacuation of that Island. . . .

Cathcart knows his "narration of facts . . . is little better than a gazette," but as the ship taking his dispatch could sail at any moment he must defer comment. Requests JM to send a credit for him to Degen & Purviance or another Leghorn firm. In a postscript states that he is forwarding a copy of his dispatch no. 8 of last year, a copy of which was also forwarded in his no. 6 of 21 May.

RC and enclosure (DNA: RG 59, CD, Tripoli, vol. 2). RC 3 pp.; docketed by Brent as received 16 Sept. Enclosure headed: "Extracts from Mr. Nissen's letters to me dated at Tripoli from the 12th. March to the 30th April inclusive recd. by me at Leghorn June 1st. 1802"; Nissen reported on events at Tripoli, including the expectation that the emperor of Morocco would send a cargo of grain, the movement of Tripolitan ships, and Swedish-Tripolitan affairs (6 pp.; printed, with second page omitted, in Knox, *Naval Documents, Barbary Wars,* 2:66–67).

1. On the last page of Eaton to JM, 4 May 1802, Cathcart wrote a note to JM dated 2 June 1802, and he appended a brief extract from Eaton's letter to him of 21 May (DNA: RG 59, CD, Tunis, vol. 2, pt. 1).

2. Eaton's 21 May 1802 letter to Cathcart is printed in full in Knox, *Naval Documents, Barbary Wars,* 2:157–58.

§ From John Mason. *4 June 1802, Georgetown.* "Mr Nicholas King of the City of Washington,[1] who will do himself the honor to hand this Letter, has requested me to make him known to you, being desirous, as he is at present out of Business, to obtain a Clerks place in your Department, should there be a Vacancy. . . . I have known Mr King for many years & can most safely recommend him as a Man of Abilities Integrity and amiable Disposition. . . . I can also speak confidently of his Industry and attention—his particular profession has been that of Surveyor & Draftsman but his Knowledge of Business is general—perhaps his Knowledge in Mecanics & Drafts may be useful in addition to the ordinary Duties—in some of the Branches of your office."

RC (ViU). 2 pp.

1. Nicholas King (1771–1812) was born in England and immigrated to the U.S. in 1794. First employed as a surveyor by the Philadelphia merchant Robert Morris, King moved to Washington in 1796 where he surveyed for Morris, the commissioners of the city, and others until 1803. That year Jefferson appointed him surveyor of the city of Washington, a position he held until his death (Ralph E. Ehrenberg, "Nicholas King: First Surveyor of the City of Washington, 1803–1812," *Records of the Columbia Historical Society*, 69–70 [1969–70]: 31–65).

§ From John Webb. *4 June 1802, Charleston.* Refers to his letter to JM of 28 Apr.[1] enclosing a certificate and a copy of his letter to J. E. Colhoun; "Mr. Calhoun has been so polite to return the Certificate, as 'it may be of service to me.'" Apologizes for this second request but explains that "the Uncertainty of my first having arrived safe, not having had the pleasure of hearing from you, & my anxiety to hear" prompted him to write.

RC and enclosures (DNA: RG 59, LAR, 1801–9, filed under "Webb"). RC 1 p.; docketed by Jefferson. Enclosures are a copy of a certificate supporting Webb for the position of commissioner of bankruptcy, signed by Thomas Bee and six others (1 p.), and a letter from Colhoun to Webb, 27 May 1802 (1 p.).

1. Webb's earlier letter to JM is dated 30 Apr. 1802.

§ From James Simpson. *5 June 1802, Tangier.* No. 40. Transmits a copy of his dispatch no. 39 [13 May 1802] and encloses a translation of the minister's response to his and the Swedish consul's 25 Apr. letter on the intended shipment of wheat to Tripoli, "by which you will see he submits the propriety of that measure to the Letter of the Treaties of Sweden and the United States, with this Country. Unfortunately neither make any provision for such a Case, nor are Blockaded Ports mentioned in them."[1] "Sunday last the Governour sent for Mr Wyk and me to shew us a Letter from His Majesty, desiring to know if we were yet authorised to grant Passports for that Wheat & the Tripoline Ship laying at Gibraltar, which of course was answered in the Negative. It did not appear he had been instructed to treat with us upon the subject, in the precise terms of the Ministers Letter." Having heard of Commodore Dale's safe arrival in the U.S., hopes to receive JM's instructions soon on the points "submitted to your consideration." The emperor is not satisfied with the "choice or quality" of the Swedish gifts; the governor "presented Mr Wyk with a very extensive and costly list of what the Emperour wishes to have in two years hence, which this Gentleman did not see himself at liberty to receive." The governor warned Wyk that should the next ambassador not bring the gifts "he had better not come." It will be some months before the two frigates launched at Rabat will be made ready for sea. Fears these ships are "intended to act against some Christian Power" and suggests stationing at least one U.S. frigate "on this Coast" to watch them. Reiterates that "nothing will tend more to keep this Government in awe" than the frequent sight of U.S. warships on its coast and in its harbors. For lack of conveyance, this letter has been delayed until 10 June, which allows him to add that the Swedish consul Wyk has been warned by the emperor that he can leave Morocco but must take his secretary and dependents; should the articles wanted by the emperor not arrive within four months, "Peace between the two Countrys would at that period cease." Hopes that the situation of Tripoli has had no share in determining the emperor's actions. Adds in a postscript that as the Swedish consul is to leave in a few days, "I do not consider it safe to freight the Ships of that Nation for Voyages to this part of the World."

RC and enclosure (DNA: RG 59, CD, Tangier, vol. 1). RC 3 pp.; docketed by Brent. Extract of RC printed in Knox, *Naval Documents, Barbary Wars*, 2:165. Jefferson communicated an extract of the RC and the enclosure to Congress with his annual message on 15 Dec. 1802 (printed in *ASP, Foreign Relations*, 2:465–66). For enclosure, see n. 1.

1. The enclosed translation of Sidi Mohammed ben Absalom Selawy's letter to Simpson and Peter Wyk, 10 May 1802 (2 pp.), described the wheat intended to be transported to Tripoli as the property of the emperor. "If you allow it to pass when the Ambassador goes . . . it will be very well. If not, you will do what is regular, and as is established by the Treaties of Peace between us and you" (printed in Knox, *Naval Documents, Barbary Wars*, 2:149).

¶ From Edward Savage. Letter not found. *5 June 1802, New York*. Acknowledged in Daniel Brent to Savage, 8 June 1802 (DNA: RG 59, DL, vol. 14). Encloses two hundred Mediterranean passports and requests a remittance of $375 to procure the parchment necessary to complete the remainder. Brent had written to Savage on 14 May 1802 (ibid.) asking him to furnish one thousand Mediterranean passports, of which two hundred were "*immediately* requisite" and the remainder were to be sent "as soon afterwards as you conveniently can, the whole to be of the old Impression." Brent wrote to Savage again on 7 July 1802 (ibid.), asking him to "lose no time in sending forward the remaining parcel."

To Ebenezer Stevens

SIR,   DEPARTMENT OF STATE June 6th. 1802.
    I duly received your letter of the 21st. Ulto,[1] and in consequence on[e] has been written to Mr. Kingston from this office,[2] informing him that I do not accede to his proposition for referring the question between the government and himself to the arbitration of persons at Philadelphia, and that you was authorized to take the necessary steps in concert with him; for

having it settled in that way at New York. I request you therefore to name some Gentleman in that City who may be entirely confided in, to act as an arbitrator, on the part of the United States, in this business, provided Mr. Kingston designates one on his part as he probably will. In that case, if these two disagree, they may call in a third or, if you can effect a compromise on equitable terms, this as it wo[u]ld be the least troublesome, might be the most advantageous way of closing the Transaction altogether.

It seems but reasonable that the owners of the Grand Turk should pay for the Cable in question, if there be not some special cause to the contrary, which is not known at this Department. I am respectfully, &ca.

JAMES MADISON.

Letterbook copy (DNA: RG 59, DL, vol. 14).

1. JM referred to Stevens's letter of 28 May 1802.
2. Daniel Brent to Kingston, 5 June 1802 (ibid.).

From Peder Blicherolsen

SIR   PHILADELPHIA 6th June 1802

In your letter of the 22d of April,[1] you have been pleased to observe Sir in answer to mine of the 12th same month concerning the capture of the Danish ship Mercator by Captain Maley of the United States, that proper instructions should be given to an attorney as soon as I had signified the District in which I wished the judicial proceeding to be instituted.

As for the present moment I reside in the City of Philadelphia where I shall be at hand to give instructions to counsel, I take the Liberty to propose that the case may be investigated in the district court of Pennsylvania, which I suppose will be so much the more eligible, in point of locality, as it is the state where Captain Maley resided at the time of the capture, and in which he may in his absence perhaps be most legally sued. I have the honor to be with the greatest esteem & consideration Sir &c &c

(signed)   BLICHER OLSEN.

Tr (DNA: RG 46, Transcribed Reports and Communications from the Executive, vol. 4). Marked "(Copy)." Enclosed in JM to the Senate, 30 Mar. 1810 (see *ASP, Foreign Relations*, 3: 344, 347).

1. JM to Blicherolsen, 23 Apr. 1802.

From Joseph Russell and Others

Sir!   Buenos Ayres June 6th. 1802

We beg leave through you to lay before the President of the United States an account of the injuries we have suffered from the government of this country & the measures we have taken in order to obtain their redress. In doing this we shall confine ourselves to a general description of those cases only which we conceive to be fairly of national cognizance not being embarrassed with illicit trade or the least violation of the laws of this province.

The most numerous class of sufferers consists of those who either in the United States or some foreign port let our vessells to freight to the subjects of his Catholic Majesty to come here & load on their account with the produce of this country. The Spanish subjects thus freighting these vessells possessed either generally as importers of negroes or specially by royal letters patent the privilege of shipping the produce of this country in foreign bottoms. It was with the knowledge of this privilege & with the full expectation that the Spanish government possessed to[o] much good faith wantonly to revoke it or to impede its free enjoyment that we let our vessells to freight in the manner abovementioned. Sad experience has however taught us that this expectation was ill founded for after our having been detained here for months beyond what was reasonable or necessary those who freighted our vessells are not allowed to load them according to their stipulations with us & as by the aforementioned privilege they had had a right to do. Encouraged by this example of injustice on the part of the government these individuals have in their turn ventured to sport with the solemnity of contracts & wherever the rate of demurrage reserved by charter party bears any just proportion to the injury occasioned by delay there they dishonorably refuse to pay it. Thus between the tyranny of government & the treachery of individuals we are compelled to remain here & behold our vessells rotting without the least prospect of indemnity.

Another class of sufferers but nearly resembling those already mentioned consists of such as having sold their vessells to Spanish agents in the United States undertook the delivery of them & agreed to receive the purchase money in these ports. The right which Spanish subjects here possess of purchasing foreign vessells is derived like their right of freighting them either from the general privilege ceded to the introducers of negroes into this colony or from the special licence of the King. The agents who purchased our vessells took good care to induce our confidence by exhibiting to us their evidence of this right & we like our defrauded countrymen abovementioned came here with the most perfect reliance on the honor of this government & the honesty of its contracting subjects—but like them we have been disappointed. Some of our vessells of this description have now been above seven months in these ports, the government unrighteously refusing or delaying to sanction the transfer & the individuals basely availing themselves of this iniquity of their rulers for a pretext to refuse payment. Hence we find ourselves among inhospitable strangers with vessells which their bad faith has turned upon our hands—without funds sufficient even to preserve these vessells in repair.

All the vessells comprised in both the aforegoing classes came here *bona fide* in ballast & we do not know that the government here has any suspicion to the contrary. There is however a third class of sufferers who have reason perhaps still more acutely to feel their wrongs. These are such as found themselves in the ports of the Brazils immediately after the commencement of hostilities between Portugal & Spain. It was then that the persons & property of Spanish subjects in those ports were menaced with arrest & imprisonment, with seizure & confiscation & it was at this perilous crisis that our countrymen were induced to relinquish their more lucrative pursuits & to rescue these persons & this property from the mischeifs with which they were threatened. This was certainly an action which gave our countrymen a right to expect upon their arrival here if not a cordial & friendly welcome at least protection & justice. Instead of this however they have been affronted with illiberal surmises—perplex'd by vexatious prosecutions & oppressed & ruined by detention. More than a year has now elapsed since some of them have been waiting here for the fulfilment of their contracts while government has stept between the parties & prevented what it was its duty to have enforced.

There is a fourth class of sufferers who although few in number find their embarrassments here equally ruinous. These are such as in the prosecution of long voyages into the Indian or Pacific oceans were forced by necessity into this river for supplies & while there waiting in hopes of hospitality were encountered & taken possession of by cruizers in the service of this government. These vessels with their cargoes which are valuable have been taken from their rightful owners without any specific cause being alleged therefor by those concerned in the depredation. No charge is exhibited against which we can direct a defence but the whole process is conducted in a dark & mysterious manner & we are left to conjecture the end in view by the general bearing merely of the interrogatories of which they extort from us the answers.

These four classes comprize most of the cases arising from injuries done to our property—injuries which we with due deference apprehend are not only in violation of good faith but in many respects of the laws of nations & of the existing treaty between the United States & Spain. You will find a particular statement of the vessells alluded to in these classes in the inclosed paper No. 1.[1] The documents & peculiar circumstances of each case will be furnished by those therein immediately interested.

In addition to these injuries done to the property there are others still more humiliating which have been inflicted on the persons of American citizens. We have seen our fellow citizens thrust into loathsome prisons where disease & chagrin have impaired their constitutions—where every species of villains which swarm in a rotten & corrupted State have been their bed & board companions & where the torn & mangled limbs of executed felons have been scattered among them to increase their disgust & horror. Yet no crime has been alleged against these unhappy sufferers—no cause assigned for their commitment & no motive can be conjectured for such barbarous treatment of men habituated to law & liberty from their infancy other than the mere love of oppression or the hope to torture them into the confession of some imaginary guilt, or to betray or falsely criminate those who have entrusted & employed them.

We are indeed all treated as the members of a weak & contemptible nation, which has neither the means nor the spirit to protect us. Our government is the sneer & scoff of those in authority here & our flag has been ignominiously hoisted with the union down on board a Kings frigate, while those of other, even of petty nations have been displayed with honor.

To obtain redress for these injuries we have given our frequent personal attendance on this government. We have endeavored to move it by individual supplication & to rouse it by general remonstrance. But to no effect. The inclosed paper No. 2 is a copy of a remonstrance which we presented now more than two months since[2] & which like all our other applications has been passed over with the most mortifying silence. Since then we have thought it prudent to address the American Minister at Madrid a copy whereof No. 3 you will receive herein.[3]

Such are the injuries we have suffered & are still suffering here & such are the measures we have heretofore pursued in order to obtain their redress. But worn down by the persevering injustice of this government— deeply wounded by what we consider a wanton & arbitrary violation of our rights, we feel at length compelled to flee for protection to the government of our own country. It is there we expect to find the prompt & powerful guardians of these rights & it is there we look with filial confidence for their vindication. In this address to you we have endeavored to employ the manly language of the injured citizens of a great & independent nation—if it may now & then appear too bold we trust you will impute it to those uncontroulable feelings excited by our wrongs. We have aimed at nothing more than the discharge of a duty which we conceived we owed to ourselves, to our employers & to our country—beleiving as we do that the interest &

dignity of the republic is deeply concerned in insuring a just & honorable treatment to its citizens in foreign countries.

You will please to accept our best wishes for your personal health & happiness & beleive us to be with the most profound respect Yr. mo. obdt. & very hble Servants

JOSEPH RUSSELL
[and thirty-three others]

RC and enclosures (DNA: RG 76, Spain, Treaty of 1819, Misc. Records, ca. 1801–24). Docketed by Wagner. For enclosures, see nn.

1. Enclosure no. 1 is a list of twenty-seven American ships in the Río de la Plata on 6 June 1802 (1 p.), with their place of origin, master, and date and reason of arrival.

2. Enclosure no. 2 is a copy of a memorial addressed to the viceroy of La Plata, dated 31 Mar. 1802 (2 pp.), protesting the detention of American vessels, the seizure of merchant cargoes, and the confinement of American citizens.

3. Enclosure no. 3 is a copy of a letter from the American claimants in Buenos Aires to Charles Pinckney, 22 Apr. 1802 (3 pp.), in which was enclosed a copy of the memorial to the viceroy of La Plata; the writers asked Pinckney to prepare the Spanish court for the "favourable reception" of the documents substantiating their grievances, soon to be collected and arranged, and called to Pinckney's attention the "mean & mercenary spirit of plunder" which characterized the conduct of the viceroy.

§ To Robert R. Livingston. *6 June 1802, Department of State*. Introduces the bearer, Captain Johnson, who goes to Paris to prosecute the claim of Mr. Dunlap, an Alexandria merchant, against France.

Letterbook copy (DNA: RG 59, IM, vol. 6). 1 p.

To Charles Willing Hare

SIR   DEPARTMENT OF STATE WASHINGTON June 7th. 1802.

I have recd. your letter of May 10th. 1802.[1] and communicated its contents to the President, as the case of Mr. Bingham has been laid before Congress and has been postponed only not discussed, it is thought not proper that the Executive, should under such circumstances, interpose any decision or instructions in relation to it.[2] In answer to your enquiry therefore whether if a comprimise should now be effected, Mr. Bingham's claim on the Government would be thereby impaired or destroyed, I cannot go farther than to express my belief that in the event of the case being left to the decision of the Executive, a compromise, with the guardian of Mr. Bingham's interests with the adverse party would not be made a bar to any claim against the United States which would otherwise be admitted. I am respectfully &ca.

JAMES MADISON

Letterbook copy (DNA: RG 59, DL, vol. 14).

1. Letter not found.

2. Hare and Robert Gilmor were agents for William Bingham in the case of the Danish brig *Hope* (see JM to Levi Lincoln, 13 June 1801, and Lincoln to JM, 21 Jan. 1802, *PJM-SS*, 1:310–11 and n. 1, 2:416). The memorial asking for relief in the judgment against Bingham was introduced in the House of Representatives on 10 Feb. 1802 and referred to the Committee of Claims. On 3 Apr. the committee postponed consideration of the petition until the next session (*Journal of the U.S. House of Representatives*, 7th Cong., 1st sess., pp. 221, 222, 418).

Proceedings of the Commissioners of the Sinking Fund

[7 June 1802]

The Secretary of the Treasury reported to the Board, that provision has already been made to meet nearly all the demands which will become due in Holland, during the course of the present year, but, that it is necessary to make immediate provision for the payments on account of principal & Interest which fall due there, during the first five months of the year 1803, and amounting to Four millions, four hundred and thirty nine thousand eight hundred & thirty Guilders, and payable at the following periods. Vizt.

1st. of January.	872,700	Guilders
1st. " February.	986,350	"
1st. " March.	601,000	"
1st. " June.	1,979,780	"

That from the great diminution of Trade, between this Country and Holland, he has ascertained during his late excursion to New York and Philadelphia, that it is impracticable to obtain bills on Holland to that amount; that the rate of Exchange is already forty one Cents ℔ Guilder, and that any attempt on the part of the Government to procure the large amount now wanted, would indubitably raise considerably, the rate of Exchange: That if it shall be attempted to remit by the way of England, the loss will be also considerable, the present rate of Exchange with that Country, being now above par and raising, and would indubitably be enhanced, should Government come into the market for large purchases; and the rate of Exchange between England and Holland, being, by the last advices ten Guilders eight Stivers per pound Sterling, nor likely to become more favorable, which, supposing the whole amount in bills on England to be procurable, (which is not believed to be the fact) at 168, would, including the commission of one ₩ Cent in England, amount to forty three and a half Cents ₩ Guilder: That the Bank of the United States having been applied to, has refused to undertake to contract for making the necessarry Remittance: And that the two only considerable offers made to the Secretary, are now submitted to the Board. Vizt.

The Manhattan Company offer to remit the whole, at the rate of forty three Cents ₩ Guilder.[1]

Alexander Baring[2] offers to remit Guilders 3,140,487.16½ payable in Amsterdam, at the following dates. Vizt.

1st. of January 1803.	605,000. Guilders
1st. " February "	685,000. do.
1st. " March "	425,000. do.
1st. " June "	1,425,487..16½.

and at the rate of forty one Cents ₩ Guilder, provided however, that the United States shall sell to him the two thousand two hundred & twenty shares of the Bank of the United States, owned by the United States, at forty five ₩ Cent advance, or at the rate of five hundred & eighty dollars ₩ Share; which last proposition is recommended by the Secretary of the Treasury as the most eligible, as, exclusively of the advantageous rate of Exchange thereby secured, the transaction will not have any unfavorable effect on the rate of Exchange generally, and by so considerably diminishing the demand, will enable the United States to obtain what is still wanted at a reasonable rate: And because in his opinion, the price obtained for the Bank shares, is more than could be obtained, were they thrown in the market for sale, and more than their intrinsic value.

Whereupon, it was resolved by the Board, "That the Secretary of the Treasury be authorized to sell the shares of the Stock of the Bank of the United States, belonging to the United States; and that the proceeds thereof be applied to the payment of the Capital or principal of any part of the Debt of the United States, which had become due to the Bank of the United States, before or during the course of the year 1796, and which remains still unpaid, in conformity to the provisions of the Act entitled "An Act making provision for the payment of certain Debts of the United States" passed on the 31st. day of May 1796."[3]

(Signed)   JAMES MADISON secretary of State
ALBERT GALLATIN secretary of the Treasury
LEVI LINCOLN Atty Genl.

Attest
EDWARD JONES
secretary to the Board
of Commissrs. of Sinking Fund.

Tr, two copies (DNA: RG 46, Reports and Communications from the Secretary of the Treasury, 7A-F2; and DNA: RG 233, Reports and Communications from the Secretary of the Treasury, 7A-E2.1). Headed: "At a meeting of the Commissioners of the Sinking Fund on the seventh of June 1802. / Present / The Secretary of State / The Secretary of the Treasury / The Attorney General of the United States." Enclosed in Gallatin's 16 Dec. 1802 report to the Senate (printed in *ASP, Finance*, 2:5–9); received by the House of Representatives on 20 Dec. (*Annals of Congress*, 7th Cong., 2d sess., 281).

1. For Gallatin's overtures to Aaron Burr and the Manhattan Company, see Kline, *Papers of Burr*, 2:681 n. 2.

2. Alexander Baring, first Baron Ashburton (1774–1848), was a British financier whose mercantile house invested heavily in American real estate. Married to the daughter of the influential Philadelphia merchant William Bingham, Baring played an increasingly important role in U.S. financial matters during the 1790s, and in 1803 the house of Baring was made the official agent of the U.S. government (Pieter J. Van Winter, *American Finance and Dutch Investment, 1780–1805* [2 vols.; New York, 1977], 2:914–16).

3. *U.S. Statutes at Large*, 1:488–89.

To Rufus King

SIR,   DEPARTMENT OF STATE, June 8th. 1802.

You will herewith receive a Commission giving you powers to adjust by proper stipulations with the British Government whatever remains to be decided in relation to the boundaries between the two nations.

In executing the first part of this trust relating to the Bay of Passama-quody you will recur to the observations contained in my letter of the 28th of July last.[1] I refer you also to a copy herewith inclosed of a letter from Judge Sullivan,[2] heretofore Agent of the United States on the controversy regarding the river St Croix, in answer to some enquiries from me on the subject now committed to you. His information and his reasoning will be useful in the discussion; and to illustrate both I also inclose herewith a copy of the Map to which he refers in the beginning of his letter.[3]

The essential objects to be secured to the United States are the jurisdiction of Moose Island and the common navigation of the Bay and of the channels leading towards the sea between Deer Island and the Island of Campo bello. To the observations of Judge Sullivan in support of the rights of the United States it need only be added that the outlet through those Islands being the only adequate communication with the sea from a great and valuable territory of the United States, they are entitled to the full use of it on that principle as well as on others; and with the less pretext for objection, as the trifling island of Campo bello is the only territory held by Great Britain on one side of the channel.

In pursuance of the next object, viz, the establishment of boundaries between the United States and New brunswick on one side and of Canada on another, it will be proper to provide for the immediate extension of the line which is to run from the source of the St Croix, and which is represented as necessary to guard against interfering or incroaching grants under american and British authorities. As the course of this line is to be due North, and is to proceed from the point fixed by a survey already made, the running of it will be sufficiently provided for by an appointment of a Commissioner by each of the two Governments, and an appointment by the two Commissioners of a surveyor. In fixing the point at which the line is to terminate, and which is referred to as the N. W. angle of Nova Scotia, the difficulty arises from a referrence of the Treaty of 1783 "to the Highlands,"[4] which it is now found have no definite existence. To cure this difficulty, no better expedient occurs than to provide for the appointment of a third Commissioner as in Art: 5th of the Treaty of 1794,[5] and to authorize the three to determine on a point most proper to be substituted for the description in the 2d Art: of the Treaty of 1783, having due regard to the general idea that the line ought to terminate on the elevated ground dividing the rivers falling into the atlantic from those emptying themselves into the St Laurence. The Commissioners may also be authorized, to substitute for the description of the boundary between the point so fixed and the Northwestermost head of Connecticut river, namely, a line drawn "along the said Highlands" such a referrence to intermediate sources of rivers, or other ascertained or ascertainable points, to be connected by straight lines, as will admit of easy and accurate execution hereafter, and as will best comport with the apparent intention of the Treaty of 1783. The remaining provision necessary to complete the boundary of the United States, will be a stipulation amending the 2d Art: of the Treaty of 1783 in its description of the line which is to connect the most Northwestern point of the Lake of the Woods, with the Mississippi. The description supposes that a line running due West from that point would intersect the Mississippi. It is now well understood the highest source of the Mississippi is South of the Lake of the Woods, and consequently that a line due West from its most Northwestern point would not touch any part of that river. To remedy this error, it may be agreed that the Boundary of the U. States in that quarter shall be a line running from that source of the Mississippi which is nearest to the Lake of the Woods, and striking it Westwardly as a tangent and from the point touched along the Water mark of the Lake to its most Northwestern point at which it will meet the line running thro' the Lake. The map in McKensies late publication is probably the best to which I can refer you on this subject.[6]

From the mutual and manifest advantage to G. Britain and the U. States of an adjustment of all uncertainties concerning boundary, it is hoped you will find a ready concurrence in all the propositions which you will have to make to the Government of the former. Should difficulties or delays threaten those which relate to the boundary connecting the Mississippi and the Lake of the Woods, or that connecting Connecticut river and the point to be established as the N. East corner of the United States, it will be proper to separate from these the other subjects of negotiation, and to hasten the latter to a conclusion. With the highest respect & consideration I have the honor to be, Sir, your Obt Sert.

JAMES MADISON

RC (NjMoHP); letterbook copy (DNA: RG 59, IM, vol. 6). RC in a clerk's hand, signed by JM; docketed as received 12 Aug. For surviving enclosure, see n. 2.

1. *PJM-SS*, 1:484.
2. James Sullivan to JM, 20 May 1802.
3. For the map, see Sullivan to JM, 20 May 1802, n. 1.
4. The second article of the 1783 treaty between Great Britain and the U.S. declared that one of the boundaries should be drawn "from the North West Angle of Nova Scotia, viz. That Angle which is formed by a Line drawn due North from the Source of Saint Croix River to the Highlands along the said Highlands which divide those Rivers that empty themselves into the River St. Lawrence" (Miller, *Treaties*, 2:152).
5. Article 5 of the Jay treaty provided for a commission to settle the question of what river was "truly intended under the name of the River St Croix." The commission was to be composed of one American, one Englishman, and a third member to be chosen by the other two (ibid., 2:249).
6. Alexander Mackenzie, *Voyages from Montreal, on the River St. Laurence through the Continent of North America* (New York, 1802; Shaw and Shoemaker 2568).

From Robert R. Livingston

No. 43.

DEAR SIR   PARIS 8th. June 1802

Enclosed is the answer of the Spanish ambassadour to my letter[1] a copy of which was forwarded on the 28 ult. It accords with the conclusions I drew from the delay of the expedition & the conduct of the Minister for exterior relations. *I have had a conversation with Collot & Adet separatly I find that tho they both consider their going in official characters to Louisiania as settled yet that* neither have seen the treaty or know precisely the boundary of the territory they have acquired Pensacola & Mobile they say are expresly given as to the rest or whether it includes west florida they can not say. That France intended that it should I have no doubt. And I still think it probable that she will make it yield to her intentions for in Europe she does what she will & it will require firmness & exertion to prevent her doing so in America. Rely not my dear Sir too much upon her affection or her justice nor neglect from œconomy every necessary means of defence, this however is by way of parenthesis. To proceed I called yesterday on the minister & again insisted upon some direct answer to my note relative to Louisania shewing that we had certain interests in the treaty that intitled us to the information. He told me that the first consul had definitively settled that Mr. Otto was to go to America—that he was expected here daily & that he would be empowerd to treat & take arrangment with me on that subject.

I then shewed him the remonstrance of the St Domingo merchants which I found in a New York paper[2] I told him that tho this was not official yet I had no doubt of its authenticity I contrasted the conduct of the United States in their exact & liberal fulfilment of the treaty with the conduct of France I told him that it was not to be expected that we would long submit to such degrading treatment but that we should be compelled to *seek for means* of repelling it—& concluded by desiring an explicit answer to my note on the subject of our claims—& information on the measures that the government had adopted for the payment of the bills forced upon our citizens.

He told me that the measures of the fleet & army were not in his depàrtment & that he could not give me any direct information on the subject nor of the means provided for the discharge of the bills tho he was assured that means had been adopted & that the [*sic*] Marbois had told him that two millions of livres were put at the disposition of Mr Pichon for this object. I replied that as it was my duty to make my inquiries thro' him & as I had received from the head of the marine nothing more than vague assurances on the subject I prayed him to take such informations as would enable him to give me an answer that I might lay before my govermt. This he promised to do—And added that with respect to my note the first consul had ordered it to be referred to the counsellor of State Flerieu[3] to report upon it as he had been one of the negotiators of the treaty & there were several points in it that had a reference to that negotiation. I asked him when I might expect an answer he told me in very few days.

My conclusion from this is that finding it too direct to evade & too strong to be easily answered it is gone in to the hands of Flerieu to give some elaborate & (as the eastern men say) some twistical answer by wire drawing the treaty. I shall however call today on Flerieu & get out of him some hint of what the final intention of the government is. In the mean time limit credit at home as much as possible & do not neglect the fortification of your harbours. Conciliate the affections of your western Country, And put your militia on the best footing circumstances may arise which you can not prevent. There are various causes of irritation at home that may compel the government to take a decisive line & where this may lead to god knows. Be explicit in your instructions to me & be assured whatever they may be they will be strictly fulfilled according to the best of my abilities. I am Dear Sir with the most respectful consideration Yrs

Draft (NHi: Livingston Papers); letterbook copy (NHi: Livingston Papers, vol. 1). RC not found but mentioned in JM to Jefferson, 11 Sept. 1802, and acknowledged in JM to Livingston, 15 Oct. 1802 (DNA: RG 59, IM, vol. 6). Italicized passages are underlined in the draft; Livingston apparently intended them to be encoded. Enclosure not found, but see n. 1.

1. In his reply of 2 June 1802, Azara informed Livingston that although he had not been involved in the affair, "it seems certain . . . that a treaty ceding Louisiana has been concluded; but I am of opinion that the Floridas are not comprised in the cession" (*ASP, Foreign Relations*, 2:519).

2. The protest of American merchants addressed to Tobias Lear was published in the *New-York Evening Post* on 10 Apr. 1802 (dated Philadelphia, 8 Apr. 1802). The merchants requested that their cargoes and vessels be free from requisition, that cargoes already furnished to the French be paid for in cash, that Americans meet with no more obstacles at customs than French merchants, and that the embargo on their ships be raised.

3. Charles-Pierre Fleurieu reported to Talleyrand on 22 Prairial an X (12 June 1802) (12 pp.; in French) his recollections—as one of the French negotiators—of the basis for discussion of articles 2, 4, and 5 of the Convention of 1800 and the French interpretation of the suppression of article 2. Fleurieu's understanding of this latter was that the U.S. could make no demands for indemnities and that the French were justified in refusing to pay them (AAE: Political Correspondence, U.S., 54:365–70).

From Albert Stevens

Sir WASHINGTON June 8th. 1802

Inasmuch as I propose to tarry some time in this City for the purpose of determining whether it will be a place suitable for my professional business and being at present not only without business but devoid of society or books I have thought whether it might not be possible that I could obtain employment in your office or in one of the other offices, during my proposed stay in this quarter or till such time as other occupations would interfere. Any thing of this kind being unthought previous to my arrival in this place, I had neglected to furnish recommendations that otherwise I should have procured. If however any assistance as abovementioned should be wanted & you should think yourself assured from the letter of Mr. Smith which I delivered the other Day[1] of my ability & qualifications to render you that assistance I should be proud to obey your commands. If, Sir, also with the same Assurance, you would be so obliging as to give me a line to Mr. Mason, the lawyer you mentioned in Georgetown—or an open letter, or both to any friend of yours to the north or eastward of this, you would recieve my sincere acknowledgments.

I hope, Sir in perusing the above you will pardon me with troubling you in this manner & believe me to be with the greatest esteem your most obdt & very humble Servt.

ALBERT STEVENS

RC (DLC). Docketed by JM.

1. Israel Smith to JM, 19 May 1802.

§ From William Eaton. *8 June 1802, Tunis.* Complains that his plans regarding Hamet Pasha of Tripoli "have undergone very severe criticism by Captains S. Barron and Bainbridge; by them reprobated in a stile of most illiberal censure; and under their influence, rejected by Capn. Murray in an air of authority and reprimand." Acknowledges his reporting that "*We are abandoned by our ships of war*" must have offended the captains but considers it his duty to report facts. The *Philadelphia* patrolled before Tripoli for "only six hours" before retiring to Saragossa for the winter. The *Essex* was stationed off Gibraltar "to watch the hull of a dismantled ship." "This is a singularly economical mode of carrying on the war." Adds that another source of grievance may have been his criticism of the degrading action of a U.S. ship forced to sail under Algerine colors.

"It is very certain that Cap. Murray has been influenced by Captains S. Barron and Bainbridge. . . . Last summer they expressed their intire concurrence in all my measures; and seemed, with me, fully persuaded that the most energetic operations would alone stamp the impression on these powers which our nation are desirous to impress." Cannot understand why they suddenly changed their minds or why Murray "should arrogate to himself the discretion to put so prompt, so rigorous a check" to the plan. The expense is paltry compared to the sum to be saved. "If he acted from want of confidence in the success of the project he was moved by a *zeal without knowledge.*" Asks whether commanders should not place their trust in those "local and proper Agents of the Government stationed here" to gather correct information rather than in "the Theatres of Saragosa, Leghorn and Malaga."

Opportunity for peace was missed last summer when the navy was unable to execute a close blockade of Tripoli. Plan involving the pasha "presented another position still more favorable; because it promised a *permanent* peace." If Dale's squadron had remained at its post and had "seized the occasion which my project with the Bashaw offered; the UStates ere this, perhaps, might have had a peace on terms equally honorable and advantageous." Is "extremely hurt" by Murray's rejection of the plan and public censure at Gibraltar, where Murray proclaimed Eaton's "reprehensibility," forbade the consul to supply the *Gloria*, and tried to take the seamen from the ship. "It is . . . a summary way of blasting men and measures, which would better become an eastern Bashaw than a citizen of the United States in command. But all this out of pure regard to the Treasury!"

Declares that "while here six days, and conversing with the utmost seeming frankness and friendship,"[1] Murray never mentioned the steps he had taken, although he initially opposed Eaton's plan on the grounds that "no construction of his orders would justify him in taking the said Bashaw out of a neutral vessel . . . nor even to fire a shot on a Tripoline town or castle"; he was to operate "solely against the cruisers at Sea." Even so, how could Murray's orders "prohibit his cooperations with a rightful Bashaw to reduce a rebel and a common enemy"? "I do believe, however premature, chimerical, or insane the project may appear on a superficial view, . . . if supported, it would have saved the United States more than a million of dollars and many lives." Plan was long digested; it was suggested by Cath-cart and developed with the advice and concurrence of Captain McNeill, Dr. William Turner, Charles Wadsworth, captains George G. Coffin and Joseph Bounds, the Swedish chargé d'affaires, and Lewis Hargreaves, "an English gentleman in my confidence, appointed to take charge of this office in case of my decease or necessary absence." If captains Barron and Bainbridge "are correct in charging *me* with insanity, those gentlemen must have labored under the same delirium." Will "adhere to the position I have taken" until Commodore Truxtun arrives. "If I have surpassed the limits of that discretion which I suppose attached to my duty I hold myself responsible alone to my government for my Conduct; not amenable to an inferior Captain of a squadron." Considers Murray's decision "premature, presumptious, the result of weakness biassed by ignorance and prejudice." Asks if Murray has "come forward vested with supreme authority to pass unqualified censure on the measures of officers long employed on this frontier; and to hold us up, unheard and unseen, in a foreign port, to public mistrust and disgrace?" If so, Eaton asks to be recalled. "There is no reason why I should be sacrificed to the convenience of gentlemen, who seem to consult their ease rather than their duty. After nearly four years exile, in a state of constant vigilance, exertion, perplexity and menace, and after having received honorable testimony of the approbation, not only of my government but of every officer serving under it who has been well acquainted with my Agency, to be condemned and published by a man just from his fire side, seems as unreasonable as it is indeed mortifying."

"During the whole time of the Squadrons being in this sea Tripoli has not been blockaded forty days until since the arrival of the Swedes and the Boston." The regencies begin to "whisper that *The Americans are playing the same farce here as the Danes!*" Unless more effort is made against Tripoli, "we shall fail in our object"; moreover, the other Barbary powers will "become insolent." The U.S. frigates, either cruising or blockading, "are inadequate to prevent the small gallies of the enemy from stealing out and doing us mischief." Two galleys passed along the coast of Tunis while the *Constellation* was at anchor in the bay.

Murray believes "we must rely on the magnanimity of Europe to regulate these States altogether. Men and nations must undergo more than a Christian regeneration before we shall see Europe volunteering in the protection of the commerce of the UStates."

"I have delivered the last regalia from England, saving the sword; they were highly acceptable." But the bey has reiterated his demand for a corvette or brig of war. "I got over this claim—at least for the present"—and also answered the bey's complaint of a neutrality violation "*without a sacrifice.*"

Reports that a large Swedish ship with military stores for the bey arrived on 5 June. No Americans had been captured by Tripoli as late as 22 May. Since the definitive treaty was signed over a hundred French citizens have arrived in Tunis to establish themselves—"a striking proof of the humane intentions of that Government to *regulate these regencies.*"

Notes in a postscript of 15 June that he has received word that Hamet Pasha is still at Malta, where he met with the Swedish admiral, who agreed to the plan, and where he awaits the juncture of the Swedish and American fleets. Hamet is so confident of success that he wrote to the bey of Tunis on the subject; "the Bey expressed astonishment." Cannot understand why those who have "*acted* on this coast" all agree to the measure, while "those only who have scarcely or never been here take on themselves to reject it!" Flatters himself that the "sink of Jewish perfidy in Algiers" will not always have the power to "blast the measures and disgrace the flag of my Country!"

RC and enclosure (DNA: RG 59, CD, Tunis, vol. 2, pt. 1); letterbook copy (CSmH). RC 11 pp.; marked "Duplicate"; docketed by Brent as received 16 Oct. Extracts printed in Knox, *Naval Documents, Barbary Wars*, 2:166–70. For enclosure, see n. 1. Filed with the RC and letterbook copy are copies of Capt. Alexander Murray to Eaton, 6 May 1802, wherein the former disagreed with Eaton's plan, claiming Eaton was "unauthorized in employing the ship Gloria on public account" (1 p.; printed ibid., 2:145); and extracts (4 pp.) of letters to Eaton supporting his plan from Cathcart, 10 Apr. 1802 and 13 May 1802, from Charles Wadsworth, 29 May 1802, and from an officer on board the *Philadelphia*, 7 May 1802 (for Cathcart to Eaton, 10 Apr. 1802, and Wadsworth to Eaton, 29 May 1802, see ibid., 2:111–12, 161). Also filed with the RC is a copy of Eaton's letter to the officer commanding the U.S. squadron in the Mediterranean, 12 May 1802 (3 pp.; printed ibid., 2:152–53), enclosing a 12 May 1802 chancery statement (3 pp.) describing a 3 May incident where an American schooner plundered a Tripolitan xebec of a total of $257.49 worth of valuables. Another copy of the RC (PHi) does not include the postscript and is docketed by Cathcart as received at Leghorn 23 July, with his notation: "Mr Eaton herein acknowl[edge]s that the project with Hassan Bashaw originated with me!"

1. Eaton enclosed a separate sheet, dated 8 June 1802 (docketed by Brent as received in Eaton's 8 June dispatch), in which he related a conversation with Murray.

"☞ While Cap. Murray was on shore he seemed willing to excite my alarm by a frightful picture of the operations of Government—Said that, *Under the influence of the present Executive, the Constitution of the United States was sapped to its base — the ablest and best men in office put down — salutary laws repealed — the military establishment almost annihilated — the best citizens generally dissatisfied — and every thing verging to disorder and anarchy in our country.*

"When I asked an explanation to this pretended violation of the Constitution He quoted the repeal of the Judiciary Act. As a common-place answer I supposed that the creative power had inherently the power of abolishing—and that this power was exercised in the establishment of the courts which formed the subject of this repeal.

"If this circumstance do not suggest what kind of support executive measures may receive from Gentlemen of this turn of thinking, it will at least show that his latitude of censure is not confined to the subordinate agents of the Government.

"I did not enter this article in the body of my communications of this day, it being irrelative to the subject."

§ From Thomas W. Fox. *8 June 1802, Falmouth.* Reports that the market for wheat and flour "at present is favourable for the produce of the U. S." Flour is scarce in northern France; "it appears that their wants are considerable—a great deal of Wheat is arrived and expected there from Dantzic and other parts of the North. . . . A great many Cargoes of Flour have arrived at this port lately for orders, and been forwarded to different ports in France and Spain. Trade in general is dull in most parts of England—there is a report of a commercial treaty being on foot between this Country and France; it is the opinion of many, that if it should take place, it will not be so advantageous for this Country as the former. Freights continue to fall; but American Vessels are sought after for many voyages, their Masters being in general active and clever men, and their Vessels sail fast." In a postscript, notes that he is signing for his brother, who has gone to the country.

RC (DNA: RG 59, CD, Falmouth, vol. 1). 2 pp. Signed by Thomas W. Fox "for Rob: W. Fox."

From Albert Gallatin

Sir   TREASURY DEPARTMENT June 9th 1802

I have the honor to transmit transcripts of the proceedings of the Circuit Court for Connecticut[1] & of the Supreme Court[2] in the case of the Schooner "Peggy" a French prize first acquitted in the district, then condemned in the circuit & finally acquitted by the Supreme Court. It appears that whilst the appeal was pending the district court, under the circumstances stated in their order, directed the one half of the nett proceeds to be paid to the Treasury of the United States, and the other half to the captors. The moiety which would have been the share of the United States was not received in the Treasury, it being known that the appeal was then before the supreme Court, and on the decree of this Court was paid by the Treasurer, (to whose credit it remained in Bank) to the attorney for the original owners. The other half having, as above stated, been paid over to the captors, Mr Pichon now claims the same under the treaty, and the instructions of the President are wanted at the Treasury on that subject.

The questions which occur are

1st. whether the owners having, by the decree of the supreme court, obtained their remedy, a remedy which they elected instead of claiming under the convention, they ought to be left to pursue the same against those to whom improper payments may have been made, or whether they have an unimpaired right to claim under the convention?

2dly. in what manner can the money be recovered, either by the United States or by the owners, from the captors or their agent?

These questions may perhaps require the decision of the Attorney general; but I wish also that the subject may be communicated to the President.[3] I have the honor to be with the highest respect Sir Your obedt. Servt.

ALBERT GALLATIN

RC and enclosures (DNA: RG 59, LOAG); Tr (DLC: Hamilton Papers). RC and enclosures docketed by Brent.

1. Gallatin enclosed a copy from the records of the U.S. Circuit Court for the District of Connecticut (13 pp.; marked in pencil by Gallatin, "To be enclosed with Mr P. Edward's letter

in letter to Secy. of State / A. G."). The court, which convened at New Haven on 15 Apr. 1801, decided that of the sum of $18,804.72, "the avails of the french prize Schooner Peggy & her cargo," one-half should be distributed among the captain and crew of the capturing ship *Trumbull* and the other half deposited into the U.S. treasury.

2. Gallatin enclosed a copy of the Supreme Court decree, dated 11 Jan. 1802 (1 p.; marked in pencil by Gallatin, "To be enclosed in letter to Secretary of State / A. G."), which reversed the judgment of the U.S. circuit court (n. 1, above) and ordered the restoration of "the said Schooner Peggy and Cargo with her apparel Guns and appurtenances" to the claimants. In accordance with the decree, payment was made to Pichon of one-half the sale price (Gallatin to JM, 19 Jan. 1802, *PJM-SS*, 2:411 and n.).

3. There is no written record that JM passed these papers on to the president, but he did request Attorney General Levi Lincoln to study and give his opinion on the legal questions of the *Peggy* affair (JM to Lincoln, 13 June 1802).

§ From William Savage. *9 June 1802, Kingston, Jamaica*. "I have this day drawn on you . . . for the Balance due me on the last Quarters Account, say Two thousand & Twelve Dollars 34/cents, to which please pay due Honour."

RC (DNA: RG 59, CD, Kingston, Jamaica, vol. 1). 1 p.; marked "Duplicate"; docketed by Brent as received 24 July.

From George W. Erving

No 7

SIR   LONDON June 10th 1802

I had the honor to address you last on the 6th March, since when a great pressure of business consequent upon the ⟨r⟩eassembling of the Board has prevented my writing to you upon ordinary occurrences; When the commissioners reassumed their ⟨f⟩unctions the state in which the cases ⟨b⟩efore them were found seemed to have ⟨r⟩esulted from an Expectation that no adjustment with this government upon the difficulties arising out of the 6th & 7th articles of the Treaty was likely to take ⟨p⟩lace, for I was called upon to furnish ⟨p⟩apers necessary for the consideration of nearly 300 Cases in which they were deficient, which shoud have been filed by my predecessor, & which indeed the long suspension of the proceedings of the board afforded ample opportunity for furnishing: Thro' the hands of our council, proctors, & the private Agents of the claimants, these documents were scattered like the leaves of the *Sibyls*, & have required almost as much care to collect & arrange; they are however in a good train & the Board is making considerable progress: The commissioners however have thought proper to defer the making any awards 'till the arrival of the ratification, but many cases have been "*decreed* to be awarded"; this distinction (perhaps unnecessa⟨ry⟩) does not retard the business of the Board & may be attended with no inconvenience unless Mr Trumbull (which I trust is not probable) shoud happen to die; in that case indeed if we were unfortunate in the choice of his successor, these decrees being subject to ⟨re⟩vision might be reversed: To avoid this chance, it woud have been better perhaps to have made awards & to have fixed the time of payment (as no precise date coud have been named) in the words of the ⟨c⟩onvention. The business of the court ⟨a⟩dvances rapidly, & their proceedings & decisions it is said have more of Equity & liberality than have heretofore characterized ⟨th⟩em; a change certainly very much to their credit: No present calculation ⟨c⟩an possibly resolve the question as to how much more than 600,000 £ stipulated to be paid by the convention, may be Expected to be recovered from the British government thro' the awards of the commissioners ⟨a⟩bove what in the present temper of the ⟨co⟩urt of appeals may be there decreed in ⟨o⟩ur favor; I shoud indeed imagine a large sum— but this however ought to be supposed to depend a great deal upon Mr Trumbulls life; an English commissioner in his place (upon the supposition that we are not intitled to name his successor, but must submit to the mode of appointment prescribed in the treaty) & it is to be presumed that the awards woud amount to very much less than may be expected to be given in the present state of the board; the *British* cases woud then doubtless be all decided against us: Considering that there is by no means a general wish in the Board to Expedite the business before them, I look at this chance (which perhaps is small) with some little apprehension, & mention it that you may Sir if you please consider whether any steps can be taken to diminish it by obtaining more frequent sittings of the Commissioners, if not by fixing upon an absolute period for the ⟨c⟩ompletion of their business. But having ⟨a⟩dverted to this tardiness of the Board, I ⟨o⟩ught in justice to Mr Pinkney to Exonerate ⟨h⟩im from any part in the charge, he has frequently Expressed to me the utmost Earnestness to bring the business to a speedy termination, & I have reason to think that he has very strenuously Exerted himself at the Board to produce a similar disposition; ⟨u⟩nfortunately without Effect; He is of an ⟨o⟩pinion with which I coincide, that if the ⟨c⟩ommissioners woud meet regularly 5 or Even four times pr Week for 12 or 15 months the whole business might be completed; At the rate of twice or three times a week, at the utmost for two or three hours, with occasional vacancies & prorogations, it may be eke'd out to three or four years.

Mr. Lenox intending to return to the United States Hath in compliance with your directions transferred the business of his agency to me, in Consequence of which I have written a circular letter to the consuls of which a copy is inclosed: I have no particular instructions as to my conduct in this department of business, therefore as respects its connection with the admiralty I follow the methods observed by Mr Lenox, & as to the disbursements for the releif of seamen I continue to make them according to the same rules & to the same Extent as before: I have thought it necessary to caution the other consuls against assuming a latitude in making disbursements which might swell the amount of our annual Expenditure in this Country, & yet the provision afforded by the law is really very inadequate to the releif of those in real distress: A longer acquaintance with the character of our sailors has however convinced me that an alteration of the law in this particular woud not be beneficial, & that a superintending discretion ⟨g⟩iven to persons in whose discretion government ⟨ca⟩n confide, woud be more likely to answer ⟨go⟩od purposes; for however valuable this ⟨c⟩lass of our citizens as a body, & however necessary therefore to extend the protection & support of government to them in foreign countries, yet there are amongst them such ⟨a⟩ proportion of dissolute idle and improvident ⟨c⟩haracters, that were they intitled by law to claim any allowance which might suffice for their support (& they most of them learn Enough of law to know what they may claim) the benevolence of government woud be abused, the extent of the charge woud be Enormous, & ⟨w⟩e shoud lose to a very Considerable degree the benefit of their services: The difficulty which Consuls have formerly found in settling their Accounts with government, has restrained them from making large disbursements—& as it is impossible for us to have in all situatio⟨ns⟩ officers who coud be induced to a strict Œconom⟨y⟩ from any other motive, perhaps to give general discretionary powers woud not be adviseable. Under the best regulations the expence of this department must always be very considerable, but permit me Sir to renew a suggestion contained in a former letter; if by legislative provision the masters of vessels coud be placed in the power of the consul, if their papers might be witheld & their ships detained till they had complied with the duties imposed upon them by the law, a great deal of Expence woud be saved & every other good purpose answered: A regular return so much desired by government of the state of our trade might al⟨so⟩ be easily obtained, which under the present state of the law as respects this port I find impracticable; Mr Maury at Liverpool writes to the Same Effect; he says that he ⟨k⟩nows "from 12 years Experience that such returns cannot be had from the masters without the means of compelling compliance." In this important port only Eleven masters have reported their Vessels since my being in ⟨o⟩ffice! I find it very difficult Even to persuade many of them to take men on board; sometimes after taking them they have set them on shore again in their passage down the river; they discharge them, leave them behind sick, & unprovided for; & are guilty of Numerous irregularities, which with all my exertions I am not able to correct: A great deal of this results from their independance of the Consul in this port, & I have reason to think that some of their consignees here have ⟨c⟩ontributed not a little to this negligence; ⟨m⟩ost or all of our Merchants have their particular correspondents & consignees here who may be presumed to be a little jealous lest the influence of the consul shoud draw some of their busines⟨s⟩ to himself; & tho such apprehensions are vain with respect to me, yet as a general principle probably they consider it wise to discourage as much as possible a communication between the consul & the masters of vessels: amongst this class of our citizens too are of course many who have no disposition but what necessity may create to contribute to any regulations, the sole object of such is their private Emolument & they cannot Extend their ideas to national advantages. Do not these things shew the necessity of some more strict regulations; I mean also Sir to suggest that the want of such regulations is more mischevious in this port than elsewhere.

Mr Lenox has made representations to you respecting the conduct of Messrs Bird & co bankers of the United States in refusing to advance upon the credit of the U. S. the sum necessary to Enable him to settle his Accounts; if on these grounds you shall see fit to change your bankers or to make any alteration in this Establishment, I woud take the ⟨l⟩iberty of recommending that the depositary of the public monies shoud be a banker by business, because the transactions of such a person being confined altogether to money, he has no objection at any time to make the advances that may be accidentally ⟨r⟩equired: Without intending any disparagement to the credit of Messrs Bird & Co it is fair ⟨to⟩ observe that the stability of a banking house Exposed to no speculations or risques, must always be less precarious than that of an house Engaged in mercantile concerns: I coud recommend as persons very proper for this trust Messrs George & Richard Lee & ⟨N?⟩iles Satterthwaite of Lombard Street, a long Established, highly respectable & substantial house.

The regulations respecting Aliens in this country still continue in force; none of our citizens can proceed after landing in the country, or go out of it, or reside in it without the Express permission of government.

As the ships of war are paid off our men are discharged with others, no general discharge of Americans has taken place; particular applications are regularly attended to by the Admiralty, & if the men applied for have proper documents, & have not Entered, they are discharged; but this is of course a slow process, & after all cannot releive nearly the whole of those which we now have in the British service, many being without documents & not in a situation to procure them, many having been induced to enter; & some doubtless who are claimed as British subjects who are on that Account detained tho they may have protections. I have the honor to be Sir With the Most perfect respect Your very obt St

GEORGE W ERVING

14 June

We have heard by private letters of the ratification of the convention. Since Writing the above I have conversed further with Mr Pinkney respecting the progress of the business at the Board; he expresses himself for the present satisfied with the attention of the English commissioners. After some discussion upon this subject it seems to be ⟨u⟩nderstood that they are to meet only twice ⟨a⟩ week, but to decide from *four to six* cases: ⟨if⟩ there shoud be no interruption of or relaxation in this plan we may Expect to see the business completed in a year & a half or two years at furthest.

RC and enclosure (DNA: RG 59, CD, London, vol. 8). Margins of RC obscured by binding. The enclosure (3 pp.; docketed by Brent) is a "Circular to the Consuls," 3 May 1802.

§ From Stephen Cathalan, Jr. *10 June 1802, Marseilles.* Mentions that he will soon send a statement of the American ships that entered and left the ports of his district between 1 Jan. and 30 June 1802. Refers to a packet he forwarded to JM on 31 May—under cover of William Lee at Bordeaux—from James Leander Cathcart at Leghorn, including Cathcart's letter of 21 May. "I have now the honor of inclosing you one from Wm. Eaton Esqre. our Consul at Tunis[1] which I have received yesterday with his Letter to me of the 28th. ulto., on which when Sealed he adds to me on the cover—'May 29th.: The Fregate Constellation Capn. Murray arrived in this bay yesterday.'"

RC (DNA: RG 59, CD, Marseilles, vol. 1). 1 p. Sent "*Viâ Bordeaux.*"

1. Eaton to JM, 25 May 1802.

§ From Rufus King. *10 June 1802, London.* No. 69. Acknowledges JM's public letter of 7 Apr. "communicating the Presidents approbation of the Convention respecting the 6 & 7 articles of the Treaty of 1794"; by "private accounts of a later date" has learned of the Senate's consent. Has no news as to countervailing duties; "their continuance or repeal is a question submitted to the decision of Congress." Does not think it expedient to broach the subject of American trade with the West Indies as Parliament is engaged in last-minute business. Encloses a copy of a House of Commons report on vaccine inoculation—"a discovery of the highest interest to humanity"[1]—and a statement of the British national debt with figures on the sinking fund.[2] Promises to send by the first ship a copy of the last British census "so far as it has been completed," with the supplement to follow as soon as printed. "As our Census is a subject of much enquiry, I shall be obliged to you to send me a dozen copies of the former, as well as of the late Census, some of which I wish to deposit in the public Museums and Libraries."[3]

RC (DNA: RG 59, DD, Great Britain, vol. 10); letterbook copy (NHi: Rufus King Papers, vol. 55). RC 2 pp.; in a clerk's hand, signed by King; docketed by Brent as received 19 Aug. Printed in King, *Life and Correspondence of Rufus King,* 4:137–38. Enclosures not found, but see nn. 1 and 2.

1. *Report from the Committee of the House of Commons on Dr. Jenner's Petition, respecting His Discovery of Vaccine Inoculation* (London, 1802) (see Sowerby, *Catalogue of Jefferson's Library,* 1:430).

2. Daniel Brent sent these "Statements concerning the funded debt and sinking fund of England" directly to Albert Gallatin (Brent to King, 23 Aug. 1802 [MiU-C]).

3. Brent sent six copies of the 1800 census to King with the promise to send copies of a reprinting of the first two censuses "in a convenient form," which was slated for publication in Philadelphia (ibid.). The census of 1800 was published in December 1801 by order of the House of Representatives (*Return of the Whole Number of Persons within the Several Districts of the United States* [Shaw and Shoemaker 1559]).

§ From O'Brien Smith. *10 June 1802, Charleston.* Writes at the request of several merchants of Charleston who wish to have John O'Hara appointed consul at Kingston, Jamaica. "He is a native of this city but has lived at Kingston sever[a]l years as a Merchant, from my Knowledge of him I am sure He will fill the appointment with propriety." Adds in a postscript, "There is a Mr. Savage who has Acted as agent these two years, but I am informd. the Merchts. of Kingston and Charleston are displeased with him."

RC (DLC). 1 p.

From Thomas Newton

DR SIR   NORFOLK June 11. 02
    I Received yr favor,[1] the wine shall be sent as you desire, of the same Cargo. I have just arived a few pipes of best quality of Brasil wine, I beleive superior to any we have yet had, if you or friends should want I shall be happy to supply you or them the quality you have had we also keep. With best wishes for your health &C I am respectfully Yr. Obt
                                                        THOS NEWTON

RC (DLC). Docketed by JM.

1. Letter not found.

From George W. Erving

Private No 9.
DEAR SIR   LONDON June 12th 1802
    My last unofficial letter was dated March 6th; not having had the pleasure of hearing from you, & always supposing that my communications may have been found deficient in interest, it is not without apprehension that I again address you: To write too much however is an Error on the right side as long as our correspondent has the priviledge of burning; I

conclude too that this may find you at Orange where your time being less occupied my intrusion may be better borne.

I have from time to time such voluminous dispatches to forward to you from Mr. King besides Newspapers, that I presume there can be scarcely an Event relating to the proceedings of this government as well as in the general affairs of Europe, of which you are not particularly informed; from the feild of intelligence therefore I can scarcely glean a flower or the humblest weed to present you. The state in which the treaty of Amiens has placed this Country, & the wise & determined stand which the French have made to the commercial Expectations of Great Britain, naturally give a proportionable importance to the connection with our Country, & induce to a language on all occasions more respectful & friendly, or to speak more properly less haughty & illiberal than formerly; & which probably relying upon our predisposition in their favor they ostentatiously draw into their public debates: You will be diverted too in observing the kind apprehensions which are entertained for us on the quarter of Louisiania by some, & with the imaginations of those who connect with a settlement of the French in that country an immediate & all commanding controul over the Union. There have been some rumours of a change in the administration of this Country & of the return of Mr Pitt into power; that there may be some change is extremely likely, perhaps it woud be wise ⟨in⟩ Mr Addington to call in some of the talent of the last administration to his support, for in this respect his is woefully deficient; but those who pretend to be in the secret, say, that the personal dislike which the king has taken to Mr Pitt deprives him of all chance; for happily such is the state of the public mind, the house of Lords so well made up, parliamentary interest so circumstanced, that the king can now chuse his own Ministers whatever their talent or degree of popularity, & this perhaps during the course of his long reign he has never before been able completely to Effect. The Parliament will in all probability be speedily dissolved; the new parliament will of course contain as many vicars of Bray as the present or any former one, therefore the same Majority in favor of Existing Ministers, & "Existing circumstances."

It was rationally Expected that the peace amongst many other attendant advantages by opening new markets woud afford a vent for the Stores of this commercial depot; but no such effect has resulted from it, & with respect to West India produce, the prices remain extremely low, & are even lower than before the peace, particularly cotton, it being found that the demand for the cotton manufactured goods of this Country is considerably less now than during the war: I take the liberty of inclosing you a general price Current which in this view is interesting; also, *what is not unconnected with it*, a statement of the public debt.[1] On the other side the channel Buonoparte seems incessantly occupied as well in the Extension of his own power, as in plans for the glory of France, & perhaps for the domestic happiness of its Citizens; & if it be of no importance that there shoud be Established in that Country principles of government beyond the controul of momentary circumstances, & unassailable by the Ambition of individuals; if national glory & governmental splendor are a good compromize for a pure & safe tho peaceful System; then indeed neither we or they have any thing to regret in their vast accumulation of power, which it must be allowed the great consul Employs for none but good purposes. We hear frequent reports of plots & assasinations from that quarter, but I have seen very intelligent persons from France who tho they allow that the proceedings of Buonoparte have created much discontent, & that all true republicans are decidedly his Enemies; yet are of Opinion that he is perfectly beyond apprehension from any combination against Either his power or his person. Indeed what coud they hope from his death.

"Deploratur in perpetuum libertas, nec vindex quisquam Exsistit, aut futurus Videtur.["]² If he shoud fall he woud be succeeded by some Equally hardy adventurer, prompted by his success & improving upon his Errors.

Buonoparte has appointed to Succeed in this Country to Mr Otto the General Andreossi a great Engineer, & a corsican:³ The English who have learnt by passed Events to apprehend danger & to suspect design from Every movement of Buonoparte, take it for granted that Andreossi is come to draw plans of their fortifications, & to survey their Coasts rather than to Exercise his diplomatic functions. Mr Otto is we understand to go to the U S, & from this Country instead of Mr Jackson lately intended, we are to have Merry now at Paris; That is a *commissary of prisoners* from Each Country. I am Dear Sir with Great respect Very faithy your obt Sevt

GEORGE W ERVING

RC and enclosure (MHi: Erving Papers). For surviving enclosure, see n. 1.

1. Erving enclosed a "State of the British Funds 1802," a broadside published on 22 May 1802 by John Luffman, London.

2. "Men mourned for liberty as for ever lost; nor did any one arise, or seem likely to do so, in its defence," Livy, *Ab Urbe Condita*, 3.28.2 (*Livy*, trans. B. O. Foster, Loeb Classical Library [13 vols.; London, 1922], 2:122–23).

3. Antoine-François Andréossy (1761–1828) was trained as an artillery officer and gained the notice of Napoleon during the Italian campaign (1796) and Egyptian expedition (1798). Named French ambassador to Great Britain in 1802, he served only a year before war between the two countries broke out once more (Tulard, *Dictionnaire Napoléon*, p. 93).

§ From Joseph Pitcairn. *12 June 1802, Hamburg.* "I have the honor to hand you enclosed a note from the Regency of Wertheim which explains that property lays there for the claim of heirs now in America. By a letter to Mr Randolph dated the 31 January 1795 from William Hendel Jur. at Tulpehoon, it seems he had discovered the family asked after—& since then nothing further has been done.¹ The Regency desires that you will have the enclosed transmitted to the interested. . . . A second affair you will find marked No. 2. which regards heirs living under the Regency of Wertheim to a person who died near Philadelphia. It requests that full information should be obtained respecting the property left and directions of the mode proper for its recovery—together with an Offer to aid in Exchanging to the one family an equivalent at Wertheim for what might be paid the other in America." In a postscript, notes that Randolph's letter to the regency was dated 17 Mar. 1795.

RC and enclosures (DNA: RG 59, CD, Hamburg, vol. 1). RC 2 pp.; docketed by Brent as received 16 Sept. Enclosures are two one-page statements (in German), both dated 23 Dec. 1801.

1. On 28 Sept. 1802 Daniel Brent requested William Hendel, Jr., of Tulpehocken, Pennsylvania, to "notify the heirs of John Christophe Shabe" of the information sent by Pitcairn and to "inform them that this Department will cheerfully render its aid, to facilitate the recovery of the property to which, it seems they are entitled by forwarding the evidences of their title to our Consul at Hamburg." In the case of "John Philip Weiss, who, it would appear, died at Reading, without Heirs in this country," Brent asked Hendel to procure "such information as may be useful towards the elucidation of the claim" (Brent to Hendel, 28 Sept. 1802 [DNA: RG 59, DL, vol. 14]).

§ From Benjamin F. Timothy. *12 June 1802, Charleston.* Encloses his account for publishing the laws of the U.S. passed during the second session of the Sixth Congress.

RC and enclosure (DNA: RG 217, First Auditor's Accounts, no. 13,519). RC 1 p. In the enclosed account (1 p.; signed by JM and dated 24 June 1802 at the auditor's office), the amount of $47.50 has been supplied.

From Thomas Sumter

Dear sir   Stateboro, 13th. June 1802

When at the seat of Governt. I mentioned to the Govr. of So. Caroa. that I had made his request known to you in regard of an authentid. coppy he Wanted, of the first return made of the Numr. of the Inhabitce. of Said State—that you had politely assured me one Should be Prepaired accordingly—but at the Same time remarked the press of business in your office was Excessive. He has lately informd Me that the object he had in View is attained or within reach Without Giving farther Trouble.

I now Sir—take the liberty conformably to your friendly offer, to convey to My Son any of my communication to him Which might be Sent to your office. I therefore beg you will have the Goodness to cause the enclosed to be forwarded as Early as may be.

Some time Since in a letter to the President of the Ud. States, I mentioned Several persons who I thought Well Quallified to act as Commissioners in cases of insolvency.[1] I Should be Gratified to Learn that it was recd. & the Characters designated approved of.

It would Seem Very extraordinary to Say, that at this time under the Greatest Drought ever known in this country, the Crops are more promising than were ever Seen in it—our large rivers for navegation—as well as Smaller watercourss. are rendered of little use—and have been in this State ever since the past Summer. Still the slight rains, or Mists, with unusual falls of dew, has Proved Sufficient to nurrish & promote Vegitation in the degree before mentioned.

I hope you had an agreable jour⟨ney⟩ to Orange and that you & Good family now enjoy perfect health. I am Dear sir With perfect respe⟨ct⟩ your obt. Servt.

Thos. Sumter

RC (DLC). Docketed by JM.

1. Sumter apparently wrote to Jefferson on 30 May 1802 (not found, but listed in Jefferson's Epistolary Record [DLC: Jefferson Papers] as received 17 June).

§ To Levi Lincoln. *13 June 1802, Department of State.* "The Secretary of State presents his compliments to the Attorney General of the United States and requests his opinion on the points stated in the enclosed letter of the 9th. inst. from the Secretary of the Treasury—all the documents relating to the case which were received from Mr. Gallatin being also herewith sent to Mr. Lincoln."

Letterbook copy (DNA: RG 59, DL, vol. 14). 1 p. For the enclosed letter and documents relating to the case of the French schooner *Peggy*, see Gallatin to JM, 9 June 1802, and nn.

§ To Charles Pinckney. *13 June 1802, Department of State, Washington.* Introduces the bearer, William Cooke, who has a claim against Spain "which he is going to Madrid to prosecute—and it will of course be patronized and urged by you as far as may be proper."

Letterbook copy (DNA: RG 59, IM, vol. 6). 1 p. This letter evidently was never delivered, for Cooke did not sail for Madrid until 1803 (see JM to Pinckney, 22 Dec. 1802 and 7 Apr. 1803 [ibid.]). For Cooke and his claim, see Cooke to JM, 27 Nov. 1801, and JM to Cooke, 3 Feb. 1802 (*PJM-SS*, 2:277 and n. 1, 438).

From Charles Simms

Sir   Alexandria June 14th. 1802

I have receivd a letter from Mr. Danl Brent requesting me to give you information respecting the conviction of Elihu Marchant.[1]

I was not present at his Trial nor have I ever seen the Information or Indictment against him, and therefore cannot precisely state his offence—but I beleive the charge against him was in substance, for clandestinely and fraudulently runing away with the Brig Ranger a Brittish privateer of which he was the first Lieutenant, of which offence he was convicted in the circuit Court for the District of Virginia in the October Term 1800, and was sentenced to Two years Imprisonment—and to the payment of a fine of Two hundred dollars. I am very sincerely and respectfully Yr. Obedt Servt.

CH: SIMMS

RC (DNA: RG 59, Petitions for Pardon, no. 50).

1. Brent's letter to Simms, 13 June 1802 (DNA: RG 59, DL, vol. 14), explained that the president had decided to pardon Marchant, "in whose behalf, it is understood, you acted as Council," but that "the papers in the case are accidentally mislaid"; Brent conveyed JM's request that Simms inform him of "the definition of this man's offence [and] the particular Court before which he was tried," so that the pardon might not be delayed.

§ From Richard O'Brien. *14 June 1802, Algiers.* Describes two Tripolitan corsairs that arrived on 10 June and departed "this morning . . . in Search of Americans and Swedes." "They Say they are about 20 days from Tripoli Sailed with 3 others, and those 2 has Coasted it down the Barbary Shore to Algiers. They report that the Swede and American frigts. Cruises a long way of[f] and durst not approach on account of the Gun boats." Has heard reports that the Swedes and Americans attacked Tripoli and destroyed its sea batteries and gunboats, but letters from Tunis of 28 and 31 May do not mention the affair. States his opinion that the U.S. should "attack [Tripoli] with force and finish at Once a *war* which on its present System will drain The UStates of Vast Sums and not be Terminated in a few years." Recounts details of the Algerine capture of the Portuguese frigate *Cisne* and lists several other Algerine captures, including a British brig at Mahón; the latter "detention is to irritate and to try to Bring About the payment on the part of the British of Old Algerine Claims" of $187,000, but the British consul warned the Algerine minister that condemnation of the brig would result in war. Should there be a "sudden rupture" with Algiers, one frigate convoying merchant vessels will not be enough to secure American trade. Complains that he cannot save U.S. vessels from condemnation when "our meditteranian passports is defective [and] our Consuls in This Sea gives American papers to Vessels which Cannot be legally Considered Americans."
    "The large Schooner built by Humphreyes & Hutton[1] is rotten & Condemned The 2d Schooner is all but gone and the Brig and frigt. is nearly in the Same prediciament. This circumstance will Enrage the dey—and he will Say we deceived him." Reports the conditions of recent peace agreement between Spain and Algiers; the result of this "Shamefull Bombast of Spain" will be increased calls by the dey for money and presents from other nations.

Under date of 21 June, relays report of the capture of an American brig and crew off the coast of Spain by one of the Tripolitan corsairs that sailed from Algiers on 14 June. In answer to his demand that the brig and crew be turned over to him, he was told that "it would be Something new and Extraordinary for one State of Barbary to take away The Christians and prizes from the power of another State." Has offered the Algerine prime minister and other officials "the Sum of . . . 7 thousd. dollars to Extricate the Brig Cargo and Crew out of the power of the Tripolines." Adds on 26 June that the Tripolitan corsair "this morning at 6 A.M. Entered the port of Algiers" with the American brig *Franklin* and its crew, the corsair carrying a reversed American flag on its prow. Reiterated his arguments to the minister of marine, who stated them to the dey. Through the minister of marine, the dey offered $5,000 to the Tripolitan captain for the nine American prisoners, the brig, and the cargo; the captain refused, saying "that it was by haveing possesion of them that his Master The Pascha would find Thereby means to Bring The Americans to a peace on Tripoli *Terms*." On 28 June the dey ordered the corsair with its prize to leave port, which it did the same day. Recommends that the U.S. attack Tripoli and make a remonstrance to Algiers "on the deys bad faith in his gaurentee of the US treaty with Tripoli." "I hope the US. has too much Spirit to be treated with Contempt by the Barbary powers. . . . We will have to take this position and The Sooner we do it the better." Reminds JM of his frequent requests for money. "I am Sorrow to add that neither Money or letters I have recd none. . . . Here I am at The Mercy of The Jew directory."

RC (DNA: RG 59, CD, Algiers, vol. 6). 7 pp.; docketed by Wagner. Below his signature, O'Brien noted: "Sent by me open for the perusl. of the American Ambasadr. at Madrid—& for him to forward for The UStates." Extract printed in *ASP, Foreign Relations*, 2:463–64.

1. Joshua Humphreys (1751–1838) and Nathaniel Hutton were Philadelphia shipbuilders. Humphreys, one of the early republic's first naval architects, served as U.S. naval constructor from 1794 until 1801. He was responsible for the superior design and construction of the first six frigates of the U.S. Navy. Of the vessels built for the dey of Algiers by the U.S., the frigate *Crescent* was constructed at Portsmouth, New Hampshire, and the brig *Hassan Bashaw* and the schooners *Skjoldebrand* and *Lelah Eisha* were built at Philadelphia by Humphreys and Hutton (Knox, *Naval Documents, Barbary Wars*, 1:232; Allen, *Our Navy and the Barbary Corsairs*, pp. 60–62).

§ From James Simpson. *14 June 1802, Tangier.* No. 41. Presumes that no. 40 [5 June 1802], which was forwarded to Gibraltar on 10 June, is still there and that "this will go from thence with it." On 13 June the governor informed him that "since Passports could not be granted for the two Cargoes Wheat he wished to send to Tripoly, His Majesty had directed the Vessels should go to Tunis; which I was happy to hear, as by that means we get rid of what threatened to be a very unpleasant piece of busyness." At the governor's request, wrote the emperor to explain again "the powerfull motives why I could not sanction Vessels going to Tripoly, but that I was ready to grant the usual Certificates for those His Majesty might direct to be laden with Cargoes his property, for Tunis." The Swedish consul's secretary has been permitted to stay and raise his country's flag as usual until further notice.

A shipment of brass cannon, mortars, fieldpieces, and ammunition was "landed at this Port from Gibraltar for His Majestys Service. . . . It is presumed these are a Present from the British Government."

RC (DNA: RG 59, CD, Tangier, vol. 1). 2 pp. Jefferson communicated an extract to Congress with his annual message on 15 Dec. 1802 (printed in *ASP, Foreign Relations*, 2:468).

To Alexander J. Dallas

SIR,   DEPARTMENT OF STATE June 15. 1802.

Mr. Olsen the Danish Minister Resident has complained of Captn. Maley in capturing a Danish vessel the Mercator, which was afterwards lost by capture, whilst under the American Flag, by a British Armed vessel, and condemnation in a British Court of Admiralty.[1] He has represented also, in behalf of the Danish owner, that Captn. Maley is both absent from the United States and in a state of insolvency; and requests that the proper mode of redress may be pointed out.

He was informed that notwithstanding the absence of Captn. Maley a judicial investigation of the case could be effected thro' an attorney of the United States, and that the necessary steps would be taken as soon as he should signify the District preferred by him.

I have just received an answer from him,[2] requiring that the judicial proceedings may be had in Philadelphia.

You will please therefore, Sir, to concur in instituting the proper proceedings, by appearing in behalf of Captn. Maley; in whose defence the United States are interested.

I inclose for your information on the subject the protest of the second Lieutenant under Captn. Maley, who was prize master of the Mercator, and of another person belonging to the Experiment; and also the decree of the British Court of Vice Admiralty which condemned the Mercator.[3] These are the only documents which I am able to forward for the purpose. I am very respectfully &ca.

JAMES MADISON.

Letterbook copy (DNA: RG 59, DL, vol. 14). Enclosures not found, but see n. 3.

1. For Blicherolsen's charges, see his letters to JM of 16 Jan. 1802 (*PJM-SS*, 2:400–401 and n. 1) and 12 Apr. 1802.
2. Blicherolsen to JM, 6 June 1802.
3. It is likely that these supporting documents were included in JM's report to the House of Representatives, 12 Apr. 1806, and were among those burned during the British invasion of Washington in 1814 (*ASP, Claims*, pp. 332–33).

To John Read, Jr.

SIR,   DEPARTMENT OF STATE June 15. 1802.

Mr. Thornton the British Chargé d'Affaires has expressed a wish that Mr. Smith the British Agent under the 6th. art: of the Treaty of 1794. may be permitted to take such copies and extracts from the American papers now in your custody as may be of use in adjusting claims of British subjects on their Government. It being considered by the President as altogether proper that the application should be complied with, you will please to give it the due effect, by opening the papers to Mr. Smith, and making his intended use of them as convenient to him as may be. I am very respectfully &ca.

JAMES MADISON.

Letterbook copy (DNA: RG 59, DL, vol. 14).

§ From John Gavino. *15 June 1802, Gibraltar.* No. 89. Reports "no Novelty here regarding Tripoly. Comodor Morris is in the Bay, & the Essex sails this day for the U. S." With regard to the emperor of Morocco, refers to "the sundry dispatches from Consul Simpson which goes by this Conveyance." Notes arrival on 14 June of Wyk, the Swedish consul at Tangier, who was expelled for noncompliance with the demands of the emperor. If demands have not been met in four months by the king of Sweden "it will be deemd a Declaration of Warr."

RC (DNA: RG 59, CD, Gibraltar, vol. 2). 2 pp. Enclosures probably included James Simpson's dispatches to JM of 5 and 14 June 1802.

To James Blake

SIR,   DEPARTMENT OF STATE June 16. 1802.

Your letter of the 17th. May was duly recd. As it appears that you have relinquished the intention of now going to Europe, and the arrangement suggested by you, of performing the duties of Consul at antwerp by the agency of another, does not coincide with the views of the President, he has thought proper to appoint to that office another Gentleman who is now in France.[1] I am &ca.

JAMES MADISON.

Letterbook copy (DNA: RG 59, DL, vol. 14).

1. In place of James Blake, Jefferson appointed Isaac Cox Barnet (*Senate Exec. Proceedings*, 1:433).

To Robert W. Fox

SIR, DEPARTMENT OF STATE June 16. 1802.

I have recd. your letter of april 10. in which you ask a decision whether you may whilst american Consul perform certain services as agent for the Batavian Government. The constitution of the U. States has left no discretion to the Executive on this point "no person holding any office of profit or trust under them shall, without the consent of congress, accept of any present, emolument, office, or title of any kind whatever, from any King, prince or foreign state."[1] You will perceive therefore that as congress alone can grant the permission, the application for it must be made by you, to that authority; which has hitherto manifested a disinclination to grant such permissions. I have the honor &ca.

JAMES MADISON.

Letterbook copy (DNA: RG 59, IC, vol. 1).

1. U.S. Constitution, article 1, section 9, clause 8.

To Louis-André Pichon

DEPARTMENT OF STATE 16. June 1802.

Mr. Madison has the honor to inform Mr. Pichon that the case of the Portuguese Brig la Gloria dal mar, recaptured by an American Ship of War from a french armed Schooner, and which is a subject of his note of the 14. day of April 1802. has been taken into consideration, and that in several views the claims of the captors against the United States do not appear to be in any respect warranted by the convention of Septr. 30. 1800.

The final disposition of the Brig having taken place prior to that date, and consequently no requisition relating to it being their [sic] depending, the case in that view alone is so clearly not within the purview of the Convention, as to render unnecessary any particular discussion of other circumstances involved in it. Mr. Madison begs Mr. Pichon to accept his respectful consideration.

Letterbook copy (DNA: RG 59, DL, vol. 14).

§ From Rufus King. *16 June 1802, London.* Acknowledges JM's private letter of 7 Apr. conveying the president's permission to visit France and neighboring countries. Has no plans at the moment; might spend a few weeks at Paris in July or August.[1] His secretary, John Pickering,[2] returned home several months earlier; "I have expected as his successor my Nephew Mr. H. Southgate,[3] who will probably arrive in the course of the summer." In the interim, John Munro of Scotland has undertaken those duties and been given the pay. If King extends his leave or goes beyond Paris, Christopher Gore will serve as chargé d'affaires during his absence with no expense to the public.

RC (DNA: RG 59, DD, Great Britain, vol. 10); letterbook copy (NHi: Rufus King Papers, vol. 55). RC 1 p.; marked private; in a clerk's hand, signed by King; docketed by Brent. Printed in King, *Life and Correspondence of Rufus King*, 4:140.

1. King and his family left England on 15 Aug. and traveled through the Netherlands, Germany, Switzerland, and France. They returned to London 17 Nov. 1802 (Ernst, *Rufus King*, p. 233).
2. John Pickering (1777–1846), lawyer, linguist, and eldest son of Timothy Pickering, had been King's secretary for about eighteen months when he returned to Boston in October 1801.
3. Horatio Southgate was the son of King's sister Mary and Dr. Robert Southgate of Scarborough, Maine (King, *Life and Correspondence of Rufus King*, 1:2–3, 4:154).

¶ From Thomas Paine. Letter not found. *16 June 1802*. Calendared as a three-page letter in the lists probably made by Peter Force (DLC, series 7, container 2). Also calendared by JM in his list of letters from Thomas Paine, 1795–1807 (DLC).

¶ From Thomas Stockton. Letter not found. *16 June 1802*. Acknowledged in Daniel Brent to Stockton, 28 June 1802 (DNA: RG 59, DL, vol. 14). Encloses his account as clerk of the U.S. district court of Delaware. In his reply Brent challenged the charge of $25 for "searching the Dockets of the Circuit Court for the District of Delaware," because it was already covered by a charge for transcribing the records of that court. Brent indicated that the account would be paid "after a reduction shall have been made agreeably to the foregoing suggestion."

From John G. Jackson

DEAR SIR,   CLARKSBURG June 17th 1802

The Public Papers having announced your arrival in the City; I take the liberty to address you upon a little business I have there which I beg the favor of you to negociate. By a Contract with the Post Master General[1] I am to receive $476 dollars per Ann. for carrying the Mail at quarterly payments; the first quarter will end the last of June; I enclose an order for the Money; which you will please send by post; after deducting the $5 advanced Mr. Smith; which I find my Father forgot to pay you; & five dollars for the subscription the ensuing Year.[2] The pleasure we anticipated of visiting you this Year; must be somewhat longer postponed on account of arrangements of my business; & some political events; which from the virulence of infuriated Federalists, will require every honorable exertion; to repel their machinations & ensure success. The Berceau[3]—dismissal of Officers[4] Continuance of a Brigadier General,[5] Refusal to diminish the salaries of Officers[6]—Repeal of the Tax on Carriages & continuing that on Salt &c[7]—Repeal of Judiciary Law[8] &c &c are among the innumerable charges which they are daily making: in spite of all we shall beat them; if we carefully attend & explain their misrepresentations, as truth and honesty are on our side & they are omnipotent.

I expected long ere this to have waited upon Mrs. Payne to this Place; but have not heard from her for about two months past; Mrs. J. also complains of the neglect of her Sisters. Adieu Your sincere Friend

J G JACKSON

PS if any deductions from the Money are required by the P. M. G. on account of delays please allow them. So far as I know they were unavoidable; but I suppose he is peremptory.

J G J

RC (ViU). Cover marked "*Private*" by Jackson. On the cover is a column of figures in JM's hand and a list of four names and amounts in an unidentified hand.

1. Jackson secured this postal contract in the summer of 1801 (Jackson to JM, 3 Aug. 1801, *PJM-SS*, 2:8).

2. The money was due to Samuel Harrison Smith for a subscription to the *National Intelligencer*. On 6 Aug. 1802 John C. Payne, charged by JM to execute Jackson's business, sent him $110 after deducting $9 for the payment to Smith (Payne to Jackson, 6 Aug. 1802 [InU: Jackson Collection]).

3. Federalists attempted to make political hay out of the $32,839.54 expended to repair the corvette *Berceau*, which had been captured by an American ship and ordered restored to France under the terms of the Convention of 1800. On 5 Apr. 1802 Roger Griswold had moved a resolution calling on the secretary of state to report whether the repairs were made "in order to equip her for the service of the United States, or for the purpose of delivering her to the French Republic." Federalists disguised this attempt to embarrass the executive as a simple request for information; Republicans impugned their efforts as an attack on the motives of the executive branch (*Annals of Congress*, 7th Cong., 1st sess., 1133–41, 1142–54).

4. The Military Peace Establishment Act of 1802 eliminated one-third of the officer positions in the army, reducing the preponderance of officers over enlisted men (Theodore J. Crackel, *Mr. Jefferson's Army: Political and Social Reform of the Military Establishment, 1801–1809* [New York, 1987], pp. 44–45).

5. In the House debate over the Military Peace Establishment Act, Federalists objected to the one remaining post of brigadier general as a "perfect sinecure," but the bill passed without amendment, 77 to 12 (*Annals of Congress*, 7th Cong., 1st sess., 431).

6. Congress had passed an act continuing for a period of two years the salaries of executive officers as they had been augmented in an act of Congress of 2 Mar. 1799 (*U.S. Statutes at Large*, 2:152).

7. The tax on carriages "for the conveyance of persons" was one of the taxes eliminated by the "Act to repeal the Internal Taxes," signed into law on 6 Apr. 1802 (ibid., 2:148–50). The

duty on salt was continued to 1807 (Dall W. Forsythe, *Taxation and Political Change in the Young Nation, 1781–1833* [New York, 1977], p. 68).

8. Jackson referred here to the repeal of the Judiciary Act of 1801 (*U.S. Statutes at Large*, 2:132).

From Levi Lincoln

SIR   WASHINGTON June 17 1802

I have the honor, in compliance with your request,[1] to submit to your consideration, my ideas respecting the case of the schooner Peggy.

This vessel, if the information I have been able to collect, abroad, is correct, for it does not appear from the papers I am furnished with, was captured in the neig[h]bourhood of a west India Island, and so near the shore, and so destitute of arms, as to render it doubtful whether she was on the high seas, or, an armed vessel, at the time of the capture, in the sense of the law which authorized the taking of french vessels. These are said to have been the questions, on which, the cause was placed, and the acquittal depended—& these are assumed as facts, in considering the cause. She was libelled in the District Court of Connecticut July 1800. and on an appeal to the Circuit Court on the 23d of Sept. following was condemned, as good prize to the Captors, one moiety to their use, & the other, to the use of the United States. The Clerk of the Court held the avails of the apprized value of this vessel, & her cargo amounting to $18,804.72 subject to the disposition of law, at the time of this condemnation.

Final decrees, and judgments, in civil actions &c. in a circuit court, the matter in dispute exceeding $2,000, may be reexamined, reversed or affirmed, by writ of Error brought to the Supreme court, within five years from the making of such a decree, the Plaintiff in Error giving to the adverse party, notice of such writ, thirty days previous, at least, to the setting of the Court to which it is made returnable, and giving also to the judge signing, the writ of error, or the citation, sufficient security for the prosecution of the writ to effect, & to answer all cost & damages, if he fail to make his plea good. Writ of Error stays Execution only in cases, where it is sued out & a copy thereof lodged in the clerks office for the adverse party within ten days from the rendition of judgt. &c. It does not appear, that this was done; It is certain, no citation was served on the adverse party— and I assume, as a fact, no bond for the prosecution of the writ of error, was ever given.

It appears tht. On the 15th of April 1801, by a representation of the Clerk to the Circuit Court which had decreed the condemnation of the Schooner Peggy & her cargo, as lawful prize, to the use of the captors &

the U. S, in moieties—that the abovementioned money was in his hands; that a writ of Error had been issued dated Octr 2d., the determination of which was unknown—that the captors had requested the moiety which had accrued to them by the sd decree; and that the President of the United States, had ordered, so far as they were concerned, the property to be delivered to the Claimants. It also appears, from an application of Mr Livingston,[2] who acted as Atty to the claimants, who were the Plaintiffs in Error, that proceedings on the sd writ in the Supreme Court were suspended for the want of a citation or notice to the adverse party, and that Mr. Edwards the Atty of the U. S for the same District, had acknowledged in writing a citation & a notice on him as atty to the U. S.

Under these circumstances the said Circuit Court on the 15th day of April 1801 order one moiety of the said avails, after deducting the cost expences &c, to be paid to the Captors, & the other, to be paid into the treasury of the U States. The Captors were paid accordingly, & the residue was lodged or deposited in the treasurer's office.

The Supreme Court, in their last December term, try the cause on the writ of Error, and decree in the following words viz—"The Court having heard the arguments of counsel in this cause, and mutually[3] considered the same do adjudge and decree, that the decree of the circuit court of the U. States in this cause be, and the same is hereby reversed, and that the Schooner Peggy & Cargo with her apparel, guns and appurtenances be restored to the sd Claimants, but without cost." On this decree the sd. moiety lodged in the treasury, has been paid, to the claimants, without any further deductions of cost, or expence. The other Moiety, Mr. Pichon now claims, as their agent, from the U. S, under the treaty.

The 4th Art: provides, "that property captured, and not yet *definitively condemned*, or which may be captured before the exchange of ratifications, shall be mutually restored"—and further, "that *this article* shall take effect from the *signature* of the convention, and if from the date of the sd signature, any property shall be condemned contrary to the intent of the sd Convention, before the knowlege of *this stipulation shall be obtained*, the property so condemned shall without delay be restored, or paid for."[4] The only effect which this article can be construed, as designed to have from its signature, is a description of the property which is to be considered within its operation.

The treaty was signed Sept 30th 1800—Judgt in Circuit Court 23d of Sept. & in Supr. Court Decr 1801 previous to which, the treaty had been ratified. The principal questions are: First, Is Govt. obliged by the treaty to restore to the claimants, the property delivered to the Captors? 2d. If not, are they obliged to do it, by the law of nations, or the Judgment of the Court, the treaty being out of the way?

The design of the convention, was to provide for such cases as were not otherwise provided for, to secure, the restoration of *such* a description of property to the original owners, as the United States were not obliged to restore, by any preexisting laws, or obligation. As to *such* property, the treaty was alone necessary[;] to other[,] nugatory. It could have for its object, only, such property, which had not been *finally condemned* at the signing [of] the treaty, or such, as without its provisions, was liable to condemnation, & it can operate alone against captors, who, independent of the treaty stipulation, would have had a right to hold these captured articles, & who, by *that*, are obliged to restore them. There could be no need for extending its provisions further. In others [*sic*] instances of captures, there were other provisions; if for a breach of the laws of trade; if without any authority; if as a trespass, in violation of the rights of individuals, or of the nation; the remedies were under the laws applicable to such subjects, & by which, the courts could restore, with damages & cost. Indeed, the terms, '*condemned*,' and which could have been, '*condemned*,' had it not have been for the treaty, are *used, in it*, as descriptive, of what is to be restored, *under it*. The preamble states, as its object, the determination of the differences, which had arisen between the two States. The words in the 4th Art are, "property *captured*, & not yet *definitively condemned*," or, "which *may be captured* before" &c—or, if any "property shall be *condemned* contrary to the intent of the sd convention, & before the knowledge of this *stipulation shall be* obtained; the *property so condemned*, shall without delay be restored, or paid for." From which, it is evident, that the property on which the treaty was meant to operate, was not, such, as had been *finally acquitted*, or, by existing laws, as would in a course of regular judicial proceedings, be acquitted, but such, as a knowledge of the treaty stipulation, would prevent a condemnation of. A French vessel, therefore, taken, not on the high seas, &, unarmed, is not to be restored under the treaty—as property within its provisions—admitting there had never been any definitive condemnation, And the proceedings of the Supreme Court, seem to have been, on this idea.

But if the Peggy & her cargo are included in the terms, '*property captured*,' in the sense of the treaty, were they not, definitively, condemned at the time of the signing of the Convention? A definitive, judgment, decree, or condemnation, are legal terms, and have a technical meaning, they are synonymous with *final* judgment, decree & condemnation. The word final, & definitive, in law, as in common parlance, have the same meaning. A final judgment, or decree, is that which puts an end to a suit, by declaring that the Plaintiff, or libellant, has, or has not, intitled himself to recover the object of his suit, and it is opposed to an interlocutory, or intermediate, judgment, or decree. In suits, in which, an appeal is given by law, it is true, the judgement is not considered as final, untill the time, allowed for the appeal, has elapsed. Within that time, no execution can issue. And the effect of the appeal, is, to suspend the judgment below. But a writ of Error, does not suspend, the judgment, even where it is a supercedeas of the Exon. In the present case, as the Exon. could issue, on the decree, in the circuit court, it is proof, that it was final, or definitive. Indeed, the very law, which gives this writ of Error, provides, that *final decrees* and judgements, in the circuit courts may be reexamined, reversed or affirmed, in the Supreme Court. It, therefore, has fixed the meaning of the word *final*, as applied to a decree of *condemnation*. The word *definitive*, is not used in our law, as *applicable* to the condemnation of captured property, but the treaty uses it, as descriptive of a judgment in our prize courts, of condemnation, of such property. It therefore can apply, only, to what our *law*, and the *courts*, consider, as *their final* judgements. The decree, on a writ of error, is a judgment, of *reversal*, or *affirmation* of a former Judgment of condemnation, not a judgment of condemnation itself. There is one further idea, on this subject. The makers of the treaty, are to be presumed to have understood the subject, about which they treated & the existing laws by which it was regulated. The sense, in which, they use the term *definitively*, is such, as not only admits of, but actually supposes some of the captured property, to have been definitively condemned. On the ground, that no judgement was to be considered as definitive, which was liable to be reexamined, by writ of error, there could [not] have been, nor can there be any definitive condemnation of French property in America under the treaty—The five years for the writ of error, not having elapsed. It is, to my mind very clear, that the owners of the captured Schooner & her cargo, cannot claim a restitution of her, under the treaty.

At law, the decision of the circuit court, determined and fixed the original owners claim to a restitution, at their own election. If they did not give bonds, the property was to be distributed. If notice of the writ of error was not given to the adverse party, they would not be bound by it. This was not done. Under these circumstances, on strict legal principles, the court below, I conceive, were justified in making distribution. They had condemned the schooner as taken, on the high seas, with arms. The treaty was not, then, ratified, & of course, not binding. And if it had been, they having rendered a definitive judgement, previous to the signature *it* could have no effect on the cause. There being no bonds, admitting there had been a citation, on the writ of Error, & the treaty out of they [*sic*] way, the captors were intitled to a moiety of the avails of their prize. This then, they have been put in the possession of, by judgement of law. If that judgement has been, regularly, reversed, on a writ of error, Those who took a benefit under it, are by law bound to make restoration, to those from whom they took it. The U S have done it, as it respects its moiety. By the judgement of the S. Court, U. S. are not answerable for the other half. This, is on the idea

316

that I am right, in considering the circuit judgement, as definitive, or the reversal, as applying to a case, not within the provisions of the treaty.

How far the captors ought to have been, or are, bound by an acknowledgement of the service of a citation, on the attorney of the U. S., to give effect to a writ of Error, as against them; whether it ought to divest them of property, that the law had vested in them, without having an opportunity to defend it; or whether the claimants have not, by their own laches, lost their law & all remedy in not notifying them agreeably to law, thirty days before the return of the writ of Error, are questions which are for the parties to attend to, & which, as they do not involve the interest of Government, I have not looked into, & am not able to decide upon. I have been thus particular, that you might possess the reasons, on which the above opinions are formed. As the letter is lengthy, and I am my own copying clerk, you will be kind enough, to excuse the many interlineations, & rasures, which would require a transcriber to cure. I am Sir most respectfully your very obedient Sevt.

LEVI LINCOLN

RC (DNA: RG 59, LOAG). Docketed by Brent.

1. JM to Lincoln, 13 June 1802.
2. Edward Livingston was mayor of New York City and U.S. attorney for the district of New York.
3. "Maturely" in the copy of the decree enclosed in Gallatin to JM, 9 June 1802.
4. For article 4 of the Convention of 1800 between France and the U.S., see Miller, *Treaties*, 2:459–62.

From Arthur St. Clair

SIR,   June 17th. 1802

In a conversation with the Secretary of the Navy, a day or two ago, on the subject of the fees which it has been said have been demanded and received by me, for which there was not warrant by Law—I asserted to him, as I had done in my general Vindication, that no fees had ever been received by me that were not expressly granted by Law, and the Laws authorising the fees for Tavern Licenses and Commissions to certain Officers were pointed out. But the two first Volumes of the territorial Laws, printed at Philada. by order of Congress under the direction of the Secretary of State, and by him transmitted to me to be distributed, are not to be found in the Office. In one of them, ⟨I am?⟩ most positive there is a Law authorising the fee for marriage Licenses, but a doubt struck across my mind that the fee

317

which had been taken for ferry Licenses was not authorised, and had been demanded on the principle of a Quantum meruit.[1] It is a doubt only, but candor obliged me to acknowledge that doubt to him and to state it likewise to you. Be pleased Sir to consider that the ferry Licenses were a public Act, under the Seal of the Territory, whereby the parties accquired a freehold in the ferries, and could not be ousted from them, but in consequence of a breach of the conditions asscertained by a Jury—that there was no Law prohibiting the taking reasonable fees for Services done, and that I knew it to be customary in some of the States, and particularly in Pennsylvania & New York, where, tho' the Salarys are very liberal, the fees amount to a large Sum—that I conceived I had a right to demand a fee, and that the fee demanded was not exorbitant, taking into view the benefits accruing to the parties paying it—that it could not have been demanded from avaricious motives, the whole amount, received by me not exceeding ten Guineas that the Salary was in fact no compensation for the labour and expense to which I was exposed, in the execution of the Office and that, when I refused to accept it at the Salary it was pressed upon me by my freinds in Congress, as a thing of no moment, as the opportunity of acquiring landed property would rendered [sic] the Office an object even without Salary. The price, however, and the terms of payment, at which the public Lands were set, put it absolutely out of my power to carry that expectation into effect. But, supposing that no Law exists to justify this demand, and that I have been mistaken in supposing I had a right to take any thing on the principle of a Quantum meruit, Bear with me, I pray you, when I take the liberty to observe that it seems hard that one mistake should cancel the merit of thirteen years Service attended with a degree of labour and difficulty that not a great many Men either could or would have gone through. Be assured, Sir, it is no easy matter to conduct and keep in order a new Settlement, composed of people gathered together from the four winds, with habits manners and customs as different as their faces and to amalgamate and reduce them to one Mass. This however and more so when they scattered over an extent of country near a thousand miles in length ⟨was in?⟩ great measure effected. I have led the Colony Sir, from thirty Men till now that they near double that number of thousand⟨s⟩ without the smallest Symptom of discontent, until about five years ago, and that discontent, confined to a small part of the territory and proceeding from a Circumstance very trifling in itself.[2] Allow me to say Sir, that had the Government been oppressive—had not the Governors conduct been generally approved, such numbers of people would not have flocked to seek protection under him, and that very circumstance is, at least, prima facie evidence that it was not ill administered.

Draft (O). Damaged by folds and tears. The editors are grateful to Gary J. Arnold of the Ohio Historical Society for his assistance in reading the damaged portions.

1. *Quantum meruit*: "as much as he deserves." The common count in an action of *assumpsit* for work and labor, founded on an implied *assumpsit* or promise on the part of the defendant to pay the plaintiff *as much as he* reasonably *deserved* to have for his labor" (*Black's Law Dictionary* [5th ed.], p. 1119).

2. The Republican opposition to St. Clair was centered in the Scioto Valley counties of Ross and Adams, and it was a 1798 altercation over the location of the county seat in the latter county to which St. Clair referred (Andrew R. L. Cayton, *The Frontier Republic: Ideology and Politics in the Ohio Country, 1780–1825* [Columbus, Ohio, 1986], pp. 59–61, 70).

From James Simpson

No. 42.

SIR   TANGIER 17h. June 1802.

Its with great concern I am under the necessity of acquainting you, that either the information given the Swedish Consul and myself on Sunday last, respecting His Imperial Majesty having consented to allow his Wheat Vessels to go to Tunis, was extremely fallacious on the part of the Governour of Tangier, or the Emperour must have very speedily repented of having taken that resolution. This morning at Nine OClock the Governour sent for me again, to say he had received fresh Instructions from His Majesty, with Orders to demand from me Passports for those Vessels to go direct to Tripoly, and in case of refusal that I was to quit the Country, adding that the Letter was written in such strong terms, as must prevent his consenting to any mitigation. After a very long conferrence, he at last however allowed me time to write to Commodore Morris at Gibraltar, which I am now about to do fully, on his answer will depend my remaining in this Country, or being compelled to retire from it.[1] As a Portuguese Brig of War is on immediate departure for Gibraltar, I must beg your excuse for not enlargeing farther, than to assure you nothing possible for me to accomplish, for good of the Public Service on this occasion, shall be neglected. I have the honour to be with sentiments of the highest respect Sir Your Most Obedient and Most Humble Servant

JAMES SIMPSON

RC (DNA: RG 59, CD, Tangier, vol. 1). At the bottom of the letter, Daniel Brent wrote: "I have in consequence of this letter, requested Mr Sheldon, at the Secy of the Treasury's Office, to suspend issuing the warrant for the Gun Carriages 'till your determination shall be known. The Gun Carriages, themselves, would not, at all events, be shipped At an earlier day." Jefferson communicated an extract of the RC to Congress with his annual message on 15 Dec. 1802 (printed in *ASP, Foreign Relations*, 2:466).

1. In his letter to Richard Morris, Simpson offered his opinion that "it is better to grant the passports than to come to a rupture with this country." In reply, Morris asked Simpson to

"urge the necessity of the Emperor's suspending his determination" until the arrival of the *Adams* with instructions from the secretary of the navy (Simpson to Morris, 17 June 1802, Morris to Simpson, 19 June 1802, Knox, *Naval Documents, Barbary Wars*, 2 : 181–82, 182–83).

§ To James Maury. *17 June 1802, Department of State, Washington.* "Your letter of the 10th. April last has been duly received. According to the rule now in practice, all such accounts as yours are to be settled at the Treasury Department. It will be proper therefore that you forward them to that Department with the requisite vouchers. As soon as the balance shall be authenticated, you may receive payment either here or in England, as you prefer."

Letterbook copy (DNA: RG 59, IC, vol. 1). 1 p.

§ From Lange and Bourne. *17 June 1802, Amsterdam.* "By the request of our friend and Partner Mr. Sylvs. Bourne,[1] we have the honor to send you hereby some Leyden newspapers up to the 15 Instt. which we hope will meet you in a perfect State of health! We are Sorry to mention at same time that Mr B: is since some time unwell of a nervous fever in Consequence of his Lady's Sickness. . . . This has induced him as his indisposition prevents a regular attention to the duties of his office, as Consul general, to give *ad interim* proper powers for that purpose to Mr. Herman Hendrik Damen and due notice is given thereof to the Collectors of the different ports of the United States." Postscript adds that "as Mr B. appears to be in a way of recovering we hope he will Soon be able to attend to the business again himself."

RC (DNA: RG 59, CD, Amsterdam, vol. 1). 2 pp.

1. Bourne's business partner was Johann Wilhelm Lange; their partnership dated from 1797 (Van Winter, *American Finance and Dutch Investment*, 1 : 432–33 n. 27).

§ From John P. Van Ness. *17 June 1802.* "The Gentlemen whose names I wish you to mention to the President for the Office of Commissioners of Bankruptcy for the State of N. York under the late Act are, in the City of Hudson David Laurence; in the City of N. York William P. Van Ness & William Paulding. The two latter, altho' not immediately within my District, I have heretofore taken the liberty to suggest to the President."

RC (DNA: RG 59, LAR, 1801–9, filed under "Van Ness"). 1 p.

§ From John Mathieu. *18 June 1802, Naples.* Takes the opportunity by the frigate *Boston,* Captain McNeill, which is about to sail, to enclose a statement of all American ships that arrived at Naples, Messina, and Palermo between 1 January and 30 June 1802. Has heard from Captain McNeill that Morocco declared war on the U.S. and has informed all U.S. consuls in the Mediterranean. Adds in a postscript that he just received the enclosed circular letter from Leghorn [not found]; "I am very unhappy to see our Commerce so interrupt⟨ed⟩ by those Barberians, but that our Frigates will give a good account of them."

RC and enclosure (DNA: RG 59, CD, Naples, vol. 1). RC 2 pp. Surviving enclosure, dated 30 June 1802 (1 p.), lists seven ships that had arrived at the port of Naples since 1 Jan. 1802.

§ From James Maury. *18 June 1802, Liverpool.* "I had the Honor of presenting you with the State of this market for American produce on the 5th ulto. In this you have the prices of the day for the same, as well as of other articles of import from the United States."

RC and enclosure (DNA: RG 59, CD, Liverpool, vol. 2). RC 1 p.; in a clerk's hand, signed by Maury. Enclosure (1 p.; docketed by Brent) is a printed form listing produce that "*May be imported for Exportation in American Ships,*" including sugar, coffee, hides, Nicaraguan wood, cotton, and indigo, with prices and remarks added by hand.

§ From Josiah Tattnall, Jr. *18 June 1802, Executive Department, Louisville, Georgia.* Encloses an act of Georgia, passed 16 June, ratifying the articles of agreement between the commissioners of Georgia and the U.S. concluded 24 Apr. 1802.

Tr and Tr of enclosure, two copies (DNA: RG 46, President's Messages, 7A-E1; and DNA: RG 233, President's Messages, 7A-D1); letterbook copy (G-Ar: Executive Department Minutes). Tr 1 p.; marked "(Copy)." Tr of enclosure 11 pp. Tattnall's letter and enclosure were transmitted by Jefferson to Congress in his message of 15 Dec. 1802. A copy of the letter in the Georgia governor's letterbook (G-Ar) is dated 12 July 1802.

To James Fairlie

Sir,   DEPARTMENT OF STATE. *19th. June 1802*
In pursuance of an Act of the last Session of Congress, authorising the President of the United States to appoint COMMISSIONERS of BANKRUPTCY in the several districts composing the United States,[1] he has selected yourself together with *John Broome, William Edgar, Jonathan Pearsee junr., Daniel D. Tompkins, Nathan Sandford, Abraham G. Lansing, Nicholas V. Quackenbush and Georg Merchant* ESQUIRES, to be COMMISSIONERS for the District of *New York*; and I have the pleasure herewith to enclose your commission. I am, very respectfully, Sir, Your obedient servant,
JAMES MADISON

RC (NjP: Crane Collection). A printed form letter, signed by JM, with date, names, and place supplied in an unidentified hand (indicated here by the use of italics). Enclosure not found. JM's subsequent letters appointing commissioners of bankruptcy will be omitted.

1. By section 14 of "An Act to amend the Judicial System of the United States," 29 Apr. 1802, the power to appoint commissioners of bankruptcy, as delineated in "An Act to establish an uniform System of Bankruptcy throughout the United States," 4 Apr. 1800, was given to the president of the U.S. (*U.S. Statutes at Large,* 2 : 19–36, 164).

Memorandum to Thomas Jefferson

June 19. 1802

The President having called on the heads of Departments for their opinion in writing whether certain charges made by Col. Worthington against Governor St. Clair, be or be not established;[1] and whether such as are established, be sufficiently weighty to render the removal of the Governor proper? the Secretary of State respectfully submits his opinion as follows;

Charge 1. Forming new Counties & fixing their seats of justice by his sole authority.

The fact is admitted and its legality contended for. The reasons given are unsatisfactory to the judgment of the Secretary of State; but he can not undertake to say that they have so little plausibility as to preclude a difference of opinion.

Ch. 2d. "Putting a negative on useful & necessary laws."

It appears that the Negative has been exercised in many cases, and in some probably, where the laws would have been salutary. The discretion however involved in the use of this power, requires stronger and clearer abuses of it, than are shewn, to justify a hasty or rigorous condemnation.

Ch. 3. "Taking illegal fees."

In the case of ferry licenses the charge seems undeniable. In that of tavern licenses, an act is found in the code of the Territory, authorizing the fees; but there is reason to believe that a latitude of construction or rather an abuse of power in which the Govr. himself participated, was employed in the adoption of the Act. With respect to the marriage fees, it is affirmed that a legal authority also exists. As the volume of laws however referred to on this point cannot be consulted no opinion will be given either on the tenor or the origin of the Act.

The taking of illegal fees is in itself an abuse of power, of so deep a die, as, unless mitigated by powerful circumstances, to justify a rigorous proceeding against the author of it and as to be altogether excusable under no circumstances.

Ch. 4. "Negativing a bill for abolishing fees, and passing one giving the Govr. a secu⟨rity?⟩ meant by the Legislature as a substitute for them."

This charge involves questions which it would be difficult to unravel, and perhaps improper to decide.

Ch. 5. "Concurring in the plan of changing the Constitutional boundaries of the proposed States N. W. of the Ohio."

The fact is certain, and the attempt of the Governor to explain obscure & unsatisfactory.

Ch. 6. "Appointing his son Attorney General, by an illegal commission during good behavior."

The fact is admitted without being palliated by the explanations given by the Governour.

⟨Ch.⟩ 7. "Attempting to influence certain judiciary proceedings."

This charge as far as it can be judged of by what appears, can not be considered as established. In one at least of the transactions referred to, the conduct of the Governor was justified by that of the Justices.

Ch. 8. "Appointing to offices requiring residence in one county, persons residing in another."

The fact here may be true, and conduct of the Govr. free from blame. If the offices were incompatible, the second appointment might be made on the presumption that the first could be relinquished. To judge fully of the case it ought also to be known what the law of the territory is with respect to the residence & deputyship of the different officers.

Ch. 9. "Neglecting to organize & discipline the Militia."

This charge is not established.

Ch. 10. "Hostility to republican form of Government."

The circumstances under which expressions to this effect are admitted to have been used, & under which the evidence of them appears to [have] been collected, render it improper to lay stress on this charge.

Upon the whole, it appears that altho' the conduct of the Governor has been highly culpable in sundry instances, and sufficiently so in the particular cases of Commissioning his son during good behavior, and in what relates to fees, to plead, for a removal of him from his office, yet considering the revolutionary & other interesting relations in which he has stood to the public, with other grounds on which some indulgence may be felt for him, it is the opinion of the Secretary of State, that it will be proper to leave him in possession of his office, under the influence of a salutary admonition.

JAMES MADISON

RC (DLC: Jefferson Papers). Docketed by Jefferson.

1. For the circumstances surrounding the charges against Arthur St. Clair, see Circular Letter from Thomas Jefferson, 29 Apr. 1802, and n. 1.

From William Madison

DR. BROTHER   19th June 1802

Mr Taylor, having had the Measles, could not draw the Bill & Answers 'till lately since which I have been indisposed myself. All the Answers are made out, except Nelly's, & hers will be ready in a few days. You, Myself &

the grand children are Dfts. and answer seperately. Mr Taylor has drawn the Bill very full & I trust will bring the case fully before the Chancellor. If Council shd. be satisfied with the decree it will be unnecessary to go to the Court of Appeals for the same reservation in favor of Infants will be made there as in Chancery. The only way to prevent the Infants reviving their Claims wd be to make them Plfts. the right to do which is very questionable.[1]

I shall forwd your answer in a few days, by the Mail. It will be unnecessary to send you the Bill as it complains generally. I am as anxious as any one for a decree. Love to all with you

WM MADISON

RC (NjP).

1. For the complex legal actions involved in the settlement of the estate of James Madison, Sr., see William Madison to JM, 22 Sept. 1801 (*PJM-SS*, 2 : 124–25 and n. 1).

From Louis-André Pichon

GEORGETOWN le 30. Prairial an 10. (19. Juin. 1802.)

Le citoyen Pichon à [*sic*] l'honneur de présenter Ses respects à Monsieur Madison et de lui adresser copie.

1e. d'une lettre qu'il vient de recevoir de l'ordonnateur en chef (quarter Master general) de l'armée de la République française à St. Domingue[1] qui répond, comme le verra Monsieur Madison, à diverses lettres écrites à l'administration de St Domingue par le Cen. Pichon au Sujet des plaintes élevées par le commerce Americain, Dans les premiers tems de l'arrivée de l'armée francaise.

2e. D'une lettre que le Cen. Pichon a écrite au Général Leclerc relativement à M. & M. Davidson et Rogers.[2]

L'objet du Cen. Pichon, en communiquant à Monsieur Madison la premiere piece, est d'instruire le Gouvernement des Etats Unis des dispositions de l'administration de St Domingue: dispositions dont la force des circonstances a pu Seule faire dévier, Dans la partie de la colonie où des catastrophes inesperées ont presque compromis l'existence des troupes et des vaisseaux de la République. Cette correspondance fera en même tems connaître à Monsieur Madison les efforts que le Cen. Pichon a faits de bonne heure pour contribuer autant qu'il est en lui au redressement des plaintes que le commerce americain a pu avoir à porter: plaintes qui d'après la lettre de l'ordonnateur général, paraissent avoir été exagerées.

Les mêmes Sentimens portent le Cen. Pichon à communiquer à

Mr. Madison la Seconde piece. Elle Servira en outre à démontrer à Mr. Le Sécrétaire d'Etat combien Sont éloignés de la vérité les bruit qui ont attribué au Cen. Pichon une part dans ce qui est arrivé à St. Domingue aux deux personnes qui en Sont l'objet.

Le Cen. Pichon doit aussi informer Mr. Le Sécrétaire d'Etat qu'il a reçu dernierement du Gal. en chef des directions relatives aux Sommes qui ont été déposées dans les caisses publiques à St. Domingue pour le compte de Mr. J. Low qui est décédé au Cap quelques Jours après qu'il eut lui même porté ces Sommes à bord d'un vaisseau de l'armée. Mr. le Sécrétaire d'Etat Se rappelera probablement que cette affaire a été présentée, dans le tems, Sous un Jour extrêmement défavorable et irritant.[3] Le Gal. en chef a invité le Cen. Pichon à prendre des renseignemens Sur les personnes ayant droit à cet argent et, Jusqu'à la réponse du Cen. Pichon, a refusé de le remettre au frère du décédé, Mr. Cornelius Low, vû que Mr. J. Low était mort en faillite. Les personnes à qui appartiens la propriété Sont des Négocians de Baltimore à qui le Cen. Pichon S'est empressé de donner les avis et les lettres propres à les diriger. Ces négocians viennent d'envoyer leurs papiers au Cap et ils n'éprouveront aucune difficulté pour recouvrer la propriété.

Le Soussigné prie Monsieur le Sécrétaire d'Etat de vouloir bien porter le contenû de ces pieces à la connaissance de Monsieur le Président des Etats Unis, et de recevoir l'assurance de Sa respectueuse et haute consideration.

L. A. PICHON

CONDENSED TRANSLATION

Pichon presents his respects to JM and encloses copies of (1) a letter he has just received from the quartermaster general of the French army at Saint-Domingue, responding to letters Pichon had written on the subject of complaints made by American merchants after the arrival of the French army at that island; and (2) a letter that Pichon wrote to General Leclerc on the subject of Davidson and Rodgers.

His object in enclosing the first letter is to inform the U.S. government of the dispositions of the authorities in Saint-Domingue, dispositions that could only be altered by the force of circumstances in the part of the colony where catastrophes have jeopardized the existence of French soldiers and ships. The letter will also inform JM of Pichon's early efforts to redress the complaints of American merchants, complaints that, according to the quartermaster general, seem to have been exaggerated.

The second letter will serve to demonstrate to JM how far from the truth was the report that attributed to Pichon a part in what happened to the two captains.

Pichon must also inform JM that he has lately received directions from Leclerc about the sum deposited in the public treasury in Saint-Domingue for the account of J. Low, who died at the cape several days after he carried this money on board a French armed ship. JM will probably remember that this affair was presented at the time in an extremely unfavorable and irritating light. Leclerc has asked Pichon to inquire about persons having a right to this money and has refused to give it to the dead man's brother, Cornelius Low, before hearing from Pichon, seeing that J. Low died in bankruptcy. Those who own the property are Baltimore merchants, to whom Pichon hastened to give notice along with the proper letters to direct them. These merchants are sending their papers to the cape, and they will have no difficulty in recovering the property.

Asks JM to inform the president of the contents of these letters.

RC and enclosures (DNA: RG 59, NFL, France, vol. 1). RC in a clerk's hand, signed by Pichon; docketed by Brent as received the same day. For enclosures, see nn.

1. Hector Daure to Pichon, 4 Prairial an X (24 May 1802) (4 pp.; in French). The quartermaster general's letter, in response to Pichon's letters of 5 and 11 Apr. 1802, explained that the violence in the days following the invasion of Saint-Domingue, especially the burning of Cap Français, forced the French to rely on American cargoes for their supplies. The embargo was enforced out of fear that these supplies would find their way to the rebel camp. Items were bought by the army, giving one-quarter of the price in cash and the balance in bills on France. The profit that resulted was far more than the Americans could have expected with the island in flames, Daure asserted, and no sooner was the army victorious than Leclerc lifted the embargo and opened all the island's ports.

2. Pichon's letter to Leclerc, dated 17 Floréal an X (7 May 1802) (4 pp.; in French) informed the general of JM's displeasure over the imprisonment of John Rodgers and William Davidson. Pichon wrote that he agreed with JM, noting that Rodgers could not be held responsible in Saint-Domingue for acts he had committed in the U.S. As for Davidson, Pichon went on, a ship's name, however suspicious, did not constitute a crime, and in any case, both men had the right to a speedy judgment; they should not be held indefinitely on vague charges.

3. For the case of Jonathan Low, see *PJM-SS*, 2:508, 513, 516.

From John Steele

SIR,   NATCHEZ. MISSISSIPPI TERRITORY. June 20th. 1802.

It is with much reluctance I prevail on myself, so far to intrude upon you, as to request your attention to a subject which concerns myself only.

Having gone nearly through a term of twenty one years in various public employments, without the *colour* of *censure*, cast upon my integrity or honour, and being desirous to preserve the small share of fame, I might thereby be entitled to, I wrote to my Friend (who I presume is known to you) on the 23rd. of January last, informing him that "*on him alone* I relied to see that no unfair advantage was taken of me."[1] This Letter he answered on the 29th. of April, as follows.

"The very day your Letter came to hand I waited on the President, and Secretary of State, expressed, to them your wishes to be continued in the Office you now hold, and urged the propriety of your reappointment by every argument which friendship and a consciousness of your merit could suggest. They assured me that they saw no objection to the application, provided you stood well with the Governor of that Territory, but as it was important that a good understanding should subsist between the Governor and Secretary, and as they had received no communication from him on the subject, nothing would be done until information on that head could be obtained. Last evening, I had some conversation with   ² from which I learned that representations have been received by the President,³ stating that you are not on confidential terms with the Governor, that you concur with Colo: Sargent in views and measures tending to lesson the influence of the Governor &c. He did not say from whom these representations came, but I fear they have made impressions unfavorable to your views and my wishes to serve you. I shall call tomorrow on Mr. Madison to know how the business stands and shall write again on this subject."

As this charge if true, would very justly tarnish or throw down, the merit of my whole life, I have taken the liberty of enclosing to you a Copy of my reply to my Friend,⁴ under a hope that it will be considered sufficient ground on which to suspend a final decision, and one that is to mark the purity or impurity of my character for ever.

I remember Sir, when it was my pride, to admire your Talents and virtues, I remember when I would have thought it highly honorable to merit your esteem. These sentiments are not extinguished, and I assure myself, that such is your love of Justice that you will take pleasure in expressing to the President of the United States my desire, that my Accuser may be made known to me, and that I may be indulged in attempting to shew the accusation is not founded in fact. For sure I am, his wisdom and humanity, will dispose him to continue open the way to a fair decision rather than hasten to close a proceeding which is to cast the first stain upon a life devoted to honorable pursuits. Had I gone out of Office without accusation, the world should not have heard from me a single murmur—now to be silent would be a crime against myself, and those who have honored me, with their friendship. With high respect and Consideration I have the honor to be Sir your Obedient humble Servant

JOHN STEELE

RC and enclosure (DLC: Jefferson Papers). Cover dated Frankfort, Kentucky, 17 Aug. 1802. Docketed by Brent as received 31 Aug. For enclosure, see n. 4.

1. Steele's friend was Senator John Brown of Kentucky. Steele had written Brown on 23 Jan. 1802 that he hoped to be reappointed as secretary of the Mississippi Territory, and he asked the senator to intervene with the administration on his behalf if necessary (DNA: RG 59, LAR, 1801–9).

2. Steele left a blank space here.

3. Jefferson had received comments from Governor Claiborne that left no doubt he wanted Steele replaced when his term of office expired (Claiborne to Jefferson, 4 Mar. 1802 [DLC: Jefferson Papers]). For Jefferson's comments, see his letter to JM, 6 Sept. 1802.

4. In the enclosed letter of 16 June 1802 (6 pp.), Steele explained the rift between Claiborne and himself as a misunderstanding, resulting from an "incident of a *private* nature" and not a difference of political opinion. He protested that he had contributed his best efforts

toward the success of Claiborne's administration despite being severely ill from August 1801 to April 1802.

§ From John Gavino. *20 June 1802, Gibraltar.* No. 90. Encloses copies of letters from Simpson of 17 and 18 June.[1] The emperor of Morocco "not only renews his Demands for Pasports for to send wheat to Tripoly, but wants to take out the Tripolin Ship blocaded here under his Flag, for particulars of which referr to Comodor Morris & Consul Simpsons Dispatches which the former Gentn will forward." Morris will go to Tangier at "the first fair wind" to consult with Simpson, but no doubt the consul will refuse the Moroccan request and in consequence be obliged to leave. The emperor has no cruisers ready for sea but may send out small ones soon. Encloses a copy of his circular to U.S. consuls on the subject.[2] Reports Algerines have taken two British ships; "a 74 with a frigate is gone up to Enquire into the business." Lord Keith "saild for England but put back & is wind bound."[3]

RC and enclosures (DNA: RG 59, CD, Gibraltar, vol. 2). RC 2 pp.; docketed by Brent. For enclosures, see nn. 1 and 2.

1. Simpson's letter of 17 June to Gavino (1 p.; printed in Knox, *Naval Documents, Barbary Wars,* 2:178–79) warned that if Commodore Morris did not grant the passports for the two ships with wheat bound for Tripoli, Gavino should "send off by very first Post Circulars East & West *to Caution our Merchant Vessels not to pass the Straits without Convoy untill they hear whither I have left Barbary or not.*" Simpson's letter of 18 June to Gavino (1 p.) requested that Morris be informed that "I have only told the Secretary [of] State the principal point, and that the issue will totally depend on the Comodors determination—which he will no doubt Communicate to Goverment" (see Simpson to JM, 17 June 1802, and n. 1).
2. Gavino's circular to U.S. consuls, dated 20 June 1802 (1 p.; printed ibid., 2:181), warned that affairs with the emperor of Morocco were in a "very Critical Situation and it would be highly imprudent that our Merchant Vessels should attempt to pass the Straits without Convoy."
3. George Keith Elphinstone, Viscount Keith, was on his way home from Egypt, where he had resigned his command of the British fleet at the close of the war.

§ From Rufus King. *20 June 1802, London.* No. 70. Has received the duplicate of JM's letter of 1 May; as soon as the original arrives, will take "immediate measures to complete the Convention by exchanging the Ratifications." The commission under article 7 is proceeding satisfactorily; more than fifty cases have been decided since it recommenced its business, and once the exchange of ratifications is made, "their respective Sums may be computed and fixed." The question of interest will be taken up once these computations are made. Since British claims for allegedly illegal captures amount to a "considerable sum" and "many of these Claims are destitute of any just foundation," they will receive "early consideration and decision." Cabot's assistance will be a "material advantage" to American claimants and to the commissioners through his knowledge of the peculiarities of the American trade. Will inform the commissioners of the president's wish to allow Cabot an annual salary of $1,500. As to the countervailing duties on American ships entering British ports, repeats that "I do not perceive that I can with propriety resume the subject, until Congress shall have come to some decision concerning it." The British intention to suspend immediately the countervailing duty on tobacco depended on reciprocal repeal of discriminating duties in America; "but as soon as I perceived that such repeal had become doubtful . . . I thought it due to a candid course of Proceeding, to intimate my doubts upon this point to the British Minister; and in consequence thereof it was determined by the Treasury to postpone the suspension until more precise information of the views of Congress should be received."

RC (DNA: RG 59, DD, Great Britain, vol. 10); letterbook copy (NHi: Rufus King Papers, vol. 55). RC 3 pp.; in a clerk's hand, signed by King. Docketed by Brent as received 14 Sept., but JM received a copy by 11 Sept. (see JM to Jefferson, 11 Sept. 1802). Printed in King, *Life and Correspondence of Rufus King*, 4:141–42.

From Dabney Carr

SIR: WASHINGTON. June 21st. 1802

I intended to have waited on you, at your Office, today, on the subject of the enclosed letter; but unluckily deferred my walk, till I found, that you had returned to your own house. I am obliged to leave the City this evening, & have therefore thought it best, to communicate with you on the subject in this mode. If in doing this, I make a *faux pas*, it will, I trust, be attributed to my entire ignorance of the etiquette of *applications*. An acquaintance of long standing, with Mr Hanson, strengthened by the uniform testimony of all unprejudiced persons, authorises me to say that he is a man, of unblemished reputation, incorruptible integrity, & of great diligence & industry in performing the duties of an office he has undertaken. Mr Hanson is considered by those who know him, as a man of fine talents, & general information—whether he be competent to supply the place of Mr Wagner, it would be presumptuous in me to undertake to decide—this however, you can easily ascertain, if you should be inclined to make trial of him.

If it were proper, I could add, that, Mr Hanson, by his difference with the Directors of the Bank of Columbia, has been thrown out of the receipt of a handsome annuity, & has now *litterally* nothing to support himself & a large family.

The letter enclosed, you will be so good as to give into the care of Capt'n Lewis. Yrs with respect

D CARR[1]

RC (DLC). Docketed by JM. Enclosure not found.

1. Jefferson's nephew Dabney Carr, Jr. (1773–1837), had been left in JM's care during his friend's residence in France as U.S. minister. Carr later served as justice of the Virginia supreme court of appeals, 1824–37 (*PJM*, 8:33 n. 6).

§ From John Steele. *21 June 1802*. Encloses a copy of a letter he wrote to the secretary of the treasury[1] for JM's perusal and asks JM to return it when convenient. "It would be agreeable . . . that the President shd. see it; but . . . the Secry. of the Treasy. may perhaps have shown to him the original."

RC (Nc-Ar: Steele Papers). 1 p. Printed in Wagstaff, *Papers of John Steele*, 1:283.

1. Steele's letter to Gallatin, 4 June 1802, commented on "the Report of the Committee of investigation which relates to the expenses of removal from the City of Philadelphia to the permanent seat of Government." The committee report had cast doubt on the legality of certain payments to executive branch officials for the removal of their offices to Washington, and Steele's letter was intended to convince Gallatin that the payments were "defensible as well in an equitable sense, as according to the strict letter of the law" (printed ibid., 1: 275–81).

From Thomas Newton

D_R S_{IR}   N_{ORFOLK} June. 22. 1802
I Received your favor[1] the wine similar & of the same cargo was shipped & expect with you before it came to hand. The Brasil wine I think superior & price $350 dollars little of such wine is imported; the President has had some of the quality, but most here, give a preferance to the last importation; what is sent, if it gets to hand as shipped, I have no doubt will please; I have some of the Brasil wine in Hds. It will give me pleasure to supply you & friends with what you may want from this place, I have some Citron with the wine ⟨in⟩ boxes of 14 lb. each it comes high, but a box will serve three or four large families & is a scarce Article, if you wish any please to let me know. I am respectfully ⟨Y⟩r. Obt Servt

T_{HOS} N_{EWTON}

RC (DLC). Docketed by JM.

1. Letter not found.

§ From Daniel Clark. *22 June 1802, New Orleans*. Informs JM of the state of affairs in Louisiana "in compliance with your direction, to point out such objects as would require the interference of our Government, with this of Spain, to ascertain our rights, and procure redress, and at the same time to have your instructions to regulate my own conduct." Notes that JM is already aware of "the disagreable predicament in which I am placed, by the refusal of the Spanish Government, to recognize a Consul for the U. S., in any port in their American dominions, and of the new order from the Governor of Luisiana, to the Vice Consul, to Suspend the exercise of his functions"; feels confident the U.S. will insist on recognition by the court of Spain of an official character to protect U.S. interests. Outlines previous regulations on U.S. trade and mentions the intendant's plan to close New Orleans to Americans upon promulgation of the definitive treaty with Great Britain, "limiting our Commerce in this quarter, to the Supplying of our own Settlements on the river, & exportation of their produce deposited in New Orleans." Complains of security deposit requirement and other impediments to trade, including a 3 percent duty on money brought into New Orleans which was ordered on 24 Mar. and has already amounted to $552 as indicated in enclosure no. 1.[1] "On no pretence whatever, can this duty be demanded. It is not warranted by Treaty. . . . It is an abuse of too great a magnitude to admit of delay, as it may take root & require a violent remedy. . . . The Paper No. 2, the Protest of a Mr. Cushing, is intended as an official document on the subject."[2] Has complained to the intendant that if persisted in, the duty "would probably occasion a very serious misunderstanding" between the two countries. "From this you may Judge, Sir! of the necessity of making such representations to the Court of Spain as will put it in mind of its engagements with us."

Assumes JM knows the situation of the residents on the Tombigbee River, who are denied the right to carry goods by way of Mobile and must instead ship from New Orleans where they are subjected to a duty of 6 percent on importation "& as much more on exportation." Discusses problem of Spanish right to embargo American shipping on the Mississippi, an example of which is set forth in enclosure no. 3, a statement of Robert Lowry of Baltimore.[3] Suggests that other points the U.S. government should raise with Spain are the passport fee required of all American boatmen and the disposition of the property of Americans who die intestate on the Mississippi. Cites impediments set up to the free movement of slaves in and out of Spanish territory. Observes that trade with Louisiana is open to the nations of Europe; "the exception seems singular in respect to us."

RC and enclosures (DNA: RG 59, CD, New Orleans, vol. 1); Tr and Tr of enclosures (DLC: Monroe Papers). RC 18 pp.; docketed by Brent. Printed in "Despatches from the United States Consulate in New Orleans, 1801–1803," *American Historical Review*, 32 (1927): 815–22. Tr and Tr of enclosures in the hand of Daniel Brent; docketed by Monroe. A letterpress copy of the Tr is in the Livingston Papers (NHi).

1. Enclosure no. 1 (1 p.) is a "Memorandum of Sums of money imported into New Orleans in American Vessels from foreign Ports & in Boats from the Settlements on the River on which a duty of three ℀ Ct. has been exacted by the Intendant of New Orleans for Liberty to deposit it, from 20th. March to 22 June 1802," totaling $18,804 for a duty of $552.12.

2. Elijah Cushing's deposition (4 pp.), taken by Clark on 21 June 1802, complained that he had been forced to pay a 3 percent storage duty on money he had deposited, according to custom, in New Orleans before shipping it to Philadelphia, and Clark added his own protest that the "aforesaid illegal and exorbitant exaction" amounted to a violation of article 22 of the Pinckney treaty.

3. Robert K. Lowry's statement, dated 28 Feb. 1802 at Philadelphia (3 pp.), described events in July 1800, when the schooner *Volunteer* was detained near New Orleans. Lowry and the captain of the ship were treated with "extreme insolence" and threatened with physical harm by Spanish officials and were forced to pay $45 before obtaining leave to clear the Mississippi River. In the Tr, Brent miscopied the signature as "Thomas Lowry."

§ From Tobias Lear. *22 June 1802, Walnut Tree Farm.* In compliance with Brent's request, transmits to JM "copies of my correspondence with General Leclerc concerning Captain Rogers and Captain Davidson, which you will find enclosed under Nos. 1. 2 & 3."[1]

RC and enclosures (DNA: RG 59, CD, Cap Haitien, vol. 4). RC 1 p. The enclosures, numbered by Lear and docketed by Brent, relate to the imprisonment in Saint-Domingue of John Rodgers and William Davidson. Enclosure no. 1 is a copy of Lear to Leclerc, 13 Apr. 1802 (2 pp.), in which Lear appealed to the French general's "justice and humanity" on behalf of the two Americans. Enclosure no. 2, a copy of Lear to Leclerc, 14 Apr. 1802 (3 pp.), is a more strongly worded complaint on the same subject. Enclosure no. 3 is a copy of Leclerc to Lear, 27 Germinal an X (17 Apr. 1802) (1 p.; in French), which officially informed Lear that Leclerc was unable to recognize him in the capacity of U.S. commercial agent in Saint-Domingue and replied to Lear's protests about the treatment of the two American captains (see n. 1).

1. JM had already seen at least part of this correspondence shortly after Lear's arrival in Washington on 5 May. On 7 May JM sent Livingston copies of Lear's 14 Apr. letter to Leclerc (enclosure no. 2) and Leclerc's reply (enclosure no. 3). JM also copied the paragraph in Leclerc's letter concerning Rodgers and Davidson and sent it to Pichon and Jefferson (see JM to Livingston, 7 May 1802, and n. 1; JM to Pichon, 6 May 1802, and n. 3; JM to Jefferson, 7 May 1802, and enclosure).

To Arthur St. Clair

SIR,   DEPARTMENT OF STATE June 23d. 1802.

The several charges against you as Governor of the North Western Territory with the vindication offered in your several communications ending 17th. June 1802. have been duly considered by the President. Altho' he is disposed to view with much indulgence the transactions of an officer, who has stood in so many honorable and interest[ing] relations to his country, he has judged it indispensible that his particular disapprobation should be expressed to you, of your conduct in granting to your son an illegal tenure of office; and in accepting yourself illegal fees, an abuse which he expects will be immediately rectified by proper notice to the agents collecting them. He has charged me also to make known to you, that in continuing, since the commencement of the Legislative power under the second grade of Government, to lay out Counties and fix their seats of justice by your sole authority, you have not pursued the construction put by the Executive on the Ordinance constituting the Territorial Government.

From the regret which the President has felt at an occasion for the animadversions now conveyed, you will be sensible how much you will contribute to his satisfaction by such a line of official conduct as may best obviate discontents among the people under your administration, foster their respect for the laws, and coincide with the benevolent policy of the federal Government towards their rights and interests. I have the honor to be &ca.

JAMES MADISON.

Letterbook copy (DNA: RG 59, DL, vol. 14).

From George Hay

DEAR SIR,   RICHMOND. June 23. 1802.

I have just now finished a letter of this date, addressed to you as the Secretary of State,[1] announcing my refusal of the office of commissioner of bankruptcy, on account of my professional pursuits. It will, probably, appear to you, somewhat singular, that I should assign as a reason for not accepting the office, the circumstance which had perhaps, most influence in producing the appointment. You will pardon me therefore, for troubling you, for a few minutes, with an explanation.

The truth is, that during the last eight years I have devoted, a great deal, of time and labor, to pursuits unconnected with my profession. The consequence is that I do not occupy the ground, on which as a professional man, I ought, *perhaps* to stand: that I have not reached the Station at the bar which, it is not impossible, if my attention had been uniformly directed to one object, I might have attained. This evil which is felt in more than one way, I am determined if possible to remove. For this purpose great and unremitted exertions are necessary. I cannot therefore engage in any business, which is not directly within the line and course of my profession, unless the profit were Sufficient to indemnify me for a total dereliction of my practice. Fortunately for the people of this State, the office of commissioner of bankruptcy holds out no such prospect here: and even if it did, my intire disapprobation of the System and of every System of bankrupt-laws, would make me unwilling to hold an office, the abolition of which my own opinion would teach me, annually to expect.

I do not know that I had a right, to trouble you with this detail; but I could not reconcile it to myself to transmit to you a letter containing nothing more than a formal and peremptory refusal of an office to which it was the pleasure of the Executive to call me, without some explanation. My motive, if ever the Subject of a moments thought, might have been Supposed to be different, from that, which I have Candidly stated it to be.

Mr. Munroe when he was making out a list of persons proper to be recommended as Commissioners, communicated with me on the subject two or three times, without the Slightest intimation however that my name was thought of by himself or any other person. Some little difficulty occurred in making out this list tho' the makers of it were on the spot: the difficulty in Washington will I presume be greater. I therefore take leave to mention George Tucker,[2] who tho not a very young man, has just commenced the practice of the law, and is every way unexceptionable. Mr. Munroe is well acquainted with him, but forgot him I presume, as I did merely because he was absent. I have said nothing on this subject to Mr. Tucker and therefore do not know that he would be willing to act: I have however no doubt that he would.

Mrs. Madison will accept *my* most respectful Compliments. I cannot offer her Mrs. Hay's. Her friendship and affections have been for Some days suspended by a raging fever & measles of the most malignant aspect. I am with very great respect Yr. mo. ob. St.

GEO. HAY[3]

RC (DNA: RG 59, LAR, 1801–9, filed under "Hay"). Docketed by Jefferson.

1. Letter not found.
2. George Tucker (1775–1861), lawyer, U.S. congressman (1819–25), and author of works on political economy and a two-volume biography of Thomas Jefferson, was professor of moral philosophy at the University of Virginia, 1825–45.
3. Jefferson appointed George Hay (1765–1830) U.S. attorney for the district of Virginia in 1803. His most significant case was the 1807 prosecution of Aaron Burr for treason. In 1808 Hay married James Monroe's daughter Eliza and became one of the future president's principal advisers. John Quincy Adams later appointed him U.S. district court judge for eastern Virginia.

From Rufus King

DR. SIR   LONDON June 23 1802
I yesterday recd. by the foreign mail the enclosed letter from Leghorn.[1] As I have no information relative to the extraordinary project of the Consul at Tunis, except what is contained in this Despatch, I can form no very precise notion of the Propriety of the means by wh. Peace is expected to be restored with Tripoli.

Whether the president has in any shape authorised the measures wh. are in view is more than I know; if not, it is to be hoped that some discreet man is the Commander of our naval force in the Mediterranean, as whatever shall be done or attempted will be ascribed to our Govt. Faithfully yr ob. Set

RUFUS KING

By the Enclosed letter from Leghorn you will perceive that this Despatch was sent open to Degen Purviance & Co.[2] who also put it in that state to me.

RC (DNA: RG 59, DD, Great Britain, vol. 10). Docketed by Brent as received 13 Sept.

1. Enclosure not found, but it was possibly William Eaton to JM, 18 Mar. 1802, which provided details of the former's plan to use the brother of the pasha of Tripoli to launch a coup d'etat in that regency. The possibility is enhanced by the fact that Eaton wrote King on the same day and enclosed the letter in his dispatch to JM. Copies of both letters were enclosed in Eaton to JM, 4 Apr. 1802.
2. The commercial firm of Degen, Purviance, & Co. was agent of the U.S. Navy in Leg-

horn, Italy (Robert Smith to James Barron, 31 Aug. 1802, Knox, *Naval Documents, Barbary Wars*, 2:260).

From Arthur St. Clair

SIR,   WASHINGTON 23d June 1802

I have been honored with your Letter of this day. It cannot be, Sir, that it should not pain me, that any part of my conduct in the Government of the western territory should have drawn forth the animadversions of the Presidt. In the affair of the Fees I believed myself acting agreeably to Law, and in that of my Son, I was very sensible at th⟨e tim⟩e, that the extraordinary tenure was nugatory, th⟨at I did n⟩ot intend, for the reasons I have assigned that it sho⟨uld⟩ [. . .] understood and this was, I own it a reprehensible fallacy. A stop shall be put to the fees immediatly. There are few instrume⟨nts so c⟩arefully drawn, that different people will not differ about their true construction. The construction of the Ordinance for the Government assumed by me, as it respects Counties, I thought right, and it has been acted upon with the single view of producing the general good of the Counties ⟨r⟩espectively without respect of persons—but, since the Executive has thought it wrong, I shall certainly correct the error in future.

I request you Sir to have the goodness to convey ⟨to⟩ the President the Sentiments of my high respect, and to ac⟨cept⟩ my thanks for the delicate manner in which you have been pleased ⟨to⟩ communicate the Animadversions, which to my extreme r⟨egret?⟩ he has had occasion to make.

Draft (O). Torn at edges.

To Martin Parry

SIR,   DEPARTMENT OF STATE June 24. 1802.

I have received your letter of the 12 Inst.[1] stating the case of your schooner the rising sun which with her cargo was condemned in New Providence for trading   [2] Teneriffe to New Orleans, and in behalf of which an appeal was instituted.

The opinion of Counsel inclosed in your letter concurs with other evidence in discourageing so much an expectation that the principle however wrong, on which the condemnation was founded, will be overuled by the Courts in Great Britain, that I am unwilling to recommend the expence of a further prosecution of the claim in that channel. It is to be apprehended also that the British Government will not easily yield to a call from ours to enterpose redress against a principle to which an attachment has been manifested. This is the course of proceeding however, next to be resorted to; and which requires that you should forward your case with the proper documents and explanations to Mr. King the Minister Plenipotentiary of the United States to Great Britain who will without question give every useful attention to the subject. I am respectfully &ca.

JAMES MADISON.

Letterbook copy (DNA: RG 59, DL, vol. 14).

1. Letter not found.
2. Left blank in letterbook.

To Louis-André Pichon

SIR,   DEPARTMENT OF STATE June 24th. 1802.

Captain Davidson, whose case with that of Captain Rodgers, was the subject of a late communication to you, has produced an order from the General then commanding at Cape Francois, by which it appears that besides the severities inflicted on him, he was peremptorily forbidden at any[1] to St. Domingo. He represents also that he has certain interests of much importance to him remaining in that Island which cannot be arranged & secured without his personal attentions.[2]

Without recurring to the transaction in a general view, or discussing any question incident to such a mode of excepting individuals from the benefit of a general regulation, I persuade myself, Sir, that in addition to public considerations, your benevolence will suggest the steps most likely to effect a recall of the order referred to, and a readmission to the footing of other american citizens one whose good character is so well known in his own country, tho' it has been so much misunderstood elsewhere.

The injurious delay which must attend the measures confidently expected from the justice of the French Government will sufficiently explain this second resort to your interposition. I am &ca

JAMES MADISON.

Letterbook copy (DNA: RG 59, DL, vol. 14).

1. JM's clerk evidently either omitted several words here or miscopied "entry."
2. Davidson was "interdicted from a personal intercourse with the Island of Hispaniola, and that under a severe penalty, no less than the pain of death," as he indicated in a memorial addressed to the president, 10 June 1802 (DNA: RG 76, France, International Commission on Claims, box 19). Davidson believed he was a scapegoat for American merchants who had

unwisely angered French officials by accusing them of bungling the invasion of Saint-Domingue. Leclerc had imprisoned him, Davidson wrote, because the commander-in-chief believed he had spread rumors of French incompetence in the U.S., "added to which the General by this time had received information that the head of my Ship was the Effigy of Toussaint and (as he told an American in a private conversation since) that he had been informed that the Ship belonged to that Chief and had brought Powder and Arms for his use."

§ To John Steele. *24 June 1802*. "Mr. Madison having perused the letter of Mr. Steele to the Secy. of the Treasury which he was so good as to communicate for that purpose, herewith returns it. Mr. M. gave the President an opportunity of perusing it also, as intimated by Mr. Steele."

RC (Nc-Ar: Steele Papers). 1 p. Printed in Wagstaff, *Papers of John Steele*, 1:283–84.

From Levi Lincoln

SIR   WASHING[TON] June 25th 1802

Since I forwarded you the papers respecting the schooner Peggy, Mr Pichon has furnished me with the opinion of the supreme Court,[1] on which, their decree was founded, and which, connects their decision with the treaty. Had I have seen this opinion before, I should [have] given my own, in defference to it, with less confidence, but still differing from it. Our convictions depend on the views, we have of a subject, and the force with which evidence & reasonings impress our minds. The Court give no opinion on the only questions which the record of the cause put in issue, between the parties. Was the Peggy armed? was she taken on the high seas? & was the decree of the circuit Court *definitive*, or final, in the sense of the treaty, were the questions argued at the Supreme Court. The negative of either of the two first, would in my opinion, have controuled the conclusion, which the court appear to have drawn from the negative of the last, and yet the court seem to infer, that the case was within the provisions of the treaty, merely, from considering the judgement which they reversed, as not being final. This could not be correct, but on the idea that the treaty was designed to embrace captures of all descriptions, & was not confined to those taken under the non intercourse laws. This construction would be injurious to sufferers who had been captured without probable cause, as it would deprive them of their claim of damages; and on the idea, of the circuits judgement's being final, of the benefit of a writ of Error, which might restore the property, on the reversal of a final judgment. [. . .][2] Going out of the meaning of the term definitive or final as fixed by its use in the law which gives a writ of error to reverse a final judgmt into the provisions of the treaty, and it appears to me to mean the same. The opinion of the Court

337

says, "the terms used in the treaty seem to apply to the actual condition of the property, and to direct a restoration of that which is still in controversy between the parties. On any other construction the word definitive would be rendered useless and inoperative. Vessels are seldom if ever condemned but by a final sentence. An interlocutory order for sale is not a condemnation. A stipulation then for the restoration of Vessels not yet condemned, would on this construction, comprehend as many cases as a stipulation for the restoration of such as are not yet definitively condemned. Every condemnation is final as to the Court which pronounces it—and no other difference is perceived between a condemnation, and a final condemnation, than that the one terminates definitively the controversy between the parties, and the other leaves that controversy still pending." It is necessary, to determine the exact force of this reasoning, to know the prize processes, and their incidents, in France as well as in this country. If in that country, there is any previous examination, which co. ¹emns, or exempts captured property, to, or from further trial it renders the distinction necessary. The opinion admits a judgment of an inferior court is final, if aquiesced in. But the foregoing construction excludes all proof of an acquiescence, if the right of bringing a writ of error militates with it, & proves it not to be final.

In cases w[h]ere there is no *limitation* for a writ of *error* there could be *no definitive* judgment. The present instance, is limited to five years on the judgt of the cir[c]uit court. But a writ of error, may be brought, on a writ of error, to correct an error, in the proceedings on the *first* writ of error—of course the judgment is not yet definitive, on legal principles, & on the above construction. If you look beyond that judgment, on which Exon. can, & does issue, & puts individuals into the possession of the property, which is adjudged to them, for a final judgment, it will be difficult to find it. To extend the treaty construction, beyound this, would be confounding all the distinctions which it seemed to make, in reference to *us*—and its *operation*, would restore the *whole* of the property, we had ever taken from France, however it might have been, before the making of the treaty, condemnied [*sic*], abandoned by its former owners, distributed, & spent. Surely our commissioners would not have stipulated to have given up *all* we had taken, & to have *received* but a *part*, of what had been taken from *us*, nor would our Government have *ratified one so unequal*, without the *attempt*, to amend it. This construction also confounds, & renders nugatory, the distinction made between national ships mentioned in the 3d., & the captured property, which is to be restored, by the 4th Article.³ The court I think are mistaken, in supposing there is no ground for a distinction on the construction which I contend for between a *condemnation* & a *final* condemnation. A libel decided upon in a district court, is liable to be carried to the circuit court, by an appeal, the judgt appealed from is final, in the first court, in reference to interlocutory Judgments—but not, as it respects the process—the same process goes to the circuit Court—no execution can issue—And the judgment which would have been final, had there have been no appeal, is as much suspended thereby, as if a new trial had been granted. Not so with a writ of error to the Supreme Court. There the judgt. is not suspended, & except in the case, of a bond's being given, within ten days, execution may issue, & the judgt be carried into complete effect. How far a bond, which would suspend the Exon., would bind together the judgt in the circuit Court, and the writ of error, which is, *quasi*, a new process, so as to make them a continued one, is not now necessary to consider, as it is not our case.

But however this general principle may be determined It can have little, or no effect on the case of the schooner Peggy. The Supreme Court who were competent to decide this principle, have determined it, in her case. It must therefore be considered as binding in this particular instance. Altho, they have fixed the principle, for themselves, & thereby bound others, in reference to the case on which they have adjudicated—It can, I conceive, extend no farther. In all other cases, in which the executive, or other courts, are obliged to act, they must decide for themselves, paying a great defference to the opinions of a court of so high an authority as the supreme one of the United States, but still greater to their own convictions, of the meaning of the laws & constitution of the United States, and their oaths, to support them.

It appears by a certificate of the Clerk, that no bond was given by the Plaintiffs in error, and indeed the distribution of the property, is proof of it, by the circuit court. I have been informed, that Mesrs. Bayard and Griswold appeared in the S Court, and argued the cause, for the Captors, If so, it [*illegible*] the want of notice to them. Government, I conceive, are now immediately, or in the event, that the owners cannot recover, from the captors the other moiety of the avails of the Schooner Peggy & her cargo, liable for it. In strictness, I beleive with the court, their judgment divest the property, and entitles the owners to recover from them, their distributed shares. How far under the circumstances of the case, it is reasonable, for Government, to make them compensation, you are much more capable of determining, than myself. Accept Sir assurance of the high esteem with which I am most respectfully your most obt Sevt

LEVI LINCOLN

Be pleased to let Mr Pichon have the copies of the courts opinion after you have done with them.

RC (DNA: RG 59, LOAG). Docketed by Brent.

1. Lincoln apparently enclosed with this letter the copy of the opinion of the Supreme Court in the case of the *U.S. v. Schooner Peggy* certified by Supreme Court clerk E. B. Caldwell

and marked by him "for Mr. Pichon" (ibid.). Caldwell appended to the six-page opinion a one-page note headed "Answer to the interrogatories of M Pichon Esqr.," in which he made two points: (1) there did not appear to be any bond filed in his office with the papers on the case of the *Peggy*; and (2) he received the writ of error—which was dated 2 Oct. 1800—with the record and other papers on 7 Feb. 1801. The opinion of the Supreme Court is printed in Johnson et al., *Papers of John Marshall*, 6:99–102.

2. Two or three words are missing here from the lower right corner of the page, which has been broken or trimmed.

3. Article 3 of the Convention of 1800 between France and the U.S. provided for the restoration of "Public Ships, which have been taken on one part, and the other." Article 4 dealt with the restoration of "property captured, and not yet definitively condemned, or which may be captured before the exchange of ratifications" (Miller, *Treaties*, 2:459).

From Benjamin Grayson Orr

DEAR SIR   GEO. TOWN 25th. June 1802.

I am greatly surprized at Mr. Merewether Jones's application to you about Plato.[1] I know not how true his accot. may be, but this I know most perfectly that one of the Gentlemen to whom he says the mortgage was given was present when the sale was made to me & when I recd. him. They both saw me very frequently about that time & the servant in my possession. Mr Skelton Jones has been often at my house within the last twelve months & Mr Mere: Jones was here whilst I was last in Kentucky. On all these occasions perfect silence has been observed & the letter you enclosed me today[2] is the first intimation I have ever recd. of a pretended right.

Ignorant of law I cannot decide what is to be done without enquiry. To yours & Mr. Walter Jones's Judgment the case shall be submitted on sunday or monday next & all that I can at present assure you, is, that no loss, (or if I can help it, inconvenience,) shall be sustained by you on the occasion. Yours Dr Sir very respectfy.

BENJ G. ORR

RC (DLC).

1. Plato was a slave leased by JM from Orr in July 1801 for a period of five years (*PJM-SS*, 1:482). See also Walter Jones to JM, 31 Oct. 1801 (*PJM-SS*, 2:213).
2. Letter not found.

§ From Sylvanus Bourne. *25 June 1802, Amsterdam.* Reports that his health is better and he is again performing his official duties. "But the Doctor strongly advises me to try to pass the seas to America before Winter with my family—as in his opinion being the best possible remedy to benefit the state of Mrs Bs mind & to give strength to my nerves. Should I resolve on this measure I shall claim & hope for the indulgence of Govt for a short absence." His consular duties will be attended to by H. H. Damen, "who had my Official powers when I last visited America." Will bring "the Gazettes you desired & full answers to your late question⟨s⟩ as to discriminating duties &c."

RC (DNA: RG 59, CD, Amsterdam, vol. 1). 3 pp.; docketed by Brent as received 16 Sept.

§ From Joseph Forman. *25 June 1802, Baltimore.* Encloses a return of American ships that arrived in the port of Rotterdam between 1 Jan. and 1 Aug. 1801. Return for the second half of 1801 will be forwarded as soon as it is sent by Lawson Alexander, who is acting as consul in his absence. Encloses also his account with the U.S. with vouchers [not found].[1] Requests that the amount due him be placed to his credit with the collector of Baltimore to enable him to close his accounts with the U.S. Will visit JM before he leaves for Holland "& take directions about some matters interesting to the Consulate & which I hope will meet with Legislative Assistance the next session of Congress."

RC and enclosure (DNA: RG 59, CD, Rotterdam, vol. 1). RC 2 pp. Surviving enclosure (one oversize page), headed, "Return of American Vessells arrived in the Port of Rotterdam since the 1st. day of Jany 1801 to the 1st. day of August same year," lists forty-three ships.

1. Joseph Forman reiterated his request for a settlement of his account in a letter to Brent of 18 Sept. 1802 (not found), to which Brent replied on 30 Sept. 1802 (DNA: RG 59, DL, vol. 14) that "a full reimbursement of the advances" made by U.S. consuls for the relief of seamen could not be made under the Treasury Department's interpretation of the current law. Brent went on to say that a new law would probably be proposed at the next session of Congress and in the meantime decisions on such claims had been postponed; "this it is that delays the settlement of your account, as it appears to be chiefly founded on advances to seamen."

Agreement with Nicholas Voss

Memorandum   June 26. 1802

J. Madison agrees with Mr. Voss to take his house at the rent of 500 drs. per year—on condition of Mr V's agreeing that J M may have it as long as J. Madison resides in the City of Washington, & may give up the House whenever he ceases to do so. It is further agreed that Mr Voss shall build a Brick Stable for four horses & a carriage before October next, in consideration of which J. M agrees to advance half a years rent in July & the other half on the first day of Ocr. or as soon thereafter as the Stable shall be finished—and as what remains to be done to the dwelling house shall also be finished

NICHOLAS VOSS
JAMES MADISON

Mr. Voss has been promised a half yearly advance of the rent and admits that he is to pay all taxes.

Ms (DLC). In JM's hand, signed by Voss and JM. Docketed by JM. For JM's previous arrangement with Voss, see William Thornton to JM, 15 Aug. 1801 (*PJM-SS*, 2:45, 46 n. 1).

§ From Patrick Mullony. *26 June 1802, Cadiz.* Forwards a packet just received from Barcelona. "I avail of the present opportunity to offer a few lines in my own behalf.... In the month of July 1797. Mr. Joseph Yznardi ... appointed me to act as Vice Consul at the Port of Algeciras under an allowance of Sixty dollars pr. month: to which I agreed. After two months had expired this small Stipend was suppressed. Notwithstanding, at the request of various Masters ⟨&⟩ Supercargos then at Algeciras, suing for property unjustly detained by French & Spanish Privateers, I continued in the Appointment ... under the most sanguine hopes of receiving Some Compensation from the Government of the United States." Refers JM to David Humphreys and his secretary of legation, Henry Preble, at Madrid for "any information you may require respecting my Conduct during my residence at Algeciras." States that he is "now destitute of means" and prays his zeal in service to U.S. will be rewarded. "The War in Europe having subsided, & my further attendence at Algeciras not being required, I have returned to this place with my family."

RC (DNA: RG 59, CD, Cadiz, vol. 1). 2 pp.; docketed by Brent.

§ From James Simpson. *26 June 1802, Gibraltar.* No. 43. Transmits a copy of his dispatch no. 42 [17 June 1802]. Is "extremely sorry" to report that he was "compelled by the Governour of Tangier to retire from thence on thursday Evening, in consequence of positive orders from His Imperial Majesty to that effect, received on the evening of the 22d, accompanied with advice of his having declared War against the United States."

As indicated in his letter of 17 June, Simpson had informed Commodore Morris of the state of affairs, and Morris arrived in the *Chesapeake* off Tangier Bay on 20 June. On 21 June "I was with him on board, when he acquainted me the reasons prevented his gratifying His Imperial Majestys wishes in regard to sending Wheat to Tripoly; which was extremely distressing, as I saw great cause to dread the consequences. At landing I had another interview with the Governour of Tangier, when I succeeded in obtaining his promise to suspend again the execution of His Majesty's Orders received on the 16th for my expulsion, untill he could represent to His Majesty, the impossibility he was then satisfied had always existed to my granting the required Passports." States that his chief aim was to gain time until the *Adams* arrived, hoping it would "bring such dispositions from Government, as would have enabled me to quiet the Emperours Irritation." On "Tuesday morning" [23 June] the governor sent a message to the emperor, but the same evening a soldier came with a second order for Simpson's immediate expulsion "*in a state of War.*"

"It appears the Emperour declared at his ... Public Audience on the 19th. that he was at War with the United States, and directed that the utmost expedition should be used, in fitting out his Cruizers." Finds it difficult to believe that the emperor would declare war over such a "trivial" object as sending "some Cargoes of Wheat, to be distributed in Charity to the poor at Tripoly" but admits that no demands had been made of him before this or any communications of an "unfriendly nature," except for the exchange with Pasha Hackmawy in December 1801 described in dispatch no. 35.[1] Thinks it best to wait for the *Adams* before writing to the emperor so that "I may not fall into the error of giving His Majesty room to hope for more, than I may be authorised by you to do." Will remain at Gibraltar until the arrival of the *Adams* and will be "extremely attentive to strive at obtaining the best information of what may happen in Barbary, respecting their sending out armed Boats, which is my chief fear; for it will be some time before either the Frigates at Rhabat, or half Galleys at Tetuan, can be ready for Sea." Encloses a copy of a circular he sent to consuls in all the main seaports of Europe advising of this "new danger" to American vessels.

Believes the property he left behind in Tangier will be safe, owing to "the very Friendly footing on which I was with the Governour." Has left his house and garden at Mount Washington in the care of the Spanish consul. "No agreement has been fixed for the House in Tangier, I was in Treaty for, which in the actual situation of Public affairs is fortunate."

RC and enclosure (DNA: RG 59, CD, Tangier, vol. 1). RC 4 pp.; marked "Triplicate." Printed in Knox, *Naval Documents, Barbary Wars*, 2:185–87. Enclosure (3 pp.) is a copy of Simpson's 25 June 1802 circular announcing Morocco's declaration of war against the U.S., with a list of cities to which Simpson sent copies (printed ibid., 2:183–84). Jefferson communicated an extract of the RC to Congress with his annual message on 15 Dec. 1802 (printed in *ASP, Foreign Relations*, 2:466).

1. Simpson to JM, 8 Jan. 1802 (*PJM-SS*, 2:378–80).

To John Rodgers

Sir,   Department of State June 28th. 1802.

I have received and laid before the President your narrative dated June 1802; of the outrages committed on you in St. Domingo, under the administration of that Island. The proper use will be made of the facts stated in this document, to support the remonstrances to the French Republic, and to urge the satisfaction due from it to the United States, and which ought equally to flow from its own sense of justice. In the mean time, I am authorized to assure you of the particular sensibility with which the President has received this detail of the injuries and indignities offered to you, and that he takes all the interest in your case which ought to be inspired by that of so respectable and deserving a citizen. I am &ca.

James Madison.

Letterbook copy (DNA: RG 59, DL, vol. 14).

From Benjamin Grayson Orr

Dear Sir!   Monday morng 28. June 1802.

The inclosed letter from Mr Walter Jones[1] is the result of my consultation with him on the subject of the negro Plato. I beg you to consult your own convenience entirely in your determination in this business—except a voluntary surrender of the property to the present Claimant, I am willing to do any thing that you will suggest. With great esteem I am Dr Sir Yr. mo Obedt Servt

Benj G. Orr.

RC (DLC).

1. Letter not found.

To Benjamin Grayson Orr

Dr. Sir   [28 June 1802]

I have just received yours of this morning inclosing Mr. Jones' opinion on the subject of Negro Plato. I am sorry on the negro's account as well as yours for the claim on him which has emerged. I admit also that having counted on his service for a particular purpose, during a given time, some inconveniency would result from a loss of that service. The course most agreeable to me would certainly be that of an amicable adjustment between you & the other party. If this cannot be done, my wish to avoid becoming a party to a legal controversy suggests the idea of my re-conveying the negro to you at the price given for him, and retaining him for the present on hire. In the event of your successful defence of your title, I can have full confidence in your reselling him to me on like terms.

In answer to Mr. W Jones letter I have written the inclosed,[1] which you will be so good as to seal after perusal, & send to the post office. I presume you will write also to Mr. Jones, without delay.

Draft (DLC).

1. Letter not found.

From Louis-André Pichon

MONSIEUR,   (le 28. Juin 1802.)

Parmi les affaires de prises demeurées pendantes Se trouve celle de la Diane, bâtiment de la République armé et commissionné à la Guadeloupe; Monsieur le Sécrétaire de la Trésorerie a différé de la regler, afin d'éclaireir la nature de quelques réclamations dont cette prise fait l'objet. Les Recherches ont fait connaitre que des Sujets Britanniques, habitans de l'isle de Nevis, ont présenté requête à la cour du district de Pensilvanie à l'effet d'obtenir la restitution du navire qui parait avoir appartenu primitivement aux réclamans: ceux ci appuyent leur demande.

1e. Sur ce que ce Bâtiment, originairement armé en course par eux avec commission de Sa Majesté Britannique, a été enlevé par partie de Son Equipage du port de Nevis, conduit à St. Eustache et de là à la Guadeloupe où il a été commissionné par les agens de la République Française.

2e. Sur ce que rien ne prouve que le bâtiment ait été condamné Judiciairement, Sous l'autorité de la france, avant d'être commissioné par elle.

La Diane a été condamnée par la cour de District le 2 9bre. 1800 (postérieurement au traité): c'est le 9. Xbre. Suivant que l'action Susditte a été intentée et, en ce moment, les demandeurs Sont occupés à recueillir les preuves nécéssaires au Soutien de leur requête.

Tel est l'éxposé que Mr. le Sécrétaire de la Trésorerie à bien voulu me transmettre et dans Sa lettre d'envoi il m'invite à intervenir dans ce procès de concert avec les Etats Unis qui Sont défendeurs, et à réclamer, devant la cour, le bâtiment comme devant être tendu à la République en vertu du traité: c'est Sur cet état de choses que Je prends la liberté, Monsieur, d'appeller vôtre attention.

L'action intentée devant la cour de district, par les propriétaires primitifs de la Diane, a pour but de prouver que ce bâtiment n'était pas *légalement* Français au moment de Sa capture et Si l'action était admise l'opinion de Mr. Le Sécrétaire de la Trésorerie semble être que les Etats Unis n'auraient rien à restituer à la France.

Vous verrez, Monsieur, au premier coup d'œil que Je ne pourrais intervenir dans un procès dont l'objet est de mettre en doute la propriété de la République Sur la Diane Sans admettre des principes que Je regarde comme dérogatoires au respect que Se doit tout Gouvernement. Je ne puis croire d'après cela que Mr. Le President des Etats Unis fasse dépendre de l'issue de ce procès la restitution à laquelle la République a droit.

Je n'entrerai point, Monsieur, dans le detail des raisonnemens qui viennent à l'appui de ces opinions. Il me Suffit de dire que l'action intentée devant la cour de district me parait être absolument étrangère à la République Française dont les droits Sont constatés par le traité, la commission du Bâtiment et la date de Sa condamnation. Si, comme Je m'en flatte, Monsieur, cette opinion est celle de Mr. le Président des Etats Unis Je vous prie de vouloir bien en obtenir les directions nécéssaires pour lever les obstacles qui S'opposent à la restitution de cette propriété. Agréez, Monsieur, l'assurance de mes Respects et de ma haute consideration.

L. A. PICHON

CONDENSED TRANSLATION

Among the prize cases still undecided is that of the *Diane*, a French public ship commissioned in Guadeloupe. The secretary of the treasury has declined to decide this case until certain claims, of which this prize is the object, are cleared up. Some British subjects from the island of Nevis have petitioned the district court of Pennsylvania for restitution of the vessel, which appears to have belonged to them originally. They support their claim with the following: (1) that the ship, originally commissioned as a privateer by the king of Great Britain, was taken by a part of its crew to St. Eustatius and then to Guadeloupe, where it was commissioned by agents of the French republic; and (2) that there is no proof that the ship was legally condemned, under French authority, before being commissioned by France. The *Diane* was condemned in U.S. district court on 2 Nov. 1800 (after the treaty); it was on 9 Dec. 1800 that the aforementioned action was brought. At this moment, the petitioners are occupied in collecting the necessary proofs in support of their petition.

States that this is the explanation given him by the secretary of the treasury, who invited him to intervene in this process in concert with the U.S., which is the defendant, to claim the ship for France by virtue of the treaty. The object of the action brought by the original owners of the *Diane* is to prove that the ship was not *legally* French at the moment of its capture. If this is the decision, then the opinion of the secretary of the treasury seems to be that the U.S. would have nothing to restore to France.

Explains that he cannot intervene in a process by which French ownership of the *Diane* is put in doubt without admitting to principles that he regards as derogatory to the respect owed all governments. He cannot believe that the president would make the restitution, to which France has a right, dependent on the outcome of this proceeding. Observes that he will not enter into the reasoning that supports this opinion but will only say that the action brought before the district court appears to be completely irrelevant to the French republic, whose rights are established by the treaty, the ship's commission, and the date of condemnation. If this opinion is that of the president, asks JM to obtain the necessary directions to restore this property to France.

RC (DNA: RG 59, NFL, France, vol. 1). Docketed by Wagner.

§ To Albert Gallatin. *28 June 1802, Department of State.* Requests that payment of $250 from the fund for Barbary negotiations be made to Thomas Thompson of Portsmouth, New Hampshire, "to enable him to pay the storage which has accrued upon a parcel of oars that he procured by the request of the late Secretary of State, and which are still on hand."[1]

RC (NHi: Gallatin Papers); letterbook copy (DNA: RG 59, DL, vol. 14). RC 1 p.; in Brent's hand, signed by JM. Reproduced in *Papers of Gallatin* (microfilm ed.), reel 7.

1. Thompson had requested payment in a letter to JM of 9 June 1802 (not found, but acknowledged in Daniel Brent to Thompson, 2 July 1802 [DNA: RG 59, DL, vol. 14]). Brent instructed Thompson to send his account and vouchers to the Treasury Department for settlement and to deliver the oars to the naval agent in Portsmouth.

§ To Ebenezer Stevens. *28 June 1802, Department of State.* "Your letter of the 22d Instant has been duly received.[1] The arrangement which you suggest for settling with Mr. Daniel Cotton, on account of the freight of his vessel, is quite satisfactory, and you will be pleased to take measures for carrying it into effect."

RC (NjP: Crane Collection); letterbook copy (DNA: RG 59, DL, vol. 14). RC 1 p.; in a clerk's hand, signed by JM.

1. Stevens's letter has not been found, but it was no doubt written in reply to a letter from Daniel Brent, 19 June 1802 (DNA: RG 59, DL, vol. 14), stating that Daniel Cotton of New York had asked JM to settle his "claim against Government, for the Charter of a vessel to Tunis" and requesting Stevens to provide "a short statement of the case, containing the material facts."

§ From Thomas Aborn. *28 June 1802, Providence.* Informs JM that he left Cayenne on 9 Apr. "On my arrival at that Port which was on the 5th. Feby 1802 I waited upon the Governor Victor Hugues and acquainted him of my appointment as Vice Commercial Agent of the United States. . . . The Governor observed to me that he was not authorised to receive an Agent from the United States, as he conceived the American Government had no Right by the late Treaty between France & the United States to send Consuls to the French Islands, he then requested of me a Copy of my Credentials in order to send to France and wait an answer from his Government. . . . On account of my ill state of health and the unpleasant situation I should have been placed [in] to have remained there unacknowledged by that Government I thought it most prudent to leave the Colony for the present." Encloses a copy of the law imposing duties on foreign vessels trading to Cayenne. Reports that American vessels are subject to "many impositions" under the present government; the people are dissatisfied, and they "expect when they shall receive from France the new laws for the Colony of Cayenne, the American Trade will be placed under the same regulations as it was previous to the Revolution."

RC and enclosure (DNA: RG 59, CD, Cayenne, vol. 1). RC 2 pp.; docketed by Brent as received 5 July. Enclosure (9 pp.; in French) is a copy of an *arrêté* issued by Hugues consisting of fourteen articles restricting foreign trade at Cayenne.

§ From John Gavino. *28 June 1802, Gibraltar.* No. 92. Informs JM that "the faltering hopes given us the 22d: Inst: by Consul Simpson & Communicated to you in mine of 24th. No: 91 [not found] respecting our affairs with Morrocco are Vanishd." Simpson arrived at Gibraltar 25 June, "fresh orders having reachd Tanger the 24th: Currt: for his quiting the Country immediately. He tells me the Empr: had mentiond in publick that his Cruisers were to be fitted out against the Americans." Refers JM to Commodore Morris and Simpson,[1] "who no doubt will inform you how he has disposed of the $1000 he called for Account publick Service, which I sent him the 23d: Inst: and drew on you for same the 24th." Sir James Saumarez in the *Caesar* arrived 25 June with "part of the Troops from Mahon, which was entirely evacuated the 17th: Ulto." The governor of Gibraltar, the duke of Kent, "is Encamping some of the Troops belonging to this Garrison." Lord Keith has gone home. Notes in a postscript that he has written circulars to all U.S. consuls "advising the Empr. of Morroccos final Determination regarding us."

RC (DNA: RG 59, CD, Gibraltar, vol. 2). 2 pp. Printed in Knox, *Naval Documents, Barbary Wars*, 2:189.

1. See Richard V. Morris to Robert Smith, 26 June 1802 (printed ibid., 2:185), and Simpson to JM, 26 June 1802.

§ From Anthony Haswell. *28 June 1802, Bennington.* Has published the laws of the last session of Congress, according to JM's order, as well as "a resolution relative to Capt. Sterritt" and the treaties between the U.S. and the Choctaw and the Chickasaw.

RC (DNA: RG 217, First Auditor's Accounts, no. 13,611). 2 pp. RC written below Haswell's account; Brent added a note dated 12 July, "The foregoing account is conformable with the direction of the Secretary of State." Brent wrote Haswell on 12 July 1802 (DNA: RG 59, DL, vol. 14) that after settlement of his account at the Treasury Department he would be paid $94.50. Brent wrote similar letters to Joseph Gales, 13 July 1802, and to Wilson & Blackwell, 24 July 1802 (ibid.), in response to letters to JM which have not been found.

§ From Louis-André Pichon. *28 June 1802, Georgetown.* Has received JM's letter on the subject of Captain Davidson and will transmit the contents to General Leclerc. Draws JM's attention to several cases about which he has received no response. The first is the affair of the corvette *Cassius*, a French property, long contested by the U.S., formally delivered to Adet, and abandoned by him long after the disagreement. Wishes restitution to be made to France, as stated in his note of 4 Jan. 1802.[1] The second case on which he asks for a response is that of Beaumarchais, as detailed in his letter of 14 Nov. 1801.[2] The third, the claim of Rayneval, was submitted in his letter of 3 Dec. 1801.[3]

RC (DNA: RG 59, NFL, France, vol. 1). 2 pp.; in French.

1. *PJM-SS*, 2:368 and n. 2.
2. *PJM-SS*, 2:241–43 and nn.
3. *PJM-SS*, 2:293 and n. 1.

§ From John Gavino. *29 June 1802, Gibraltar.* No. 93. "After referring you to mine No. 91 & 92 ⅋ this Conveyance, still detaind by Contrary Wind, have now to inform you that Yesterday Saml: Moor Commander of the English Brig Mary from Mahon, who parted Company on the 24th: Inst: to the Eastward of the Rock with the American Brig Rose whose Commander deliverd him the following note, Vizt: 'Captain Andrew Morris, Brig Franklin bound to Martineca, belonging to Summaril & Brown of Philadelpa: taken the 17t: June Inst: off Cape Palos in Compy: with the Rose—signd Willm: Whitehead.'

"Capn: Moor further told me . . . that the Capturing Vessel was a Galliott with three Latin Sails. . . . We have also accot: of a Galiott boarding a Swedish Schooner. . . . A Gibraltar armed Vessel being in Sight Cheased the Galiott, but she got off, after which took the Schooner into Port, from which Circumstances it is Supposed the Galiott is a Pirate."

RC (DNA: RG 59, CD, Gibraltar, vol. 2). 2 pp.

§ From William Kirkpatrick. *29 June 1802, Málaga.* Forwards a copy of his 10 May dispatch and encloses a return of U.S. shipping that arrived at Málaga between 1 Jan. and 29 June. Commodore Morris has sailed from Gibraltar to Tangier "on some Business of Consequence Which you must Already be acquainted with, I sincerely Wish He may . . . prevent a rupture With the Emperor of Morocco." Reports that "there has been for some time past, a coolness between this Government, and the Regency of Tunis, [and] I am informed some Spanish Frigates are now fitting out with an Intention to cruise on the Coast of Barbary, and be prepared to Act, in Case of the Worst." Encloses ship's register, Mediterranean pass, and sea letter of the brig *Two Friends,* John Magrath, master, which was stranded on the coast near Málaga in December 1801. Thinks proper to inform JM that the ship and cargo belong not to Magrath but to a Spanish merchant at Cadiz. Also encloses papers for ship *Astrea* of New York, which was disposed of by its owner. In a postscript, states that John Watkins, mate of the *Two Friends,* drowned while attempting to reach shore. "As it is supposed by his Relations at Bristol, [England,] that He was married in New york I give you this Information, that the proper Representative may come forward, and demand [his] Property."[1]

RC (DNA: RG 59, CD, Málaga, vol. 1). 3 pp. Enclosures not found.

1. On 15 Oct. 1802 Daniel Brent sent David Gelston an extract from Kirkpatrick's dispatch relating to Watkins and asked him "to give [it] such publicity . . . as the nature of the case may render proper and necessary" (DNA: RG 59, DL, vol. 14). Gelston replied on 18 Oct. that he had not placed a newspaper advertisement, having ascertained that Watkins had never married and had no relatives in the U.S. (copy enclosed in JM to Kirkpatrick, 21 Nov. 1802 [ibid.]).

To Roger Gerard van Polanen

SIR   DEPARTMENT OF STATE June 30th. 1802.

The ship Mary, belonging to Mr. Jeremiah Yellott of Baltimore,[1] whereof Isaac Phillips was master, was, with a very valuable cargo, captured on the 4th. of February. 1800. by a French privateer, & carried into Curracoa. As the ship was bound from Batavia, a Dutch port, to Baltimore, a neutral port, restitution was due, and was claimed from the Governor of Curracoa but without effect, under the articles of the proclamation of the intermediate Executive power of the Batavian republic dated august 12. 1798. In pursuance of instructions given to the American Minister at the Hague, he represented the case to the Batavian Government, & in September last received from the Minister of Foreign relations, an answer assuring him that a just attention should be paid to the subject as soon as a report of the proceedings at Curacoa which had been called for, should be transmitted.[2] By information lately recd. from that Island, by the parties interested, it is found that this report which was made by the Batavian Government, a preliminary to its discussion, had never been forwarded.

The object of this letter Sir, is to request that the claim in question may have the benefit of your favorable interposition in stimulating a transmission of the report by the Governor of Curracoa, as well as in promoting an early decision of your Government in behalf of the sufferers. Persuading myself that your regard for justice and for the cordial relations subsisting between the United States and the Batavian republic, will under[3] this interposition as ready, as I trust, it will be effectual, I have the honor to remain &ca.

JAMES MADISON.

Letterbook copy (DNA: RG 59, DL, vol. 14).

1. Jeremiah Yellott (d. 1805) emigrated in 1774 from Great Britain to Maryland, where he built a fortune as a privateer and trader during the Revolutionary War. He solidified his position as one of the foremost merchants in Baltimore in the postwar period and served as naval agent in that city during the Adams administration (John Bosley Yellott, Jr., "Jeremiah Yellott—Revolutionary War Privateersman and Baltimore Philanthropist," *Md. Historical Magazine*, 86 [1991]: 176–89).

2. The U.S. minister to the Netherlands, William Vans Murray, informed Secretary of State John Marshall on 1 Oct. 1800 that he had received instructions regarding the *Mary* and had passed the case on to the Batavian minister of marine (DNA: RG 59, DD, Netherlands, vol. 4). On 10 Nov. 1800, Murray wrote Marshall that he believed the Batavian government would restore to Yellott the money from the sale of the ship and cargo (ibid.).

3. JM's clerk no doubt should have written "render" here.

To Jeremiah Yellott

SIR   DEPARTMENT OF STATE June 30th. 1802.

Your letter of May 30th. with the documents to which it refers were duly received.[1]

The case of the ship Mary, I find, was committed to the patronage of Mr. Murray, the Minister of the U. States then resident at the Hague, by a letter from this Department of June 16. 1800.[2] A letter from Mr. Murray of Septr. 2. 1801.[3] shews that he had repeatedly pressed the claim on the Batavian Government, and that he had just received from the Minister of foreign relations an answer expressing the strongest disposition to do whatever right might require, as soon as the Government should receive from Curacoa a report which the Governor had been instructed to forward, of the proceedings which had then taken place your efforts therefore to stimulate the transmission of this report were well directed. Perhaps they may be repeated now with more effect, the change of circumstances having removed the obstacles or the pretexts heretofore existing, with a view to the same object, as well as to promote an early & favorable decision by the Batavian Government. I have stated the transaction to Mr. Van Polanen the Batavian Minister resident in the United States, and have requested his co-operation. I have &ca.

JAMES MADISON.

Letterbook copy (DNA: RG 59, DL, vol. 14).

1. Letter not found.
2. John Marshall to William Vans Murray, 16 June 1800 (DNA: RG 59, IM, vol. 5).
3. William Vans Murray to JM, 2 Sept. 1801 (*PJM-SS*, 2:80).

From Edward Thornton

SIR,   PHILADELPHIA 30th June 1802.

You were so good as to promise before my departure from Washington, that you would give me a definitive answer on the subject of the Transport Ship Windsor in time for the sailing of the July Packet. I propose to dispatch my final letters on the 7th of next month, and I am anxious to learn the decision of the President on this matter.

I have already had the honour of mentioning to you verbally, that the Ship has been transferred by sale more than once contrary to the express stipulations of the Treaty of 1794, and I cannot forbear to repeat my hope that the President will see in the original irregularity of the capture and in the illegal proceedings subsequent to it sufficient motives for making adequate compensation for the loss of the vessel to the original proprietors. I have the honour to be with perfect truth and respect, Sir, Your most obedient humble servant,

EDWD THORNTON

RC (DNA: RG 59, NFL, Great Britain, vol. 2).

§ From Isaac Cox Barnet. *30 June 1802, Bordeaux*. Addresses JM "on the subject of various claims mentioned in my former letters from 25th September 1800 to 24 December 1801,[1] to none of which I have yet received an answer." Requests JM's attention to the accompanying accounts and vouchers. "I have presumed upon the validity and justice of these claims, by drawing on the Department of State for my reimbursement in the following Bills of this date," amounting to $3,578.62; hopes that in consideration of the services he has rendered to his fellow citizens these bills will be honored. His hopes of obtaining an appointment and his "state of suspence from receiving no answer to my numerous letters" have prevented him from settling in business, and he has a large family to provide for. Will delay drawing for the balance of his account until he hears from JM. Refers to his letter of 25 Sept. 1800 on the subject of a salary or compensation and asks JM to support a petition he intends to submit to Congress next session for his services as agent for prisoners between November 1796 and April 1801; "certainly I have an equal claim with Mr. Skipwith to whom Congress has rendered that justice." Asks for a determination from the president on his request for an appointment to another post. "My Agent, Mr. Aubrée, still acts at Brest—his services since my departure, have been wanted in only one instance. . . . That agency therefore has produced nothing." Sends under separate cover eight memoirs of the council of commerce at Bordeaux on the subject of French trade. "I received them from the Council as a new mark of the good opinion of the authorities of Bordeaux."

RC (DNA: RG 59, CD, Bordeaux, vol. 1). 4 pp.; docketed by Brent as received 15 Sept. Enclosures not found.

1. For Barnet's letters to JM between 20 Mar. and 24 Dec. 1801, see *PJM-SS*, 1:32, 257–58, 312–13, 364, 2:18–19, 211, 317, 337.

§ From William C. C. Claiborne. *31* [sic] *June 1802, "Near Natchez."* Acknowledges JM's letter of 11 May enclosing the opinion of the attorney general. Observes that the Spanish governor was "extremely liberal in his donations, after the promulgation of the treaty between the United States, and Spain. And there is no doubt but many tracts of land in this District are claimed by antidated grants; and I believe the fraud may be proved without any difficulty." The compromise between the U.S. and Georgia is regarded "in this quarter" as "just and liberal"; if Georgia accepts it and the terms of the land sale are moderate "this Territory will, in a few years become strong in population." The Spanish are friendly neighbors; if the French were to take Louisiana, "I should regret the exchange. . . . I wish to God the U. States could possess themselves of East & West Florida, including the Island of

Orleans. The bounds of our Country would then be sufficiently extensive, and the chain of the American Union rendered too strong to be weakened for several centurys."

Letterbook copy (Ms-Ar: Claiborne Executive Journal). 2 pp. Printed in Rowland, *Claiborne Letter Books*, 1 : 139–40.

From Charles Pinckney

DEAR SIR   MADRID 1st July 1802

In my last, I inclosed you all the correspondence, I had then had, with Mr Cevallos the first Secretary of State here, on the several Subjects committed to me. At that time I had considered the Subject of our Claims for Spoliations as agree'd to be submitted to arbitration by Commissioners, upon those general principles which would include every description, and so supposing, I drafted the inclosed Convention,[1] agreeing to insert two, instead of one Commissioner, as the Spanish Government wished it—to which draft no objection being made, (except as to the place of their sitting): for the reasons given in my last, I consented that Madrid should be inserted—had two fair Copies of it made out and prepare'd for signing and transmitted them to the Secretary. To my surprise however instead of naming a time when I should call to sign the Convention, as I had requested—I received from him the inclosed Letter marked No 1 requesting an explanation of my meaning of the words "*y otros en sus Dominios*"[2] previously to the signing. Immediately upon the receipt of this Letter I furnished him with the explanation he desire'd (inclosed & marked No 2) and requested a conference with him.

He appointed the Wednesday following at the Palace in Aranjuez at which day I attended him, and entered fully into an explanation of the nature of our Claims as well for Spoliations made by the Subjects of Spain, as by the Subjects or Citizens of other powers, who had been permitted to arm & equip their Privateers in Spanish Ports and condemn & Sell the Vessels they had taken, under the authority of French Consulates exercising the powers of Courts of Admiralty—that this permission to arm & equip, & to condemn and sell had for the reasons I stated to him, rendered the Spanish Government responsible to our Citizens for all the Losses accruing thereby to innocent & legal Traders—that precisely the same thing had occurred at the commencement of the War between England & France, in some of the American Ports—that our Government as soon as they were informed of it, had interfered & prevented it, and agree'd to pay for such as had been previously taken and brought in & condemned, and that having done so themselves they had a right to expect it from oth-ers—particularly from a Government whose Justice & Honor they had al-ways held in the highest Respect.

He replied that it certainly was very honorable and generous in the American government to do this; but he did not conceive they were bound to do it by the Laws of Nations or agreeably to the dictates of Justice—that His Majesty had fully considered the Subject, and was ready to submit all the Captures, Detentions or other Acts committed by Spanish Subjects, to arbitration, but that he could not consent to do so, with respect to the Cap-tures by French Privateers—and that he was ready to sign a Convention with the exclusion of the words *y otros en sus Dominios.*

I answered, I was extremely sorry to find His Majesty had thus deter-mined, because our Government held a very different opinion on the Sub-ject of the Captures & condemnations by the French Privateers equipped in Spanish Ports, and where opposite & different opinions of such impor-tance were held by nations having equally a right to think & judge for themselves—I saw no amicable mode of determining the dispute, but by arbitration—that as my powers did not extend to the surrendering of our claims for the Captures made by the French, and he said His Majesty was determined not to include them, I wished to know if His Majesty would consent to a convention for the appointment of commissioners to arbitrate the Spanish Spoliations, and insert an article expressly reserving to the American Government the right to demand and negotiate hereafter on the Subject of the French Spoliations. He said he would mention it to His Maj-esty and send me his answer. Upon my return however to my House I thought it adviseable to make another attempt to procure the admission of such words as might enable the Commissioners to arbitrate all our claims, and I wrote him the Letter a copy of which is inclosed (No 3) and thus this affair stood at the end of the conference.

I then stated to him the anxiety of our Government to be informed of His Majestys determination on the subject of the Floridas—that I had in my Memorial to him[3] very fully gone into the reasons which made the United States wish the cession and Sale of these Provinces, and that I was sure His Majesty could see in the offer, nothing but the sincerest wishes on the part of our Government to remove all grounds of difference on these important Subjects either with the Spanish or French nations—that in this memorial I had mentioned to His Excellency our information respecting the cession of Louisiana and requested him to inform me officially of the nature of the Treaty as it respected the Limits of Louisiana, and that I was particularly anxious to know whether in the cession to the French His Maj-esty had stipulated for the undisturbed exercise, by the United States of their right to navigate the Mississipi, which His Majesty had by his Treaty confirmed to them, so far as he could, or Spain, or those to hold under her were interested, and also the right to deposit our Merchandize and Produce at New Orleans, or some other convenient place on its banks—that His Excellency must certainly suppose, we viewed these Rights as so vested that Spain could not properly cede Louisiana to another Power, without ceding it subject to the Exercise of these Rights by us—that if he would have the goodness, to examine the Treaty he would find the Articles so clear on these points of the right to navigate and deposit,[4] as not to admit a doubt—that at the time France received them, she received them subject to these limitations—that however the best and most certain way, was to have their free exercize recognized by France, and that we hoped His Majesty had done so, and that not having received any answer to this part of my Memorial, I would now be much obliged to His Excellency to inform me verbally whether in the cession of Louisiana to France any Notice had been taken of our right to Navigate the Mississipi and deposit our Merchandize and Produce on its banks, as had been stipulated by His Majesty in his Treaty with us—he replied *No*, that nothing had been said in the Treaty ceding Louisiana on that Subject, and added that with respect to the Sale of the Floridas & their limits, which was the other subject of my enquiry His Majesty had directed the Governor of the Florida's and the Persons concerned in the administration of that country to be written to, for all the Information necessary to enable him to form a correct and proper Opinion, on the Nature of our proposition to purchase them, and that as soon as they could receive Answers, he would inform me—that it was an affair of such great Importance, our Government, he was sure, could not expect an Answer in so short a time; but assured me repeatedly it was His Majestys wish upon all occasions to manifest the highest Esteem, and most sincere affection for the American Government whose true Interest he would always consider as inseparable from his own.

I shall continue my communications on the 6th by Mr Gibson & in the interim I remain With much respect & regard Dear Sir Yours Truly

CHARLES PINCKNEY

RC (DNA: RG 59, DD, Spain, vol. 6A, misfiled at end of 1803). In a clerk's hand, except for last paragraph and signature in Pinckney's hand. Enclosures not found, but see n. 1.

1. See Pinckney to JM, 20 Apr. 1802, n. 14.

2. "And others in his dominions."

3. For Pinckney to Cevallos, 24 Mar. 1802, see Pinckney to JM, 6 Apr. 1802, n. 3.

4. Article 4 of the 1795 Pinckney treaty guaranteed the free navigation of the Mississippi River to the subjects of the two countries. Article 22 permitted Americans to "deposit their merchandize and effects in the Port of New Orleans," or after a three-year period Spain would provide "on another part of the banks of the Mississipi an equivalent establishment" (Miller, *Treaties*, 2:321–22, 337).

From Stephen Pleasonton and Others

SIR   DEPARTMENT OF STATE July 1st. 1802

With great reluctance we take the liberty of appealing to your candor, in laying before you a Statement of our situation as clerks in this Department. The Congress not being able to discriminate between the merits of the inferior officers in the various Departments, & yet being fully impressed with the propriety of making provision more adequate to the support of the public servants, very wisely left the distribution to the Heads of the Departments. They have acted accordingly, & have generally increased the salaries of their agents. There were many years in this Department eight clerks. The duties no doubt increase in proportion to the increase of our Foreign & Domestic Relations. We are at present but four in number & the duties have required unremitting attention. Of this we shall never complain, but we submit to your candor & liberality whether an increase of duty, more than double, does not demand a consideration, & whether we may not be deemed, in strict justice to the Public, duly entitled to as liberal compensation as the Congress have authorized, & have left to your discretion.[1] We submit this with great deference, not doubting that while you are strictly conforming to your official duty, you will keep in view the justice due to faithful public servants. We are Sir with the highest consideration Your Obedt Servts.

STEPHEN PLEASONTON
WILLIAM CRAWFORD
CHRISTOPHER S. THOM

RC (DLC). Docketed by JM.

1. In May 1802 Congress appropriated $11,360 for the compensation of State Department personnel (*U.S. Statutes at Large*, 2:184).

From Charles Simms

SIR   ALEXANDRIA July 1st. 1802

I have been informd that Doctr Rose, has receivd assurances from the President, that if he would remove to this Town, he would appoint him Collector of the Customs.

I do not give full credit to the report, because, I am persuaded, that, the Secretary of the Treasury, and the other Officers of Government, to whom my accounts are renderd and my returns are made, will do me the Justice to say, that they are correctly and promptly renderd and made, and that the duties collected by me are punctually paid to the Treasurer of the United states. I have also the satisfaction of beleiving that no person who ever transacted business in my office, ever left it dissatisfied. And I have never yet beleived, that an officer who faithfully discharges the duties of his office would be removed from office, merely because he was denominated a Federalist.

I confess however that the report has given me some uneasiness.

To enable me to pay that attention to the duties of the Office of Collector, which was realy necessary, I have been obliged to relinquish a considerable portion of my practice at the bar, and a practice once lost is not easily regaind, especially at my time of life. My Family is large and would feel very sensibly the loss of my present office.

I hope you will pardon the liberty I have taken in addressing you on a subject which does not come properly before your department of office.

The apology I have to offer for this intrusion is, the long (tho not intimate) acquaintance I have had with you—and the knowledge I have of your friendly character and your love of Justice.[1] I am most respectfully Yr. Obedt. Servt.

CH: SIMMS

RC (DLC); draft (DLC, vol. 91). Draft undated. Minor variations between the RC and draft have not been noted.

1. In the draft, the last paragraph reads: "The only apology I have to offer for the intrusion is, the long (tho not intimate) acquaintance I have had with you—and the conviction on my mind that you are not one of those, who consider public offices in the united States as the property of men in power, to be disposed of by them to gratify either their partialities or prejudices."

To Charles Simms

SIR   WASHINGTON. July 2. 1802

In answer to your letter of yesterday, I am enabled to assure you that the report to which it alludes is entirely destitute of foundation. I am very respectfully Yr. obedt. servt.

JAMES MADISON

RC (RPJCB).

From Albert Gallatin

Sir,   Treasury Department July 2d. 1802.

In the case of the Snow "Windsor," the Collector of Boston was, in conformity to the Presidents instructions, directed in September last, to order her to depart.[1] She was at that time abandoned by her Crew, and a mere hull. A compliance was physically impossible. She was not repaired nor fitted for sea, untill after the preliminaries of Peace had been signed between Great Britain and France. No obligation of restoration or indemnifaction [sic] can attach to the Government of the United States on that account. It is true that she has been sold by the Captors, and was by last advices, in possession of Messrs. S. Higginson & Co. That sale being contrary to the Treaty with Great Britain, and that Treaty being the law of the land, the sale is considered by the executive Officers, and will be considered by the Courts as a nullity. Her present pretended owners will therefore receive neither clearance or any Kind of Papers from the Custom house Officers, in their own name. But that sale being only a nullity and no penalty being affixed by law to the nugatory attempt of selling, the United States have no claim or plea under which they can arrest or libel the vessel. It is the business of the original British Owners to libel the vessel before our courts, if, on account of the pretended sale, and consequent abandonment by the Captors, they are entitled to her under the Treaty. That Treaty is binding on the Federal and State Courts, and there is no doubt of their carrying it fully into effect. The attorney General is of opinion that the remedy is at common Law, before the State Courts; in as much, as Messrs. Higginson & Co. the present Possessors cannot plead against the British original owners, the title of the Captors, which is not vested in them.

It is proper to add that we cannot be answerable for the departure of the vessel without Papers or clearance. I have the honor to be with respect Sir, Your obdt. Servant

                                                    Albert Gallatin

RC (DNA: RG 59, ML). In a clerk's hand; signed by Gallatin.

1. For Gallatin's order to Benjamin Lincoln, dated 3 Sept. 1801, see The Struggle to Maintain Neutrality, 8 June 1801 (*PJM-SS*, 1:270–71). See also JM's letter to Gallatin, 29 Aug. 1801, requesting the departure of the *Windsor*, and Gallatin to JM, 23 Sept. 1801 (*PJM-SS*, 2:73 and n. 1, 129–30 and n. 1).

From Edwin Gray

SIR   JERUSALEM. 2d. July. 1802

I take the liberty to enclose to you at the request of the friends of
Mr Benjamin Wood, a certificate of his being a Citizen of the United states.

Mr Wood states by letters recently received from him that he is at this
time detained against his will onboard an English Ship of War, having been
impressed into that service some time past. Presuming that he can be
speedily released, thro' your Official aid; and understanding that an application to the British Government, can not with propriety be made but thro'
the Secretary of State, I have taken the liberty to trouble you on this occasion, requesting the enclosed letter may be permitted to accompany such
communication as you may think proper to send forward in behalf of the
unfortunate young man.[1] I have the honor to be sir, with sentiments of
great respect Yr. Obt Sert

EDWIN GRAY[2]

RC and enclosure (DNA: RG 59, Records of Impressed Seamen, 1794–1815, box 11). RC
docketed by Brent. For surviving enclosure, see n. 1.

1. Gray enclosed a letter from Mary Wood to her son Benjamin Wood, dated July 1802 at
Southampton County, Virginia (1 p.). In it, she acknowledged her son's letters of 12 Aug.
1801 and 15 Mar. 1802, informed him of his father's death, and assured him that a certificate
of citizenship obtained by Gray would accompany her letter, "so that I doubt not but you will
be set at liberty."

2. Edwin Gray (1743–1814?), a former burgess from Southampton County, Virginia, and
later member of the House of Delegates and state Senate, was elected to the U.S. House of
Representatives in 1799 as a Federalist. He served in the House until 1813, supporting, along
the way, James Monroe's challenge to JM's election to the presidency in 1808 (Fischer, *Revolution of American Conservatism*, pp. 373–74).

From James Monroe

DEAR SIR   RICHMOND July 2. 1802

It is understood that the functions of the marshall here ceased on the last
of June, by virtue of the late law repealing the former Judiciary law of the
UStates. By the former Law this State was divided in to two districts, an
Eastern and a western district, & Major Scott was appointed marshall of
the Eastern. By the 13. Sect: of the last Law that division is abolishd,[1] the
whole State is made but one district and otherwise designated in reference
to the general system of districts & circuits, so as to make his commn. totally inapplicable to the present state of things. His delicacy has prevented
his writing to you on the subject, for reasons wh. will readily occur to you.
But hearing the above, as that he had not written, I take the liberty to com-

municate it to you, that you may examine into the affair, and apply with the least possible delay the remedy wh. the case requires.[2] You will readily perceive the inconvenience attendant on such a state of affairs. All Judicial process is suspended &ca. The merits of Major Scott are too well known to require commendation from me. If he was not in the office he is precisely the man who ought to be called into it, or some office which is due to extry. merit, in a person who is still capable of performing the duties of any he wod. undertake. Sincerely I am yr. fnd.

JAS. MONROE

RC (DLC). Docketed by JM.

1. Section 13 of the "Act to amend the Judicial System of the United States," signed into law 29 Apr. 1802, provided for the removal of all marshals and district attorneys from "districts which were divided or within the limits of which new districts were erected" by the Judiciary Act of 1801 (*U.S. Statutes at Large*, 2:156, 164).

2. Jefferson made an interim appointment of Joseph Scott to be marshal of the district of Virginia on 8 July 1802; he submitted this appointment to the Senate on 11 Jan. 1803, and that body confirmed Scott a week later (Jefferson to Daniel Brent, 1 Aug. 1802 [DNA: RG 59, ML]; *Senate Exec. Proceedings*, 1:433, 437).

§ From Stephen Cathalan, Jr. *2 July 1802, Marseilles.* Encloses lists of American vessels that entered and cleared the port between 1 January and 30 June 1802 [not found]. Last vessels left under Swedish convoy. States that on 10 June 1799 he sent Timothy Pickering "an account of my disbursements for printing Consultations of Doctors on The yellow feaver &ca." but Pickering never acknowledged receipt of it. Encloses an account [not found] of disbursements he made on behalf of the U.S. "down to this day," amounting to 900 francs, and requests reimbursement. Reports that he sent the U.S. minister at Paris copies of his memorials to the first consul and minister of foreign relations relative to his commission as commercial agent and his exequatur; "this matter has not yet been settled but I Still Continue to be acknowledged in the full Exercise of my functions." Encloses an *arrêté* of the French government regarding the port of Marseilles,[1] "but it appears some amendments will be made to it, as the administrators of the Custom house are Claiming against it." Tonnage duties on foreign vessels have been increased by one-half.

RC and enclosure (DNA: RG 59, CD, Marseilles, vol. 1). RC 2 pp. For surviving enclosure, see n. 1.

1. The *arrêté*, dated 10 June 1802 (4 pp.; printed in French; docketed by Wagner as received in Cathalan's 2 July dispatch), required all ship captains to present manifests to the customs agents within twenty-four hours of arrival at the port of Marseilles. In addition, certain items were required to be off-loaded, weighed, and stored by French customs before being released for sale or reexport.

§ From Israel Whelen. *2 July 1802, Philadelphia.* "A draft in favour of Steven Kingston for $5,200 at 15 days sight, drawn by Ebenezer Stevens Esqr. of New York, was this day presented for acceptance, accompanied by a letter from Mr. Stevens enclosing sundry documents, and stating that in obedience to Instructions from you he had refered the dispute with Mr. Kingston to Arbitration, and in consequence of the Award had given the above draft. I enclose the documents, and if you are pleased to order the draft to be paid, request you will direct the amount to be remitted to me for that purpose."

RC (DNA: RG 59, ML); letterbook copy (DNA: RG 45, Purveyor's Office, Philadelphia). RC 1 p. Enclosures not found, but listed in the letterbook: "Consul at Tunis Rect. for the Cargo & certificate of 8 days demurage. / Do. at Algiers Certificate of the Ships detention at that place. / Do. Do. Letter to Capt Wood respecting the same. / Stephen Kingstons Accot. for Demurage. / Do. Bond & Receipt—with the Award of the Arbitrators."

§ From Frederick Jacob Wichelhausen. *2 July 1802, Bremen.* "My last respects waited on you the 6th. Janr. last.[1] . . . Inclosed I now do myself the honor, of transmitting you again the semi-annual List of american arrivals at this port, the number of which you will observe is very inconsiderable, the commercial adventures from the United States to this place having greatly decreased since the event of peace."

RC (DNA: RG 59, CD, Bremen, vol. 1). 1 p. Enclosure not found.

1. Wichelhausen probably referred to his dispatch of 25 Jan. 1802, in which he enclosed his report of American shipping for the second half of 1801 (*PJM-SS*, 2:421).

¶ From John Willard. Letter not found. *2 July 1802.* Mentioned in Daniel Brent to Willard, 21 July 1802 (DNA: RG 59, DL, vol. 14), as a request to be furnished with a set of the laws of the U.S. Brent replied that JM had directed him to point out that a congressional resolution of 3 Mar. 1797 required the marshal's predecessor to hand over any and all materials he had received from the State Department.

To Edward Thornton

SIR   DEPARTMENT OF STATE July 3d. 1802.

Your favor of June 30th. found me preparing to fulfill the promise of which it reminds me on the subject of the ship Windsor. The delay has proceeded from other demands which fell on the attention of the attorney General, and from the necessity of some additional enquiries within the Treasury Department.

It appears that before the order for the departure of this vessel could be carried into execution, certain repairs were absolutely necessary to fit her for sea; that before the repairs were compleated, the preliminaries of peace took place; that the vessel was sold, but being refused the necessary papers of clearance, was at the date of the last information still within the United States.

In this posture of the case, it is considered by the President that the Government of the United States is not obliged farther to interfere. In ordering the vessel to depart the most was done that could be expected; and the delay for repairs,[1] in consequence of which the chance of recapture was lost, having been necessary, the case is the same as if no such delay had taken place, and the peace had inte[r]posed immediately on the arrival of the vessel in our ports. Whatever question therefore may now remain seems to be a question between those who owned and those who seized the vessel, in deciding which the sale can be no obstacle, inasmuch, as being contrary to the Treaty of 1794. it is to be regarded a mere nullity. With sentiments of great respect &ca.

JAMES MADISON.

Letterbook copy (DNA: RG 59, DL, vol. 14).

1. In transmitting this letter to Lord Hawkesbury, Thornton commented, "It is for Your Lord⟨ship⟩ to judge, how far these pretended repairs will tend to relieve the United States from the cha⟨rge⟩ of neglecting to enforce the stipulations of the Treaty of Amity, and from the responsibility they incur to make a proper satisfaction to the original proprietors" (Thornton to Hawkesbury, 6 July 1802 [PRO: Foreign Office, ser. 5, 35:279]).

From Levi Lincoln

SIR   WASHINGTON July 3d 1802.

I have the honor to submit to your consideration my Ideas, generally, on the questions which arise, in the case of the Brig Los Amigos, without being able finally, to form an opinion, satisfactory to myself, on all of them.

It appears from the papers,[1] that this Brig was owned by a spanish subject, and in the prosecution of a voyage, from Jamaica to Cabello, was captured by Capt Maly of the public armed schooner Experiment, carried in to Cape Francois, and afterwards sent to America, for adjudication, In july 1800, she was libelled, in the District Court of Pennsylvania, as a vessel owned, hired & imployed, wholly, or in part, by some person resident in the United States, in a trade against the non intercourse laws. It appears, she had been purchased, not long before her capture, of an American citizen; and that the judge, finding no grounds for the capture & seisure, under the acts of Congress mentioned in the libel, and finding the alligations therein not supported, decreed, a restoration of the vessel & cargo, to the owner, with cost.

The owner, states that he has sustained great damages by the capture, but, made no claim of them, at the district Court, and he now claims them, from the U. S.[2]

The question is, if they a[re] bound, by the law of nations, to recompense the owner for these damages.

Vessels rightfully captured, under the non intercourse law, are to be distributed, one half, to the U. S, the other, to the captors. Public armed vessels are by law, directed & authorized, to seise every vessel, which there is reason to suspect is engaged, contrary to this law in commerce, and on examination, it appearing that she is so engaged to send her to the nearest convenient Port, of the U. S to be there prosecuted &c &c.

The libel, as it ought, appears, to be a prosecution in behalf of the United States, & the captors, in the shape of a qui tam,[3] in which, Govt., in case of failure, in ordinary cases, never pays cost, or damages.

To secure peace between nations not involved in an existing wa⟨r,⟩ and to guard against frauds in the collection of duties, & to enforce commer⟨cial⟩ regulations, it seems to be admitted, that a ship of war, or other authorized vessel, may bring to, an unarmed vessel, & examine her, and if she appears to be liable to capture & condemnation, to send her in. All nations, especially, commercial, have an interest in the admission of, & support of these principles, however individuals of their subjects may, in some instances, suffer by their operation.

The Ship experiment, was authorized by the Govt, to capture & send in for prosecution *such* vessels *only*, as, on examination, were engaged in a traffick, in violation of the non intercou[r]se law, It is the fault, or misfortune, of any vessel, to place herself under circumstances, to furnish reasonable presumptions of her being thus engaged when in fact, she is not. In such a case, the captured vessel ought to suffer the damages resulting from her own acts, or omissions, & not the captors, or their Govt. who have done, or caused to be done, only what they had a right to do. If there is a capture when there is not an apparent probable cause, the captor is the wrong doer. He captures at his peril; no blame can attach to the Nation. They have neither directed, nor authorized such a capture, as is made. The captor has violated this trust, reposed in him, by his Govt. as well, as the rights of individuals; and is liable for all the consequent loss, or damage, for which he may be assessed, by the decree on a libel, or, by an action at law.

In the present case, It does not appear there was probable cause, nor, clearly, that there was not, no claim in the district court, on the part of the owners, no damages, and it is certain, the Brig was not long before her capture, an American vessel, and had she in fact continued American & been covered, her papers would have probably been, as they were.

But the question still is, admitting the owner is entitled to Dam[a]ges, are the U. S. held to pay them—the captor having refused, or being unable.

I can find, neither principle, or precedent, which will support this position as a matter of rigid right. Nations may, in some instances, have practiced on this principle from national policy, when it, has been, demanded, by the Goverment of a suffering subject—or, in conformity to the practice, of some particular country. But never, I beleive, as a matter of national justice. The usages & customs of nations, seem to go no further, in ordinary cases of suffering neutrals, than to secure to them, fairly, the benefit of resorting to competent courts, and that remedy & redress of injuries, which can be obtained, in the ordinary course of justice. These usages, I conceive, no more recognize the principle, or obligation, to indemnify, a suffering subject of a foreign nation, against the insolvency of their own subjects, than they do, one individual of their own subjects, against the insolvency of another. If foreigners have the same measure of justice, and the same remidies, as citizens, ought they to complain? It, may be said, It is more reasonable, that a Government should suffer, from the misconduct of One of its subjects, than that the subjects of foreign Govert should. Perhaps, the idea, of the subjects of all Governments, which are subject, to a common principle, or to one code of national laws, forming one great society, will furnish an answer to the remark. It is beleived, when one nation, makes compensations, for *such* injuries as are done by its subjects to the subjects of another & which involve no insult to the nation; it is always done in pursuance of some treaty, or on mere principles of policy; and not, as demanded, by the law of nations.

This law, seems to be satisfied, by the punishment, or the giving up, for punishment, offenders against it; By a nation's not conniving at the injuries of its subjects; by taking every seasonable measure, & making reasonable provisions, to prevent them, or to redress them, in a regular course of judicial proceedings.

These, are my general impressions, on the subject, & as to the strict principles of the law of nations from the investigation I have been abble to make—I am sensible, yours are, in some respects different, I therefore express mine, with reluctance, & great diffidence. I had gone into a more lengthy disquisition, But was not satisfied with it, on reflection—I reviewd it, revised it, disapproved of it, and burnt it. I am Sir with the Greatest respect your most Obt. Sevt

LEVI LINCOLN

RC (DNA: RG 76, Spain, Treaty of 1819, Misc. Records, ca. 1801–24).

1. The papers referred to probably included the protest by William G. Latimer on behalf of Robert C. Latimer of Philadelphia, agent for Don Luis Garcia of Porto Cabello (present-day Colombia), dated 12 Sept. 1800 (ibid.). Garcia, owner and commander of the brig *Los Amigos*, protested against the action of Capt. William Maley of the U.S. armed schooner *Experiment* in capturing the brig and taking it first to Cap Français and then to Philadelphia. The brig had been ordered restored to its owner by U.S. district court judge Richard Peters in 1800, but the protest asked for payment of costs and damages. JM subsequently informed Latimer that the case should have been pursued in the judicial system and that the executive

was powerless to grant the requested relief (Knox, *Naval Documents, Quasi-War*, 5:219–20; JM to Robert C. Latimer, 11 Jan. 1803 [DNA: RG 59, DL, vol. 14]).

    2. Filed in the State Department records is Robert C. Latimer to William Jones, 2 Mar. 1802, enclosing a "Statement of Loss on the Brig Los Amigos" amounting to $4,400.13 (DNA: RG 59, ML).

    3. *Qui tam*: "an action brought on a penal statute by an informer, who sues for the penalty both on his own behalf and on that of the crown" (*OED*).

From Robert R. Livingston

No. 46

DEAR SIR   PARIS 3d July 1802

The letter from Genl Le Clerk which you will find in the Moniteur[1] having excited some emotition [*sic*] here I thought it proper to address the enclosed note to the Minister to which I recd the reply also enclosed.[2] As this was put in to my hands just as I was going into his house I replyed to it verbally. I took notice that the compt of Genl Le Clerc related to supplies furnished before his arrival that any interposition of the American government was rendered at that time impossible from the Congress not being in session but if otherwise that it would have been very extraordinary in them to volunteer in a business of that nature without any request on the part of the french government—that Toussant professed to hold his powers from them that he was acknowledged by them that any opposition on his part could not be forseen by the American government—that under these circumstances to have laid restrictions upon the commerce of their citizens would have been equally invidious to them & to France in case which there was every reason to suppose no opposition had been made—that the free commerce between the United States & the Islands had alone preserved them to France & that as no peace was definitively concluded a check on their supplies might have had in the Eyes of france herself an unfriendly appearance. He admitted the force of these observations & in some sort appologized for his note. We have been much injured here by a publication of Duanes relative to the conduct of the late administration with regard to St Domingo & a detailed account of all the causes of irritation we had given to France.[3] Foreign nations will not enter into distinctions between one administration & another they consider every act of government as the act of the whole people. Our affairs stand as they did when I wrote you last except that I have Tallerands most solemn assurances that they shall meet with the earliest consideration he added that I knew that in all governments money matters go slowly but that he hopes to have them satisfactorily settled & that my notes shall certainly go into the hands of Flerieu in a few days. He yesterday informed me that he was going to drink the waters &

would be absent tho not long this I suppose will put another stop to our business. I shall call upon Flerieu this morning & see whether he has yet got my papers if not I shall make a full statment of the business & apply directly to the first Consul if I find I am any longer put off tho I know such a step will not be well recd. by the minister. It will however be necessary for my justification & perhaps for yours that we take measures to convince our people that nothing has been neglected on the part of Government to obtain Justice for them.

Many of the St Domingo bills have arrived they give me the most positive assurances that they shall be paid. Mr Marbois called upon me a few days ago to inform me that he had remitted 1000000 frs. to Mr Pichon thro an english house to whom he was compelled to give the security of some bankers here as a counter security for the money—two pr Ct. for their credit & the usual commission in America which he complained of as a loosing bargain tho I think on the whole it is one that they shd. be satisfied with considering the state of their credit. In a conversation with Tallerand relative to Lousiania I could get not thing [*sic*] positive but I think I collected from him that at least West florida was not yet theirs. I have some projects on that presumption that I only wait to hear from Mr. Pinkney to determine whether it will be proper to bring forward.

I shall draw upon our banker for the price of two Swords ordered by Govr. Monroe on account of the State of Virginia & for which he says that he has loged 300$ in yr hands[4] I have not yet got the accounts but they will fall short of that amount. Enclosed is a memorial of an unfortunate gent. who has been in our service[5] He is now here with a family of Children such were his necessities that I have advanced him ten guin[e]as as the facts stated in his memoire are vouched to me by Genl Le fayette I have no doubt that Congress will at least give him pay for the time he was in our service. He was a man of great property & is now absolutly without a farthing. I have taken his note for the money advanced & shall draw for it if however the president thinks it can not be paid I shall be content to loose it, tho I should wish to have his permission to keep this family from starving till some thing was done with his memoire.

I have yet recd no answer as to the permission I solicited to make an excursion to England or elswhere not remote from this capital I shall only avail myself of it when I can be well spared & as it is not my intention to stay long in Europe I could wish to be indulged with this permission as early as possible.

Bonaparte has just concluded a treaty with the porte by which france gains some important commercial advantages & the free navigation of the black sea.[6] This will furnish them with naval stores of the best quality upon much more advantagious terms than they can be got for from the Baltic or America. Every thing succeeds in Bonapartes hands. The business of the indemnities which occasioned so much difficulty in Germany—Was settled by him here in a few days.[7] We are to have a great fete on the 14h when many look for changes in the government.[8] They will come but not so soon as I am assured that the first Consul has not yet sufficiently matured them. An abuse by which our commerce with the Batavian republic greatly suffers has just come to my knowledge but to which some immediate remedy should be applied, and I doubt not will be found if either myself or any other minister is empowered to take the necessary steps for that purpose. By our treaty with them our trade is put upon the footing of that of the most favoured nation. Yet we have constantly paid & still continue to pay nearly twice the duty that is paid upon the same articles brought from any other country. The Goods being entered at the west india company & at the admiralty. The pretence for this is that this company once held possessions in the now territory of the United States. This company is at present rather nominal than existant—they having no exclusive trade but becoming bankrupt were allowed the priviledge of collecting certain duties on goods coming into holland from places that had once been within their charters & on this shadow pretence they have collected a tax upon our commerce which has exceeded a million of dolls. & still continue this oppression. I enclose a list of the duties now collected compared with those paid when imported from any place in Europe.[9] I am surprized this matter has remained so long unnoticed[10] & if it is tho't that I can be of any use in negotiating this business either here or in Holland I shall with pleasure undertake it. It will not I believe be sufficient to leave a matter of this importance to be treated by the consul whose commerce renders him in some sort dependant for favors. Nor is it likely to be effected unless the United States should appear to attach such importance to it as to induce a belief that they will retaliate or take measures to do themselves justice in case it shd be denied. I am Dear Sir with the most perfect consideration Your Most Obt hum: Servt

RRL

Draft (NHi: Livingston Papers); letterbook copy and copies of first and second enclosures (NHi: Livingston Papers, vol. 1); third enclosure (DNA: RG 59, DD, France, vol. 8). RC not found but acknowledged in JM to Livingston, 15 Oct. 1802 (DNA: RG 59, IM, vol. 6). For first and second enclosures, see n. 2; for third enclosure, see n. 5.

1. General Leclerc's letter to Napoleon, dated 18 Floréal an X (9 May 1802) appeared in the Paris *Moniteur universel*, 24 Prairial an X (14 June 1802). Leclerc accused U.S. government agents of being in the service of Toussaint and insisted that his measures regulating U.S. commerce had been necessary because American merchants were supplying the rebel forces with guns, cannon, powder, shot, and other military supplies, as well as forcing the French army to pay ludicrously high prices for needed goods.

2. Livingston's letter to Talleyrand of 15 June 1802 (3 pp.) protested the publication of Leclerc's letter (see n. 1) as "calculated to make improper impressions on the public mind."

He argued that Talleyrand was fully aware of Tobias Lear's instructions to cooperate with French officials in Saint-Domingue because he himself had given Talleyrand Lear's original letter of 5 Mar., which the French minister still retained (see Livingston to JM, 10 May 1802 [first letter], and n. 3). Livingston also enclosed copies of JM's letters to Pichon and Villaret as evidence that "no agents authorized by the american government could be justified by their principal in giving improper advise to Toussaint" (see JM to Livingston, 26 Mar. 1802, and n. 6). Talleyrand replied on 9 Messidor an X (23 June 1802) (2 pp.; in French) that he had forwarded Livingston's complaint to the minister of marine. He noted in Leclerc's defense that no American commercial agents were authorized in Saint-Domingue, that the extreme measures used by the resisting blacks might explain in part the harsh actions taken by Leclerc, and that given the friendly relations between the U.S. and France, the U.S. government would have been better advised to forbid Americans all contact with the rebels.

3. The editors have been unable to identify this publication, but it may have been William Duane's *A History of the French Revolution . . . Containing a Free Examination of the Dispute, between the French and American Republics* (Philadelphia, 1798; Evans 48414).

4. On the swords ordered by James Monroe for John Jouett and William Campbell, see Monroe to JM, 17 Nov. 1801 (*PJM-SS*, 2:246–47 and n. 2); for delivery of and payment for them, see Livingston to Monroe, 3 July 1802, and Monroe to Livingston, 4 Nov. 1802 (NHi: Livingston Papers).

5. Livingston enclosed in this letter the marquis de Vienne's petition to the U.S. Congress (6 pp.; in French; docketed by Brent) asking for reimbursement of the cost of his Revolutionary War service in the Continental army of 1778 (1,900 guineas), a *gratification* of 75 guineas, and a pension of 70 guineas per year. Initially a volunteer aide-de-camp of Lafayette's, he received no salary while serving in the Monmouth campaign. Congress appointed him a colonel, and he later fought at Newport, Rhode Island. A bill for his relief was reported to the House of Representatives, 11 Dec. 1818 (*ASP, Claims*, p. 614).

6. The treaty between France and the Ottoman Empire was signed on 25 June 1802 (de Clercq, *Recueil des traités de la France*, 1:588–90).

7. The annexation by France of the German states on the left bank of the Rhine River had introduced the question of compensation into the complicated calculus of the relations between the larger states of the Holy Roman Empire. The indemnities problem would be used by Napoleon to reduce the number of polities in the empire and to reorder the balance of power among Prussia, Austria, Bavaria, and other German states (Deutsch, *Genesis of Napoleonic Imperialism*, pp. 38–55).

8. A review and presentation of the colors was held on 14 July, the national day of celebration. The political changes Livingston anticipated took place some weeks after, when Napoleon was elected first consul for life (Thompson, *Napoleon Bonaparte*, pp. 204, 205).

9. The list of duties has not been found, but according to Livingston's "Journal of correspondence with the Secretary of State" (NHi: Livingston Papers, vol. 7), he enclosed with this dispatch "an extract from Mr. Ridgeways letter from Holland respecting abuses on the American trade."

10. Sylvanus Bourne had already brought this matter to JM's attention (see Bourne to JM, 20 Jan. 1802, *PJM-SS*, 2:412).

§ From Peter Foster. *3 July 1802, Havana.* Refers JM to his application to government in December 1801 for "a short detail of my Sufferings; that then existed, & which at this remote period of almost eight Months, have not ceased to pursue me, with unrelenting Cruelty." Has been released from prison but his case is still pending and his "little Funds have at length become entirely exhausted, in the payment of Lawyers, & expences of collecting Testimony." Asks JM to inquire into the affair "as far as is consistent, with the existing connections, between the two Countries" and help him obtain a release from the charges against him. In a postscript states that he also wrote to JM on 26 June.[1]

RC (DNA: RG 59, ML). 3 pp. Cover postmarked at Savannah, Georgia, 23 July. Docketed by Brent as received 5 Aug.

1. Letter not found. Foster renewed his application for help in a letter to JM of 1 Apr. 1803 (not found), to which JM replied that he was in the process of making inquiries (JM to Foster, 8 Apr. 1803 [DNA: RG 59, DL, vol. 14]).

§ From James Simpson. *3 July 1802, Gibraltar*. No. 44. Transmits a triplicate of his no. 43. Informs JM that "yesterday I received a Letter from the Governour of Tangier dated 30th. June, advising that His Imperial Majesty (in answer to the Letter he wrote on the 22d) had directed I might be permitted to remain [in Morocco] six Months. . . . Had this order arrived in time to prevent my expulsion, all would have been well; as in the time mentioned a negotiation might have been carried on, and any differences accommodated." Believes however that after a declaration of war and expulsion of the U.S. consul "something beyond this Letter from a Governour will be highly necessary." No reason is given for the six-month limit, but it appears that the emperor expects "some certain thing should be done in that time." Thinks that "as the Emperour has been guilty of so flagrant a breach of the Peace, subsisted between the Countries, that he should write a Letter, or give some other Public testimony of his being in Peace & Friendship with the United States as heretofore, before I can consistently return to his Country in my public capacity." Wishes to consult with Morris on a "matter of such magnitude." Morris sailed "thursday to Cruize off the Straits & Coast of Barbary." Has sent the *Enterprize* in search of the *Chesapeake* with a letter requesting the commodore to return "as soon as he conveniently can; when this point will be deliberated on, and such measures pursued as shall appear most consistent with the dignity of the United States, always having due regard to the Commercial Interests." Believes there is "a very fair opening, for comeing to an Explanation with the Emperor, and for doing away those pretensions . . . of more frequent Presents being made him. . . . On this occasion it would be a happy circumstance if Commodore Morris could shew himself in force off the Emperours Ports, for as I have often since Summer 1795 had the honour of stateing in my dispatches, there is not any thing has such weight, as shewing the Moors that a Naval force is at Hand, to act against them in case of need."

Before he left Tangier, Simpson drew on Gavino for $1,000, "which he sent me, and drew Bills on you for that sum, which I entreat may be paid; and the Amot. charged as a supply towards the Contingent charges of the Morocco Consulate." Has also "claimed fulfillment of the 24th Article of the Treaty" on behalf of U.S. citizens who might be at Mogador; hopes they have been allowed to depart with their property. The emperor has ordered that "a Frigate which has layen some years neglected at Larach . . . shall be fitted out, but I think it is scarce possible she can be made fit for Sea."

RC (DNA: RG 59, CD, Tangier, vol. 1); Tr (DLC). RC 4 pp. Printed in Knox, *Naval Documents, Barbary Wars*, 2:190–91. Tr in Brent's hand, with his notation, "July 3d & 16th

1802 / Originals received Sepr. 1st."; docketed by JM (see Brent to JM, 3 Sept. 1802). Jefferson communicated an extract to Congress with his annual message on 15 Dec. 1802 (printed in *ASP, Foreign Relations,* 2:466).

§ From James Leander Cathcart. *4 July 1802, Leghorn.* No. 8. Enclosures A[1] and B,[2] along with his dispatch no. 7 which was forwarded by the *Liberty* on 3 June, relate all information of importance on U.S. affairs with Tripoli and Tunis. Tripolitan cruisers have been frequently at sea since the war began, and this at a time when the extent of American commerce "never was so valuable." Has seen twenty-four American ships "in this port at once last year—two thirds of whom were unarmed." Wishes something may be done "to prevent . . . our merchant ships from passing up the Mediterranean unarmed & without convoy." Suggests that this could be effected "by govt. declaring, that the seamen captured under certain predicaments would not be redeemed at the publick expence."

"The Bashaw of Tripoli seems disposed to enter into a treaty with us, but upon what terms he has not yet declared; Mr. Eaton informs me that a proposition of peace on the part of the Bashaw of Tripoli came thro' the Bey of Tunis, when it was proposed that the latter should be mediator & Guarantee; Mr. Eaton answd. that we prefer peace to war—when we can obtain it upon honorable terms, but not otherwise. . . . But I presume that the President will not find it conducive to our interests to admit any other mediators. . . . We would do well to confide in the strength of our own arms only, any other dependence . . . will ultimately prove fallacious & we shall undoubtedly become the dupe of our own credulity."

Believes the "National dignity" was wounded by the Swedish admiral's declaration that the U.S. could not negotiate with Tripoli without consulting Sweden, while at the same time he was trying to conclude a separate peace; "this Stratagem . . . was as mean as unjustifiable." Nissen has rendered the U.S. "as great Services as we had any right to expect from the Agent of a foreign Nation, but it is by no means ungenerous to beleive that . . . he would be happy if we would continue the war until Denmark concluded on terms of permanent Peace with Tripoli." Nissen fears that U.S. peace negotiations might "either serve to precipitate the war with Denmark or oblige them to Concessions." Notes that in these negotiations "the most intelligent Officer who has not a knowledge of the Language & manners & Customs of Barbary may be led astray by specious pretences," despite the best intentions. Requests "instructions founded on fix'd principles & couched in terms explicit & concise." Repeats his request for credit to furnish him with cash. Notes in a postscript his receipt of "the pamphlets alluded to in your last."

RC and enclosures (DNA: RG 59, CD, Tripoli, vol. 2). RC 4 pp.; marked "*Duplicate*"; in a clerk's hand; docketed by Brent. Extract transmitted by Jefferson to Congress on 15 Dec. 1802 and printed in *ASP, Foreign Relations,* 2:462.

1. Enclosure A is a private letter from Cathcart to JM, 4 July 1802 (2 pp.; docketed by Brent as received 6 Oct.), in which Cathcart wrote that the bey of Tunis "seems determined to exclude me" as Eaton's replacement and requested that "no delicacy on my acct. may influence the nomination." For Cathcart's wish to be named consul at Tunis, see his letter to JM, 5 Mar. 1802.

2. Enclosure B (5 pp.) is headed "Extracts of letters from Mr. Nissen to Mr. Cathcart dated at Tripoli May the 10th. & 22nd. 1802." In the first letter Nissen reported the Tripolitan declaration of war against Sweden on 5 May and included "confidential communications" on Danish policy not to pay Tripoli's "extravagant demands even if War should be the immediate consequence" and suggestions about the coming peace negotiations between the U.S. and Tripoli, one of which was the conviction that only Cathcart would be able to make peace "on terms that will insure to your nation the advantages which you have created" (printed in Knox, *Naval Documents, Barbary Wars*, 2:148–49). In his 22 May letter Nissen repeated his opinion that U.S. negotiations with the pasha should be postponed until Cathcart's arrival, described the circumstances of an "unfortunate accident" that resulted in the imprisonment of eleven Swedes, reported having seen one American and three Swedish frigates offshore, and related the pasha's threat that if the Swedes "burn his ships & the town . . . he will burn their prisoners."

§ From Robert W. Fox. *5 July 1802, Falmouth.* Reports the arrival of a great number of American ships with cargoes of wheat and flour, "part of which has been forwarded to London, Nantz, Barcelona &ca., but the greatest part for Havre de Grace, where a very large quantity of Grain and Flour is already arrived; and . . . the price has fallen." Trade in Great Britain is "very dull, and freights low and scarce." Hopes to send the returns for the district up to 30 June shortly.

RC (DNA: RG 59, CD, Falmouth, vol. 1). 2 pp.

§ From Rufus King. *5 July 1802, London.* No. 71. Reports that the loan recently obtained by the Dutch government at a rate of interest "hitherto unknown in that frugal and industrious Country" has "excited a good deal of curiosity." It is believed that part of the loan, in the amount of 15 million guilders, has been paid to France to secure release from the claims of the Prince of Orange, pursuant to the separate agreement signed at Amiens between the French and Dutch ambassadors. "The plan of indemnities about which the Princes of Germany have been so long amused, is supposed to be settled between France Russia and Prussia, and without the assistance of Austria.[1] We are told that the Prince of Orange is to receive his Indemnity in Germany, and that Austria will . . . acquiesce in a Settlement made under the influence of France, and sanctioned by her most powerful Neighbours." Commercial negotiations between Great Britain and France have made little progress; meanwhile France is aggressively pursuing its interest in ways not entirely congruent with its professions regarding European peace. Otto still awaits his successor. This will probably delay his arrival in the U.S. until spring.

RC (DNA: RG 59, DD, Great Britain, vol. 10); letterbook copy (NHi: Rufus King Papers, vol. 55). RC 2 pp.; in a clerk's hand, signed by King; docketed by Brent as received 23 Sept. Printed in King, *Life and Correspondence of Rufus King*, 4:144–45.

1. For the reorganization of the German states by Napoleon, see Robert R. Livingston to JM, 3 July 1802, and n. 7.

To Robert R. Livingston

Sir   Department of State July 6th. 1802.

I have been lately furnished by Capt. Rodgers and Davidson, with their respective narratives of the outrageous treatment which they suffered from the French Administration at St. Domingo. These documents are now forwarded to you,[1] and will enable you to press the subject on the French Government with the advantage to be derived from an accurate knowledge of its details. The insulting cruelties practised on these respectable Citizens, and the absurd pretexts for them alledged by the General in Chief, have produced irritations and disgusts in this Country which the French Government will not disregard, if it sincerely means, as we are willing to believe it does, to concur with the Government of the United States, in consolidating the friendship between the two Nations, by the exercise of reciprocal justice & respect. We trust that your claims of satisfaction in this case, will meet with the most candid and ready attention; and that besides the reparation of losses in property which as they relate to Davidson, are stated at 1196 Dollars, such animadversions will fall on the guilty as will heal as far as possible, the personal indignities offered to the American Citizens.

The affinity subsisting between General Le Clerc, and the Chief Consul, has probably emboldened the former to overleap the barriers which his duty opposed to his power, and may be now much relied on by him as an asylum against the consequences due to his excesses. This supposition is strengthened by the resentment he has expressed at the interposition & expostulations of Mr. Pichon, with whom he will no longer communicate, and whose letter he has transmitted with a complaint to the French Government. A copy of this letter is herewith sent to you.[2]

On another hand it would seem that he is anxious to exculpate himself in the eyes of his own Government; or to divert its attention from his own misconduct, to causes of resentment which he is imputing to the United States. With the first view an attempt was lately made at Cape Français to engage the Americans there to sign a paper certifying that General Le Clerc had in no instance given just ground of dissatisfaction. Not a name I am told could be obtained.

To the other view, Viz: of diverting resentment from himself may be ascribed, 1st. the loud complaints with which he is said to dwell on the freedom of the American presses, in reproaching French transactions, and particularly his own. 2d. his charge against this Country of supplying or attempting to supply the party of Toussaint with the implements of War. 3d. the suggestion of a covert acknowledgment of Toussaint's usurped authority, now observed in the form of the Commission given to the Commercial Agents of the United States, last sent to St. Domingo.

It will not be difficult to reply to these charges, if they should shew themselves in your communications with the French Government. The presses and even the parliamentary Debates in Great Britain, since the Definitive Treaty of peace use as unrestrained and as offensive a language as the Newspapers of the United States. It cannot be unknown that our presses are not under the regulation of the Government, which is itself, constantly experiencing more or less of their abuse; and that besides the ordinary excesses to which all free presses are liable from the passions or indiscretions of Citizens, those of the United States may for obvious reasons, be easily made the vehicle of insidious publications by persons among us who are not Citizens, and who would gladly kindle animosities between France and the United States. It is a fact, that some of the most offensive accounts which have been printed of the proceedings in St. Domingo, are now known to have been written from the spot, by British Subjects, not by American Citizens.

With respect to supplies of Military articles to the party of Toussaint, the answer is obvious and must be satisfactory. Without admitting the fact that any such articles were at any time so supplied, it may be observed that the French Government can have no desire to recur to past periods as criteria of present dispositions; and that it is the duty and the interest of both Countries not to remove the veil which the reconciliation so happily concluded, has thrown over preceding occurrences. The conduct of the American Administration since that event cannot be even suspected of the slightest irregularity or unfriendliness on this subject; nor, as is believed, has a single instance happened since the arrival of the french armament, and the regulations by General Le Clerc, adapted to the revolt which ensued, in which an American Citizen has engaged in Commerce of any sort, with Toussaint or his adherents. The precautions taken by the French Commanders were a sufficient bar to such an attempt; and had it been otherwise, it was explicitly declared to the French Minister here and to Admiral Villaret, as you will have seen by communications already made to you, that our offending Citizens would be considered by the President as fairly subjected to the penalties of their illegal conduct.[3]

As to the complaint against the form of the Commissions given to Mr. Lear and the other Agents in St. Domingo, of which a copy is herewith enclosed,[4] it is proper to observe that when Mr. Lear presented his to General Le Clerc, no objection or criticism was made. The first objection accompanied the order of departure given about the beginning of June to Mr. Caldwell the Commercial Agent at St. Domingo, by the Officer commanding the Spanish part of the Island.[5] From the language used on the occasion, which violated decorum not less than truth, and from other circumstances; it is inferred that the cavil was not made without the authority of General Le Clerc, and consequently that it will enter into the complaints which he may find it convenient to present to his Government against that of the UStates. On this subject observations of great force might be drawn from the very peculiar situation in which St. Domingo seemed to be left by the temporary and accommodating policy of the French Republic itself; which, finding it inconvenient to enforce its authority over the Island and to furnish it with subsistance from its own sources, was anxious, of course, that it might be fed from neutral sources, in other words from the UStates, and with every relaxation of ordinary forms necessary for so essential a purpose. But it is not necessary to resort to this consideration. The form of the Commission which refers generally to the authority over the Island, without naming the french Republic, is understood to have been copied from the usage of other Countries, and has been long, though not invariably, practised by the Government of the United States. More than a dozen instances might be specified; one of which is as far back as the year 1792, and several as the year 1794, and for places, such as Trieste, Hamburg, Bremen &c, where there could be no other inducement to such a form, than the presumed regularity of it. In truth, it has from the commencement of the present Administration, been a principle with the President, which has been as strictly observed, as it has been sincerely declared, to avoid, in the intercourse with St. Domingo, every measure and circumstance, which might controvert the authority of the French Republic, or give ground of umbrage to the French Government. On this principle is founded particularly every instruction given to the Commercial Agents sent to that Island. With sentiments of great respect and consideration, I have the honor to be, Sir, Your very Obt. Servant

JAMES MADISON

RC and enclosures (NHi: Livingston Papers); letterbook copy (DNA: RG 59, IM, vol. 6). The RC is a letterpress copy in a clerk's hand, signed by JM; filed with it are the last two pages of the original RC, docketed in an unidentified hand, "U letter No. 5 from Secretary of State / Red. 2d. Septr. 1802." The enclosures are letterpress copies (see nn. 1, 2, and 4).

1. See John Rodgers to JM, June 1802. JM also enclosed a copy of William Davidson's affidavit, certified by Edward Roche at Wilmington, Delaware, 2 June 1802 (19 pp.), describing experiences similar to Rodgers's as a prisoner in Saint-Domingue. Davidson visited Washington in June, when he apparently handed the document to JM. Appended to the affidavit is a statement of the losses sustained by Davidson, totaling $1,196 (1 p.; in Brent's hand).

2. JM enclosed a copy of Pichon's 7 May 1802 letter to Leclerc (4 pp.; in French); for the contents, see Pichon to JM, 19 June 1802, n. 2. Leclerc's reply, dated 6 June 1802, protested that Pichon had given credence to American complaints against the French army and that the tone of his letters to Leclerc was indecent. In a letter to Napoleon of the same date, Leclerc was less restrained, calling Pichon "un fripon" (a swindler), who profited from every transaction made for the benefit of the army, and "un misérable." In another letter of 6 June, Leclerc wrote the minister of marine requesting that Pichon be replaced (Roussier, *Lettres du Général LeClerc*, pp. 158–59, 164).

3. See JM to Livingston, 26 Mar. 1802, and n. 6.

4. JM enclosed a copy of Lear's commission of 26 Jan. 1802 (1 p.). He had already provided Livingston with a copy of Lear's interim commission, dated 11 May 1801 (see JM to Livingston, 28 Sept. 1801, *PJM-SS*, 2:146; for JM's concern over the wording of the interim commission, see JM to Lear, 1 June 1801, *PJM-SS*, 1:243).

5. See Caldwell to JM, 2 June 1802, and n. 3.

From Levi Lincoln

Sɪʀ   Wᴀsʜɪɴɢᴛᴏɴ July 6th 1802.

I have the honor to forward a letter recd by the last mail from the District attorney of Vermont respecting the strange affair referred to in the accompanying papers which you some time since enclosed to me.[1] I am Sir most respectfully yours

                                                        Lᴇᴠɪ Lɪɴᴄᴏʟɴ

RC and enclosure (DNA: RG 59, LOAG). RC docketed by Brent. For the enclosed letter from David Fay to Lincoln, 29 June 1802 (3 pp.; docketed by Brent), see n. 1. The "accompanying papers" have not been found.

1. Sometime in December 1801 Edward Thornton informed JM of the lieutenant governor of Lower Canada's disquiet over reports of "some ill-digested plots to disturb the tranquillity" of that province. In the course of the conversation, Thornton dropped the names of "person⟨s⟩ of some influence in the States bordering on Low⟨er⟩ Canada, who had been pointed out as engage⟨d⟩ in exciting disaffection and revolt in the province." Among these were William Hull and Ira Allen, both of whom had been involved in a previous attempt to subvert British authority in Canada (Thornton to Hawkesbury, 27 Dec. 1801 [PRO: Foreign Office, ser. 115, 9:173–75]; Chilton Williamson, *Vermont in Quandary, 1763–1825* [Montpelier, Vt., 1949], pp. 223–41). JM passed the information on to Levi Lincoln, who wrote the district attorney for Vermont, David Fay, and asked him to investigate the rumors. Fay concluded that no conspiracy existed, blaming some of the agitation on a confidence man named Rogers who "had devised a plan for swindling money from the ignorant and credulous in and near the vicinity of Montreal." As for Ira Allen, Fay wrote, he had been in a French prison "in the winter of 1800 when it is said this combination commenced," returning to America in early 1801 (Fay to Lincoln, 29 June 1802).

From Charles Pinckney

Dᴇᴀʀ Sɪʀ   Mᴀᴅʀɪᴅ July 6th 1802

In my last I acquainted you with the state of our negotiations respecting the Claims of our Citizens up to that time. I have now the Honor to inclose you Mr Cevallos Letter of the 26th Ulto marked No 1[1] in reply to mine of the same month. In consequence of this I drafted the Letter No 2[2] and

requested another conference with him on that Subject, and also on that of
Louisiana & Florida on which latter he had informed me he prefered to
reply verbally, to my repeated applications to know what were the Boundaries of Louisiana & the Florida's—and His Majestys intention with respect
to our rights of Navigation and Deposit—he appointed yesterday and I
attended him. I begun the conference by apologizing for troubling him, so
soon after his return to Madrid; but that as our affairs were important &
pressing, and I had the opportunity of a Gentleman returning to america—I wished very much to transmit to my Government the Ultimate determination of His Majesty on the Subject of our Claims. That as he had
agree'd so far as his own Subjects were concerned, to refer them to arbitration—I wished, if in my power, to endeavour to convince his Excellency,
that the Honor and Justice of Spain required, that our Claims for French
Spoliations should also be included—that in the latter part of his Letter,
he had agree'd to include the words "*de otros*"[3] which was all we wished;
but had clogged them with an explanation totally unusual and inadmissible—this was the insertion of the words "Segun los principios que constituyen la moralidad de las acciones y su responsibilidad"[4]—that I had no
objection to insert the words *Segun los principios que constituyen su responsibilidad*[5] but that those of "*la moralidad de las acciones*"[6] would lead to discussions & explanations, which would embarrass & probably defeat the whole
arbitration—that we all knew what the words the Laws of Nations & the
Stipulations of our Treaty and the principles which made Spain responsible
for the acts of others, meant; but that the Morality of actions was a field so
extensive, and the meaning so difficult to define when applied to these
cases—that I could wish His Excellency would leave the whole Business to
the Commissioners, to determine, upon the principles of Justice & Equity—the Laws of Nations, and the Stipulation of our Treaty—that it
would be easily in my power to convince him that upon these stipulations
& principles Spain was liable for those Captures by the French, which had
been made by Privateers equipped & manned in Spanish Ports & for those
American Vessels & Cargoes which had been brought in and sold in the
same. I then went into a train of reasoning to shew that "as strangers can
do nothing in a Country against a Sovereigns will"[7]—that therefore the
equipping & manning these Privateers, bringing in & selling the Prizes,
to the amount of more than one hundred Sail was not a thing to be done
in a moment, or concealed from the Eye or Knowledge of the Government—that being thus known, it was fair to conclude it was permitted and
countenanced, and that being so, if unlawful Spain was bound to compensate. That the arming and equipping vessels in the Ports of Spain to cruise
against the United States with which Spain was at peace, was certainly a
violation of the Territorial Sovereignty of Spain, and that if she had not

prevented it, when it was in her power to do so; but winked at it to the injury of the United States she is bound to repair. That by the Law of Nations it is not permitted to a Stranger, nor can any Foreign Power or Person levy Men within the Territory of an Independent Government, without its consent: that he who does it may be rightfully & severely punished—that as Spain had the right to refuse the permission to Arm Vessels & raise men to man them, within their Ports & Territories—they were bound by the Laws of Nations to exercise that right, and prohibit such armiments and enlistments and the condemnation and Sale of our Vessels—and that not having done so she was liable to compensate & make reparation.

I then stated the reasoning of Vattell[8] & Wolf[9] on this subject and those excellent ones of the President, when Secretary of State, in his Letters to Mr Genet[10] & Mr Morris.[11] I also informed him that I had written a Letter in answer to his of the 26th Ulto & had therin mentioned the only explanation, I thought myself authorized to enter into with respect to the French Spoliations—that I would read it to His Excellency & hoped he would still consent to sign the convention in the manner it was drawn and sent to him. After reading the Letter to him he replied he was sorry I considered the words "la moralidad de las acciones"[12] so inadmissible, that however certain he was that Spain was not bound by the Laws of Nations to make reparation in these cases—yet to shew she was willing to submit *the whole* of her Conduct to arbitration, he would consent to sign the Convention with the insertion of these words—that he did not suppose without them the whole Business would be properly before the Board—that when thus called upon to pay or to risque the being liable to pay large sums, by not one shilling of which, the Spanish Government had ever been benifited, Spain had the right to the insertion of such clauses, as would authorize the full investigation of her *then Stituation* [sic], Conduct, and Motives, as it would only be upon a thorough examination of the whole, that the Commissioners would be enabled to Judge, whether according to Justice, Equity, and the faith of Treaties or what he considered, ought to be as fairly before the Board as any of them, the principles which constitute the Morality of actions, or her responsibility, she ought to be really responsible for the acts of Foreigners in her Dominions, under the circumstances of these cases—that he had fully considered the Subject and could only sign that part of the Convention, with the insertion of these words. Finding him not to be brought to a change of his opinion I told him the claims were so important, and my Instructions, so clear & positive, that I did not conceive myself authorized to depart from the Proposition I had made or to insert words unusual & difficult to define, & which might tend to emba[rra]ss & defeat the arbitration. That I preferred closing with him on the ground of the Spanish Spoliations, inserting a clause, reserving to us a right to re-claim & demand for the French, in the same manner as if this Conven-tion had not have been made, and referring the whole Business as it now stands respecting the French Spoliations to my Government for their de-cision. That if they viewed it in the same light I did, they would probably direct some other mode to be proposed for adjusting these claims, or at any rate instruct me what was farther to be done. That for the present I would draft & send him another Convention, confine'd to the Spanish Spoliations, which is now doing, and will be transmitted to him as soon as finished.

My own Opinion is that Mr Cevallos has heard of the Senate's striking out that Article of the Convention with France, which respected our claims for Spoliations,[13] and that he thinks it hard, Spain should be obliged to pay for violations of her Territorial Sovereignty, which it might not have been prudent for her, or was not perhaps, then, in her power to prevent, and for claims arising from acts committed within her Dominions by the French, which if they had been committed in their own, would have been relin-quished—he never mentioned this to me, nor did I think it prudent to do so to him, because it was possible he might not be fully possessed of the facts, and being extraneous to our discussions I took care to avoid it.

The next point we discussed was the subject of my Letter requesting Official Information on the bounds of Louisiana & Florida, and the Rights of the United States to Navigate freely the Mississipi, and deposit their Produce & Merchandize on its Banks. I told him I would not enter into the Subject of our Right to Navigate the River, as on that, Spain & the United States had already agree'd, and the former had entered into Stipulations with us, on the Subject of the Deposit of our Produce & merchandize at New Orleans or some other convenient place on the banks of the Missis-sipi. That His Excellency was well aware how important it was to us to know what were the Boundaries of Louisiana as intended to be ceded to France—whether they included both banks of the River, & whether, as I had understood him on a former occasion, there being no Stipulations in the Treaty ceding Louisiana to France, respecting our right to Navigate & deposit our Merchandize on its Banks, His Majesty did not mean before the delivery of Louisiana, to instruct his Minister at Paris to apply to the French Government on that subject, and obtain from them a Stipulation that they received Louisiana subject to the Conditions & Stipulations of his Catholic Majesty's Treaty with the United States and the free & unmo-lested exercise of *their Rights* to Navigate & Deposit. That I wished such Instructions to be sent as soon as possible to the Chevalier D'Azzara at Paris, and that when sent, I would be much obliged by being favoured with a Copy of them, for the purpose of transmitting them to Mr Livingston urging him to join & aid Mr D'Azzara in the Negotiation. That I applied to His Majesty to direct this, because I apprehended we had some right to expect it from his Justice & Friendship—it being established by the Laws of Nations, that when once a nation has entered into engagements by Treaty, it is no longer at liberty to do in favour of others (contrary to the tenor of the Treaty) what it might otherwise have granted to them, agreeably to the Duties of Humanity or to the general Obligation of reciprocal commerce: being to do for others no more than what is in its power—having deprived itself of the Liberty of disposing of a thing—that thing is no longer in its power—that this was the case of Spain with respect to Louisiana & the Mississipi. That we considered the *confirmation* of our Rights under the Treaty with Spain *as irrevocably fixed* in the United States, and that she could only therefore cede Louisiana, subject to the same free & unmolested exercise of them by us when France held Louisiana that Spain had stipulated, had she continued to possess it. That I was sure His Excellency viewed it in the same light, and that if thro: accident or mistake the Stipulations respecting our Rights to navigate & Deposit had been forgotten or omitted, it was not yet too late to obtain it, and that I was sure His Majesty would instruct his Minister at Paris to use his influence in the manner I had with much deference proposed. Mr Cevallos replied that he hoped the United States would feel no uneasiness on this Subject—that he was charged by the King his Master (to use his own words) to assure me, and desire'd me to assure my Government that if the King did think proper to part with or cede Louisiana, it should never be done to the prejudice of the United States, and that the cession & Delivery would be made in a manner to secure to the United States the free & unmolested exercise of all the rights & privileges confirmed & secured to them by their Treaty with His Majesty.

He did not reply explicitly to my Question respecting the Boundaries—although I asked him repeatedly—which makes me suppose there is still some difficulty between them & France respecting the Limits of Louisiana.

On the Subject of the Sale of the Floridas or West Florida he made me the same answer he had done before—that as soon as they obtained the necessary information from their Governors and Officers in those Provinces his Majesty would reply to the Proposition.

I shall write again on the 8th & in the interim remain my dear sir With regard & much respect Yours Truly

CHARLES PINCKNEY

RC (DNA: RG 59, DD, Spain, vol. 6). In a clerk's hand, except for Pinckney's corrections and additions, last paragraph, and signature. Spanish phrases translated interlinearly by Jacob

Wagner. Docketed by Brent. Wagner noted on the verso of the last page, "No enclosures contained in this letter," but see nn. 1 and 2.

1. In his letter to Pinckney of 26 June 1802, marked no. 1 (ibid.; 2 pp.; in Spanish), Cevallos reiterated what he had said "in our conference of Wednesday"—"that the captures of American vessels made by French privateers in violation of Spanish territory did not impose on Spain any further obligation than to declare them of no effect . . . [and] that this proposition follows from the principle that no sovereign is responsible for the wrongs of the subjects or members of another." Cevallos signified his willingness to sign the convention with Pinckney only if the expression "or others" was amended to read "or others whose wrongs may be imputed to the Spanish government according to the principles which constitute the morality of actions and a responsibility on her part" (editors' translation).

2. In an undated letter to Cevallos, marked no. 2 (ibid., vol. 6A, misfiled at end of 1803; 2 pp.; docketed by Brent), Pinckney stated that since he was "confident it is not the wish of my Government that any claims which are not supported by the Treaty between the two Countries or the Laws of Nations, or the principles which constitute the Morality of Actions, or such as ought to make Spain responsible, should be allowed by the Commissioners—I am content to submit the whole Business to the fair & equal arbitration which has been proposed, & I thought agree'd to." He asked Cevallos to "sign the articles as transmitted."

3. Wagner here supplied an interlinear translation: "[of others]."

4. Wagner translated this phrase interlinearly: "[according to the principles, which constitute the morality of actions and a responsibility on her part]."

5. Wagner translated this phrase interlinearly: "[according to the principles which constitute a responsibility on her part]."

6. Wagner translated this phrase interlinearly: "[the morality of actions]."

7. In the long-standing controversy between Spain and the U.S. on American claims, JM himself would make this point several times, as he did in his letter to Pinckney of 6 Feb. 1804: "If his Catholic Majesty be sovereign in his own dominions, aliens within them are answerable to him for their conduct, and he, of course, is answerable for it to others. This is a principle founded too evidently in reason and usage to be controverted" (*ASP, Foreign Relations,* 2 : 615).

8. "They who undertake to enlist soldiers in a foreign country, without the sovereign's permission; and, in general, whoever alienates the subjects of another, violates one of the most sacred rights both of the prince and the state . . . and accordingly is punished with the utmost severity in every policied state" (Vattel, *The Law of Nations* [1820 ed.], p. 366).

9. "No one is allowed to enrol soldiers in a foreign territory without the consent of the ruler." Should a "foreigner" dare to do it, "he can be arrested and punished" (Christian Wolff, *Jus Gentium Methodo Scientifica Pertractatum,* trans. Joseph H. Drake [2 vols.; London, 1934], 2 : 387, 388).

10. On 5 June 1793, Jefferson, then secretary of state, wrote Edmond Genet, the French minister to the U.S., that the outfitting of French privateers in American ports and the commissioning of Americans into the service of France would not be tolerated by the U.S. government. "It is the *right* of every nation to prohibit acts of sovereignty from being exercised by any other within its limits," he wrote. "The granting military commissions, within the United States, by any other authority than their own, is an infringement on their sovereignty" (*ASP, Foreign Relations,* 1 : 150).

11. Jefferson, in his letter to Gouverneur Morris of 16 Aug. 1793, refuted, among other points, Genet's assertion of France's right "of arming in our ports, and of enlisting our citizens" in the war against Great Britain (ibid., 1 : 168).

12. Wagner translated this phrase interlinearly: "[the morality of actions]."

13. As a condition of ratification, the Senate had expunged article 2 of the Convention of 1800 between the U.S. and France and replaced it with one limiting the agreement to eight

years. Article 2 had provided for further negotiations on the subject of previous treaties between the two countries and American merchant claims against France. The French government agreed to the change "*Provided*, that by this retrenchment the two states renounce the respective pretentions which are the object of the said article," that is, that the U.S. renounce its commercial claims against France (Miller, *Treaties*, 2:458–59, 480, 481–82).

§ From John M. Forbes. *6 July 1802, London.* "I have this moment learned that the French Government have refused an Exequatur to Mr. Cathalan who was appointed American Consul for the Port of Marseilles. You may, perhaps, recollect the apprehensions I have frequently expressed of the effects of the Climate of Hamburg on my health. . . . It will be particularly gratifying to me . . . to be appointed to the Agency at Marseilles, where, from a familiar Knowledge of the language, I flatter myself I Could be at least as useful to the Commerce of our Country as at Hamburg—to which Post I shall repair and attend the disposition of Government. Marseilles, it is said, is to be a free port, and will probably be the Emporium of the Mediterranean Commerce."

RC (DNA: RG 59, CD, Hamburg, vol. 1); copy (DNA: RG 59, LAR, 1801–9, filed under "Forbes"). RC 1 p.; docketed by Brent as received 3 Oct. Copy varies in wording; docketed by Jefferson.

From William Eaton

Sir,   Tunis 7. July 1802.

Though the inclosure[1] of this date needs no comment I cannot forbear remarking that it exhibits a melancholly proof of the truth of my apprehensions and of the necessity of more energy.

I should be more in detail; but this goes off immediately viâ Leghorn, and I have not yet possessed myself of whole facts. The *slaves* will be marched to this city tomorrow, and probably hence by land to Tripoli. I have the honor to be most respectfully Sir, your very obed. Servt.

WILLIAM EATON

P. S. July 10. By my circular of yesterday[2] it is shewn that the Brig is of Philadelphia. The corsaire took in provisions at Bizerte, and departed 8th. inst. on another cruise. This Bey has objected to the *American slaves* marching through his country—says he does not wish to get himself into an embroil. They will be carried along the coast in a row-boat. I am not permitted by the Captors to have any communication with the captives—consequently do not know what treatment they suffer.

W. EATON

RC and enclosures (DNA: RG 59, CD, Tunis, vol. 2, pt. 1); letterbook copy (CSmH). RC marked "Duplicate."

1. In the letterbook copy, Eaton wrote "inclosures" followed by an asterisk and added in the left-hand margin, "*Letter from my vice Consul at Bizerte—and my circular." The translated copy, enclosed with the RC, of a letter to Eaton from Guiseppe Manucie at Bizerte, 7 July 1802, reported that "last night entered this port a Tripoline Xebec, having with him an American Brig and nine men which he captured off Cape Pallos" (1 p.; printed in Knox, *Naval Documents, Barbary Wars*, 2 : 194). For Eaton's 7 July circular letter announcing the capture of the U.S. brig *Franklin*, see Cathcart to JM, 6 Aug. 1802, and n. 2.

2. Filed with the RC is a copy of Eaton's circular letter dated 9 July 1802 (1 p.), containing the same information as in his 7 July circular and adding that the captured brig came from Philadelphia.

From William Henry Harrison

SIR   July 7th 1802

The mail which will carry this letter is the first from this place—since the month of March last—Or I should before have done myself the honour to write to you—altho I had nothing material to communicate. This barrenness of events still continues, with the exception of such as come under my notice as Superintendant of Indian affairs & these as has been the custom will be detailed to the Secretary of War.

The Secretary of this Territory will transmit you a Copy of our procee[d]ings from the commenc[e]ment of the Government to the 4th Instant, & a Copy of the Laws adopted by the Governor and Judges during the last Winter.[1] The expence of print[ing] laws adopted in the Territory has usually been borne by the United States, & I believe that part of the Contingent money voted annually by Congress is intended for this purpose. If I am correct will you pleas[e] to inform me, Sir, whether it will be done under your direction at the seat of Government, or will you authorise me to employ some one of the printers in Kentucky to do this and other trifling articles in the Printing line—Such as land Patents, Civil and Military Commissions &c. The Citizens of the Territory suffer great inconveniance for the want of Printed Laws[2]—& I shall shortly be ready to issue Patents for such of the land claims as have not been decided on by the former Governor. My proceeding on this subject shall be transmitted to you as it is brought to a close—which I hope to be able to effect in the course of one year from the present time. My labour in this business would be much lightened and the chance of making blunders rendered much less; If I could procure from Governor St. Clair certain Records in his possession, which exclusively relate to the land business in this Country. I have enclosed an extract of his answer to my application for these papers—in which he declares he does not think himself authorised to deliver them, without an order for that purpose from the President.[3] I am with respect &c.

Tr (In: Lasselle Family Papers). Enclosure not found.

1. No letter from John Gibson to JM enclosing these documents has been found.

2. The laws adopted at the January 1802 session were not printed until 1804 (*Laws Adopted by the Governor and Judges of the Indiana Territory, at Their Second and Third Sessions* [Vincennes, Indiana Territory, 1804; Shaw and Shoemaker 6536]).

3. JM had written Arthur St. Clair on 6 Nov. 1801, instructing the governor to hand over the land records to Harrison "immediately" (*PJM-SS*, 2:226–27).

§ To Israel Whelen. *7 July 1802, Department of State.* Acknowledges Whelen's letter of 2 July. Has directed that a remittance of $5,200 be made to him "to answer the Bill which you give notice of Mr. Stevens's having upon me for this sum, payable to Mr. Kingston, being the amount of the late award in his favor, in the case of the Peace and Plenty."

Letterbook copy (DNA: RG 59, DL, vol. 14). 1 p.

§ From Richard O'Brien. *7 July 1802, Algiers.* Reports a message from the dey telling him "to write and directly Bring to Algiers The large Ship, *The Washington*, that he the dey would send her to Constantinople to bring to Algiers A Quantity of masts and other articles."[1] "*Force* only Can Errace those *ideas* from the Brain of the dey." Suggests the U.S. be ready for war "if the dey does not renounce his *Don Quixotte* Ideas." For eighteen months the dey has been ordering the Danes "to Bring Vessels to go for those Masts &c. They have Bribed of[f] his ideas." In a postscript, recounts events following the capture and arrival at Algiers of the Philadelphia brig *Franklin*. "I Claimed the Vessel Cargo & Crew of this govt. as the Gaurentee of our treaty with Tripoli but to no Effect. I requested the interferance of the regency to ransom the Brig Cargo and Crew but Could not prevail on this Govt. to do me that favour. . . . As yet I have a distant hope." Reports terms of Spanish agreement with Algiers, listing five conditions. In a 22 June audience with the British consul, the dey threatened that if payment of an old claim of $187,000 was not made in five months "he the Potent Dey would make war with the British. His Efforts would be like unto a wasp disturbing the repose of a lion." On 30 June the dey demanded of Bonaparte's agent Thainville repayment of a $200,000 loan and a $300,000 tribute promised two years earlier; "the dey has given the french Agent 40 days to Comply with These *demands*—& if not *War War War*."[2] States that in the evening of 7 July the dey withdrew his demand for the ship *George Washington*, informing O'Brien he would "demand the favour of the Consul of a nation More adjacent." In a postscript of 13 July observes that Algiers and Tunis are on the verge of war; "this is good news."

RC (DNA: RG 59, CD, Algiers, vol. 6). 3 pp.; docketed by Brent. O'Brien may have enclosed with this dispatch a three-page document (ibid.) dated 10 July 1802; the first page is headed "Statement of Particulars relative to The Regency of Algiers in July 1802," the second page, "Statement of exactions and Captures demands &c. of Algiers in April May & June 1802," and the third page, "Statement of Spoilations on the underwritten nations by Algiers in 4 years &c."; addressed to "The Honourable James Madison Secretary of State of The UStates & for The information of Commodore Morris & US Navy"; printed in Knox, *Naval*

Documents, Barbary Wars, 2 : 198–200. Two other copies of the document (DNA: RG 59, CD, Algiers, vol. 6) are addressed "for The information of The Govt. of The united States of America"; the first is docketed by Wagner as received 23 Nov., and the second, also docketed by Wagner, bears Eaton's notation that copies were forwarded to the U.S. minister at Madrid on 19 July and to the U.S. minister at Paris on 25 July.

1. In 1800 the dey of Algiers had commandeered the U.S. ship *George Washington* for his own use over the protests of its captain and the U.S. consul. JM's instructions to O'Brien in 1801 explicitly forbade a repetition of such an act of hostility against the U.S. (*PJM-SS*, 1 : 82 n. 4, 214, 425).

2. Another copy of the RC (DNA: RG 59, CD, Algiers, vol. 6), which varies considerably in wording, concludes here with a description of the dey's harsh treatment of Portuguese officers.

¶ From Thomas Stockton. Letter not found. *7 July 1802*. Mentioned in Daniel Brent to Stockton, 14 July 1802 (DNA: RG 59, DL, vol. 14), as a request for JM to pay money due Stockton to Caesar Rodney. Brent replied that since Rodney had already left Washington to return to Delaware, Stockton would have to either authorize someone else to receive the money or "sign the enclosed receipt, and forward it to the secretary of State, in which case the money, will be transmitted to you by Mr. Thom, who acts as the Accountant to this office."

From William Nelson, Jr.

DR. SIR   VIRGA. YORK TOWN July 8th. 1802

I understand that a new District for the collection of duties has been established in Matthews County and perhaps a part of Glo[uce]ster. If no person has been appointed collector, or if no one of more experience and better pretensions has been thought of for the office, I take the liberty of mentioning as a candidate Mr. Thos. Nelson junr. of this town, son of Hugh Nelson decd.[1] He has had the usual College-education, has lived some time in a counting house, and has since attended a course of lectures on law; and I believe him to be a young man of correct demeanor. He will in few months attain his twenty second year. I am, with great respect, Dr. Sir, yr. obedt St

WM. NELSON JR.[2]

RC (DNA: RG 59, ML). In the lower margin JM wrote in pencil, "Francis Armistead is appointed."

1. Thomas Nelson, Jr. (1780–1859), was a member of the wealthy and influential Nelson family of York County, Virginia. His father was Col. Hugh Nelson (1750–1800), his uncles, Gen. Thomas Nelson, a signer of the Declaration of Independence and a governor of Virginia, and William Nelson, Jr. Thomas Nelson, Jr., was appointed collector at Yorktown in 1807; JM appointed him commissioner of loans for the state of Virginia in 1809 (Richard

C. M. Page, *Genealogy of the Page Family in Virginia* [New York, 1893], pp. 161, 172–73, 181–82; *Senate Exec. Proceedings,* 2:57, 63, 119, 120).

2. William Nelson, Jr. (ca. 1754–1813), served as a judge of the General Court of Virginia from 1791 until his death (Page, *Genealogy of the Page Family,* p. 162; *PJM,* 6:500 n. 2).

From Charles Pinckney

(Private)

DEAR SIR   July 8: 1802 IN MADRID

Mr Gibson[1] going to morrow affords me an Opportunity of sending you a line in addition to the Dispatches I have delivered him for your Department. These are voluminous & will inform You of our affairs as they stand at present. My private Opinion is that on the subject of Louisiana & the Floridas this Court is & has been for a considerable time governed by France & this Opinion I have given to Mr Livingston[2] urging him to use his influence & exertions at Paris in such manner as to place our citizens in that neighbourhood in the situation with France they now are with Spain. Mr Cevallos has promised me Louisiana will only be delivered to France subject to the conditions of our treaty with Spain. I am now urging him to give me this Declaration, (which he made verbally), in writing & I trust he will as soon as the celebration of the Princess[']s Wedding is over, which now occupies their whole attention. I have often told you that I believe Spain has been led into the Business of Louisiana against her Will & that the whole has been very reluctantly agreed to by her—that she does not act from her Own Opinions. This induces me to make great allowances for her & to hope in *the End,* as much compensation from her for our claims, as We could reasonably expect. I believe the only true mode to obtain it is the one pointed out by my Instructions & which my own Opinions persuade me is the right one, & that is Moderation. Indeed I know of no other that can be pursued at present with prudence or any probability of producing its effect. Some of the Americans here at different times have held different Opinions & supposed a strong or perhaps threatening language might produce an immediate compensation, & an agreement to our propositions & wishes. But as this was neither consistent with my instructions or my own opinions I have adopted a different & a mild one, well knowing that it is easier to irritate than to reconcile & that more is generally to be obtained by prudence & an appeal to the honour & Justice of a nation, than to its fears, unless you are in a situation very much to over-awe them. This cannot be said to be our situation at present with Spain, who is at peace with all the World & has France constantly ready to Support & assist her. For any attack on Holland or Spain would immediately produce a rupture with

France. This is not what we want & therefore I believe the mild & persua-
sive tone of moderation to be the true one not only to make friends &
obtain Justice but also favours. A nation will do the one & grant the other
with a bad grace after being threatened & it is not always prudent to
threaten unless prepared to strike. It is therefore with pleasure I have continued & I trust with no *inconsiderable industry* to pursue every moderate
means in my power to obtain what We wish. I believe I shall do so as to the
Spanish Spoliations. You will judge & determine whether I ought to agree
to the including the French, with the insertion of the Words "*segun los principios que constituyen la moralidad de las acciones*," & instruct me whether I am
to consent to accept the agreeing to arbitrate those on that ground, or what
further you wish to be done. In the meantime I shall continue to endeavour
to get them included on the same general principles with the Spanish, by
annexing another article to the Convention, & this although not probable,
I do not yet despair of. Believing that things are often granted to a Minister
who stands well with a court, which would be refused, if disagreeable to
them, it has been my endeavour to make myself as agreeable to the Court
here as possible & I trust I have succeeded, so far that I believe it gives
Mr Cevallos pain to refuse, or evade the requests of the United States
whenever he is obliged to do so. He contends the insertion of the Words,
will not confine the Powers of the Commissioners or defeat the Arbitration
& that the Commissioners thus appointed may well take up the french
claims. You will be so good as to determine, & if you see it in *that Light*, to
give me your Opinion. I thought it too important to decide myself, but at
the same time to give you these Opinions as to the propriety & policy of
pursuing mild & moderate Measures with this Court, who I am persuaded
have the Wish to do us Justice when in their power, but at present do not
find it convenient to oppose the Wishes of others, who have much influence in their councils & go the Lengths of using it as forcibly as they can.
It has been thought extraordinary while they were telling us they would
consent to an Arbitration, that still their Courts were condemning or rather
confirming condemnations of their inferior maritime tribunals, for Cases
which occurred during the War. I enquired into the reason of this & was
informed that the course of their Tribunals in Spain was regular & uninterrupted—that the King never interfered to stop them—that they were open
to all who had cases depending in one regular uniform mode & could not
be stopped—that it had been the case for a great length of time in Spain
that the Monarch never interrupted the course of their Tribunals, & in
return I was asked, if our Executive *could*, or ever did stop the Trial of prize
causes, or whether this was not left entirely to the Judges to act according
to known & *established rules*.

    I shall pursue the Subject of endeavouring to obtain full Compensation with Zeal & discretion & will thank you for your Opinions. They are always very valuable to me. In the case of Louisiana & the Floridas & the Misissipi We are particularly concerned in Georgia & South Carolina & the southern states, it therefore always has & will continue to claim my most serious attention. I have written to the Minister again to endeavour to obtain from him in writing the declaration he made to me respecting Our Rights of Navigation & of Deposit & of Louisiana being delivered subject to the conditions of our Treaty. At present the Court are & have been for sometime engaged in celebrating the double marriages of the Prince of Asturias with the young Princess of Naples & the Princess Maria Isabel (Infanta) & Daughter of the King of Spain to the Hereditary Prince of Naples & this so totally engrosses their time that some allowances are to be made for their not being able to attend very closely to Business during these festivals. It has brought on the Court & Nation great Expence & such is the magnificence & stile here upon these occasions that it has also brought considerable Expence on the foreign Ministers who were all invited to the Wedding.

Considering the length of my public Dispatches by Mr Gibson, I fear you will view this private letter as a long one, but I thought it necessary to give you my opinions on the probability of things being better arranged here by moderate & friendly measures, than by those irritating ones which ought never to be resorted to but in the last extremity & where you have a rupture in View. I know some of my countrymen for whom I have great Esteem & regard differ from me & think strong language & measures best, but I thought it my Duty to give you the Opinions I have & whenever it appears to me they ought to be changed you will hear from me the reasons. Please present me affectionately & respectfully to the President & our friends at Washington & believe me with very sincere & affectionate regard & respect & with my best Wishes Dear Sir Yours Truly

CHARLES PINCKNEY

RC (DLC).

1. This may have been William Gibson of Charleston, South Carolina (*PJM-SS*, 1:460).
2. Pinckney to Livingston, 30 June 1802 (NHi: Livingston Papers).

From Charles Pinckney

DEAR SIR   July 8: 1802 IN MADRID

Since closing my Dispatches by Mr Gibson this morning, I have recieved a letter from Commodore Morris commanding our Ships in the Mediterranean informing me of the Arrival of Mr Simpson at Gibraltar with the intelligence of the Emperor of Morocco having declared War against the United States. No doubt Commodore Morris has taken the first opportunity to communicate this to you, but lest an accident might happen to his dispatches I hasten to do the same & have directed circular letters to be Written to all our Consuls in Spain, & Italy & Portugal for the information of our Merchants & masters of Vessels. The Commodore does not mention to me the cause of the War, but I am afraid from this, it is more than probable we shall be engaged in War with the whole of the Barbary Powers & be obliged to keep a stronger Squadron in the Mediterranean.[1] With regard & respect & my best wishes I remain dear Sir Yours Truly

CHARLES PINCKNEY

P S I have just recieved a Visit from one of the foreign Envargado de Negotion. here & from his conversation with me I find that the Swedes & Danes & many other nations have numerous claims on this Government similar to our own for captures by the french equipped in Spanish Ports & Vessels condemned therein & that they *are merely waiting to* see the *issue of* our negotiations. This I told you before was one of the causes which increased the difficulty of our Negotiation for this class of our claims, but I did not know before that the claims of other Nations were to the extent I now find they are. The moment I make any arrangement with the Government here, the others will produce their claims. Mr Cevallos knows this & it is one of the reasons which makes the adjustment of the french spoliations a Question of such magnitude that Spain with all her resources would find it very difficult to meet them, for the greatest part of the claims of other nations are for Violations of the Spanish Territory by the French Privateers equipped in Spanish Ports.

I sent yesterday to Mr Cevallos the draft of another Convention for his Signature & a request to him to know his ultimate determination. This is the third I have sent him.

RC (DNA: RG 59, DD, Spain, vol. 6). Marked "(Duplicate)." Docketed by Brent as received 3 Oct.

1. In JM's absence from Washington, Brent wrote to inform Pinckney that two U.S. frigates were about to leave for the Mediterranean Sea, to which he added that "it is very much to be hoped that this reinforcement will prove an effective aid to the force already in that sea" (Brent to Pinckney, 6 Oct. 1802 [DNA: RG 59, IM, vol. 1]).

§ From John Gavino. *8 July 1802, Gibraltar.* No. 94. Encloses copy of a letter from O'Brien, dated 23 June,[1] confirming that the brig *Franklin* was captured by a Tripolitan vessel and that there were four others out; they had since been seen off the coast of Spain. Encloses also the terms of the settlement between Algiers and Spain and another letter from O'Brien dated 13 June.[2] Dey of Algiers has returned the British ships taken by his vessels. Emperor of Morocco has recalled Simpson, "alowing him Six Months for Answers from the U. S.—for particulars thereof referr to said Gentleman & Commodor Morris." Sir James Saumarez has gone home, "and the remainder of the Troops that Evacuated Mahon have passd by, also those that left Elba, when the French imediately hoisted their flag." Reports passage of "a large French Convoy with upwards of 3000 Polanders" and a French squadron of six ships of war, reportedly destined for Saint-Domingue.

RC and enclosures (DNA: RG 59, CD, Gibraltar, vol. 2). RC 2 pp.; docketed by Brent. Printed in Knox, *Naval Documents, Barbary Wars*, 2:195–96. For enclosures, see nn. 1 and 2.

1. In his 23 June letter to Gavino (2 pp.), headed "Circular," O'Brien reported seeing a three-lateen-sail Tripolitan corsair with an American brig in tow just off the port of Algiers; the corsair had been one of two Tripolitan ships that had sheltered at Algiers between 10 and 14 June. In a postscript, O'Brien outlined the terms agreed to by the Spanish, which included payment to the dey of $60,000 and, within forty days, another $42,000 in presents. Spain was also to renounce any claim to three Spanish vessels and their cargoes held by Algiers.

2. In his letter to Gavino of 13 June (2 pp.; marked "Copy of this letter forwarded to Department of State"; printed ibid., 2:172–73), O'Brien warned of the movements of five Tripolitan corsairs, two of which—galliots with three lateen sails and four guns each—had arrived at Algiers and would soon leave for the coast of Spain to harass American and Swedish shipping. After describing the taking of the Portuguese frigate by the Algerines, O'Brien reported that the "second division of Corsairs is most all returned and in a few days the Grand fleet will prepare for sea to make some one miserable, of course. They are here dashing away at a great rate, bastinading the french at Tunis, condemning Spaniards at Algiers taking Neopolitans and Genoese within one mile of the Coast of france and Spain."

§ From Edward Jones. *8 July 1802, Pointe-à-Pitre*. Forwards a copy of his last dispatch [10 May]. "Since then for nearly 30 days we were prohibited from exporting any kind of produce except Rum & Molasses." Restrictions were recently taken off, and all exports are allowed if the following duties are paid: 10 percent on sugar, 5 percent on rum and molasses, 4½ sous per pound on coffee, and 4½ ₶ per hundredweight on cotton, "with an addition of 10 ₱ Ct. on amount of Duties." Articles of the "first necessity, that is all kinds of provisions and Lumber," may be imported duty free. Expects to leave Guadeloupe for the U.S. in about a month. "This Island may be said to be restored to perfect tranquility, the Brigrands [*sic*] are all Distroyed except 100. to 150 Headed by Palerme who has taken refuge in the Mountains of Guadeloupe."

RC (DNA: RG 59, CD, Guadeloupe, vol. 1). 2 pp.

§ From Daniel Sheldon, Jr. *8 July 1802, Treasury Department*. "By direction of the Secretary of the Treasury, I have the honour to enclose a Copy of a Letter from him to the Comptroller of the Treasury, dated July 7th. 1802, respecting the British trade through the territories of the United States in the vicinity of the Lakes;[1] and some observations submitted by him with the said Letter, to the President of the United States."[2]

RC and enclosures (DLC: Gallatin Papers). RC 1 p. For enclosures, see nn. 1 and 2.

1. In his 7 July letter to Comptroller John Steele (4 pp.; printed in Carter, *Territorial Papers, Indiana,* 7:58–60), Gallatin explored the meaning of article 3 of the Jay treaty, which exempted from duty any goods carried over portages along the borders of the U.S. and Canada for the purpose of reembarkation. Gallatin maintained that the article applied to portages only, not to traffic along the rivers, and pointed out as a case of particular abuse the claim of British merchants "to transport goods without paying duties, through the Miami of the lakes, or other waters emptying into lakes Erie or Michigan, and thence across by land to the Wabash or other rivers, emptying in the Ohio." "Goods transported through those waters are exclusively intended for the consumption of the Indians living within the Territory of the United States, and even of the American settlements on the waters of the Ohio," Gallatin wrote, so that to admit this construction of the treaty "would render all the provisions of our revenue Laws nugatory, so far as relates to that consumption." He concluded that "nothing must be done, which may admit a right to use that navigation, without conforming to our revenue Laws."

2. Gallatin's memorandum to Jefferson of 6 July 1802 (1 p.; printed ibid., 7:57) asked the president to examine three questions: (1) "Shall Portages be construed to mean only *Land carriages* from a part of the boundary to another part of the same as at Niagara"; (2) "Does the Treaty by Portages mean to include any communication by land or water leading in a straight direction from the Lakes to the Mississipi"; and (3) "Is it best only to exclude, as not being Portages, those communications which cannot be embraced by any construction, (those leading by Wabash & other rivers to the Ohio)—and to suspend covering the whole ground which the 1st definition contemplates." In the lower margin, Jefferson added a note dated 7 July 1802: "As the discussion of these questions, should any arise with Great Britain, will devolve on the Secretary of state, will he be pleased to consider & give his opinion on them?" For the administration's determination on these questions, see JM to Rufus King, 20 July 1802, and nn.

§ To Presley Carr Lane. *9 July 1802, Department of State.* "The President of the United States having continued the Marshal for the Eastern District of Pennsylvania, your appointment for the Western District is of course discontinued, Under the late act of Congress for amending the Judicial system of the United States. You will please therefore to deliver over to Mr. [John] Smith all the papers &ca. &ca. which may be in your possession according to the directions of the said Act."

Letterbook copy (DNA: RG 59, DL, vol. 14). 1 p. JM wrote similar letters on this date to Hermanus H. Wendell of New York directing him to deliver his official papers to John Swartwout and to Andrew Moore of Virginia instructing him to turn his papers over to John Scott (ibid.).

§ From Roger Gerard van Polanen. *9 July 1802, Philadelphia.* States that "a Severe fit of illness" prevented him from answering JM's 29 June letter before this. Will attempt to "hasten the transmission" of the report in the case of the ship *Mary* from the governor of Curaçao to the Batavian government; will also inform the Batavian minister of foreign relations of JM's request.

RC (DNA: RG 59, NFL, Netherlands, vol. 1). 1 p.; docketed by Brent as received 11 July.

§ From Thomas Appleton. *10 July 1802, Leghorn.* Reports that on 8 July he was informed by the Danish consul of the arrival of two armed Tripolitan galliots in Algiers; encloses a translation of a letter on the subject[1] and declares that he "lost not a moment" in warning American ships at Leghorn. Encloses a copy of a letter from O'Brien at Algiers,[2] received 9 July, which he forwarded to "all our Consuls on the European side of the Mediterranean." Suggests that all American ship captains entering the Mediterranean stop at Gibraltar to "inform themselves ⟨i⟩f Danger exists, and where?" No important political events have occurred in Italy since his last dispatch on 1 June. Encloses a translation of the Ligurian constitution established by Bonaparte [not found]. "Continually are we told that a Port must be found for the Italian republic, and . . . the opinion hourly gains credit that Leghorn will probably be preferred." The king of Etruria continues in poor health and announced in a recent edict that the queen will have a voice in all important matters. On 3 June the king of Sardinia abdicated in favor of his brother, the duke of Aosta. The king of the Two Sicilies is to make a triumphal march into Naples shortly. "The emperor at Vienna has re-established all the monocal institutions which had been suppressed by Joseph and even the order of Mendicant friars are declared not without their use in Society."

RC and enclosures (DNA: RG 59, CD, Leghorn, vol. 1). RC 4 pp.; docketed by Brent as received 6 Oct. For surviving enclosures, see nn. 1 and 2.

1. The extract of a letter from the Swedish agent at Algiers, Norderling, to the Swedish consul at Genoa, 14 June 1802 (2 pp.), announced the arrival at Algiers of two Tripolitan galliots that had escaped from Tripoli despite the blockade and warned of their intention to cruise for Swedish and American ships (printed in Knox, *Naval Documents, Barbary Wars,* 2:174).
2. Richard O'Brien's circular letter of 26 June 1802 (1 p.), reported the arrival at Algiers of a Tripolitan corsair with the captured American brig *Franklin,* the efforts he was making to ransom the crew, and the rumor that six Tripolitan corsairs had evaded the blockade (printed ibid., 2:187).

§ From Joseph Pulis. *10 July 1802, Malta.* Takes advantage of the departure of the frigate *Boston* to report that he delivered to the commander of the frigate a dispatch left by the schooner *Enterprize,* which arrived at Malta on 27 Apr. The brother of the pasha of Tripoli remains at Malta, awaiting a meeting with the commander of the U.S. squadron in the Mediterranean; his arrangements with his brother are not yet settled, so that he has postponed his proposed voyage to Bengasi. The Order of St. John of Jerusalem has not yet taken command of Malta as stipulated by the definitive treaty. A British frigate has just arrived with Mr. Ball, the king's minister, who carries instructions for handing over the island to the order. The British governor, Charles Cameron, received permission to resign and leaves 12 July for Great Britain. Encloses a list of all American ships that entered the port between January and June 1802. Has assisted all U.S. captains who stopped at Malta to their entire satisfaction.

RC (DNA: RG 59, CD, Malta, vol. 1). 3 pp.; in French. In a clerk's hand, signed by Pulis. Docketed by Brent as received 16 Oct. Enclosure not found.

§ From John Hall Rogers. *10 July 1802, Alicante.* Mentions that he wrote to JM on 18 Aug. 1801 from Boston, enclosing a letter from William Hull of Newton "on the subject of the Consulate of Alicante and its vicinity; which in case of vacancy or removal [I] take leave to offer myself as a candidate."[1] Intends to reside at Alicante and offers to send "any wines, trees, fruits or seeds peculiar to this province or Spain in general that would be acceptable" to JM or the president.

RC (DNA: RG 59, LAR, 1801–9, filed under "Rogers"). 1 p. Docketed by Jefferson.

1. Rogers's letter has not been found, but see Hull to JM, 12 Aug. 1801, recommending Rogers for the post at Alicante (*PJM-SS*, 2:37).

From James Sullivan

SIR   BOSTON 12th July 1802
I have never been in the habit of seeking for offices for myself, or for my friends. I have given a number of Sons all the advantages which can be derived from the modes of education among us, and have been, as yet, rendered happy by their conduct. Had I wished any thing for them under the late administration, Mr Adams and his party would have treated a proposition in that way with contempt, on account of my childrens father. They must be much more mortified when they see their clas[s]mates noticed and themselves neglected by the present government. I should be greived to see them deprived of advantages on my account, or because I do not make the usual attempts to bring them into notice.

There are calls for Services, under the bankrupt, and other Acts, and to which men and the sons of men, who have not had so much concern in the revolution as I have had are called. I make no claim, however, on the score of merit, nor do I make any engagement in the political disputes of the day. I have my sentiments fixed on the consideration of the Presidents personal qualifications and his habitual virtues; and his firm republican principles. But if ever he was to attempt to assimilate the constitution of our nation to that of great Britian I should firmly oppose him. You will be so obliging as to excuse this intrusion and to beleive me to be with the most perfect respect to your character Your most humble Servant

JA SULLIVAN

RC (DNA: RG 59, ML).

§ From John Blake. *12 July 1802, Charleston.* Acknowledges JM's letter of 22 June [not found] enclosing a commission as commissioner of bankruptcy for the district of South Carolina, "which I am very sorry it is out of my power to accept."

RC (DNA: RG 59, LAR, 1801–9, filed under "Blake"). 1 p.; docketed by Jefferson. JM received another letter of this date from Simeon Theus of Charleston, also declining appointment as a commissioner of bankruptcy, "as my personal avocation employs so much of my time" (ibid.; 1 p.; docketed by Brent). Dominic A. Hall declined the appointment as well, in a letter written from Charleston on 15 July 1802 (ibid.; 1 p.; docketed by Brent).

§ From Ebenezer Stevens. *12 July 1802, New York.* Knowing that the U.S. government often has occasion to send supplies to the Mediterranean, offers the use of "a Ship of 290 Tons, a New & fine Vessel, which the owners are desirous should have a freight for the Meditaranean." Asks JM to communicate this offer to secretary of the navy. "I have been defeated in being able to purchase a required Cargoe for this vessel & My only chance of now getting her there, is by a freight." Thanks JM for the "friendly Civilities I recd. from yourself & family while in your City."

RC (DNA: RG 59, ML). 1 p.

§ To Thomas McKean Thompson. *13 July 1802, Department of State.* "Your letter of the 3d. Inst: [not found] with the 4th. Vol. of the laws of Pennsa., has been duly received."

Letterbook copy (DNA: RG 59, DL, vol. 14). 1 p.

§ From Elias Vander Horst. *13 July 1802, Bristol.* Wrote last on 15 May. Fears uncommonly cold weather will harm crops, especially wheat. Encloses accounts of all imports and exports by American ships in his district for the six months ended 30 June, a report on the Bristol infirmary, newspapers, and a London price current.

RC (DNA: RG 59, CD, Bristol, vol. 2). 1 p. Enclosures not found.

§ From Ebenezer Stevens. *14 July 1802, New York.* In accordance with JM's instructions of 18 Feb.,[1] submitted the papers in the case of the ship *Grand Turk* to the district attorney for his opinion on whether the owners were entitled to demurrage for the time the ship was detained at Gibraltar. Encloses a copy of the attorney's written opinion that the claim should not be allowed.[2] "I am sensible that the Owners will not abide by this decission, as they have suffered materially, on Account of the detention, having engaged a freight for the Ship, up the Mediteranean, which was lost on Account of her not arriving in Season.[3] . . . I have reason to fear they may cause me trouble in this business, and will thank you to inform me what in your opinion will be best to have done on the occasion."

RC and enclosure (DNA: RG 59, ML). RC 2 pp. For enclosure, see n. 2.

1. *PJM-SS*, 2:475.
2. Stevens enclosed a copy of Edward Livingston's letter to him, 13 July 1802 (1 p.), which stated that "as there is no Stipulation for this payment in the Charter party, nothing obligatory in the Instructions, and as the delay seems to have been a measure calculated as well for the benefit of the Ship Owners, as the United States, I cannot advise you to allow the Claim."

3. The owner of the *Grand Turk*, John Coles, petitioned Congress on 25 Jan. 1803 to be reimbursed $4,280, the cost of 107 days' demurrage at Gibraltar and Tunis in 1801. Coles maintained that he entered into the contract with the U.S. government without knowledge of the situation in the Mediterranean and that detention of his ship in the two ports lost him a freight worth $11,000 (DNA: RG 233, Committee on Claims, Petition of John Coles, 8A-F1.1). The House passed a bill on 30 Dec. 1803 allowing Coles demurrage at Gibraltar with interest on the sum; the Senate followed suit on 12 Jan. 1804 (*Annals of Congress*, 8th Cong., 1st sess., 791, 794, 230).

§ From James Leander Cathcart. *15 July 1802, Leghorn.* No. 9. Cannot find "words expressive of my feelings" about the capture of the brig *Franklin* by the Tripolitans. "It proves that we cannot evade the depredations of the most insignificant cruisers of the most insignificant Barbary State. What? after the pains that had been taken to defeat the projects of the Bashaw of Tripoli . . . had been attended with success . . . & we were upon the eve of concluding a treaty upon terms which would not only have been honorable . . . but would have establish'd a precedent worthy the imitation of other nations, . . . to be lull'd into a false security which has in a great measure blasted our most sanguine hopes is distressing beyond parallel. . . . You may depend Sir that this event small as it may appear will produce an entire change of sentiment in that Bashaw, . . . & nothing but the capture of one or two [Tripolitan cruisers] will place us in the same point of view that we were in before this misfortune happen'd."

"No pains or expence ought to be spared" to prevent the crew of the *Franklin* from being taken to Tripoli, but ransoming the brig and cargo would establish a "pernicious precedent." Article 9 of the U.S. treaty with Algiers prohibits the sale of captured American vessels in Algerine ports, and with the Swedish and American squadrons at sea "it is more than probable that [the *Franklin*] may be recaptured before her arrival at Tripoli. . . . Besides it is attended with this consequence, it will be apparently lessening the risque of navigating those seas by assuring our fellow Citizens that govt. will redeem both them & their property when captured." On 10 July he and Appleton "endeavor'd to dissuade the Masters of vessels now in port from sailing until some of our Frigates or those of Sweden arrives to take them under convoy, but with out effect, they seem at present as they ever have seem'd, intent upon gain only, without properly appreciating the risque." Has been "indefatigable" in warning ship captains of the danger and in giving them "timely information in order to prevent them from rushing inconsiderately upon ruin & what is worse, Slavery." In a postscript, relays an unofficial report that Commodore Morris has arrived at Gibraltar and reiterates his request for a credit for cash.

RC and enclosures (DNA: RG 59, CD, Tripoli, vol. 2). RC 4 pp.; docketed by Wagner as received 5 Oct. Printed in Knox, *Naval Documents, Barbary Wars*, 2:204–5. Extracts of RC and second enclosure transmitted by Jefferson to Congress on 15 Dec. 1802 and printed in *ASP, Foreign Relations*, 2:462. Both enclosures docketed by Wagner as received in Cathcart's 15 July dispatch. Thomas Appleton also sent JM copies of both enclosures (see Appleton to JM, 10 July 1802, and nn.). The first enclosure (2 pp.), an extract in French of a letter from the Swedish consul at Algiers, Norderling, to the Swedish consul at Genoa, 14 June 1802, bears a note from Cathcart to JM attesting that he had received it from Appleton on 7 July 1802 and expressing surprise that "our Consul at Algiers has been silent on an occasion so very interesting to our commerce." The second enclosure (2 pp.) is a copy of Richard O'Brien's circular letter of 26 June 1802, below which Cathcart wrote, "By comparing this with Mr. Nordelings letter it would appear that more Cruisers than the two galleys are out but I can hardly beleive it possible that they could evade the diligence of two Squadrons, or that they have enterprize to attempt it in anything but row boats such as the Gallies"; Cathcart also relayed an unofficial report that Captain Sterett in the *Enterprize* had "recaptured a Swede."

From John T. Mason

DEAR SIR   GEORGE TOWN 16th July 1802
   I am by no means satisfied with myself for the trouble I give you in addressing to you this letter. I am apprized of the two applications made to you, the one by Mr S. Hanson in person, the other through Mr Dab. Carr to appoint the former Chief Clerk in your Department, and of the answer by you given to each application. I know nothing of the duties appertaining to the Office, and consequently can know not what talents are requisite to fill it, but I can readily suppose that there are many quallities desirable in an Officer of this kind, besides the bare capacity to discharge the duties of the office, and therefore had I been in Mr Hansons place, I should have understood enough from your answers to make me cease to look for or expect the appointment. He however sees the subject differently, and can discover nothing in your answers but a doubt as to his capacity, and a reluctance to receive into the office a man, who from incompetency you may be compelled to remove. So rivetted is he to this opinion, that nothing will satisfy him but an answer from you to a proposition of the following nature "to receive him into your Office for a fortnight, or even for a week, upon trial, without a previous appointment, and if upon that trial you should be willing to trust him with the appointment, he will at all times hold himself bound to resign, upon the slightest intimation of your wish that he should do so." Through me he has insisted that this proposition should be made to you. In better circumstances he was justified in beleiving me his friend, now that he is reduced to the most abject poverty and threatened want, I feel myself unable to deny him that which under different circumstances I might possibly have refused. These considerations will I trust excuse the liberty I take in thus addressing you.
   This evening Mr Hanson will call on me, and if it be not improper to ask it, I shall be very glad of an opportunity to say to him, in any way that you shall think proper, that he may, or that he may not expect to have his wishes gratified. With great respect & real esteem I am D Sir Your Obedt Servt
                                                        JOHN T. MASON

RC (DLC). Docketed by JM.

From Louis-André Pichon

G. Town 16th. july 1802

Mr. Pichon takes the liberty to Sollicit of Mr Madison a decision in the case of the *Peggy*, Cape. Buisson, which is pending on this issue whether the owners, after the judgment of the Supreme court, will have to prosecute the Captors or will receive their property from Govmt. Mr. Madison will please to recollect, altho those circumstances may be considered as foreign to the merits of the case, that of all the cases of french Captures this was the most favorable: & Mr. P. begs leave to represent that by the different obstructions it has met with, the owners have lost nearly 6,000 Doll out of the 9,000 released by Govmt. The order at first given by the President of the U. S. as early as march 1801 for the delivery of this last Sum being the moiety appertaining to the United States, appears to evince that *at that early Stage of the business there was not the least doubt but the case came fairly under the Treaty.* It is really difficult to conceive that after so positive a decision on the part of the President of the United States, the indemnification for the other moiety may be considered as not coming within the treaty. When the first order was given no trial had taken place in the Supreme court, it seems to Mr. Pichon that the circumstance of the trial had posteriorly and of the sentence of the Supreme court, cannot have an effect to invalidate the claim under that instrument. The owners in france have made to Mr Pichon several applications & he begs Mr Madison will endeavour before the impending recess to put it in Mr P. power to give an answer to the owners and direct their attorneys in New York how to act.

RC (DNA: RG 59, LOAG). Docketed by Brent as received the same day.

From Charles Pinckney

Dear Sir   July 16: 1802 In Madrid

A few days after Mr Gibson left us I recieved the inclosed from Mr: Montgomery who had recieved it inclosed from Mr Obrien at Algiers.[1] This is the third I have forwarded to you from him & I am hopeful it will arrive in time to go by Mr Gibson. The intelligence of War being declared by Morocco I forwarded, Via Cadiz in the beginning of this Month. If it should be necessary for me to interfere in this Business or take any Steps in it you will please instruct me as I shall always with pleasure give every aid in my power. I have sent in a fourth draft of a Convention to the secretary of state here on the subject of our Claims & other Business. I am now waiting his Decision & as soon as I recieve it you will hear from me fully. I still hope the best, although they are so extremely dilatory in their proceedings, it is impossible to calculate when a thing can be drawn to a conclusion. In the interim I am pursuing every probable mode in my power to ensure success to the propositions I have submitted. With great regard & respect I am dear sir Yours Truly

CHARLES PINCKNEY

RC (DNA: RG 59, DD, Spain, vol. 6). Docketed by Brent as received 27 Oct.

1. See O'Brien to JM, 14 June 1802, and n.

§ From William Baker. *16 July 1802, Washington.* "I am apprized that you have received already, through several channels, Colo. Hanson's application for the chief clerkship in the department of State; & I know too, that your answer has been unfavorable. . . . If it were believed, that you are in possession of all the circumstances which induce this application . . . you would not again have been importuned upon this subject. . . . An intimate acquaintance with the deplorable situation of Colo. Hanson, & a natural hope & anxiety, arising from my near connection with him, that through you his situation may be bettered, form at once the apology & object of this letter. . . . I would barely suggest that upon the procurement of appointment under the government, the family of Mr. Hanson depends for the means of existence; & that the conferment of an office equal to their support, would be an act of real charity. . . . Mr. Hanson only solicits a trial to be made of him. He is willing to risk all he hopes for, upon a faithful & competent discharge of his duty. . . . I have supposed that you were unacquainted with the extent of his misfortunes, & that you will believe me when I say, that he is at this moment without a shilling."

RC (DNA: RG 59, LAR, 1801–9, filed under "Hanson"). 3 pp. William Baker (ca. 1749–1812) was a Georgetown physician and brother-in-law of Samuel Hanson of Samuel (Papenfuse et al., *Biographical Dictionary of the Maryland Legislature*, 1:111).

§ From Sylvanus Bourne. *16 July 1802, Amsterdam.* Transmits latest issues of Leiden *Gazette*; "those you desired for the last years are all packed & only want a Conveyance to Baltimore—my house here will continue to forward those which succeed." Expects to embark for the U.S. within the month, "as the most probable means of restoring the physical & intellectual health of Mrs B.," and has made arrangements for filling his place during his absence.

RC (DNA: RG 59, CD, Amsterdam, vol. 1). 1 p. Mistakenly docketed by Wagner, "16 Jany. 1803," and filed under that date.

§ From Thomas Bulkeley. *16 July 1802, Lisbon.* Refers to his dispatches of 2, 5, and 10 Feb.[1] "The Schooner I mentioned to have been lost on the Coast of Faro has

397

been claimed by James Philips & Co. of Philadelphia and delivered to them. . . . I have obtaind an order for the restitution of the Duties imposed on the Cargo of Fish by the Hope. . . . The duties were demanded on an old law which has never been revoked." Reports that since the arrival of the crew and supercargo of the schooner *Samuel*, the captain, crew, and supercargo of the schooner *Pilgrim* arrived from Rio de Janeiro, and the confiscation of both ships is under appeal; will send JM the documents in the cases following the prince regent's decision. "The Cases of these vessels are nearly alike. . . . The confiscation is founded on their clearances and the Sea Letters being filled up to Rio de Janeiro only, but not the least accusation of illicit trade brought forward." Encloses copies of letters "which will show you the state of affairs in the Mediterranean."[2] In a postscript, notes that John Watson, supercargo of the *Samuel*, "has just brought me the inclosed Translation of his case."[3]

RC and one enclosure (DNA: RG 59, CD, Lisbon, vol. 1). RC 3 pp.; docketed by Brent as received 10 Sept.

1. *PJM-SS*, 2:436, 437, 446, 456.
2. Bulkeley enclosed a seven-page transcription of letters that included John Gavino to Bulkeley, 20, 24, and 28 June 1802; a circular letter from James Simpson, 25 June 1802 (see Knox, *Naval Documents, Barbary Wars*, 2:183–84); F. A. Kantzou, Swedish consul general at Lisbon, to Bulkeley, 2 July 1802; Richard O'Brien to Robert Montgomery, 16 June 1802; the captain of the British ship *Fortune* to the British consul at Alicante, 16 June 1802; and W. May of the British brig *Cameleon* to Bulkeley, 13 and 15 July 1802.
3. Enclosure not found, but see William Jarvis to JM, 3 Aug. 1802, for a copy of the translation in Jarvis's hand. The Boston owners of the *Samuel* were notified of the ship's detention earlier in the year when Bulkeley forwarded a copy of a letter from the ship's captain in his 10 Feb. 1802 dispatch to JM. Bulkeley suggested they could send JM the needed documentation. Owners Thomas Arnold, Arnold Wells, and Peter C. Brooks wrote JM on 6 Aug. 1802 (not found), and Daniel Brent forwarded their letter to JM in Virginia. When Bulkeley's 16 July dispatch was received at the State Department, Brent sent an extract to the owners "on account of the information which it affords, with respect to a case that is interesting to you" (Brent to Arnold, Wells, and Brooks, 22 Aug. 1802, and Brent to Brooks, 11 Sept. 1802 [DNA: RG 59, DL, vol. 14]).

§ From Rufus King. *16 July 1802, London.* No. 72. Reports that he exchanged ratifications of the convention on 15 July with Hawkesbury. An original copy of the British ratification and certificate of exchange will be delivered to JM in Washington by Gabriel Christie, a former U.S. representative from Maryland.

RC (DNA: RG 59, DD, Great Britain, vol. 10); letterbook copy (NHi: Rufus King Papers, vol. 55). RC 1 p.; in a clerk's hand, signed by King; docketed by Brent as received 23 Sept. Printed in King, *Life and Correspondence of Rufus King*, 4:148.

§ From James Simpson. *16 July 1802, Gibraltar.* No. 45. Transmits a duplicate of his no. 44 and encloses a copy of his letter to the governor of Tangier and an extract of a letter from the Danish consul at Tangier "containing substance of what the Governour encharged him to communicate by way of reply to my Letter to him."

Thought it best to wait for the *Adams* and instructions from JM "before I closed with the Governours proposal of returning to Tangier or entirely reject it." Has received a report from Rabat indicating that the fitting out of the two frigates there goes slowly, "but at Tetuan I find they make all dispatch with the two Galleys." Has communicated this information to Commodore Morris.

RC and enclosures (DNA: RG 59, CD, Tangier, vol. 1); Tr and Tr of enclosures (DLC). RC 3 pp.; docketed by Brent as received 1 Sept. Printed in Knox, *Naval Documents, Barbary Wars*, 2:205–6. Tr and Tr of enclosures in Brent's hand (see Simpson to JM, 3 July 1802, n.). Enclosures are a copy of Simpson to Hajj Alcayde Abde-Rhaman Hashash, 5 July 1802 (2 pp.), acknowledging the governor's letter informing him of the emperor's order allowing him to remain in Tangier for six months and indicating that he would write to the emperor after the arrival of the *Adams* (printed ibid., 2:192); and an extract of a letter from the Danish consul to Simpson, 9 July 1802 (1 p.), describing his conversation with the governor of Tangier after presenting Simpson's letter of 5 July; the governor said that he found Simpson "in the right" and would inform the emperor that he had written Simpson "a very good Letter, and . . . got still a better answer." Jefferson communicated extracts of the RC and enclosures to Congress with his annual message on 15 Dec. 1802 (*ASP, Foreign Relations*, 2:466).

§ To Ebenezer Stevens. *17 July 1802, Department of State*. Acknowledges Stevens's letter of 14 July. Concurs in the opinion of the district attorney on the claim of demurrage for the *Grand Turk* but thinks it proper that the claimants should be referred to Treasury Department for a settlement of the question; "this is in fact the most regular course in such cases." The claim of Stewart & Company should be submitted with supporting documents to the accounting department, "which will liquadate [*sic*] and decide thereon, according to the tenor of the contract legally entered into in behalf of the public."

Letterbook copy (DNA: RG 59, DL, vol. 14). 1 p.

§ From Charles Peale Polk. *18 July 1802, "near the Old Bridge," Washington*. "I take the liberty of writing a few lines soliciting your Patronage to procure a Clerkship, as Copyist, in the Office of the *Treasurer*. . . . I am told that the duties are extremely easy, and can be performed by a Common Capacity. . . . I have long depended on *Your humanity* for being placed in a Situation more permanent than Painting for my Support."

RC (DNA: RG 59, LAR, 1801–9, filed under "Polk"). 2 pp.

To Louis-André Pichon

S<small>IR</small>   D<small>EPARTMENT OF</small> S<small>TATE</small> July 19. 1802.

Having laid before the President the subject of your Note of the 16th. instant, I am charged to acquaint you, that under the circumstances of the case of the Peggy, Capt. Buisson it rests with the claimants of restitution to pursue their object, by judicial proceedings against the captors for the moiety distributed to them according to a decree of an inferior court reversed by the Supreme Court of the United States. This course is rendered particularly proper by the consideration that the actual distribution resulted from the failure of the claimants to interpose the legal means of preventing it, at the proper stage of the trial. Accept assurances of the high consideration &ca.

JAMES MADISON

Letterbook copy (DNA: RG 59, DL, vol. 14); Tr (DLC: Alexander Hamilton Papers).

From Jonathan Bull

S<small>R</small>   HARTFORD July 19th: 1802

I receiv'd your favour of the 6th. Instant with its inclosure.[1] I feel very sensible of the respect paid me by the President of the United States, in being selected to be one of the Commissioners of Bankruptcy for the District of Connecticut, and beg through you, to return him my gratefull acknowledgments. I should most cheerfully have accepted the appointment had I not been particularly circumstanced. I hold Offices under this State, which are annual, and although not very lucrative, are necessary to aid me in the support of a large Family. My Political sentiments being obnoxious to the ruling party here have already bro't me into Jeopardy, and should I accept of the Commission now offerd me, It might be deemed a relinqu[i]shment of my present State Offices and would probably pave the way for my removal—the Duties which will ⟨fair⟩ly attach to the whole might be executed by one Person, and not even engross the whole of his Time—yet under the present virulence of my adversaries, I have no right to expect any indulgence. It is the opinion of my Friends here that the cause in which we are engaged will not be advanced by my acceptance, but the reverse. I therefore find myself under the necessity to decline the Honour intended me. I am Sr with the highest respect your humble Servant

JONTH: BULL.[2]

RC (DNA: RG 59, LAR, 1801–9, filed under "Bull"). Docketed by Brent.

1. Letter not found.

2. Jonathan Bull (ca. 1747–1825) was a Yale graduate and Republican politician who served as judge of probate for the Hartford district (1790–1808) and as judge of the Hartford county court (1798–1807) (Kline, *Papers of Burr*, 1:545 n. 13).

Memorandum from Thomas Jefferson

July 19. 1802.
Henry Warren (of Mass) to be Collector of Marblehead v. Samuel R. Gerry.[1]
William Lyman of Massachusetts to be Collector of Newbury port, vice Dudley A. Tyng[2]
William R. Lee of Massachus: to be collector of Salem & Beverley vice Joseph Hiller[3]
Peter Muhlenberg of Pensylvania to be Collector of   [4] vice George Latimer
John Page of Virginia to be Collector of Petersburg v. William Heth.[5]
Tenche Cox of Pensylvania to be Supervisor of Pensylvania v. Peter Muhlenburg.[6]

Perhaps it may be better to inclose blank commissions to mr. Gallatin in all the above cases, to be filled up & sent out by him, all together, on his return.

TH: JEFFERSON

FC (DLC: Jefferson Papers).

1. Henry Warren, son of the Revolutionary War politician James Warren and the historian Mercy Otis Warren, was appointed collector of customs and inspector of revenue for the port of Plymouth in 1803 (*Senate Exec. Proceedings*, 1:453). Joseph Wilson was named to the post at Marblehead in place of Samuel R. Gerry, the brother of Elbridge Gerry, who had been removed for incompetence (ibid., 1:432; George Athan Billias, *Elbridge Gerry: Founding Father and Republican Statesman* [New York, 1976], pp. 305–6).

2. William Lyman (1755–1811), of Hampshire County, Massachusetts, served as a Republican in the U.S. House of Representatives, 1793–97, but declined this appointment. In 1804 he was appointed U.S. consul at London. Ralph Cross, who had been dismissed as weigher and gauger of customs in 1792, was appointed collector of Newburyport after Dudley A. Tyng was removed for political reasons (Carl E. Prince, *The Federalists and the Origins of the U.S. Civil Service* [New York, 1977], pp. 35–36; *Senate Exec. Proceedings*, 1:432, 476; Samuel Spring to JM, 20 Oct. 1801, *PJM-SS*, 2:187–88 and n. 1).

3. William Raymond Lee (1745–1824), Revolutionary War veteran, merchant, and land speculator, served as collector of Salem and Beverly from 1802 until his death (Thomas A. Lee, "The Lee Family of Marblehead," *Essex Institute Historical Collections*, 53 [1917]: 155–68). Joseph Hiller was a prominent Salem Federalist and contributed both financially and editorially to the anti-Jeffersonian Salem *Gazette* (Prince, *Federalists and the Origins of the U.S. Civil Service*, pp. 31–33).

4. Left blank by Jefferson. Peter Muhlenberg was appointed collector for the district of Pennsylvania (*Senate Exec. Proceedings*, 1:432).

5. John Page (1743–1808), a former congressional colleague and longtime friend of JM's, declined the appointment due to bad health. John Shore was chosen in his stead to replace the Revolutionary War veteran and Federalist William Heth (1735–1808), who was removed (Daniel Brent to JM, 3 Sept. 1802, and n. 5; *Senate Exec. Proceedings*, 1:433; Lyon Gardiner Tyler, ed., *Encyclopedia of Virginia Biography* [5 vols.; New York, 1915], 2:172).

6. Tench Coxe's struggle to obtain a position in the Jefferson administration is described in Coxe to JM, 22 Nov. 1801, Editorial Note (*PJM-SS*, 2:258–59). Coxe's unhappiness with the post he took up was evident from the soothing letter John Beckley wrote to him on 28 Mar. 1802. Beckley assured Coxe that he had "held full and free conversations with Mr: Madison and Mr: Jefferson on the subject—they have both explicitly declared their high regard and determination to . . . do something adequate to your merits & services" (*Papers of Tench Coxe* [PHi microfilm ed.], reel 74).

From John Steele

DEAR SIR,   Monday Morning [July 19. 1802][1]

I beg leave to put into your hands the enclosed letter from General Davie recommending Mr. Barnet and Mr. Montflorence to the notice of Government.[2] As I am not at all acquainted with the former, and but slightly with the latter, I wish to be understood as not offering an opinion concerning the pretensions of either: Indeed I would not have put you to the trouble of even reading the letter but to satisfy the importunity of Genl. Davie, who in a late letter which I received from him continues to expect that I should do something, and I know of nothing else that I can do with propriety. In reply I informed him that I would hand the enclosed letter to you, or to the President as his recommendation. You need not therefore be at the trouble to return it. Accept the assurance of my highest esteem and respect.

                                                  JNO. STEELE

RC and enclosures (DLC); FC (NcU: Southern Historical Collection). RC docketed by Brent. FC marked "*Private*" by Steele. For enclosures, see n. 2.

1. Date in brackets supplied by JM.
2. William R. Davie's letter, dated 30 Jan. 1802 (2 pp.), recommended Isaac Cox Barnet and James C. Mountflorence for U.S. vice-consulships in France. Both had been removed from offices there by the Jefferson administration, and Davie objected to the "injustice and hardship" of Barnet's treatment and insisted that Mountflorence had "real claims upon the attention and patronage of our Government." In addition, Davie enclosed a copy of a letter of 10 Oct. 1801 he had received from Barnet (4 pp.), complaining of his misfortune at being replaced and presenting his "just pretensions to public confidence."

To John Steele

DEAR SIR   WASHINGTON July 19. 1802

I have recd. your favor inclosing a letter to you from Genl. Davie on the subject of Mr. Barnett & Mr Mountflorence. It may not be improper to enable you to inform General Davie, that Mr. Barnett has been appointed

Consul at Antwerp, a place not unlikely to become soon of importance, & for which there have been sundry candidates. It is not known whether it will be acceptable to him or not. Should a vice Consulate at Paris be deemed expedient by the President, the pretensions of Mr. Mountflorence, with the recommendation of Genl. Davie, will of course be brought to his view. With great respect & esteem I remain Dr Sir Your most Obedt. servt.

JAMES MADISON

RC (Nc-Ar: Steele Papers).

§ To Clement Humphreys. *19 July 1802, Department of State.* "I have duly received your letter of the 12th. Inst. [not found] enclosing one from Mr. Pinckney and another from the Consul of the United States at Madrid,[1] for which I return you my thanks."

Letterbook copy (DNA: RG 59, DL, vol. 14). 1 p.

1. Probably Charles Pinckney to JM, 20 Apr. 1802, and Moses Young to JM, 26 Apr. 1802 (not found) (see JM to Pinckney, 26 July 1802, and JM to Young, 28 July 1802).

§ From John Dodd. *19 July 1802, Hartford.* Acknowledges JM's letter of 6 July [not found] informing him of his appointment as one of the commissioners of bankruptcy for the district of Connecticut, "but as I had no previous knowledge of any Such thing being about to take place, and having made arangements of a different kind; duty to my self and in my opinion to the Public require me to decline accepting the appointment."

RC (DNA: RG 59, LAR, 1801–9, filed under "Dodd"). 1 p.; docketed by Brent.

§ From Rufus King. *19 July 1802, London.* No. 73. Reports receipt of 25 June letter from Commodore Morris at Gibraltar[1] announcing Morocco's "unexpected declaration of war" on U.S. Has notified U.S. consuls in Great Britain so that American ships might be forewarned. Does not know why "this unjust Proceeding has arisen," having "no exact information either concerning the internal condition of Morocco, or of the State of our Relations with this Power." The event confirms his belief that "our security against the Barbary Powers must depend upon Force and not upon Treaties." Owing to dry weather followed by wet hay season, the hay crop is "not only short in quantity but ill cured; old Hay has in consequence thereof risen in the London Market." Prospects for grain are better, but "the Continuance of rainy weather" makes the corn harvest uncertain.

RC (DNA: RG 59, DD, Great Britain, vol. 10); letterbook copy (NHi: Rufus King Papers, vol. 55). RC 2 pp.; in a clerk's hand, signed by King; docketed by Brent as received 23 Sept. Printed in King, *Life and Correspondence of Rufus King,* 4:148–49.

1. Printed in Knox, *Naval Documents, Barbary Wars,* 2:184.

§ From Thomas Newton. *19 July 1802, Norfolk.* "The wines & Brandy lie ready for an opty. to Fredricksbg. & will be shipped the first. The Madeira is cased as you desired & is very fine so is the brandy & Sherry having got some very old."

RC (DLC). 1 p.

To Rufus King

SIR,   DEPARTMENT OF STATE, July 20th. 1802.

A case has lately been stated to the Treasury Department by one of the Northwestern Collectors of the Customs, which turns on a construction of the Treaty of 1794, between the United States and Great Britain, in relation to "portages or carrying places."[1] I inclose a copy of a letter from the Secretary of the Treasury to the Comptroller, which conveys the sentiments of the President on that subject.[2] It seems no less obvious than it is important, that the meaning of those terms should be limitted to cases, where the waters forming a boundary between the parties become unnavigable, and where a transit by land is thence required and used, in order to re-enter the common waters where they are again navigable. Had no obstructions to the navigation existed, no portages or carrying places would have been established. These portages or carrying places, therefore, are essentially connected with those obstructions, and co-extensive only with them. Any departure from this idea of a portage or carrying place, is inconsistent with the usual acceptation of the terms, and with the manifest import of the Treaty. But a latitude of construction which would open our Country to the free passage of foreign merchandize, from the waters forming a boundary with Great Britain, without regard to distance or direction, and without distinction of roads, rivers or lakes, wholly within our limits, or rather linking all of them together, as a portage or carrying place, is as absurd in itself, as it would be pernicious in its effects. At present, as is observed by the Secretary of the Treasury, the inconvenience in allowing British Traders to pass with their goods thro' our territory to the Indians beyond the Mississippi, either by the way of Lake Michigan and the rivers Fox and Ouisconsing, or by way of the Miami and Illinois rivers, is not very material. But in the trade by way of the Wabash, the abuses are already such as to call for immediate interposition. And even in the other cases, it is to be considered that the advantage enjoyed by the Canada traders in conveying to the Indians beyond the Mississippi goods which have paid no duty, over the american traders through the same channels, whose goods are loaded with american duties, affords just ground of complaint to the latter, and is besides a real sacrifice on the part of the United States. A further consideration at this time is that the indulgence of a passage thro' our country, for foreign merchandizes into the Mississippi, favours the introduction of them among our settlers on this river, in violation of our laws, and at the expense of our revenue.

From this view of the subject it is fairly presumed that whatever pretensions or expectations may be entertained by interested individuals, the British Government will in no way patronize them, as within the meaning of the Treaty. The President has thought it proper nevertheless that the present explanation should be communicated to you, that you may the more easily correct any misrepresentations or misconceptions existing on the subject; and may have an occasion of preparing that Government for the regulations which cannot be distant, by which the use of portages and carrying places within our limits, will be reduced to a conformity with the true meaning of the Treaty.

I inclose also a late Act of Congress,[3] the 8th Section of which exempts from tonnage duty, all vessels (including British) not above 50 tons burden, trading between the ports of the Northern and Northwestern boundaries of the United States and the British provinces of upper and lower Canada. In the British ports within the same waters, vessels of the United States, we understand, are subject to a duty of six cents ℔ ton. The disposition lately manifested by the British Government to concur in equalizing the situation of vessels of the two Countries, and to do it rather by abolishing, than assimilating the duties on them, justifies the expectation of the President that you will find no difficulty in drawing its attention to the measures proper to be taken in the present case. With sentiments of great respect and consideration, I have the honor to be Sir, your most Obt Sert.

JAMES MADISON

RC (PP: Jay Treaty Papers, William M. Elkins Collection); letterbook copy (DNA: RG 59, IM, vol. 6). RC in a clerk's hand, signed by JM; docketed as received 10 Sept. Enclosures not found, but see nn. 2 and 3.

1. British violations of article 3 of the Jay treaty were brought to the administration's attention by Mathew Ernest, collector and inspector of the revenue at Detroit (John Steele to Ernest, 6 July 1802, Carter, *Territorial Papers, Indiana*, 7:57–58; Miller, *Treaties*, 2:248; *Senate Exec. Proceedings*, 1:332).

2. See Daniel Sheldon, Jr., to JM, 8 July 1802, and n. 1.

3. "An Act to provide for the establishment of certain districts, and therein to amend an act intituled 'An act to regulate the collection of duties on imports and tonnage'; and for other purposes," 1 May 1802 (*U.S. Statutes at Large*, 2:181–82).

§ From William Lee. *20 July 1802, Bordeaux.* "The bearer hereof Mr Kidder[1] of Massachusetts has been Secy. to this Agency for some months. He is a young man of good abilities & strict integrity and has had the advantage of being educated at

Cambridge. He will answer any questions you may please to put to him concerning the affairs of this agency and will be able to give you considerable information respecting the state of things in this Country."

RC (DNA: RG 59, CD, Bordeaux, vol. 1). 1 p.

1. This was probably John Kidder, a Boston merchant (Stinchcombe, *The XYZ Affair*, p. 136).

§ From William Savage. *20 July 1802, Kingston, Jamaica*. States that he last wrote on 9 June, since which he has received JM's letter of 29 Apr. "I am sorry to find my services here are not entitled to any Compensation, I will hope was the question to come before Congress they would acquiess in my Wishes." Encloses his account up to 30 June, amounting to £366 13*s*. 5*d*. "I am well aware of the rigid economy that may be necessary in the Goverment but at the same time I cannot refrain from expectations when the question is properly laid before the nation in their Legislative Capacity."

RC (DNA: RG 59, CD, Kingston, Jamaica, vol. 1). 1 p.; docketed by Brent as received 24 Sept. Enclosure not found.

§ From Carlos Martínez de Yrujo. *20 July 1802, Mount Pleasant, near Philadelphia*. Informs JM of the exchange of ratifications of the treaty of peace between Spain and Russia.

RC (DNA: RG 59, NFL, Spain, vol. 2). 1 p.; in Spanish; in a clerk's hand, except for Yrujo's complimentary close and signature.

From Bird, Savage, and Bird

SIR,   LONDON 21 July 1802.

The last time we had the honor to address you was on the 29th. April last by the William via New York & copy by the Juno via Philadelphia.

We have by this opportunity transmitted to the Secretary of the Treasury copies of our various half yearly accounts with the United States to the 30 June 1802 viz:

Our Acct. with the United States, Diplomatic fund to
which we have made an advance of £1000.— on loan,
& the balance of which is transferred to our debit in
new acct. in   £ 248.10. 8.
Our dtto. British Treaty Fund the balance of which is
transferr'd to our Debit in new acct. in   " 104.16. 1.

Our dtto. Barbary Treaty Fund to which we have made
an advance of £2700.— on loan, & the balance of
which is transferr'd to our debit in new acct. in   " 278.17. 6.

Our dtto. Fund for the relief & protection of Seamen
the balance of which is transferr'd to our debit in new
acct. in   " 10. 1. 9.

Our dtto. Fund for the prosecution of claims in Prize
causes, balanc'd   —.—.—.

Our dtto. Suspense acct. for articles paid by order of His
Excellency Rufus King, without assignment to any of
the above accts. to which we have made an advance of
£300.— & of which the balance is transferr'd to our
debit in new acct. in   " 67. 8.10.

Our dtto. For money advanced by us on loan the amount
of which to our Credit is   4000. . .

In making these advances we have follow'd the plan agreed on with
Mr. King of advancing £1000.— at a time when the accounts were deficient
of cash, on the principle that as Bankers to the United States we ought not
to be without cash in hand. On this principle we have on the 18th. inst.
made a further advance of £1000. on loan to the British Treaty Fund to
provide for the payment that day of a quarter's Salary to C. Gore Esqr.
The payment of £500.— to Mr. Trumbull the 5th. commissioner on the
2d. Feby. last is on the receipt of Mr. Moore the Secretary to the board on
acct. of the contingent expences & the Salary of the 5th. Commissioner.
We have been applied to by Mr. Gore & Mr. Pinkney the two American
Commissioners to know if we wou'd advance £375. towards a further payment for the contingent expences & the 5th. Commissioner. On thr. stating that the British Government had advanced its proportion, & that if we
did not make this advance the business of the board must Stop, we have
consented to make this further deviation from the instructions we had received from the Secretary & shall advance this amount.

We hope in all the instances in which we have deviated from these instructions to make no disbursements beyond the Sums remitted, we shall
be justified by the nature of the case & our Knowledge that the articles for
which we paid were authoriz'd by law & the services perform'd or at least
performing. An additional motive was our inclination to attend to the personal accomodation of the Gentlemen here who would have been much
incommoded by not receiving their salaries regularly.

In cases where it wou'd have been presumption in us to have assum'd a
judgement whether services had been perform'd, till you or the Secretary
of the Treasury provided for them, we have declined making advances desired both by Mr. King & your Consul Mr. Erving.

We are however placed in a Situation of great difficulty & delicacy by not having received any answers from you or the Secretary ⟨of⟩ the Treasury to our various letters, asking for remittances & further instructions, & we are apprehensive that by some means or other our letters do not regularly come under your notice. We will therefore recapitulate the dates of them that you may have them laid before you:

13 Jany. 1802
21 Feby. 1802
13 March 1802
22 dtto. "
29 April 1802

In this last we stated that our advances in May would Amount to £4102.7.5. including a payment not yet made of £766.15.4. to Mawhood & Co. on the Barbary Treaty Fund, which we suppose that knowing the State of the accts. Mr. King has postpon'd applying to us for. [. . .] present State of the accts. requires a remittance of [. . .] ⟨a⟩dvances, besides providing for the salaries &a. [. . .], & for such contingencies as Mr. King & Mr. Erving [. . .] pointed out including the £766.15.4. to Mawhood & Co. & the large demands of the Proctors in the Prize causes.

We flatter ourselves that you will fall on some plan to keep us in future in remittance for all these demands, with a fund in hand for unavoidable contingencies,[1] & we are with sentiments of high respect Sir, Your most obedient Servants

BIRD SAVAGE & BIRD

We are just inform'd that the payment of the £766.15.4 will be wanted.

RC (DNA: RG 59, Letters Received from Bankers). Docketed by Brent as received 3 Oct., with his note: "Remittances, amounting to 60. or 70.000 Dollars, have been made in the course of this year, of which the receipt is not acknowledged in this letter. Most of this sum must have long since got to hand; and Mr Gallatin is now taking measures for making a further remittance. I have informed Messrs B, S & B of this last Circumstance. DB." Ms torn by removal of seal.

1. Daniel Brent replied on 4 Oct. 1802 (DNA: RG 59, IC, vol. 1), in JM's absence from Washington, assuring the bankers that "the Secretary of the Treasury will immediately take measures for causing a remittance, of fifty odd thousand dollars, to be made to you" and that "this sum with the others that will have reached you beforehand, will relieve you from the difficulties and perplexities which you state in the many letters quoted in the one of which I . . . acknowledge the receipt."

From Albert Gallatin

DEAR SIR   NEW YORK July 21st 1802

Having neither the law authorizing the Commissrs. on the Georgia business to enquire into the claims of individuals, nor the compromise with
Georgia, I cannot frame a satisfactory advertisement till my return which I
expect to be before you shall have left the city.[1] But as those documents are
not necessary at least to enable me to convey my ideas on the subject of the
letter to Gov. Claiborne; and as this does not admit of further delay, I will
submit to your consideration what seems to me necessary to be written
to him.[2]

The information to be obtained from the Governor relates
1st. to the extent of Territory both on the Mississipi & on the Mobile to
which the indian title has been extinguished.
2dly. to the extent of the claims recognized & secured by the compromise
with Georgia.
3dly. to the nature & extent of the claims not recognized by that compromise but which may be embraced by Congress & satisfied out of the five
millions of Acres reservation.
4thly. to the intrusions on the lands of the U. States, which are not coloured
by any claim or title whatever.
On the first & last points, general information only can be expected & he
may only be requested to collect & transmit such as it may be in his power
to obtain.

The claims secured by the compromise with Georgia are those of persons settled on the lands on the day fixed in the compromise, & who were
embraced by the Bourbon County act,[3] or who had complete grants derived
from the British Government of West Florida or from the Spanish Government prior to the date of the Treaty of 1795 with Spain. In relation to
these the Governor should by public advertisement invite all the claimants
to file before 1st. Nover. next, with such county officers as he may designate, the nature & extent of their claim, together with a specification of the
original grant under which they claim and of the chain of title as derived to
the present claimants from that original grant. And the Governor should
transmit to the seat of Government by the time that Congress will meet,
the substance of the information thus obtained, and also whatever other on
that subject he may obtain. He should be particularly requested to state in
his communications to the Dept. of State, in what manner grants were
made and *completed* under both the British & Spanish Governments—this
information being essentially necessary in order to enable Congress at their
next session to pass a law carrying into effect that part of the compromise
& therein designating what shall be considered as a *completed* grant secured

by such compromise. His not being able to give a full statement of the extent of such claims should, by no means, induce him to delay that necessary information concerning their return.

The claims not secured by the compromise, but which may be satisfied by Congress, provided they shall do it at their next session, are 1st. those of the Yazoo companies, or speaking more generally those derived from Georgia subsequent to the Bourbon County act. Of these the Governor should be instructed to take no public notice whatever, as we will do it ourselves in our general advertisement; but he may be desired to communicate whether any steps have been taken by the Agents of those companies towards settling, selling or surveying any part of the land, & particularly whether any tract is now occupied by such claimants. 2dly. those derived under the French Government previous to the peace of 1763. 3dly. those derived under the British Govt. of West Florida or the Spanish Govt. before the treaty of 1795, but where a settlement did not exist on the day specified in the compromise. 4thly. those derived under the Spanish Government by grants made subsequent to the treaty of 1795. The claimants of the three last classes should be also invited to present their claims by 1st Nover. to the Governor that he may transmit the same to Government, and they should be particularly informed that, as their claims are not yet secured like those recognised by the compromise, it is essential, if they mean to avail themselves of the benefit accruing from the five millions of acres reservation, that their claims should be presented without delay. It is possible that the last class is the only one under which claims will be made; it is certainly the only one under which any considerable grants were issued. Although it is clear that they have no colourable foundation, yet policy may dictate a very liberal conduct towards the inhabitants of the Mississipi territory, and the advertisement of the Governor in relation to those claims (not secured by the compromise) should, without committing Government be so framed as not to convey an idea that they are considered as altogether groundless. For the same reason, it is necessary that the Governor should transmit early & full information of the nature & extent of those claims, of the number of persons who will be affected by a decision, and of the general expectations entertained on that subject in the Territory. It has struck me that in relation to that class of claims, which I know to have been a mere speculation carried on by Don Minor[4] & other individuals favorites of the Spanish Governors, a right of pre-emption would be sufficient.

Whilst the attention of the Governor is drawn towards those particular points, he may be desired generally to communicate all the information in his possession relative to the extent of the territory not claimed by the Indians—to the aggregate quantity of land covered by claims secured under the compromise with Georgia—to the aggregate quantity of land covered by any other claims whatever, those derived from Georgia only excepted—to the nature of claims to land in the territory of every description.

It will be necessary in order to give him a full view of the subject, that copies should be enclosed to him—of the section of the law which authorizes the Commissioners to enquire into individual claims—of the compromise with Georgia now binding on both parties⁵—and of the Bourbon County Act. This last you will find in the Georgia digest of laws & is no otherwise necessary than as the titles therein recognized are secured by the compromise. I do not recollect precisely its provisions, but think it includes some settlers whose claims might not be derived from Spain & may not have been completed, perhaps also those, if any such do exist, who had claims under the old French Government. It will be necessary for you to read the law before you write to the Governor, as you may thereby be better enabled to describe the several species of claims secured by the compromise.

I do not recollect any other thing material on the subject: only when requesting information from the Governor on the *nature* of the claims, he might be particularly desired to state whether there are any public records of the grants made, and in that case to transmit such extracts from these as may be necessary. Your's

ALBERT GALLATIN

P. S. As I contemplate two advertisements by the Governor, or an advertisement to two different descriptions of claimants, it may be necessary to designate with precision the distinction; and for want of the Bourbon County act, I cannot well do it. My idea is to describe those secured by the compromise, in the words of the compromise, substituting only to the general expressions of, "recognized by the Bourbon County act" the description of claims, recognized by that Act, which are not included within the other classes secured by the compromise—and, as to claims not secured by the compromise, to embrace them under the general words of "all other claims not derived from Georgia" intending to exclude by the word "other" those which are secured by the compromise & by those "derived from Georgia"—the Yazoo grants.

A. G.

RC (DLC). Docketed by JM.

1. JM and his family left Washington on or about 1 Aug. 1802 (see JM to Jefferson, 30 July and 11 Aug. 1802).
2. See JM to William C. C. Claiborne, 26 July 1802.
3. The 1785 act for laying out Bourbon County, Georgia, reserved land "by right of preference," in the absence of a land office, "to any, all, and any honest and friendly possessor and possessors of the said Lands" who were U.S. citizens or friendly aliens, provided "such persons do actually live on and cultivate the said lands" (Rowland, *Claiborne Letter Books*, 1:180).

4. For Stephen Minor, see Andrew Ellicott to JM, 29 Dec. 1801 (*PJM-SS*, 2:347, 349 n. 5).

5. See JM and others to Jefferson, 26 Apr. 1802, and n. 1.

§ **From William Bainbridge.** *21 July 1802, U.S. Frigate* Essex, *Quarantine Ground, Staten Island.* Informs JM that "Samuel Helsdon, an impressed American Seaman, was discharged at Gibraltar on the 14t. June last, from His Brittainick Majesty Ship Triumph; and returned to this place in the United States Frigate Essex under my command."

RC (DNA: RG 59, Records of Impressed Seamen, 1794–1815). 1 p.; docketed by Brent as received 25 July.

§ **From Joshua Carter.** *21 July 1802, Newburyport.* "Inclosed is a Commission recd. from you this day; and which I have taken the liberty to return, as it is not in my power to receive the appointment."

RC (DNA: RG 59, LAR, 1801–9, filed under "Carter"). 1 p.; docketed by Jefferson. Enclosure not found.

§ **From George W. Erving.** *21 July 1802, American Consulate, London.* Acknowledges receipt of his consular commission and returns his bond. Encloses his account as consul and as agent for the relief and protection of seamen from the time of Lenox's resignation to 30 June. The balance due him is £186 14s. 5½d. sterling. King refused his application for reimbursement of this amount on the grounds that "he has no longer any controul over our Funds enabling him to provide for the disbursements of this Agency." Bird, Savage, and Bird have also declined, "for the reason set forth in their letter, a Copy of which is inclosed." Also encloses his account to 30 June as agent for claims and appeals, with the amount due to the U.S. of £52 17s. 4d., and his spoliation account with Bird, Savage, and Bird. A bill for £175 will be debited to that account when paid. The proctors are uneasy about payment; his funds are, and will be, inadequate to satisfy them. Encloses a letter from Slade on this subject. The ratifications of the convention were exchanged on 15 July, "since when I have concluded to forward no more Processes to the *West Indies*; nor to extract any where there is not a prospect of receiving immediate payment; for the Expences of serving them are very considerable." The board is now "proceeding in their business with much more dispatch" than anticipated; will forward list of decisions when they begin to make awards. "I herewith also inclose a List of th⟨e⟩ Ships of which the Masters have reported to me on their arrival, and lament that it is . . . absolutely impossible to obtain such a Statement as is desired without some strong legal controul over the Masters."

RC and enclosures (DNA: RG 59, CD, London, vol. 8). RC 5 pp.; in a clerk's hand, signed by Erving; docketed by Brent as received 23 Sept. Surviving enclosures are copies of Robert Slade to Erving, 12 July 1802 (3 pp.), enclosing a copy of his 18 July 1801 letter to Samuel Williams (4 pp.) and complaining that his accounts as a proctor employed in prosecuting American appeals had never been settled; and Bird, Savage, and Bird to Erving, 16 July 1802

(2 pp.), stating that the bankers could not reimburse Erving for his accounts "without funds in hand thereto specially appropriated."

§ From Joshua Gilpin. *21 July 1802, Philadelphia.* Wishes to make a recommendation for the post of consul at Barcelona. "The recess of Congress prevents my addressing you thro the introduction of many of my friends who attend there." Refers JM to his uncle George Gilpin of Alexandria and his friends William Thornton and Dolley Madison for personal references. "The application I wish to make is, for Mr Joseph Teasdale, (now Mr Joseph Burn) having within a short time past changed his name by Act of Parliament in order to inherit an estate in England of which he is a native." Teasdale, a young man about twenty-seven years old, "has long resided at Barcelona & has conducted business there with uncommon propriety, especially American business, of which he has transacted more than any other house during the War: he has resided in Spain as an American Citizen which I beleive he is entitled to, but I am ignorant whether by residing in the United States or no." Suggests that Teasdale's services would be valuable "in a city remote as Barcelona, where few reside who possess such a knowledge of American manners, & its language."

RC (DNA: RG 59, LAR, 1801–9, filed under "Teasdale"). 3 pp. Joshua Gilpin (1765–1841) was a director of the Chesapeake and Delaware Canal Company, 1803–24, and a member of the American Philosophical Society (Van Horne, *Papers of Benjamin Henry Latrobe*, 1:319 n. 1). George Gilpin (1740–1813) was an Alexandria merchant and active member of the Potomac Company (Jackson and Twohig, *Diaries of George Washington*, 4:141).

§ From Rufus King. *21 July 1802, London.* Explains an item in his contingent account relating to the publication of Robinson's admiralty reports.[1] Decisions of British prize courts are not published by the government. Observes that although it is a "pretty general opinion" that Great Britain "administers the Law of Nations in matters of prize with great rigour, Englishmen have uniformly asserted that these Tribunals have manifested greater moderation" than those of any other nation. When Sir William Scott[2] was appointed judge of the High Court of Admiralty, King persuaded the government to allow the admiralty cases to be reported and published so as to end this "Disagreement." Believed that publication would give "this important branch of public Law, a fixed character in place of the uncertain and contentious Reputation it has hitherto possessed." Since anticipated demand was not sufficient to defray expense, he subscribed for fifty copies; has sent them to the State Department, except for a few copies he distributed to U.S. ministers in Europe. Hopes with this explanation the expense will meet the president's approval. Expects an appendix to be published containing examples of all documents used in the prize courts.

RC (DNA: RG 59, DD, Great Britain, vol. 10); letterbook copy (NHi: Rufus King Papers, vol. 55). RC 4 pp.; marked private; in a clerk's hand, signed by King; docketed by Brent as received 23 Sept. Printed in King, *Life and Correspondence of Rufus King*, 4:150–51.

1. Sir Christopher Robinson, *Reports of Cases Argued and Determined in the High Court of Admiralty* (6 vols.; London, 1799–1808).

2. Sir William Scott (1745–1836) was judge of the High Court of Admiralty from 1798 to 1828. His decisions, such as in the cases of *Immanuel* (1799) and *Polly* (1800), which established rules of conduct for neutral trade, profoundly affected American commerce and formed the basis for a code of maritime law (R. G. Thorne, ed., *The History of Parliament: The Commons, 1790–1820* [5 vols.; London, 1986], 5:113–15; Bradford Perkins, "Sir William Scott and the *Essex*," *WMQ*, 3d ser., 13 [1956]: 169–83).

To Albert Gallatin

DEAR SIR   WASHINGTON July 22. 1802

It has been concluded by the Secy. of the Navy that the public ship the General Greene, can be advantageously sent with the provisions intended for the squadron in the Mediterranean, and the gun carriages promised to the Emperor of Morocco. I have proposed to the President by a letter of this date that 30,000. dollars be tendered, by this opportunity, to the Dey of Algiers, who will be entitled on the fifth of Sepr. to an annual remittance of tribute. Should the President sanction the measure, he will let you know it.[1] In the mean time you will be so good as to take preparatory steps for having the money delivered according to the order of the Secy. of the Navy. The ship will sail in about 20 days from this place, & will take on the provisions at Norfolk. The money therefore may be delivered either here or at Norfolk as may be most convenient. If equally convenient at this place, it will perhaps be preferable. On this subject you will of course correspond with the Secy. of the Navy.

The President left us yesterday for Monticello. It will be 5 or 6 days before I follow him. Yrs. respectfully & affey.

JAMES MADISON

RC (NHi: Gallatin Papers). Addressed by JM to Gallatin in New York.

1. Jefferson directed Gallatin to "take such measures as may be necessary, in conjunction with the Secretary of State, for remitting that sum to Algiers" (Jefferson to Gallatin, 28 July 1802 [ibid.]).

To Thomas Jefferson

DEAR SIR   WASHINGTON July 22. 1802

On consultation with the Secretary of the Navy, it has been concluded that the public service will be favored by sending the ship the General Greene, with the provisions & gun-carriages destined for the Mediterranean, instead of chartering a private vessel for the occasion. It has occurred also that as the period at which an annual remittance to Algiers will become due, will arrive before the ship will get to that place, it may be found proper that another thirty thousand dollars should be sent as an experimental measure for avoiding the stipulated & expensive tribute of Stores. Should the substitute be accepted, it will be a saving to the U. States. Should it be rejected, time will be gained for the other remittance. I have written to Mr. Gallatin on the subject, and requested him to make preparation for having the money ready in case your approbation should be signified to him. You will recollect no doubt that if a letter from you to the Emperor of Morocco, should be decided on, as a companion to the Gun carriages, it must be forwarded in time for the sailing of the Ship. May I ask the favor of you to leave it open for the perusal of Mr. Sampson, that it may serve as an explanation & instruction to him in the case. The ship will probably sail from this place in about 20 days from this date.

I observe in the papers that one of the Commissrs. of Bankruptcy for Philada. has been taken off by the fever.[1] I have not heard lately from Mr. Wagner, but think it not improbable that the vacancy will attract the attention of himself & his friends, and that it may be properly bestowed on him, if no particular claim to it be in the way. With the most respectful attachment I remain Dr. Sir Yrs.

JAMES MADISON

RC (DLC: Jefferson Papers). Docketed by Jefferson as received 25 July.

1. The death notice of John Vancleve was printed in the Philadelphia *Aurora General Advertiser*, 20 July 1802.

From Jacob Wagner

DEAR SIR   PHILADA. 22 July 1802

A relapse of my complaint prevented me from sooner rendering my best thanks for the favor of your last[1] and expressing my sensibility at the obliging expressions it contains.

The habits I have contracted by a long employment in the Department of State and the additional attachment produced by the personal qualities of its head, made my retirement a painful event to myself: and could I anticipate such a stability of health, arriving within a reasonable time, as would enable me to resume my functions, I would not hesitate to promise a return. I flatter myself however that I shall have it in my power to visit the City of Washington at the meeting of Congress, and to render some assistance to my former colleagues in the pressure of business it will occasion. In the mean time I cannot expect my salary to continue while I am not performing the duties it requires.[2] With the highest respect & esteem I have the honor to remain, Dr sir, Your most obed. servt.

JACOB WAGNER

RC (DLC). Docketed by JM.

1. Letter not found.
2. The account listing salaries paid to State Department personnel for the quarter ending 30 Sept. 1802, dated 8 Oct. 1802, shows no payment to Wagner for the period (DNA: RG 217, First Auditor's Accounts, no. 13,827).

§ From Samuel Brown. *22 July 1802, Boston.* Has received JM's letter of 12 July [not found] with appointment as commissioner of bankruptcy for the district of Massachusetts but declines, "as the attention to be given to my existing engagements does not admit of my devoting the portion of time which appears to be requisite."

RC (DNA: RG 59, LRD, 1789–1827, filed under "Brown"). 1 p.; docketed by Brent as received 31 July.

§ From Jacob Crowninshield. *22 July 1802, Salem.* Acknowledges JM's letter of 12 July [not found] enclosing a commission for him as a commissioner of bankruptcy for the district of Massachusetts. Regrets he cannot accept the office owing to pressing commercial business that would make it "*extremely inconvenient.*"

RC (DNA: RG 59, LAR, 1801–9, filed under "Crowninshield"). 1 p.; docketed by Jefferson.

§ From William Lee. *22 July 1802, Bordeaux.* Reports that since his last dispatch he has been "obliged to leave the Consulate for six weeks owing to the failure of John Fry Junr. of London with whom the House of Perrot & Lee were closely connected." Hopes "the necessity of the case" will excuse his absence. Calls JM's attention again to the distressing situation of American seamen at Bordeaux. For the last three months there have been over two hundred American sailors in his care; he has "supplied about Eighty of them every day with bread and 'soupe economique.'" Had hoped to escape "being harassed by these though[t]less beings" by requiring every American ship that sails to the U.S. to take two sailors for every hundred tons of weight; "still from the many Vessels which are sold and by the great number of Men who collect here from Havre, Nantz, and all parts of France and Spain (for they even cross from the Mediterranean) the Office is continually surrounded with them." Encloses a letter from the Bordeaux commissary of police on the subject [not found]. Refers to the enclosed semiannual return of ships from 1 Jan. to 30 June [not found] for a "more striking point of view [of] the situation of our Seamen here." The figures show 399 sailors at Bordeaux who are "totally destitute of employment and without the means of subsistence." Urges legislation to prevent owners and masters of vessels from discharging crews in foreign ports. "Almost every Sailor will consent to be discharged if the Captain will give him four or five dollars to spend on shore." Has ordered that ship captains not discharge their men without his consent. "Most of the Masters (particularly those from New England) . . . discharge their Men just when they please, always taking care to get a receipt of the sailors, who from ill treatment, & confinement on board, while in port, & short allowance is willing to do any thing to get clear of his opressors." Encloses a list of seventy-one sick and distressed seamen sent in the ship *Jefferson*, Captain Gross, to Baltimore [not found], for whom he put all needed provisions on board; an account of his disbursements for the voyage is also enclosed.[1] "I should feel very thankful for a line from you on the subject of present and future advances. I have convers'd with Mr. Livingston on the business but he declines giving me any instructions." Notes that many vessels arrive without bills of health, despite the Treasury Department circular of July 1801. Has received his commission. Encloses a copy of a letter from Charles Pinckney.[2]

RC and enclosures (DNA: RG 59, CD, Bordeaux, vol. 1). RC 6 pp.; docketed by Brent as received 16 Oct. For surviving enclosures, see nn.

1. An account listing goods Lee supplied to the *Jefferson* for the voyage, totaling Fr 7,447.24, is dated 20 July 1802 (1 p.; in French).
2. The letter from Pinckney to Lee, dated 10 July 1802 (1 p.), is a circular informing the latter of the declaration of war on the U.S. by the emperor of Morocco.

§ From Littleton Waller Tazewell. *22 July 1802, Norfolk.* Has received JM's letter of 12 July [not found] enclosing a commission to act as a commissioner of bankruptcy for the district of Virginia. Declines the appointment "because the duties which it woud impose, I consider as incompatible with other avocations more important to myself."

RC (DNA: RG 59, LRD, 1789–1827, filed under "Tazewell"). 1 p.; in a clerk's hand, signed by Tazewell. Docketed by Brent as received 24 July.

§ From Anthony Terry. *22 July 1802, Cadiz.* Reports that Yznardy arrived from Philadelphia on 20 July. "The Quaranteen to which American Vessels [are] here subjected & which Mr: Yznardy is now performing, imposes on me the unwelcome Duty of informing you of the Capture of the Brig Franklin of Philadelphia by a Tripolitan Corsair: the particulars . . . are contained in the inclosed Copy of a Letter from Mr: J: Gavino.[1] . . . Permit me Sir, to suggest that according to the prevailing Opinion amongst the well informed here, the protection of our Commerce against the Ravages of these Pirates would be more efficaciously accomplished by light Brigs well mann'd & armed than by larger Vessels, which from their to great Draught of Water are incapable of approaching the Coasts within a sufficient degree of proximity." Reports that the royal wedding of the prince of Asturias to the princess of Sicily, daughter of the king of Naples, and that of the prince of Naples and a Spanish infanta, will take place at Barcelona late in September. The court, foreign diplomats, and others, numbering about twelve thousand people, will leave Madrid on 12 Aug. "Vast preparations are makeing & an enormous expence will be incurred in this Celebration, while the long accumulating Arrearag⟨es⟩ of the Navy are to remain unpaid."

RC and enclosure (DNA: RG 59, CD, Cadiz, vol. 1). RC 3 pp.; docketed by Brent as received 3 Oct.

1. Gavino's letter to Terry, 12 July 1802 (1 p.), reported the capture of the *Franklin* and added that "probably one of our State Ships will shortly call off your Port in order that our trade may come out & go some distance with safety."

To Rufus King

SIR,   DEPARTMENT OF STATE July 23d. 1802

Your three letters of May 3, 5 & 7 have been duly received.

On the subject of the first, to wit, the refusal of Byrd, Savage and Byrd to make an advance on your requisition in favour of Mr Lenox, I find on conferring with the Secretary of the Treasury, that the rule laid down by that Department for limitting their disbursements, has been misunderstood. The rule was not meant to interfere with the usual course of advances made with your sanction. Mr. Gallatin will write to Byrd, Savage and Byrd, if he has not already written, in order to rectify their misconstruction of his former letter on this subject.[1]

The bill imposing a greater duty on British exports to America, than on like exports to other places, which is the subject of your letter of the 5th May, is regarded by the President in the same light in which your comments place it. It is impossible indeed not to see in it an infraction of the Treaty of 1794, which expressly prohibits such discriminations against the United States;[2] and it may be fairly expected from the good sense and good faith of the British Government that the just and strong ground of complaint given by this regulation, will be removed on the earliest opportunity that can be found. This unjustifiable step, is the more remarkable, as it is so much at variance with the spirit of the British Government towards this Country, manifested in other instances; as it is so evidently and so utterly destitute of the plea for the convoy-discrimination, of which it is to take the place; and as it departs so widely from the ordinary policy of that Government, which systematically invites instead of taxing the demand of distant markets. The only explanation that can be given of this experiment is, that it is tempted by a peculiar incapacity ascribed to this Country, of rivalling the manufactures of Great Britain, and by the supposed security with which she may therefore levy an extra tribute on our consumption. But besides the restraint which good faith imposes on the attempt in the present case, the British Government is too enlightened not to perceive on reflection, that every duty which it imposes on her exports to the United States, is a bounty on the exertions of her manufacturing rivals; and co-operates with our own duties on her manufactures and with the charges incident to the distance between the two Countries, in stimulating the progress of this branch of industry in the United States. And altho for reasons sufficiently obvious, our demand of British manufactures is not likely to be superseded, or in an absolute sense, may not be lessened by moderate impositions of this sort; yet it is certain that their effect in stimulating american manufacturers, and, in the same proportion checking the growth of demand for British, must outweigh the advantage accruing to her Treasury. It will only be added that it deserves the serious consideration of the British Government, also how far so naked an effort to draw revenue from American pockets into her own Treasury may add the force of resentment and indignation to other motives for lessening the dependence of our consumption on a country disposed to make such a use of it.

The subject of your letter of May 7th namely your correspondence with Lord Hawkesbury on the Cession of Louisiana and the Floridas, to France, will receive from the President all the consideration which its great importance demands; and as soon as an answer can be founded on the result of his reflections, no time will be lost in transmitting it. With very great respect and consideration &c &c &c.

JAMES MADISON

Letterbook copy (DNA: RG 59, IM, vol. 6). RC offered for sale in Stan. V. Henkels Catalogue No. 1290 (1921), item 315. A typescript of the RC supplied in 1959 by James G. King of New York City indicates that it is docketed as received 13 Sept.

1. See the extract of Gallatin to Bird, Savage, and Bird, 6 July 1802, in *Papers of Gallatin* (microfilm ed.), reel 7.

2. Article 15 of the Jay treaty states that "no other or higher Duties shall be paid by the Ships or Merchandize of the one Party in the Ports of the other, than such as are paid by the like vessels or Merchandize of all other Nations" (Miller, *Treaties*, 2:257).

To Rufus King

SIR,   DEPARTMENT OF STATE July 23d 1802

The enclosed letter of Jacob Peterson of the American armed ship Asia[1] and copy of the Protest of Peter Sutter chief Officer thereof,[2] on the subject of an affair in January 1802 between the Asia and the British ship Walker of London, John Nichols, Master, are forwarded to you for the double purpose of enabling you to give any explanations which may be proper, and of leading you to aid in obtaining any redress which may be justly sought, in the case. With very great respect & consideration, I have the honor to be Sir Your Obt Set.

JAMES MADISON

RC and enclosures (DNA: RG 76, British Spoliations, 1794–1824, Ship "Asia"); letter-book copy (DNA: RG 59, IM, vol. 6). The RC is a letterpress copy marked "(Duplicate)"; in a clerk's hand, signed by JM; docketed as received 23 Sept., with a penciled notation, "Nothing done by Mr. G." Letterbook copy dated 26 July. Another copy dated 23 July, probably the original RC, was offered for sale in Parke-Bernet Catalogue No. 1064 (3 May 1949), item 338. A typescript of the RC supplied in 1959 by James G. King of New York City indicates that the RC is docketed as received 13 Sept. For the enclosures, see nn. 1 and 2. The "Asia" file also includes letterpress copies of transcripts of the enclosures.

1. Jacob Peterson to JM, 13 Apr. 1802.
2. For Peter Sutter's affidavit, see John Elmslie, Jr., to JM, 29 Mar. 1802, and n. 1.

From Albert Gallatin

(Private)
DEAR SIR   NEW YORK 23d July 1802

I received yesterday six blank commissions for offices of collector &a.[1] But one has been omitted; the Collector of Marblehead should also be commissioned as inspector of the revenue for that port. The President should also have left a commission of collector for Massac in lieu of W. Chribs whose character is infamous.[2] If he is yet in town, will you be good enough to apply for those Commissions, and if he is already gone, to have them prepared and sent to him for his signature. The collector of Massac must also receive a commission as inspector of the revenue for that port. Please to let me know the day when the President left Washington, as from that day the commissions must bear date. Do you know whether Henry Warren the intended collector of Marblehead, and W. Lyman intended for Newbury port will accept, whether they will be ready to go and take possession of their offices at once (for they do not reside at the places where these are kept) and what is the place of their residence? Gen. Dearborn might write to them; otherwise they may not be ready to go and take possession, and their predecessors may refuse to act. Do you also understand whether Mr Page is ready to go to Petersburg. Your's

ALBERT GALLATIN

RC (DLC). Docketed by JM.

1. See Memorandum from Thomas Jefferson, 19 July 1802.

2. Jefferson appointed William Chribbs collector and inspector of the port of Fort Massac, Indiana Territory, during the congressional recess of 1801. Formally nominated and approved by the Senate in January 1802, Chribbs was replaced by Daniel Bissell, whose appointment was approved in January 1803 (*Senate Exec. Proceedings*, 1:401, 405, 433, 437; Gallatin to Jefferson, 6 July 1802, *Papers of Gallatin* [microfilm ed.], reel 7).

From Robert Smith

SIR   BALTO. July 23. 1802

I have received from a friend intimations which induce me to think that the son of G. Christie is not qualified for the appointment of Consul.[1] This may be a subject of some delicacy. But to such unpleasant situations we are frequently exposed. With great Esteem I am sir, Y st.

RT SMITH

RC (DNA: RG 59, LAR, 1801–9, filed under "Christie"). Docketed by Jefferson.

1. For Gabriel Christie's efforts to obtain a position for his son in the consular service, see his letters to JM of 20 Mar. and 14 Apr. 1802.

§ From Anthony Terry. *23 July 1802, Cadiz.* "I had the honor of writing you yesterday and the Vessel being still detain'd I have now to inclose you Copy of a letter I have just received from Mr. Wm. Kirkpatrick our Consul at Malaga."[1]

RC and enclosure (DNA: RG 59, CD, Cadiz, vol. 1). RC 1 p.; in a clerk's hand, signed by Terry.

1. Terry enclosed a copy of a circular letter from Richard O'Brien to William Kirkpatrick, 30 June 1802 (1 p.; docketed by Brent as enclosed in Terry's 23 July letter), announcing the capture of the American brig *Franklin*.

To Louis-André Pichon

SIR   DEPARTMENT OF STATE July 24. 1802.

The Newspaper herewith inclosed contains a translation of an instruction from the Minister of Marine in France to a maratime prefect,[1] in which if the translation be correct, the Minister has fallen inadvertently into a mistatement of the tenor of a regulation within the United States concerning certificates of health. The error lies in transposing the collectors and naval officers, as you will observe on a comparison of the latter [*sic*] of the Minister of Marine with the printed copy also inclosed of the regulation as communicated by the Treasury Department to the collectors of the customs.[2] Will you be so obliging Sir, in case you have a French copy of the letter of the Minister to inform me whether the error lies in the letter itself or in the translation; and in case of its lying in the former, to aid in guarding agai[n]st its effects, by whatever interposition you may deem requisite. Accept assurances &ca

JAMES MADISON.

Letterbook copy (DNA: RG 59, DL, vol. 14). Enclosures not found, but see nn.

1. Denis Decrès to Auguste Bergevin, maritime prefect at Rochefort, 23 Pluviôse an X (12 Feb. 1802) (Philadelphia *Gazette of the U.S.*, 7 July 1802).

2. Gallatin's 1801 circular to collectors of customs stipulated that the certificates of health issued to U.S. vessels be signed by the collector at the port of embarkation and countersigned by the naval officer, except for those ports without the latter, where "the bill of health can only be certified by the Collector" (see Gallatin to JM, 22 July 1801, *PJM-SS*, 1:453–54 and n. 1). In Decrès's letter to the maritime prefects, he transposed collectors and naval officers, leaving the impression that there was a naval officer in every port and that all bills of health must be signed by one of them.

To John Steele

DEAR SIR   July 24. 1802

I inclose a paper* in which you will find a translation of the Document referred to in Mr. Mclane's letter to you. If the translation be correct, the French Commissary of Marine, has inadvertently transposed the Collectors & naval officers. The error can scarcely have failed to excite the attention of the American functionaries in France, and to have been rectified on their interposition. It may notwithstanding be well to ask of Mr. Pichon whatever information he can give on the subject, and such interposition on his part as may aid in preventing consequences of the error. For these purposes I will drop him a line without delay.[1] With great respect & esteem I am Yrs.

JAMES MADISON

*instead of inclosing the paper I beg leave to refer you to the Gazette of the U. S. July 13. 1802.[2]

RC (Nc-Ar: Steele Papers).

1. See JM to Pichon, 24 July 1802, and nn.

2. The items referred to were printed in the *Gazette of the U.S.* on 7 July 1802.

From Nathan Dane

SIR   BEVERLY July 24. 1802

The inclosed commission and letter have Just been handed to me—
which I return to you. I doubt if [I] am the person intended. And if I am,
such a commission could not induce me to change a resolution not to accept any appointment. Your obedient servant

NATHAN DANE[1]

To Mr. Madison—*private.*

I am exceedingly sorry you and the presidt. have been so misinformed as to
one or two of the characters on the list—party politics out of the question
they are Justly considered fitter subjects of guardianship than of appointments—whatever may be the present state of politics good men can have
but one object—and that is the union, prosperity, and respectability of a
common country.

RC (DNA: RG 59, LAR, 1801–9, filed under "Dane"). Docketed by Jefferson. Enclosures
not found.

1. Nathan Dane (1752–1835), a lawyer and former Continental congressman (1785–88)
who attended the Hartford Convention in 1814, refused the office of commissioner of bankruptcy (Fischer, *Revolution of American Conservatism*, pp. 247–48).

From Charles Pinckney

DEAR SIR   MADRID 24th July 1802

Some time since I received a Letter from Thos. Clifton, praying that I
would take measures to release him from confinement in Coruña, where he
had been detained a Prisoner, by the Orders of Mr Robert Montgomery of
Alicante. In consequence of this Letter I wrote to Mr Montgomery to give
me a statement of the transaction. I annex his answer, as also Cliftons account of the Affair, thinking it the best means I have, of laying this Case
before you, on which I ask your Instructions.[1]

I do not find that the Laws of the United States make any provision for
it, I therefore do not feel myself at Liberty to proceed, without your advice,
more particularly as it involves private Rights, and as the measures adopted
now, may hereafter be drawn into precedent, on similar occasions. It is to
be lamented that this poor man should be detained so long without a trial;
but I do not feel myself authorized to bring him to a trial in Spain, and I
was fearful if I sent him Home in a Merchant Vessel, he might make his
Escape, and avoid that punishment which ought to be inflicted on him, if
he is guilty of Barratry.

The Letters annexed to this contain all the material information, I have been able to collect on this Subject, excepting that Mr Montgomery has withdrawn the support hitherto allowed by him to Clifton, and of consequence until your directions are received, he will be maintained at the expence of the United States. With great respect & regard I am dear sir Yours Truly

CHARLES PINCKNEY

RC and enclosures (DNA: RG 59, DD, Spain, vol. 6). RC in a clerk's hand, except for Pinckney's complimentary close and signature. Enclosures 7 pp.; docketed by Brent (see n. 1).

1. Pinckney enclosed copies of two letters to him from Montgomery. The first letter, dated 27 Apr. 1802, described Clifton as "a fellow running off with a ship & cargo" entrusted to him by Montgomery on behalf of the owners, Loving and Curtis of Boston; Clifton "was first apprehended by our friend Barnet at Bordeaux, having transformed the American ship into a Swedish brig, but escaped from thence as he did afterwards from San Sebastian, & was finally detained, where he now is." Montgomery "declined bringing him to Trial in Spain, where, if prosecuted, he must be hanged, . . . nor do I think myself at liberty to let him have his liberty. . . . Now that you are induced to take notice of the business, I leave him with much pleasure at your disposal." Montgomery added that the stolen ship and cargo were worth $19,000, "of which nothing has been regained but the empty vessel in very bad condition," and he suggested that Clifton might "buy himself from the Gallows" by making restitution to the owners. The second letter from Montgomery to Pinckney, 11 June 1802, covered a letter from Clifton to Pinckney of 15 May 1802. In it Clifton maintained his innocence in the affair, claiming that a series of accidents and misfortunes had led to the allegedly criminal acts. JM passed the matter on to Attorney General Levi Lincoln, who decided that "the authority of the general government to take, forcibly detain in custody, and bring to this country, from Europe, a person charged with barratry on private property" was doubtful, and "the controversy" appeared to be of a "civil nature, between private persons; and, like all such cases, to be left to their own course, on the ordinary principles of law" (Lincoln to JM, 29 Oct. 1802, Hall, *Official Opinions of the Attorneys General*, 1:123–24).

§ From Elias Vander Horst. *24 July 1802, Bristol.* Transmits a copy of his letter of 13 July. Despite cold, wet weather, reports of approaching harvest are "not unfavorable." "You will no doubt before this can reach you have heard that the Emperor of Morocco has compelled Mr. Simpson the American Consul, to quit his dominions & declared War against the United States." Forwards a letter from Rufus King and encloses newspapers and a London price current.

RC (DNA: RG 59, CD, Bristol, vol. 2). 1 p. Enclosures not found.

To John Steele

DR SIR   [ca. 25 July 1802]
Mr. Fairfax[1] who waits on you wishes to know whether the Treasury Dept. is [in] want of bills on London. He will himself explain an offer he

will in that case make. In the absence of Mr. Gallatin,[2] I have taken the liberty of referring him to you for information. Yrs very respectfully

JAMES MADISON

RC (Nc-Ar: Steele Papers). Undated. Conjectural date supplied here on the basis of circumstances described in n. 2.

 1. His Republican leanings and prior correspondence with JM make it probable that this was Ferdinand Fairfax (see *PJM-SS*, 1:308–9 and n. 3).
 2. Steele's departure on 5 Aug. and his subsequent resignation places the date of this letter sometime during Gallatin's absence from Washington between 17 July and 1 Aug. 1802 (Gallatin to Jonathan Burrall, 17 July 1802, and Gallatin to Jefferson, 9 Aug. 1802 [DLC: Gallatin Papers]; Steele to Oliver Wolcott, 5 Aug. 1802, Wagstaff, *Papers of John Steele*, 1:307).

§ From Sylvanus Bourne. *25 July 1802, Amsterdam.* "This will serve to inclose the two latest Leyden Gazettes & to confirm my decision of embarking in course of 10 days for the U States with Mrs B. . . . Craving the kind indulgence of Govt. for my absence I shall endeavour to make it as short as possible while in the interim I have made every proper arrangment for the affairs of the Consulate."

RC (DNA: RG 59, CD, Amsterdam, vol. 1). 1 p.

§ From John Elmslie, Jr. *25 July 1802, Cape Town, Cape of Good Hope.* Encloses a duplicate of Asa Bordwell's note, the original of which was enclosed in his 29 Mar. dispatch. Also encloses lists of American ships that entered the ports of the Cape of Good Hope between December 1801 and June 1802. "I have had frequently to observe to Government the remissness of many Masters of Vessels in not ⟨c⟩alling on their arrival to report their Vessels, as well as in departing from the Ports without notifying the same; A late Case in which Captn. Tibbetts of the Merchant Ship Hazard from New York bound to the Cape who was entrusted with Duplicate of Papers from the Owners of the Pacific to Claim the Cargo of that Ship and for want of which the Cargo has been Condemn'd in the Cape Vice Admiralty Court of which I advised Govermt. in March last. Captn. Tibbetts arrived here in Septr. last, but neither Call'd to report his Vessel nor deliver'd any papers; The Consequence of which I am afraid will be the loss of large property to the Owners of the Pacific." These difficulties would be avoided if ship captains were required, under penalty of law, to report to consuls and not to depart without a consular certificate.

RC (DNA: RG 59, CD, Cape Town, vol. 1). 2 pp. Enclosures not found.

To William C. C. Claiborne

SIR   DEPARTMENT OF STATE July 26. 1802.

 Herewith inclosed is a copy of the agreement entered into on the 24. April last between the Commissioners on the part of the United States

425

and those on the part of Georgia, duly authorized for that purpose, which agreement was ratified by the Legislature of that state on the 16. of June last.[1]

According to the Act of Congress of May 10. 1800 The commissioners of the U. States authorized to settle the terms of a compromise with the State of Georgia, are further authorized to enquire into the claims which are or shall be made by settlers or any other persons whatever, to any part of the lands in question, and to receive from the claimants propositions of compromise and lay a full statement of the claims and propositions, together with the opinion of the commissioners thereon, before congress for their decision.[2]

Of the claims to be made, a part is defined and recognized in the 2d. article of the agreement, under the kind[3] of grants legally executed to actual settlers within the territory ceded to the U. States prior to the 27. octr. 1795. by the former British Government of West Florida, or by the Government of Spain, and under the head of claims derived from any actual survey or settlement made under the law of Georgia passed February 7. 1785. entitled "An Act for laying out a district situate on the river Mississippi, and within the bounds of the State into a county to be called Bourbon." An extract from this Act is also herewith inclosed.[4]

To enable the commissioners to make the proper report to Congress on this part of the subject, you are requested to furnish them with the best information you can obtain, first with respect to the extent of territory both on the Mississippi and the Mobille, which has been relinquished by the Indians, secondly with respect to the claims recognized by the 2d. Article of the agreement with Georgia. To make this last information as accurate and full as possible, it may be well to invite the claimants by public advertisement to file prior to the 1st. of November before the proper County officers, the particular authority and extent of their respective claims and the chain of title derived to the present claimants from the original title.[5] The Commissioners hope that you will be able to state to them particularly the manner in which grants were made and *compleated* under both the British and Spanish Governments, this information being necessary for the use of Congress in carrying the 2d. Article of the agreement into due effect. Should it be found impossible to render the information on these points compleat, you will notwithstanding be pleased to forward the best you can collect.

The other claims to be enquired into, and which tho' not recognized fall within the report to be made to Congress, are first and principally such as are grounded on alledged grants of Georgia subsequent to the Bourbon County Act. With respect to these claims, it is not desired that you should make any public call for information; but you will oblige the commissioners by enquiring and communicating what or whether any steps have been taken in behalf of the claiming companies towards settling selling out, or surveying, any part of the land; and particularly whether any tract is now actually occupied by any of their claimants: secondly claims if any, derived under the French Government previous to the peace of 1763. Thirdly claims derived under the British and spanish Governments previous to the Treaty of 1795; but unaccompanied by actual settlement at the date of the Treaty. Fourthly claims derived under the Spanish Government by grants made subsequent to the Spanish Treaty of 1795. fifthly claims founded on the 3d. section of the Bourbon County act of Georgia, the four last descriptions of claimants may also be publickly invited to give in the state of their respective claims, by the 1st. of November that they may be transmitted by you in due time with the others. It is proper that the claimants in their cases should be aware, that their claims not being included in the guaranty of the 2d. article of the compromise with Georgia, the consideration of them by Congress will be barred by the 3d. article, after the period of one year from the assent of Georgia to the instrument of compromise.

In calling for the information wished from the claimants not included in the guaranty, it will occur to you as proper to use a language neither committing the Government on one hand, nor dampling [*sic*] expectations too much on the other. It being uncertain what degree of strictness or liberality may be exercised by Congress, the present measure must be limited to the collection of such information as may enlighten or influence their decision. With this view, you cannot be too particular in explaining the nature and extent of the several classes of claims; to which may be added the number of persons who will be affected by the decision on each class; It may be satisfactory also to know, the general sentiments and expectations prevailing in the territory on this subject.

Should there be claims of any sort within the Territory which escaped the above enumerations, you will oblige the commissioners by adding a particular account of them: as well as by communicating your estimates of the General extent of Territory not claimed by the Indians of the aggregate quantity of land covered by claims under the 2d. article of the compromise, and of the like aggregate, of all other claims.

It need not be suggested to you that where records of claims exist, suitable extracts from them will [be] proper: nor that it will be expedient to compleat and transmit your communications with as little delay as possible.

It only remains for me to ask your excuse for the heavy task which is imposed on you, and to assure you of the great respect and esteem, with which I have the honor to be &ca.

JAMES MADISON.

Letterbook copy (DNA: RG 59, DL, vol. 14); Tr (Ms-Ar: Claiborne Executive Journal). Enclosures not found, but see nn. 1 and 4.

1. The "Articles of Agreement and Cession" are printed in *ASP, Public Lands*, 1 : 125–26.

2. JM was referring to section 10 of "An Act supplemental to the act intituled "'An act for an amicable settlement of limits with the State of Georgia; and authorizing the establishment of a Government in the Mississippi territory'" (*U.S. Statutes at Large*, 2 : 70).

3. Tr reads "head."

4. For the Bourbon County act, see Gallatin to JM, 21 July 1802, and n. 3.

5. Claiborne published a handbill to this effect on 9 Sept. 1802 (Rowland, *Claiborne Letter Books*, 1 : 177–80; Claiborne to JM, 12 Sept. 1802).

To Charles Pinckney

SIR,   DEPARTMENT OF STATE July 26th 1802

Your several letters now to be acknowledged are of March 20th. April 6 and April 20.

The President has learnt with much satisfaction the readiness manifested by the Spanish Government to concur in establishing a Board for deciding on the indemnifications claimed by our citizens. My letter of Feby. 5th suggested an improvement in the definition of the powers of the Board, of which I hope you will not lose sight.[1] As that letter is not acknowledged in any yet received, from you, a copy of it is now inclosed.

The last information from Paris renders it certain that the Cession of Louisiana to France has actually been concluded, and that the Cession comprehends the two Floridas. In this state of the business it seems unnecessary to decide on the price which Spain might be led to expect, for a cession of the Floridas including New Orleans to the United States; and the more so as it would be of use for us previously to know the value she places on the guaranty proposed in my letter to you of 25th of September last.[2] For the present the Cession wished by the United States, must be an object of negotiation with the French Government. It will notwithstanding continue to be proper for you to cultivate the good dispositions of Spain in relation to it, both as they may not be entirely disregarded by France, and as in the turn of events, Spain may possibly be extricated from her engagements to France, and again have the disposal of the Territories in question.

The repugnance of the Spanish Government to the residence of an American Consul at New Orleans is to be regretted. It may be hoped however when the special grounds on which it may be rightly claimed by the United States, and safely yielded by Spain without infringing the general principle of her Colonial policy on this point, are more fully explained in the second representation proposed by you, that a more favourable determination will take place.

The complaint against Capt. Mallowny communicated in your letter of

April 6 has been long since brought to the attention of the executive by the Spanish Minister here. On recurring to your instructions of June 9th 1801 you will find the subject noticed, and the proper assurances to the Spanish Government with respect to it, authorized and explained.[3] I have now only to add, that the regular steps have been taken for enquiring into the allegations against him, and doing whatever right shall be found to demand.

As a supplement to the case of Joseph Dunlap and others forwarded in My letter of May 10th, I inclose a copy of a letter from Mr Ross, a Senator of the United States from Pennsylvania, with certain documents accompanying it, in support of the claim of the injured parties, on the Spanish Government, to all which I rely on your giving the due attention.

I inclose also a copy of a letter from James L. Cathcart Consul at Tripoli, which explains the nature and amount of a claim on the Spanish Government in behalf of the United States, which has long been postponed, but which appears to be so just and so clear that there can be little doubt of its being immediately admitted and satisfied.

You already know that W. Willis the Consul for Barcelona, suddenly withdrew from that place last year. That and other circumstances have made it a proper subject of consideration whether his Commission should be revoked or continued. The President wishes you to enquire into his conduct and character, and to forward the best information with respect to both that you can procure.

I did not fail to lay before the President your wish to have his permission to make an excursion into Italy, from Barcelona, whither the Court is to proceed in the Month of September. I need not assure you of his disposition to afford every indulgence in such cases which a due attention to the public service will allow. Of this condition you can under existing circumstances best judge yourself. To yourself therefore he leaves the decision; not doubting that it will be made under the due influence of every public consideration. With the highest respect and consideration &c. &c. &c

JAMES MADISON

Letterbook copy (DNA: RG 59, IM, vol. 6). Enclosures not found.

1. In his letter of 5 Feb. 1802, JM had reminded Pinckney that U.S. claims against Spain should not be restricted to captures but should include "injuries received from the officers of Spain in attaching [U.S. merchants'] property for supposed breaches of its fiscal regulations: and examples are not wanting of unjust and ruinous prosecutions against our citizens upon criminal allegations." He penned an example of a general provision that would include these cases, instructing Pinckney to add it to the Spanish-American claims agreement (*PJM-SS*, 2: 441–42).

2. JM had suggested that Pinckney might discuss, but not agree to, a U.S. guarantee of Spain's American possessions (JM to Pinckney, 25 Sept. 1801, *PJM-SS*, 2:132).

3. For Yrujo's complaint of 4 June 1801 and JM's instructions to Pinckney on the matter, see *PJM-SS*, 1:262, 276.

§ To Rufus King. *26 July 1802, Department of State.* "Agreeably to a suggestion in a letter from you to Mr Elias Vanderhorst, of the 5th January last, a copy of which he has forwarded to me,[1] you will please to pay him the sum of Twelve pounds, sixteen shillings and ten pence, and charge it to your contingent account with the United States."

Letterbook copy (DNA: RG 59, IM, vol. 6). 1 p. RC offered for sale in Parke-Bernet Catalogue No. 1064 (3 May 1949), item 339. A typescript of the RC supplied in 1959 by James G. King of New York, N.Y., indicates that it was received 13 Sept. JM also wrote to Vander Horst on 26 July to inform him that the money would be paid (DNA: RG 59, DL, vol. 14).

1. See Vander Horst to JM, 12 Feb. 1802 (*PJM-SS,* 2:464).

§ From Moses Myers. *26 July 1802, Norfolk.* Acknowledges JM's letter of 12 July [not found] appointing him a commissioner of bankruptcy. Declines the post because he is "not well calculated to fulfill the duties."

RC (DNA: RG 59, LAR, 1801–9, filed under "Myers"). 1 p.; docketed by Brent and Jefferson.

To Richard O'Brien

SIR,   DEPARTMENT OF STATE July 27. 1802.

In my letter of May 21st. 1801.[1] accompanying the remittance of 30,000 dollars as a commutation of the current annuity of stores, you were requested to use your endeavours to bring about this mode and rate of paying the annuity, as a permanent regulation. It has been some disappointment not to have learnt by any of your subsequent communications, whether such an experiment had been made, or how far another remittance of a like sum, would be likely to be accepted by the Dey. From your silence it has been inferred that the Dey did not enter fully into the plan of a permanent commutation, but from his acceptance of the payment for one year, in money when placed before his eyes, and from the motives which his advisers probably feel to favour that mode of payment, the President has determined to remit another sum of 30,000 dollars, as a commutation for the current annuity in stores. The money will be conveyed to Algiers in the ship General Green, commanded by Lieutenant Chauncey,[2] and will be delivered to you on her arrival there. You will take the occasion to renew to the Dey assurances of the friendly dispositions and good faith of the United States, and of their confidence in his; will inform him that the remittance in money is made in the expectation that he will find it not less acceptable than in the former instance, as well as from an anxiety to avoid the unpunctuality sometimes inseparable from the transportation of stores; and in case he cannot be prevailed on to receive payment in this mode you will assure him that the letter of the Treaty shall be complied with, as soon as the President shall know his refusal, and the stores can be transmitted. You will also avail yourself of the occasion, if it should prove favorable, for another attempt to draw the Dey into a permanent regulation for satisfying the Treaty by an annuity of 30,000 dollars in place of stipulated stores. The evident advantages of such a change in our engagements; will call for your best exertions to accomplish it.

In case the Dey shall positively refuse to take the money in lieu of the stores, you will deliver the 30,000 dollars back to Lt. Chauncey, unless one of our frigates should happen to be with you. In that case it will be better because safer, to place the money in charge of the Captain of the frigate. I have the honor to be &ca.

JAMES MADISON.

P. S. August 22d. Since the above was written the Navy Department has concluded to send to the Mediterranean the Frigate New York Captain James Barron, instead of the ship General Greene. As it may not be convenient for this frigate to proceed to algiers with the remittance it will be left to the discretion of Commodore Morris to forward it as he may find most eligible, and to point out to you the mode of returning the money in case the Dey shall not accept it.

Letterbook copy (DNA: RG 59, IC, vol. 1). Addressed to "James L. Cathcart Esqr. or in his absence Richd. O'Brien Esqr.," with Wagner's notation, "this direction should be reversed."

1. *PJM-SS*, 1:212–15.
2. Isaac Chauncey (1772–1840) was a career naval officer who served in the war against Tripoli, 1802–5, commanding at various times the *Chesapeake*, *New York*, and *John Adams*. In 1812 JM appointed him commander of naval forces on lakes Ontario and Erie, a position he held until 1815.

To James Simpson

SIR,   DEPARTMENT OF STATE July 27. 1802.
Since my last which was of april 20th. and went by the Adams Frigate, I have received your favors of May 13. and June 5th. & 14th. which arrived in the Essex Frigate.

It affords pleasure that the Emperor of Morocco has withdrawn his inadmissible request of passports for vessels freighted with supplies of wheat for Tripoli. In refusing to sanction such a communication with Tripoli as well as to comply with the request relating to the Tripoline vessel at Gibraltar, you pursued a plain course of duty, in which you justly counted on the approbation of the President. Your readiness to grant the usual certificates in favor of vessels bound with Morocco property for Tunis, was equally proper.

Should the certificates be perverted into a cover for an illicit trade with the enemy, it will be a just ground of subsequent complaint, but could not be refused either of right or at the present crisis particularly, in sound policy, on the mere presumption that such a use would be made of them.

My letter by the Adams informed you of the intention of the President to compliment the Emperor with one hundred gun carriages. They are now forwarded by the Ship General Greene. It is hoped that they will be found of the right sort and sizes. As far as they may fail in either of these respects, you will make the best apologies you can; and otherwise render them as acceptable as possible. The President being at his seat at present, and being myself on the point of leaving Washington, I cannot inform you with certainty whether you will receive with the Gun carriages a letter from him to the Emperor. In case he should chuse to write one, and can convey it to this place in time for the sailing of the ship Lieutenant Chauncy will be charged with it.

It is proper to inform you that Mr. Cathcart is commissioned by the President to take advantage of the impression which may be made on the Bashaw of Tripoli by a rendezvous of the American squadron before that place, by meeting him in negotiations for peace. This consideration will add force to others which will be felt by you, for studiously cultivating harmony with Morocco at so interesting a moment. Mr. Cathcart is also appointed to succeed Mr. OBrien in the Consulate at Algiers, who has long asked and is now permitted to retire.

As soon as I can have an interview with the Secy. of the Treasury who is at present not in Washington I will propose to him an arrangement for lodging a fund for your salary in London as you wish. With sentiments &ca.

JAMES MADISON

Letterbook copy (DNA: RG 59, IC, vol. 1). Another copy of the letter, printed in Knox, *Naval Documents, Barbary Wars*, 2:207–8, is dated 22 July 1802.

§ From William Burley. *27 July 1802, Beverly.* Acknowledges JM's letter of 12 July [not found] appointing him a commissioner of bankruptcy for the district of Massachusetts. Declines the appointment but recommends Daniel Kilham of Wenham for the position.

RC (DNA: RG 59, LAR, 1801–9, filed under "Burley"). 1 p.; docketed by Brent as received 2 Aug.

§ From John Nicoll. *27 July 1802, New Haven.* Has received JM's letter of 6 July [not found] appointing him a commissioner of bankruptcy for the district of Connecticut. Declines the appointment; "I am so frequently absent from the State, that it will be out of my Power to pay the requisite Attention to the Duties of the Office." Recommends John H. Lynde for the position.

RC (DNA: RG 59, LAR, 1801–9, filed under "Nicol"). 1 p.; docketed by Brent as received 31 July.

§ From James Simpson. *27 July 1802, Tangier.* No. 46. Acknowledges JM's letter of 30 Apr., received from Captain Campbell of the *Adams,* and reports that he "landed here last Night" under a flag of truce to "more speedily and effectualy" make the communications JM charged him with for the emperor of Morocco. The governor is absent in Tetuàn, "whither I shall follow him tomorrow, and after the necessary interview send a Messenger with an Address to His Majesty on the subjects you have directed." The frigate at Larache "lays quite ready for Sea," and its commander "left this place on Sunday, fully authorized to capture American Vessels"; has informed Commodore Morris "& entreated of him to employ the Adams in preventing her puting to Sea." Adds that the "Armament of the Emperor" is aimed not only at Americans but at "all other Nations, who have not actualy Consuls resident with him."

RC (DNA: RG 59, CD, Tangier, vol. 1). 2 pp.; marked "duplicate." Printed in Knox, *Naval Documents, Barbary Wars,* 2:211. Jefferson communicated a brief extract to Congress with his annual message on 15 Dec. 1802 (*ASP, Foreign Relations,* 2:467).

To Joshua Gilpin

Sir   Department of State July 28. 1802

I have reced. your letter of the 21st. instant. The Consulate at Barcelona is not at present considered as vacant, Mr. Willis having returned thither, and no answer having been yet recd. to the enquiries made by this Department relating to his continuance in that station.[1] Should these result in a vacancy, or should a vacancy otherwise happen, Mr Burne with your recommendation & any others that may be added, will be presented to the consideration of the President, and be brought into due comparison with other candidates for the same appointment. In the mean time as citizenship will probably have an influence on the selection, it may not be amiss to ascertain the date and legality of that of Mr. Burne. I am Sir respectfully Your Obedt. servt

James Madison

RC (courtesy of an anonymous collector). Addressee not indicated.

1. See JM to Pinckney, 26 July 1802.

To Moses Young

Sir,   DEPARTMENT OF STATE WASHINGTON July 28th. 1802.
Your letter of the 26th. April has been duly recd.[1] It is to be regretted that the circumstance of your being continued Consul of the United States should have induced an expectation of your receiving a salary as such, especially as it appears you have remained at Madrid, under this impression, contrary to your private Interest. The remuneration of our consuls proceeds from the weight of commercial character, which, it is supposed, the appointments give, and the fees they are authorized to charge for official acts—in no instances from fixed salaries, but to those in the Barbary States. Regretting, as I do, that peculiar circumstances should have deprived you of these advantages, it is not in my power to encourage a hope that the emoluments of your office will be encreased by any act of the Government, as the laws of congress on the subject give no authority for countenancing such expectations. With much respect &ca.

JAMES MADISON.

Letterbook copy (DNA: RG 59, IC, vol. 1).

1. Letter not found.

From Christopher Gore and William Pinkney

Sir,   LONDON July 28th. 1802
The unavoidable Expences of the Board of Commissioners to which we belong make it necessary that the two Governments should from time to time be required to furnish as heretofore the means of defraying them; and as it would greatly embarrass the proceedings of the Board, and materially retard the so much to be desired Conclusion of its Labours if the arrangements which it is presumed the United States have made for this purpose should be inadequate, or their Execution much longer delayed, we take the liberty of calling the attention of the Government to this subject.

As there are strong Grounds for expectation that the Business of the Commission may be completed, and the Commission itself closed within 15 or 18 months it need not be mentioned that at the expiration of that Time any Deficiency in the Fund intended to answer the engagements of the Board would be extremely undesireable. But however carefully such future Deficiency may, and we doubt not will be guarded against, it is in the meantime manifestly indispensable that we should be placed in a situation to meet the ordinary Charges of the Commission as they occur; Such as the Salary of the fifth Commissioner, those of our Secretary, Clerks &c. House-Rent, Stationary &c. These are already in arrear, and some of them are of a nature obviously to require the promptest attention to their payment. The Salary of the fifth Commissioner is peculiarly of this Description. His public Trust engrosses his Time, and his Dependance is consequently upon his Salary. This, we believe, has never been paid with any sort of Regularity, and for sometime past has not been paid at all.

Upon applying to Messrs. Bird & Co. to know the precise state of the Fund appropriated by the Government of the United States to the purposes of the Commission under the Title of the British Treaty Fund, we have found that Fund (as well as the others) totally exhausted; and their Instructions appear to forbid them from aiding this or any other appropriation by *advances*. We have however thought it[1] our Duty (and we Trust that our Conduct will be approved by the President) to request that they would advance such part of the arrearages of the Salary of the fifth Commissioner as is payable by the United States, and from a Conviction of the evident propriety and even necessity of it they have consented to do so. But as to the other ordinary Charges above mentioned they must remain unsatisfied until the Fund is made competent to their payment.

In making provision for the Expences of the Board, it cannot have escaped observation that, exclusive of those which are regular and constant, and therefore demand immediate Funds (with the nature and amount of which the Government is already sufficiently acquainted) a considerable Sum will soon be wanted to enable the Board to comply with its Contract with its assessors. Of the probable amount of this Sum we cannot at present give any thing like an accurate Estimate; but it would undoubtedly be proper to make the provision for it so ample, as not to incur the Hazard of being short of its object.

It may perhaps be worthy of consideration whether, if a Contingent fund shall not be placed at the Disposal of the American Minister, it might not be prudent to secure to the British Treaty fund a certainty of being adequate by giving Directions for the eventual Re-inforcement of it by a part of the money hereafter to be retained by the public Agent for Disbursements in prize Causes out of the first Installment of our awards. Such an arrangement certainly would not in itself, or in the first instance be suitable Provision for the objects of that Fund or any of them; but, as calculated to avoid any possible Deficiency from short Calculations it might be desireable.

We take this occasion to mention that the Board has decided 92 Cases in favor of the Claimants since its re-assembling in February; in 52. of which, heretofore reported on by our Assessors we shall probably soon make

Awards: that the Residue of the Cases decided have been referred to Messrs. Cabot and Glennie, and that in these our Awards will immediately follow the Return and Examination of their Reports. As soon as we shall have made Awards to any Extent, a List will be forwarded.

We have the Honor to enclose herewith an Extract from the Proceedings of the Board on the 13th. day of this month relative to the salary allowed to Mr. Cabot.[2] The condition upon which this Compensation seems to have been granted makes it proper for us to state that the British Commissioners have not disapproved of it, but have on the contrary expressed their Regret that it should have been found expedient to lessen the salary heretofore received by this truly useful and meritorious officer, with the knowledge and entire approbation of every Member of the Board. We have the honour to be, with great Consideration, Sir, Your most ob. and hum. servants

C. GORE
WM. PINKNEY

P. S. Since writing the above we have received a Letter from Mr Trumbull in relation to his Salary copy whereof we take the liberty herewith to enclose.[3]

RC and enclosures (DNA: RG 76, Great Britain, Treaty of 1794 [Art. 7], Papers Relative to the Commissioners, vol. 4). RC incomplete (see n. 1). The remainder of the letter is supplied from a letterpress copy of the RC (ibid.; docketed by Brent as received 2 Oct.). In a clerk's hand, signed by Gore and Pinkney. For enclosures, see nn. 2 and 3.

1. RC ends here.
2. The enclosed extract of the board's minutes, 13 July 1802 (2 pp.), included a copy of a letter from Rufus King to the Board of Commissioners, 29 June 1802, announcing that the president had granted Samuel Cabot a salary of $1,500 per year for his services as assessor.
3. John Trumbull to Gore and Pinkney, 28 July 1802 (4 pp.). The fifth commissioner wrote that his salary had been paid by the British government through 5 July, so that an advance by Bird, Savage, and Bird for that purpose was unnecessary; however, he requested a payment from the U.S. bankers for the contingent expenses of the board and warned that should his salary not be paid punctually, he would be justified in "consulting my own convenience, and engaging in such pursuits as I may find necessary."

From Samuel A. Otis

SIR   BOSTON July 28th 1802
    I take this opportunity to acknowledge the honour of an official communication from the Secretary for the department of State,[1] with a commission from the President of the United States; And altho the more

obliged by this mark of his confidence as it was unsolicited & unexpected, permit me respectfully to state my doubts as to the propriety of holding this office, together with that of Secy of the Senate, without the permission of the Senate; And which cannot be obtained until they are in Session.

If holding both offices should be deemed incompatible, I hope it will hardly be necessary for me to apologize for my candid declaration of a preference, for *an office*, the duties of which, from long practice, have become familiar to me, to which, I feel myself fully competent, the salary too of which, is a principal article of, altho not adequate to my support, to *one*, of less emolument, precarious from liability to repeal & alterations in the law; An office whose duties are probably laborious, & in which I am without experience.

On the other hand should the honourable Body whose officer I am, from preference to a more meritorious person, or other cause, think fit to dismiss me their service, in the habits of business, necessary too for the subsistence of my family, I should regret being wholly out of employ. I hope therefore under all the circumstances, it will not be thot indelicate or disrespectful in me to ask permission, to consider of a reply, to your official communication until the Session commences; More especially as no injury can result to the public, there being a number of Commissioners already employed in the execution of the business. I have the honour to be With every sentiment of respect & esteem Your most obedient humble Servant

SAM A. OTIS

RC (DNA: RG 59, LAR, 1801–9, filed under "Otis"); Tr (DLC: Jefferson Papers). RC docketed by Jefferson and by Brent as received 2 Aug. Tr dated 14 July 1802 and marked "Copy."

1. Letter not found. Jefferson had appointed Otis a commissioner of bankruptcy for the district of Massachusetts (*National Intelligencer*, 16 July 1802).

From Louis-André Pichon

GEORGETOWN le 9. Thermidor an 10.
MONSIEUR,   (28. Juillet 1802.)

J'ai reçu les lettres que vous m'avez fait l'honneur de m'écrire Sous la date des 19 et 24. Juillet. La premiere a pour objet de me faire connaître la décision portée par Mr. le Président des Etats Unis Sur l'affaire de la Peggy. Il me reste a regretter, Monsieur, que cette décision inespérée, et, en apparence, contraire aux principes qui ont dirigé le Gouvernement des Etats Unis dans les restitutions antérieures et même dans celle de la premiere

Moitié de cette propriété, n'ait pas été prise plûtot, Depuis le mois de Décembre dernier où la Sentence de la cour Suprême a été rendue. Ce delai ne peut qu'être extrêmement préjudiciable aux interessés qui ont déjà eu beaucoup à Souffrir des incidens qui ont empêché l'execution des ordres donnés par Monsieur le Président dès le mois de mars de l'année dernière.

L'objet de la Seconde lettre étant, Monsieur, de prévenir les inconvéniens qui pourraient résulter de la meprise qui S'est glissée dans les instructions du Ministre de la Marine de France relativement aux précautions à prendre contre l'introduction de la fievre Jaune, Je m'empresserai, Monsieur, autant qu'il Sera en mon pouvoir, de concourir à la rectification de cette erreur. Agréez, Monsieur, mes respects.

L. A. PICHON

CONDENSED TRANSLATION

Acknowledges JM's letters of 19 and 24 July. The first informed him of the president's decision in the case of the *Peggy*. Regrets that this unexpected decision, which appears to be contrary to the principles that guided the U.S. in earlier restitutions and even in that of the first half of this property, was not taken sooner, since the Supreme Court judgment was delivered in December 1801. This delay can only be extremely prejudicial to the interested parties, who have already suffered greatly from the circumstances that have prevented the execution of the president's orders of March 1801.

The object of the second letter was to warn of the inconveniences that could result from the mistake that slipped into the minister of marine's instructions on precautions to take against yellow fever. Will do all in his power to rectify this error.

RC (DNA: RG 59, NFL, France, vol. 1). In a clerk's hand, signed by Pichon.

§ From Louis-André Pichon. *28 July 1802, Georgetown.* Encloses a copy of a letter from the minister of foreign relations announcing the signing of the definitive peace between France and Great Britain; adds a copy of the treaty [not found] and requests that both documents be brought to the president's attention. Would have had the pleasure of sending this interesting communication sooner had the packet that contained it not been mislaid at Norfolk, where it arrived a long while ago.

RC and enclosure (DNA: RG 59, NFL, France, vol. 1). RC 2 pp.; in French. In a clerk's hand, signed by Pichon. Surviving enclosure is a copy of Talleyrand to Pichon, 5 Germinal an X (26 Mar. 1802) (1 p.).

§ From Lewis S. Pintard. *28 July 1802, Madeira.* Forwards copies of James Simpson's letters. Reports that on 12 July two American ships arrived from Mogador, "which Port they had left three days before in consequence of Mr. Simpson's letter." He recommended that they not return to Mogador; "notwithstanding which, as they had left a considerable proportion of their property there, they resolved on returning, and sailed from hence on the 21st. inst." Suggests stationing a U.S. frigate or cruiser off Madeira owing to its proximity to Mogador, where many Barbary cruisers will be fitted out; "it would certainly be attended with great advantage to our Trade." Reports the death of John Joyce on 23 July, a sailor from Brattleborough, Vermont, the only death that has occurred in the marine hospital in five years. Encloses an inventory of Joyce's belongings, "which are really not worth his friends looking after."[1]

RC (DNA: RG 59, CD, Funchal, vol. 1). 4 pp.; docketed by Brent. Printed in Knox, *Naval Documents, Barbary Wars*, 2:216. Enclosure not found.

1. On 13 Oct. 1802 Daniel Brent wrote the Brattleborough postmaster (John Halbrook), asking him to "communicate to the friends of John Joyce" the news of his death (DNA: RG 59, DL, vol. 14).

To Robert Smith

SIR   DEPARTMENT OF STATE July 29th. 1802.
    It being thought proper that $30,000 should be transmitted to the Consul at algiers, by the ship General Greene, I request that you will please to give the proper instructions to Lt. Chauncy to receive that sum from the orders of the secretary of the Treasury, and deliver it at algiers to the American Consul there, with a further instruction to receive the money back from the Consul, if not applied as intended, and to place it as soon as he conveniently can, on board one of our Frigates to be returned to the United States under the arrangements and directions of Captain Morris, I request also that you will please to instruct Lt. Chauncy to take on board the ship commanded by him, one hundred Gun carriages intended by the President for the Emperor of Morocco, and to deliver the same at Tangiers to the order of James Simpson Consul of the United States at that place. I have the Honor to be &ca.

                                                    JAMES MADISON.

Letterbook copy (DNA: RG 59, DL, vol. 14).

From Louis-André Pichon

                                          G. TOWN 29th july 1802
Mr. Pichon with his respects incloses to Mr. Madison some letters under the Seal of the National institute, adressed to the President, which he found

among his dispatches from france,[1] in the package which has been so long coming from Norfolk.

The inclosed extract of a dispatch of Mr. P. to the minister of foreign affairs, Mr. Pichon confidentially communicates to Mr. Madison and desires that it may be forwarded to the President.[2] It was written, as the extract itself shows, in consequence of an intimation given to Mr. P. on the subject to which it relates.

RC and enclosure (DNA: RG 59, NFL, France, vol. 1). For enclosure, see n. 2.

1. No doubt these included François-André Vincent's letter to Jefferson of 5 Nivôse an X (26 Dec. 1801) announcing Jefferson's election to the Institut National de France, which the president received on 31 July 1802 (Jefferson's Epistolary Record [DLC: Jefferson Papers]; Malone, *Jefferson and His Time*, 4:178–79).

2. This extract of a letter from Pichon to Talleyrand, 29 Messidor an X (18 July 1802) (4 pp.; in French; mistakenly docketed by Brent as enclosed in Pichon to JM, 28 July 1802), explained the workings of the U.S. press, especially the brutal treatment often given to France and French officials.

§ From Peder Blicherolsen. *29 July 1802, Philadelphia.* "I take herewith the liberty to lay before You the enclosed *seven powers*, directed to an equal number of Danish Vice Consuls for the States of New-York, Pensylvania, Mary-Land, District of Columbia, North & South Carolina, and Georgia—to which I respectfully beg, You will have the goodness to cause the necessary Exequatur's to be respectively annexed [and] . . . order them to be returned to me. . . . I shall probably be under the necessity on some futur[e] day to occasion a repeated trouble with still other powers of the same kind, for those States, where I have not yet been able to meet with suitable Subjects, willing to take upon them the burthen of a charge destitute of salary and holding out but an indifferent prospect of any other emoluments or advantages whatever."

RC (DNA: RG 59, NFL, Denmark, vol. 1). 2 pp.

§ From George W. Erving. *29 July 1802, American Consulate, London.* No. 9. Encloses copies of letters from Simpson and the U.S. consul at Gibraltar announcing the declaration of war against the U.S. by the emperor of Morocco. Has published the information for American citizens in Great Britain and sent word to U.S. consuls in Germany and Holland. Believes the time is "peculiarly favorable for the Extirpation of those hordes of pirates upon the African coast." The French "undoubtedly meditate an attack upon Algiers under pretence of supporting the honor of their flag, but with a view doubtless of making a permanent settlement on that important part of the Barbary Coast." There is no "pretext" for any European power to intervene in such an affair, except Turkey. Believes such a plan on the part of France is the more probable because French policy "must necessarily be . . . to obtain possession of Ægypt; in the division of the Turkish Empire which is manifestly intended, Candia & Cyprus if not the Morea also, will naturally fall to her share." It was probably for this reason that Marseilles was made a free port; "to what purpose it will be said have we opened this port if a banditti are to be suffered at the very door to intercept our customers & friends." As to the British reaction, "it is probable that (without a pretext for assisting the Barbarians,) they may resort to the next best ⟨m⟩easure of dividing their spoil; they may gain some of ⟨o⟩ur good will by joining us in an attack upon the Moors, & locate themselves opposite to their own Gibraltar." British will be watchful of French movements, and "every project of this sort will doubtless be beneficial to us." Bonaparte's "grand speculations" in Africa will divert his attention from Louisiana, nor will he be eager to interfere with the U.S. in that quarter because of "the necessity he will be under of receiving from us for a long time the means of supporting" French forces in Saint-Domingue and Guadeloupe.

RC and enclosures (DNA: RG 59, CD, London, vol. 8). RC 3 pp.; docketed by Brent as received 23 Sept. Enclosures are copies of circulars from James Simpson, 25 June 1802 (2 pp.; printed in Knox, *Naval Documents, Barbary Wars*, 2:183–84); and from John Gavino, 28 June 1802 (2 pp.). The second enclosure is similar in substance to Gavino to JM of the same date, with a postscript asking Erving to communicate the circular to consuls in Holland and the North Sea and informing him of the capture of Capt. Andrew Morris and the brig *Franklin* off Cape Palos on 17 June.

§ From Benjamin R. Morgan. *29 July 1802, Philadelphia.* "Mr. William Dewees being desirous of obtaining the appointment of Commissioner of Bankruptcy in the place of Mr Van Cleve lately deceased has requested me to . . . sollicit on his behalf your friendly interference in obtaining the object of his wishes." Dewees is a Philadelphia attorney whose family has "long been established here."

RC (DNA: RG 59, LAR, 1801–9, filed under "Dewees"). 2 pp.; docketed by Jefferson. JM also received a letter from John Dawson, 16 Aug. 1802 (ibid.; 1 p.), recommending Dewees for the position.

§ From Fulwar Skipwith. *29 July 1802, Paris.* Introduces John Jones Waldo of Massachusetts and recommends him for "one of the vacant commercial Agencys of this Country."

RC (DNA: RG 59, LAR, 1801–9, filed under "Waldo"). 1 p. Addressee not indicated. Skipwith wrote a similar letter to Jefferson on 30 July (ibid.).

To Thomas Jefferson

DEAR SIR   WASHINGTON July 30. 1802

I inclose several letters for you put into my hands by Mr. Pichon, with some communications of his own,[1] which are proper to be forwarded along with them. I inclose also a letter from Mr Jones at Gaudaloupe,[2] and two others declining commissions of Bankruptcy.

My departure from this place, suspended for a day by preparations for the Mediterranean business stated in my last, has since been prevented by the lameness of a horse which obliges me to leave him behind & to purchase another. Having been thus long detained, & understanding that Mr Gallatin will be here to night or tomorrow, I am induced to submit to a little further delay for the chance of seeing him. By sunday at farthest I hope to be on the road, and in about 10 days from that date to be at home.

Nothing has occurred at this place since you left it which deserves mention. With the most respectful attachment I remain yours

JAMES MADISON

RC (DLC: Jefferson Papers). Docketed by Jefferson as received 31 July.

1. For these letters, see Pichon to JM, 28 July (two letters) and 29 July 1802, and nn.
2. Edward Jones to JM, 8 July 1802.

From Thomas Jefferson

DEAR SIR   MONTICELLO July 30. 1802.

Your's of July 22. came to hand on the 25th. the day of my arrival here. I think the proposition to tender another 30,000. D. to Algiers a very judicious one, and have therefore written to mr. Gallatin to take measures in conjunction with yourself to make the remittance by the General Greene.[1] I have not yet written to the emperor of Morocco; because when one has nothing to write about it is difficult to find the end to begin at. I will sketch something before next post, and inclose it for your alteration with a blank sheet signed, over which they may write the letter.

You are now I presume in the middle of your journey & must have had a good deal of rain. This will be directed to await in Orange for your return. Present me respectfully to the ladies, & be assured of my affectionate esteem.

TH: JEFFERSON

P. S. Not knowing whether the inclosed letters have past through your hands I forward them to you instead of returning them to the office from whence I recieved them.

RC (DNA: RG 59, ML); FC (DLC: Jefferson Papers).

1. See JM to Albert Gallatin, 22 July 1802, and n. 1.

From Robert R. Livingston

Duplicate No. 18

Dear Sir,   Paris 30 July 1802

I have recieved your dispatches ⟨& the Presidents by Mr. Du⟩pont de Ne⟨mours.⟩[1] I shall reply more particularly to them at the next opportunity as I am now very much engaged in preparing a lengthy memoir on the subject of the mutual interests of France & the United States relative to Louisiana by which I hope to convince them that both in a commercial & political view the possession of it would be disadvantageous to france. In my last I hinted to you my suspicions that France & Spain did not understand each other on the subject of Louisiana and communicated to you my letter to the Spanish Ambassador calculated to sound this business and interpose some difficulties to its execution.[2] His answer confirmed my opinion. I have since verbally his explicit assurance that the Floridas are not included in the cession, and I have been applied to by one of the Ministers here to know what we understand in America by Louisiana you can easily concieve my answer. I have just recieved a letter from Mr. Graham in which he communicates the Spanish Ministers answer to Mr. Pinckneys application upon the same subject in these words "If the King should think proper to cede *Louisiana* he will take care that the interest of the United States shall not be affected by it.["][3] It appears also by the 5th. Article of the treaty of Madrid 21 March 1801 that the cession had been made of Louisiana generally. The french you know have always extended the term to South Carolina and all the Country on the Ohio since the possession of the Floridas by britain and the treaty of 1763 I think there can be no doubt as to the precise meaning of the terms. I find a certain degree of roideur[4] in the Spanish Ambassador on that subject which it will be our interest to cherish at the Court of Spain unless we should have a prospect of purchasing the Floridas—in the present state of things and till this point is settled I think it probable the expedition to Louisiana will be postponed. In the meantime all that can be done here will be to endeavor to obtain a cession of New Orleans either by purchase or by offering to make it a port of entry to France on such terms as shall promise advantages to her commerce—And give her hopes of introducing her manufactures and wines into our western country. An arrangement of this sort if they listen to it would certainly be beneficial to both countries and only hurtful to Britain if to this we could add a stipulation that she shall never possess the Floridas but on the contrary in case of a rupture with Spain and a conquest of them cede them to us our affairs in that quarter would stand as well as I would wish & the Colonies that France might attempt to establish on the west side of the Missisippi would be too feeble to injure us. I find them very anxious to have the ports of Pensacola & Augustine as they dread our having the command of the gulph.

I confess this appears to me no very important object and if they would be content with these and give us west florida and New Orleans even at a *large price* we should not hesitate. I am sorry that you have not communicated to me what are precisely, the utmost limits of the sum I may venture to offer in cash or in our own demands. As the Minister has been absent some time & has but just returned I can not state precisely to you what we may hope on this subject but be persuaded that I am fully impressed with the importance of the subject and that nothing will be left undone which I can do to effectuate your wishes. I saw him last night and was very cordially recieved, his health is so much mended by the waters that I hope he will be able to go through business more speedily than he has done. On the subject of our demands nothing is yet done owing to his absence. I have however rather better prospects than I have hitherto had. The St. Domingo bills have been accepted as presented & they still continue to assure me that they shall be paid. Enclosed is my note on the subject of our officers confined by Genl. Le Clerc.[5] I yet have recieved no answer.[6] You have probably heard more directly of the war that the Emperor of Morocco has declared against us.[7] I sent notice of it immediately to our Consuls in the different ports of France & Holland & also to Mr. King who I presume will give the necessary information in Britain and the Northern ports.

I have since advices from Mr. Obrien that a vessel from Philadelphia—Capt. Morris is taken by a Tripolitan & carried into Algiers. Her crew consists of nine men. It is necessary if the war continues to have a number of small armed vessels in the Mediterranean as the corsairs will always be able to elude the vigilance of the large ships whom they see at a distance but on these subjects you will have better and more direct information from Mr. Pinckney. Mr. Paterson is now here he says that if his relinquishment of the place of commercial agent at L'Orient will in the least contribute to the public interest he will do it with pleasure—in the hope that the President will still retain him in mind in case of any other vacancy. Nantes is vacant And Cadiz in the hands of Mr. Iznardi and exercised by a Spanish deputy who I am informed is not only a bankrupt but a dishonorable one and who also labors under the imputation of having been concerned in privateering upon our commerce. As I expect Mr. Vail here every hour I have taken no steps in the business but I much wish to retain him as a worthy officer and a very decided republican if any other provision could be made for Paterson. I have the honor to be dear Sir, with the highest esteem your Mo. Obt. Hle. St.

RC (NHi: Livingston Papers); draft (ibid.); letterbook copy and copies of first and second enclosures (NHi: Livingston Papers, vol. 1); third enclosure (DNA: RG 59, DD, France, vol. 8). The RC is a letterpress copy in a clerk's hand, unsigned; docketed by Brent, "No 18. July 19 1802." Words in angle brackets are obscured by a fold in the RC and have been supplied from the letterbook copy. Letterbook copy dated 29 July 1802. For first and second enclosures, see nn. 5 and 6; for third enclosure, see n. 7. According to Livingston's "Journal of correspondence with the Secretary of State" (NHi: Livingston Papers, vol. 7), Livingston also enclosed a "Copy of note from the Helvetic Minister on establisht of a constitution" (see JM to Livingston, 15 Oct. 1802 [DNA: RG 59, IM, vol. 6]).

    1. DuPont carried JM's dispatches to Livingston of 1 and 7 May 1802, JM's private letter of 1 May 1802, and a private letter from Jefferson of 18 Apr. 1802 (see JM to Livingston, 1 May 1802 [second letter], and n. 1).

    2. For Livingston's unofficial letter to Azara and the response, see Livingston to JM, 28 May and 8 June 1802.

    3. Graham actually wrote (in code): "*if the king does think proper to part with Louisiana he will do nothing to the prejudice of the United States.*" He went on to say that he feared the U.S. had "*little to expect from the friendship or even justice*" of Spain (John Graham to Livingston, 12 July 1802 [NHi: Livingston Papers]).

    4. *Raideur:* inflexibility.

    5. Livingston enclosed a copy of his letter to Talleyrand, 19 July 1802 (2 pp.), protesting the imprisonment of the American captains Rodgers and Davidson in Saint-Domingue and communicating his instructions from the U.S. government "to apply to the justice of that of France for the immediate release of these persons and such satisfaction as shall compensate their sufferings."

    6. In the letterbook copy, Livingston's secretary placed an asterisk here and wrote in the margin, "see No. 48. the answer came the day this was written." No. 48 in the letterbook is Talleyrand to Livingston, 10 Thermidor an X (29 July 1802) (2 pp.; in French), in which the French foreign minister defended Leclerc's actions by insisting that the general would not have arrested Rodgers and Davidson without good cause. He noted also that under Leclerc's rules of commerce a great number of American ships had traded in Saint-Domingue, that Americans were not discouraged from commercial ventures with the island because of the arrests, and that Leclerc's actions could be explained only in terms of the particular cases of the two ship captains and were not indicative of the general treatment of Americans.

    7. Livingston enclosed with this dispatch, according to Daniel Brent's docket, a letter from Commodore Richard Morris, 25 June 1802 (1 p.), informing the minister of the Moroccan emperor's declaration of war on the U.S. and the arrival of U.S. consul James Simpson at Gibraltar after his expulsion from Morocco. A nearly identical letter of the same date to Rufus King is printed in Knox, *Naval Documents, Barbary Wars*, 2:184.

From Roger Gerard van Polanen

SIR   PHILADELPHIA, July 30th. 1802.

    I have recieved the official intelligence, of my being appoint⟨ed⟩ a Member of the Supreme Council of Government at the Cape of Good hope. The Batavian Government has authorised me at the same time, if I should accept of the said promotio⟨n,⟩ to take my leave of the American Government, and to depar⟨t⟩ from here for Holland, or for the Cape, by the first opportunity.

Having accepted the office of Counsellor at t⟨he Cape,⟩ I am thereby recalled from the Station ⟨I have the honor⟩ to hold near the Government of the U⟨nited States of America, and⟩ I take the liberty, Sir, to request Y⟨ou, to acquaint the⟩ President thereof.

I am at the same time auth⟨orised to declare, the wish⟩ of the Batavian Government, ⟨to cultivate, whenever occasions⟩ may offer itself, the friend⟨ly relations, subsisting between⟩ the Batavian Republic, & ⟨the United States of America.⟩ And I indulge myself wit⟨h the hope, that altho'⟩ the American⟩ Executive has thought proper to withdraw his Minister from the Hague, and my recall is a consequence thereof, the cordial sentiments of mutual good-will between the two Nations, ⟨w⟩hereof my Nation has given an early and striking proof, in being almost foremost in acknowledging the independence of the American Republic, will suffer thereby no diminution.[1]

In addressing you, Sir, for the last time, permit me to assure ⟨y⟩ou of my high & sincere regard, & for my best wishes for ⟨your⟩ welfare & happiness. Beleive me to be, with perfect esteem ⟨& considera⟩tion sir Your most obedient Servant

⟨R. G.⟩ van Polanen.

⟨I have further the honor to inform you, that as my acceptance of the new appointment, Could not h⟩ave been recieved ⟨by the Secretary of State⟩ for foreign ⟨affairs, when his last dispa⟩tches to me ⟨were sent of[f], the Customary⟩ Letters of ⟨recall have not been sent to me,⟩ but will ⟨be forwarded to you, as soon as⟩ my Departure ⟨from here, shall be known at⟩ home.

RC (DNA: RG 59, NFL, Netherlands, vol. 1); Tr (AR). RC torn and obscured on verso by lamination; words and parts of words in angle brackets have been supplied from the Tr.

1. In the Tr, the paragraph written as a postscript in the RC follows this paragraph.

§ To Edward Thornton. *30 July 1802, Department of State.* "I have the honor to enclose a copy of a letter from the District Attorney of Vermont reporting the result of the enquiries he was directed to make on the subject of a communication some time since received from you."[1]

Letterbook copy (DNA: RG 59, DL, vol. 14). 1 p.

1. For David Fay's letter, see Levi Lincoln to JM, 6 July 1802, and nn.

§ From John Gavino. *30 July 1802, Gibraltar.* No. 95. Acknowledges JM's letter of 11 May enclosing letters for O'Brien and Eaton. Simpson returned to Tangier on 26 July "to conferr with the Bashaw who had then sett out for Tetuan for whence Mr: Simpson was also to sett off the 27th: as you will see by the annexd Paragraph of his Letter to me." Also encloses a letter to JM from O'Brien "in the state it [was] received." The *Chesapeake, Adams,* and *Enterprize* are all at Gibraltar. "Should the Emperour of Morrocco Persist in his hostil Intentions 6 or 8 light Sailing Vessels such as the Enterprize I think would be very usefull to Protect our Trade." A Dutch squadron of three sail of the line, a frigate, brig, and schooner, passed Gibraltar for Málaga. The Dutch also have two corvettes in the Mediterranean. Notes in a postscript that the Dutch fleet is commanded by Admiral de Winter.

RC and enclosures (DNA: RG 59, CD, Gibraltar, vol. 2). RC 2 pp.; docketed by Brent as received 8 Oct. 1802. Enclosures are an extract of Simpson to Gavino, 27 June 1802 (1 p.), stating that he was following Alcayde Abde-Rhaman Hashash to Tetuán in expectation of receiving the emperor's decision on peace or war with the U.S. and warning that "the Capn. of the frigate that lays ready for Sea at Larach carrys orders to take American Vessels, which you will please Communicate to whom it may Concern coming in your way"; and O'Brien to JM, 20 May 1802 (2 pp.).

§ From Thomas Sumter, Jr. *30 July 1802, Paris.* Introduces [John Jones] Waldo, "the same gentleman for whom Mr. Livingston made a conditional application to you, last winter, supposing, then, that the french government would not agree to recieve Mr. Cathalan as commercial Agent & which he has since informed you was determined on." Repeats his recommendation of Waldo for Cathalan's post "or any other place, as agreeable to Mr. Waldo as Marseilles."

RC (DNA: RG 59, LAR, 1801–9, filed under "Waldo"). 1 p. Addressee not indicated. For Livingston's recommendation, see his letter to JM of 31 Dec. 1801 (*PJM-SS,* 2:360, 361 n. 6).

§ From William Buchanan. *31 July 1802, Ile de France.* Encloses a list of "the American Vessels, which have arrived at this port up to the 30 June, as pointed out in your orders." Notes that the list is incomplete; "it frequently happens, that the Consul never sees the Capn. during the time he is in port; and he is indebted to others for the informations he receives." Believes the island's administration would assist in getting the information, "but the proposition would draw upon me, the displeasure of all the american masters: as well as that of the French Merchants residing here, who are very jealous of the few Americans, who are established at this Place."

RC (DNA: RG 59, CD, Port Louis, vol. 1). 1 p.; docketed by Brent as received 20 Nov. Enclosure not found.

§ From Edward Livingston. *31 July 1802, New York.* Encloses a letter from Colonel Weissenfels written on behalf of his son-in-law Mr. Baker.[1] Indicates that the latter is "well acquainted with several of the Modern languages and I think he might be useful in the Office he solicits."

RC and enclosure (DLC: Jefferson Papers); FC (NjP: Edward Livingston Papers). RC 1 p. RC and enclosure filed with JM to Jefferson, 20 Aug. 1802. For enclosure, see n. 1.

1. Frederick Weissenfels to Livingston, 28 July 1802 (1 p.), recommended John Martin Baker for a consulship at Bordeaux or Gibraltar. Frederick Weissenfels (d. 1806) served as an

officer in various New York regiments of the Continental line during the American Revolution, rising to the rank of lieutenant colonel (Abbot, *Papers of Washington: Presidential Series*, 2:203 n.).

§ From John J. Murray. *31 July 1802, Glasgow.* Acknowledges JM's letter of 18 Mar. [not found] enclosing another commission for him as U.S. consul, confirmed by the Senate. Transmits a renewal of his bond for $2,000. Reports that he arrived at Glasgow on 29 June and received his exequatur on 25 July, "since which nothing has transpired ⟨w⟩orth communicating to you except an account of the Declaration of War by the Emperor of Morocco against the united states." Requests permission to appoint a deputy at the port of Leith. "My doubts respecting the propriety of mak⟨ing⟩ such an appointment originates in the knowledge that Mr. Grant some years ago received from the United states the appointm⟨ent⟩ of Consul for Leith[1]—since which however, he has not . . . resided within his consulate making Londo⟨n⟩ or Paris, where he is now, his place of res⟨i⟩dence. I have had an application from Leit⟨h⟩ for a deputation which inclines me to believ⟨e⟩ that there is no American Agent there at all."

RC (DNA: RG 59, CD, Glasgow, vol. 1). 2 pp.; docketed by Brent.

1. John Adams's appointment of Harry Grant of South Carolina as consul at Leith was confirmed by the Senate on 14 July 1798 (*Senate Exec. Proceedings*, 1:286).

§ From William Willis. *31 July 1802, Barcelona.* "I arriv'd here on the 23d inst and on the following day wrote to our minister at Madrid a Coppy which letter I now enclose to you as it contains something respecting the Clamor that has been rais'd in my absence which as I expected has ceas'd and those that have been so active in their Clamor begin now to be sensible that their reward will be nothing but shame and disgrace and some of the most violent of them have met me with hipocriti[c]al apologies for their Conduct. I also enclose you my second letter to our Minister—by which you will also see some of the most agravating parts of the treatment I have met with. . . . In my journey through france I discover'd nothing remarkable. The people seem in general friendly to the United States." Forwards a letter from O'Brien. Hopes soon to conclude the case of Captain Mills of the ship *Catherine*.[1] "The case of this Vessell is Certainly a hard one as the inocence of the Captain has been made manifest and the Spanish Government seem sensible of it or otherwise they Certainly would have condemnd him."

RC and enclosures (DNA: RG 59, CD, Barcelona, vol. 1). RC 3 pp.; docketed by Brent. Enclosures (4 pp.) are copies of Willis to Charles Pinckney, 24 and 28 July 1802.

1. The case of the *Catherine* stemmed from an incident in September 1800 in which the captain of the ship, James Mills, was accused by the Spanish of complicity in the capture of two Batavian frigates by British ships in Barcelona harbor. The *Catherine* was detained in Barcelona despite the protest of David Humphreys, then U.S. minister to Spain (Humphreys to Urquijo, 17 Sept. 1800 [DNA: RG 59, DD, Spain, vol. 6], and Yrujo to John Marshall, 2 Jan. 1801 [DNA: RG 59, NFL, Spain, vol. 1]).

§ From Joseph McLellan. *August 1802, Portland.* Has received JM's letter of 12 July [not found] enclosing a commission for him as a commissioner of bankruptcy "but must decline accepting the trust, on Account of my being so far advanced in years—& being deprived in a great measure of my eye Sight." Wonders if the commission was meant for his son, Joseph McLellan, Jr., who is a merchant in the nearby town of Gray. "*He* as well as myself, are warm & Steady friends to the President, . . . and I have a right to suppose—he would accept the Office if appointed."

RC (DNA: RG 59, LAR, 1801–9, filed under "McLellan"). 1 p.; in a clerk's hand, signed by McLellan; docketed by Jefferson.

To Edward Livingston

SIR   DEPT. OF STATE Augst. 1. 1802
    I have duly recd. yours of the 28 Ult:[1] inclosing a protest of James Hopper commander of the private English ship James, against James McCall capt: of the Diana, an American armed ship.[2]
    In the absence of the President, I can only offer my own opinion that the object in taking the bond of the latter to the U. States, makes it proper, that it should be put in suit in behalf of the former; on the condition you suggest, of security to the U. States against costs. I remain very respectfully Sir Your most Obedt. servt.

                                                    JAMES MADISON

RC (NjP: Edward Livingston Papers); letterbook copy (DNA: RG 59, DL, vol. 14).

    1. Letter not found.
    2. For Hopper's case, see JM to Rufus King, 28 July 1801, and King to JM, 31 Dec. 1801 (*PJM-SS*, 1:485, 485–86 n., 2:356).

From Fulwar Skipwith

SIR   PARIS 1 Augt. 1802
    Under cover of my last letter of the 14th. March I had the honor of inclosing to you two seperate statements of the American claims in my charge, the first comprehending those commited to me while in the Office of Consul General, and the other those that have lately been placed in my hands as Agent of Claims for the United States. I informed you of my having submited both descriptions of said claims to what is called the Commission of Comptabilité Intermediaire for liquidation, who notwithstanding my daily and pressing solicitations for the final adjustment of them, I

am sorry to add, have made but little progress to that effect. There has however lately been a new organization of this Commission, and a Counsellor of State, Mr. Defermond,[1] placed at their head under the denomination of the Council of liquidation of the Public debt, and from his assurances, I hope in the course of one month more to be enabled to anoun⟨ce⟩ to you the liquidation of such Claims as are intrusted to my Agency, and have been accompanied by regular and substanti⟨al⟩ documents. Such as are not thus supported must remain unsett⟨led⟩ untill they be furnished me by the Parties concerned therein. As yet this Government maintain their long and obstinate silence on the subject of Interest, and the mode and time of making payment; but the prevailing opinion is that the Principal will be either funded on the footing of the national debt, or paid by instalments, bearing Interest, annually from one to ten years.

It was my intention, as mentioned in my letter of the 14th. March, to pass some months of this year in Virginia, but the prospect of seeing something decissive effected in the adjustment of my Countrymens claims, added to the ameliorating state of my health, has induced me to defer my project of returning to the United States.

Inclosed is an Arreté just published of the 1st. Consul fixing the duties of entry on French and foreign Colonial produce; and also I inclose a tariff of the new weights and measures of France. Some particular Ports, namely, Bordeaux, L'Orient, and Dunkerque are endeavoring to obtain of this Government the exclusive priviledge of the East India and Tobacco trade, while most of the others are remonstratring [sic] against the justice and policy of granting them. The ultimate conduct of the Government in this affair is yet doubtful.

I have the honor of sending herewith my Bond required for the performance of my official duties and am with great consideration, Sir, Your Mo Ob Servt

FULWAR SKIPWITH

RC (DNA: RG 59, CD, Paris, vol. 1). Enclosures not found.

1. Jacques Defermon (1752–1831) was an early participant in French revolutionary politics where he gained a reputation as a financial expert. After the coup of 18 Brumaire an VIII (9–10 Nov. 1799) Defermon became president of the commission of finances within the Council of State (Tulard, *Dictionnaire Napoléon*, p. 582).

§ From Fulwar Skipwith. *1 August 1802, Paris.* "The foregoing[1] being from a very respectable merchant of Philadelphia, and on a subject in my opinion of sufficient importance to shew the expediency of there being as speedily as may be a Commercial Agent at Antwerp, I beg leave to recommend its contents to your attention."

RC (DNA: RG 59, LAR, 1801–9, filed under "Skipwith").

1. Skipwith wrote this note to JM on the last page of a copy of Leopold Nottnagel to Skipwith, 2 July 1802 (3 pp.; in French; docketed by Brent as enclosed in Skipwith's 1 Aug. dispatch). Nottnagel wrote at the behest of a number of Americans in Antwerp. Using the example of the ship *Voltaire*, he explained that the complexity of commercial regulations at Antwerp and the merchants' ignorance of them meant that shippers risked the confiscation of their cargoes, an action that could be avoided if a U.S. commercial agent were appointed.

From Aaron Burr

Sir   Nyork 2 Augt. 1802

At the request of Col. Weissenfels I transmit the enclosed Certificate.[1] Having served with the Colonel during the revolutionary War & knowing him to be a brave & Valuable officer, a Man of integrity & honor, I could not refuse to him this Civility. I have no personal acquaintance with Mr Baker, but from my knowledge of two of the persons attesting in his favor, I cannot doubt of the truth of their Certificate. It may be proper to add that Mr. Baker is the son in Law of Col. Weissenfels. I have the honor to be with great respect Your Ob St

A; Burr

RC and enclosure (DLC: Jefferson Papers). Filed with JM to Jefferson, 20 Aug. 1802.

1. Burr enclosed a one-page certificate, dated 30 July 1802 and signed by Frederick Weissenfels, William Tredwell, and John Casenave, attesting to John Martin Baker's character and knowledge of English, French, Spanish, and Italian.

§ From Frederick Weissenfels. *2 August 1802, New York.* "Permit me to recomend to your Notice and patronage the Bearer hereof my Son in Law, John Martin Baker, Whose object to your City is, to obtain an appointment from our Government, in the Consular department, your Interest Joined with the two Eminent Characters Who are engaged in his behalf, leaves not the least doubt of its Success."

RC (DLC: Jefferson Papers). 1 p. Filed with JM to Jefferson, 20 Aug. 1802.

§ From William Jarvis. *3 August 1802, Lisbon.* Reports that he arrived on 1 Aug. and wrote the enclosed letter to the minister of foreign affairs the next day.[1] Acknowledges JM's letter of 6 May, which he received on his arrival; will "pay particular attention to the several claims against this Government for the Vessels siezed in the Brazils." Notes that the quarantine "laid last winter" has been taken off. Has just received a letter from John J. Clark of Providence, who "acquaints me of the siezeure of his schoon⟨er⟩ Pilgrim, Saml. Staples Master, in Rio Janiero upon suspicion of intending to carry on an illicit Trade, & has requested me to pu⟨r⟩sue the business." Both the *Pilgrim* and the *Samuel* "have been condemned for a breach of

451

the Law of the realm." Encloses a copy of the condemnation in the *Samuel* case.[2] "I am much mortified at the situation of our Affairs with the powers of Barbary, which appear from the inclosed papers to be in the most disagreeable posture; Mr Bulkeley has to day put them into my hands; part of which he informed me he had communicated to you, but . . . I thought it most desireable to Copy & forward the whole,[3] well knowing from the interest Government takes in those affairs, how desirable is the most speedy & correct information on the subject. I shall not make any remarks on any of the letters except that from Bonaventura ⟨on⟩ page 12, which it is possible might not have been any thing but a friendly Vessel. . . . I have agreeable to your wishes been particularly careful that Mr Bulkeley shall have no cause to complain of a want of delicacy on the part of Government or myself, of which he appears to be fully sensible." In a postscript, notes that he is forwarding a letter just received from James Simpson.

RC and enclosures (DNA: RG 59, CD, Lisbon, vol. 1). RC 3 pp.; docketed by Brent as received 6 Oct.

1. Jarvis's letter to João de Almeida de Mello e Castro, 2 Aug. 1802 (1 p.), announced his arrival to take up his post as U.S. consul and requested an audience.
2. The enclosed translation of the 3 Dec. 1801 court decision in the case of the *Samuel* (1 p.) is certified by Jarvis as a true copy.
3. Jarvis enclosed a twelve-page transcription of documents that included the letters Thomas Bulkeley had already sent JM (see Bulkeley to JM, 16 July 1802, n. 2) as well as Capt. Alexander Murray to Bulkeley, 18 May 1802 (printed in Knox, *Naval Documents, Barbary Wars*, 2:155), which forwarded information from Richard O'Brien at Algiers on the "Terrible Marine of the potent Algerines"; John Gavino to the U.S. minister at Lisbon, 28 June 1802; a circular letter from O'Brien, 30 June 1802; a certificate forwarded by Gavino from Charles Clarby of the ship *Rose*, warning of pirates in the area of the "Western Isles"; Robert Montgomery to Bulkeley, 10 July 1802, which enclosed the 16 June letter from the captain of the *Fortune*; and a translation of a letter from Bonaventura José Moreina to Bulkeley, 20 July 1802, describing the pendants and rigging of a probable pirate cruiser.

§ From James Simpson. *3 August 1802, Tangier.* No. 47. "Last Night I returned from Tetuan after having had an interview with Hadge Abdarhaman Hashash, who confirmed to me that the Ship mentioned to be at Larach, was destined to detain American Vessels, as well as others; and shewed me His Majestys original Letter . . . authorising Hashash to give directions to the Captain for that effect. . . . Happily Commodore Morris being at hand with the Adams & Enterprise, the prevailing oppinion in this Country was against risquing the Ship at Sea, which circumstance has aided me on this occasion, beyond what I can express." Hashash proposed to "withdraw the authority he had given for the Larach Ship takeing Americans" if Simpson would grant consular certificates allowing the cruiser to put to sea, "but that I positively refused . . . untill such time as His Majesty should see proper, to give the most positive declaration of his being at Peace" with the U.S. "After many arguments on both sides," Hashash agreed to recommend to the emperor that he "desist from his hostile intentions" against the U.S. "As I perfectly believe he was the chief Instigator with the Emperour for makeing the essay he has done for War, I considered that as a great point gained." Encloses a copy of his own letter to the emperor. "I enjoy great hopes of a speedy accommodation, . . . yet I must candidly say had there not been a Naval force at hand . . . I very much doubt if all I could have done, would have been attended with that success, I now so much hope for. The intelligence I was enabled to give Muley Soliman of The Presidents resolution of sending the Gun Carriages came most opportunely." Anticipates hearing from the emperor "about Sunday next." Hashash also requested a passport for an unarmed schooner to carry wheat from Rabat to Tunis, to which Simpson agreed, "seeing him so much disposed for an accommodation." Notes that Ragusa has granted the emperor two ships for transporting wheat to Tripoli.

Does not have JM's letter of 30 [20] Apr. at hand; "I cannot however excuse saying with how much Affliction I observed my claim to an encrease of Salary, equal to the actual expences attendant on my residence in this Country, beyond what was first alloted for the Consul of Morocco, had not met The Presidents immediate approbation." Requests that his case be reconsidered.

RC and enclosure (DNA: RG 59, CD, Tangier, vol. 1). RC 5 pp.; extract printed in Knox, *Naval Documents, Barbary Wars*, 2:221–22. The enclosure is a copy of Simpson to the emperor of Morocco, 31 July 1802 (4 pp.; docketed by Brent), in which Simpson communicated the contents of JM's letter, expressing high regard for the emperor's "faithfull observance of the Peace" and announcing the president's decision to give the emperor one hundred gun carriages as a token of friendship; Simpson added that he intended to wait in Tangier for the emperor's answer to these overtures for peace (printed ibid., 2:219–20). Jefferson communicated an extract of the RC and a copy of the enclosure to Congress with his annual message on 15 Dec. 1802 (printed in *ASP, Foreign Relations*, 2:467–68).

§ From Robert Smith. *3 August 1802, Navy Department.* Acknowledges JM's letter of 29 July and informs him that Lieutenant Chauncey will be instructed to deliver $30,000 to Algiers. "In the event of the money not being applied as intended, Commodore Morris will be instructed with respect to receiving it back. . . . Mr. Chauncey will also be instructed to receive and deliver the Gun carriages as you request."

RC (DLC); letterbook copy (DNA: RG 45, Letters to Secretary of State). RC 2 pp.; in a clerk's hand, signed by Smith. Docketed by Brent as received 6 Aug.

§ From Carlos Martínez de Yrujo. *3 August 1802, Mount Pleasant.* Has previously complained of the insulting and indecorous behavior of Captain Mullowny of the U.S. ship *Ganges*,[1] not only in the attack and seizure of a French corsair off the coast of Cuba near Matanzas but also in having arranged the escape of his prize after entering the port of Havana. Has had no satisfactory response from the U.S. government in this matter and has received orders to renew his complaint. Hopes the U.S. will reprimand or punish the captain.

RC (DNA: RG 59, NFL, Spain, vol. 2). 2 pp.; in Spanish; in a clerk's hand, except for Yrujo's complimentary close and signature.

1. See Yrujo to JM, 4 June 1801 (*PJM-SS*, 1:262). Charles Pinckney also relayed complaints from the Spanish government about John Mullowny (see Pinckney to JM, 6 Apr. 1802, and n. 1).

From Smith Thompson and Others

GENTLEMEN,   POUGHKEEPSIE 4th. August 1802.

We have observed by the public prints, that the President of the United States, has pursuant to a late Act of Congress, appointed three setts of Commissioners of Bankruptcy for this State; two in the City of New York and one in the City of Albany.[1]

The distance between these two Cities is one hundred and sixty miles —and in the intermediate Country, on both sides of the river Hudson, are a number of flourishing Towns and Villages, particularly in the County of Dutchess. Poughkeepsie, the shire Town of Dutchess, is situated on the east bank of the Hudson, midway between the two Cities mentioned above; it is rapidly increasing in commerce & population and forms a convenient centre for transacting the business of the neighbouring Villages. Induced by these circumstances, we beg leave to offer through you an opinion to the President, that the appointment of a sett of Commissioners at this place would be an accommodation to the Citizens of the Middle parts of the state[2]—and we take the liberty, in the event of the Presidents deeming it expedient to appoint a sett of Commissioners here, to name the following Gentlemen as suitable characters for the purpose—vizt. Col. Aaron Stockholm, who resides in the vicinity of our Village (formerly a Merchant and now one of our most respectable Farmers) And Samuel Hawkins & James Tallmadge Junr. Esquires Attornies at law of this place. All these Gentlemen are of a reputable standing in the Community, and in our Judgment highly trustworthy, and fully competent to discharge the duties which will be required of them under this appointment. And we do not hesitate to vouch for the soundness of their morals and republican principles. We have the honor to be with much respect Your most Obedt. and hume. Servants

SMITH THOMPSON
BROCKHOLST LIVINGSTON
EDW LIVINGSTON

Note—The two latter Gentlemen have been heretofore recommended to the president for the appointments expressed.

RC (DNA: RG 59, LAR, 1801–9, filed under "Stockholm"). Addressed to JM and Albert Gallatin. Docketed by Jefferson and Gallatin.

1. For the names of the nine commissioners, see JM to James Fairlie, 19 June 1802. The announcement of the New York appointments was first made in the *National Intelligencer*, 18 June 1802.
2. This request was indicative of the pressure on the Jefferson administration to appoint commissioners of bankruptcy in small towns and rural areas. Both JM and Jefferson understood the problem, but they wished to avoid the proliferation of government appointments.

They considered the need for a general regulation but postponed action until the fall (Jefferson to JM, 16 Aug. and 6 Sept. 1802, and JM to Jefferson, 3 Sept. 1802).

§ From John Lowell. *4 August 1802, Boston.* "I am unacquainted with the forms which it is incumbent on me to pursue to obtain a ballance due to the Estate of my late lamented father.[1] Perhaps the application should be to a different department, but knowing that my father had the honor of an acquaintance with you, I flattered myself that you would excuse any mistake I may make on this subject. I believe but am not certain that my father received his salary up to January last, & I now inclose an account to the time of his death."[2] Will be indebted to JM for informing him if "further powers or other measures" are necessary to collect "this small ballance."

RC and enclosures (DNA: RG 217, First Auditor's Accounts, no. 13,696). RC 1 p.; docketed by Brent as received 10 Aug. For enclosures, see n. 2.

1. John Lowell, Sr., was chief judge of the first U.S. circuit court at his death in 1802. He served in the Continental Congress with JM in 1782 and 1783.
2. Lowell enclosed an account (1 p.; docketed by Brent) of salary due his father from 1 Jan. until his death on 7 May 1802 in the amount of $705.16. A note appended by a clerk in the auditor's office explained that John Lowell, Sr., had already received his first quarter's pay, and the sum due was adjusted to $203.30. Also enclosed was a certificate of Lowell's appointment as administrator of his father's estate (1 p.; docketed by Brent).

¶ From Clement Biddle. Letter not found. *4 August 1802, Philadelphia.* Mentioned in Daniel Brent to Biddle, 12 Aug. 1802 (DNA: RG 59, DL, vol. 14), as a request for information about a claim for flour furnished by Thomas Truxtun to the French republic in 1794. Brent informed Biddle in JM's absence that "a full and careful search among the Reports to this Department from our Agents at Paris" had not revealed anything about the claim.

From Carter Bassett Harrison

DEAR SIR,   RICHMOND August 5th. 1802
    Since I had the pleasure of se[e]ing you I have received a letter from my Brother William Harrison in which there is the following passage "I know that you are upon intimate terms with Mr Madison & I believe with Genl Dearbourn, should you not think it improper I wish you to write to each of those Gentle[men] & request them to take me under their Patronage so far as to give me their private advice and assistance should it at any time in their opinion be necessary & if you please you may inform them that if my conduct deserves censure I shall consider it as the greatest proof of their friendship if they will condescend to point out my errors" now my good

Sir if there be nothing wrong in the request you will confer a favor also on me by being the adviser of this young Man; should this request however be improper I pray you to reject the proposal without hesitation. I am not sufficiently acquainted with the S at War to write to him on the subject but you may if you please mention it to him with my compliments.

I shall hope to hear from [you] whilst I am in the Inda. Territory whither I am now bound. Wm Short arrived here a few days ago from France, he is now with the Govnr who has injured his leg a little & is somewhat lame. Present me respectfully to Mrs Madison & assure yourself of my esteem & confidence I am your friend & hble Servt

CARTER B HARRISON

RC (DLC). Docketed by Brent as received 9 Aug., with his note, "I have shewed this letter to General Dearbourne. DB"; also docketed by JM.

§ From William Eaton. *5 August 1802, Tunis.* Encloses copies of letters received from chargé d'affaires at Tripoli,[1] Captain Morris,[2] and Hamet Pasha.[3] Has heard from a Tripolitan merchant that the presence of the latter at Malta has excited alarm at the Tripolitan court and "Universal discontentment and revolt pervade all clases" there. "The reigning Bashaw has caused as many shirts, or robes to be constructed as he has prisoners, payed with pitch and sulpher, and he swears he will burn every American and Swede he shall have in possession the moment a shot is fired on the town. Shall such a monster live, and dictate laws to nations who could crush him!"

"This morning the Algerine Jew, Azulai, informed me that, a few days ago, letters passed through his hands from the Dey of Algiers to the Bashaw of Tripoli, demanding the immediate release of the American Captives . . . and that these dispatches were accompanied by letters from Mr. OBrien. I have received no communications from this Genn. since the 15. May—and, if Azulai's statement be true, I should be at loss to account for his taciturnity on the subject with me if I did not percieve in the transaction a perseverance of the original progect of placing the affairs of the UStates in these regencies in the controle of a cordon of Algerine Jews stationed at the different capitals. . . . I apprehend the Dey's claim will succede like his guarantee of the peace: it is possible however that the Bashaw's dependence on the Dey for supplies may induce him to concede. . . . I have put in a claim for our prisoners in exchange for those which Commodore Dale released last summer, taking the Bashaw's promise for seven Americans when captured."

Notes that there is "some misunderstanding" between Hammuda Bey and the regency of Algiers, evidenced by the bey's "having formed a camp of three thousand men which will march tomorrow towards the frontier of Constantine to observe the motions of an Algerine camp." Reports a conversation with the bey after the *Franklin*'s capture: "'You keep' said he 'a very close blockade before Tripoli—your frigates appear to be very vigilant—But supposing you were to undertake to blocade a thousand miles seacoast how many such vigilant frigates would you employ on the service?' I answered this sarcasm by saying that the enemy had not much to boast of in having picked up, after more than a year's warfare, one poor brig and nine defenceless seamen."

Complains of lack of cooperation from Captain Murray. "The procedure of this commander respecting my measures has thrown me into great embarrassments and obvious disgrace here." Wishes to be replaced if the U.S. government will not support his measures. "But let not my successor be an *Algerine Jew*."

States that Lewis Hargreaves, whom he had named "to take charge of this office in case of my decease or necessary absence," is moving to England; "I shall name Captain Holck, his Danish Majesty's Consul, to this trust." Reports "some misintelligence between the french Government and the Dey of Algiers—the English also." Spain threatens Tunis with its "*whole naval force*" if the bey "persists in his demands." The bey "answered laconically 'Let them come.'" Has received a 16 July letter from Pulis at Malta stating that the emperor of Morocco has declared war on U.S. but hopes this information is unfounded.

RC and enclosures (DNA: RG 59, CD, Tunis, vol. 2, pt. 1); letterbook copy (CSmH). RC 4 pp.; docketed by Wagner. Printed in Knox, *Naval Documents, Barbary Wars*, 2 : 223–25.

1. The enclosed letter to Eaton from Nicolai C. Nissen in Tripoli, 21 July 1802 (1 p.), announced the arrival of a Tripolitan corsair with Capt. Andrew Morris and eight seamen as prisoners and forwarded Morris's letter of the same date.

2. Andrew Morris was captain of the brig *Franklin*, which was owned by Summert and Brown of Philadelphia and was captured by three Tripolitan corsairs off Cape Palos on 17 June. In the enclosed 21 July 1802 letter (3 pp.), Morris informed Eaton of the circumstances of his capture and Nissen's intervention on his behalf. He complained that an American frigate and a Swedish frigate off the port of Tripoli had watched the progress of the Tripolitan corsair carrying him and his crew into the port but "never made the smallest effort to obstruct our progress." He warned that the three corsairs were ready to sail again under the command of Murad Rais. Eaton appended a note requesting that "this copy may be forwarded to Messrs. Summert and Brown."

3. In his letter to Eaton, 15 July 1802 (1 p.; in Italian), Hamet Qaramanli requested a living allowance to maintain himself in exile.

§ From Rufus King. *5 August 1802, London*. No. 74. Requests that the president accept his resignation and permit him to return home.[1] Had originally intended to serve no more than four years, but the war and subsequent negotiations kept him in Great Britain for six. Believing there is "nothing very material remaining to be discussed, in which I can flatter myself with being able to render any important Service," wishes to be relieved in April. Asks permission to transport his family and personal possessions in a U.S. frigate, which would be safer and less expensive than passage in a private ship.

RC (DNA: RG 59, DD, Great Britain, vol. 10); letterbook copy (NHi: Rufus King Papers, vol. 55). RC 2 pp.; in a clerk's hand, signed by King; docketed by Brent as received 27 Sept. Printed in King, *Life and Correspondence of Rufus King*, 4 : 154–55.

1. King was frustrated by the Jefferson administration's refusal to begin negotiations to revise the soon-to-expire commercial provisions of the Jay treaty. Realizing he had little influence with Jefferson and JM, he complained to Alexander Hamilton that he was not willing to

be "a mere figurant" of the administration. Hamilton advised him to return home. In December 1802 JM sent King official permission to return (King to Hamilton, 8 Apr. 1802, Syrett and Cooke, *Papers of Hamilton*, 25:598; Hamilton to King, 3 June 1802, and JM to King, 16 Dec. 1802, King, *Life and Correspondence of Rufus King*, 4:132, 200).

§ From Rufus King. *5 August 1802, London.* Suggests that if the president consents to his return to the U.S., the same public ship could bring his successor and return King home. Realizes it is unlikely a frigate from the Mediterranean would be convenient, since "coming from that Quarter she might be liable to perform Quarantine which would occasion a long detention, as well as great Expense." Requests to be informed as soon as possible of the president's decision so that he might make arrangements to decrease his baggage if a public ship cannot be made available.[1] Also requests that Nicholas Low[2] of New York be notified so that if necessary "he may execute a Provisional Order I have given him, to prepare and send from New York a Vessel to carry me and my family home." In a postscript asks to be allowed to bring home "a few Sheep of the Breeds most esteemed here" and his carriage horses if a public vessel is sent.

RC (DNA: RG 59, DD, Great Britain, vol. 10); letterbook copy (NHi: Rufus King Papers, vol. 55). RC 2 pp.; marked private and duplicate; in a clerk's hand; docketed by Brent. Printed in King, *Life and Correspondence of Rufus King*, 4:155–56.

1. JM refused King the use of a public ship for his return home. Although the stated reason was that "the Quarantine obstacle which you suggest to the return of our Frigates from the Mediterranean by way of England, cuts off the only resource which it is supposed could be made anywise consistent with the public conveniency," the real reason was given by Jefferson in a letter to James Monroe some months later—"to reform the prodigalities of our predecessors" (JM to King, 9 Oct. 1802 [typescript supplied by James G. King, New York, N.Y., 1959]; Jefferson to Monroe, 13 Jan. 1803, Ford, *Writings of Jefferson*, 8:191).

2. Nicholas Low was a New York merchant and King's financial agent. He had been a director of the Bank of New York, a director of the New York Office of Discount and Deposit of the Bank of the United States, and from 1793 to 1801 supervisor of the revenue for New York (Syrett and Cooke, *Papers of Hamilton*, 26:27 and n. 3).

§ From George Washington McElroy. *5 August 1802, Philadelphia.* Urgent personal business required his "leaving without permission my place of residence to return in about six weeks." Reports that he was received with courtesy and attention in Tenerife by the governor; has consequently forwarded his exequatur to Madrid "to be recognized at Coart [*sic*]." Wishes consuls had "some defined instructions printed and signed by the Secy. of state to be placed in a conspicuous part of their offices; specifying their duties in an official capacity toward Masters of vessels, as also that of Capns. toward Consuls, . . . as I am sorry to observe o⟨ur⟩ Captains Alone have assumed to themselves the liberty of abusing Consuls in the most shocking manner." Such conduct toward consuls "affords food for a number of English emissaries . . . to render ⟨our⟩ republic contemptable in the eyes of other nations," and it reflects badly on the honor of the U.S. government. "Mr. Ralph Fuentes formerly acting pro-Consul . . . declined acting as vice Consul, and my intention is to appoint Mr. Robert Power of Sta. Cruz Teneriffe a Merchant much respected."

RC (DNA: RG 59, CD, Tenerife, vol. 1). 3 pp.; docketed by Brent as received 9 Aug.

To Willink and Van Staphorst

GENTLEMEN,   DEPARTMENT OF STATE August 6th. 1802
I have this day drawn upon you, at fourteen days sight, in favour of Thomas T. Tucker Esq Treasurer of the United States, for twenty thousand current Guilders, being the sum received from the Batavian Government on account of the condemnation of the cargo of the ship Wilmington Packet, at St Martins, on the 30th Sept. 1793 and placed by Mr Murray late Minister Resident of the United States at the Hague, in the Hands of Messrs. Wilhem and Jan Willink, Nicholas and Jacob Van Staphorst and Hubbard, bankers of the United States at Amsterdam, on the 19th January 1800: and I request you to honor my bill without further advice. With much respect I am &

JAMES MADISON

Letterbook copy (DNA: RG 59, IC, vol. 1); letterbook copy (DNA: RG 59, DL, vol. 14).

From Elias Boudinot

MINT OF THE UNITED STATES
SIR   PHILAD. 6th. August 1802
I am sorry to inform the President of the United States through you, that a malignant fever now spreading through this City leaves the Mint little hope of keeping the workmen of the Mint many days longer.[1] It being within about 500 yards of the Mint has greatly alarmed us. Indeed, such is the state of men's minds on the occasion, that I think it neither advantageous nor safe to keep the Mint open, unless the disorder should suddenly disappear. My present expectations are, that all the public offices will remove the next week.

As it is proper the President should know all our movements, I enclose a rough copy of the Orders I shall issue in case my fears are verified,[2] that if any alteration should be agreeable to Government, it may be made. There is a very large sum in both Gold & Silver in the Mint, that cannot be worked up under four or five weeks. I have the honor to be with great respect Sir, Your very humble servant

(signed)   ELIAS BOUDINOT D. M.

Letterbook copy (DNA: RG 104, Letters Sent by Director of Mint, vol. 1); letterbook copy (DNA: RG 104, Domestic Letters and Statements of Mint).

1. The "malignant fever" was probably the yellow fever, which had struck Philadelphia repeatedly in the 1790s. In 1802 the death toll reached almost three hundred (Rowe, *Thomas McKean*, p. 332).

2. Boudinot's proposed orders have not been found. In a letter of 9 Aug. 1802 (DNA: RG 59, DL, vol. 14), Daniel Brent informed Boudinot that JM and Jefferson were absent from the capital but that Albert Gallatin "approves of the arrangement you propose." Brent added that he would forward Boudinot's letter and enclosure to JM, "but before his answer can well be received, I very much fear, from present appearances, you will have found it necessary to take a definitive step, & to abandon the City."

From Thomas Jefferson

DEAR SIR   MONTICELLO Aug. 6. 1802.

I now return you the letters of mr. Pichon, and of Jones; also those of Van Polanen & Thos. Sumter. The letter to be written to Van Polanen should be so friendly as to remove all doubt from the Batavian government that our suppression of that mission proceeds from any other motive than of domestic arrangement & e[c]onomy. I inclose you a draught of a letter to the emperor of Morocco, which make what it should be and send to your office to be written over the blank I have signed. A letter from mr. Short, dated Norfolk July 29. gives me reason to expect him here hourly. Present my respects to the ladies, & accept assurance⟨s⟩ of my constant & affectionate esteem & respect.

TH: JEFFERSON

RC (DNA: RG 59, ML); FC and FC of enclosure (DLC: Jefferson Papers). FC of enclosure (1 p.) is a letterpress copy of Jefferson's draft letter to the emperor of Morocco. The copy sent to JM with the signed blank paper has not been found. The letter was never sent.

§ From James Leander Cathcart. *6 August 1802, Leghorn.* No. 10. Has received circulars from Gibraltar announcing the Moroccan declaration of war against the U.S. "By my Circular of the 11th. of Septr. 1801[1] copy's of which were forwarded to the Department of State and to Comodore Dale I foresaw this event, & I hope I will not be thought presumptuous should I assert that it might have been prevented." Encloses Simpson's answer to the circular [not found]. "The above event is the more distressing as it may influence the other Barbary States to follow the example & it divides our force in such a manner that nothing decisive can be done at Tripoli this year"; but Moroccan forces are "so contemptible" that if American merchant ships would arm and sail in convoy there would be "little to fear." Encloses a circular from Eaton reporting that the captured brig *Franklin* had arrived at Bizerte and the vessel and cargo were put up for sale at Tunis;[2] "no doubt the crew will be march'd overland to Tripoli." Has informed Eaton of his opinion as stated in his dispatch no. 9. "I hope it may induce him to redeem our Citizens even at an exorbitant ransom if practicable on any terms which to me seems doubtfull." The *Boston* arrived at Leghorn 27 July and sailed for the U.S. on 30 July. Refers JM to Captain McNeill "for intelligence relative to our opperations before Tripoli."

RC (DNA: RG 59, CD, Tripoli, vol. 2); enclosure (DNA: RG 59, CD, Tunis, vol. 2, pt. 1). RC 2 pp. For surviving enclosure, see n. 2.

1. Cathcart's circular letter of 11 Sept. 1801 informed U.S. consuls in the Mediterranean that the pasha of Tripoli had sent an ambassador to the emperor of Morocco to curry favor with and procure provisions from the latter (see Cathcart to JM, 27 Sept. 1801, *PJM-SS*, 2: 141 and n.).

2. Eaton's circular letter of 7 July 1802 (2 pp.; docketed by Cathcart as received 28 July) also relayed a report that five Tripolitan corsairs were at sea and advised that American vessels be prevented from sailing without convoy; Cathcart added a note stating that Eaton's circular "as well as several others anterier to this . . . produced no effect whatever, three Americans saild after we had recd. intelligence of the capture of the Franklin two unarm'd entirely & one mounting four guns" (printed in Knox, *Naval Documents, Barbary Wars,* 2:194).

From William Eaton

S‍ir,   T‍unis 7th. Aug. 1802.

Since closing my dispatches of day before yesterday I have received official information of the hostile menaces of the Emperor of Morocco, and of Commodore Morris being detained in that quarter to wait the result. In consequence of this intelligence I have written to Mahamet Bashaw and Consul Pulis, inclosures 1. & 2.[1] It is now become, in my view of our actual situation, more important than ever to retain, if possible, this Bashaw in our interest; because if the project with him succeed, it will defeat at once those of his Brother and the Emperor. It was an unlucky circumstance that our *good friends* the English set the Tripoline equipages of the ship and brig at Gibr. on the Morocco coast. Not less so that they gave convoy to the escape of Morad Rais. Have we still in America any body who believes in *English Magnanimity!*

Inclosures 3. & 4.[2] require no explication.

Last spring this Bey peremptorily demanded my passports for his merchant vessels to Tripoli. I as peremptorily refused. He ordered me to quit the regency in the first American ship which should appear. I came to the right about; and, returning to my office, forbade my secretary filling any more passports for cruisers. The Bey's commercial Agent soon appeared at the Amn. house; and begged, in God's name, that I would retract from this resolution. I answered, the Bey had chosen his position. I had taken mine; which I should hold so long as he persisted in his. This produced a message from the Bey for me to appear at Bardo. I went. An amnesty was agreed on. And a discussion entered upon on the relative advantages and disadvantages of peace and war. The minister acknowledged their inferiority of fighting our ships of war—But, added, "you cannot do us any hurt. We will lay up our large ships and send out our small cruisers to distress your commerce. A fly in a man's throat, said he, though it will not kill him, will make him vomit. But, continued he, it is not our object to provoke a war by sending you away:³ we only want a Consul of more accommodating disposition—more *friendly to the Barbary interests.*" That is to say, who will yield implicitly to all their demands and receive *gratuities* in return.⁴

When the Bey's demand for a sloop of war was in discussion, the winter after my arrival here; and when menace had failed, he sent a renegade to me with a tiskery, permit, to ship a thousand caffices (14,000 bushls.) of wheat. As tiskeries then sold this was worth little less than ten thousand dollars. I had occasion for it, and indeed, had asked for it on the terms of other purchasers. On receiving it I asked the messenger the price? He said, his master sent it as *an expression of friendship!* I returned it into his hands, with a compliment of twelve dollars for his trouble, and told him to say to his Master that, We did not do business in that way. Consequence, the Bey refused me the tiskery for payment. This circumstance produced the observation, I conjecture, at Bardo last summer, when it was proposed to offer me a consideration for passports to Tripoli, that *The English and Americans never took bribes.* The postures I have taken and held here, since the war, have kept me in continual perplexity and embarassment. Why? I have been badly supported—or rather not supported at all. It is to be hoped this will not always be the case. National Honor, interest, economy dictate otherwise. Gentlemen late in command say I am too fast. Capn. Murray *likewise.* Perhaps it is because they are too slow. A decisive blow must be struck here. The interests, as the habits, of these States are the same. And, notwithstanding any friendly professions they may utter while a douceur still rests unliquidated on their tongue, they will ultimately drop the mask, except restrained by an impression of fear. It cannot but occur, that the issue of this war will serve as precedent for ages. I am a too well wisher to present administration,⁵ apart the interests of my country, not to hope that it will be honorable. This is an expression which modesty, perhaps, should cherish and conceal. But it is presumed my tedious communications are not for the criticism of the world. Besides, I am happy to learn that the term *Republi-*

can[6] is no longer opprobrious in our country. I have the honor to remain with perfect respect Sir, your Mo. Obed Servt

WILLIAM EATON

RC and enclosures (DNA: RG 59, CD, Tunis, vol. 2, pt. 1); letterbook copy (CSmH). RC docketed by Brent.

1. In his letter to Hamet Qaramanli, 6 Aug. 1802 (2 pp.; printed in Knox, *Naval Documents, Barbary Wars*, 2:227), Eaton acknowledged the pasha's 16 July letter and informed him that Joseph Pulis would give him $2,000 to tide him over until the arrival of Commodore Morris and the execution of the planned attack on Tripoli. Eaton urged the pasha to be patient and "remember that your brother thirsts for your blood." Eaton's letter to Pulis, 6 Aug. 1802 (1 p.), requested him to make the money available to Hamet on condition that he remain in Malta.

2. Eaton's enclosures 3 and 4 were probably the copies, filed with the RC, of his letter to Danish consul Holck, 5 Aug. 1802 (1 p.), requesting the latter to "take charge of this office and the affairs of the United States" with Tunis in case of Eaton's death or absence, and Holck's affirmative reply of 6 Aug. 1802 (1 p.).

3. In the letterbook copy, Eaton interlined here: "we are willing to maintain the peace with you on the footing of other small christian nations."

4. In the letterbook copy, Eaton wrote in the margin opposite this sentence: "See P. S. to letter of Feb. 1. 1803."

5. Eaton placed an asterisk here in the letterbook copy and wrote at the bottom of the page: "*If a sense of national honor and interest cannot excite the energy of Govt. I will try what individual pride can effect!"

6. Eaton placed an asterisk here in the letterbook copy.

§ From Thomas G. Addison. *7 August 1802.* Resigns his post as justice of the peace, "as I shall be no longer a Resident in the District of Columbia, after to day." Suggests that another magistrate be appointed, since he was the only magistrate on the south side of the Eastern Branch.

RC (DLC). 1 p. Cover postmarked Alexandria, Virginia, 8 Sept. Docketed by Brent as received 9 Sept.

§ From Elias Vander Horst. *7 August 1802, Bristol.* Transmits a copy of his last letter of 24 July. "Warm weather has at length commenced here," and crops are expected to be "of fine quality as well as plentiful." Encloses newspapers and a London price current.

RC (DNA: RG 59, CD, Bristol, vol. 2). 1 p. Enclosures not found.

¶ From William Gibb. Letter not found. *7 August 1802, Accomack County, Virginia.* Mentioned in Brent to Gibb, 18 Aug. 1802 (DNA: RG 59, DL, vol. 14), as enclosing documents proving the citizenship of John Elliott, an American impressed seaman, as well as information on the ship to which he had been transferred. Brent assured Gibb that "no time will be lost in making the proper application for his discharge."

§ From John Dawson. *8 August 1802, Fredericksburg.* "At the request of some of the lawyers and merchants at this place I state to you that they recieve great inconvenience for the want of some commissioners of bankruptcy, and to mention John Minor, Hugh Mercer, Benjamin Day, Stephen Winchester, and Thomas Goodwin as proper persons, shoud it be determind to appoint. I expect to leave this today & will thank you to direct your answer to Colo: F. Brooke."

RC (DNA: RG 59, LAR, 1801–9, filed under "Mercer"). 1 p.; docketed by Jefferson.

§ From Robert W. Fox. *8 August 1802, Falmouth.* Encloses a list of American vessels that arrived in his district between 1 Jan. and 30 June 1802; "many more have touched off this port for orders and immediately proceeded on their Voyage whose names I could not procure." Price of wheat in France has fallen. "On hearing of the Barbary Powers being hostile towards the Ships of the United States, I immediately communicated the intelligence as far as I could." Trade in Great Britain "continues at a low ebb."

RC (DNA: RG 59, CD, Falmouth, vol. 1). 2 pp. Enclosure not found.

§ From Fulwar Skipwith and Others. *8 August 1802, Paris.* "Mr. Dobell lately appointed by the President, to the Commercial Agency of Havre, has declined accepting that Office." Recommends John Lyle of New Jersey, "one of our best Republicans, an excellent Citizen, a Gentleman of very amiable mind, and as a Merchant, completely calculated to discharge the duties of the Office he now solicits with advantage to the Public."

RC (DNA: RG 59, LAR, 1801–9, filed under "Lyle"). 2 pp. Signed by Skipwith, Joel Barlow, and Thomas Melville. While Dobell had accepted the position of commercial agent in his letter to JM of 5 Oct. 1801 (DNA: RG 59, CD, Havre, vol. 1) and had announced his acceptance of the post to his friends, he never took up his duties in Le Havre (*PJM-SS*, 2: 296; JM to William Jones, 28 Feb. 1803 [offered for sale in Parke-Bernet Catalogue No. 2297, 13 Oct. 1964, item 26]).

From Thomas Jefferson

Dear Sir   Monticello Aug. 9. 1802.

The inclosed letter from mr. Simpson our Consul in Marocco was forwarded to me from your office by yesterday's post.[1] The demand of the emperor of Marocco is so palpably against reason & the usage of nations that we may consider it as a proof either that he is determined to go to war with us at all events, or that he will always make common cause with the Barbary powers when we are at war with any of them. His having ordered our Consul away is at any rate a preliminary of so much meaning, that the draught of the letter I had forwarded you for him, as well as the sending him the gun carriages, are no longer adapted to the state of things. On this subject I should be glad of your opinion, as also of what nature should be the orders now to be given to our officers in the Mediterranean.[2]

The Boston frigate is expected to return: there will then remain in the Mediterranean the Chesapeake, Morris, the Adams, Campbell, & the Constitution Murray; one of which perhaps would have been recalled, as two are thought sufficient for the war with Tripoli, especially while Sweden cooperates. In the present state of things would it not be adviseable to let the three remain? or does it seem necessary to send another?

I inclose you a letter from Richard Law dated New London.[3] I suppose he may be the District judge & should be answered. The proper notification of the Commrs. of bankruptcy to the judges seems to be their commission exhibited by themselves to the court, as is done in the case of a Marshal, the only other officer of a court appointed by us. Accept assurances of my constant & affectionate esteem.

Th: Jefferson

P. S. A letter from Capt Morris informs us he had gone over to Tangier, but had not yet had any communication with the government: but that he should absolutely refuse the passports.

RC (DNA: RG 59, ML); FC (DLC: Jefferson Papers).

1. This was probably James Simpson's dispatch no. 42, to which Daniel Brent added a note (see Simpson to JM, 17 June 1802, and n.).

2. On this date Jefferson sent letters to Robert Smith and Gallatin, the contents of which were nearly identical to this paragraph (DLC: Jefferson Papers).

3. The letter from Richard Law, dated 29 July 1802, has not been found (see JM to Law, 14 Aug. 1802). Richard Law (1733–1806), of New London, Connecticut, served in the Continental Congress and compiled, with Roger Sherman, the *Acts and Laws of the State of Connecticut* (1784). In 1789 Law was appointed U.S. district judge for Connecticut, and he held that post until his death.

§ From William Eaton. *9 August 1802, Tunis.* Encloses copies of letters from chargé d'affaires at Tripoli[1] and Captain Morris.[2] These letters "serve to corroborate an opinion I have steadily entertained, and repeatedly stated to our commanders, of the necessity of having small vessels of war off and on this coast." Points out that "there is no article in our treaty with this Bey which prohibits the sale of enemy prizes in his ports" and suggests that this could be advantageous "because it induces an idea of Security to the Tripoline Cruisers with prizes coming in here. The bay of Tunis is peculiarly favorable for intercepting these cruisers passing and repassing." Has had no communication from any U.S. commander since the *Constellation* sailed from Tunis on 3 June. "And Captain McNiell being ordered home without touching here seems to me something extraordinary. Whatever may be Cap. Murray's opinion of my measures, he ought not to sacrifice the interest of service to individual resentments. Government may as well send out *quaker meeting-houses* to float about this sea as frigates with Murrays in command. . . . Have we but one

Truxton, and one *Sterret* in the United States?" Reports that "the arab camp called to the defence of Tripoli has undoubtedly been collected to defeat the project of Mahamet Bashaw. . . . If so, this amounts to unequivocal evidence of the influence that measure might have had in the war with Tripoli, if pushed to effect." Has not informed Nissen of the project; "he appears totally uninformed of it." The regency of Tunis is making new demands on the U.S., "among them the original demand of a vessel of war." Will "yield no concessions." Regrets that "our ships of war do not oftner show themselves here. The vicinity of this Regency to Tripoli, and their mutual commercial interests cannot leave the events of the war indifferent to the former."[3] Observes that he has received no advice from the U.S. since October 1801.

RC and enclosures (DNA: RG 59, CD, Tunis, vol. 2, pt. 1); letterbook copy (CSmH); Tr (NN: Cathcart Papers). RC 2 pp. Both RC and Tr marked duplicate. Extract from RC printed in Knox, *Naval Documents, Barbary Wars,* 2:229.

1. Nissen's letter of 27 July 1802 (3 pp.; docketed by Wagner) informed Eaton of the release of five of the eight crewmen of the captured brig *Franklin* and of the imminent departure of three or four Tripolitan galleys. He advised that if the pasha of Tripoli persisted in his refusal to exchange the remaining American prisoners according to an agreement made with Commodore Dale the previous year, Commodore Morris ought to inform the pasha that he could not negotiate for peace "or pay any further attention to what the Bashaw might promise when he thinks so little of a former engagement. . . . The Bashaw, desirous of a peace, will comply." Nissen added that Tripoli was "entirely surrounded by Camps of Arabs, all the different tribes that acknowledge the authority of the Bashaw are here"; and the grain harvest was so good as to make the blockade not "of much service." For another copy of this letter, see ibid., 2:212–13.

2. Andrew Morris's letter to Eaton of 28 July 1802 (2 pp.) described the Tripolitan galleys and their methods of operation and suggested the means by which the U.S. could prevent the capture of merchant vessels like his own. For another copy of this letter, see ibid., 2:214–15.

3. Eaton placed an asterisk here in the letterbook copy and wrote at the bottom of the page: "*In all my communications there is not a more accurate remark than this. The Bey of Tunis would join Tripoli immediately if he had no apprehensions of loosing rather than wining by the game!"

§ From John Morton. *9 August 1802, Newport, Rhode Island.* Reports his arrival in the U.S., having departed from Havana on 15 July. As he informed JM in his letter of 24 May, he left Vincent Gray provisionally charged with U.S. affairs in Cuba; encloses a copy of his letter of instructions.[1] States his opinion that "the residence of a public Agent (if it should continue to be desired by my Government) would in future be more readily effected thro' a person already established there, than by one going from the U;States newly clothed with such authority." Although American concerns in Cuba have nearly ceased, the residence of a public officer there might still be useful. Encloses a third proclamation of the Cuban government, published 4 July, on the residence of strangers.[2] Only one instance involving the enforcement of the former decree of May 1802 required his intervention. The term of limitation expired on 12 June; Robert Read arrived on 14 June; on 15 June Read presented JM's 7 Apr. letter to Morton; and on 16 June Read was ordered to leave the island within a few hours. On Morton's application to the governor, Read was granted permission to remain. Notes that the enclosed decree will be fully enforced. In the enumeration of foreigners required by the decree, "it was discovered how small was the proportion of American to that of other foreign residents." Foreigners were ordered to appear before the assessor general (who is also the lieutenant governor) and receive permission for further residence; "in the distribution of those indulgencies there appeared, so far as I could learn, no exercise of partiality or favor to those of one, more than of another nation." In his conferences with the governor, the latter claimed to have "no discretionary powers whatever," as the decrees were dictated by the court at Madrid. Reports that a large number of merchants and planters had petitioned the court for trade to be continued in a few American articles and in the exportation of molasses, but no answer had been received. "The partial admission of our Vessels, since the Peace, as effected mostly thro' corruptive influence with the Intendant, . . . occasioned a formal Impeachment of that Officer by the Governor & Council; the result of which was not fully known on my departure." Observes that "in all those wavering and distracting opinions, & Contentions, among the Heads of Departments, the American Trader has been subjected to variable & frequently unjust & rigorous measures; and the Island left to suffer under the most pressing wants."

RC and enclosures (DNA: RG 59, CD, Havana, vol. 1). RC 9 pp.; docketed by Brent as received 16 Aug. For enclosures, see nn. 1 and 2.

1. In his 15 July letter to Vincent Gray (2 pp.), Morton formally named Gray to be provisional commercial agent of the U.S. for Havana, referred him to the State Department instructions for guidance, and charged him with the care of the records of the office.
2. The enclosed printed proclamation, dated 1 July (1 p.; in Spanish, with Morton's translation written in lower margin and on verso), announced that foreigners should present themselves to the assessor general for examination eight days after publication of the proclamation, on penalty of a fifty-ducat fine.

¶ From Alexander Moultrie. Letter not found. *9 August 1802, Charleston, South Carolina.* Mentioned in Brent to Moultrie, 21 Aug. 1802 (DNA: RG 59, DL, vol. 14). Brent promised to forward Moultrie's letter to JM at Montpelier, and "in the mean time I will take the liberty of communicating it to the Secretary of the Treasury, who is, as well as the Secretary of State, a Commissioner on the part of the United States, with regard to the lands in question."

From Robert R. Livingston

No 1⟨9⟩
DEAR SIR,   PARIS 10 August 1802
    On the 15 Thermidor when the Ministers had a public audience the Senate were ⟨announced⟩—they entered the ⟨circle with⟩ their President Barthelemi at their head. He presented the decree declaring Bonaparte Consul for life as the result of the vote and made an address in writing upon the

occasion which was answered by the first Consul from a paper he held in his hand so that it appears the moment had been concerted in order to render the act public both are contain⟨ed in the⟩ enclosed Moniteurs[1]—two days after was published the new french constitution also enclosed.[2] But what is a little extraordinary this is not considered as a new constitution (*tho it alters every tittle of the old but the names of the constituted authorities*) but merely as an explanation or exposition of it. It is evident that ⟨this constitution must form⟩ the basis of a *violent aristocracy* whenever the executive power shall fall into less energetic or less popular hands than those by which it is now administered. The power of the senate is *unlimited & undefined*. The two Consuls (who have in fact *no real place in the constitution*) together with the Corps of honor will naturally *combine to perpetuate their rule* & to render the *first consul a mere doge. The measure is not popular* but it will meet with *no opposition nor would it* in the present disposition *of the people* if it had created the most *absolute despotism*. Our own affairs have advanced but little since the whole attention of those in power are turned to objects nearer home. I have had several conferences on the subject of Louisiana—but can get nothing more from them than I have already communicated. I have thought it best by conversation and by writing to pave the way prior to any direct application till I know better to what object to point. For this purpose I have written the enclosed essay which I have had translated and struck off 20 copies.[3] I have just got them finished. I have placed some of them in such hands as I think will best serve our purposes. Taleyrand has promised to give it an attentive perusal after which when I find how it works I will come forward with some proposition. I am very much however at a loss as to what terms you would consider it as allowable to offer if they can be brought to a sale of the Floridas either with or without New Orleans—which last place will be of little consequence if we possess the Floridas because a much better passage may be formed on the east side of the river. I may perhaps carry my estimate of them too high but when I consider first the expense it will save us in guards and garrisons, the risk of war, the value of duties and what may be raised by the sale of lands I should think them *a cheap purchase at twenty millions of dollars*. I trust however that you will give me some directions on this head & not leave the responsibility of offering too much or too little entirely at my door. I speak in all this business as if the Affair of the Floridas was arranged with Spain which I believe is not yet the case. But I took occasion to touch on the subject three days ago with the *Spanish embassador* ⟨with⟩ whom I was dining & think he appeared to have somewhat relaxed on that ground but would say nothing decisive nor were the time and place proper to press him. Such is the power of this Nation over her neighbors that if she chuses to give her own construction *to the treaty they must submit*. Mr. Paterson and Mr. Vail are both here—the first considering the claims of Mr. Vail as best founded is willing to withdraw in his favor—in hopes that the President will consider him in the appointment to one of the places now vacant in addition to those I have mentioned is Hâvre by the resignation of Mr. Doble[4] who has not been there these six months residing as I believe at Bour⟨deaux—this⟩ appointment would be very acceptable to Mr. Paterson. Enclosed however is a recommendation of Mr. Lyle for that place.[5] I have told him that I would transmit the letter but that I believed if the President had made no other provision for Mr. Paterson that as he resigned from public Motives he would merit a preference. Mr. Lyle bears a fair character but has been unfortunate in commerce his house has failed, the president will judge what weight ought to be given to this circumstance. Mr. King is I believe at present in Holland from letters I have lately recieved from him he proposes to pay Paris a visit in his route. My postage bill will I fear appear very extravagant but this can not be avoided as it arises from two causes quite out of my power to correct. The first is that every american having a correspondent at Paris sends his letters under cover to me and that too frequently a mere blank cover so that I know not whence the letters come. Others having accounts or ship claims &c. send them to me and request me to be their Agent or to appoint one for them. These too often come in duplicates each of which some times amounts to 30 livres & often even more for postage as they are marked *Colonies*[6] & charged on that account with a double postage—it is impossible for me to open accounts with all these persons for trifling sums & they accordingly are paid by my Porter & enter into my postage bill. Perhaps on the whole—though these are private concerns yet they are so far interesting to the public as to justify this trifling expense which I see no way of avoiding. It will however be proper to direct all packages of Newspapers and pamphlets to be so put up as to shew what they are—for want of this I have paid 10 dollars postage upon a single set of Newspapers. I have the honor to be dear Sir with Much esteem your Mt. Hle. St

RC (NHi: Livingston Papers); draft (ibid.); letterbook copy (NHi: Livingston Papers, vol. 1). The RC is a letterpress copy marked "duplicate," in a clerk's hand, unsigned; docketed by Brent. Unless otherwise noted, italicized words are those encoded by Livingston's secretary and decoded here by the editors. RC decoded interlinearly in an unidentified hand. Words and parts of words in angle brackets are obscured by folds in the RC and have been supplied from the letterbook copy. For enclosures, see nn. 3 and 5.

1. François Barthélemy (1750–1830), diplomat, former director, and exile, had been welcomed back to France by Napoleon and made a senator (*Biographie universelle* [1843–65 ed.], 3:182–87). His address as president of the delegation that offered Napoleon the first consulship for life was printed, with Napoleon's reply, in the Paris *Moniteur universel*, 16 Thermidor an X (5 Aug. 1802).

2. The new French constitution—*Constitution de l'an X*—was published in the *Moniteur* twice, on 17 and 18 Thermidor an X (6 and 7 Aug. 1802).

3. Livingston apparently sent JM an English version of his essay, a copy of which is printed, with an extract from his dispatch, in *ASP, Foreign Relations*, 2:520–24. Livingston's thirty-three-page draft (NHi: Livingston Papers) varies somewhat in wording. The essay examined the question, "Whether it will be advantageous to France to take possession of Louisiana?" Livingston argued that due to France's economic state—its lack of both surplus population and capital—Louisiana would prove a drain on its resources rather than an economic benefit. The colony's enterprises would require a heavy investment that would take years to turn a profit. Even then, its products duplicated those of the islands of the West Indies, so that increased production would only lower prices. Nor would Louisiana provide much of a market for French manufactures. Western demands were few and simple, and French goods were too expensive for western purses. Besides, traffic on the Mississippi River ran north to south, not the reverse. Politically, Livingston went on, the proximity of a French possession to the U.S. would create friction and disputes that would only drive the Americans into the arms of the British. He closed with the argument that it was in the best interest of the French to cede New Orleans to the U.S.

4. Peter Dobell.

5. The letter recommending John Lyle may have been that of Fulwar Skipwith and others to JM, 8 Aug. 1802. Lyle was the bearer of this dispatch (see Livingston's "Journal of correspondence with the Secretary of State" [NHi: Livingston Papers, vol. 7]; Livingston to JM, 19 Aug. 1802).

6. Underlined in RC.

§ From Samuel Fulton. *10 August 1802, New Orleans.* Has written to JM "from Diffrent quarters of The world" offering his services to the U.S. "I presume it has been my peculiar Situation of being tosd. from one Country to another that has prevented me from receiveing any answer. I am now in this Country for a few months. Should my Request have been rejected by the President and the French get possession of this Country I must Reclaime a Continuance of my imploy.... I Should much Reather Serve my native Country than any other. Probably in the Mobille Country I might be more Usefully imployd. than almost any person from having Lived in it for a Considerable time & haveing had much intercourse with the Creek Indians During the Time of McGillvery." His last letter was sent by Tobias Lear, "who promised me to Speak to you particularly on the Subject."[1]

RC (DNA: RG 59, LAR, 1801–9, filed under "Fulton"). 2 pp. Cover marked, "Honod. by Col. Gaither."

1. No earlier letters from Fulton to JM have been found.

§ From William Jarvis. *10 August 1802, Lisbon.* No. 2. Forwards a duplicate of his last dispatch of 3 Aug. and part of the accompanying documents. Mentions that an American ship which arrived after a twelve-day voyage from Cadiz spotted nothing suspicious. "A letter from a private House in Cadiz" informed him that the emperor of Morocco had suspended hostilities against the U.S. for six months. "Another private letter dated the 5 Inst from the same place mentions that the 22 gun ship from Larach had saild, but is silent as to the foregoing report." Describes his audience on 8 Aug. with the Portuguese minister, who "received me with politeness." In a conversation about the quarantine, "I inform'd his Excellency of the Regulations that had been adopted at home, which would prevent Foreign Nations from being in any sort of danger from our Vessels; for if any disorder existed even of a suspicious nature it would be inserted in the Bills of Health of all Vessels comeing from such place." Reports that a misunderstanding has taken place between the Portuguese court and the French ambassador General Lannes;[1] "it is said to have arisen from the refusal of the Intendant of Police who is also Comptroller of the Customhouse to let the Genl.'s effects come on shore before the Vessel in which they came was entered, when he first came here, & the like difficulty has in one or two instances taken place since." After the ambassador's demand for the intendant's dismissal was refused, he suspended all communication with the Portuguese government and determined to quit the country. "It is hinted by some that he has taken this measure in hopes to force the Court to acquiesce in his demands & that it is not his real intentions to go farther than the borders of the Kingdom." Adds in a postscript of 11 Aug. that "the Ambassador absolutely left here yesterday without takeing leave at Court."

RC (DNA: RG 59, CD, Lisbon, vol. 1). 7 pp.; docketed by Brent.

1. Jean Lannes, duc de Montebello (1769–1809), began his military career as a volunteer in 1792, rose to brigadier general in 1797, and was named marshal of the empire in 1804. He was appointed minister to Portugal in November 1801 and served in that post until 1804, achieving some success in increasing French influence in that traditionally pro-British country (Chandler, *Napoleon's Marshals*, pp. 192–202).

§ From Rufus King. *10 August 1802, London.* No. 75. Reports on a conference with Lord Hawkesbury on trade and navigation in the West Indies and the Maryland bank stock. Hawkesbury said that measures would be taken to transfer the bank stock to the Crown. Although he indicated that there were other claims besides Maryland's, Hawkesbury seemed to think that after the stock was transferred "there would be no Difficulty of importance in the way of a satisfactory Settlement." King tried, "without success, to obtain from him an explicit Engagement that the Stock should be transferred to me, after its Transfer to the Crown." On West Indian–American trade, the minister made no commitment owing to the "unsettled as well as uncertain Condition of the West India Colonies" and the region in general. King argued that "on account of our just claim to an equal participation" in the West Indies trade, no decision meant a return to the old "unequal and injurious" system, the result of which would be passage by the U.S. of anti-British trade regulations. "These Countervailing Regulations would prove mutually . . . inconvenient" and might "disturb the harmonious and beneficial intercourse" between the two nations. Hawkesbury repeated that no decision could yet be made because of the "pressure of affairs of greater Interest." King observed that although the question might not appear important to the British, it had excited "a lively Interest" in the U.S., and it would afford him "some satisfaction" were it to be settled, along with that of the Maryland bank stock, before his departure next spring. Hawkesbury vaguely assured him there should be no reason to delay decisions beyond that time. Hawkesbury also indicated that the French expedition to Louisiana would proceed and that France was preparing another against Algiers with the active support of

Spain. King assured Hawkesbury that before his departure for the Continent he would introduce Christopher Gore, who would act as chargé d'affaires during his absence.

RC and enclosures (DNA: RG 59, DD, Great Britain, vol. 10); letterbook copy (NHi: Rufus King Papers, vol. 55); partial Tr (MdAA: Blue Book 2). RC 7 pp.; in a clerk's hand, signed by King; docketed by Brent. Printed in King, *Life and Correspondence of Rufus King*, 4: 156–59. Enclosures are copies of King's 30 July 1802 request to Hawkesbury for a conference before his departure (1 p.), and Hawkesbury's assent, 2 Aug. 1802 (1 p.) (both printed in *ASP, Foreign Relations*, 2:501).

§ From William Kirkpatrick. *10 August 1802, Málaga.* Transmits duplicates of 29 June dispatch and return of U.S. shipping. Has received letters from Gibraltar indicating "that some Hopes still exist of Mr Simpson's succeeding in arranging the actual differences, with the Emperor of Morocco." In the meantime, "Commodore Morris remains at Gibraltar with the Frigate Adams and Schooner Enterprize." Encloses for JM's information a copy of a letter just received from Richard O'Brien. Admiral de Winter proceeded to Algiers on 9 Aug. to settle matters between the Batavian government and the regencies of Algiers, Tunis, and Tripoli. Swedish frigates continue to convoy Swedish and American merchantmen.

RC (DNA: RG 59, CD, Málaga, vol. 1). 2 pp. Enclosure not found.

§ From William Lee. *10 August 1802, Bordeaux.* Reports that since his letters of 22 July and 2 Aug.[1] another seventy-three distressed seamen "have been thrown on my hands." "I thought proper to state this to you that you might see the necessity of instructing me on this head." Encloses tariff of new duties.

RC (DNA: RG 59, CD, Bordeaux, vol. 1). 2 pp. Enclosure not found.

1. Letter not found.

§ From Mr. L'Hospital. *10 August 1802, Le Havre.* Transmits a number of registers, certificates, and other ship's papers delivered to his office of ships sold at Le Havre and currently sailing under French flags: the ship *James and William* of Portsmouth, New Hampshire; the ship *Boston Packett* of Nantucket; the ship *Elizabeth* of New York; and the brig *Reunion* of Charleston. Includes also the register of the brig *Felicity* of Baltimore, "cast away in last Dber. on this coast." Requests JM to give orders to cancel the bonds of the aforesaid ships.

RC (DNA: RG 59, CD, Havre, vol. 1). 2 pp. L'Hospital signed as "Chancelor of the commal. agency of the United States" for Peter Dobell, the U.S. commercial agent at Le Havre.

§ From Josef Yznardy. *10 August 1802, Cadiz.* Informs JM of his safe arrival at Cadiz and his plan "to proceed to Madrid when I shall re[e]stablish myself of my health." Encloses "Copies of what has passed since my arrival regarding the embarasmts. of our Vessels, in consequence of the troubles with the Moors." Little or nothing will be done in foreign affairs at the court of Madrid for the next six months owing to the royal wedding. "It is for certain the ceading over to the French the Louisian⟨na⟩ and New Orleans; a large Convoy with French Troops on board has left this last week for some secret Expedition in the West Inds., but I think they are gone for the Louisianna, . . . as I do not see any other object in view."

RC (DNA: RG 59, CD, Cadiz, vol. 1). 3 pp.; in a clerk's hand, signed by Yznardy. Docketed by Brent. Enclosures not found, but see Yznardy to JM, 13 Aug. 1802, and n. 1.

To Thomas Jefferson

DEAR SIR   ORANGE Aug. 11. 1802

I reached home just before dark this evening, after the most fatiguing journey I ever encountered, having made the tour I proposed over the mountains, and met with every difficulty which bad roads & bad weather could inflict.[1] As this must be at the Court House early in the morning, I have only time to inclose you some despatches from Mr. Livingston which I recd. the night before I left Washington, and decyphered on the journey,[2] with some others which I found here on my arrival & have but slightly run over. The inclosed patent may [be] sent with your signature to the Office without returning thro' my hands.[3] Your favor of the 30th. Ult: I also found here on my arrival. Yrs. with respectful attachment

                                    JAMES MADISON

RC (DLC: Jefferson Papers). Docketed by Jefferson as received 12 Aug.

1. It is more than likely that this trip was a family visit to George Steptoe and Lucy Washington's estate, Harewood, near Charles Town, Virginia (now West Virginia). Lucy was Dolley Madison's sister, and despite the "painful journey" Dolley described to a friend, the Madisons "spent three happy days" there (Ketcham, *James Madison*, p. 381; Anna Maria Thornton to Dolley Madison, 24 Aug. 1802 [ViU]).
2. These were probably Robert R. Livingston to JM, 27 Mar. and 10 (two letters), 12, and 20 May 1802.
3. The sole surviving record of a patent issued during this period was for Jacob Idler's cotton press, which was patented on 24 Sept. 1802 (DNA: RG 241, Restored Patents, vol. 1).

From Archibald Roane

SIR   KNOXVILLE 11 August 1802.

When Doctor Dickson our Representative was on his return from Congress he gave me reason to expect that Copies of those papers or books in your office, which had respect to the titles of land in this state would be forwarded on here as soon as convenient. Permit me again to remind you that such Copies particularly those of the entries in Carter's office will be very beneficial to many of the Citizens in support of their titles as the originals are lost or destroyed. A considerable number of suits have been delayed and probably will be farther delayed or lost should they not arrive in the course of a few months. Your attention is therefore respectfully sollicitted to the business.[1] I have the honor to be &c

(signed)   ARCHIBALD ROANE

Letterbook copy (T: Governor's Letterbook).

1. For Tennessee governor Archibald Roane's request for the copy of a book containing land entries for Washington County, Tennessee, supposedly lodged in the State Department, see Roane to JM, 28 Nov. 1801 (*PJM-SS*, 2:285). Roane reiterated his request in a letter to JM of 1 Sept. 1802 (not found), to which Daniel Brent replied in JM's absence that he would "procure an examination of the copy of the Book in question to be commenced, and when it is compleated, the Secretary will, no doubt, ca[u]se it to be forwarded to you" (Brent to Roane, 4 Oct. 1802 [DNA: RG 59, DL, vol. 14]).

¶ From Elisha Fisher & Company. Letter not found. *11 August 1802, Philadelphia.* Mentioned in Brent to Elisha Fisher & Co., 18 Aug. 1802 (DNA: RG 59, DL, vol. 14), as enclosing "two accounts against the Governor of the Indiana Territory for printing." Brent replied that in JM's absence he had sent the documents to the Treasury Department for settlement "but they have just been sent back, with a note, of which I subjoin a copy"; he returned "the account in question, that you may if you think proper, procure the necessary assignments, to entitle you to the benefits of them." Brent wrote to the company again on 9 Oct. 1802 (ibid.), acknowledging a letter of 25 Sept. (not found) and stating that the amount due would be remitted by the U.S. treasurer "in the early part of next week."

§ From John Cowper. *12 August 1802, Norfolk.* "I have taken the liberty to trouble you with the inclosed for Mr. Short—it is from a very particular friend of mine and upon an interresting subject to him and neither knew Mr. Short's address. Knowing he will be at Washington, I was certain you would see him."

RC (DNA: RG 59, ML). 1 p.

§ From Thomas Moore. *12 August 1802, Retreat.* "Enclosed is a Certificate from the Farmers Society in this neighbourhood."[1]

RC and enclosure (DLC). RC 1 p. Cover dated "Brookeville 8th mo 14th. 1802." Docketed by Brent as received 16 Aug.

1. The enclosure, dated 8 May 1802 (1 p.) and signed by Joseph Elgar, president, and Thomas Moore, secretary, certified that JM was, "in confidence of his zeal to promote Agricultural knowledge, and in testimony of esteem for his character, duly elected an Honorary Corresponding member of the Farmer's society established at Sandy Spring in Montgomery county Maryland."

§ From James Simpson. *12 August 1802, Tangier.* No. 48. "Original of No 47 [3 Aug. 1802] was forwarded by way of Lisbon, duplicate and triplicate under cover of Mr Gavino at Gibraltar; each accompanied by a copy of the Letter I wrote the Emperour from Tetuan. I have now the honour of encloseing with this, translation of the answer I received last night, to that Letter; by which I am concerned to find new ground taken, likely to be productive of some trouble with His Imperial Majesty."[1] Declares that "the pretention of frequent Embassys is totally founded in error, for no such arrangement as is pretended, was . . . moved or hinted at, since the period alluded to, namely 1795." His every transaction at that time with former minister Sidi Mohamet ben Ottman is described in his dispatches to the State Department. His only letter to the minister on the subject declared "in the most positive terms" that the U.S. "would not consent to give this Country any thing whatever at stated periods." Observes that the emperor does not ask for an immediate decision but leaves room for negotiation. Will write immediately to the minister that "no such engagement as he alledges, was at any time made on the part of the United States." Commodore Morris wrote him that "very urgent Service required his passing up the Mediterranean," leaving only one frigate at Gibraltar. In consequence, has decided "to close with the Emperours wish of my remaining in this Country, as thereby we are to consider Peace restored." Hopes to receive the president's approbation for this step. "This day I have addressed twenty two Circulars to the Consuls in Europe, advising them that Peace is again restored with the Emperour."

RC and enclosure (DNA: RG 59, CD, Tangier, vol. 1). RC 3 pp.; marked "*duplicate*"; docketed by Brent as received 16 Oct. Extracts printed in Knox, *Naval Documents, Barbary Wars*, 2 : 231. Jefferson communicated an extract of the RC and the enclosure to Congress with his annual message on 15 Dec. 1802 (printed in *ASP, Foreign Relations*, 2 : 468). For enclosure, see n. 1.

1. Simpson enclosed a translation, dated 12 Aug. 1802, of a 6 Aug. letter to him from Moroccan minister Sidi Mohammed ben Absalom Selawy (3 pp.), stating that the emperor "still adheres to what you stipulated" with Sidi Mohamet ben Ottman, "which is, that your Nation shall send each year one of your people . . . with your Present; but if it be difficult for you to come every year . . . you will come once in every two Years." Selawy asserted that it was on this basis the convention and treaty with the U.S. had been signed, and "if you abide by this agreement and fulfill it, you will be as you were, . . . and if you do not fulfill it, youll see how you will have to settle your matters. What has happen'd to you now, has been occasioned by your own tardyness and neglect in this particular, but Our Master (whom God preserve) now forgives all that, and do you on your part as Justice directs, and God will assist you" (printed in Knox, *Naval Documents, Barbary Wars*, 2 : 226–27).

To Roger Gerard van Polanen

SIR   VIRGINIA Augst. 13. 1802

I have received & communicated to the President your letter of the 30th. Ulto: giving information of your appointment to another public station which terminates that which you have held near the United States.

The President receives with much satisfaction the assurance that the disposition of the Batavian Republic to cultivate friendship with the United States, will suffer no diminution from the mutual recall of their Diplomatic functionaries; and I am charged to say in return, that as the step taken in this case, on the part of the United States, had its origin altogether in considerations of domestic arrangement & œconomy, your Goverment may be equally assured of the constancy of the U. States, in their cordial dispositions towards a nation whose early & welcome proofs of good will strengthen its other titles to their confidence, their esteem & their cultivation of the friendly relations which subsist between the two countries.

I have the pleasure to add that the personal merits exemplified during your residence in the U. States, have obtained for you the sincere esteem of the President. Be persuaded, Sir, that you will carry with you not less the regards & good wishes, which I beg leave to offer you with the sentiments of great respect & consideration, with which I have the honor to be Your most Obedt. humble servt.

Draft (DLC); letterbook copy (DNA: RG 59, DL, vol. 14).

From Thomas Jefferson

Th: J. to mr. Madison   Monticello Aug. 12. [13] 1802.
The post having made it night before his arrival yesterday and my mail extraordinarily voluminous, I have been able to read & now return you the inclosed papers only. Mr. Livingston's shall come by the next mail. I do not like this mistake of Capt. McNiel's, and fear it will be very embarrassing.[1] Other d⟨is⟩patches oblige me to close here with assurances of my affectiona⟨te⟩ esteem & respect.

FC (DLC: Jefferson Papers). Dated 12 Aug. in the *Index to the Thomas Jefferson Papers*. Date assigned here on the basis of Jefferson's Epistolary Record (DLC: Jefferson Papers), which lists a letter of 13 Aug. but not 12 Aug., and JM to Jefferson, 14 Aug. 1802, which acknowledges a 13 Aug. letter from Jefferson.

1. JM had received a report that the *Boston* frigate, captained by Daniel McNeill, had attacked some Tunisian vessels, a circumstance that might have expanded the Barbary war. The report proved untrue (JM to William Eaton, 22 Aug. 1802, and n. 1).

From John Porter, Jr.

Honored Sir   Louisa County August 13th. 1802.
I Received your letter November 25. 1801[1] and do take it in the most kindest part for your advice on the Subject as I am at a lost how to proced

in Respect of this petition that you advised me to lay before Congress Respecting my Claim I have against the United States for Services done in the Regular War Six months as a Waggon Conductor, you will be pleased to Write me by Mr Stephin Watkins and you Will be kind a Nuph to form me a petition to lay before the house I Shall think it Very hard Should I loose that Money for Services becusse I was not able to attend to the Business and that Certificate Was handed in to Mr Dunscombs office Sixteen or Seventeen years ago if it was not Cared to the Department before the Limited time Run out it must have been Neglect of Mr Duncomb becusse it was handed in to his office in due time therefore I hope the Gentle[men] of Congress will Consider my long Confindment and will make provision for that Service to an old Soldier that has Served my Country better than fours years in the Regular War where I Ventured my life in three ingagements Jarman Town Battle Brandy Wine and Blufords Defeat Am Dear Sir your frend & hubl sert

JOHN PORTER, JR[2]

RC (DLC). Addressed to JM in Orange County, "To the Care of Mr S Watkins."

1. Letter not found.
2. For Porter's claim, see his letter to JM, 31 July 1809 (*PJM-PS*, 1:315 and n. 1).

§ From Stephen Cathalan, Jr. *13 August 1802, Marseilles.* His last was of 2 July. Reports arrival on 4 Aug. of the U.S. frigate *Boston* under Capt. Daniel McNeill, "who sailed with 4 american Merchantmen under his Protection on the 6th. ditto for Barcelona, Alicant &ca. down the Streights." Received on the same day a packet of dispatches for JM from Cathcart, which he sent to Robert R. Livingston to be forwarded. Transmits a packet from William Eaton to JM received 12 Aug. "It is very unfortuna⟨te⟩ indeed that Capn. Andrew Morris of the Aman. Brig Franklin has been taken by the Tripolines—I have Since the beginning of the war with Tripoly prevented as much as in my power the American Masters to Venture at sea without the protection of an American or Sweed Freegate, but I was not aut[h]orized to Lay their Ships under an Embargo. . . . We the American Consuls or Agents in the Mediterranean, keep ourselves regularly advised of all the news or Events interesting our navigation and safety during this Barbarian War." Sends this dispatch via William Lee at Bordeaux.

RC (DNA: RG 59, CD, Marseilles, vol. 1). 2 pp.

§ From Josef Yznardy. *13 August 1802, Cadiz.* "At the other side you have Copy of the Circular receiv'd by William Willis Esqr. Consul of the United States at Barcelona, from Mr. Stephen Cathalan Junior at Marseilles,[1] & which I transmit to you without loss of time for government."

RC (DNA: RG 59, CD, Cadiz, vol. 1). 1 p.; in a clerk's hand, signed by Yznardy; docketed

477

by Brent. On the verso of the RC is an undated letter signed by Yznardy, stating that in inspecting the papers of the American ship *Hampshire*, Capt. Samuel Chamberlain, he found that the Mediterranean pass "does not Correspond in the least, as it is for the Ship Mac." Despite his warnings of the risk, Yznardy wrote, the captain insisted on proceeding up the Straits; "therefore I avail myself of the first oppy. to advise you of this occurrence."

1. On the verso of the cover is a copy of Richard O'Brien's circular letter of 26 June 1802 (see Thomas Appleton to JM, 10 July 1802, and n. 2); the circular was countersigned by Cathalan on 22 July and Willis on 30 July.

To Thomas Jefferson

DEAR SIR   ORANGE Aug. 14. 1802

I red. last evening your two favors of the 9 & 13th. Before I left Washington I wrote to Simpson approving his refusal of passports in the cases required by the Emperor,[1] and understood that the instructions from the Navy Dept. to Commodore Morris were founded on the same principle. It is to be inferred therefore that we are no longer on a footing of Amity with Morocco: and I had accordingly retained your letter, and concurred in the provisional step taken for stopping the Gun carriages. As it is possible however that things may take a more favorable turn in that quarter, I have desired Mr. Brent to forward, with the qu[i]ckest attention, whatever accounts may arrive, and also to let me know the day, as soon as it can be done, on which the General Greene is to sail. Should it be found that peace with Morocco cannot be preserved or restored without the concession demanded by him, my opinion decides that hostility is a less evil than so degrading an abandonment of the ground rightfully taken by us. As a consequence of this opinion, I concur in that which your quere intimates, that neither of the frigates in the Mediterranean in a condition to remain ought to be recalled. I should prefer if circumstances admitted, that the force there ought rather to be increased, and with the greater reason as the blunder of McNeil may endanger the footing on which we stand with Tunis. May it not be proper, as soon as authentic information of this occurrence comes to hand, that something of a healing nature should be said from the Govt. to the Bey; in addition to the explanations which will no doubt be made from the naval Commander.

The letter from Law the District Judge of Connecticut,[2] was preceded by one to me from a Commissr. of Bankruptcy at Boston,[3] representing the objection of Davis the D. Judge there, to proceed without such a notification as is proposed by Law. Viewing as you do the Commission itself, as the most authentic of all notifications, I did not give any answer, presuming that the scruples of the Judge would yield to further reflection. The letter from Law shall be answered to the effect which you suggest.

Among the papers now inclosed are applications from the Mechts. of Boston & Philada. for an interposition in behalf of their vessels &c detained in Spanish America.[4] This is a delicate subject, and must be so handled as well for their interest as for the honor & dignity of the Govt. I suppose they may be told that Spain does not object to a Board for deciding on our complaints & that Mr. P. will endeavor to give it latitude eno' for all just cases. The sending a public ship, as suggested by Fitzsimmons seems to have no national object, and to be of an injurious tendency. Yrs. with respectful attachment

JAMES MADISON

RC (DLC: Jefferson Papers). Docketed by Jefferson as received 16 Aug.

1. JM to James Simpson, 27 July 1802.
2. See Jefferson to JM, 9 Aug. 1802, and n. 3.
3. Letter not found. John Davis (1761–1847) was a Harvard-educated lawyer who served as U.S. attorney for the district of Massachusetts, 1796–1801, and as judge of the same district from 1801 to 1841.
4. JM referred to letters to him from Stephen Higginson and other Boston merchants, 23 July 1802, and from Thomas FitzSimons, 6 [Aug.?] 1802. The letters have not been found, but see JM's replies of 6 Sept. 1802.

To Richard Law

SIR   VIRGINIA Aug. 14. 1802
The President has received your letter of the 29th. Ulto. He considers the proper notification of the Commissioners of Bankruptcy to be the exhibition of their commissions, as in the case of Marshals, whose appointment is no otherwise officially notified; and on this ground no collateral and inferior evidence of the appointments of the Commissioners was officially added.

Draft (DLC); letterbook copy (DNA: RG 59, DL, vol. 14).

From Charles Pinckney

DEAR SIR   August 14: 1802 IN MADRID
I had the pleasure to write you some weeks agoe on the subject of your mercantile enquiries respecting Spain & to send you a Book which I hope you will recieve safe. Lest however you should not I now send you another & such information as I have been able to collect.

The Spanish Government has on every occasion shewn a great predilection in favour of her colonies & with the view of their enjoying every possible advantage in the Mother country has imposed such duties on all the productions of the West Indies by foreign Vessels as to amount to a total prohibition: during the late War as the Spanish Navigation was entirely done away certain modifications took place on the introduction of colonial produce by neutrals, but from the moment the preliminary articles of Peace were notified to the Custom houses in Spain these Privileges have subsided. The following are the duties now paid

By American or any other foreign Vessel on		By Spanish Vessels from Spanish Colonies	
	cents	cents	
White Havana Sugars pr q: of 100 lb	$5.65	$1:86:	whether white or brown
Brown Do pr Do	$5.50		
Indigo pr quintl of do	$90:60	$2	
Cocoa of all Qualities pr fanega¹ of 110 Wt	$66:55	$7.60	for Caracas
		5.75	for Guayaqil
Coffee pr quintl of 100 Wt:	$23.—	65	cents for Coffee
Cotton pr ditto	$10.8	4½	cents for Cotton

Such a material difference exists as to prevent American or other foreign Vessels from ever bringing Colonial Produce into Spain. However some licenses granted by Government to a few individuals for the importation of Cocoa & sugar by foreign Vessels in paying only the spanish duties are still admitted which the importers of the articles generally purchase as they require them & by that means avoid disbursing the extravagant duties demanded particularly on Cocoa. The same maxim is not adopted for what regards the productions of the United States of America for they pay exactly the same duty when imported by an American or Spanish Vessel, although it will be proper to observe that an American or any other foreign Vessel bringing to this Country articles that are not the produce of the nation such vessels belong to pay an extraordinary contribution of two per centum on the value of the goods under the denomination of "Habilitation Duty" to which those by Spanish Vessels are on no occasion subjected. It may also be necessary to remark that all the articles of Exportation from hence pay exactly the same duties when shipt by an American or Spanish Vessel, Wine alone excepted which by the former or any other foreign Vessel is subject to an exaction of $1:96 cents per quarter cask of about Thirty Gallons whilst it contributes 53 cents per said Quarter Cask when loaded on board a spanish Vessel from hence for a foreign market.

The Port Charges on foreign Vessels are very trifling and are paid equally by the Spanish. The Tonnage duty is only five cents per Ton on the quantity loaded here. None is paid on the cargo inwards. For all the information you wish to have concerning the American Vessels & duties exacted upon their cargoes I beg leave to refer you to the Book I give Mr Codman[2] for you intitled Almanac mercantil o guia de Comerc por D D M G.[3] There you will find the Difference of duties on goods or produce imported in Spanish or foreign Bottoms. Extra of the Duties marked in this Book are some others: to wit Internation, abilitation Consulado antiguo & moderno &c & also arbitrio temporal or consolodacion of Vales. These duties upon calculation are an overcharge of about 75 per centum upon those stated in the Almanac mercantil. Most of the privileges granted during the War being exhausted it is the general opinion that new ones will not be granted & that in future the commerce of this country with foreign nations both in Europe & America will be put on the same footing it was before the War. I inclose an Order that has been passed to the Custom houses granting certain premiums on the productions of Spain and her Colonies when shipt to a foreign port by Spanish Vessels. This is a new one & dated so late as in April 1802.[4]

I have endeavoured to obtain as much information on this subject from Portugal as I could & I now inclose you a regulation or ordinance of that Kingdom made in October 1783 as well as the 8th: article of the Treaty with Russia.[5] In the former the commerce of Portugal in Portuguese Vessels for certain articles has an exclusive privilege & in the latter it is confined to Russian & Portuguese who alone favour the Portuguese more than any other nation in their commerce & some advantages are to be derived, yet so little is the animation amongst the Portuguese Merchants to carry on foreign commerce in their own Bottoms, that no inconvenience has arisen to foreign Bottoms. The Tonnage Duties, Lighthouse duties & other pasport & Anchorage charges are alike to themselves as to other nations & are as follow—

Vessels that arrive & sail with the same cargo.
Tonnage—fees 440 Rs: Lights 200 Rs pr Ton—fees 2385 Reis
Passport & anchorage for every Ship that comes in & goes out—1820 rs:
Vessels that discharge & take entire cargoes out Tonnage 100 Rs pr Ton Fees Rs: Lights 50 Rs. pr Ton—Fees 2385 Rs.
Vessels that discharge Cargoes & sail with ballast. Tonnage about 60 Rs: pr Ton—fees 440 Rs: Lights 200 & Fees 2385 Rs:
Vessels that enter in Ballast & take out cargoes: Tonnage [. . .] Reis pr Ton—fees 440: Lights 50 Rs pr Ton: fees 2385.

Vessels that enter & sail with Ballast. The same as When they carry out the same cargo.

N: B: Vessels only pay Lights & Tonnage once on the same Voyage to Portugal. For example a Vessel going from Lisbon direct to Oporto by presenting a certificate of having paid the Lights in Lisbon is exempted paying at Oporto.

The Portuguese Vessels pay the same. I ⟨am⟩ endeavouring to collect all the information in my power on these subjects from Italy for y⟨ou⟩ & as soon as I recieve it you shall hear from me again. With affectionate regard I am dear sir Yours Truly

CHARLES PINCKNEY

RC and enclosures (DNA: RG 59, DD, Spain, vol. 6). For enclosures, see nn. 4 and 5.

1. A *fanega* is a grain measure equaling about 1.5 bushels.

2. This was probably Richard Codman, a Boston merchant resident in Paris (William Stinchcombe, *The XYZ Affair* [Westport, Conn., 1980], pp. 85–86).

3. *Almanak mercantil, ó Guia de comerciantes para el año de 1801* . . . (Madrid, 1801). This guidebook for merchants contained, among other things, information on consulates in Spain and the Americas; weights, measures, and currency converted to those of Castille; days of arrival and departure of the mails; and a list of the duties paid on Spanish, colonial, and foreign goods on arrival at and departure from Spanish ports (Dionisio Hidalgo, *Diccionario general de bibliografía Española* [1862; 7 vols.; New York, 1968 reprint], 1:50).

4. Pinckney enclosed a printed statement, dated 14 Apr. 1802 at Aranjuez (5 pp.; in Spanish), that included a list of commodities and merchandise, ranging from olive oil to sarsaparilla, and the premiums to be granted to Spanish ships exporting these articles.

5. Pinckney enclosed a copy of a Portuguese law passed 25 Nov. 1783 (3 pp.), which stipulated that most Portuguese goods exported in Portuguese ships be subject to half the usual duties and which granted a 3 percent compensation for certain goods imported into the kingdom in Portuguese ships. He also enclosed a copy of article 8 of the 1787 treaty between Russia and Portugal (1 p.), which cut Portuguese customs duties by half on certain goods imported directly from Russia in the ships of either nation. The treaty is printed in Borges de Castro, *Collecçao dos Tratados*, 3:428–71.

§ From William Jarvis. *14 August 1802, Lisbon.* Refers to his letters to JM of 10 and 13 Aug.,[1] "each incloseing Copies of letters from the several Consuls in the streights & a dispatch from Mr Simpson." Has learned by a 10 Aug. letter from Cadiz that "the 22 gun ship from Larach had sail'd, but head winds had obliged her to put back again." "By my last I acquainted you with the departure of Genl. Lannes from here. . . . The Public paper has in consequence fallen from ten ℔ Cent to fourteen ℔ Cent discount. It excited so much sensation that the reasons were published yesterday in a Supplement to the Official Gazette, of which the original & translation are inclosed.[2] Since the Generals departure the French Citizens assign as the causes beside what was beforementioned, that the Portuguese Government has refused to comply with the Commercial part of the treaty in the sense the Genl. received it. . . . In fine they wished to put the French on the same footing with other nations. It is also said that the Genl. had reason to suspect that some new Commercial arrangements were makeing between this Govmt. & the English Minister." The Portuguese insist that all differences have been amicably adjusted, a point which the ambassador would not acknowledge. "Not any Vessels haveing arrived from New York, I cannot say what will be done relative to the quarantine, those from other ports have been freely admitted." Adds in a postscript that on 13 Aug. he forwarded a letter from William Willis at Barcelona.

RC and enclosures (DNA: RG 59, CD, Lisbon, vol. 1). RC 3 pp.; docketed by Wagner.

1. Jarvis's 13 Aug. dispatch has not been found.
2. Jarvis enclosed a one-paragraph newspaper clipping (in Portuguese), with an English translation in Jarvis's hand stating that Lannes's departure was "entirely of his own accord" and was "the more unexpected as the civilities and attentions shewn the Said Minister were repeated, in demonstration of the constant friendship, good harmony and perfect intelligence subsisting between this Monarchy and the French republic; there not existing actually any object of discussion between the two Governments which might impede their friendly intercourse."

§ From Josef Yznardy. *14 August 1802, Cadiz.* Reports that since his last letters of 10 and 13 Aug., he has received a packet from John Gavino for JM, "which I dont loose a moment in forwarding you, as likewise Copy of the answer from Commodore Morris which you will find herewith."

RC and enclosure (DNA: RG 59, CD, Cadiz, vol. 1). RC 1 p.; in a clerk's hand, signed by Yznardy. Docketed by Brent as received 25 Oct. Enclosure is a one-page letter from Richard Morris to Yznardy, 11 Aug. 1802 (printed in Knox, *Naval Documents, Barbary Wars*, 2:230).

¶ From John McAllister. Letter not found. *14 August 1802, Jonesborough, Tennessee.* Acknowledged in Brent to McAllister, 18 Aug. 1802 (DNA: RG 59, DL, vol. 14), and mentioned in Brent to Joseph Anderson, 18 Aug. 1802 (ibid.), as a letter informing JM that a commission for Thomas Stuart for the position of U.S. attorney for the district of Tennessee had been mistakenly sent to a man of that name in Jonesborough who returned it to the post office. Brent directed McAllister, the postmaster at Jonesborough, to send the letter and commission to Joseph Anderson in Jefferson County, Tennessee, who "has just been requested to deliver them to their proper address." In his letter to Anderson, Brent requested the Tennessee senator "to cause the letter containing the Commission to be delivered to the Gentleman for whom it was intended, as we are entirely ignorant of his address at this place, and it is more than probable that it is known to you."

From Charles Pinckney

DEAR SIR   MADRID 15th August 1802
Mr Codman going to the United States I avail myself of so safe an opportunity to write you. My last by Mr Gibson[1] will inform you of the difficulties I have met with in my endeavours to persuade the Spanish Govern-

ment to consent to an Arbitration which should include all our claims as well for Spanish as French Spoliations.

Notwithstanding all my efforts you will find that Mr Cevallos the first Secretary of State, and appointed as the Plenipotentiary on this occasion has continually refused the insertion of any clause worded as I felt authorized to agree to, which would include the arbitration of the Prizes made under French commissions or condemned by French Consuls. For these he thinks we ought to go to the French Government—in his Letter to me while I was with the Court at Aranjuez of the 26th June he has repeated in writing what he frequently told me in conversations—a Copy of this I sent by Mr Gibson, and a duplicate accompanies this.[2] In one of my former I detailed to you the arguments I had used with Mr Cevallos to induce him to consent to the insertion of a clause including the French captures; but all that I could after many efforts bring him to consent to, was the arbitration of the excesses committed by Foreign Vessels within *the respective Territories of Spain and the United States*—to this I told him I would consent if he would add after the words ["]*Corsarios Estrangeros*" the following "*ó Agentes, Consules ó Tribunales.*"[3] You will find by his Letter of the 7th Inst: he expressly refused this addition, and as the excesses committed within their respective Territories by Privateers would include but a few cases, and exclude the most numerous and important classes, I informed him I was not authorized to consent to any Convention which might in the remotest degree weaken or abridge the right of the United States and their Citizens to urge these Claims as they should hereafter think proper—that the honor & character of our Country were deeply involved in the event, it being as much their Duty to feel the Insults offered to the rights of their Citizens, as it was to assert and defend them—that on this question I had made the only offer in my power—that if he continued to decline it on the ground that Spain was not liable under the Laws of Nations or the Treaty to make reparation that I would communicate his answer to our Government and it would remain for them to determine what was best to be done—that as his Majesty had said he would consent to a Convention for the purpose of arbitrating all the Excesses committed during the late war by the Citizens and Subjects of the United States & Spain—that knowing the friendly disposition of my Government towards Spain, and their confidence in the Justice & Honor of the King ultimately to arrange & adjust their Claims upon Honorable & Equitable principles—I would consent to a convention which should be so worded as to include the arbitration of every Claim arising from the Excesses of the Subjects or Citizens of either party, contrary to the Laws of Nations or the existing Treaty, and which should also by a clause to be therein inserted, reserve to the United States and to Spain, all the Rights they now have to claim reparation for the Excesses committed within their respective Territories, by the Corsairs, Agents, Con-

suls, or Tribunals of Foreign Powers. This Convention we signed on the
11th Instant, and I have delivered it to Mr Codman of Massachusetts to
give you.[4]

My Reasons for signing it were as follows & I trust they will meet the
approbation of the President & Senate. That upon examining the Returns
in the Consular Office here, I find the Number of Vessels taken or detained
by Spaniards up to the 7th Octr last with their Cargoes were 101—to which
are to be added 12 taken jointly by the French & Spaniards and 12 Cargoes
seized or embargoed by Spain making in the whole One Hundred &
Twenty five sail of Vessels & Cargoes. A few of them have been acquitted;
but on all of them will arise claims for damages. To these considerable
Claims for Captures, are to be added all our other Claims arising from the
Excesses of Individuals, contrary to the Law of Nations or the Treaty,
which I am informed are to an amazing amount, particularly from South
America. On the latter Subject it was impossible for me to obtain exact
accounts; but from every information I have received, and particularly from
a Gentleman who brought me a Letter from you[5] and who has lately been
in that Country, I learn that the Claims which our Citizens have are so
great as to amount to a Sum of not less than five Millions of Dollars, and
he beleives probably eight Millions, most of which he thinks, from a knowledge of their particular circumstances may be arbitrated under this Convention, the wording of which I shewed him in confidence, in order that I
might determine how far it was sufficiently general to include every case
within his knowledge, which might be said to be contrary to the Laws of
Nations & the existing Treaty. These added to the 125 Sail of Vessels and
their Cargoes, and all the other claims arising in the Spanish, European &
West India Dominions amount in the whole to so considerable a Sum, that
finding Spain inclined to agree to the immediate arbitration of them, I did
not feel myself authorized to withhold from such of our Citizens as were
interested, the only mode of repairing their Losses, which at this time is
practicable. I was urged to this from a conviction that it is not our wish to
go to war and that there can be little doubt of Spains hereafter agreeing to
an Arbitration of the French Spoliations. At present out of the whole number of Vessels captured by the French Seventy one only have been condemned, and it will require very able and Minute Investigation to decide
how many of these have been legally or otherwise condemned—that it is
not unlikely when the true amount is ascertained for which the Citizens of
the United States may have a right to compensation, the claims arising
from French Spoliations will be far short of our claims for compensation
on account of the Excesses of Spanish Subjects. If this should prove to be
the case, Spain after having agree'd to arbitrate the larger Sum, will not
hesitate to add the other, rather than proceed to extremities.

I shall continue to urge her to consent to some agreement to this effect authorizing the Commissioners to be named, to arbitrate the French Spoliations at the same time, and should I not be able to effect it before I can hear from you I will thank you for your Instructions, or any plan or modification you may think proper. It appears to me to be wise in us to prevent as much as possible the accumulation of our Claims against Spain, for the more she is in arrear, or the more extensive our Claims are against her, the more unwilling & unable will she be, to adjust them. Take however from the present aggregate all our Claims for Spanish Spoliations & Excesses and the residue will be such as she can meet without difficulty—at least with much less difficulty than a war with the United States. Another reason also had great weight with me which is the Policy of being at this time on good terms with Spain, from whose Government we wish to obtain the cession of Florida, in consequence of the cession she made in 1800 of Louisiana to France. On this Subject I have frequently conversed with the Secretary, who informs me, the Moment they hear from America, he will send me an Answer to the proposal I made in consequence of your Instructions & on which I am very anxious to hear from you, as to the Sum I am to offer should they be inclined to sell.

Knowing the importance our Government annex to this acquisition it would be with great regret I should see the Spanish Cabinet unfriendly or even cool to us at this time, and being certain that some amicable Arrangement of the French Spoliations, or of such of them as Spain *ought* to make compensation for, will hereafter take place, I thought it upon the whole the best thing I could do at present, to sign the Convention I have the Honor to send you: and particularly so as the day after its signature the King and all his Ministers were to leave Madrid on a Tour to Barcelona and that part of his Dominions, and to be absent several months during which little or no business can be done with them, and so much time would have been lost.

I beg leave to introduce to your acquaintance & to the President the Bearer Mr Codman whose good sense & knowledge of Europe, particularly of France & Spain will enable him to give you much useful information. I hope he will have the honour of delivering these Dispatches in person. I am with affectionate regard dear sir Yours Truly

CHARLES PINCKNEY
August 16: 1802
IN MADRID

RC (DNA: RG 59, DD, Spain, vol. 6). In a clerk's hand, except for last paragraph, signature, and second date in Pinckney's hand. Docketed by Wagner as received 24 Nov.

1. Gibson apparently carried Pinckney's dispatches of 1, 6, and 8 July 1802 (see Pinckney to JM, 8 July 1802 [first letter], and n. 1).
2. Probably enclosed with this dispatch was a packet consisting of copies of Cevallos's letters to Pinckney of 26 June, 13, 19, and 26 July, and 3 and 7 Aug. 1802 and an undated letter

from Pinckney to Cevallos, apparently written 2 Aug. 1802 (ibid.; 10 pp.; partly in Spanish; translated interlinearly by Wagner). All the letters discussed the wording of the spoliations convention. For the copy of Cevallos's 26 June letter that Pinckney sent JM earlier, see Pinckney to JM, 6 July 1802, and n. 1.

3. Wagner translated this phrase interlinearly: "[or Agents, Consuls or tribunals]."

4. "A Convention between His Catholic Majesty and the United States of America, for the indemnification of those who have sustained losses, damages, or injuries, in consequence of the excesses of individuals of either nation, during the late war, contrary to the existing treaty, or the laws of nations," as signed on 11 Aug. 1802 by Cevallos and Pinckney, is printed in *ASP, Foreign Relations*, 2:475–76. Article 6 stipulated that "it not having been possible for the said plenipotentiaries to agree upon a mode by which the above mentioned Board of Commissioners should arbitrate the claims originating from the excesses of foreign cruisers, agents, consuls, or tribunals, in their respective territories," both parties reserved the right to bring these claims forward at a later time.

5. This was probably James Yard (see JM to Pinckney, 27 Mar. 1802).

From Daniel Clark

(Private)

SIR   NEW YORK 16 August 1802

A Business of very considerable importance calls me suddenly to England, for which I shall embark immediately. I had not an Opportunity to advise you of my intention of leaving Orleans before I sailed for this Place where I have been but a few days. The Situation of affairs in Luisiana is such that my presence except as an influential private Character can be of no service to my Country, the Government of Spain persisting in its refusal to acknowledge a Consul in that Province. In my absence, the Vice Consul who has afforded his assistance on all occasions to his Countrymen where the interference of the Spanish Government was unnecessary, will continue to act, so that no Complaints will arise, or any one meet with delay or disappointment. I calculate on returning to Orleans in December as my Stay in Europe will be very short. Should such Circumstances occur in my absence as to render the appointment of another Officer necessary I have to request you will in that case intreat the President to accept my resignation but still retain the right of commanding any Services in my Power to render.

The alarm occasioned in Luisiana by the report of the Cession to France had increased, and all the People of Property were indignant at it. Many intimations were given me of the general wish that the U. S. should get Possession of the Province and it would only require a hint from hence that such a measure would meet encouragement to induce the leading Characters to take the Government into their own hands & put themselves under the Protection of the U. S. & form an integral part of it. In proof of what I

487

advance I now forward you a Memorial which has been inclosed to me here, with a request that I should lay it before the Executive. The Characters by whom it was transmitted are leading & influential men. I have not acknowledged the receipt of it in order not to encourage expectation; and request that as the thing is of a delicate nature and might commit the Lives & fortunes of Hundreds you will not suffer this Paper to get to Light. I would not have hesitated to destroy it myself, but that I thought it a Pity the Wishes of a People so desirous of uniting their fate with ours should be concealed from Government. They perceive & tremble at their destiny in the Hands of France.

I am in possession of some other Papers relative to former transactions in that Country which I shall take an Opportunity of shewing you when I return from Europe, I would have sent them for your perusal but am fearful of accidents on the Road as the Loss of them would commit those from whom they were received, these Papers will I think tend to elucidate past events & may serve as a Caution in future.

The Chicasaw Chief Ugulucayabé,[1] the head of the Party in that Nation attached to Spain, was in New Orleans since the treaty with our Commissioners,[2] his object was to express his dissatisfaction with it & to request the interference of Spain that nothing further should be attempted by our Government. On his arrival he saw the Governor whose Age & infirmities incapacitate him from attending to the duties of his Government[3] & who besides had no idea of the manner in which the Indians had always been treated by his Predecessors. He consequently in a fit of impatience received the Chief very ill & scarce listened to him, his Pride was wounded, he retired in disgust & before he went away made a voluntary surrender of an annual Pension of 500 dollars which has been constantly & regularly paid him by order of the Court of Spain, saying that as he was to become an American he would do so in earnest. These dispositions ought perhaps to be encouraged at this juncture. The ignorance, incapacity, & dotage of the old Spanish Governor have thus effected a Breach with those Indians whom his Predecessors have so long courted & which his successor will make the greatest efforts to repair. Respecting the allowance of the annual Pension I have proofs in my hands which I mean to communicate to you.

If your Friendship for & confidence in me will authorise you to write a Line in my favor, which may serve me as an introduction to Mr King our Minister in London, in case I should find it necessary to call on him I would thank you to forward it as soon as possible to my Friend Mr Daniel Wm Coxe of Philadelphia who will transmit it to me by first Opportunity.[4] I have the Honor to remain with Sentiments of respect & Esteem Sir Your most obedient & most humble Servant

DANIEL CLARK

RC (DNA: RG 59, Territorial Papers, Orleans, vol. 1). Marked in an unidentified hand, "Enclosure missing."

1. From the 1780s on, the Chickasaw nation was divided into a number of factions, including a Spanish party, headed by Ugulaycabe (Wolf's Friend), and an American party, led by Piomingo (Mountain Leader). The U.S. and Spain vied for Chickasaw friendship, and each faction signed treaties with its patron. Ugulaycabe had granted the Spanish permission to build a trading post at Chickasaw Bluffs in 1795, but it was abandoned after 1797 according to the provisions of the Pinckney treaty and replaced by an American outpost in 1802. As the fortunes of the Spanish declined in North America, so did those of Ugulaycabe's Spanish party (Arrell M. Gibson, *The Chickasaws* [Norman, Okla., 1971], pp. 80–105).

2. A treaty was negotiated between the U.S. and the Chickasaw nation in October 1801 that permitted the former to construct a wagon road through the territory of the latter from Natchez into Tennessee (*ASP, Indian Affairs*, 1:648–49).

3. Manuel de Salcedo, "a well-meaning nonentity who had fallen into senile decay," was Spanish governor of Louisiana from 1801 to 1803 (Whitaker, *Mississippi Question*, pp. 159–61).

4. JM obliged Clark by forwarding to Coxe a letter of introduction to King (see Coxe to JM, 8 Oct. 1802 [DLC: Gallatin Papers]).

From Albert Gallatin

SIR, TREASURY DEPARTMENT Augt. 16th: 1802

I have the honor to enclose a Letter from the Auditor in which he expresses his doubts of the legality of the Expenditures incurred for the relief of Seamen subsequent to the year 1799,[1] beyond the allowance of twelve cents ℔ day, established by the Act of 14th: April 1792.[2] I have had a verbal communication on the subject, with the Comptroller of the Treasury, have carefully examined the Laws, and have no doubt whatever of the illegality of that expenditure. The Law of 14th: April 1792, is the only permanent Law authorizing any expense for the relief of Seamen abroad.

The Law of 18th: April 1798,[3] authorized the reimbursement of the reasonable expenses, which had been made, or during that year should be made for the relief of such Seamen beyond the sum already allowed by Law (viz. by the Act of 14th: April 1792) for that purpose. The Law of 19th: Feby: 1799[4] authorizes the reimbursement of similar expenses which may be made during that year. From the date of the last mentioned Act, no other Law authorizing expenses for that object has been made; from whence it follows that the annual appropriations since made, can be applied only in conformity to the provisions of the permanent Law of 14th: April 1792.

It is apprehended that the Consuls have not been duly informed of that circumstance, and have thought themselves Justifiable in continuing the Expense at the same rate which had been allowed for 1798 & 1799. The consequence is that, a number of Bills drawn by them, on the Department of State, and which have been paid by your direction, ought not to have been honored, as the Accounts on which they rested cannot pass, and that in several instances balances claimed by them cannot be admitted. The only manner in which to remedy that inconvenience will be an application to Congress for a Law which, like that of 18th: April 1798, may have a retrospective effect; but, I loose no time in communicating the information, in order that the Consuls may be apprized that, hereafter, they must strictly conform to the provisions of the Law of the 14th: April 1792.[5] This indeed is in itself reasonable, since we are restored to a state of Peace; and a general caution on the score of expense may not be improper, as I am verbally informed that the Accounts of some of them, particularly that of Mr. Lee, at Bordeaux,[6] amount to much larger sums than could, under any possible circumstances, have been expected, or allowed. I have the honor to be, very respectfully Sir, Your Obedt. Servt.

ALBERT GALLATIN

RC and enclosure (DLC: Gallatin Papers). RC in a clerk's hand, signed by Gallatin. Docketed by Brent as received the same day. Another copy of the RC (ibid.), in the same clerical hand and signed by Gallatin, is also docketed by Brent. For enclosure, see n. 1.

1. Gallatin enclosed a copy of Richard Harrison's 11 Aug. 1802 letter to him (4 pp.; docketed by Brent), in which Harrison requested "the Sentiments of the Secretary of State on the point, before any of the accounts are taken up for settlement."

2. Section 7 of "An Act concerning Consuls and Vice-Consuls" laid down the rules for the relief of U.S. seamen "in cases of shipwreck, sickness or captivity." In addition to a per diem payment provided by the U.S. government, the act required all masters of American ships, at consular request, to transport unengaged American seamen to the U.S. in the ratio of two seamen for every "hundred tons burthen." Refusal was punishable by a fine of $30 per seaman. Section 8 of the same act required masters of ships sold in a foreign port to provide the crew "with means sufficient for their return" (*U.S. Statutes at Large*, 1:256–57).

3. Section 1 of "An Act authorizing an expenditure, and making an appropriation for the reimbursement of monies advanced by the Consuls of the United States, in certain cases" (ibid., 1:551).

4. "An Act to authorize the reimbursement of monies expended in rendering aid to sick and destitute American Seamen, in foreign countries" (ibid., 1:617).

5. A circular to this effect was sent to U.S. consuls and commercial agents by Daniel Brent on 26 Aug. 1802 (ICHi).

6. For the extent of Lee's problem with U.S. seamen, see his letters to JM of 20 Jan. and 18 Feb. 1802 (*PJM-SS*, 2:414, 479).

From Thomas Jefferson

DEAR SIR   MONTICELLO Aug. 16. 1802.

I now return all the papers recieved from you by this post, except those relative to our affairs at Buenos Ayres.

Mr. Boudinot's provisional measures for taking care of the Mint on shutting it up appear entirely proper.[1] The 5th. alone seems imperfect, as I do not see why a positive conclusion should not have been formed as to the care of the bullion, the most important part of the charge. I presume the bank of the US. would have recieved that as well as the papers, keys &c. However it is too late to say any thing on that subject, and I have no doubt that effectual care has in the end been taken.

With respect to Commissioners of bankruptcy at Fredericksburg,[2] you are sensible that if we were to name Commissioners over the whole face of every state in the Union, these nominations would be infinite, & 99 in 100. of them useless. To draw some line therefore was necessary. We have accordingly confined our nominations to the greater commercial towns only. I am sensible however that bankruptcies may happen in small towns and even in the country, and that some regulation should be provided to which resort may be had more conveniently than to that of referring the case to the commissioners of the large cities who may be distant. What would you think of writing a circular instruction to the district attornies of the US. to notify us when any case arises too distant for the established commrs. to take up, sending us at the same time a recommendation of proper persons to act in that case, whom, or such others as may be preferred, may be commissioned to act in that special case? He should inform the judges of this instruction so that they will apply to him to procure commissioners in any case before them. The delay of this will be trifling. Or will you propose any thing you may like better? Accept assurances of my affectionate esteem & respect.

Th: Jefferson

RC (DLC); FC (DLC: Jefferson Papers).

1. See Elias Boudinot to JM, 6 Aug. 1802, and n. 2.
2. For the complaints of merchants that no commissioners of bankruptcy had been appointed for Fredericksburg, see John Dawson to JM, 8 Aug. 1802.

From Robert R. Livingston

No. 20

Dear Sir   Paris 16th.[1] Augt 1802

I informed you in my last that I found some relaxation on the subject of the floridas in my last conversation *with the Spanish Minister I have reason* to think that within this few days they have come to a settlement with France on that subject what it is I can not precisely say but I presume that it is whatever France wishes it to be. *I find all the old French maps mark the river*

Perdigo as the boundary between Florida & Louisania it is possible that this may have been insisted upon if so the remainder was hardly worth the keeping. Whatever it is the project of taking possession has resumed a certain degree of activity Genl. Victour is appointed[2] he is to have under him a genl. of division two genls. of brigage [*sic*] & 3000 men only no more than 2000000 frs. are allowed to this service *so that they must starve or find resources in the country. Saturday* the Genl. was all day with the minister of marine arranging the inferior appointments to be submitted to the first consul. I have been pressing for some time past *with every body that I thought could have any influence on this business — And as I have been happy enough to convince most of them I do not absolutely despair tho* I am much discouraged by this last arrangment. The same silence is observed by the Minister I can get him to tell me nothing. I shall see him this morning again & if I can not induce him to speak on the subject more plainly than he has done I will put in a note insisting on our claims under the Spanish treaty & demanding an explicit recognition of them. On this I believe there will be little difficulty as they have always agreed that the cession must be subject to the restrictions under which Spain held the territory.

There are obvious symtoms of ill humour between this country & Britain[3] *& I think it will not be long before they assume a serious asspect. Good may arise out of this evil if it shd. happen.* The enclosed Letter from Obrien will shew you the state of our affairs with the Barbary powers.[4] France has sent two ships & a frigate to Algiers to demand satisfaction for the insult to their fishing vessels. I believe however that the government will not chuse to enter into a war tho it is evidently much the wish of the people about court particularly the military men. A report for the discharge of our demd is before the first consul if adopted it is *all I can ask & more than I hoped it is very pointed as to the justice* of our claim & the national disgrace that would attend its farther neglect.[5]

We yesterday had a grand fete in honor of the Consuls birth day & the extention of his powers—*there are many discontents & there was I am told much more expression of it among the people that crowded the streets than could* have been expected. I have the honr. to be Dr. Sir With the highest consideration Your Most Obt hum: Servt

Draft (NHi: Livingston Papers); letterbook copy (NHi: Livingston Papers, vol. 1). Italicized passages are underlined in the draft; Livingston apparently intended them to be encoded.

1. In the draft, Livingston first wrote "12th." and later wrote "16" below it. The letterbook copy is dated 16 Aug., as is an extract from the missing RC printed in *ASP, Foreign Relations*, 2:524.
2. The commander of the French army in the Batavian Republic, Claude-Victor Perrin (known as General Victor), had been named on 27 Apr. 1802 to head the French expedition

to occupy Louisiana. The force was delayed by a lack of funds, French reverses in the battle to regain control of Saint-Domingue, and North Sea ice, and it never left Holland (Tulard, *Dictionnaire Napoléon*, p. 1717; E. Wilson Lyon, *Louisiana in French Diplomacy, 1795–1804* [Norman, Okla., 1974], pp. 129–44).

3. Among the "symtoms of ill humour" that soured Anglo-French relations in the summer of 1802 were the continued British support for French émigrés, the seizure of British merchant ships by the French, and the signing of a treaty between France and the Ottoman Empire in June 1802 (Michel Poniatowski, *Talleyrand et Le Consulat* [Paris, 1986], pp. 700–722).

4. This may have been O'Brien's 10 July 1802 statement on the situation at Algiers, a copy of which was sent to Livingston (see O'Brien to JM, 7 July 1802, n.).

5. Livingston referred to Talleyrand's "Rapport au premier Consul de la République," submitted to Napoleon circa 29 Floréal an X (19 May 1802) (AAE: Political Correspondence, U.S., 54:343–46).

From Thomas McKean

S<small>IR</small>   L<small>ANCASTER</small> August 16th. 1802

As soon as I received your Letter of the 11th. of May last an enquiry into the representation of the Minister of Spain to the Department of State of an indignity offered to his Sovereign and of certain violences committed on a number of Spanish Sailors in Philadelphia was instituted but from a variety of untoward circumstances, such as the absence of the Cheif-Justice, the Attorney General, The Counsel for the Ship Carpenters, and the Sailors, upon the Circuit, it was not completed until the latter end of last Month. Indeed it was with some reluctance, these Gentlemen undertook the business, as it had been fairly and fully heard before the constituted authorities, and at the instance of the Counsel for the Sailors upon their making satisfaction to the persons injured a nolle prosequi was granted by the Attorney General.

On the whole I have good reason to beleive that the Minister of his Catholic Majesty is now persuaded no indignity to his Sovereign or wrong to his Subjects was contemplated or committed. The whole misunderstanding appears to have arisen from the zeal of the Consul General of Spain who as yet seems to be unacquainted with our Language and Laws and is but a young Officer, though advanced in years.[1] I conceived it proper to give you this information, and have the honor to be with great regard, your most obedt. humble Servant

T<small>HOS</small>. M<small>C</small>K<small>EAN</small>

Letterbook copy (PHarH: Secretary of Commonwealth Letterbooks, vol. 5).

1. Valentín Tadeo Echavarri de Foronda (b. 1751), a writer on political economy and a member of the American Philosophical Society, began his term as Spanish consul general in

Philadelphia in 1802 and later served as chargé d'affaires in Washington (Robert S. Smith, "A Proposal for the Barter and Sale of Spanish America in 1800," *Hispanic American Historical Review*, 41 [1961]: 275–76; Yrujo to JM, 22 Jan. 1802, *PJM-SS*, 2:416).

From Richard O'Brien

ESTEEMED SIR   ALGIERS The 16th. of August 1802

On the 5th. Inst. arrived here 2 french 74 Gunships a Brig and Corvetta under the orders of a rear admiral haveing on board General Hulen as Ambasador of Bonapt.

On the 6th. he demanded of the dey to renounce all money Claims on france

to admit of the free navigation of The Italian republic—

to punish with Severity 2 algerine Captains for over acts against france That france will give no passport to any of her national Vessels whatsoever demands 3 Neopolitan Vessels Cargoes and Crews Captured by Corsrs. of Algiers on the Coast of france—Captives 45 Neopolitans.

To those demands The dey with reluctance acquised. The Algerine Corsairs 8 were under way when the french hove in Sight They returned and did not Sail untill The 14th.

On the 11th. Inst. arrived here a french Brig of war with letters in 12 days from Paris brought by an aid of Bonapts. wherein the great Consul tells the dey that he will double his Vengance on this regency if he ever hears Any more of its abuse or irritations—that he will Errace Algrs from the list of pirate nations. This was a bitter pill to the dey whom had no alternative but to Grumble and promise respect and friendship with Obedience to Bonapt.

The two Algerine Captains has been put in prison and Severely punished they would have lost their heads, but pardoned by the Ambasador.

The french is to have LeCall and their other Commercial privilages as Specifyed in the treaty made december last further Bonapart. insists on fortifying LeCall and it is further Said that The french demands to have a fortifyed factory at Bona.

On the 15th Inst. a french Brig of war with The ambasador and aid of Bonapt. left this place destined for toulon or Marseilles. The french admiral and division will leave this place this day for Tunis—Where no doubt They will Carry all before them on all tacks.

By The italian republic haveing a free Commerce The Neopolitans Genoas &c. will be able to obtain passports and Colours and will be nearly The Same thing as if all italia had a peace with Barbary.

I find That all these Circumstances is to Turn out only to The interest of france nor have I perceived anything as yet on the reform or Generl. System as Specifyed jointly in the Articles of the Genrl. peace.

The ambasador told me that hereafter Something would be done on this tack whether by the Christian powers or by their request to The Grand Signior he Could not Say.

There is as yet here 54 french of Oran and I doubt not but that they and a peace for Genoa will be The next demand.

The British has not Shown themselves Since June last They will in My Opinion neither give the dey Money or yet Change their passports—but will act as france did—& do right.

The dons has acquised to The arrangement of giveing the dey The 160 fathoms ½ that Sum is paid and The presents and greasing feese will Come with The new Expected Consul.

As the dey has failed in his attack on the french I presume he will meet the Same fate with the British—As he is now despised by his own people that he will Search for a rupture with Either The deans[1] Swedes dutch or U States.

I hope that Mr Simpson will gain time with Morrocco. I hear of nothing of what The americans and Swedes are doing before Tripoli relative to the ransom of Capt Morris and Crew I wait with Anxiety to know what has been the result of the deys application to ransom them.

The dey is halling in his horns relative to Tunis. If france fortifies LeCall & Bona They will drain Algiers and Tunis and do away their political exis-tance. Sir I am respectfully Your Most Obt Servt.

RICHD. OBRIEN

PS. The ministry has Enquired If I had no acct. of the Vessel with The annuities from The U States.

On the 19th of August The algerine Corsairs returned into port as the dey remains Suspicious of the french haveing a design to invade him further he has ordered in The out Militia &c. Haveing wrote Sundry letters This yr. of importance to The ambasador of The U S. at Paris & forwarded many through that Conveyance Under Cover & unsealed for The Secretary of State I am Sorrow to add—that they have not one been Ansd. I shall for Once Enquire if it is Beneath The dignity or Contrary to The Official duty of An American Ambasador at paris to not Ansr. The letter of A Consul of the U S. At Algiers.

[Addendum]

ALGIERS The 22d. of August 1802

Articles to be insisted on by The Governments of The United States Sweden and Denmark in order to reform existing abuses of The Govt. of Algiers and to extend to The Same Effect with Tunis Tripoli and Morrocco. As Viz—

495

1st. A Cash payment of The Stipulated Annuity which is 21600 dollars or the full Value of Stores Sent here together with a full and raisonable freight.

2d The Biennal presents to be made in Cash to The amount of 12.000 dollars.

3d No arbitrary employment of Vessels Coming here but full freight to be Agreed on between The regency and the Consul master and Supercargo of the Vessel and no demands for Vessels to Come here and be Sent on The regencies Errands or affairs.

4th. No reponsibility for Cargoes Shiped on board our Vessels by The regency its agents or Subjects for any part of The world.

5th. No Condemnation or Bringing in of Vessels and Cargoes On any Suposed deficiency in The pass—or other documents.

6th. No Exaction of any presents whatever on any promotion or Change of Ministers or the other officers in this regency or on any Change in our own Governments—or on the Occasion of a new dey—no presents of Any description whatsoever to be asked for or Given.

7th Instead of A Consular present—for every new Consul Comeing here The sum of 16.000 dollars to be given every 10th. year—and no detention of the Consul or his family or of Any Citizen or Subject of the Contracting parties but in Case of hostilities 6 months is to be allowed before the declaration of the Same—or any Capture to be made— with Such other reforms That our respective Governments may think proper to insist on. The three nations to make The Above A Common Cause and be responsable one for all and all for one and to Consider what would be The requisite force to furnish Each of The three Contracting parties & in what manner most Effectual to Employ Said force to obtain & Sustain The desired Effect. Sir I am respectfully Your Most Obt Servt.

RICHARD OBRIEN

Here is The Squadron of admirl. de Winter he has gave the dey 200 Barrels of powder as a present.

RC and addendum (DNA: RG 59, CD, Algiers, vol. 6). RC and addendum sent in multiple copies (ibid.), all of which vary in wording and content; "6th. Copy" of RC docketed by Wagner as received 17 May. Two copies were sent under cover to Livingston at Paris. One copy of the addendum is docketed by Wagner, "Mr. OBrien's proposals for amending the treaty with Algiers."

    1. Danes.

§ From Israel Smith. *16 August 1802, Rutland, Vermont.* Recommends Samuel Prentiss of Rutland for the post of commissioner of bankruptcy. "P⟨r⟩entiss is about thirty five ⟨years o⟩f age has been Educated ⟨in⟩ the profession of the Law—is a man of good morals and good habits and in my opinion very capable of discharging the duties of a Commissioner."

RC (DNA: RG 59, LAR, 1801–9, filed under "Prentiss"). 1 p. Docketed by Brent and Jefferson.

¶ From Samuel Marsh. Letter not found. *16 August 1802, Norfolk.* Mentioned in Brent to Marsh, 21 Aug. 1802 (DNA: RG 59, DL, vol. 14), in which Brent promised to forward the letter to JM and noted, "it does not appear that any further step is requisite on your part as agent of Mr. Blanchard, with respect to the Commission in question."

From Thomas Jefferson

DEAR SIR   MONTICELLO Aug. 17. 1802.
    I now return you the papers forwarded by the merchants of Philadelphia and Boston on the subject of the wrongs they complain of at Buenos Ayres. I observe that they have not gone into a developement of the subject. Two or three cases are opened with some degree of detail; as to the rest we have only a list of the ships for which our interference is claimed. But in cases where a hair's breadth of difference makes the thing right or wrong, full details are requisite. I think we ought to be informed what was the extent and what was to constitute the termination of the indulgences granted to Neutrals under which these vessels have ventured there: as also the specific circumstances under which every vessel went. Spain had a right, according to the practice established, to give to those indulgences what duration she thought proper, only not withdrawing them so suddenly and on such short notice as to make the indulgence a trap to catch our vessels. Reasonable time should be allowed them to settle their affairs. On this last ground only can we urge any claim against Spain. We should therefore have a precise statement of the case of every vessel, and strike off from the list all those which cannot be brought within the limits of the indulgences, urging, under the authority of the government, only such cases as are founded in right. There seems to have been a great breach of faith by individuals, Spanish subjects: for these their courts should be open to us: or perhaps these cases could be got before the Commrs. proposed by mr. Pinckney in the Algesiras depredations. I hazard these reflections that you may consider whether a detailed statement of cases should not be called for from the merchants, lest we should be committing ourselves in behalf of mere interloping & contraband adventures. Accept assurances of my constant affection & respect.

                                        TH: JEFFERSON

RC (DNA: RG 59, ML); FC (DLC: Jefferson Papers).

§ From David Lenox. *17 August 1802, New York.* Notifies JM of his arrival in New York after a passage of fifty-seven days from London; "I shall conc[e]ive it my duty to proceed to the Seat of Government when I am advised of your being there." Asks JM to "direct a remitta⟨nce⟩ to me here of three or four thousand doll⟨ars⟩ which I expect will [be] due to me on a settlemen⟨t⟩ of my Accounts."[1]

RC (DNA: RG 59, CD, London, vol. 8). 2 pp.; docketed by Brent as received 19 Aug.

1. Daniel Brent informed Lenox that he had forwarded this letter to JM in Virginia "and I have just got his instructions to inform you in reply, that he had made a requisition on the Treasury in your favor for Three thousand dollars, which will accordingly be remitted to you from that Department, in a draft on New York. I have it in charge from him likewise to signify to you on this occasion, that it is desireable your accounts should be forwarded hither with all convenient dispatch." Lenox replied that he would prefer to bring his accounts and vouchers to Washington himself after JM's arrival there but he would forward them if instructed to do so (Brent to Lenox, 9 Sept. 1802 [DNA: RG 59, DL, vol. 14]; Lenox to Brent, 13 Sept. 1802 [DNA: RG 59, CD, London, vol. 8]).

To Thomas Jefferson

DEAR SIR   ORANGE Aug. 18. 1802

Your favor of the 16th. came duly to hand with the papers to which it referred. I now forward others recd. by the last mail.

I have signified to Mr. Sumpter that his resignation was acquiesced in, and have used a language calculated to satisfy him that he retains the good opinion of the Executive.[1] What is to be said to Mr. Livingston on his request that he may appt. a private Secretary, and fill provisionally consular vacancies? Considering the disposition of a Secretary of Legation, acting as private Secy. to view himself on the more important side, and of the Minister to view & use him on the other, it is to be apprehended, that there may be difficulty in finding a successor to Mr. Sumter who will not be likely to be infected with the same dissatisfaction. I am not aware that the other proposition of Mr. L. is founded in any reason claiming equal attention. Yours with respectful attachment

JAMES MADISON

RC (DLC: Jefferson Papers). Docketed by Jefferson as received 19 Aug.

1. JM's reply to Thomas Sumter, Jr.'s letter of 18 May 1802 has not been found.

From Rufus King

Private

Dear Sir   Rotterdam August 18. 1802

Since I left London I have received your letter accompanying the instructions & authority concerning the settlement of our Boundary with Great Britain[1]—and in consequence thereof have written to Mr Gore, desiring him to communicate to Lord Hawkesbury that powers have been sent to me for this purpose, and to request his Lordship to put the business in such a train as to be settled upon my return.[2] I shall moreover write a Letter to the same Effect to Lord Hawkesbury from the Hague or Amsterdam. The principal object of my troubling you with this letter, is to beg of you to give me the earliest information of what the president shall decide respecting the accommodation I have taken the Liberty to ask for in regard to my return to america, and I hope you will excuse my praying you to advise my agent Mr Low of New york of the Presidents determination, as he may otherwise be embarrassed respecting the Execution of my Instructions.

I earnestly hope I shall be relieved in season to embark in Apl. which will give me a good probability of arriving in June. Very faithfully Yr. Ob. Ser.

Rufus King

RC (DNA: RG 59, DD, Great Britain, vol. 10). Cover addressed to JM "Viâ Boston / Ship Mary / Capt Emery," with a note indicating that the letter was received and forwarded by Lawson Alexander, U.S. commercial agent at Rotterdam. Postmarked Boston, 1 Nov.

1. JM to King, 8 June 1802.

2. Christopher Gore informed Hawkesbury of JM's instructions and King's power to settle the boundary question in his letter of 24 Aug. 1802 (King, *Life and Correspondence of Rufus King*, 4:159–60).

§ To Peder Blicherolsen. *18 August 1802, Department of State, Washington.* "The Secretary of State of the United States presents his respects to Mr. Olsen, and does himself the honor to forward herewith to him Exequators for the Gentlemen whose names are subjoined, . . . agreeably to Mr. Olsen's letter of the 29th. of last month to the Secretary of State. The delay unavoidably incurred in procuring the necessary signatures [on] these Exequators from the absence of both the President and Secretary of State has thus long retarded the transmission of them." Returns commissions for John Spindler (New York and Connecticut), Erich Bolman (Pennsylvania), Peter Collin (Maryland), John Boritz (North Carolina), Joseph Winthrop (South Carolina), William Scarborough (Georgia), and Jonathan Swift (District of Columbia).

Letterbook copy (DNA: RG 59, DL, vol. 14). 2 pp.

§ From John Bulkeley & Son. *18 August 1802, Lisbon.* Mentions that they last wrote on 31 Dec. 1801 and 29 Jan. 1802,[1] "the contents of both which, we now confirm, and herewith beg Permission to hand you extract of our account to this day, on which, the Balance due to us is Rs: 42,211$ 815, & having Occasion for this Property in Europe, we have for some time endeavoured to pass our Bills on you, but the low rate of dollars here, inducing those who have Funds to remit to America, to send them in Specie, we have been unsuccessful." Requests JM to "establish a Credit in our Favor with your Bankers in London or Amsterdam, for the above Balance, & the Interest that may further become due thereon," and to reply through Jesse and Robert Waln of Philadelphia, who have "frequent opportunities of writing us."

RC and enclosure (DNA: RG 59, Letters Received from Bankers). RC 2 pp.; docketed by Brent as received 15 Oct. Enclosure (1 p.) is a statement of Bulkeley & Son's account with the State Department, 31 Dec. 1801 to 18 Aug. 1802.

    1. *PJM-SS*, 2:361, 429.

From Robert R. Livingston

No. 21

Dear Sir,   Paris 19 August 1802

    I write in haste in hopes that this may overtake Mr. Lyle and correct an error in my last. Notwithstanding the appointment of Genl Victor & several other officers for Louisiana, among others a Compt[r]oller of the forests, no Prefet is yet appointed—nor is *the difference relative to the Floridas settled. Spain insists that they are not ceded and I have certain information that two days ago the minister of marine wrote to the minister of foreign affairs that without the Floridas there could be no Louisiana.* Nothing shall be *neglected on my part to keep up this difference* for while it *lasts there will I believe be no expedition and time and change may work in our favor.* I am, Dear Sir, with the most perfect esteem Your Mo He. St.

RC (NHi: Livingston Papers); draft (ibid.); letterbook copy (NHi: Livingston Papers, vol. 1). The RC is a letterpress copy marked "(duplicate)," in a clerk's hand, unsigned; docketed by Wagner. Italicized words are those encoded by Livingston's secretary and decoded here by the editors. RC decoded interlinearly in an unidentified hand. According to Livingston's "Journal of correspondence with the Secretary of State" (NHi: Livingston Papers, vol. 7), he enclosed with this dispatch a copy of his 19 Aug. note to Talleyrand on Louisiana. The note stated the rights of the U.S. in regard to the free navigation of the Mississippi River and the deposit of American goods in New Orleans and requested an answer as to whether France would respect those rights (ibid., vol. 1; 3 pp.).

§ From William C. C. Claiborne. *19 August 1802, Natchez.* "In a former letter I stated to you the want of confidence on the part of many of the Citizens of this

Territory in their Supreme Judiciary; the deficiency of legal talents in two of the Judges; and the propriety there was, in supplying the first vacancy with a character of good law information.[1] It is now reported that Judge Tilton has resigned. . . . But there is another report which I believe more certain, 'That this gentleman has gone to Europe on some Commercial business.'" Thinks it his duty to relay this report, since such conduct can be considered "an abandonment of office." Tilton left Natchez in January or February "and has been attending to his private business, at Orleans until his late departure from that Port." Recommends David Ker of the Mississippi Territory,[2] "an able lawyer & an amiable man," to replace Tilton. States that Steele's commission as territorial secretary expired 7 May 1802, "since which he has not considered himself bound to transact any public business"; requests that an appointment "be speedily made."

Letterbook copy (Ms-Ar: Claiborne Executive Journal). 3 pp. Printed in Rowland, *Claiborne Letter Books*, 1:161–62.

  1. See Claiborne to JM, 8 Jan. 1802 (*PJM-SS*, 2:377–78 and n. 1).
  2. David Ker (d. 1805), a graduate of Trinity College, Dublin, who helped found the University of North Carolina, moved to the Mississippi Territory in 1800. He offered his services to Jefferson in October 1801, conscious of "the opportunity which a public station affords of spreading information & cultivating the love of Republican governments." Jefferson appointed him a territorial judge on 11 Jan. 1803 (Ker to Jefferson, 3 Oct. 1801, and Ker to David Stone, 3 Oct. 1801, Carter, *Territorial Papers, Mississippi*, 5:129–30, 130–31; *Senate Exec. Proceedings*, 1:433, 437).

§ From John Gavino. *19 August 1802, Gibraltar.* No. 96. Encloses Simpson's dispatches reporting the settlement of difficulties between U.S. and Morocco; the emperor has withdrawn orders for cruisers to attack American ships. "Comodor Morris in the Chesapeake & the Schooner Enterprize Saild yesterday for Leghorn with about 11 Sail of our Vessels, & near as many Swedes, he is also to take up those that are detaind on the Coast of Spain." Five Tripolitan cruisers are still out. The *Adams* is "Cruising behind the Rock"; the *Boston* is "coming down" with several American and Swedish ships in convoy. The Portuguese squadron, consisting of two seventy-four-gun ships, four frigates, and three brigs, is reportedly going to cruise off the coast of Algiers. Encloses list of arrivals at Gibraltar during last six months [not found].

RC (DNA: RG 59, CD, Gibraltar, vol. 2). 2 pp. Printed in Knox, *Naval Documents, Barbary Wars*, 2:241–42. Enclosures probably included Simpson's dispatches to JM of 3 and 12 Aug. 1802.

To Thomas Jefferson

DEAR SIR   Aug. 20. 1802
   The inclosed letters will shew the object of the Bearer Mr. Baker.[1] From his conversation, I find that, placing Bourdeaux & Gibralter out of view, he

wishes to be appd. as Consul, to Minorca, where he says a Consul will be admitted, now that it is again under the Spanish Government, and where he observes a consul may be of use to the U. States, particularly during our bicker⟨in⟩gs with the Barbary powers. I find from his conversation also that he is a native of Minorca, whilst under British Govt. but that he has been in the U. States about six years & is an American Citizen. Nothing has passed between us that can influence his expectations or calculations, of the result of his pursuit.[2] Always with affectionate respect, Yrs.

JAMES MADISON

RC (DLC: Jefferson Papers). Docketed by Jefferson as received 21 Aug. For enclosures, see n. 1.

　1. See Edward Livingston to JM, 31 July 1802, and n. 1, Aaron Burr to JM, 2 Aug. 1802, and Frederick Weissenfels to JM, 2 Aug. 1802.
　2. Jefferson appointed Baker U.S. consul for the islands of Minorca, Majorca, and Iviza in February 1803 (*Senate Exec. Proceedings*, 1:441).

From John Steele

SIR   MISSISIPPI TERRITORY 20th. August 1802
　Herewith enclosed you will receive a Copy of the Journal of proceedings in the Executive Department of the Government of this Territory from the first of January to the 6th of May of the present year.

　I had at a period early enough applied to Governor Claiborne for his letter Book, that I might be able to make up the Journal by the end of my term of appointment, the 6th. of May. Notwithstanding repeated Applications, it was for some Cause withheld from me until after I was out of Office. He then Said I was not bound to make it up. I replied that I had no doubt I was bound to make it up, and that a prosecution would lay against me for not making it up: But that being out of Office at the end of the first Six months of the year I would not consider myself bound to transmit a Copy to the Department of State, because I could not give it the Authenticity required by Law. His letter Book was Accordingly delivered to me on the Second day of June. Since that period the whole of the Business has been recorded, and I continued to Compare the proof Sheets for the Printer with the original Laws in my possession, until the fifteenth instant, when they were finished—And also Sealed All Commissions pardons &c. wanted by the Governor. With high respect and personal esteem, I have the honor to be Sir your Obedient humble servant

Signed   JOHN STEELE

Tr (DNA: RG 233, Committee on Claims, Petition of John Steele, 8A-F1.1). Marked "No. 14." Enclosed in Steele's petition to Congress, 5 Oct. 1803 (see Carter, *Territorial Papers, Mississippi*, 5:241–61). Enclosure not found.

§ From John M. Forbes. *20 August 1802, Hamburg.* "I have at length the satisfaction to announce to you my arrival here and recognition by the Government of this City as Consul of the United States of America. Having announced my establishment here to a very extensive Circle of mercantile friends, I prefer encountering all the severities of this Climate to incurring the inconveniences which would attend a Change of residence. I beg leave, therefore, to relinquish the application I made from London for the Agency at Marseilles."[1]

RC (DNA: RG 59, CD, Hamburg, vol. 1). 1 p.

1. Forbes to JM, 6 July 1802.

From Wade Hampton and Fontaine Maury

DEAR SIR,   NEW YORK Augt. 21st. 1802

Some little time ago three French ships of War arrived at this Port from Guadaloupe via Carthagena where they touched with a view to sell, or otherwise dispose of a number of renegado negroes they have on board, but the Spanish Government not permitting them to be landed, they proceeded hither, and dispatched a vessel to Gel. Le Clerc for further instructions as to the mode of disposing of them, which they daily expect to receive. The number of these unfortunate half starved wretches already arrived, and momently expected in three other ships of War, amount to about 1500, and from the best information we can collect after having been at much pains to procure it, we have little doubt but they will attempt to disperse them clandestinely along the Southern coast, they have in many instances offered to sell them in this City, in open violation of the laws. 60 of them have been taken sick and thrown into the Marine Hospital, to which number, daily additions may well be expected. Altho' this information may not in every respect be correct, yet we believe it nearly so, and from the extreme agitation which exists in the public mind, we have deemed it expedient to give it to you, with a view, that you make such use of it as you think proper to guard against a measure which if carried into effect may considerably endanger the peace and tranquillity of the Southern States. We are very respectfully Dear Sir, your Obt Sert.

(Signed)   W HAMPTON
FONTAINE MAURY

Tr (NHi: Gallatin Papers). Marked "(Copy)"; docketed by Brent, "Copy of a letter from Mr Hampton & Fontaine Maury to the Secy. of State."

§ **From Josef Yznardy.** *21 August 1802, Cadiz.* "I have just this moment receiv'd from Mr. simpson of Tangiers the agreable news of War having terminated with the Moors to entire satisfaction, as you will be informed by the within Copy of the Circular & Letter received from him. . . . I have only time to advise you that said Simpson's Dispatch for you Sir, has been delivered to Capn. Silas Crowell of the Schooner Happy Return & will follow in a few days for Philada."

RC and enclosures (DNA: RG 59, CD, Cadiz, vol. 1). RC 1 p.; in a clerk's hand, signed by Yznardy; docketed by Brent. Enclosures (2 pp.) are copies of Simpson's 12 Aug. 1802 circular announcing the establishment of peace and a 14 Aug. 1802 letter to Yznardy covering a dispatch for JM.

To James Leander Cathcart

SIR,   VIRGINIA, August 22d 1802

Your letter of May 21st. 1802 with a copy of that of July 2d. 1801 has been duly received.

I hope that before the receipt of this you will have been successfully engaged in making peace with Tripoli. The late conduct of the Emperor of Morocco, and the effect which may be produced on the disposition of the Bey of Tunis by the rencounter reported to have happened between the Boston Frigate, and some of his cruizers, add fresh motives, at the same time that they may embarrass the means, for putting an end to the war with Tripoli. To provide for any contingency to yourself which might produce disappointment or delay, Commodore Morris will be instructed, should the negotiation not be over, to carry it on himself if necessary; and as he will be in a manner the center of information, and will have a certain relation to all the measures connected with our Mediterranean affairs, the President thinks it proper, that the proceedings which may remain for the fulfilment of your instructions, should be concerted with him and receive his sanction.

According to information given by Mr Eaton, he has prevailed on the brother of the Bashaw of Tripoli to repair to Malta, with a view to be with our squadron before Tripoli, and to be made use of against the Bashaw. At this distance it is difficult to judge accurately of the project, or to give particular instructions for the management of it. Altho' it does not accord with the general sentiments or views of the U States to intermeddle with the domestic controversies of other Countries, it cannot be unfair in the prosecution of a just war, or the accomplishment of a reasonable peace, to take advantage of the hostile cooperation of others. As far therefore as the views of the Brother may contribute to our success, the aid of them may be used for the purpose. Should this aid be found inapplicable, or his own personal object unattainable, it will be due to the honor of the U. States and to the expectations he will have naturally formed, to treat his disappointment with much tenderness, and to restore him as nearly as may be, to the situation from which he was drawn or to make some other convenient arrangement that may be more eligible to him. In case of a treaty of peace with the ruling Bashaw of Tripoli, perhaps it may be possible to make some stipulation, formal or informal, in favour of the Brother, which may be a desirable alleviation of his misfortune.

This will be sent by the New York, a Frigate Commanded by Captain James Barron. She will reinforce our Squadron in the Mediterranean at the same time that she conveys supplies for it, and $30 000 to be offered to the Dey of Algiers in place of the annuity of Stores. She also conveys to Gibraltar an hundred Gun carriages prepared as a compliment to the Emperor of Morocco before his hostility was declared, and which it is possible may now be usefully employed in some stage of a reconciliation with him. With much respect I am, Sir, your Obt Set

(Signed)   JAMES MADISON

Under discretionary powers from the President to the Heads of Departments who were at the seat of Government when this letter reached it, they have determined to withdraw ⟨the⟩ Gun carriages referred to; which are accordingly not sent by the New York.

DEPARTMT OF STATE 31st Augt 1802
(Signed)   DANL BRENT

RC (NN: Cathcart Papers); letterbook copy (DNA: RG 59, IC, vol. 1). RC marked "(Copy)"; in a clerk's hand; docketed by Cathcart, "Per the Enterprize Sterret recd. at Malta the 6th. of December 1802." Postscript not on letterbook copy. Extract transmitted by Jefferson to Congress on 4 Feb. 1806 and printed in *ASP, Foreign Relations*, 2:701.

To William Eaton

SIR,   VIRGINIA, Augt. 22d 1802.

Not having your last letters by me I cannot refer to their dates, nor particularly to their contents. The most important part of them communicated the plan concerted with the brother of the Bashaw of Tripoli for making use of him against the latter, in favour of the U. States. Altho' it does not accord with the general sentiments or views of the United States to intermeddle in the domestic contests of other countries, it cannot be unfair, in the prosecution of a just war, or the accomplishment of a reasonable peace, to turn to their advantage the enmity and pretensions of others against a common foe. How far success in the plan ought to be relied on, cannot be decided at this distance, and with so imperfect a knowledge of many circumstances. The event it is hoped will correspond with your zeal and with your calculations. Should the rival brother be disappointed in his object, it will be due to the honor of the U. States to treat his misfortune with the utmost tenderness and to restore him as nearly as may be to the situation from which he was drawn; unless some other proper arrangement should be more acceptable to him. This wish of the President will be conveyed to Commodore Morris, and Mr. Cathcart, with a suggestion that in the event of a peace with the ruling Bashaw, an attempt should be made to insert some provision favourable to his Brother.

Late letters from the Consul to Morocco, have brought us the disagreeable information that a rupture with the U. States has been declared by the Emperor. We learn at the same time by reports from Gibraltar that an encounter has unfortunately taken place between the Boston frigate[1] and some of the Cruizers of the Bey of Tunis, which may endanger our good understanding with that power. The importance of providing peace for our Commerce in the Mediterranean makes it a painful reflection, that at the moment chosen for the experiment, occurrences should not only favour a continuance of the War already on hand, but threaten to multiply our enemies in that quarter. Every proper step will be taken to parry the evil on the side of Morocco; and the President expects the utmost that your prudence and exertions can contribute to heal the wound that may have been given to the pacific dispositions of Tunis. Not being yet acquainted with any of the circumstances of the encounter; nor being even certain that it has taken place explanations and apologies, as far as they may be proper must be left to your own discretion, aided by the Communications which may be received from Commodore Morris. Among the soothing considerations urged on the Bey, you will be able to appeal to the elegant presents lately furnished by the U. States as an unquestionable proof of their esteem, and their desire to cultivate his friendship; and you are particularly authorized by the President to give him the strongest and most frank assurances that rigorous enquiry will be made into the conduct of the American Officer, and that every satisfaction will be rendered to the Bey which justice and respect shall require.

You are sufficiently aware of the motives to circumscribe expence as much as possible in our Mediterranean transactions. It is hoped that no money will be required by the present occasion, nor is any remitted to you for it. Commodore Morris will indeed have in his hands a fund of about $20,000, of which some part may be spared to you, in case he be led to see the necessity of it as an ingredient in the preservation of peace with Tunis.

I trust however, that your good management of other means will render them sufficient for the object. With much respect I am Sir, your Obt Sert.

(Signed)   JAMES MADISON

RC (CSmH); letterbook copy (DNA: RG 59, IC, vol. 1). RC marked "(Copy)"; in a clerk's hand; docketed by Eaton as received 22 Feb. 1803 "by Commodore Morris, who arrived 8. A.M. same day."

1. Eaton placed an asterisk here and wrote on the last page of the letter: "*I could never satisfy myself whence this report took its rise; believe it however a fabrication for the express purpose of blasting Captain Mc.Neill: an officer not very popular among his brother commanders—but as well qualified, perhaps, as any of them for a *Barbary coast!* There was not a syllable of truth in the report. W. Eaton." The report of the action between McNeill and five Tunisian cruisers, taken from a 19 June letter from an officer on the U.S. frigate *Chesapeake*, was published in the *Washington Federalist*, 11 Aug. 1802.

To James Simpson

SIR. VIRGINIA August 22d. 1802.

Your two letters of June 17. & 26 have been duly received. The hostile result of the deliberations of the Emperor of Morocco, notwithstanding your endeavor to give them a more favorable turn, is made particularly unwelcome by the moment at which it has occurred. All that remains now is to meet it in a proper manner by opposing force to force, without losing sight of the interest we have, in restoring a state of peace, as soon as an honorable one can possibly be effected. Commodore Morris will receive from the Secretary of the Navy, the instructions under which his arrangements will be formed. It will be your duty, whilst you aid him with all the useful information you may possess, to continue your endeavors, as far as circumstances will justify to convey to the Emperor the regret of the U. States, at his unexpected and unprovoked conduct, and their disposition to renew the friendship which has been unhappily interrupted taking care in whatever steps you may pursue for that purpose, to consult with and receive the sanction of Commodore Morris whenever he shall be within a communicating distance.

In my letter by the Adams,[1] you were informed of the intention of the President to compliment the Emperor with one hundred Gun Carriages, and that they would probably be accompanied by a letter. Notwithstanding the hostile declarations of the Emperor it is hoped that an advantage may flow from your possessing these conciliatory tokens of the esteem and good will of the U: States towards him. They are accordingly sent by the New York. How far it may be best, in case use can be made of them at all, to tender the Carriages, or send the letter or both, or to communicate only on your receipt of them, must be decided according to circumstances of which yourself & Commodore Morris can best judge. Should it be thought improper to make the tender of the carriages, or should the tender be refused, Gibraltar will probably be the most convenient depository for them, under a permission which will no doubt be given by the proper authority, on a proper application.

Commodore Morris will receive for certain contingent purposes, about 20,000 Dollars. Should a part of this money be indispensably required in any of your conciliatory measures, he will open the resources to you, on being satisfied with the occasion of resorting to it. Your draft for 1000 Dols. will be honored.

I have thought it not amiss to forward a letter of July 27th. altho' written with reference to a state of things different from that presented in the last communications; remarking only, that in case the question should again arise on the request of the Emperor of Morocco, to receive under his flag, the Vessel left at Gibraltar by the Tripolines, it is deemed proper, by the President, that the permission should be granted on reasonable appearances, that he has become the real owner of the Vessel, and that his flag is not meant to protect the return of the Vessel to Tripoli. I am &c.

JAMES MADISON.

This letter was sent to me by the Secretary of State, some days ago, to be forwarded with other dispatches from him for the Mediterranean, by the New York frigate, which is now on the point of departure. The Heads of Departments, who were at the seat of Government, when it reached me, under discretionary powers from the President to stop the letter referred to for the Emperor of Morocco, and the Gun Carriages, if the state of things should in their judgment, render such a step advisable, have determined that it would not be proper to send either; and they are both accordingly witheld.

DEPT. OF STATE, Augt. 31st. 1802.
DANIEL BRENT.

Letterbook copy (DNA: RG 59, IC, vol. 1). Misfiled in August 1805.

1. JM to Simpson, 20 Apr. 1802.

§ From William Jarvis. 22 *August 1802, Lisbon.* No. 4. Acknowledges JM's letter of 12 May 1802. "The determination of the Insurance Company to send some person here gave me much pleasure, since the importance of the object required the evidence of a person in so elevated a station as is Don Juan de Almeida & as it will prevent my being implicated by a want of success which I am apprehensive will be the case, it being almost impossible in any cases whatever to obtain the attestation of Officers in a much inferior station." Encloses a dispatch received 21 Aug. giving a "disagreeable account" of U.S. affairs with Tripoli, which was accompanied by a circular from Simpson that announced the end of hostilities with Morocco. Reports that the *Antelope* from New York was quarantined on 16 Aug. owing to a notice in a Portuguese gazette, copied from an English newspaper, that yellow fever had broken out in New York. The ship was released on 21 Aug. after Jarvis met with the officer of health and submitted a petition made out in the captain's name and a copy of the U.S. government's circular letter to collectors, both in Portuguese; encloses a copy of his covering letter. "The noise that was made in the affair of Genl. Lannes has pretty much subsided, by its being announced to the Public that the Genl. was appointed Inspector Genl. of the Armies of France. It is sd. that Brune or Augereau will succeed him." On 18 Aug. "an order was received at the Customhouse from the Minister of the Interior, to prohibit altogether the importation of Cordage for home Consumption. In consequence of which an American Vessel that was freighted in St. Petersburg on account of an English House here & had discharged about one half of her Cargo was prevented from dischargeing the rest." The protests of the British and Russian ambassadors against the order were unsuccessful. "I hope this Govmt. will no longer suffer in the opinion of Foreigners, for an indolent procrastinating disposition, for certainly here is promptness & decision enough. . . . I am afraid that after their granaries are well supplied, our flour will exhibit another specimen of their promptness." Unverified reports circulate that France has declared war on Algiers. Notes in a postscript that he has employed a lawyer in the cases of the schooners *Samuel* and *Pilgrim* "who has been remarkable for his success in those kind of affairs."

RC (DNA: RG 59, CD, Lisbon, vol. 1); enclosures (DNA: RG 59, CD, Tunis, vol. 2, pt. 1). RC 4 pp.; docketed by Wagner. The enclosures, misfiled with William Eaton's 7 July 1802 dispatch, are a copy of Eaton's circular letter of 9 July 1802 (1 p.) announcing the capture of the American brig *Franklin* and, on the verso, an undated copy of Jarvis's letter to the Portuguese officer of health asking that the quarantine on the *Antelope* be raised. Extract from RC printed in *National Intelligencer*, 22 Nov. 1802.

From Thomas Jefferson

DEAR SIR   MONTICELLO Aug. 23. 1802.

Yesterday's post brought me, as I suppose it did you, information of the Emperor of Marocco's declaration of war against us,[1] and of the capture of a merchant vessel of ours (the Franklin, Morris) off cape Palos, by a Tripoline as is said in a New York letter; but a Marraquin as I am in hopes from the place, & the improbability of a Tripoline being there. The letter to the Emperor, & the gun carriages are of course to be stopped, and I have approved a proposition from mr. Smith to send another frigate, which he says can be ready in two weeks, in addition to the New York.[2] These with those already there, & the Swedes, are surely sufficient for the enemies at present opposed to us. These are the only alterations made in the arrangements we had agreed on. I have desired mr. Smith to recommend a liberal attention in our officers to the interests of Sweden in the Mediteranean, and if peace with Marocco does not take place this year, I should think it proper that we should undertake the forming a permanent league of the powers at war, or wh: may from time to time get into war with any of the Barbary powers.[3] Accept assurances of my constant & affectionate esteem.

Th: Jefferson

FC (DLC: Jefferson Papers).

1. News of the declaration of war by the emperor of Morocco was announced in Robert Smith's letter to Jefferson of 20 Aug. 1802 (DLC: Jefferson Papers).

2. Smith's idea to send an additional frigate to the Mediterranean was proposed in his letter to Jefferson of 20 Aug. 1802; the president agreed in his letter to Smith of 23 Aug. 1802 (ibid.).

3. On 30 Sept. 1802, Edward Thornton reported to Lord Hawkesbury that after a conversation with JM, he could see no foundation to rumors that the U.S. was joining a northern European confederacy to repress the piracy of the Barbary States (PRO: Foreign Office, ser. 5, 35:321).

§ From William Eaton. *23 August 1802, Tunis.* Reports on a personal interview with an acquaintance, Mr. DeWitt, which took place 22 Aug. on a Danish frigate twelve days from Tripoli. DeWitt said that the pasha of Tripoli "was desirous of peace; the subjects more so: but that the capture of the American brig had greatly elevated his pride." The threat of an attack by his brother in company with the Americans and the Swedes had led the pasha to collect "with all possible expedition the whole force of his kingdom about the city," reported to be about 60,000 men, but they had dispersed to the mountains on 8 Aug. for lack of provisions. DeWitt also said that the American and Swedish blockade of Tripoli was "no real impediment to the entry and departure of vessels."

Relates his first dragoman's assertion "that the number of men above stated to have come to the assistance of that Bashaw must be greatly exaggerated; and that the whole number of fighting men whom he can bring to his obedience cannot exceed ten[1] or eleven thousand: that it is impossible to keep them in the field any considerable time for want of provisions; that being chiefly mounted and totally undisciplined they are extremely terrified at the appearance of artilery."

"If to coerce Tripoli be an object with our government . . . the position I have taken with Mahamet Bashaw is well calculated to secure that object. . . . We are contending with a perfidious usurper whose rightful sovereign may be used in our cause. If we suffer the occasion to be lost . . . what alternative shall be adopted equally promising? Is it not a circumstance, which should interest the friends to present administration, that the issue of this war will in some measure, stamp the character of the Executive? . . . Can an occasion more favorable than the present offer to consolidate the affections and interests of the American people? In the present war . . . there can be but one mind and one voice. It is only to be feared that the enemey are thought too contemptible to rouse exertion. But it ought to be considered, that we are combatting the commercial policy of all Europe. It is not only then in Barbary that we are about to fix a national character—it is in the *world!* . . . The question now at issue is, Whether we will defend our right of free navigation, or hold this privilege as *tributaries* and as *tenants at will* at the discretion of a Barbary pirate?"

Has learned from his dragoman that the bey of Tunis intends to renew his demand for a small frigate "in terms which could not admit of a refusal!" To this "I shall yield no concessions. But, one of two events must result from this posture of affairs—concession, or war."

Mentions reports that France and England have made their peace with Algiers. "If true, Spain, of course, will compromise with Tunis. No longer held in check by those *magnanimous powers*, the field is open for these marauders to coersce the Americans into their views."

States that "our operations of the last and present year produce nothing in effect but additional enemies and national contempt"; his "obstinate posture and affected indifference to menace" are no longer effective. "The minister puffs a whistle in my face and says, '*We find it is all a puff! We see how you carry on the war with Tripoli!*'" Has "never ceased" to provide reports, warnings, suggestions, and advice. "I have now the melancholy reflection that my apprehensions have been but too well founded, and my predictions but too accurate."

"My exile is become insupportable here. Abandoned by my countrymen in command—no advice from government to regulate my conduct—and my own exertions failing of effect—I am left subject, though not yet submissive, to the most intolerable abuse and personal vexation." Cites damage to his health, "dispositions in this court to distress me in my personal concerns," an inadequate salary, and attacks by Captain Murray on his public character. "Are such the rewards of my services? To be branded, unheard in my own defence, and by a solitary captain of a frigate, with speculation [and] insanity?" Requests the president's permission to resign unless "more active operations shall be resolved on against the enemy."

Notes that only one American frigate has appeared at Tripoli since the *Boston*'s departure, that he has received no information from any of the American naval commanders since 3 June, and that five Tripolitan galleys are at sea. Adds in a 28 Aug. postscript that on 27 Aug. the Tunisian minister "formally demanded of me a frigate of 36 guns. It need not be thought strange to see me in America this winter. I can neither yield to nor get rid of the demand."

RC (DNA: RG 59, CD, Tunis, vol. 2, pt. 1); letterbook copy (CSmH). RC 5 pp. Letterbook copy incomplete. Extract, which varies in part from the RC, printed in Knox, *Naval Documents, Barbary Wars*, 2:248–49.

1. Eaton placed an asterisk here in the letterbook copy and wrote in the margin: "*By a mate of a swedish vessel, captive from Tripoli I learn that the number did not exceed six thousand! I might have mistaken *sixty* for *six* from Mr. DeWitt."

From Charles Pinckney

Dear Sir   August 24: 1802 In Madrid

Mr Codman by whom I proposed to send the inclosed[1] being taken ill I think it best to send Duplicates to give you the earliest intelligence of what I have been able to do here. The original will go by him to Washington. I still hope to be able to bring this Court to agree to an arbitration by the same Commissioners of the french spoliations, & of the claims for Vessels condemned by their consuls in Spanish Ports. It will be with great reluctance but I still think they will agree to it. The Spaniards, I mean *private individuals*, in speaking of this claim of ours complain of it as one of the hardest cases that can possibly occur—that just emerging from a War with their all powerf⟨u⟩l neighbour (France) in which they had been unsuccesful & were in fact obliged to wink at this conduct of the french consuls ⟨for⟩ fear of irritating their Government & renewing the War, they could not have beheld this violation of their territorial sovereignty either with pleasure or indifference—it could not certainly have been agreeable to them—the Americans were their friends & their commerce was useful & valuable to Spain—the capture & condemnation of our Vessels was therefore a loss & inconvenience to Spain—not one shilling of the prizes ever went into the Pockets of the King or his subjects, & it was with pain they saw their condemnation & sale. For Spain, they say to be obliged, under these circumstances to pay for them, appears as they continually repeat, to be one of the hardest cases that can possibly occur. Mr Cevallos (the Secretary) or the Government do not avow to me that this is their motive for declining to include them in the convention. He says that neither the laws of Nations or the Treaty oblige them, but no doubt the reasons I have stated as coming from individuals, have also their Weight.

I however find since forming the Convention, it will be much more extensive in its Operations & effects than I at first supposed. All the cases of Mr Higginson will come clearly under the Convention & so will a number of others which have been heretofore supposed *entirely french*. The Variety of very important claims from South America, Europe, & the West Indies not only for captures but the illegal interferences of Governors, Generals, & other officers acting under the authority of the Spanish Government will swell the list to an enormous amount & there can be no doubt that in a number of the french cases there have been such illegal interferences of Spanish Officers in the different ports as to bring them within the Convention & subject them to the decision of the Commissioners. If we get the fifth Commissioner I have little Doubt that most of the cases will be included now supposed entirely french.

On the subject of Florida & Louisiana I have frequently written you lately. To my Enquiries on the subject of the Floridas Mr Cevallos always replies that as soon as the King recieves answers to the letters he has directed to be Written on this subject he will give an answer whether he is willing to sell or not. The Business of Louisiana has long since been decided. Whatever you may hear on this subject the following is the true state of facts. That so long since as 1800 General Berthier was specially appointed & sent on to Madrid to negotiate this cession which he effected & Spain at that time completely ceded all her rights according to the antient Boundaries of Louisiana when held by France. That in the year 1801 & *very early* in it, (in March) Lucien Bonaparte in a new treaty recieved a confirmation of this right[2] & that ever since that period the Spanish commanding officers in Louisiana have held orders to deliver it to the french whenever they would send to take posession of it. The War with England & the difficulty of sending troops to posess it were no doubt the only reasons they have not posessed it before. I have repeatedly been with Mr Cevallos to know if there was any menti⟨on⟩ in the Cession of our right to navig⟨ate⟩ the Misissipi & deposit our produce on its Banks. In our first conversations he told me no. But afterwards he assured me Louisiana should not be delivered to the French to the prejudice of the United States but subject to the Conditions of our Treaty with Spain. This I requested him to reduce to writing to send you—but for some reason he has not done so explicitly. I shall continue to write & urge an explicit answer & if it can be obtained in Writing I will send it to You. You may be assured that long before I arrived here every thing *was irrevocably* fixed about Louisiana & finding it so I wrote to Mr Livingston at Paris that whatever was necessary must be done by him there. That even in the affair of the purchase of Florida—the influence of France was extremely important. In short it appears to me to be irresistible in the south of Europe. I have therefore Written to Mr Livingston that it would be very important for him to know from the french Government whether any express stipulation is made by them respecting the Navigation of the Misissipi & the right to deposit our produce & merchandize on its Banks & if not to know whether they are ready to make in form a proper declaration that they consider France as recieving Louisiana from Spain subject to the conditions of the Treaty of the Latter with the United States. That it would not do for the United States to hold the navigation at the Will or by the permission of France. It would not only be derogatory to them to do so but should the Western inhabitants ever have the Opinion or entertain the idea that it was to France they were to look for the permission to navigate & deposit & not to their own Government it would be a most unfortunate one indeed & might ultimately produce a Separation. By Mr Codman I am to send the Original Convention

& several letters I recieved from Mr Cevallos & in the interim with my most affectionate & sincere respects & good Wishes to the President I remain dear sir always Yours Truly

CHARLES PINCKNEY

RC (DNA: RG 59, DD, Spain, vol. 6). Damaged by tears at folds. Enclosure not found.

1. Pinckney no doubt enclosed a copy of the spoliations convention (see Pinckney to JM, 15 Aug. 1802, and n. 4).

2. For the negotiations of Lucien Bonaparte, see David Humphreys to JM, 23 Mar. 1801 (*PJM-SS*, 1:36).

§ From Thomas Auldjo. *24 August 1802, Cowes.* "Our Crop of Corn is half saved in these parts & in exceeding good order from our having had no rain for these three weeks & we only want a Continuance of favorable weather to secure abundance. Our prices are now nominal, there being little grain of any Sort at market. . . . Every thing goes on as usual. I pay due attention to your Circular of 1st Augt 1801 & the papers it refers to."

RC (DNA: RG 59, CD, Southampton, vol. 1). 1 p. President Washington appointed British subject Thomas Auldjo U.S. vice-consul at Cowes in 1790 (*Senate Exec. Proceedings*, 1:48, 50, 52).

§ From Elisha Hyde. *24 August 1802, Norwich.* Has received a commission to act as a commissioner of bankruptcy for the district of Connecticut but declines the appointment, "as it will preclude me from a seat in our Legislature which place I have been Honour'd with many years." Explains that "there are too many who feel very uncandid towards the present Administration of the United States that I may have an opportunity to be more active in favour of the present measures of the General Government is my only reason for declining this Office."

RC (DNA: RG 59, LRD, filed under "Hyde"). 2 pp.; docketed by Jefferson.

§ From John Lamson. *24 August 1802, Trieste.* Since his dispatch of 22 May, "some events have taken place which appear to threaten the ⟨tota⟩l annihilation of our commerce in these seas." They are the declaration of war by the emperor of Morocco, the threat of war by the other Barbary States, and the capture of the brig *Franklin* by Tripoli. "As the commerce of this country with their own Ships is allmost entirely confined to the Levant and Medeteranean seas they depend wholly upon foreigners for their supplies of East and West India produce of which there is an immense consumption. . . . If therefore the Navigation of the Medeteranean could be free'd from its present embarassments, I think [the U.S.] might employ a portion of their shipp⟨ing⟩ in this trade to very good account."

RC (DNA: RG 59, CD, Trieste, vol. 1). 2 pp. Damaged by removal of seal.

514

§ From Elkanah Watson. *24 August 1802, Albany.* Encloses a letter from Lieutenant Governor Van Rensselaer,[1] "who has the honor of a personal acquaintance with you." Wrote to the president on the same subject on 1 June, together with Van Rensselaer and state comptroller Jenkins, but they have had no reply. Solicits "the appointment of Consul for the Port of Nantes in behalf of my worthy friend Simon Lynch Esqr. a respectable mercht. of that City." Transcribes an extract from his letter to the president.

"During five years I Resided in Nantes in Our Revolution, . . . I was Well acquainted with the father of Mr. Lynch, who was esteemed one of the Most respectable Merchants there. He was of Irish extraction, of Course the English Language is in a Manner the Mother tongue of Mr. L—altho' born in Nantes. He has made the Tour of the United States, . . . has an extensive & personal Knowledge & correspondence with Our principal Merchants a'Long our Sea bord; & from my personal Knowledge of him . . . I am confident No person Can better Supply the Vacancy. . . . The last Consul Mr. Dobrée who lately died was a Guernsey Man. . . . I am a'ware that the Government have wisely adopted a prefference to American Characters, but . . . I presume the prefference alluded to, cannot in this Instance impair my hopes in favr. of Mr. L."

Encloses a circular dated 14 June [not found] just received from Lynch that "will afford Some important commercial Information." Quotes from a private letter from Lynch of the same date.

"I persuade myself, that my Situation will enable me to discharge the duties incumbent on that respectable Station, with all the Zeal, fidelity & attention, which the American Government has a right to expect. Since the death of the respectable Mr. Dobrée . . . the American Nation, has Not been represented by any One. There are Now in Port 10 or 12 Sail of Americans, & No agent to assist, dispatch & protect them."

RC (DNA: RG 59, LAR, 1801–9, filed under "Lynch"). 4 pp.; docketed by Jefferson. For surviving enclosure, see n. 1. Elkanah Watson (1758–1842) was a prominent Albany merchant and canal promoter. He later moved to western Massachusetts where he concentrated his energies in agricultural pursuits, among which was the establishment of the first county fair in the U.S.

1. Jeremiah Van Rensselaer to JM, 25 Aug. 1802.

§ From Josef Yznardy. *24 August 1802, Cadiz.* Transmits duplicates of his correspondence since his arrival. Also forwards the dispatch from James Simpson mentioned in his 21 Aug. letter as having been delivered to Captain Crowell; Crowell did not sail as expected because of contrary winds. "Looking over & examining the Books of this Consulship I find that a great number of Vessels have been sold during my absence; & having called for their respective Registers from Mr. Anthony Terry the Vice Consul, he answered me that he only had the five following in his possession." Lists names of five ships and their captains. Encloses a list of those ships for which Terry has been unable "to get the Captains to deliver [the registers]"; "fearing that they or the Owners may make bad use of them, . . . I avail of the first opportunity to acquaint you thereof."

RC and enclosure (DNA: RG 59, CD, Cadiz, vol. 1). RC 2 pp. Enclosure (1 p.), headed "List of Vessels sold in this Port, and their Registers were carried to America by their respective Captains," is dated 22 Aug. 1802 and lists fifteen ships.

To Thomas Jefferson

Dear Sir   Aug. 25. 1802

Yours of the 23d. has been duly recd. Mr. Brent had informed me that copies of the letters from the Mediterranean had been sent to you by Mr. Smith, and therefore I did not send the originals by express.[1] The declaration of a rupture by the Empr. of Morocco, put me at a loss what to say to Simson on the subject of the Gun carriages, and how to decide as to the letter you left with me. As the event however was anticipated when you were here, as a necessary consequence, of Morris's concurrence in the refusal of Simson, and of the instructions sent from the Navy Dept. by the Adams, I concluded that the Gun carriages ought still to go, subject to the discretionary & conciliatory use of Morris & Simson, and have written to Simson on that supposition. I was the more inclined to this opinion, by the anxiety & the ideas of the Secretary of the Treasy. Reasoning in a similar manner, I sent on to Mr. Brent your letter to the E. of M. with an erasure of the last paragraph, & some little alteration besides, & a request that the Secretaries present would decide what ought to be done;[2] and have in my letter to Simson given him like discretion over it, as I gave him with respect to the Gun carriages. In pursuance now of your decision agst. sending either, I shall write by the next mail to have a post[s]cript added by Mr. Brent signifying the change that has taken place. Nothing appears in the communications to me, relative to the affair between the Boston & the Tunisian cruisers. In my letters to Cathcart Eaton OBrien & Simson,[3] I have spoken of it as report believed here, and have fashioned my instructions accordingly particularly those to Eaton. I find from Gavino's letters to me, that the capture of the American vessel, was ascribed to a Pirate, and not to a cruiser of Tripoli or Morocco.[4] With most respectful attachment I remain Yrs.

                                                                    James Madison

RC (DLC: Jefferson Papers). Docketed by Jefferson as received 27 Aug.

1. Brent's letter to JM has not been found.
2. JM's 23 Aug. letter to Brent has not been found (see Brent to JM, 25 Aug. 1802). For the president's letter to the emperor of Morocco, see Jefferson to JM, 6 Aug. 1802.
3. JM wrote to Cathcart, Eaton, and Simpson on 22 Aug. and added a 22 Aug. postscript to his letter to O'Brien of 27 July 1802.
4. JM apparently misread Gavino's 29 June 1802 dispatch.

From Daniel Brent

Dear Sir,   Washington, Augt 25th 1802.

I have duly received your favor of the 23d Inst.,[1] with the several papers enclosed in it, which were immediately given to the Secretaries of the Treasury and Navy, agreeably to your direction. The latter having just returned them to me, copies will be forthwith made of all of them but of the letter to the Emperor of Morocco, (which does not go) as well for the Office, as for Mr Smith, who is to send them to Commodore Morris. The necessary orders are to be given by Mr Gallatin and Mr Smith concerning the 30.000 Dollars, and they both say, that nothing more will be required of you, or your Office, at least for the present, about this money. Mr Smith tells me that the New York frigate will be hawled off to morrow, and that she will probably move down the River the next day. I enclose a Copy of his Instructions to Commodore Morris.[2] He desired me to inform you that his engagements unluckily prevent him from writing to you to day. I am very sorry that my silence concerning the affair of the Boston frigate should have at all embarrassed you. No official Confirmation of the truth of the Report on that subject had been recd. here when I wrote, nor has any been since received of it. I enclose a requisition on the Secy of the Treasury for 400 Dolls., founded upon a Bill of Mr Gavino for an advance to Mr Simpson, of which you are already advised. Mr Barnes, of Geo Town, is the Holder of this Bill. The letter from Mr Moultrie, herewith sent, together with the printed papers accompanying it, were recd. some time ago,[3] & immediately put into the hands of Mr Gallatin, who has just returned them to me. I received on Thursday your note of the 21st by Mr Woodward, enclosing a reprieve for McGirk, which has been delivered to the Marshal.[4] I understand from Mr Smith that the Jno. Adams will soon follow the New York. I have the Honor to be, with the highest Respect & most sincere esteem, Sir, Your Obedt & faithful servt.

                                                            Danl Brent.

RC (DLC). Docketed by JM. Enclosures not found, but see nn. 2 and 3.

1. Letter not found.
2. The instructions are printed in Knox, *Naval Documents, Barbary Wars*, 2:257–58.
3. See Alexander Moultrie to JM, 9 Aug. 1802.
4. Letter not found. A reprieve for convicted murderer James McGirk, dated 21 Aug. 1802, postponed execution of his sentence until 28 Oct. 1802 (DNA: RG 59, PPR).

From Samuel Sheild

D<small>EAR</small> S<small>IR</small>   Y<small>ORK</small> C<small>OUNTY</small> V<small>IRGINIA</small> August 25th. 1802.

The Office of Collector of the Port or District of York-Town having lately become vacant by the Death of Mr. Wm. Reynolds,[1] I have taken the Liberty to write to the President of the United States on the Subject and to recommend Mr. William Cary of that Town,[2] as a proper Person to supply the Vacancy. To address the Head of the Treasury Department also rather than the Secretary of State might be most proper on such an Occasion; but as I have no Acquaintance with Mr. Gallatin, I have ventured to trouble you and to request that you will be so kind as to interpose your good Offices both with the President and Mr. Gallatin. I verily believe that it is a fortunate Circumstance, that so respectable a Man as Mr. Cary will accept the Office, as other wise it would in all Probability fall into the Hands of some young Man, who might occasion considerable Trouble to the Treasury-Department. Mr. Cary is one of the oldest Inhabitants of the Town, quite easy in his Circumstances, of strict Integrity and has all his Life been remarkable for his Punctuality in the Discharge of any Business which he undertakes. Antirepublicanism, I must confess, has always been and still is too prevalent in York; but so moderate has this old Gentleman ever been, that he has uniformly voted for me, even in the most trying Times. Please to present my best Respects to Mrs. Madison and to be assured that I am with the greatest personal Esteem Yr. most obdt. Servt.

S<small>AML.</small> S<small>HEILD</small>[3]

RC (DLC: Jefferson Papers). Filed with Albert Gallatin to Jefferson, 9 Sept. 1802.

1. William Reynolds (d. 1802) was born in Yorktown, Virginia, but received a mercantile education in the house of John Norton & Sons, London. He returned to Virginia in 1771 and served as a paymaster of state troops in 1777 and as a justice of the peace. He was appointed collector and inspector of the revenue for Yorktown in 1794 and served in that capacity until his death (Frances Norton Mason, ed., *John Norton & Sons, Merchants of London and Virginia* [New York, 1968], pp. 518–19; *Senate Exec. Proceedings*, 1:165).

2. William Carey was appointed to the post but resigned almost immediately. Thomas Archer, a Revolutionary War veteran, was appointed in Carey's place (Jefferson to Albert Gallatin, 13 Sept. 1802, *Papers of Gallatin* [microfilm ed.], reel 7; Gallatin to Jefferson, 5 Oct. 1802 [DLC: Jefferson Papers]; *Senate Exec. Proceedings*, 1:433; Heitman, *Historical Register Continental*, p. 65).

3. There were several Samuel Sheilds prominent in Tidewater affairs, but this was probably the Samuel Sheild (or Shield) who died in York County, Virginia, in 1803 and was "for many years a member of the General Assembly" (*Marriages and Deaths from Richmond, Virginia, Newspapers, 1780–1820* [Easley, S.C., 1988], p. 140).

§ From James Leander Cathcart. *25 August 1802, Leghorn.* No. 11. During his residence at Tripoli, transmitted to the State Department a history of the reign of Ali

Pasha, father of the reigning sovereign, including the "different revolutions in that State," the murder of Mohammed Bey, and the usurpation by Yusuf Pasha Qaramanli of the throne of his brother Hamet Pasha. Is convinced that the inhabitants of Tripoli hold the present pasha "in the greatest degree of horror imaginable" and would support restoring Hamet Pasha to the throne. Yusuf is aware of this, so that "when ever he goes out of the city he carries all his treasure & jewels with him in chests mounted on Mules"; he has alienated the Grand Signior, who "only waits for a proper opportunity" to chastise him. "No act could be more just than the re-instating Hamet Pacha on the throne of his forefathers, & no act could insure the Grand Signore a revenge so prompt & efficacious & attended with so little expense both of blood & treasure; nor so effectually insure the gratitude & future obedience of Hamet & his family, as well as set a precedent to the other states of Barbary whose incorrigible insolence has become unsupportable at the sublime Port." Yusuf, who understands these circumstances, tried to entice Hamet to come to Tripoli "under the specious pretext" of giving him the governorship of Derna and Bengasi, a post which the latter refused. Hamet demanded instead that Yusuf free his wife and children and give him a small annuity, "promising that he would then live & die at Tunis."

"In the above train were affairs at Tripoli when I left it." Quotes from his letter to Eaton of 15 June 1801, where he observed that "'if [Hamet] was a man of understanding & enterprize I would stake my soul that with the assistance of four of our Frigates that I would effect a revolution in his favor and place him on the throne of Tripoli.'" Thought at the time it was "a moral impossibility that it would take fifteen months to draw out the energy's of an injured nation, or that motives of humanity would so far preponderate in our councils as to induce us to postpone our vengeance." In a letter of 29 June, Cathcart forwarded to Eaton the outlines of his dispatch no. 8, dated 2 July 1801,[1] and asked him to find out "how far said Hamet would be willing to engage in an expedition of that nature." Cathcart's intention was to send Hamet in a U.S. ship to Constantinople to gather Ottoman support for a coup in Tripoli, while taking the opportunity to conclude a commercial treaty with the Sublime Porte; "by procuring the Grand Senior's sanction to this expedition would effectually prevent any coalition taking place unfavorable to our interests, & that the Grand Senior still intends to revenge the insults he has receiv'd you will be inform'd by Mr. Nissens communications dated Tripoli April 22nd. 1802 forwarded in my dispatch No. 7."[2] In March, however, Yusuf succeeded in persuading the bey of Tunis to deny his protection to Hamet, who was then obliged to accept the governorship of Derna "& embark'd onboard a russian ship bound to Malta (but supposed to have been bound to Derna) where he arrived the 11th. of April." This event "induced Mr. Eaton to take the measures which he no doubt has detail'd to government in the amplest manner," measures he normally would not have taken without the president's instructions but which Cathcart judges to have been "judicious [and] dictated by imperious necessity & an honest zeal for the success of an enterprize which promised such vast advantages to our Country." This was the situation when the *Constellation* arrived, "when it seems by Mr. Eatons communications to me, that Captn. Alexr. Murray arrogated to himself the presumption to discard measures . . . in a stile of the most illiberal censure, without even observing the common respect due from public Officers in difft. departments to each other." Cathcart's object in making this report is to ask that the president "draw a line of distinction between the relative dutys of the Consuls residing in Barbary & the Commanders of our vessels of War, for I cant suppose it conducive to the public interests to subject men (who have spent the best parts of their lives in the public service & who have been several years acquiring knowledge in the Country's where they reside) to the caprice of every gentleman who may command our vessels of War. . . . I presume we had much better stay at home than subject ourselves to this additional degradation. The situation of a Consul in Barbary . . . is of all others the most humiliating & perilous, exiled ('tho honorably) from his dearest connections, doom'd to breath an air contaminated by plague & slavery, subject even in our beds to the mortal stings of scorpions, exposed to every species of insolence & degradation that a fertile brain'd Mohammetan can invent to render the life of a christian superlatively miserable."

Captain McNeill has had several conferences with Hamet Pasha at Malta and, in conjunction with Admiral Cederström, "has made some arrang⟨e⟩ments with him the particulars of which are to me unknown." Requests JM to present the subject of this dispatch to the president "in such a manner that in future a line may be drawn between our relative duty's."

RC (DNA: RG 59, CD, Tripoli, vol. 2); FC (NN: Cathcart Papers); FC (CSmH). RC 9 pp.; docketed by Wagner; printed in Knox, *Naval Documents, Barbary Wars*, 2:250–54. Both FC's marked duplicate. First FC in Cathcart's hand; docketed by Cathcart, with his later notations: "By this despatch will be seen that the plan of engaging Hamet Bashaw in our interests originated with me, & not with Consul Eaton as is generally believed, he got home before me, & not only got the credit but likewise 10,000 Acres of land from the State of Massachusetts as a reward for it, but more of this will be seen in the publication which is now preparing for the press, where the injustice I have received in many instances will be made manifest, & those concern'd in it pourtray'd in their proper colours. / There is no other proof necessary that I received my appointment as Consul genl. for Algiers prior to the date of this despatch, had I not I would not have had power vested in me to write it." Second FC in a clerk's hand, signed by Cathcart. Extract of RC transmitted by Jefferson to Congress on 4 Feb. 1806 and printed in *ASP, Foreign Relations*, 2:700–701.

1. *PJM-SS*, 1:370–72. Cathcart's letter to Eaton of 29 June 1801 is printed in Knox, *Naval Documents, Barbary Wars*, 1:493–95.

2. "There is a report that the Capt. Bashaw is expected here from Constantinople with five ships of war. The Bashaw is arming all his Subjects, without distinction of Persons, he has prohibited the Inhabitants of the town to leave it. Most of the Caids or Governors of Villages are changed & his Measures of defense are really calculated to make a vigorous defense by Land. This seems to indicate that he dreads some other force more formidable than the Americans & Swedes" (extract of Nissen to Cathcart, 22 Apr. 1802, enclosed in Cathcart to JM, 3 June 1802).

§ From Jeremiah Van Rensselaer. *25 August 1802, Albany*. "Some time since I wrote the President of the United States by the request of my particular friend (as well in social as in *political* life) Elkanah Watson Esqr. of this City, for the purpose of recommending to the notice of Goverment Mr. Simon Lynch. . . . I have no personal knowledge of Mr. Lynch; but from the long and intimate acquaintance I have had with Mr. Watson, . . . his representations on that head I am persuaded will be found to merit the respectfull attention of government."

RC (DNA: RG 59, LAR, 1801–9, filed under "Lynch"). 2 pp. Mistakenly docketed by Brent, "Augt 15th 1802."

To George Simpson

SIR   DEPT OF STATE Aug. 26. 1802.
I request that the Proceeds of the enclosed Bill of the Treasurer of the United States, for Eight thousand two hundred dollars, may be placed to the Credit of the Secretary of State of the United States, for the time being, in the Bank of the United States, for the benefit of Jeremiah Condy and Company and others, interested in the Ship, Wilmington Packet, and her Cargo.[1] With respect, I am, Sir, Your Very Obedt Servant,

JAMES MADISON

RC (NN: Myers Collection); letterbook copy (DNA: RG 59, DL, vol. 14). RC in a clerk's hand, signed by JM; month and day in dateline supplied by JM. JM probably enclosed a bill of exchange dated 6 Aug. 1802 (1 p.), drawn on Willink and Van Staphorst for 20,000 guilders ($8,200); on 16 Aug. Daniel Sheldon, Jr., noted on the bill that it had been purchased by the secretary of the treasury on account of diplomatic expenses (DNA: RG 217, First Auditor's Accounts, no. 13,708).

1. George Simpson was cashier of the first Bank of the United States from 1795 until 1812 (James O. Wettereau, "New Light on the First Bank of the United States," *Pa. Magazine of History and Biography*, 61 [1937]: 277). For the disbursement of the sum awarded in the case of the *Wilmington Packet*, see JM to Gallatin, 20 Sept. 1802, and Gallatin to JM, 6 Oct. 1802.

§ From James Leander Cathcart. *26 August 1802, Leghorn.* Submits for the president's decision a plan to coerce Yusuf Pasha of Tripoli to agree to a permanent treaty with the U.S. and "perpetual protection" for his brother Hamet by threatening him with the "use of such means as God had already placed in our hands . . . join'd to our influence at the sublime Port." Encloses William Eaton's letter to him of 12 July "with my addition to it which I have made circular" as well as another from Algiers given to him by Appleton. Has received no other news from Barbary worth mentioning.

RC (DNA: RG 59, CD, Tripoli, vol. 2); FC (NN: Cathcart Papers); FC (CSmH). RC 2 pp.; docketed by Wagner as received with Cathcart's 25 Aug. dispatch; printed in Knox, *Naval Documents, Barbary Wars,* 2:254. First FC in Cathcart's hand. Second FC in a clerk's hand, signed by Cathcart. Enclosures not found.

§ From John J. Murray. *26 August 1802, Glasgow.* Reports problems carrying out the law of 2 Mar. 1799 regulating the collection of duties on imports and tonnage.[1]

Some captains consider it a hardship to travel to Glasgow from Greenock "for the sole purpose of taking & subscribing the Oaths required before me." Believes they have no grounds for refusal, as neither Greenock nor Port Glasgow "is above two hours by Land or Water Conveyance from this place." Encloses a notice he has circulated to importers in the Clyde River. "Should you sir disapprove of my construction of the Law quoted be pleased to signify the same—if not, . . . to prevent irregularities in future, will you be good enough to guard the Collectors particularly against the injustice pointed at." Expresses doubts about the claims to American citizenship made by some owners of American vessels and asks two questions: if a foreigner becomes an American citizen but after some years returns to his native land with the intention to remain and a fortune earned in the U.S., is he an American citizen and can he own American vessels?[2] If not, would establishing a mercantile house in the U.S. enable him to own American vessels during his residence out of the U.S.?[3]

RC and enclosure (DNA: RG 59, CD, Glasgow, vol. 1). RC 6 pp.; docketed by Wagner. Postmarked New York, 22 Oct. Enclosure (1 p.) is a printed circular dated 24 Aug. 1802, informing masters and mates of American ships entitled to drawbacks that oaths must be taken before Murray, "but it is not necessary to be done by the different Officers at the same time."

1. *U.S. Statutes at Large*, 1:627–704.
2. In the right margin, Albert Gallatin wrote: "Answer—*No*."
3. In the right margin, Gallatin wrote: "Answer—Yes, provided that he can be considered as an American citizen & not as an English subject."

From Thomas Jefferson

DEAR SIR   MONTICELLO Aug. 27. 1802.

I inclose you a letter from W. Hampton & Fontaine Maury on the subject of apprehensions that the negroes taken from Guadaloupe will be pushed in on us.[1] It came to me under the superscription of mr. Brent, so may not have been seen by you. Would it not be proper to make it the subject of a friendly letter to M. Pichon. Perhaps Govr. Clinton should also recieve some mark of our attention to the subject.

I received under the same cover a letter from Israel Smith to you on the subject of Commrs. of bankruptcy for Vermont.[2] I had been expecting a General recommendation from him & Bradley. I therefore make this the occasion of reminding them of it.[3]

Of the blank commissions of bankruptcy which came to me with your signature, I signed & send two to mr. Brent to be filled with the names of Wm. Cleveland &   [4] Killam of Salem. The rest you will recieve herewith. I have no further news from the Mediterranean. Genl. Dearborn has been unwell & quitted Washington. Gallatin not well and gone to New York. His 2d. clerk sick, Miller also, and Harrison unwell and gone away.

There seems to be much sickness begun there. Mr. Short left Washington on Saturday last, & comes here by the way of the Berkley springs. Pichon does not come. Accept assurances of my affectionate esteem & respect.

TH: JEFFERSON

RC (DLC); FC (DLC: Jefferson Papers).

1. Wade Hampton and Fontaine Maury to JM, 21 Aug. 1802.
2. Israel Smith to JM, 16 Aug. 1802.
3. Jefferson wrote letters to Stephen R. Bradley and to Smith on 27 Aug. 1802 (DLC: Jefferson Papers), requesting them to name three or four persons, "lawyers or merchants, of republican principles," to be commissioners of bankruptcy. Smith replied in a letter to JM, 13 Sept. 1802.
4. Jefferson left a blank space here.

From Edward Thornton

SIR,   WASHINGTON 27th August 1802.

I am sorry to be obliged to call your attention once more to the subject of the Transport Ship Windsor in consequence of additional information, which I have received from His Majesty's Consul at Boston, and which, as I have no doubt of its correctness, seems to impeach in a high degree the accounts, which the officers of the United States in that port have given you on the subject of the repairs of that vessel.

It is only necessary to enumerate to you the circumstances under which it stood to convince you of this position.

Without dwelling on the presumable condition of a vessel sent on a voyage from the West Indies, and which after her capture by the prisoners experienced no disaster on her passage to the United States, I have to observe—That on her arrival at Boston the Captain, having reason to expect from the promises of the captors that the Ship would be freely restored to him, informed the Consul that he should proceed immediately to sea, not thinking that she stood in need of any repairs: That the latter afterwards employed a Gentleman, well skilled in naval matters, to examine the state of the vessel, who pronounced that she might be got ready for sea in a week, and that a fortnight would be a very ample allowance: That notwithstanding the Windsor remained in Boston without alteration from the end of June or the beginning of July to the 27th of August, when she was transferred by sale to a Mr. Marston—in direct violation of the Treaty of Amity: That from the latter period to the receipt of the order for her departure in the middle of September (you must have the goodness to set me right, if I mistake the date of your order)[1] and from thence to the intelligence received in November of the signature of the preliminary Articles, she remained equally without repairs and without attention from the officers of the Custom: And that in fine no alteration at all took place until the month of March of the present year, when being transferred by the bankruptcy of Mr Marston to other hands, she was converted from a snow to a ship, and after some delay dispatched to the East Indies without any regular papers from the Custom House.

Perhaps few instances occurred during the late war of more irregular proceeding on the part of the officers of the United States; and I cannot forbear re-urging the expectation of His Majesty's Government, that the President having due regard to the double violation of the Treaty of Amity (first in the sale of the vessel and afterwards in the perfect neglect of his orders for her expulsion) will be pleased to think the original owners entitled to a proper compensation for her loss.[2] I have the honour to be with perfect truth and respect, Sir, Your most obedient humble servant,

EDWD THORNTON

RC (DNA: RG 59, NFL, Great Britain, vol. 2). Docketed by Brent.

1. For the date of the order for the *Windsor*'s departure, see Gallatin to JM, 2 July 1802, and n. 1.

2. Even as Thornton made this argument, he conceded to his superiors in London that "there is ⟨little?⟩ room to hope, that any arguments will b⟨e⟩ able to extract from the present economic⟨al⟩ government a pecuniary compensation ⟨or⟩ even a promise of endeavouring to obtain ⟨it?⟩ at the approaching meeting of the legislatu⟨re⟩" (Thornton to Hawkesbury, 29 Aug. 1802 [PRO: Foreign Office, ser. 5, 35:310]).

To Thomas Jefferson

DEAR SIR   [ca. 28 August 1802]

Yours of the 27. came duly to hand. I had recd. the letter from W. Hampton & F. Maury. I had proposed to observe to them, that the case fell wholly within the State laws, & that it was probable the several Governors would be led to attend to it by the correspondence between the Mayor of N. Y. & the French consul & Admiral.[1] It had occurred also that it might not be amiss for the President to intimate to the Secy. of the Treasury, a circular letter from that Dept. to the Officers of the Customs, calling on their vigilance as a co-operation with the State authorities in inforcing the laws agst. the smugling of slaves.[2] As a further measure a letter may be written to Mr. Pichon as you suggest, and whatever else you think proper from me shall also be attended to.

I inclose several land patents which you will please to send, with your sanction, to Mr. Brent; also a letter from Govr McKean & another from James Yard; to which is added a letter from a Mr. Cochran, which give some ideas & facts which will repay the perusal.[3] I need not observe that the answer to his inquiry will transfer his hopes of patronage from the Genl Govt. to the State Govts.

What is decided on the subject of our Tobo. by Leiper, and what are to be the price & paymts. if he is to have it?[4] Yrs. always with respect & attachment

JAMES MADISON

RC (DLC: Jefferson Papers). Undated; docketed by Jefferson as received 29 Aug.

1. New York mayor Edward Livingston had sought assurances from the French consul in New York, Louis Arcambal, that none of the West Indian blacks on board the French frigates in the harbor would be landed in the city and that security on board ship was tight enough to prevent a mutiny. After consulting Admiral La Caille, Arcambal insisted that Livingston had nothing to worry about. The exchange of letters was published in the N.Y. *American Citizen and General Advertiser*, 17 Aug. 1802.

2. Jefferson made this suggestion to Gallatin in his letter of 30 Aug. 1802 (*Papers of Gallatin* [microfilm ed.], reel 7).

3. Thomas McKean to JM, 16 Aug. 1802. The letters from Yard and Cochran have not been found.

4. Philadelphia tobacco merchant Thomas Leiper informed Jefferson that he would not buy the president's tobacco crop at the price Jefferson specified, mentioning Jefferson's own opinion that it was "not of the first quality" and quoting the current prices of different grades of tobacco (Leiper to Jefferson, 26 Aug. 1802 [DLC: Jefferson Papers]). For JM's previous dealings with Leiper, see *PJM*, 14:20 and passim.

From Charles Pinckney

(Private)

DEAR SIR   August 28: 1802 IN MADRID

I send you my account for the last three months. The only charge of consequence is for the Post Office which is to me a very disagreeable one because they will give no Voucher. I have applied to them repeatedly & they always say they never do. While almost every American who has friends or Business in Madrid incloses his letters & packets under cover to me & particularly while large Bundles of Newspapers & Documents are sent by Post it will always be the case. I do not know how to remedy it, for the regulations here oblige you to take *every thing* directed to you, otherwise they refuse to deliver you any You may wish to take.

In the course of the last three months my extra Expences have been enormous, on account of the Wedding of the Kings Daughter to the heir of the Two Sicilies—being invited to the Wedding I was of course exposed to them, but not knowing whether this ought to be considered as a Contingency I have made no charge nor can I unless you should think I ought to be entitled to them—nor have I done so for all my extra expences in attending the Court at the Sitios except for mule hire although I understand many other ministers are allowed to charge their extra expences for that, or have a fixed extra allowance on that account.

I know how much they talk of money in America & how narrowly public Expenditures are examined & finding that I am not unfrequently the object of censure from those who do me the honour to suppose I have had some hand in putting a stop to their infamous & malicious designs against the honour, the peace & the liberties of their country, I am to request should any charge at any time appear to you improper or such as ought not to be charged to contingencies, immediately to deduct it & charge it to my account for Outfit & salary of which I have yet recieved but little. My confidence in your friendship is such that I am ready to be bound by your Opinion, nor would I have it supposed for millions that I had charged one cent improperly—pursuing the prospects I now have Money is with me a very secondary object. I write you no opinions on France & her politics. You will hear all & judge for yourself. I am sure our Opinions are in unison & not wishing to commit myself to paper where there is a possibility of the Letters being lost I conclude with my best Wishes to yourself & Lady & my most affectionate respects to the President. I am dear Sir With regard & esteem Yours Truly

CHARLES PINCKNEY

RC (DLC). Enclosure not found.

§ From John M. Forbes. *28 August 1802, Hamburg.* Calls JM's attention to "a Subject which has been frequently urged upon the former Administration, without effect, by my Predecessor Mr. Pitcairn. From the great variety of petty Sovereignties which divide the Circumjacent Country and particularly the Shores of the Elbe, a general imbecility in the execution of the Consular functions and, in many instances, Serious inconveniences to our Commerce result from our Consular District being limited to the Hamburgh Territory." Cites a recent case of the ship *Hercules;* "wrecked in this River, her valuable Cargo was Saved by Danish subjects and the Captain was obliged to resort to Copenhagen and demand the interference of our Consul there." Proposes that his consular district be extended " 'to the Circle of Lower Saxony' which is the only political division of Country, which embraces all the Sovereignties bordering on the navigable Elbe." Reports that the provision made by the U.S. for destitute seamen is inadequate; twelve cents per diem is not enough for shelter.

RC (DNA: RG 59, CD, Hamburg, vol. 1). 3 pp.; docketed by Wagner as received 19 Nov., with his notation, "Extension of his consular district necessary." An abbreviated version of the letter (ibid.), marked "*Triplicate*," bears a postscript in which Forbes recommends that an express right be granted him to name vice-consuls or agents "in the several ports of the Circle"; this has been "a Subject of some discussion between the British Consul and the Senate of Rostoc, but the latter has ceded the point."

From Thomas Jefferson

Dear Sir   Monticello Aug. 30. 1802.

Your two favors of the 25th. & blank¹ were recieved yesterday; and all the papers forwarded me are returned by this post. I must pray you to direct an extract from so much of mr. Clarke's letter as relates to the dissatisfaction of the Chickasaw chief with the Spanish governor, to be taken & sent to Genl. Dearborn to whom I have written on the subject.² Mr. Clarke's letter cuts out a considerable job for us, but the several matters are so important that I think a detailed instruction should be sent to be [*sic*] mr. Pinckney.³ Indeed I wish we could once get the European powers to give to their diplomatic representatives here such provisional authorities as would enable them to controul the conduct of their governors in whatever relates to us. We are too far from Europe to dance across the ocean for attendance at their levees whenever these pigmy kings in their colonies think proper to injure or insult us. Be so good as to order a commission from your office for John Shore of Virginia as successor to Heath at Petersburg.⁴ The stile of the office must be obtained from the treasury: also a Commission for Abraham Bloodgood for Albany, for which mr. Gallatin will apply.⁵ On the suggestion in the newspapers that Simpson is recalled to Marocco, I have suggested to mr. Smith, *if it be known certainly before the John Adams sails*, to consider whether we ought not to retain her. Tho' armed by Congress to employ the frigates largely, it was in confidence we would not do it lightly. I wish you to consider whether it would not be useful, by a circular to the clerks of the federal courts, to call for a docket of the cases decided in the last twelvemonth, say from July 1. 1801. to July 1. 1802. to be laid before Congress. It will be satisfactory to them, & to all men to see how little is to be done by the federal judiciary, and will effectually crush the clamour still raised on the suppression of the new judges. I think it a proper document to be furnished annually, as it may enable us to make further simplifications of that corps. I have written to mr. Gallatin respecting the Guadaloupe negroes. Accept assurances of my affectionate friendship.

Th: Jefferson

⟨P. S. I before mentioned to you what I had written to Lieper on the subject of our tobo. I have recd no answer. The same letter said something of his disappointment of office. I suspect it has not pleased him. I own I have thought something of his silence, were it only on account of the use Callender is making of his name.)[6]

RC (DLC); FC (DLC: Jefferson Papers). The postscript, which is missing from the RC, has been supplied from the FC (see n. 6).

    1. JM to Jefferson, ca. 28 Aug. 1802.
    2. See Daniel Clark to JM, 16 Aug. 1802. Jefferson wrote to Henry Dearborn on 30 Aug. 1802 (DLC: Jefferson Papers).
    3. In his letter of 25 Oct. 1802 JM wrote Pinckney to pursue his standing instructions on Louisiana but did not add anything to them (DNA: RG 59, IM, vol. 6). By the time he wrote next, matters were superseded by the closing of the deposit at New Orleans (JM to Pinckney, 27 Nov. 1802 [ibid.]).
    4. For the removal of William Heth as collector at Petersburg, see *PJM-SS*, 1:144–45 and n. 1.
    5. Abraham Bloodgood's appointment as surveyor and inspector of revenue for the port of Albany was confirmed by the Senate in January 1803 (*Senate Exec. Proceedings*, 1:432).
    6. The postscript is a letterpress copy, written on a separate sheet and misfiled with the FC of Jefferson to JM, 30 Apr. 1801 (DLC: Jefferson Papers).

§ From Charles Pinckney. *30 August 1802, Madrid.* "By Mr Gibson & Mr Codman you will receive full accounts of every thing up to this time. . . .[1] We have nothing new here except that the Emperor of Morocco has permitted Mr Simpson to return to Tangiers & means to be at peace with us."

RC (DNA: RG 59, DD, Spain, vol. 6). 4 pp. Docketed by Wagner as received 24 Nov.

    1. The body of this letter is substantially the same as that of Pinckney to JM, 24 Aug. 1802.

From Daniel Brent

DEAR SIR   WASHINGTON, August 31st 1802.

Your letter of the 27th Inst.[1] was duly received by me, with the draft of the Treasurer on the Cashier of the Bank of the United States and a letter to Mr Simpson, directing him what to do with the proceeds of this draft, and I have accordingly sent on the letter and dft.

You will have been informed that the letter and Gun Carriages intended for the Emperor of Morocco are witheld. I have accordingly added short postcrips to the letters for Mr Simpson and Mr Cathcart, explaining the Circumstance. No Official account of the recall of Mr Simpson is reced., and the truth of the report on this subject is not at all relied upon. You will see, by an Article in the National Intelligencer of yesterday, that the account communicated in Mr Gavino's letter of June 29th, Concerning the capture of the Rose by Pirates, is untrue; as that vessel has actually arrived at Martin[i]que, whither the account states she was bound. Nothing further is known about the rencountre which the Boston is said to have had with the Tunisian vessels. But it would seem, from the silence of your own and Mr Smith's Mediterranean letters to the 29th June, nine days after the date of the private ones from the same quarter which brought the account of this affair—and from Mr Eaton's not mentioning a word about it, in his letter of May 25th, herewith sent—that the Report is entirely groundless. I received the Copy of Mr Smith's instructions to Commodore Morris just as I was about to close the last letter which I had the honor of writing to you, and had not time then to read them. But it does not appear to me now, since I have seen and read the original at the Navy office, that these instructions contain such precise orders about the 30.000 Dollars as your letter of June 29th to Mr Smith requested, and as I counted upon from other Circumstances. I have suggested to Mr Smith the propriety of his giving further instructions conforming with your wishes to have the money returned to the US in the event of its not being recd. at Algiers, but he does not think that it would be proper for him to do so, and of course declines it. It remains for you, therefore, under a view of all the Circumstances of the case, to give such further directions as you shall think proper. The New York has just got out of the Eastern Branch, and it is said that she be at least a fortnight at Norfolk before she gets to Sea. The letter from Mr Cathalan enclosing Mr Eaton's was forwarded on the 18th June; by our Consul at Bordeaux. I have the Honor to be, with great Respect & sincere esteem, Sir, Your Obedt & faithful servt.

DANL BRENT.

I send to the President a Copy of Mr Eaton & an Extract from Mr Cathalan's letters.

RC (DLC). Docketed by JM.

1. Letter not found.

From Robert Taylor

DEAR SIR   August 31st. 1802.
    The deeds requested accompany this.[1] I know nothing of yours & miss Nelly's title—but if the smallest doubt attends it, as the decree directs the

warranty to be general—perhaps it would have been best to suffer the plt's title to have rested on the decrees & to have made no deeds. I have understood the manner of authenticating deeds in Kentucky was the same as here which you will see in the last revised code pages 165 & 341.[2] The most usual mode is to acknowledge the deed or have it proved by 3 witnesses in the county court where the grantor resides and have such proof or acknowledgment certified by the clerk under the county seal. I am Yr. Obt.

ROBERT TAYLOR

RC (DLC). Docketed by JM.

1. These deeds to Kentucky lands once held by JM and Ambrose Madison were issued pursuant to a decree obtained by William Croghan and Richard Taylor and delivered to JM by Denis Fitzhugh (Croghan to JM, 7 Apr. 1802, and n. 1). Apparently Fitzhugh's request that JM send him the deeds for safe passage to Kentucky went unheeded, for Croghan complained in May 1803 that he had never received them (Fitzhugh to JM, 10 July 1802 [misdated 10 July 1801 in *Index to the James Madison Papers* and in *PJM-SS*, 1:394–95]; Croghan to JM, 22 May 1803 [DLC]).

2. Taylor referred to section 5 of "An Act for regulating Conveyances," which explained how deeds could be authenticated and deposited with the "proper Court" within eight months if by a resident or eighteen months if by a nonresident of the state, and section 2 of "An Act to amend the act for regulating Conveyances," which extended the period of deposit for nonresidents to two years (*A Collection of . . . Acts of the General Assembly of Virginia, of a Public and Permanent Nature . . .* [Richmond, 1794; Evans 27999], pp. 165, 341).

To Thomas Jefferson

DEAR SIR   Sepr. 1. 1802

The mail not having returned from Milton when my messenger left the Court House on monday evening, & it having been inconvenient to send thither at any time since, I can not now acknowledge any favor which may have come from you since my last. Among the letters inclosed is one from Higginson seconding the application from Philada. for your patronage to a demand on the vice Govt of the La plata provinces.[1] The measure as proposed seems to be inadmissible on several grounds; but I shall be glad to have your sanction if you think it proper, to a refusal. Yours with respectful attachment

JAMES MADISON

RC (DLC: Jefferson Papers). Docketed by Jefferson as received 2 Sept.

1. The letter to JM from Stephen Higginson and other Boston merchants, 11 Aug. 1802, has not been found. It was acknowledged by Daniel Brent on 28 Aug. 1802 (DNA: RG 59, DL, vol. 14) and by JM on 6 Sept. 1802.

From George W. Erving

DEAR SIR   LONDON Septr 1st. 1802

The return of Mr Lewis to Washington affords me an opportunity of acknowledging the rect of your private & friendly letter (May 3d)[1] upon the subject of the assessorship to the board of commissioners; It is unnecessary I hope for me to assure you that I feel on all occasions the most perfect disposition to acquiesce in, & chearfully conform to, the Opinions & wishes of the President & of yourself: On this particular occasion I find additional reasons to be satisfied with the arrangement made, in the nature of the Office in question the duties of which merely clerical are but little adapted to my taste, perhaps less to my habits; its dependance upon the board, & in the probability of the frequent dissatisfactions & misunderstandings which might thence naturally arise, (if not studiously occasioned by the individuals of that body) to the great delay & perhaps material prejudice of the public business.

The board have hitherto proceeded in their decisions with a great deal of spirit, all which however has been infused into them by Mr Pinkney: The omission in the convention of a stipulation for interest upon the instalments payable on awards, seems to have been rectified, & a rule for allowing it Established by the award in the case of the Pigou-Lewis, the only one yet completed;[2] But another oversight in our negotiator hath created a difficulty at the Board which for the present has prevented the completion of any further decrees; it is the question whether interest shall be allowed for the time during which the functions of the Board were suspended: To enable the British Commissioners to digest this point the Board has adjourned to the 12th Inst.

Mr King has gone for a tour on the continent; he proposes to return in a few Months, to wind up his negotiations here, & to return about this time 12 mos to the U. S.—there to be held up as the federal candidate for the Presidency! Previous to his departure he gave me no intimation as to the person whom he meant to charge with the affairs of the U. S, I have since accidentally heard that *Mr Gore* is his locum tenens; but I presume that it is not so. It has appeared to me a duty in my situation here to commit a violence on my feelings sufficient to enable me to preserve a decent & respectful intercourse with Mr King; as I have rarely seen him however but on business have had no opportunities of becoming intimate with his private character, as a public man I have had repeated cause both personal & official to be disgusted with him; there is no sincerity no loyalty in that character: My letter goes by a hand so perfectly safe that I am tempted to give a loose to my pen in treating of this candidate for the presidency, in the confidence that you will indulge me in the free expression of my opinions: If however I err in this, you will at least attribute the defect of my judgement to the excess of my zeal; I submit no sentiment to you but with the utmost deference, yet am irresistably impelled to say more than may be prudent; I am sure that my motives will not be impeached; I have no personal view no wish unconnected with the support of genuine republican principles & the success of Mr Jeffersons administration. The general principle of Mr Kings ministry here seems that of accommodation to the British govermt, every thing he does is precisely in the form most agreeable to them, nor will he consent to give them any trouble unless by particular instruction, or to carry some point favorable to his own popularity: When the peace was concluded between this country & France I foresaw that great numbers of our sailors detained on board Men of war woud of course be discharged, that they woud spend their Wages as sailors usually do, & fall a burthen upon the U. S. or become Vagabonds in this metropolis, & therefore thought it proper to make an application to the admiralty with a view of procuring passages & maintenance for them to their several homes; considering that it woud be highly reasonable to ask this aid in favor of such men as they might acknowledge to be Americans & whom they had compelled into their service: as a negotiation however with the Admiralty promised to be dilatory I requested Mr King to assist me by an application thro' an higher department of the government, this he declined; I was of course left to make my own way, & according to the method of doing business here the negotiation *is in train*; when it comes to a point I shall forward the Official details, I mention this circumstance at present as one instance calculated to shew the apathy of Mr King as to the public interest; the object surely was sufficiently great to engage his attention; but no popularity was to be gained by it, & the application was to harrass & embarrass this government. Few situations afford more opportunities of cultivating popularity than this of Mr Kings; he sees all who arrive from every part of the Union, he selects for his particular attentions those who may have it in their power to do him the most service on their return, he calculates his conversation & his communication to the temper, the opinions or the situation of Each individual; he maintains a perpetual Correspondence with influential men at home, & he acquires credit & reputation as a statemans [*sic*] from the wise dispositions of the government; & by maintaining the most perfect personal understanding with the ministry here, he secures all the English interest directed by their Agents in the United States. Mr King has therefore become the most likely man for a federal candidate, I do not know whether there is any thing openly said upon this subject in the U. S. but from what I have heard here there can be no doubt but that Mr King has entered fully into the views of the federal party in their intended opposition to Mr. Jefferson on the next Election, & that he is their candidate. I trust that there is nothing to be apprehended from any opposition, and if the republicans do not neglect their own interests, & lose ground by too much confidence in their strength, or too much generosity towards the adverse party, the victory may be so signal as to discourage any future attempts. It is now very manifest that federal rancour is not to be soothed by moderation, that measures of conciliation or concession on the part of a republican administration cannot mitigate the inveteracy of a spirit hostile to every republican principle; a confidence in the generosity gratitude or public spirit of federalists will be certainly abused, & the influence which they acquire or preserve thro' your liberality, they will not fail to Employ in hostilities against you. Mr King has obtained it appears considerable reputation from the negotiation of the late convention; such as it is, I have the best opinions here to confirm my own that by a proper Exertion on his part it might have been settled long ago, & I presume he woud have been in negotiation upon the subject at this moment but for the explicit directions which he received from you contained in the dispatches which I had the honor to take from you; thus he has positively no merit in this affair, & the discredit of having overlooked or neglected one or two important points. Previous to Mr Kings final departure from this country he will exert himself to secure an interest in the state of Maryland by obtaining a favorable conclusion to that hitherto woefully neglected business respecting the Bank stock; woud it not be well if this & every thing else which may probably add to his popularity or credit might lay over for his successor? Mr Pinkney I find is a decided enemy to Mr King, & disapproves of his ministerial conduct here; he has told me that he considered him Extremely unfit for his situation, & that he will always be a most determined opponent to his political views: I beleive that you do not personally know this gentleman, & as he may probably one day make himself of very considerable political importance, it may not be improper to say something of him also. That he is a man of unquestionable abilities I presume you may have found from his official communications; he is certainly the very soul of the board of commissioners, nothing woud be done without him in fact he may be said almost to do all the business himself; feeling that the time of his activity & usefulness was wasting here, he has exerted himself most strenuously & with great effect to push forward the decisions of the board, & to bring to a conclusion this business over which his colleagues woud be content to sleep for years: As our object is the same, in the prosecution of his views my assistance is necessary, & I have given him continual proofs of my disposition to second his zeal & exertions, we have therefore as far as relates to this always preserved the best understanding: In politics he has the appearance of candor, but at the same time some fixed opinions, with a temper so uncontroulable as to afford little hope of his ever being a supporter of the present administration, tho the violence & depravity of the opposition will be very likely to neutralize him; In conversation his language is correct & even Elegant, his conceptions remarkably quick, but he has the fault of forming his Opinions too suddenly, & does not give his judgement time to mature propositions; this gives him the air of inconstancy; he appears to have an high sense of honor & a determined spirit, perhaps not a good temper: I have been told that he is extremely indolent, but that report does not agree with any observation which I have made, or with the impression which one must receive from his conversation.

As to the general state of things here, every day seems to add something to the degradation of this country, & the supremacy of Buonoparte; they are waiting with the utmost anxiety for some commercial advantages which they vainly expect to derive from an Arrangement with the french government; in the mean time their funds continue low, perhaps 18 out of 25 Millions of their last loan is mortgaged to the Bank; they seem hitherto not to have realized any great advantages from the peace, or to have any ⟨v⟩ery promising prospects as to the future. The late general Elections wherever the popular Voice has had an opportunity of declaring itself have been in favor of Opposition; I do not say in favor of liberty, for that is out of the question here, if there ever was any disposition that way Buonoparte has entirely destroyed it; their constitution as they call it will therefore be coeval with their public credit which will not die a sudden death: Ireland is yet dissatisfied; subdued perhaps, but not conciliated.

Mr Lewis whose delay here has been occasioned by the difficulties which he has met with in Establishing his claim before the Board of commissioners, returns now to the Seat of government as a matter of duty, having been refused an Exequatur upon his commission as consul to Calcutta. He is a man of very good sense, full of spirit & activity, of a very firm & Energetic character, & a sound republican: He will be able to give you some interesting details respecting our proceedings here, that is if you encourage him in such conversation; otherwise his apprehensions that it may not be acceptable will prevent his offering you even his information.[3] Mr Lewis may probably solicit another consular appointment, & from the manner in which the President bestowed the last upon him, I presume he will succeed: since he & myself were at Washington together I have known him still more intimately, & am well convinced of his firm attachment to government, & that any trust may be safely reposed in him: But the navy department is that in which he woud be most Serviceable, his particular information in every branch of which added to his other qualities woud there make him really a valuable acquisition, he is fit Either for the command of a frigate or the direction of a navy yard. Beleive me Dear Sir with perfect respect & attachment always most sincerely yours

GEORGE W ERVING

PS I have forwarded my Accts up to 30th June to your department, will you be so good as to instruct me whether in future they shoud be sent to the Treasury & by what vouchers they shoud be accompanied.

GWE

Septr. 3d.

DEAR SIR

The principal subject of the foregoing letter leads me to add the mention of a conversation which took place between Mr Pinkney & myself last Evening, at which Mr Lewis (who went with me to take leave of Mr P having received considerable attention from him in his claim before the Board) happened to be present: It commenced by my enquiring whether what I heard was true as to Mr Gore's having been left chargé d'affaires by Mr King, he assured me that it was so; I expressed my surprize at the thing itself, & at Mr King's making no communication on this subject to me, & from thence took occasion to make some remarks upon his general conduct as Minister; this induced Mr Pinkney without any reserve to express his opinion against Mr Kings conduct, & against the conduct & policy of the administration in continuing him in Office; he said that the federalists attributed this to a fear of Mr King, that it was a *weakness*[4] from which Mr K's party derived strength, that he had not only been kept in Office but complimented & flattered by the administration, & that they were Even now charging him with commissions from the Execution of which he woud derive credit & popularity; I asked whether he thought Mr K. woud be able to settle the business respectg Maryland Bank stock; he answered "if he does negotiate successfully upon that subject he certainly will be president, I will insure him." That he had known a long time since of Mr Kings plan, that when Mr Jefferson came to the chair Mr King laid himself out to court the administration, but that latterly his conduct was extremely altered, & that he talked in a very independant manner (eve[r]y person who has been lately in the habit of seeing Mr King must have made this observation). Without being more minute (& I fear you are long since fatigued) such was the Stile of his conversation; which I have repeated principally because his opinions support some of the suggestions which I have ventured to make. I wish that I may not have risqued something of your good opinion by writing with so little reserve, I make a great demand upon your candor, but I trust that you will attribute this to the motives which really & which only influence me a perfect devotion to Mr Jeffersons principles & administration. With true respect Dear Sir Your Very faithl & obt St

GEORGE W ERVING

PS.

It will not impeach Mr Pinkneys integrity or the force of his opinions, to surmize, that his wish may probably be that government shoud intrust the negotiation respecting the Maryland Bank Stock to himself; I suspect this is so; the popularity which he might in this way acquire in his own state woud be very important to him, & perhaps less dangerous to the general interest.

RC (MHi: Erving Papers).

    1. Letter not found.
    2. On the question of allowing interest on claims, see Moore, *International Adjudications,* 4:109–20.
    3. Erving might have been referring to his own experience when he first met JM at Montpelier in 1800 (Monroe to JM, 6 Nov. 1800, and JM to Monroe, 10 Nov. 1800 [two letters], *PJM,* 17:431, 432 n. 3, 434, 435).
    4. Erving here interlined: "want of confidence in themselves (the administration)."

From Robert R. Livingston

(No. 22)

DEAR SIR,   PARIS 1st. September 1802

I yesterday made several propositions to the Minister on the subject of Louisiana. He told me frankly that every offer was premature, that the French Government had determined to take possession first—so that you must consider the business as absolutely determined on. The armament is what I have already mentioned and will be ready in about six weeks. *I have every reason to believe the Floridas are not included.* They will for the present at least *remain in the hands of Spain.* There never was *a government* in which *less* could be done *by negotiation than here.* There is *no people no legislature no counselors one man* is every thing—*he* seldom asks *advice and never hears it unasked—his ministers are mere clerks* & *his legislature* & *counselors parade of⟨ficers.* Tho the sense⟩ of every *reflecting man about him is against this wild expedition no one dares to tell him so.* Were it not for the *uneasiness it excites at home it would give* me none for I am persuaded that the whole will end in a relinquishment of the country and transfer of the Capital to the United States. Their islands call for much more than France can ever furnish. The extreme *hauteur of this government* to all around them will not suffer *peace to be of long continuance.* The French Minister at Lisbon it is said is coming home without taking leave. *England is very sour.* The debts due the Northern powers unpaid as well as ours tho' their justice is admitted. Helvetia is still in arms the little Cantons not acceding to the new form of government.[1] I propose to make an excursion of about 15 days into the low countries—as I find nothing pressing at this moment here that I can forward by my stay. I am Dear Sir, with much esteem and respect your Obt. Hle. St.

RC (NHi: Livingston Papers); draft (ibid.); letterbook copy (NHi: Livingston Papers, vol. 1). The RC is a letterpress copy marked "Duplicate," in a clerk's hand, unsigned; docketed by Wagner. Italicized words are those encoded by Livingston's secretary and decoded here by the editors. RC decoded interlinearly in an unidentified hand. Words in angle brackets are obscured by a fold in the RC and have been supplied from the letterbook copy.

1. The French conquered Switzerland in 1798 and imposed a regime and a constitution similar to their own. Swiss resistance to the country's reorganization as the Helvetic Republic was fierce, if sporadic, and once French troops were withdrawn from the country in May 1802, the government was overthrown. This provoked the French to reoccupy the country in October 1802 (James Murray Luck, *A History of Switzerland* [Palo Alto, Calif., 1985], pp. 305–12).

§ From Joseph Pitcairn. *1 September 1802, Hamburg.* Encloses the list of American vessels that arrived at Hamburg from 1 Jan. to the end of June, "but you will observe that none came in here the first month of the Year." Will send account of money paid to sick and distressed sailors to the U.S. minister in Paris as instructed in JM's 1 Aug. 1801 circular. "My Successor Mr. Forbes being some time arrived I refer you to his Correspondence for the situation of trade &c."

RC (DNA: RG 59, CD, Hamburg, vol. 1). 1 p.; docketed by Wagner. Enclosure not found.

§ From George Simpson. *1 September 1802, Bank of United States.* "I have been honord with yours of 26th. Ulto. enclosing the Treasurers Check for eighty two hundred dollars—which amount is credited to the Secretary of State for the time being &c—as requested."

RC (DNA: RG 59, ML). 1 p.; docketed by Brent as received 6 Sept.

To Thomas Jefferson

DEAR SIR   Sep. 3. 1802

I have duly recd. yours of the 30th. Ulto. with the several papers to which it refers. I have directed the commissions for Shore & Bloodgood to be made out, and have sent the extract from Clark's letter as you required to Genl. Dearborn. He had however been made acquainted with it by Mr. Brent, before the letter was forwarded to me. May it not be as well to let the call for the Dockets be a rule of Congress, as there is no specific appropriation for the expence, and a regular call by the Ex. might not be regarded as within any contingent fund? to this consideration it may be added that the Ex. have no power over the Clerks of the Courts, & that some of them might refuse to comply from a dislike to the object. When the object was not known, there was a manifest repugnance in some instances. Your final determination in the case shall be pursued. I have thought also that it might be as well to postpone till the reassembling at Washington any general regulation with regard to the appointment of Commissioners of Bankruptcy; but shall in this case also cheerfully conform to your pleasure.

Mr. Brent informs me that he has sent you copies of Eaton's letter of May 25–27. & Cathalan's of June 10. It does not seem necessary that the communications of the former should be made the subject of further instructions till we receive further accts from other sources. Thornton you will see is renewing the subject of the Snow Windsor;[1] May he not be told that the remedy lies with the Courts, and not with the Ex. The absence of the Vessel can no more be a bar to it, than the sale was. It seems proper however that the irregularity in sending the vessel out without the legal clearance should be prosecuted. The law is I believe defective on this point. The Correspondent referred to in Steel's letter is, I take it, Mr. Brown the Kentucky Senator.[2] Yours with respectful attachment

JAMES MADISON

RC (DLC: Jefferson Papers). Docketed by Jefferson as received 5 Sept.

1. See Edward Thornton to JM, 27 Aug. 1802.
2. See John Steele to JM, 20 June 1802, and n. 1.

From Daniel Brent

DEAR SIR,   WASHINGTON, September 3d 1802.

I have duly received your letter of the 30th Ulto.,[1] with a Requisition on the Treasury Dept in favor of Mr Barnes, to satisfy one of Mr Gavino's Bills for an advance to Mr Simpson. A Copy of your letter to Mr Fitzsimons concerning the Georgia lands is herewith forwarded.[2] I send likewise two letters from Mr Simpson, of the 3d & 16th July and the Copies therein referred to. You will perceive that the Report of his Return to Tangier is not destitute of some Circumstance for its foundation; tho' that event had not actually taken place. These two, I understand, are the only official letters from the Mediterranean; and I do not learn that any private ones by the vessel that brought them, which left Gibraltar about the date of the last, strengthen the Report of the Affair of the Boston frigate, or give any color to the rumor of the Enterprise's having had an engagement with a Tripolitan. I send Copies to the President, as I do of every thing interesting from the same quarter. The letter from Mr Elkanah Watson, herewith sent, solicits the appt of Commercial Agent at Nantz, in France, for a Mr Simon Lynch, who resides there; and a recommendatory letter from

Mr Van Ransaelaer in favor of this Gentleman accompanied Mr Watson's, and is also sent to you. Mr T P Gantt, of the neighbourhood of this place, was Appointed on the 20th July last, and the Senate confirmed the President's Act at its last session. But I learn that Mr Gantt has not yet been in France, and that he has no intention of going thither. It seems necessary, under these Circumstances, that some other person should be appointed without delay. I have written to Mr Watson, informing him of your absence, and barely stating the appointment of Mr Gantt.[3] The President, it appears, has been already Applied to on this subject. You will receive herewith a letter from Mr Biddle, with a Protest concerning the recapture of the Portuguese vessel, La Gloria de la Mar.[4] This Instrument was sent, I suppose, merely to Answer a purpose which its receipt will have accomplished. Mr Page states, in a letter to the Comptroller of the 25th Augt, that the state of his health will not permit him to accept the appointment of Collector for the District of Petersburg, and he accordingly sent back his Commission. I forward his letter to day to the President.[5] The New York frigate yesterday dropped down to Alexa, and is still there. She will probably, as I have intimated to you already, be detained some days at Norfolk, having a considerable number of men and a large portion of her stores to ship at that place. The Adams is to follow next Sunday week. The Circular letter for our Consuls and Commercial Agents was prepared some time ago, and is now sent off, after having been seen & approved of by Mr Gallatin.[6] Doctor Thornton, with his family, sat out for your House this morning. Mr Ed. Thornton, the English Chargé d'Affaires, sets out to morrow from this place, I hear, for the Sweet Springs, the Natural Bridge &&, in Virga. Mr Pichon is still in Geo. Town. I learn that he has had, and continues to have, a vast deal of perplexity about the negroes from Guadeloupe, who are still, I believe, at New York. This Circumstance is said to have prevented him from taking an excursion, likewise, as he intended. I have the Honor to be, with great Respect & sincere esteem, Dear Sir, Your Obedt & very faithful servant,

Danl Brent.

RC (DLC). Docketed in error by JM, "Sepr. 30. 1802."

1. Letter not found.
2. Letter not found.
3. On 1 Sept. 1802, Brent wrote Watson that his 24 Aug. letter had been forwarded to JM and informed him that "a Mr. Gantt in this neighbourhood was appointed Commercial Agent of the United States at Nantes some time ago, tho' he has not repaired to that place" (DNA: RG 59, DL, vol. 14). For Thomas T. Gantt's appointment, see *PJM-SS*, 1:404 n. 2. Gantt subsequently resigned his agency at Nantes owing to "an unexpected call to the West Indies" (Gantt to JM, 5 Oct. 1802 [DNA: RG 59, LRD]).
4. Letter not found.
5. John Page declined the office in a short note dated 25 Aug. 1802 (DLC: Jefferson Pa-

pers). His wife, Margaret, wrote a longer letter of explanation to Jefferson on 23 Aug. 1802, which Jefferson docketed as received 3 Sept. (ibid.).

6. For the circular, see Gallatin to JM, 16 Aug. 1802, and n. 5.

From James Leander Cathcart

Dispatch No. 12

SIR   LEGHORN Septr. 3rd. 1802

Enclosures No. 1: 2: 3, are letters which I have receiv'd since my last from Tripoli. No. 3 informs us of the Bashaws great desire to come upon terms which he may suppose to be favorable to us, but from the stile of the letter it is pretty evident that he still expects we will purchase our peace. I am really at a loss how to act for want of knowing the pleasure of government, not having receiv'd a line from you since yr favor accompanying the communications made to Congress on the 6th. of Feby. For the present I shall state my opinion only to Mr. Nissen & endeavor to make him as well as the Bashaw believe that we will never conclude on terms of Amity with that Regency until we are placed exactly on the same scale that France & Great Britain is, & are equally respected with those nations.

It occurs to me that the Arabs being encamp'd round the City indicates that Jouseph really suspects the designs of his brother Hamet & his keeping their Shieks in the City is through policy to insure the fidellity of their tribes, but neither the one or the other will remain there longer than they are paid & maintain'd which it is impossible for Jouseph to do long his whole wealth when I left Tripoli not being more than 270,000 dollars & from the hatred the Arabs in general bear to Jouseph it is not improbable that the very means that he has used of defense will eventually produce his ruin which the Lord in the infinitude of his mercy permit. If the above supposition is founded on fact, it accounts at once for the Bashaws b⟨e⟩ing desirous to negociate with us upon what he calls favorable terms.

Some days ago I saw in a Newyork paper of the 8th. June that the President had thought proper to appoint me Consul at Algiers, Vice Richd. OBrien resigned,[1] I return the President my most sincere thanks for this fresh mark of his & my countrys approbation & he may depend that the whole study of my life shall be to merit a continuance of the confidence they have pleas'd to repose in me.

I have receiv'd other letters from Barbary which contains similar intelligence to what is contain'd in the enclosed despatches from Mr. Eaton which goes Via Marseilles—there being no American vessels in this Port at present consequently no direct conveyance to America. I have the honor to remain with the greatest respect Sir Yr. most Obnt. Servt.

JAMES LEAR. CATHCART

RC (NN: Cathcart Papers). Docketed by Wagner, with his note, "Mr. Pulis was the late Vekil of Tripoli at Malta." JM wrote in pencil on the verso, "Quer. has his commission been forwarded," above another note in an unidentified hand, "Mentions having seen in a New York paper his appt to Algiers." For enclosures, see Cathcart to JM, 4 Sept. 1802, n. 1.

1. The announcement was made on 11 June 1802 in the N.Y. *American Citizen and General Advertiser*. JM forwarded Cathcart's commission in his letter of 9 Apr. 1803 (DLC: Cathcart Papers).

From Thomas Jefferson

Dear Sir   Monticello Sep. 3. 1802.

Yours of the 1st. was received yesterday. I now return the letters of Higginson, Davis &c. praying that a public vessel may be sent to demand their vessels of the Viceroy of La Plata, indemnity for the detention, & a full performance of existing contracts with the Spanish merchants of La Plata. It would certainly be the first instance of such a demand made by any government from a subordinate. Certainly we have never sent a ship on such an errand. I cannot also but repeat the observations made in mine of the 17th. that among the papers sent you by the merchants there were but two or three cases so specified as that we could form any judgment about them, & even for these some very material information was wanting to shew that they went under license, all commerce with a Spanish colony being primâ facie contraband. As to the other cases they named only the ships & masters, which cannot but excite some doubts of contraband. I see no reason for departing from the regular course and committing our peace with Spain by a vapouring demand of what, for any thing which has been shewn, may turn out to have been smuggling adventures. The merchants must pursue their own measures in the first place, and for such cases as they shall shew to have been contrary to right, we must aid them with our interposition with the Spanish government. In the mean time mr. Pinckney should be desired to look into the cases should they go there, satisfy himself of those which are right, ask redress for them, abandoning those evidently illicit: except indeed so far as sudden changes of their regulations may have entrapped a bonâ fide trader.

I send you an answer from Lieper recieved yesterday.[1] I suppose he meant the answer to my proposition as an answer to your's also, altho' the cases differed in a material circumstance. Accept my affectionate esteem & respect.

Th: Jefferson

RC (DLC); FC (DLC: Jefferson Papers).

1. For Thomas Leiper's 26 Aug. letter to Jefferson (docketed by Jefferson as received 2 Sept.), see JM to Jefferson, ca. 28 Aug. 1802, and n. 4.

From James Simpson

No. 49.

SIR   TANGIER 3d Septemr 1802

No 48 dated 12h. last Month was forwarded in triplicate by way of Lisbon—Cadiz & Gibraltar, each accompanying a translation of the answer, received to the Letter I wrote His Imperial Majesty Muley Soliman from Tetuan, which I hope will reach you safe. I have now the honour to acquaint you that after sending away No. 48, I reflected it would be best [to] delay writing the Minister again, untill after departure of the Frigate, then generaly believed to be about to sail from Larach; lest the Emperour disapointed by the resistance it was natural I should make to his groundless pretensions, should recall the order given the Captain for respecting the Flag of The United States. An uncommon delay happening 'ere application was made for my Passport for that Ship, offered a farther inducement for me not to hazard giving Umbrage at that moment; however the first Lieut arrived from Larach on the 21st. Ulto, when I delivered him the usual Passport & they put to Sea on the 26th.; said to be destined to run as far as the Canaries, and thence to the Coast of Cantabria to establish their Cruize. It now appears the Captain of the Frigate resisted the order sent him by Alcayde Hashash on my arrival at Tetuan, alledging that altho' he admitted he had authority for directing him to take American Vessels, yet he doubted if once given if he could do away that order; of consequence it became necessary to apply to His Majesty, on receipt of whose answer Captain Lubarez sent for my Passport. The Ship carrys 22 Guns & only 93 Men, part of the Crew having been landed at Larach Sick.

With this I have the honour of transmiting copy of the Letter I wrote the Minister on the 1st. Inst.[1] It will afford me much satisfaction, to know what I have said on subject of the Emperours pretension, meets the approbation of His Excelly The President. I have stated only facts, and thought best to reserve copy of my Letter of the 18h. July 1795 to the then Minister, and that of Muley Solimans to The President on the 18th. August following,[2] as Vouchers more proper to be exhibited in support of my arguments, and in opposition to what farther may be alledged on the part of this Governmt. on subject of what they have thought fit to advance, rather than now. I confess I am almost at a loss to assign any more probable reason for that measure, than that either they are ignorant of what actualy passed between the Minister and myself in 1795, and are desirous of comeing at such facts as we may be able to substantiate; or that they have asserted an arrangement then took place such as they now wish to establish, and by that finesse conceive they take a more plausible mode for bringing it forward, than a new pretension would be.

In either case I shall conceive it my duty to resist it by every means in my power, untill I shall be honoured with His Excelly The Presidents Commands on the occasion, which I persuade myself you will have the goodness to transmit, in the most probable speedy Channel.

The busyness of bringing the Tripoline Ship from Gibraltar under the Emperours Flag, has been again agitated, and a general application made by Alcayde Hashash to the Consuls here for Passports for her as belonging to His Majesty, to sail from hence for Tripoly; I positively refused mine in these terms, nor do I find any has been granted; but it is certain Men are ordered from Tetuan for her, and that she is to hoist the Emperours Colours at Gibraltar, so soon as the Weather will allow these people to get over. I have acquainted Captn Campbell of the Adams Frigate, that in my private oppinion the whole is a colourable busyness; but if the Emperour announces to the Body of the Consuls that the Ship is his, and demands Passports accordingly, merely to go to Sea, and Navigate as his, I realy do not see how I dare venture to contest the matter; or from circumstances to express doubts on what is stated by the Sovereign of the Country as a fact, without runing a great risque of drawing serious resentment on the Commerce of The Unit⟨ed⟩ States. At this trying moment I pray His Excelly The President will be perfectly assured my best exertions shall be called forth for the good of the Service I have the honour of being entrusted with; but I cannot help repeating tha⟨t⟩ nothing can give me such aid as a Naval force being se⟨en⟩ on the Coast, or known to be in the Neighborhood, for tha⟨t⟩ alone is the terror of these people. Altho' I would glad⟨ly⟩ hope matters may yet be accommodated, yet lest the Emperour should persist in the demands he has at last brought forward, which I conclude will not be granted him, I would beg with due submission to recommend that the Commanding Officer of the Ships of War of the United States in these Seas, be instructed to act with energy against this Country, but especialy against its Cruizers, so soon as the Emperour shall repeat his late hostile conduct in sending your Consul from hence, or by any other means authorise a violation of the Peace now subsisting. A first grand point in War against this Country, is to be extremely carefull to prevent their Cruizers being sent to Sea, for as they seldom go out in quest of but one Nation, he who blocks up their Ports, is considered to fight the Battles of all; and are accordingly feared or respected, which appear to have become synonymous here. On my late return to this Country, finding the Frigate at Larach was certainly destined to act against us, I earnestly entreated Commodore Morris to send one of the Ships under his Command to watch her; I was so confident he would do so, I ventured to say he had, which certainly had a good effect for it was generaly believed, as fortunately a fresh Gale at East daily presented Vessels beating in sight of the Port. Nothing is more easy than to prevent Cruizers geting out of Salle & Larach, for being Bar Harbours they can only sail with a fair Wind, and Vessels of War can but very seldom pass them with all their Stores in. A few Frigates would be sufficient to deprive this Empire of that part of its Trade at Mogadore—Saffi—Sallé—Larach—Tangier & Tetuan done on a great scale, the three first enjoy almost the whole of that description, save in time of export of Grain when Mazagan and Darelbeyda become the chief; but these being dangerous roads & Vessels laying in them out of all sort of protection from the shore, none would venture to Trade there were they declared to be in a state of Blockade. Tangier & Tetuan almost exclusively supply the Live Stock carried to Portugal & Gibraltar, and Spain also when it takes any; it might be difficult to prevail on those to forego the conveniency they enjoy in this particular, but they might be restrained to the carrying funds to Barbary for this purpose in Specie. If all other Exports & Imports were interdicted & the Blockades well attended to, the Emperour would speedily feel the consequence in his Treasury, his people of the Provinces [that] supply the chief exports would become troublesome to him, and the whole Nation be made sensible of the superiority of the Power who should so chastise them. The Chief thing after this, would be to station six small Vessels in and about the Straits for counteracting Boats fitted out from hence, & with these well managed Commerce would have ample protection.

Whilst I presume to throw out these hints as my oppinion, on the principal outlines of the best mode of Warfare and defence against this Country, I most sincerely wish I may never see a necessity for e[i]ther being carried into effect. John Hill and Samuel Bowyer, the two Men mentioned in my Letter to the Minister to be at Tarudaunt,[3] were part of the Crew of the Ship Oswego of Hudson, cast on shore near Cape Nun in April 1800. I cannot doubt but the order for their release will be sent me, and then I shall soon have the satisfaction of restoring them to their Country and their Friends. It has been impossible to get them freed before, as untill they reached Tarudaunt, they have constantly been in the possesion of people, who do not acknowledge allegiance to this Emperour, and where money could not be sent to pay for them, with any the smallest chance of its being applied for that purpose.

All the others have already been redeemed except two free Negroes, who by every Account I have been able to trace of them, voluntarily remained with the Arabs & got married. I have the honour to [be] with great respect and esteem Sir Your Most Obedient and Most Humble Servant

JAMES SIMPSON

RC and enclosure (DNA: RG 59, CD, Tangier, vol. 1). RC marked "Duplicate"; docketed by Brent as received 16 Oct. Jefferson communicated an extract of the RC and the enclosure to Congress with his annual message on 15 Dec. 1802 (printed in *ASP, Foreign Relations*, 2: 468–69). For enclosure, see nn. 1 and 3.

1. Simpson's letter of 1 Sept. 1802 to Sidi Mohammed ben Absalom Selawy (4 pp.) informed the minister that he had hoisted the flag of the U.S. again at the consulate and notified the president and the U.S. commander in the Mediterranean of the return of peace. But he went on to express surprise and concern at the emperor's expectation that annual gifts would be presented by the U.S., explaining that the treaty the emperor had ratified in 1795—"without any addition or alteration; in fulfillment of His Fathers engagement"—contained no stipulation for such tribute (printed in Knox, *Naval Documents, Barbary Wars*, 2:262–63).

2. Simpson's 18 July 1795 letter to Sidi Mohamet ben Ottman responded to Ottman's inquiry as to "what sum of money it would be agreeable to the United States of America, to pay to His Majesty annually" by asserting "that the United States of America never have, and I am satisfied never will, engage to pay any Subsidy whatever, by way of Tribute" (DNA: RG 59, CD, Gibraltar, vol. 1). Emperor Mawlay Sulaiman's subsequent letter to President Washington offered assurances that "we are at Peace, Tranquillity and Friendship with you in the same manner, as you were with our Father" (ibid.; printed in *ASP, Foreign Relations*, 1: 526–27).

3. In his 1 Sept. 1802 letter, Simpson informed Selawy that two American seamen who had escaped after three years of captivity by the Arabs were at Taroudaunt, and he requested a letter directing the governor there to allow them to proceed to Mogador.

§ From John Gavino. *3 September 1802, Gibraltar.* Refers JM to his last dispatch, no. 96 [19 Aug.]. A Moroccan crew arrived on 1 Sept. from Tetuán; "the report is they come to take away the Tripolin ship (laid up here) with the Emperours flag as his Property." Has no late news from Simpson. The *Boston* is expected; the *Adams* is in port for repairs. "It is currently aserted that the Algereens have declard Warr Against France."

RC (DNA: RG 59, CD, Gibraltar, vol. 2). 1 p.

§ From Robert Morris. *3 September 1802, New Brunswick.* "I will thank you for a certificate from your office, by the mail, of the names of the General Commissioners of Bankruptcy appointed by the President of the United States for the New Jersey District, if any such are appointed, no notice thereof having reached me."

Draft (NjR). Robert Morris (ca. 1745–1815) was federal judge for the district of New Jersey, 1789–1815. On 6 Sept. Stephen Pleasonton replied to Morris in JM's absence, informing him that commissions dated 6 July had been sent to Thomas Ward of Newark, Phineas Manning of New Brunswick, John Cobb and Josiah Shinn of Woodstown, Abraham Brown of Burlington, and Anthony F. Taylor of Bordentown. Pleasonton added that only Ward and Brown had as yet acknowledged receipt of the commissions and both had consented to serve (ibid.).

¶ From Nathaniel S. and Washington Peirce. Letter not found. *3 September 1802, New Hampshire.* Mentioned in Daniel Brent to N. S. and W. Peirce, 13 Sept. 1802

(DNA: RG 59, DL, vol. 14), as an inquiry about payment for printing the acts of the first session of the Seventh Congress. Brent replied that "your publication of them was made without authority from this department entitling you to any compensation from the Government for the work; unless in its progress you shall have become the owners of one of the papers officially made use of," in which case payment would be "50 cents pr. page for 189 pages." The Peirces had purchased the Portsmouth *N.H. Gazette* in February 1802 (Brigham, *History and Bibliography of American Newspapers*, 1:473; see also Woodbury Langdon to JM, 6 Feb. 1802, *PJM-SS*, 2:449).

From James Leander Cathcart

Dispatch No. 13

SIR   LEGHORN Septr: 4th: 1802.

Having found an assistant I am enabled by this Post to forward the enclosed letter, and my answer to and from Mr: Nissen at Tripoli with my answer to his letter of the 8th: of July.[1] I refer you to my dispatch No: 12. of last year dated September the 27th. 1801,[2] for the reason which induced the Danish Comodore to adopt this pusillanimous conduct, he thinks he has effected a great deal by arranging the affairs of his nation under the Guns of the Frigates of the United States and of Sweden, he certainly must have been convinced that it is the Bashaw's interest to conclude upon any terms with Denmark as certainly in the present moment he would endeavour not to add to his enemy's but so sure as he concludes treaties with the United States and with Sweden he will immediately originate fresh demands upon Denmark, and then Spoliation, Slavery, and other concessions will succeed. I cant help observing the difference of conduct between Comodore Koefoed in agreeing that Mr: Nissen should no longer be encharged with our affairs at Tripoli and that of his Danish Majesty as expressed by his orders in a letter of thanks from the Chamber of Commerce at Copenhaguen to Mr: Eaton at Tunis last year.

The Swedes will act similar to the Danes, and ultimately we will be left to ourselves, and those nations will enjoy the benefit of an uninterrupted commerce, but no longer than they derive protection from our being at war, I can See no alternative at present, but either to send more force into this Sea, and Strike some brilliant blow either at Tangiers or Tripoli, or have recourse to negociation. I presume four Frigates and four small vessels would be Sufficient with a fund or credit of about twenty or thirty thousand dollars to be at the disposals of our Comodore to purchase Bomb Ketches, gunboats &ca as circumstances required, adverting that mortars, Shells and twelve pound brass Cannon ought to be sent out in our Frigates with every necessary apparatus which may be on hand in order to economize as much as possible. Submiting those observations for your consideration I have the honor to subscribe myself with very great respect Sir Yr very Obnt. Servt.

James Lear. Cathcart

RC and enclosures (DNA: RG 59, CD, Tripoli, vol. 2); FC (CSmH). RC docketed by Brent. For enclosures, see n. 1.

1. Among the enclosures sent with this dispatch and Cathcart's 3 Sept. 1802 dispatch were apparently copies of two letters from Nissen to Cathcart and Cathcart's replies. Nissen's letter of 8 July 1802 (2 pp.) communicated a confidential message from Tripolitan minister Sidi Mohammed Dghies that a change had taken place in Tripoli's attitude toward the U.S. and "it is his opinion that this moment would be the most advantageous to negotiate a peace" (printed in Knox, *Naval Documents, Barbary Wars*, 2:195). Cathcart's reply, dated 31 Aug. 1802 (1 p.), asked Nissen to inform Dghies that the U.S. would not enter into negotiations until the pasha of Tripoli carried into effect "the convention agreed on by his certificate" and released Captain Morris and three of his crew (printed ibid., 2:261). Nissen to Cathcart, 10 Aug. 1802 (2 pp.), reported that Danish negotiations with Tripoli had concluded favorably but the pasha had stipulated that Nissen cease acting as chargé d'affaires for the U.S.; "I must henceforth demand the greatest Secrecy in our correspondence" (printed ibid., 2:229–30). Cathcart's reply to this letter, also dated 31 Aug. 1802 (1 p.), complained of the pasha's "inconsistency of character" and his "unworthy behaviour relative to the Exchanges of prisoners by convention with Comodore Dale" and asked Nissen to provide Captain Morris and crew "with whatever they may want."

2. *PJM-SS*, 2:141.

§ From Robert W. Fox. *4 September 1802, Falmouth.* "I am much obliged to thee for thy favor of the 16th June; prior to the receipt of which I had desired my Freinds to recommend another Person to the situation proposed for myself. I assure thee I wou'd not intentionaly do any thing or accept any public situation, that wou'd be improper for a Consul of the United States of America to hold. . . . I beg leave to assure thee that if I can at any time render thyself or Friends acceptable Services hereaway, it will give me great pleasure."

RC (DNA: RG 59, CD, Falmouth, vol. 1). 1 p.

§ From David Lenox. *4 September 1802, New York.* Transmits a copy of his 17 Aug. letter "on the supposition that it may not have reached you" and requests an answer. "The prevalence of the Fever in Philadelphia has hitherto prevented me from proceeding there with my family, you will therefore be pleased to direct to me at this place."

RC (DNA: RG 59, CD, London, vol. 8). 1 p.

§ From Nathaniel Macon. *4 September 1802, Buck Spring, North Carolina.* Notes that the appointment of the present marshal for North Carolina will expire in December. "If he wishes to be reappointed, I have no doubt but he ought to be contin-

547

ued.[1] If however he should not, I do not now know, but it would be adviseable to appoint Mr. Lockhart.[2] I will however make the necessary enquiry before the meeting of Congress, and inform you the result on my arrival at Washington." Encloses two letters recommending Lockhart; "Mr. Baker is our attorney general, and Mr. Plummer is the person named to the president last winter for the district Judge of this state."

RC and enclosures (DNA: RG 59, LAR, 1801–9, filed under "Lockhart"). RC 1 p.; docketed by Jefferson. Enclosures are Blake Baker to Macon, 3 Sept. 1802 (3 pp.), and Kemp Plummer to Macon, 3 Sept. 1802 (1 p.).

1. John Spence West was appointed marshal for the district of North Carolina in May 1798; Jefferson reappointed him on 20 Dec. 1802 (*Senate Exec. Proceedings*, 1:278, 426).
2. John Lockhart was appointed marshal for North Carolina in 1806 (ibid., 2:45).

¶ From Stephen Kingston. Letter not found. *5 September 1802, Philadelphia*. Mentioned in Kingston to John Quincy Adams, 24 June 1822 (DNA: RG 76, Spain, Misc. Records, ca. 1801–24), as his first letter of complaint against the Spanish government on the subject of the detention of his ship *Three Sisters* in the Río de la Plata, which began, "I beg leave to lay before the government a statement of the following facts & to solicit that interest which is due to cases of hardship imposed upon their citizens."

¶ From Samuel Morey. Letter not found. *5 September 1802*. Acknowledged in Daniel Brent to Morey, 9 Oct. 1802 (DNA: RG 59, DL, vol. 14). Brent informed Morey that his letter had arrived in JM's absence "and I have just received his directions, since his return, to forward the enclosed exemplification of the Patent alluded to, to you, and to return you fifty cents, and I herewith do so." Samuel Morey (1762–1843) was an inventor who held a number of patents, including a steam-operated spit (1793), a windmill (1796), a steam pump (1799), and the internal combustion engine (1826). He began steamboat experiments in 1790 and was awarded a patent in 1803 for improvements on a steam engine.

To Thomas FitzSimons

Sir   Virginia September 6th. 1802.
    I duly received and laid before the President your [*sic*] of the 6th.   .[1] His sentiments on the subject of it, are explained in an answer to two letters from a Committee of Merchants at Boston, of which as it will serve as an answer to yours, I enclose a copy:[2] and am very respectfully &ca.
                                                              James Madison.

Letterbook copy (DNA: RG 59, DL, vol. 14).

1. Left blank in letterbook. FitzSimons's letter has not been found.
2. JM to Stephen Higginson and others, 6 Sept. 1802.

To Stephen Higginson and Others

GENTLEMEN   VIRGINIA Sepr. 6th. 1802

I have received your two letters of July 23 & Aug. 11;[1] the former requesting the interposition of the Executive with the Government of Spain
for redressing injuries suffered by American Merchants in Spanish Colonies; the latter suggesting that in the mean time, a public vessel be dispatched thither with an Agent authorized to demand a more prompt justice
from the local authorities.

The President feels every disposition to patronize the commercial rights
of his fellow Citizens; but he sees very strong objections to the latter expedient of a formal mission to a subordinate authority; especially with the
imperfect means as yet possessed for supporting our demands by referring
them specifically to the sanctions under which the Several voyages were
undertaken.

The mode of interposition pointed at in your first letter, being the more
regular one, had been anticipated not only by general instructions to the
Minister Plenipotentiary of the United States at Madrid to charge himself
with the just claims of American Citizens on the Spanish Government;[2]
but by a further instruction transmitted in Feby. last,[3] reminding him of the
complaints founded on detentions of their property and other unjust proceedings in Spanish America, and making it his duty, to comprehend if
practicable, all such cases, by terms sufficiently general, within the cognizance of a Board of Commissioners which he had been previously instructed to propose, in conformity to the model in the Spanish Treaty of
1795. At the date of the last letters from Mr. Pinkney he had not recd. this
additional instruction; but he had himself adverted to the expediency of
enlarging the purview of the article in the Treaty of 1795; and there can be
little doubt that the instruction itself would arrive before the negocation
for a Board of Commissioners, into which the Spanish Government readily
entered, would be brought to a conclusion.

As it is possible however that the negocation for a Board of Commissioners may fail, as it is not certain that Spain will concur in a sufficient
latitude to its powers and as considerable delay may attend this mode of
redress, it seems adviseable for those interested in the subject of your letters
to follow up the representation sent from the spot, with a particular statement to Mr. Pinkney of their respective cases accompanied with whatever
documents in support of them may be attainable. To enable him to proceed

549

with the greater precision and effect, in his discussions and reclamations, it is recommended that the several cases be so discriminated by their circumstances as to shew, how far they rest, on general regulations or special licences from competent authorities; how far on licences reasonably presumed to be competent, though in strictness not so; how far on sudden & ensnaring repeals of general regulations, or discontinuances of special indulgences; how far on the calculation from existing circumstances, that the ordinary Colonial policy of Spain would be relaxed; and how far on fraudulent proceedings of Spanish subjects. As in this last case, the claimants may be required to shew that satisfaction has been sought in vain from the regular Tribunals of the place, it will be prudent for them to be prepared to meet such a preliminary.

I shall be glad to receive a copy of the Statement here recommended, as soon as it shall have been prepared. It may furnish a ground for more particular instructions to Mr. Pinkney; and may be made one, for asking the interposition of the Spanish Minister Plenipotentiary to the U. States, with the Vice Government of la Plata. I am Gentlemen very respectfully Your Obedt. hble servt

JAMES MADISON

RC (owned by Philip D. and Elsie O. Sang, River Forest, Ill., 1958); letterbook copy (DNA: RG 59, DL, vol. 14). Addressed to Higginson "& others of the Committee of Merchts. at Boston."

1. Letters not found. For the contents, see JM to Jefferson, 14 Aug. and 1 Sept. 1802, and Jefferson to JM, 17 Aug. and 3 Sept. 1802.
2. JM to Pinckney, 9 June 1801 (*PJM-SS*, 1:273–74).
3. JM to Pinckney, 5 Feb. 1802 (*PJM-SS*, 2:441–42).

From Thomas Jefferson

DEAR SIR   MONTICELLO Sep. 6. 1802.

Your's of the 3d. came to hand yesterday. I am content that the questions relative to Commissioners of bankruptcy and dockets should remain until we meet: altho' I think there are reasons of weight for not leaving the latter for Congress to do, for that would be abandoning it. The repeal of that law has been unquestionably pleasing to the people generally; and having led Congress to it, we owe to them to produce the facts which will support what they have done. It would rally the public opinion again to what is right, should that any where have been shaken by the volumes of misrepresentation which have been published, and shew we are not to be dismayed by any thing of that kind. Perhaps our directions may better go to the district attornies to procure the dockets. They have a right as individuals to demand them. I believe we need ask only the *cases determined* during the year. This would be very short indeed. I do not sufficiently recollect the particulars of the Snow Windsor to be exact on that subject. But I know that I had not a doubt as to the justice of what we concluded before, nor do I see any thing in mr. Thornton's letter to create a doubt. We did our duty in ordering the vessel away. The delays which followed were such as the vigilance of no government can prevent: and the treaty at length placed her at liberty. If delays are to be paid for by a government, what have we not to demand from Great Britain? I think with you we should shew our sincerity by prosecuting for the departure of the vessel without a clearance, as far as the laws justify.[1] I have written to mr. Smith to stop the John Adams.[2] The war being returned to it's former state against Tripoli only, we should reduce our force to what had been concluded on as to that power, as soon as we learn the state of things with Tunis. In the mean time the New York will go on. Mr. Steele's labours to shew he is agreeable to the Govr. shew pretty clearly the reverse, independent of the Governor's own evidence. Accept my affectionate esteem & respect.

TH: JEFFERSON

RC (DLC); FC (DLC: Jefferson Papers).

1. See Thornton to JM, 27 Aug. 1802. On 27 Sept. Thornton wrote Hawkesbury that he had spoken with JM at Monticello about the *Windsor* case and that JM's views on the subject had not changed. "He told me plainly that he did not regard the neglect of the Officers of government as founding a just claim for compensation on the government itself; and that in short as the whole proceedings in the pretended condemnation, sale and transfer of that vessel were perfectly irregular and illegal, they formed no bar to the prosecution of the right⟨s⟩ of the original proprietors, which might therefore ⟨be⟩ investigated in a Court of justice, whenever the vessel should return within reach of its jurisdic⟨tion⟩." Thornton was "unwilling," he wrote, "to lay any fa⟨rther⟩ stress upon the culpable negligence, if not the intentional misconduct, of the Officers of the Customs at Boston in this transaction, as ⟨they⟩ belong to the party called federal, and as the President might avail himself with alacrity of ⟨an⟩ accusation coming from such a quarter to incr⟨ease⟩ the number of removals from office, which ha⟨s⟩ already sufficiently depressed that party" (PRO: Foreign Office, ser. 5, 35:319–20).
2. Jefferson to Robert Smith, 6 Sept. 1802 (DLC: Jefferson Papers).

From Charles Pinckney

DEAR SIR   September 6: 1802 IN MADRID
I have the honour to inclose you the Duplicate of a complaint made by the Spanish Government respecting an insult alledged to have been offered the Spanish Flag in Philadelphia.[1] To this I have replied that not know-

ing the circumstances I could only assure his Majesty I would transmit the complaint & that his Majesty would certainly recieve every reparation the nature of the case would admit—that Philadelphia was at a distance from the seat of the general Government & that in large commercial cities such Outrages would frequently occur among the mariners of different nations—that our laws were very strict with respect to the rights & protection of foreigners in amity or in treaty with the United States, & that although from the nature of our Government & the established forms of Justice, it could not generally be quite so speedy as in some other countries, it was nevertheless always certain & commensurate to every Event—that the delays however were not great & were only occasioned by the tribunals having stated Sessions at which alone such charges could be examined, or by the time it might be necessary to allow the accused to prepare for their Defence or produce their Witnesses.

The Court as I informed you have gone to Barcelona to meet the Naples family & exchange princesses—the Neapolitan princess to mount the Spanish Throne & the Spanish the Sicilian.

It is now some months since I have had the pleasure of a line, nor have I yet been acquainted with the proceedings of the last session of Congress. I am in daily or indeed hourly expectation of hearing from you & as the season is past for my going to Rome for a few weeks during the Courts absence, I give up the idea for the present. Please present me affectionately to the President & Believe me with sincere respect & attachment Dear Sir Yours Truly

CHARLES PINCKNEY

RC and enclosure (DNA: RG 59, DD, Spain, vol. 6). RC marked "(Duplicate)"; docketed by Wagner as received 24 Nov. and marked in pencil, "To be answered." For enclosure, see n. 1.

1. The complaint was made in a letter from Cevallos to Pinckney, 20 June 1802 (1 p.; in Spanish). For the incident at Philadelphia, see Yrujo to JM, 3 May 1802.

§ From Stephen Cathalan, Jr. *6 September 1802, Marseilles.* Notes that he last wrote to JM on 13 Aug. via Bordeaux. On 15 Aug. he wrote to Capt. Andrew Morris by his "particular Friend" Citizen Beaussier, the French commissary at Tripoli, who sailed for Tripoli 16 Aug., and he charged Beaussier with supplying clothes and provisions to Morris and his crew if other arrangements had not been made. Encloses copies of two letters from Morris, dated 22 and 30 July at Tripoli.[1] Transmits two packets of dispatches for JM from William Eaton, which were received with letters dated 8 and 9 Aug. from Eaton to Cathalan. Has forwarded letters from Captain Murray of the *Constellation* to the secretary of the navy by way of William Lee at Bordeaux; "this will reach you by the Same way for want of opportunities direct from this port." Encloses copies of the correspondence between himself and

W. Y. Purviance and related letters on the subject of the latter's appointment as U.S. naval agent for the Mediterranean.[2] Cites letters from JM and from Mackenzie and Glennie of London, "both ordering me to assist and Supply the american Squadron when it Should or any of their Ships of War appear on this Coast," and declares that he will continue to offer his services. "It will be [up] to them to accept of my offers or to Apply to Mr. Purviance's Agents here; in this last Case I will, However give every aid and Assistance to them." Does not believe he deserved such a "Severe Letter" from Purviance. Asks JM to transmit the entire correspondence to the secretary of the navy after reading it. "You will Judge in this affair and determine with him what is the most Convenient for the interest . . . of the United States; observing, I doubt not, how it would be unconvenient for the agents in Marseilles, Toulon, Cartagena, Malaga Gibraltar &ca. to Correspond and act under the agency of the navy Situated into Leghorn for Such Supplies; while Leghorn is well Situated to do it with Naples, Palerma, Syracusa, even Malta &ca. which it appears are the ports which the Secretary of the Navy has pointed by his orders to Messrs. DeButts & Purviance."

RC and enclosures (DNA: RG 59, CD, Marseilles, vol. 1). RC 3 pp.; docketed by Wagner.

1. Cathalan enclosed correspondence (2 pp.) reporting Andrew Morris's capture by a Tripolitan corsair and warning of Tripolitan ship movements, including an extract of a letter to him from James Leander Cathcart, 28 Aug. 1802, in which Cathcart quoted from Morris's letter of 22 July 1802, and a copy of a letter from Morris to his consignees in Marseilles, 30 July 1802. For another copy of this correspondence, see William Willis to JM, 15 Sept. 1802, n. 1.

2. These numbered enclosures (8 pp.) include copies of (1) Cathalan to William Y. Purviance, 7 Aug. 1802, in which the former indicated he had learned that Purviance had been appointed U.S. naval agent in the Mediterranean and that "our mutual Friend Mr. Schwartz of this place had offered his Services as your Agent here in that line, to Capn. MacNeill, . . . but it would make a bad Effect here Should any other than the american Agents (or Consuls) assist our Navy"; (2) Purviance to Cathalan, 20 Aug. 1802, expressing surprise at Cathalan's "interfering with my appointment" since "this business . . . belongs wholly to the Department of the Navy from which I have received the Appointment" and declaring that "I Cannot, Therefore, allow any one to Encroach on my rights, or to meddle with the duties imposed on me by my office"; (3) Samuel Smith to DeButts and Purviance, 20 May 1801, authorizing the latter to supply the U.S. squadron and draw on Mackenzie and Glennie for funds (see Knox, *Naval Documents, Barbary Wars*, 1:462–63); (4) an extract of Cathcart's letter to Cathalan, 18 Aug. 1802, giving his opinion that since Cathalan's commission came from the president of the U.S. it was superior to that of naval agent and advising Cathalan to present the case to the government; (5) Cathalan to Cathcart, 30 Aug. 1802, complaining of the manner in which Purviance had answered his letter requesting a "fair and friendly Explanation" of his agency and informing Cathcart he was referring the matter to JM; (6) an extract of JM to Cathalan, 21 May 1801 (see *PJM-SS*, 1:209); and (7) Mackenzie and Glennie to Cathalan, 8 July 1801, authorizing Cathalan to supply Commodore Dale's squadron.

§ From George W. Erving. *6 September 1802, American Consulate, London.* No. 10. "I have just received from our Consul at Cadiz, a Circular letter of which the inclosed is a Copy; since my last of 29th. July upon this subject no other authentic information has been received here."

RC and enclosure (DNA: RG 59, CD, London, vol. 8). RC 1 p. Enclosure (1 p.) is another copy of Richard O'Brien's circular letter, 26 June 1802, countersigned by Stephen Cathalan and William Willis (see Thomas Appleton to JM, 10 July 1802, and n. 2; Josef Yznardy to JM, 13 Aug. 1802, and n. 1).

§ From William Jarvis. *6 September 1802, Lisbon.* Refers to his last dispatch of 22 Aug. reporting the prohibition on importing cordage and his fears of a similar order against flour, "which I am extremely sorry is so soon verified." Encloses a copy of an order issued 4 Sept. by the inspector general of the corn market. "Not being perfectly satisfied as to the meaning of that part relateing to the Consumption, I sent to request an explanation & received for answer that the Consumption as well as the importation of all foreign flour after the 4th January next was forbidden & that what was then on hand must be exported." Has little hope the ban will be rescinded given "the determination shewn by this Government, in adhereing to the Prohibition of Cordage, notwithstanding the exertions of the English & Russian Ministers, . . . [who] finally could only obtain permission to unload the Vessel that was half unloaded when the order was issued & such others as were then actually in port." States in a postscript that "not being perfectly satisfied with the explanation sent me by the Administrator of the Cornmarket I sent up again to the Judge who entirely differed in opinion from the former, the latter conceiveing it was intended only to prohibit the importation, but the former still insists that the importation & consumption were both intended."

RC and enclosure (DNA: RG 59, CD, Lisbon, vol. 1). RC 4 pp.; docketed by Brent. Enclosure (2 pp.) is a translation in Jarvis's hand of a 4 Sept. 1802 order from João de Saldanha de Oliveira e Souza prohibiting the importation into Portugal of flour from foreign countries and declaring that "the space of four months is allowed for the consumption of the flour existing, as well as for what may arrive, counting from the date hereof." Extract of Jarvis's letter and enclosure are printed in the *National Intelligencer*, 22 Nov. 1802.

¶ From John Condit. Letter not found. *6 September 1802, Newark, New Jersey.* Mentioned in Daniel Brent to Condit, 13 Sept. 1802 (DNA: RG 59, DL, vol. 14), as a request for a land patent. Brent replied in JM's absence, forwarding to the New Jersey congressman a patent "for Three hundred eighteen Acres and fifty perches of land granted to Joseph Cone out of the reservation for satisfying the claims of the Refugees from Canada."

To Thomas Jefferson

Dear Sir   [ca. 7 September 1802]
    Yours of the 6th. instant was duly brought by the last mail.
    I inclose under cover to Mr. Brent, the answers to the Merchts. of Boston & Philada., which if approved you will be so good as to seal & send on to

him. I inclose also a letter from Mr. Brent to me, for the sake of the explanation it gives relative to the consulate at Nantz. If Mr. Grant[1] should not go, it is to be recollected that the vacancy there has been thought of for Mr. Patterson whose appointment to l'Orient interferes with the situation of Mr. Vail.

Docr. Thornton & his family are with us; and I believe mean to pay their respects to Monticello before their return. We shall ride up at the same time if my absence from home should not be forbidden by circumstances which I am endeavoring to defuse of that tendency. With respectful attachment I remain Yours

JAMES MADISON

RC (DLC: Jefferson Papers). Undated; docketed by Jefferson as received 9 Sept.

1. Thomas T. Gantt (see Brent to JM, 3 Sept. 1802, and n. 3).

From Daniel Brent

DEAR SIR   WASHINGTON Sepr 7th 1802.

Your favor of the 3d with its enclosures duly came to hand.[1] I will endeavor to make the best use of your Requisition on the Treasury Department in favor of Major Lenox, and hope to succeed in satisfying him at the same time that I coincide with your wish on the subject. The extract from Mr Clark's letter has been delivered to General Dearborne, according to the President's desire. A Commission for Mr Shore has been filled up, and sent to the Sey of the Treasury's Office, whence it will be forwarded. One for Mr Bloodgood was sent some time ago, by the request of Mr Gallatin.

I fear that you will be a good deal puzzled in the reading of the press Copies of Mr Livingstons letters, from their faintness. I forward an extract to the President from that part of one of them which relates to Mr Sumpter, and an entire Copy of Mr Sumpter's own letter, herewith sent to you.[2]

I understand that the Continuance of the french frigates, with the Guadaloupe negroes, at New York, gives great displeasure there. A Representation on the subject of these negroes has just been made to the Secy of War by the Mayor of New York, an extract from which I will subjoin to this letter. Mr Pichon intends, if he can effect it, to send the Ships and Negroes to France, and he sat out for New York this morning with that view. But I know not how he will do this, destitute, as he has told me he is, of the means of victualling the vessels.

I have just received a letter from Mr Wagner, in answer to one that I had written to him, on the subject of the obscure note in several of Cap:

555

OBrien's letters, that you recollect.[3] I will send this letter to you by the next post. I will communicate the names of the Comms. of Bankruptcy in Connecticut to Judge Law by this day's mail. I forward a letter herewith, just reced. from him.[4] I have the Honor to be, Dear Sir, with great Respect & sincere esteem, your Obedt & faithful servt.

DANL BRENT

Copy of a letter from the Mayor of N York to the Secy of War, dated Sepr 1st 1802.

SIR

You have probably heard that a french squadron is now in this port having between eleven and twelve hundred black prisoners on board—they are now at the quarantine ground, and being very much crowded on board, their sick and wounded have been received into the State hospital—this is by no means equal to their reception without totally abandoning the principal object of the institution, which was to provide for the numerous emigrants on board of private ships at this season daily arriving. I think therefore that the General Government ought to take some measures to provide accomodation for these people, or make arrangements with the French Minister to that effect, the more particularly as their stay is indefinite, and the season will augment the number of the sick.

The President has power by special act the [*sic*] employ the garrison troops in executing the quarantine laws—and as numbers of these blacks are daily escaping from the hospital and the Ships—I could wish that an order might be sent to Cap: Ingersol to furnish a proper guard to prevent their taking refuge in our Country. I am &&a

(signed)   EDW. LIVINGSTON.

PS I have thought it would be more satisfactory to you to have a Copy of the whole letter, which I have accordingly made—General Dearborne has given the order asked for to Cap: Ingersol.

D B.

RC (DLC). Docketed by JM.

   1. Letter not found.

   2. See Livingston to JM, 12 May 1802, and n. 2, and Sumter to JM, 18 May 1802.

   3. Wagner's letter to Brent has not been found, but for the "obscure note," see Richard O'Brien to JM, 14 May 1802, and n. 1.

   4. Letter not found.

§ From Henry Potter. *7 September 1802, Raleigh.* Recommends John Lockhart for the position of marshal for North Carolina. "Of Mr. Lockhart's politics I have no knowledge.... As to his qualification, there is no man in the State within my knowledge & recollection, who I think is better fitted for the discharge of the duties of Marshall than he is."

RC (DNA: RG 59, LAR, 1801–9, filed under "Lockhart"). 2 pp. Potter was appointed a U.S. circuit judge by Jefferson in January 1802 and a U.S. district judge three months later, a position he held until his death in 1857 (*Senate Exec. Proceedings*, 1:401, 405, 418, 419; Wagstaff, *Papers of John Steele*, 1:451 n. 3).

¶ From Philip Wilson. Letter not found. *7 September 1802*. Mentioned in Daniel Brent to Wilson, 11 Sept. 1802 (DNA: RG 59, DL, vol. 14), as an inquiry about Wilson's claim against the British government on account of his ship. Brent replied in JM's absence that "the dispatches of Mr. King which were brot. by Major Lenox, contain no intelligence concerning your claim, . . . but I will lose no time in examining some of his antecedent ones, and in communicating the result of my search to you, if it shall prove successful."

From James Leander Cathcart

Dispatch No. 14

Sɪʀ   Lᴇɢʜᴏʀɴ Sepr. 8th. 1802

I conceive it my duty to forward Copy's of all my correspondence that conveys the least intelligence to the department of State; however disagreeable this line of conduct may be on several occasions, I prescribed the rule myself, & from it I am resolved not to swerve, 'tho I am convinced it will procure me many private enemies, but at the same time I flatter myself it will promote the general good of the service & I assure you that only is my reason for forwarding the enclosed letter from Captn. Andrew Morris as it contains the most severe & pointed censure on the conduct of one of our gentlemen in command.[1]

Enclosed is a copy of my dispatch No. 13 & its inclosures.[2] I hope the measures their [*sic*] delineated will meet the approbation of government; I have read of my appointment to the Consulate of Algiers in a Newyork Newspaper, for which fresh mark of the Presidents & my Countrys approbation give me leave to return my most sincere thanks, & to assure you that the whole study of my life will be to merit a continuance of their confidence.

I have receiv'd no news from Barbary since my last, but by a letter from our Consul at Malta dated the 6th. of August I am inform'd that Hamet Bashaw the brother of the reigning Bashaw of Tripoli was preparing to depart in a few days for his government of Bengasi & Derna where undoubtedly he will be murder'd in less than six months.

I am in anxious expectation for instructions & a credit—to answer my expenditures here which I requested some months ago & remain with sentiments of the greatest respect & esteem Sir Your most Obnt. Servt.

JAMES LEAR. CATHCART

RC and enclosure (DNA: RG 59, CD, Tripoli, vol. 2). For enclosure, see n. 1.

1. Andrew Morris's letter to Cathcart, 22 July 1802 (6 pp.; docketed by Brent as received in Cathcart's dispatch no. 14), repeated the substance of his letter to Eaton of 21 July (see Eaton to JM, 5 Aug. 1802, n. 2) and added more suggestions about how the war with Tripoli should be conducted. After describing his capture, Morris criticized the navy command in general for not guarding the waters off Cape Bon, "a place that the necessity of strictly guarding, must appear to every naval Commander at War with Tripoli." But Morris reserved his worst scorn for the captains of the American frigate and Swedish frigate blockading Tripoli, who during the five hours while the Tripolitan ship approached the harbor "never made the least effort to obstruct our progress when it was certainly in their power to Capture or run the Pirate on Shore before it was possible for them to be protected from their batteries" (printed in Knox, *Naval Documents, Barbary Wars,* 2:176–78).
2. See Cathcart to JM, 4 Sept. 1802, and n. 1.

From Charles Pinckney

DEAR SIR   September 8: 1802. IN MADRID.

In addition to my letters by Mr Codman I am to inform you I have this day recieved intelligence from Algiers that France by sending some 74 Gun ships & other armed Vessels to that place with a Plenipotentiary on board has forced the Dey to submit to such terms as Bonaparte thought proper to prescribe.

The Dey has been obliged to renounce all old claims for money on France.

To release three Neapolitan Vessels Cargoes & Crews taken near the french shore & punish the Algerine commanders who took them very severely

To admit the free navigation of the Italian Republic. To pass all french Vessels without passports—& it is said to give to the French the place called Le cal who are to fortify it. It is added that at the time the French Envoy demanded & the Dey was obliged to submit to these terms, that the Envoy told him he was charged by Bonaparte to inform him, if ever Algiers committed the least outrage or in any degree insulted the flag or injured the commerce of France, he would erase her name from the list of nations. Such is my intelligence from Algiers & having reason to confide in it I hasten to transmit it to you.

England will certainly do the same & it will then be seen on what power the Dey will endeavour to depredate; for the freedom of the Navigation of the Italian Republic will enable them to cover under their flag both the Neapolitan & Ligurian commerce. Indeed it is expected that France considering Liguria & Batavia as much her children as the Italian Republic will very soon stipulate or insist that their Navigation shall be equally free. I am told the Dey has lately been enquiring about our annuities. I have Written lately to Mr O'brien in answer to his Letter, but owing to some difficulty I cannot get an answer from him, although no doubt he Writes to you via Gibraltar & Cadiz. My instructions saying nothing to me on the subject of the Barbary States, I do not consider myself as authorised to interfere further than in the transmission of intelligence or letters. Please present me respectfully to the President & Believe me dear sir with sincere regard Yours Truly

CHARLES PINCKNEY

RC (DNA: RG 59, DD, Spain, vol. 6). Docketed by Wagner as received 23 Nov.

§ From Thomas Appleton. *8 September 1802, Leghorn.* "The unhappy situation to which the ships of the UStates are exposed in these seas, has put a stop to almost all our Commerce with this place for the last month." Forwards letters from Captain Murray of the *Constellation* to the secretary of the navy and dispatches from Cathcart and refers JM to them for the "actual position" of the U.S. with Tripoli. "The Affairs of Italy have experienced no essential change of late whatsoever. The King with all his family are now here in order to embark . . . to Barcelona to be present at the Nuptials—the health of his Majesty is beyond example wretched having been seized with two epileptic fits in as many days. It is in truth difficult to Conceive that an object of no greater magnitude, than being a witness to a Ceremony of marriage, should be sufficient to induce him to leave his Kingdom, if he Considers the present unstable foundation of most of the governments of Italy." The British continue to garrison Malta and Alexandria. Asks JM to accept a small bust of General Washington. "It was made by my directions at Volterra, the only place where the stone is found. . . . The smallness of the intrinsic value, will I presume, do away the Necessity of further apologizing for the liberty I have taken. It is contained in a small box and addressed to the Care of the Naval Officer at New-York."

RC (DNA: RG 59, CD, Leghorn, vol. 1). 3 pp.; docketed by Brent.

§ From William Buchanan. *8 September 1802, Ile de France.* Refers to his last dispatch on 31 July enclosing a return of the American vessels that had arrived through 30 June. U.S. laws defining the powers of consuls are so limited that "it has not been in my power to make the return agreeably to your instructions, as I have no authority to demand from the American Captains the necessary informations." During the war frauds were perpetrated by which persons "not entitled to own American ships, have enjoyed all the benefit of American Registers, which it was impossible for the Consuls to prevent, as they were not empowered to demand a Sight of the ship's papers." "It has frequently happened, that Ships have been Sold at this port, and the Registers used to trade between this Port, and India and sometimes for the slave trade to the River la Plata." Since he last wrote, "the assembly of this Island have passed a law compelling all Consuls to procure exequaturs from France, before they can be acknowleged by the Administration of this Island." Requests JM to forward his commission to the American minister at Paris so that his exequatur can be procured and sent to him.

RC (DNA: RG 59, CD, Port Louis, vol. 1). 1 p.; docketed by Wagner as received 16 Dec.

From John Graham

(private)

DEAR SIR   MADRID 9th Sepr 1802

Some time since I had the Honor of addressing you, to return my thanks for the Kentucky Papers which you had the Goodness to send me; and also to express my mortification for having troubled you with a request concerning pecuniary matters on which the Law had not given you power to decide.[1] Since then I have not taken the Liberty to write to you; but as Mr Codman offers to me a safe conveyance for my Letter, and as it appears to me that you will be particularly anxious, on the receipt of the Dispatches which he takes over, to gain full information of the state of our affairs at this Court, I will venture to communicate to you what little I have been able to collect; and I will even venture to express to you my opinions— more particularly as they differ from those of Mr Pinckney.

The Mississipi Business is, I fear all at an end here. Mr Cevallos has ever avoided any candid communications on that Subject—and to this Moment Mr Pinckney has not been able to get any satisfactory Information from him; but from an other source I have learnt (and I beleive the intelligence may be depended upon) that in July last, the definitive arrangements were settled between the French Embassador & Mr Cevallos for the Cession & Evacuation of Louisiana—this was in compliance with a Treaty made in 1800, in which it was stipulated that Louisiana should be returned to the French at the close of the War. The Spaniards wished to evade this Treaty but they were not permitted to do so. I am told the Ancient Boundaries of the Provence are adhered to, these, on the East of the Mississipi are, I beleive the Iberville, and the Lakes Maurapas and Ponchatrain, at least these are pointed out in the Treaty of 1763 as dividing the French from the British Possessions, in that quarter of the World.[2] I have no possitive information on this point, and as the French say that they get back Louisiana as of right belonging to them, and as some of their Geographers have extended this provence as far as the Mobile it is very possible that they have now fixed upon that River as their Eastern Boundary, more particularly as they have it in view to supply our western Country with European & other Goods, which can be done more conveniently by the Mobile than the Mississipi. To us it is not very material which of these is to be their Boundary, for either the one or the other would cut off West Florida from any point on the Mississipi conveniently accessible to vessels from the Ocean. I very much lament that this is the case, not that I conceive there is any probability of our getting Florida; but because I am told there is no stipulation made with the French that we shall enjoy the same Rights & Privileges in the country ceded to them, which we have hitherto enjoyed there, under our Treaty with Spain. This information was given to me by a French Gentleman who had it from his Embassador. Various reasons would induce me to credit it, even if the silence of Mr Cevallos on that Subject did not carry to my Mind a Conviction of its truth. On this I have written two Letters to Mr Livingston,[3] for which I hope my peculiar situation will plead my Apology.

As to the Convention which Mr Codman takes over to America it is not for me to give an Opinion, I can only say that the Negotiation has been conducted in such a way as to throw very little light upon the Subjects of difference between the two Governments. Mr Cevallos has contrived without using a single Argument to spin out the Negotiation for five months, and has I think succeeded in his Object, which appears to have been, to do as little as possible, and to do that little as slowly as possible. I am by no means so sanguine as Mr Pinckney, in my Expectations that this Government will go farther than they have gone, except in the cases of direct violation of Territory. This is to be lamented as from the returns in the Consular Office here, it appears that our Claims upon them for French Spoliations are more numerous than those on any other account,[4] some few of these may come under the Convention; but not many. As to the Claims from South America we know very little of them here; but from what I have heared, we can have no possitive right to demand satisfaction for them because the Trade to that Country to have been legal must have been in the name of Spanish Subjects.

You will see that I do not place our Affairs in the same favourable point of view that Mr Pinckney does. I wish I could think with him; but as I do not, I conceive it my Duty to state to you that in my Opinion, nothing will be done here advantageous to the United States unless an other Minister is sent out pointedly charged to speak boldly—with this Government, I beleive no other plan will succeed—and I have my doubts whether this will for they look upon it as degrading to pay for the Excesses committed by the French when the French themselves were not obliged to pay—and independent of this they have not money I am told to meet their necessary Expendatures. It strikes me however that should a Man of Talents & Address be sent out & not be able to obtain direct compensation for our Losses, he might, in lieu thereof secure some commercial advantages, which in a national point of view, would be more than equivalent. I think this a very favourable time to propose a Measure of the kind for the Spanish Merchants are not able to carry on their own Trade as appears by a Remonstrance of the Inhabitants of the Havanna to the King—and it is said that this Government will do any thing rather than part with Money. I have reason to think that they wish to make some commercial arrangement with us—for Mr Cevallos has applyed to an acquaintance of mine to give him a detailed view of the Trade between the two countries which might no doubt be made mutually beneficial in a high degree.

I have thus, Sir, given you my Opinions with a Candour which springs from a desire of being useful & I trust you will not look upon it as infringing that Respect with which I have the Honor to be Yr mo: Obt Hume. Sert

JOHN GRAHAM

RC (DLC).

1. JM's letters to and from Graham have not been found.
2. Article 7 of the Treaty of Paris of 1763 between Great Britain, France, and Spain defined the boundaries between the then British and French territories in North America (Davenport and Paullin, *European Treaties*, 4:94).
3. See Graham to Robert R. Livingston, 12 July 1802 (NHi: Livingston Papers). As Graham noted in this letter, he feared that Cevallos had not been candid when asked about the guarantee of American rights on the Mississippi River, and he added that, as to Spain, "*we have but little to expect from the friendship or even justice of this nation*" (italics indicate code).
4. This judgment contradicted that of Pinckney, expressed in his letter to JM, 24 Aug. 1802.

§ From George W. Erving. *9 September 1802, American Consulate, London.* Encloses a copy of a letter from the U.S. consul at Tangier "announcing the establishment of peace" between the U.S. and Morocco. Has forwarded "proper notice of this pleasing circumstance" to U.S. consuls in Great Britain, Holland, and Germany.

RC and enclosure (DNA: RG 59, CD, London, vol. 8). RC 1 p. Enclosure (1 p.) is a copy of a circular letter from James Simpson, 12 Aug. 1802 (a copy addressed to Josef Yznardy is printed in Knox, *Naval Documents, Barbary Wars*, 2:232).

§ From William Willis. *9 September 1802, Barcelona.* Encloses a copy of a letter just received from O'Brien.[1] Believes U.S. shipping would be safeguarded by "a regular System of Convoy" but as yet there is none. Suggests that U.S. ships of war are too large for the mission of suppressing the Tripolitans; "but had we a few Schooners of 14 to 16 Six pnd. they would be of sufficient force to defeat any one of the Cruizers of that Power."

Assures JM that "notwithstanding the severe losses of property, I have met with I am still posses'd of sufficient funds, to support a Commercial House, and for answering all the purposes of advancing for the necessary Service of the United States, and am happy to find that all the officers of the Spanish Government treat me with every degree of friendship and respect." Cites an instance where he has been of service to consuls of other nations. Because of the great number of people arriving at Barcelona to attend the king, there has been a shortage of housing. An order was issued to quarter government officials in all of the houses, including those of the consuls. "I resisted the demand; not so much on account of the inconvenience, as on account of its being an infringement on the customs and usages of Nations. I made an immediate representation to the Captain General of this province, and . . . he immediately gave orders that no Consul whatever should be molested by the requisition."

States that the reports of his financial difficulties are false, being circulated by those who are in debt to him to a great amount. A New York mercantile house and their agent in Barcelona, Benjamin B. Mumford, "have done all in their power to injure me" but have "not been able to impair my Credit, with individuals, nor with the Government." Observes that he is one of only two American citizens serving as consuls in Spain; "and this is a sufficient reason for those Consuls that are not so, to try to make an impression, and raise a prejudice against me, with my government, in order if possible to impress the Idea, that Foreigners, will generally be more respectable, and usefull consuls, than native American Citizens. . . . This leads me Sir to make some remarks on the unequal manner in which the Consuls of the United States Compensate themselves for their trouble. You will see by the enclos'd letter from Robert Montgomery Esqr[2] that some Consuls take what they call Consulage & Vice Consulage on Each American Vessell, which I know of no law to Authorise."

Encloses a list [not found] of all American ships that entered and cleared the port of Barcelona since his arrival in 1799; believes there were only two ships from the American Revolution until his arrival, proving "how much an enterprising Commercial Consul may cause the commerce of the United States to be extended." The case of Capt. James Mills of the ship *Catherine* of Baltimore "still remains in suspence. He has remain'd already two years detain by the Spanish Government upon an evidently false charge." Notes in a postscript that some dispatches from O'Brien of a later date than the enclosed letter have arrived but "I fear by some mistake they are sent to some other Place this sometimes happens."

RC (DNA: RG 59, CD, Barcelona, vol. 1). 13 pp.

1. Probably enclosed with this dispatch was a copy of Richard O'Brien's letter of 20 Aug. 1802 (ibid.; filed at the end of 1802) discussing U.S. relations with Morocco, Tripoli, and Algiers and the concessions made by the dey of Algiers to the French (1 p.; docketed by Willis, "Copy of a letter from Consul Obrien").

2. Willis apparently enclosed a copy of a 31 Mar. letter from Montgomery written to Peter Stirling at Barcelona during Willis's absence (ibid.; filed at the end of 1802). Montgomery wrote that it was the custom at Alicante "to charge masters of American Vessels five Dollars for Consulage & Three Dollars for Vice Consulage and assistance" and inquired what the usual charges were at Barcelona. On the verso is a copy of Stirling's 10 Apr. reply, stating that

during his time as vice-consul he had never known Willis to charge such fees. The copies are docketed by Willis, "Coppy of letter from Robert Montgomery Esq. Consul of the United States of America at Alicant and Answer."

To Albert Gallatin

DEAR SIR   Sepr. 10. 1802
    Docr. Thornton wishes to dispose of a bill of Exchange for five hundred pounds sterling, on Quintin Dick Esqr London. The bills are at 60 days sight, and are sent with blanks, to Mr. Riddle of Alexandria, who is authorized to sell them. Should your department be in want of money in London, he wishes you to be acquainted with the opportunity. He has satisfied me that the draught is made on solid pounds, and you may retain this letter as equivalent to my endorsement of the Bills. They bear date the 3d. instant. The payment for them will be wanted about the first of next month. Sincerely & respectfully Yours

                                        JAMES MADISON

RC (NHi: Gallatin Papers).

From Daniel Brent

DEAR SIR,   WASHINGTON, September 10. 1802.
    I have had the Honor already of acknowledging the receipt of your last letter, which was of the 3d Inst. Considering every thing, it appeared to me best that Major Lenox'es request should be complied with, and I have accordingly made use of your requisition upon the Treasury in his favor for that purpose, to the extent of the sum, 3000 Dollars, which it directs to be paid to him.[1] Similar payments, which it has become necessary to procure a law to be passed to sanction, have been repeatedly made to him and others, with the Concurrence of the Department of State, under Circumstances much less pressing; and there seemed to be no impropriety, therefore, in adding this case to the list, especially as the advance is Chiefly intended for the reimbursement of a sum which Mr Lenox was under the necessity of borrowing, and actually did borrow, on public account. I have written to him, requesting him to send forward his accounts without delay.
    Captain Davidson has three bills of Isaac Cox Barnet, late Consul of the U. S at Bordeaux, altogether for Three thousand, five hundred, seventy nine Dolls. and 64 Cents, on the Secy of State. He presented them yesterday at your Office for acceptance. They are at 30 days sight, and were drawn

on the 30th June last. No advice has been received from Mr Barnet on the subject of these Bills, tho' they are in the usual form, and refer to advice. I told Cap. Davidson that it was very doubtful whether they would be paid in any event—but that I was well assured you would not pay them without advice. They will doubtless be brought forward again. From the appearance of the Drawer's Accounts at the Auditor's office, which remain unsettled with a great mass of others of the same kind, I presume these Bills are founded upon a supposed balance in his favor, on a settlement.

I have not met with the Certificate alluded to in Mr Wagner's letter, herewith sent, but hope to find it in the next search I make, which will be to day.[2] The account mentioned in Mr Montflorence's letter, herewith likewise sent to You, will be forthwith settled at the Treasury, and the sum found due paid to Mr Forman, as requested.[3] It is said that the John Adams will not get off 'till next Sunday week. I have the Honor to be, with great Respect and sincere esteem, Dear sir, Your Ob. & very faithful servt.

DANL BRENT.

RC (DLC). Docketed by JM.

  1. See Lenox to JM, 17 Aug. 1802, and n. 1.
  2. See Brent to JM, 7 Sept. 1802, and n. 3.
  3. In his letter to JM of 12 Oct. 1801, James C. Mountflorence enclosed his account for maintaining the U.S. consulate at Paris, which he asked JM to "cause to be paid to my friend Mr. Joseph Forman" (see *PJM-SS*, 2:174). Brent wrote to Forman on 15 Sept. 1802 (DNA: RG 59, DL, vol. 14), offering to send the money to him at Baltimore on settlement of the account.

From Henry Dearborn

DEAR SIR   WASHINGTON Septr. 10th. 1802
   In establishing a trading house with the Chocktaws, we find from the best information, that a site on the Tombigby will be much the most convenient in every point of view,[1] but as such an establishment would probably interfere with the trade of the House of Panton & others of Pensacola,[2] their influence with the Spanish Government may produce an opposition to our navigating the river, it may therefore be adviseable to take some measure for counteracting any such influence. I consider it a delicate subject & therefore submit the letter to Govr. Claiborn, for your opinnion, will thank you for your opinnion on the subject as early, as convenience to yourself will permit.[3] Please Sir to present my most respectfull compliments to Mrs. Madison & family and believe me to be with esteem Your Humbl. Servt

H. DEARBORN

RC and enclosure (DLC). Docketed by JM. For enclosure, see n. 3.

1. For the decision to build a trading house for the Choctaw nation and for the discussion over where to site it, see Henry Dearborn to William C. C. Claiborne, 7 and 11 June 1802, and Claiborne to Dearborn, 20 July, 6 and 19 Aug. 1802 (Rowland, *Claiborne Letter Books*, 1: 149–50, 150–51, 153, 158–59, 159–60).

2. The British firm of Panton, Leslie, and Co. was an influential merchant house in Pensacola that controlled much of the Indian trade in the Floridas and enjoyed special privileges granted by the Spanish government (William S. Coker and Thomas D. Watson, *Indian Traders of the Southeastern Spanish Borderlands* [Pensacola, Fla., 1986], pp. 363–70).

3. Dearborn enclosed a letterpress copy of his letter to Claiborne, 10 Sept. 1802 (3 pp.), requesting Claiborne to "sound the Governor of the Floridas" about the possibility of Americans navigating the Tombigbee River "until more permanent arrangments between the two Governments can be made." Dearborn warned that "it may not be proper to intimate that we have any doubts of the right of navigating any of the Rivers, which pass out of the United States and through the Spanish Territory, but perhaps you may ascertain their present disposition, by intimating that you presume there will be no objection to our furnishing the posts ⟨on⟩ the Mobile & our Indian Agency at Tombigby through their Territory." No reply from JM to Dearborn's letter has been found. Dearborn's letter to Claiborne was sent without alteration and was acknowledged by Claiborne on 16 Nov. 1802 (Rowland, *Claiborne Letter Books*, 1:226–27, 229).

From Thomas Jefferson

DEAR SIR   MONTICELLO Sep. 10. 1802.

Yours by yesterday's post is recieved. The letter to Higginson & others is entirely approved, and is sealed & forwarded to mr. Brent. The Consulate at Nantes must be disposed of according to our former arrangement. I do not know whether the mr. Lynch recommended is the one who was living at Nantes when I was in France, or his son. Of that one there is something not favourable resting in my mind, altho' I cannot recollect the particulars. But Patterson's claims are certainly superior. I recd. from mr. Brent extracts from the letters of Chancr. Livingston & Sumpter concerning the resignation of the latter. I presume he does not wait for a formal permission. But suppose it had better be sent. I inclose you a commission of bankruptcy for your signature. It is to correct an error of having given a former one to a person of the same surname, for which this is now substituted. Mr. Brent reminds me of a parcel of blanks he sent for signature. I remember signing them, & sending them either to yourself or him.

We shall be very happy to see yourself, family, & Dr. & mrs. Thornton here. The Govr. is up at present; goes down on Thursday (16th.) and returns on Tuesday (21st.). When you get to the forks of the road at Will Becks's, the other side of Milton, a turn of the road forces you to the river at Milton, & when there it is better to cross there & come round along the public road on this side the river, my private one being hardly wide enough & safe for a carriage, altho' my waggons & carts do pass it. This adds a couple of miles to the length of the journey. With my best respects to the ladies accept assurances of my constant & affectionate friendship.

TH: JEFFERSON

P. S. I notify the offices at Washington that the post which leaves that place on the 24th. inst. is the last by which any thing should be forwarded to me here.

RC (DLC); FC (DLC: Jefferson Papers).

§ From Isaac Cox Barnet. *10 September 1802, Bordeaux.* Has received JM's letter of 22 June [not found] enclosing his commission as commercial agent for Antwerp. "I am preparing to leave this and expect to be at my post by the beginning of October. . . . The post assigned me equals my highest wishes." Will sign the necessary bonds and transmit them to his uncle, Dr. Barnet of New Jersey, for the signatures of his sureties. "The receipt of your pacquet Sir, excited my highest sensibility—and persuaded that your kind suffrage has emminently contributed towards restoring me to Presidential favour, . . . I beg you will accept my grateful acknowledgements."

RC (DNA: RG 59, CD, Bordeaux, vol. 1). 1 p.

§ From William Kirkpatrick. *10 September 1802, Málaga.* Forwards copy of his letter to JM of 10 Aug. Since then "you will have been advised thro' Gibraltar, that Matters had been arranged between James Simpson Esqr. and the Emperor of Morocco, for a Continuance of Peace; I hope it may prove of long duration, tho', the Conduct of the Emperor does not seem to be so friendly, as might have been expected after such a solemn Engagement." A Moorish vessel loaded with wheat that called at Málaga on 28 Aug. was reportedly on its way to Tripoli, and a 2 Sept. letter from John Gavino notes that a Moorish crew had arrived at Gibraltar to take possession of the Tripolitan cruiser blockaded there and sail it to Tetuán. Encloses copy of a letter just received from Richard O'Brien "by which you will observe, that the French have forced the Dey [of Algiers], to Come into their Terms in every Respect." Commodore Morris sailed from Málaga on 26 Aug. with the *Enterprize*, convoying twenty-eight American and Swedish ships to Leghorn. The *Boston* arrived the same day; "after taking a Supply of Spirits Water &ca." it proceeded on 3 Sept. to Gibraltar to procure provisions for the voyage home.

RC (DNA: RG 59, CD, Málaga, vol. 1). 2 pp. Enclosure not found.

§ From Josef Yznardy. *10 September 1802, Cadiz.* Transmits a copy of his letter to JM of 23 Aug. and a packet from Charles Pinckney; encloses a list of arrivals at Cadiz from 1 July 1800 to 30 June 1802 [not found] and a copy of circular from

John Gavino.[1] Advises JM of "the rumour spread about here of the Algerins having, or being on the point of declaring War against Great Britain."

RC and enclosure (DNA: RG 59, CD, Cadiz, vol. 1). RC 1 p.; in a clerk's hand, signed by Yznardy. Docketed by Wagner as received 23 Nov.

1. The surviving enclosure is a copy of a circular from Gavino to Yznardy, 6 Sept. 1802 (1 p.), reporting the arrival at Gibraltar of "36. Moorish Seamen for the Tripolin Ship laid up at this Port, among them is the Commander of the late Tripolin Brig sold here. The report is that she is the Emperor of Moroccos property, and goes from hence to Tetuan for Provisions & from thence to Tripoly."

¶ From John Barber. Letter not found. *10 September 1802, Albany.* Mentioned in Daniel Brent to Barber, 20 Sept. 1802 (DNA: RG 59, DL, vol. 14), as a request for payment for publishing the laws of the last session of Congress in the *Albany Register.* Brent replied in JM's absence that $94.50 would be remitted "after the account shall have been liquidated and passed."

To Thomas Jefferson

DEAR SIR   Sepr. 11. 1802

Yours of the 10th. is duly recd. I answered by duplicates Mr. Sumter's resignation as soon as it had been submitted to you. Mr. Livingston's request that he may appt. a successor has not yet been answered. It is probable he will expect to know your determination in the first letter that may be written to him. The blanks of which Mr. Brent reminded you, came to me from you some time ago, and were sent on to him with my signature.

You will receive herewith two letters from Mr Livingston of May 28. & June 8th. and one from Mr. King of June 20th. I am glad to find that Otto is to share in the negociations concerning Louisiana, because it is probable he may retain the original policy of France on that subject, and because his destination to this country gives him an interest in a policy that will be welcome to us. The arrival of Dupont also will be very apropos. The reasoning of Mr. L. to the Spanish Minister, has a certain degree of force, but if not managed cautiously may commit us in other points of view.

We can not yet fix the day of our visit to Monticello. Yours as ever

JAMES MADISON

RC (DLC: Jefferson Papers). Docketed by Jefferson as received 12 Sept.

§ From William Jarvis. *11 September 1802, Lisbon.* No. 6. His last dispatch of 6 Sept. informed JM of the "contradictory answer of the Judge & administrator of the Corn Market" regarding the prohibition on foreign flour. Made inquiries of the inspector general and was referred to "his representatives in the Corn Market, who were as divided in sentiment as were the Judge & Administrator; from which I concluded, that the order was worded so ambiguously on purpose to prevent, or allow, the consumption, as there should be a plenty or scarcity of grain on hand." Encloses a copy of his communication to the minister "attempting to prove, what I really believed, that it was for the interest & policy of this Government to admit our flour freely." Supporters of the prohibition told the prince regent that as long as foreign flour was allowed to be imported, the grain cultivated on the royal estates could not be sold and his revenue would suffer. "It is unfortunate for a People when the Prince believes his interest different from theirs, & their misfortunes are like to be perpetuated, when the only persons who have his ear are of the same opinion; nor under those circumstances is there much probability that any representations however just will convince them of their error, which I am apprehensive nothing will do short of a general scarcity." Encloses a copy of the original order and a letter dated 16 Aug. from Richard O'Brien.

RC and enclosures (DNA: RG 59, CD, Lisbon, vol. 1). RC 3 pp.; docketed by Brent. Enclosures are copies of Jarvis to Almeida, 9 Sept. 1802 (7 pp.), arguing against the order prohibiting the consumption and importation of foreign flour; the 4 Sept. 1802 order (2 pp.; in Portuguese); and O'Brien's letter of 16 Aug. 1802 (1 p.) reporting the arrival in Algiers of a French squadron, which exacted a number of concessions from the dey.

§ From Hans Rudolph Saabye. *11 September 1802, Copenhagen.* Refers to his last letter of 26 Mar.; "the two points therein mentioned, have since been settled favourably." Sugar imported in American bottoms will pay only 1 percent more duty than that imported in Danish ships, and the Danish government has given up its claim to one-third of the cargo of the *Hercules*, wrecked on the Elbe. Encloses the "Semi-annual List of the Ships, that have passed the Sound" [not found]. Although trade in general has been "very dull" since the peace, Copenhagen has been the best market in Europe, "and several of the Ships bound for this place, have made great Voyages, particularly when loaded with Rice and Rum." Encloses a price current.

RC and enclosure (DNA: RG 59, CD, Copenhagen, vol. 1). RC 2 pp. Surviving enclosure is a one-page price current.

From William Bingham

SIR, LONDON Septemr 12th 1802

I had the Honor of addressing you under Date of the 19 July[1] & having then wrote you a very long Letter, must apologize for again troubling you on the Same Subject.

I therein mentioned that the Plaintiffs in the Action in Massachusetts concerning the Brig Hope & her Cargo, had produced on the Trial, Proof that the Cargo was British Property. But however natural, Such an Inference, knowing that they were in Possession of Such Proof, yet I find I was mistaken.

By their Exertions in procuring every Species of Intelligence in Europe (after they had commenced their Action in 1793) which could benefit their Cause, they had obtained in August 1793 of the Same Year, ample Testimony to that Effect. But, on inspecting a Copy of the records of the Trial, before Judge Cushing in June 1794, it is found they made no Use of this Proof.

The Reason for their Suppressing this important Evidence, would appear inexplicable, if there was not a Clue, which unravels the Mystery.

From the Enquiries which have been made on this Subject, there is reason to Suppose, that the Destination of these Funds, being known to the Owners of the Cargo in Europe, an Application will be made for their Surrender, Supported by the Proof which the Owners of the Vessel will produce, of her being Danish Property—about which there is no doubt.

It will be observed that by the Proclamation of Congress of May 9. 1778,[2] as well from the Policy of conciliating the Good Will of the maritime Neutral Nations of Europe, as with a View of curbing those licentious & flagrant Aggressions on the rights of Neutral Nations, as had been recently committed, the United States very early adopted the Principle of free Ships making free Goods, which afterwards became Part of the maritime Code of Europe. They in this Proclamation, prohibited their Cruizers from molesting any Neutral Vessels on the high Seas, except they were laden with Contraband Goods, or were carrying Soldiers to the Enemy.

The Commission of this Privateer was not granted untill Sept 1778, as will appear by the records of the Trial.

It is therefore on the Plea of having placed implicit Faith on the Ordinances of Congress, that this Claim will be Supported. The Danish Vessel in Consequence thereof having loaded with British Property—& the Underwriters who are the Representatives of the Owners, as far as the Cargo was insured, having in the Same Confidence made the Insurance proportionably low.

It will be found that the Plaintiffs, aware of the Force of this Plea, had instituted a Suit for the recovery of the Vessel likewise (for which the United States are equally responsible) claiming her as Prize, & therefore, not Neutral.

By Mr Davis's Letter to the Secretary of State, as late as Nov 1 1796, it will be Seen that the action for the recovery of this Vessel Still continued.[3]

Now long before this Period, they were in Possession of a Document, which afforded incontrovertable Proof of the Vessel being Danish, derived from the Same Authority, which had informed them that the Cargo was British, as you will observe by the enclosed Copy of the Answers to their

Queries, which they had (thro their Correspondent) put to the Shippers of the Cargo at Cork.[4]

And there is no doubt that this Testimony obtained in Augt 1793, was the only Proof they have ever acquired of the Cargo being British.

But on consulting the records of this very extraordinary Suit in the Circuit Court in 1794, it will be found that this important Proof of the Cargo being British, So calculated to make an Impression, was never produced to the Court or Jury.

The Reason is evident. It would have altogether defeated their Hopes— as well with respect to a Judgment for the Vessel, which was the Object of our Suit, as for the Value of the Cargo, which was the other Point in View—for it will be observed, that the Same Document, that proved the Cargo British, contained the fullest & most unequivocal Testimony that the Vessel was Danish.

Now, Under the Authorities they derived from their Commission, they had no right to molest or capture this Cargo, Sailing under the Protection of a Neutral Danish Flag. On the Contrary there was a Strict Prohibition against it.

In order therefore to obtain Judgment, in the Suit for the Cargo, they relied Solely on the Evidence of a Witness who deposed, that whilst acting in a public Character, I had been in possession of this Property, which their Privateer had Captured, & that I refused to deliver the Same, when he was authorized to receive it from me—& on this Exhibition of Evidence, without any Proof of Prize, was the Verdict of the Jury, under the Direction of the Court, founded. All Testimony to prove by what Authority it came into my Possession, the Destination of the Proceeds, after it was Sold, by order of the General, the release of the Vessel being Neutral, by the Same Orders, & the Papers found on board which ascertained this Point, were all offered by the Council & rejected by the Court.

With Such feeble & unsubstantial Testimony, & a Court & Jury Similarly constituted, & the Same Prejudices excited, they will likewise recover from the United States, the Value of the Vessel—for She too had been captured, & She had been in my Possession. But it is unnecessary to dwell on these Points at present, as they will probably form a Subject of Serious Enquiry.

It is not unlikely that Application from the Claimants of the Proceeds of this Cargo may be made in the first Instance to me, after they have heard of the Destination of these Funds. To be prepared for Such an Event, I must request that you would be So obliging as to enclose to me an authenticated Copy of the Certificate of the Marquis de Bouille,[5] which will exhibit the Conditions of the Trust, & will authorize me in referring the Parties to Congress, who will after an Investigation of the respective Claims of the Parties, before a competent Tribunal, form their Decision, & give their Orders for the Delivery of the Balance, (according to the Words of the Trust) to whomsoever they may of right belong.

For my own part, I am most anxious to disburthen myself of these funds, which it is evident I accepted with reluctance, & which have been, Since they were brought back into my Possession, a Source of great Trouble & Vexation. I have the honor to be respectfully sir Your obedt hbe ser

WM BINGHAM

RC and enclosure (DNA: RG 76, British Spoliations, 1794–1824, Unsorted Papers). Docketed by Wagner.

1. Letter not found.
2. Worthington C. Ford et al., eds., *Journals of the Continental Congress, 1774–1789* (34 vols.; Washington, 1904–37), 11:486.
3. John Davis, then U.S. district attorney for Massachusetts, represented the government against the Cabot family claimants in the *Hope* case (Alberts, *Golden Voyage*, pp. 365–66).
4. Bingham enclosed a "Copy of the Answers of Denroches & Thompson, Shippers of the Cargo of the Brig Hope, of Arundel, to the Queries of the Owners of the Privateer Pilgrim, as presented to them by their Correspondent at Cork," 31 July 1793 (2 pp.).
5. JM enclosed a certified copy of the marquis de Bouillé's certificate in a letter to Bingham of 14 Apr. 1803 (DNA: RG 59, DL, vol. 14).

From William C. C. Claiborne

MISSISSIPPI TERRITORY TOWN OF WASHINGTON

SIR, September 12. 1802

On the 8th Instant, I had the honor to receive your Communication of the 20th of July,[1] and on the next day, I published a hand Bill, addressed "to persons Claiming Lands within the Mississippi Territory,["] and of which the enclosed is a Copy.[2]

In my publication, I have endeavoured to comply literally with your instructions, and I trust the Language which is used, cannot be construed "as Committing the Government on [one] hand, or damping expectations, too much on the other."

There exist a variety of Tittles for Land in this Territory, and I fear, it will not be in my power, to detail them with accuracy, but I shall carefully collect the best information, within my reach, and will make a General Communication to you, on the subject early in November.

I find that some designing men are endeavouring to impress upon the Citizens an opinion, that the filing of their Claims will be injurious to them; I do not yet know, how far they may succeed; It is however probable, that they may excite some alarm, and prevent a General return of Claims.

Under Cover of a letter, which I addressed to you, on the 20th of January last³ was inclosed a Communication made to me, by Mr Harding, at that time, the Attorney General for this District, stating the situation of some Claims for Land: A Copy of Mr Harding's Communication having been mislaid in my office, I will thank you to furnish me with *one* from your files. With great respect and Esteem I am Sir Your most obt. Servt

(Signed)   WILLIAM C. C. CLAIBORNE

Letterbook copy and copy of enclosure (Ms-Ar: Claiborne Executive Journal). Enclosure (4 pp.) printed in Rowland, *Claiborne Letter Books*, 1:177–80.

1. Claiborne referred to JM's letter of 26 July 1802.
2. *To Persons Claiming Lands within the Mississippi Territory . . . William C. C. Claiborne. Town of Washington, Sept. 9th, 1802* (Natchez, Miss., 1802; Shaw and Shoemaker 2676).
3. *PJM-SS*, 2:413.

§ From Stephen Cathalan, Jr. *12 September 1802, Marseilles*. Mentions that this dispatch will be sent to JM via William Lee at Bordeaux as was his last of 6 Sept. Transmits three packets of dispatches from James Leander Cathcart for JM and a letter to Messrs. Sammert and Brown, which Cathcart in a letter of 3 Sept. asked Cathalan to forward "to Some port of the Atlantic ocean . . . to prevent the possibility of their falling into the hands of any of the Barbarians." On 9 Sept., received a 12 Aug. letter from James Simpson with news of the reestablishment of peace between the U.S. and Morocco. Reports that on 9 Aug. a Swedish frigate arrived with a convoy of Swedish merchantmen and two American ships, the *Venus* of Newport and the *Columbia* of Providence. An eleven-day quarantine was required for all the ships, which had been at Gibraltar, but the Swedish frigate and merchantmen took on provisions and sailed after five days. The American ships completed the quarantine with no sickness on board; however, within a few days three crewmen from the *Columbia* fell sick, two of whom died. A diagnosis was made of "Malignant Fever with Symptoms of the yellow Fever," and the *Columbia* was ordered to return to quarantine. The ship was subsequently released and then quarantined again after two more men became ill. Of the fourteen crewmen on the *Columbia*, five fell sick and three died; this "may be Deemed Sufficient to alarm the French aut[h]orities and this populous City." Encloses a copy of his official correspondence on the subject.¹ "All the French or neutral merchantmen from the West indie⟨s⟩ on their arrival here are Submitted to a quarantine, and precautions are not Spared to prevent the introduction in This place of the yellow Fever or any other Epidemical disease." Describes the case of a newly appointed commercial agent of Russia who, as a native of France, was reportedly apprehensive he could not get an exequatur but "he obtained it without the least difficulty. The question is whether the Minister was or not informed he is a french Native." Once he is able to question this man, Cathalan will make a new application for his own exequatur through the offices of his patron, Joseph Bonaparte, "stating this fact as it is."

RC and enclosure (DNA: RG 59, CD, Marseilles, vol. 1). RC 5 pp.; docketed by Wagner. For enclosure, see n. 1.

1. The enclosure, "A Copy of the official Correspondance which has taken place relatively to the Ship Columbia of Providence, G. A. Hallowel Master," 12 Sept. 1802 (6 pp.; partly in French), includes Samuel W. Greene to Cathalan, 31 Aug. 1802, announcing the return of the *Columbia* to quarantine and complaining that the commissary of police had stationed a number of soldiers on board ship; Cathalan to Greene, 31 Aug. 1802, promising to "do the Needfull near the proper aut[h]orities" of Marseilles; Cathalan to the commissary of police, 31 Aug. 1802, enclosing Greene's letter and objecting to the posting of armed men on the ship as being contrary to the 1778 convention between France and the U.S.; commissary of police to Cathalan, 31 Aug. 1802, defending his decision to place five soldiers on board the *Columbia* for the duration of the quarantine; Cathalan to the commissary of police, 9 Sept. 1802, requesting a meeting with the latter. The enclosure ends with Cathalan's note, "I am, now, Making proper applications to obtain if there is no more danger, the free pratick of the Columbia and Crew."

§ From William Eaton. *12 September 1802, Tunis.* Has suggested in former communications that "when these regencies prevail on a tributary national Agent to state a demand to his Gov. they raise an assumpsit on this compliance. I have consequently been uniform in refusing to state their demands. Steady to this resolution I now refuse to write for a thirtysix gun frigate." The bey decided to write demanding the ship himself but requested that "I should *make a form* of the letter which he would send the President under his signature." Has refused.

In a 29 Aug. conversation at the palace, tried to discourage this demand by pointing to "our late delivery of regalia" and the terms of U.S. treaty with Tunis. "I asked the minister, If he was not ashamed to make the demand after having received such valuable presents from the UStates, and so lately? He answered in substance—'The presents already received were mere *peace stipulations*, which ought to have been delivered years ago. . . . It is six years since your peace negociation was begun. We expected full payment in a year. You came out with nothing. . . . You have made us no consideration for this forbearance. . . . We shall expect a different answer to this request. His Excellency, my master, is a man of great forbearance; but he knows what steps to take with the nations who exhaust his patience with illusive expressions of friendship—as you have learnt from the Danes, Spaniards, and others. . . . We shall expect therefore that you will give us your influence to obtain us a frigate. . . . And should a rupture happen and [the president] be made acquainted with your neglect of duty, he must impute the cause to you alone!' To which I answered—Let the Bey write the President. He can undoubtedly state his pretensions with more perspicuity than I can."

At the palace on 2 Sept. the demand was repeated to Eaton's dragoman who replied that Eaton would not write either directly or indirectly. "The Minister said 'It is what all the tributary Consuls do—and the American is in an error if he thinks to break our established customs!'" Eaton met with the minister on 4 Sept. when the latter again demanded, "in an imperious tone," a form of a letter to the president. "I asked again on what pretext he founded his claim for a frigate and why he so strenuously insisted on my forming the letter? . . . Said he—'We must have this expression of *friendship*, as you have given the Dey of Algiers. My master . . . don't know what stile would be agreeable to your master. You therefore must form the letter . . . to insure our object.'" Eaton continued to refuse, offering to send the letter if the bey wrote. "'He will write,' said the Minister, irritated, . . . And ordered the Dragoman to come on the 7th. and receive the letter 'Which' said he to me 'you will send off by your Ship express!'" Eaton eventually received the enclosed letter, marked D, on 10 Sept. "There can be little doubt that this demand of the Bey has for its object a pretext of rupture, in case circumstances should encourage his hope of plunder or of greater concessions. He certainly cannot be stupid enough to suppose it will be yielded him. He is penetrating and subtile as he is avaricious; . . . witness the surprize of the Danes in 1800. . . . He certainly starved Mahamet Bashaw out of his kingdom to force him into the hands of his brother. I once thought him partial to the exile, . . . but state policy has outweighed individual attachment. These regencies, though always jealous of and freequently bickering with each other, are one in principle, interest and pursuit; and, of course, either openly or covertly allied in their measures against the Christian nations who furnish them tribute or booty. We find that their arrogance increases in proportion to the moderation of the nations they dare insult." The bey is angered by Eaton's refusal to grant passports to Tripoli for Tunisian merchantmen, although for all the good the blockade has done, he might as well have consented.

On 5 Sept. the *Constellation* arrived off Tunis and Eaton received the enclosed letter, marked A, "from which it will appear that the coast of Tripoli is now totally abandoned by our ships of war. Thus ends the expedition of 1802!" Agrees with Captain Murray that "to *keep up the blockade*, in the manner it has been kept up, is of no avail" but thinks Murray's abandonment of the coast goes too far. "The circumstance however furnishes additional evidence of the accuracy of my uniform opinion that *our present mode of warfare is not sufficiently energetic.* The idea of 'giving security to our trade by frequent convoy' will be found as unavailing as the blockade. Our merchantmen, impatient of long delay, will hazard themselves at sea; and the enemy, finding no impediment before his port, will become more enterprizing." The expense of this measure would be great and last indefinitely. "Would it not be more safe and less expensive to buy a peace? . . . But are the Government and people of the UStates prepared for this abasement!"

On 8 Sept. the *Constellation* appeared again. The following day the bey sent Eaton a message: "'Tell the American Consul I will not suffer the ships of war of his nation to cruise in my harbor. If they enter here they shall anchor, their commanders come ashore, according to custom let me know their object and their wants—and pay me and the neutrality of my port the respect due to a sovereign!' I returned the message 'Tell the Bey . . . when he will pay our ships of war the same respect as those of other nations in amity I will . . . be responsible that the civilities shall be reciprocated. But so long as he refuses the *usual* salute to our flag, and withholds the customary present of provisions to our ships of war, as has hitherto been the case, if he expects gratuitous compliments he must be disappointed. . . . In the mean time our ships of war would cruise on his coast and look into his ports whenever circumstances rendered it expedient.'"

States that "on delivery of the regalia from London last spring I proposed some alterations in the treaty; particularly the articles of duty and salutes" but the dey said he was "satisfied with the treaty as it is." The minister added that if the treaty was renewed, more "peace presents" would be expected. Notes that commercial prospects have changed in the last year, as the French "are binding these regencies to conditions which will secure to themselves the exclusive Commerce of this Country." The French pay 3 percent on imports; Americans by treaty pay 10 percent. "This however is not a very weighty matter: the commerce of the UStates with this country will never be likely to become an object: These people flatter themselves of profiting of our commercial enterprizes on easier terms."

Encloses triplicate copy of 18 Aug. letter from Murray, marked B, the original of which he received 2 Sept., "by which it will appear that notwithstanding he *differed much with regard to my ideas* on the project with Mahamet Bashaw when at Gibraltar, he has at length come into the General measure and taken the most direct steps to defeat the object." Asserts that all his efforts have gone to prevent the pasha from going to Derna; yet Murray has offered to take him there in the *Constellation*. "It is singular that the Capn. should not have apprehended that the circumstance alone of the Bashaw's going to that place in an enemy's frigate would excite a just suspicion of treachery!" Besides, Derna is a fortified town and the frigate would have been seized in port. If the pasha proceeds to Derna "he will certainly be put to death." The captain's letter is "evidence of a conviction of the error of his judgement, passed on this measure at Gibraltar," but his compliment of "*respect for my unwearied zeal to serve my Country* is not sufficient indemnity" for the injury caused by the mistake.

Also encloses depositions, marked C, taken two days after receiving Murray's letter of 18 Aug. "They place his declarations relative to taking the Gloria's men in a doubtful point of view."

Observes that since Murray's arrival in the Mediterranean "he has taken steps tending to defeat measures calculated to distress the enemy and effect an honorable and secure peace to the UStates; countenanced conduct tending to encourage sedition and mutiny in the merchant vessels of the UStates; neglected his duty in suffering all vessels to pass unvisited from Gibraltar to this place; and finally abandoned his post before the enemy without orders, and thereby left the coast clear for the departure of cruisers of any force and for the entry of all prizes they may make, to the disgrace of the arms and prejudice of the interests of the UStates." Makes these points to show that the U.S. needs more commanders like Truxtun, Shaw, and Sterett, whom Murray refers to as "*mad-men*." When the U.S. squadron first appeared, the enemy's naval force was at sea, their shore defenses in disrepair, and "scarcely a sentinel on their ramparts," but Commodore Dale did not take advantage of the situation and the occasion was lost. Then the project to capture the Tripolitan admiral failed, and the U.S. warships abandoned the coast. Next, the "strategem" of using the pasha's brother was resorted to. "But this project is finally lost also. It has been sacrificed to a punctilio—or disconcerted through weakness."

"During these transactions the enemy has gained more than a year to strengthen himself at home—to attach allies to his cause abroad—and to fortify his arrogance by capture of our citizens! And what have we acquired? National contempt! We must now, as it were, begin the war anew.... Or we must subscribe to a peace which will entail on posterity eternal humiliation and unlimited pecuniary sacrifices."

On 28 Aug. four French warships arrived at Tunis from Algiers, having settled their differences with Algiers "*à l'amiable!*" However "humbled by the french," the dey "is left intire in all his resourses to humble smaller nations." On 31 Aug. the

French admiral and suite presented the bey with a gold saber studded with diamonds worth about $2,160. The same day the bey proclaimed "*That no turk insult a Frenchman on pain of death!*" Four Turkish armed watchmen were condemned for trying to arrest a number of French officers in the streets the evening of the same day; they were reprieved through the intervention of the admiral. "When shall we see these distinctions paid to an American squadron!"

The French mission's object is not yet clear. It is rumored that the French demand an indemnity for ships captured at Tunis by the British on 9 Mar. 1796 and the liberation of 150 Sardinian slaves, "descendants from Piedmont." "Whatever is demanded will be yielded. . . . But a most important article of this convention, as it effects us, is that the flag of the Italian and Ligurian republics shall be free! I am told the same article is yielded to by Algiers. This deprives the regencies of a grand source of plunder."

The Danes have renewed their peace with Tripoli for $20,000 and an annual payment of $5,000. A stipulation of the convention, according to the enclosed letters from Nissen of 16 and 24 Aug., is that the Danish consul "*shall not interfere in the American affairs.*" This contradicts the assurances given by the king of Denmark through an 11 July 1801 letter from the board of Barbary affairs in Copenhagen, a copy of which Eaton forwarded to the State Department. "The same document shows that this is a project concerted with a view of placing the affairs of the UStates at Tripoli under the influence of an *Algerine Jew* and *a Spaniard!* . . . I believe there can be no doubt that the Jews at Algiers influenced the rupture with Tripoli with a view of getting Mr. Cathcart out of the Country. . . . Both Farfarra and DeSouza (the Spaniard) are known enemies to Mr. Cathcart. How long will Government suffer foreigners, whose interests are so much opposed to those of the UStates as these, to intermeddle with our affairs?"

The bey expects the *Gloria* to be sent to the U.S. with his letter, but Eaton will send the ship to Leghorn for sale. Has instructed Captain Bounds to proceed directly to the U.S. and deliver the bey's letter. "I really do not know what measures to adopt to meet the exactions, importunities and arrogance of these people. If my resistance should influence a rupture I am apprehensive I may incur the disapprobation of my country. If I should yield to their instances I am conscious I should merit it."

RC and enclosures (DNA: RG 59, CD, Tunis, vol. 2, pt. 1); letterbook copy and copies of enclosures (CSmH). RC 10 pp.; docketed by Wagner as received 18 Mar. Extract from letterbook copy printed in Knox, *Naval Documents, Barbary Wars*, 2:271–73. Enclosures are copies of (A) Alexander Murray to Eaton, 5 Sept. 1802, stating that he had given up the blockade of Tripoli and was proceeding to Naples and Leghorn (2 pp.; for another copy, see ibid., 2:266); (B) Murray to Eaton, 18 Aug. 1802, objecting to comments about him and the ship *Gloria* made by Eaton in a letter of 11 July but praising Eaton's efforts, reporting on naval action at Tripoli, and informing Eaton that he "had a communication with the Legal Bashaw of Tripoli, & offered to take him to Derne, & to aid him in any measures he chose to pursue, but he thinks it will be more to our advantage, as well as his, to go there in an English Brig that he hath Chartered & to try what force he can raise there, in as private a manner, as possible" (3 pp.; for another copy, see ibid., 2:238–39); (C) depositions dated 4 Sept. 1802 by Capt. Joseph Bounds, mate Michael McKee, and seamen John Waller and William Martin of the *Gloria*, testifying to the actions of Murray in regard to the ship (4 pp.), and a certification by

George G. Coffin and Charles Wadsworth, 22 Aug. 1802, signifying their support of Eaton's plan and his enlistment of the *Gloria* (3 pp.; not in CSmH; printed in *ASP, Claims*, p. 330); (D) the bey of Tunis to the president of the U.S., 8 Sept. 1802, expressing his pleasure at the stores and jewels sent by the U.S. to confirm the peace with Tunis and asking for an additional present of a thirty-six-gun frigate (2 pp.; in French; translation printed ibid., p. 331); Nissen to Eaton, 16 Aug. 1802, reporting that the American prisoners were being taken care of but that the pasha had made it an article of his convention with Denmark that Nissen was not to interfere in any nation's business but his own (4 pp.); and Nissen to Eaton, 24 Aug. 1802, announcing that the pasha was sending peace overtures to O'Brien at Algiers through the dey (1 p.).

From Thomas Jefferson

Dear Sir   Monticello Sep. 13. 1802.

I now return you the papers which came in your letter of the 11th. I am not satisfied that the ground taken by Chancellor Livingston is advantageous. For the French government & the Spanish have only to grant him all he asks (and they will in justice & policy do that at once) and his mouth must be shut: because after-sought objections would come from him to great disadvantage. Whereas the true & solid objection remains in full force, after they shall have the merit of granting all he asks.

Judge Law's letter can be nothing more than an effort to save himself from the appearance of retreating.[1] The Commrs. will surely exhibit their appointments to him, in the expectation of being called into action. If they do not the District attorney (according to what I propose) will on the application of the judge ask appointments from us.

I inclose you a letter from the Mayor of New York, who asks a guard or guards from us to prevent the French blacks from escaping into the country.[2] If a guard to their hospital would suffice, that could be admitted under the provisions of the Quarantine law: and Genl. Dearborne (with whom I concur) seems disposed to this. I think therefore to leave to his discretion to order the guard. But I think it would be well that you should write a friendly explanation of the measure to mr. Pichon, to whom it might otherwise wear an unfriendly aspect. I cannot but view this case as still lying substantially within the police of the states, and that we have only small & incidental relations with it; viz. as within the cases of contraband or smuggling. Colo. Monroe has in contemplation to carry his family down on Thursday, not to return. Mr. Short & Bp. Madison arrived here yesterday. We shall hope to see you here before Monroe goes, as I think an interview with him would not be unuseful. Will you be pleased to order a commission for Wm. Carey to be collector of York vice Wm. Reynolds dead? Accept my affectionate salutations.

Th: Jefferson

P. S. Return Livingston's letter to the War office.

RC (DLC); FC (DLC: Jefferson Papers).

1. See Brent to JM, 7 Sept. 1802, and n. 4.
2. The letter enclosed by Jefferson has not been found, but it was no doubt Edward Livingston's letter to Henry Dearborn, which Dearborn sent to Jefferson, noting that "an extract . . . has been transmitted to the Secretary of State, conceiving that the subject generally came more immediately under the direction of his Department" (Dearborn to Jefferson, 8 Sept. 1802 [DLC: Jefferson Papers]). For the copy sent to JM, see Brent to JM, 7 Sept. 1802.

§ From Israel Smith. *13 September 1802, Rutland.* Has received the president's letter of 27 Aug.[1] concerning recommendations for commissioners of bankruptcy; "it is the first intimation which I have received that the President wished me to make a recommendation." Suggests the appointment of six general commissioners—three in the vicinity of Rutland and three near Windsor. Believes Attorney General Bradley is more qualified to nominate from the eastern district. Recommends Samuel Prentiss, Darius Chipman, a Rutland attorney, and Richard Skinner, a Manchester lawyer.

RC (DNA: RG 59, LAR, 1801–9, filed under "Chipman"). 2 pp.; docketed by Jefferson. Chipman was appointed but declined serving (Chipman to JM, 6 Dec. 1802 [ibid.]). Richard Skinner (1778–1833) held a number of state and federal offices in his political career, including terms in the U.S. House of Representatives, 1813–15, and as governor of Vermont, 1820–23.

1. See Jefferson to JM, 27 Aug. 1802, and n. 3.

§ From Elias Vander Horst. *13 September 1802, Bristol.* Since his last letter of 1 Sept. [not found], has received JM's of 26 July[1] "and thank you for the order you have been so kind as to give Mr. King for payment of my small demand." Reports that the harvest is near completion "and is undoubtedly very abundant, & which is said to be the case also on the European Continent in General." Begs reference to the enclosed paper and congratulates JM on "the happy termination of the dispute with Morocco."

RC (DNA: RG 59, CD, Bristol, vol. 2). 1 p. Copy (ibid.), written on the verso of Vander Horst to JM, 25 Sept. 1802, is docketed by Wagner as received 20 Nov. Enclosure not found.

1. See JM to King, 26 July 1802, n.

§ From Josef Yznardy. *13 September 1802, Cadiz.* Has heard from the British consul general at Madrid, John Hunter, newly arrived from Lisbon, "that the Portugues Government have determin'd to deny entrance to all American Produce in that Kingdom."

RC (DNA: RG 59, CD, Cadiz, vol. 1). 1 p.; in a clerk's hand, signed by Yznardy. Docketed by Wagner as received 26 Nov.

From Daniel Brent

DEAR SIR,   WASHINGTON, September 14. 1802.

Your two letters of the 7th Inst. reached me yesterday,[1] with the several enclosures to which they refer. The letters to Mr Fitzsimons and the Boston Commee. of Merchants are sent on, copies having been first taken for the Office: A Copy likewise of that to Higginson and others was forwarded to Mr Fitzsimons. I have not heared a word about the french negroes arrived at New York, since the date of my last, nor of any measures on the part of the Commanders of the frigates to prevent their dispersion within this Country. General Dearborne is equally uninformed on the subject. Mr Pichon is still at New York. I learnt from him, before his departure, that the Interdiction to land these Negroes at Carthagena, whither they were sent from Guadaloupe, had been altogether unforeseen, and that the Commodore of the Squadron, in consequence thereof, immediately dispatched one of the frigates under his Command to Guadaloupe for orders, to be brought to him at New York, where he has since rendezvoused. Mr Pichon told me also, as no orders were then received from Guadaloupe, he should send the vessels and negroes to france, and I suppose he is now taking measures for that purpose. Under these Circumstances it is hardly worth your while, I presume, to give yourself any trouble on the occasion, 'till some formal Representation shall be made that may require the further Interference of the General Government. The Report concerning our Collision with Tunis has never been cleared up. The letter from Eaton, herewith sent, which came through Mr King's hands[2] (and was accompanied by Triplicates of his Correspondence, which you have seen, respecting the Rival Brother of the Bashaw of Tripoli) gives little or no satisfaction on this point. But Mr Gavino's letter, herewith likewise forwarded, confirms the Truth of Another very unpleasant article of Intelligence—that of the Capture, by the Tripolitans, of an American Merchantman.[3] The Dispatches from Mr Simpson consist of Duplicates & Triplicates of letters that you already have. The Navy Department has received no late letters from the Mediterranean. I have furnished Mr Brooks, at Boston, with an extract from Mr Bulkley's letter, herewith sent, so far as it relates to the Schooner Samuel, in which he is interested.[4] I am, Dear sir, with sincere esteem and Great Respect, Your Obedt & very faithful servt.

DANL BRENT.

RC (DLC). Docketed by JM.

1. Letters not found.
2. See Rufus King to JM, 23 June 1802, and n. 1.
3. See John Gavino to JM, 8 July 1802.
4. See Thomas Bulkeley to JM, 16 July 1802, and n. 3.

§ From James Maury. *14 September 1802, Liverpool.* Has received JM's letter of 17 June and will "make application in the manner you have been so obliging as to point out." "Wishing much to have you furnished with the particulars of Imports & Exports as ℔ your circular of 1st Augt 1801, I applied to the person who has the exclusive privilege of granting such information from this Custom House. He informed me . . . that he could not undertake it for less than sixty pounds ℔ annum. I did not consider myself warranted to pay such a sum for it, & therefore have made it out in the best manner I could from such documents as I could obtain." Encloses a statement for the six months ending 30 June [not found]. Most of the traffic is in exports by American vessels; "it may be said we monopolize that branch of the carrying trade." Encloses an act of Parliament allowing the importation in American ships of "certain articles not the produce of the U.S.A. to be warehoused for exportation" until January 1804; "but it is important to the Merchants to know that Cotton not the produce of the U.S.A. can no longer be admitted in our vessels for home consumption as it was during the late war."

RC and enclosure (DNA: RG 59, CD, Liverpool, vol. 2). RC 2 pp.; in a clerk's hand, signed by Maury; docketed by Wagner. Surviving enclosure (3 pp.) is *An Act for Repealing Several Acts . . . Relating to the Admission of Certain Articles of Merchandize in Neutral Ships . . .* (London, 1802), passed 22 June 1802.

§ From James Simpson. *14 September 1802, Tangier.* No. 50. "I have this day taken the liberty of drawing a Bill on you to order of Mr Edward Humphry, payable thirty days after presentation for Two thousand dollars, on Account of Sallary; which request you will be pleased to direct being paid. Including this Bill, I have since my appointment to this Consulate, drawn for Ten thousand dollars in all, on Account of Sallary."

RC (DNA: RG 59, CD, Tangier, vol. 1). 1 p.; docketed by Wagner as received 8 Apr. 1803.

To Thomas Jefferson

DEAR SIR   Sepr. 15. 1802

I have duly recd. yours of the 13th. I had been apprised of the application by the Mayor of N Y. for a guard. Considering as you do, that the federal Govt. have only an incidental connection with the case of the French Negroes, I have waited for more particular information concerning them, before writing to Pichon, who I learnt from Mr. Brent, and also from himself, was exerting himself to get them away.[1] His plan was to ship them to France, but he was at a loss for the means. I had my fears that if prematurely pressed on the subject, it might lead to applications for aid. The mail of tomorrow, I hope will bring me from Mr. Brent an answer to some enquiries which will assist in framing a proper letter to him.

I am sorry to learn that Col. Monroe is so soon to leave Albemarle with his family. I had assured myself that I should see him on our visit to his neighbourhood, as your letter intimated that he would not leave it till tuesday next. We propose to be with you, accompanied by Dr. Thornton his lady & her mother, on saturday evening, and still hope, that the oppy. may not be lost. It will add to the satisfaction, to find Bishop Madison as well as Mr. Short at Monticello. I shall direct a commission to be made out for Mr. Cary to take the place of Mr. Reynolds. Yours as ever

JAMES MADISON

RC (DLC: Jefferson Papers). Docketed by Jefferson as received 16 Sept.

1. See Brent to JM, 7 Sept. 1802. Pichon's letter has not been found.

§ From William Willis. *15 September 1802, Barcelona.* Encloses copies of letters "giving information of the affairs of Tripoli, with the objects the Triplins Seem to have in view."[1] Commodore Morris in the schooner *Enterprize* passed within sight of Barcelona on 12 Sept., "and I Extremely regret his not Calling, because but three or four days before, there was a Tripoline Cruiser of About thirty Tons on this Coast." Has been investigating reports that some counterfeit American ship's papers were made in Barcelona. "Although some Circumstances have furnished strong presumptions, I have not yet been Able to obtain any positive proof of it. . . . I Gave orders to my Vice-Consul Mr. Stirling to investigate it . . . in my Absence, . . . but on Demanding of Mr. Stirling whether he had obeyed my orders, I found he had not, and he has given me no very Satisfactory reasons, why he did not. . . . The most Certain information I have, of the Existence of false Papers, is, through Mr. Adams, whose affidavit I enclose you,[2] and Also the information of Mr. Kirkpatrick,[3] who, I think did not act properly in Shewing my official Letter to the Capn., . . . and in Neglecting taking his Oath upon the Subject, and not taking the name of the Person he Receiv'd these Papers from. Capn. Lee Seems very Angry at my enquiry, and insinuates to Mr. Kirkpatrick quite a different name from those he told Mr. Adams, . . . as Mr. Adams could never have mistaken the Name of Samadet & Cushing for Lewis, and a Mercantile house no way Ressembles a master of a Ship. . . . But Capn. Lee Seems in his Anger to have insinuated the name of Lewis, in order to bring Suspicion on me if possible, because no doubt he had understood I had a Share in the Ship Lewis Commands, which I have. This Ship was fitted out in my Absence and Sailed from this Port while I was in france. . . . I Shall Continue my investigation and give you the result of it in a few days, as well as a Copy of all the Documents I have Relating to the Subject. . . . The fitting out of the Ship Pomona originated with Mr. Benjamin B. Mumford of Rhode island, Mr. Wm. Baker of Boston, and Capn. Thomas Lewis, and it was with much Persuasion that I took a Small Share of ¼₀th. part. . . . [I] have Since found to my Cost that it was little better than a Swindling trick, of the two first, for having Confided the fitting out of the Ship to them in my Absence to france, and particularly to Mr. Mumford, they hurried away the Ship and brought my house into the Advance of Abt. fifteen thousand Drs. which I have not Since been Able to get, and Almost despair of ever getting it. How many other tricks of vilany were played by

Mr. Mumford, I know not, but know him very Capable of them, for he has Even Seduced one of the Clerks of my house to falsify my books."

RC and enclosures (DNA: RG 59, CD, Barcelona, vol. 1). RC 4 pp.; in a clerk's hand, signed by Willis. Docketed by Wagner as received 25 Nov. Brief extract printed in Knox, *Naval Documents, Barbary Wars*, 2:275. For enclosures, see nn. Also filed with the RC are copies of other letters concerning the counterfeit ship's papers, including Willis to William Kirkpatrick, 17 Aug. 1802 (1 p.), which stated that Capt. George G. Lee in the brig *Joseph* was bound for Málaga and related the information provided by John Adams, "in order that you may do what you think proper"; George Lee to Willis, 1 Sept. 1802 (2 pp.), denying that he received the false papers from Samadet & Cushing, protesting that the papers were not the business of U.S. consular agents, and expressing surprise that Willis was questioning a matter which "if properly investigated, would Redound so little to your honour"; and Willis to Kirkpatrick, 15 Sept. 1802 (2 pp.), protesting his showing the letter to Lee and not getting a sworn statement from him.

   1. The enclosed correspondence (3 pp.), dated by Willis at Barcelona, 15 Sept. 1802, and certified as a true copy, was another copy of the correspondence relating to Andrew Morris's capture that Stephen Cathalan had sent JM (see Cathalan to JM, 6 Sept. 1802, n. 1). Extracts of the copy sent by Willis are printed in Knox, *Naval Documents, Barbary Wars*, 2:259.
   2. In his affidavit to Willis, 16 Aug. 1802 (1 p.), John Adams, an American citizen in Barcelona, testified that about 26 July on board the brig *Joseph*, George G. Lee showed him what seemed to be exact reproductions of blank American ship's papers and that he thought Lee said he got them from Samadet & Cushing of Marseilles, who had told Lee they were made at Barcelona.
   3. Kirkpatrick's letter to Willis, 1 Sept. 1802 (2 pp.; docketed by Wagner as received in Willis's 15 Sept. dispatch) reported that Lee had shown him a set of counterfeit American ship's papers and told him he was carrying them to Boston to show some friends; when Kirkpatrick subsequently showed him Willis's 17 Aug. letter, Lee "very Candidly Confessed that Samadet & Cushing did not give them to him, but that an American Capn., I think of the Name of Lewis, had done it, . . . that he was informed they had been made at your place, [and] that he was now determined to forward the Papers to the Secretary of State on his Arrival at Boston" (extract printed ibid., 2:263).

¶ From Lewis G. Gobs. Letter not found. *15 September 1802*. Acknowledged in Daniel Brent to Gobs, 12 Oct. 1802 (DNA: RG 59, DL, vol. 14). Brent informed Gobs that JM had directed him to say that "he sincerely sympathises with you in your misfortunes, and regrets exceedingly that it is not in his power to serve you—no opportunity being known to him, by which he can render you the assistance which seems to be the object of your letter."

§ From Peder Blicherolsen. *16 September 1802, Philadelphia*. "The undersigned having received from his Court the enclosed ordinance, with an order to cause the same to be translated and made publicly known throughout the United States, he thinks it his duty respectfully to offer a copy of the translation to the Department of State previous to the publication."

RC (DNA: RG 59, NFL, Denmark, vol. 1). 1 p.; addressed "To the Department of State." Enclosure not found.

§ From Richard O'Brien. *16 September 1802, Algiers*. Acknowledges JM's letter of 10 May "recd this day inclosed to me Open in one from Consul Gavino of the 30th. Of July." Observes that while he will try to obtain such vouchers as are available, he can get none but what consuls of other nations get—"the Circumstances and System of transacting affairs in this Country will not admit of it." This was fully explained in his dispatches to the State Department and in person to Pickering and Wolcott before he took up his post as consul at Algiers. Has Turkish certificates for the peace stipulations and the first two years of annuities and one for the "Settlement of The 4 years Annuities in November last as detailed in my dispatches & Statements which you acknowledge to have recd." His November dispatches explain the disbursement and expenditure of money "so as to remove every difficulty on this Subject with the Secretary of the treasury."[1]

"You will please Sir to look at yr. letter which accompanied the 30 thousd dollars for the Cash payment of one yrs. annuities,[2] and had I not there done as I did—The Amt. of The Cargo of the Washington would not have turned out to more on the annuities then The One half which it cost in Philadelphia—it was by my haveing it in my power On the Cash paymt to *Bribe* The *Ministry* &c. That gave me The *Opportunity* of Obtaining extra prices on the articles which Composed the Cargo of The Wn. & the Same System I had adopted in Settleing The peace Stipulations & the first 2 yrs. Annuities."

States that a consul who comes to Algiers must give presents of $17,000 to $21,000 and perhaps more "to keep impending difficulties at a distance." No receipt is given by the government. The biennial presents amount to $15,000 to $17,000 if procured in Algiers. "No receipts is given for the Same but they are noted in The books of the regency the time They are given So that they should know when they become again due. All other Occasional and extraordinary presents feese gratuities &c. of every description given by a consul to The dey Ministry &c. no receipts whatsoever for the Same is given—The Consul Only Stateing The motive and amt. and necesity he was under for So Doing to The Govt. he represents."

Asks why an Algerine official would provide him with a receipt when "one did not know what the other did—nor yet knew What The other recd. . . . His receipt in my power . . . would be in this Country Equal to putting his life & property into my power & possesion." Besides, business of this nature is managed through intermediaries such as the Jews, who move like "ferryboats between The Consuls, The dey and Ministry, on all like Occasions of Bribes gratuities &c. on great affairs would the Jews put Themselves in the power of the Consl. to give him receipts that They were a party in bribeing The ministry & that they recd. allso a gratuity for their Services and aid on the business." In Algiers a person's house and papers are subject to search and seizure, and discovery of vouchers such as those required by JM "would be The destruction of The Ministry Jews directory and all persons Concerned."

Nor is it safe for a consul to record this business, although it is his official duty. "If discoverd. it might throw him into Chains And his Country into A Sudden and destructive War." Thus, "this whole business Must depend On the Honour Honesty & Patriotism of The Consul. . . . If I have ever deviateing [*sic*] from my true Course in Studying & Steering for the interests of the UStates it has been owing to Contrary winds Currents &c. that would make & Oblige me to fall of[f] 3 or

5 points but whenever Circumstances permitted I Clung as Close to my Course as posibly in power and has never failed to detail the necesity of thus deviateing, to my Owners The Govt of The US—and I trust that on reviewing my whole conduct in this long Voyage to Barbary That They and all Concerned will Consider that I have not made them a bad voyage."

When the present dey took the throne he demanded a present of maritime and military stores equal to the U.S. peace stipulation, but O'Brien and the Swedish consul managed to put him off, saving the government great expense. Observes that he also saved a valuable cargo of cherry wine carried by the brig *Mary* of Philadelphia. "I did my duty but those affairs with many others Seems to be buried in Oblivion in The department of State."

"I shall presume to ask you Sir If you ever Seen the instructions which was given to me by the *Ex* Govt. for Conducting their affairs in Barbary." The powers of a tributary consul to Algiers are difficult to define. He is to act for the interests of his country; "this Sir I have not deviated from So far as has been in my power in order to Save the peace & prevent The US. from a Sudden War."

Hopes the presence of U.S. frigates in the Mediterranean will induce Tripoli to terminate the war. "But the Misunderstanding between the US. and Morrocco keeps ½ our Meditteranian force in the Vicinity of Gibraltir—this with the Success of the tripoli Corsairs in Captureing Swede &c Americans will induce the Pascha of tripoli to demand perhaps more then the Govt. of The US. has authorized to give. Further last yr. tripoli offered to make a truce with Commodore Dale but it was rejected. . . . If we now purchase the peace with tripoli it is The Same thing as giveing A bounty to Algrs & Tunis to do over acts and make extra demands." Had his advice been followed, as detailed in his dispatches received by the State Department in December 1800,[3] the war might have been avoided. For the U.S. to sue for peace after receiving "Such Gross insults" from Tripoli, "the most insignificantest power in The world, . . . must be Humiliateing & dishonourable in a great degree to The Citizens in general of a great & riseing nation—however all in my power Shall be done to Contribute to The will & desire of The President of The UStates."

"*Relative to keeping The dey of algiers in proper temper* towards The UStates nothing Shall be Omited on my part, . . . but I am sorrow yr letter is so barren or makes no mention of The Vessel & Stores on the Annuities being forwarded for Algrs. . . . Those articles is much looked for &c. Expected—the detention of them at this crisis might leave it out of my power . . . to keep the dey & ministry in proper temper." For intervening on behalf of the U.S. with Tripoli the dey "would expect a gratuity for his letter &c. Services—& he would first ask me where is the Stores on the Annuities. . . . Therefore I have not thought it good policy to wake a sleeping *Lyon*—it might be the means of avoiding A small evil and running us on to a great one—nor do I renounce the Orriginal Idea that the influence of Algiers with Tunis & Particularly with Tripoli—on or relative to our Affairs Should not be omitted or abandoned."

Believes there will be some difficulty in the appointment of Cathcart as U.S. consul at Algiers for several reasons. First, in 1787 Cathcart received "500 Bastenados" for a transgression with a Moorish woman and would have lost his head but for the influence of Capt. George Smith. Second, the dey believes that in 1800 Cathcart intrigued with a Portuguese officer to defraud the pasha of Tripoli, and "all My reasoning arguments & Justification in favour of Mr Cathcart that he was innocent of this malicious Charge . . . could not Errace the idea or stain from the Mind of the dey." Third, "it is not Customary at Algiers to receive a Consul that has been a Consul with A moorish govt. as Morrocco Tunis or Tripoli—Algiers being A turk govt. Considers it to be beneath their dignity." Cites examples, such as the rejection of the Danish consul who had served at Tunis. "Under These Considerations which in general must be unknown to you and the president will not The appointment be Considered here more as an affair to insult & irritate Then to Consolidate friendship between this regency & the US.? . . . I do not pertend to Say that those objections Cannot be overcome, . . . but I have my fears that they Cannot be removed even in A temporary manner with out money and presents, perhaps—from 8 to 12 Thsd dollars." Even if Cathcart should be received and the presents accepted, these objections would continue to be a pretense for removal.

"I Shall Secure myself with Such Vouchers as will in every respect Justify my conduct and prove that I left no Stone Unturned on my part to do What yr. letter of the 10th. of May requires—and Shall not Consider myself Justifyable in resideing Any longer in Algiers, if Mr Cathcart Shld. be rejected, Only in Case that my departure Should endanger the peace." Has no desire to remain in Algiers, but Cathcart's appointment "might throw me and yr affairs into a disagreeable Situation." Will provide Cathcart or any other person the president sends "every information in my power relative to The Conducting in the best manner The affairs of the UStates with This regency—but Sir I think it incumbent on me to keep possesion of all My own papers, Journals dispatches &c. to Ansr. in A Chiefe respect As Vouchers & Testimony of My Conduct in this Country."

Observes that the lack of funds "will be the ruin of our affairs—except The US establishes directly a Shure Credit Somewhere adjacent to Algiers Where the Consul will have it in his power to draw on." Repeats his warning that if there should be peace between the U.S. and the Barbary States "it will be requisite to keep in this Sea 4 frigates—without them what Security from Barbary Caprice will A Valuable and Extended Commerce of the US. have." The capture of the Portuguese frigates and the arrangement Spain made with Algiers in June were detrimental to the affairs of the Danes, Swedes, Dutch, and Americans, but the actions of the French in August have in some respects "*humbled* the *pride* of the dey." Four Portuguese warships are cruising off Algiers, but none of the Algerine corsairs are at sea; the object of the Portuguese is "to try to Catch Some Algerine Corsair or Cargoes of Merchandize—or a load of turks recruits from the levant" in order to exchange them for the four hundred Portuguese captives in Algiers. The dey demands one million dollars ransom, "which with the Usual 15 pr. cent presents & comisions will amt to nearly 1½ Millions of dollars." If Portugal should succeed in making peace "the W. Ocean is free to Them And our Commerce As well as other nations is exposed in both Seas." Presumes under this consideration the president will see the necessity of keeping a U.S. squadron in the Mediterranean.

"You mention That my bill in favour of Capt Shaw is paid & one in favour of my mother for 200 dollars you will observe Sir that the first is a public affair The latter is a private one out of my salary." Will draw on JM for the whole amount of his salary and wishes to be informed what sums are paid out of his salary by the State

Department as he will want to pay a debt owed for money advanced to him on his private account.

Has reviewed his letters from the State Department and concludes that the U.S. government does not pay that attention to Barbary affairs "which The magnitude of the business requires." JM's letter of 10 May has left him without credit or word of the annuities. If this open letter had fallen into the hands of the dey "he would Conclude that the US. did not intend to Send the required Stores on the Annuities and had in a manner protested or Quarrenteened the accts. of yr. own agent." This might have meant war with Algiers. Trusts that in the future "those requisite affairs—relative to Barbary will be fully attended to." Should there be a war, "would not The US. make an Enquiry [in which] The Consuls dispatches & the letters he recd in Ansr. from The department of State would come before The Public That Great Tribunal which would Judge"? Informs JM that in Sweden, Denmark, and Batavia committees are established to aid the State Department on Barbary affairs. "I am in Some respects Sensible of the Multiplicity of business which you have to Attend to, but being fully Sensible of my official duty . . . I am under The necesity of Stateing to you those facts and Circumstances. . . . Our affairs with Barbary as yet has not been fully discused in order to establish A System. On my arrival at The departmt. of state I hope I shall be able to inform you of many particulars which will promote our affairs much in this Country."

"The US. named first a Norfolk Capt as Consul for Algrs. he was not to be found, next Sent or named an ambasador he went to his long home. Next appointed Paul Jones he died in Paris. Next the mision of Mr Lamb and Randel well known to The prest. Presidt. next Col. Humphreys Mr. Donaldson Skjoldebrand Junior & Mr Barlow—Mr. famin Mr. Clarke as Charge des affairs—untill I have been the first Consul of The US. regularly established at Algiers." His reasons for requesting a replacement are his bad health, the fact that the U.S. left him without funds or credit, and his young family, "which in Case of extraordinary events and the Custom of this barbarous Country would be The Victims of Slavery and Despotism." Prays that JM will "View The purport of this long letter in a true and favourable light That nothing has induced me to its Contents—but to Serve and Contribute to The interests of The US."

RC (DNA: RG 59, CD, Algiers, vol. 6). 14 pp. Copy of RC (ibid.), in a clerk's hand, is docketed by Wagner as received 19 May.

1. See O'Brien to JM, 8 and 25 Nov. 1801 (*PJM-SS*, 2:231–32, 272).
2. JM to O'Brien, 21 May 1801 (*PJM-SS*, 1:212–15).
3. On 22 Oct. 1800 O'Brien advised the secretary of state to send "a fleet of six of our best and fastest sailing frigates into this Sea, under the command of such an active man as Commodore Truxton" to forestall Tripolitan aggression (Knox, *Naval Documents, Barbary Wars*, 1: 388–89).

§ From Josef Yznardy. *16 September 1802, Cadiz.* Transmits copies of his letters to JM of 10 and 13 Sept. "The purport of the present is to inclose you Half of the Register of the American Ship Columbia of Glastenbury Capt. Samuel Naylor that has been Sold in this Bay; the other half the owner Mr. Elisha Hale takes with him to America." Also encloses an affidavit of Capt. Mark Collins of the *Fame*, "which intelligence I do not loose a moment to communicate you."

RC (DNA: RG 59, CD, Cadiz, vol. 1). 1 p.; in a clerk's hand, signed by Yznardy. Docketed by Brent. Enclosures not found.

From Thomas Jefferson

DEAR SIR   MONTICELLO Sep. 17. 1802.

I recieved yesterday your's of the 15th. In the hope of seeing you here tomorrow I return no papers. I will pray you not to fail in your visit. I have recd a letter from mr. R. Smith disapproving of the countermand of the John Adams for reasons detailed;[1] & one from mr. Gallatin disapproving of the original order for her sailing.[2] (He had not then, Sep. 9. heard of the countermand.) The vessel now awaits our decision, which I have delayed till the next post, in order to consult with you on the subject. This renders it interesting that you should preserve your purpose of coming tomorrow, when I shall be happy to recieve your's & Dr. Thornton's families & friends. Bp. Madison is gone. Colo. Monroe was to go off yesterday; but I have not heard whether his family is gone or not. If not, he will be back on Tuesday. But I rather expect they are gone. Dr. Bache has broken up house-keeping, ready for his departure.[3] Accept my affectionate salutations.

TH: JEFFERSON.

FC (DLC: Jefferson Papers).

1. For Jefferson's order, see his letter to JM, 6 Sept. 1802, and n. 2. Smith replied on 14 Sept. that, since the crew of the *John Adams* had already been engaged and advanced two months' pay, and a short delay might bring more certain news about the intentions of the emperor of Morocco, he was taking "the liberty to suspend the execution of your Orders until I Shall have the satisfaction of being favored with another letter expressing your determination" (DLC: Jefferson Papers).

2. Gallatin thought that not only was sending an additional frigate unnecessary but "the appropriations for that object were exhausted" (Gallatin to Jefferson, 9 Sept. 1802 [ibid.]).

3. For William Bache's appointment as director of the Marine Hospital at New Orleans, see *PJM-SS*, 2:70 n. 1.

From Robert Taylor

DEAR SIR   Septr. 17th. 1802

I received yours with the papers sent,[1] but own that I do not sufficiently comprehend what it is expected Doctr. Rose is to convey to you to enable me to prepare the proper conveyance. I wish you would make a particular memo: so that no mistake can arise in drawing the deed—no copy of your fathers Will is in my hands. I still think you had better postpone the conveyance to Mrs. Rose until a division has been made when each can convey more definitely what is intended. I am Yr. affte friend

ROBERT TAYLOR

RC (DLC). Docketed by JM.

1. Letter not found. These papers probably pertained to the exchange of property pursuant to the informal addenda to James Madison, Sr.'s will that was challenged by the executor, William Madison (see JM to Isaac Hite, 24 Nov. 1801, *PJM-SS*, 2:268 n. 3).

¶ From Edward Carrington. Letter not found. *17 September 1802*. Mentioned in Daniel Brent to Carrington, 22 Sept. 1802 (DNA: RG 59, DL, vol. 14), as an inquiry about land patents. Brent replied that he had opened the letter in JM's absence and that "the patents in question will be compleated, and sent to you in a few days, the obstacle alluded to being now removed." On 29 Sept. Brent wrote Carrington again (ibid.) explaining that the secretary of war could not certify one of the patents owing to "a defect in the survey of the 1367 acres of land, as this survey does not mention the parts of Warrants, Nos. 73 & 1792, respectively, which were taken for its completion"; he returned the documents for correction and added that the other patent for 1,000 acres would be sent after signature by Jefferson and JM.

§ From William P. Gardner. *18 September 1802, Demerara*. Reports his arrival on 14 Sept. after a passage of forty days from Philadelphia.[1] Met with Nicholas Rousselet, the former U.S. consul, who informed him that the British governor had refused to recognize him in his official capacity because the Jay treaty "made no provision for the Residence of American Consuls in their foreign possessions." Rousselet "further inform'd me that he has written to the Department of State ⟨by⟩ several Conveyances." Has announced his arrival to the governor by the enclosed letter but deems it "inconsistent with the Dignity of the United states to repeat the Application" for recognition.

"The British have still possession of all the Dutch settlements on this Coast. They are now making preperations to evacuate this, as well as their other Conquests in this part of the Globe. Citizen Marteens, the new Governor, appointed under the Batavian Government is expected here in the Course of a very short time to take possession of the Colonies of Demerary and Essequebo." The Americans in both colonies express satisfaction at the appointment of an American "and not a foreigner to represent their Nation."

RC and enclosure (DNA: RG 59, CD, Paramaribo, vol. 1). RC 2 pp. The enclosure is a letter from Gardner to Gov. Anthony Beaujon, 18 Sept. 1802 (1 p.), announcing his arrival but declining to present his commission because of the governor's refusal to recognize Rousselet.

1. Some contemporaries viewed William P. Gardner's appointment as U.S. consul at Demerara and Essequibo in March 1802 as a reward for passing Treasury Department records to

William Duane, editor of the Republican Philadelphia newspaper *Aurora General Advertiser* in 1800. Gardner, a clerk in the auditor's office at the time, furnished Duane with accounts that the editor used to charge Timothy Pickering, Oliver Wolcott, and Jonathan Dayton with misuse of public funds (Kline, *Papers of Burr*, 1:528–29 and n. 1, 530 n. 3).

¶ From Thomas FitzSimons. Letter not found. *18 September 1802*. Acknowledged in JM to FitzSimons, 9 Oct. 1802 (DNA: RG 59, DL, vol. 14). Requests that JM instruct Charles Pinckney to intervene with the Spanish government on behalf of the agent to be sent to Madrid to prosecute American claims in Spanish America.

From Thomas Sumter, Jr.

No. 23
SIR,   PARIS 19 September 1802
   The Minister of the United States left this City on the 1st. inst. on a tour through the Belgique & Holland. I transmitted to you on the same day, his letter No. 22 of that date (a duplicate of which is now enclosed) together with a duplicate of his note to the Minister of Exterior Relations dated the 19 of August on the cession of Louisiana from Spain to France: urging the latter to a recognition of our rights in the Missisipi &c.[1] No notice has been taken of this note; or any one which has pointed to that subject. On the 2d. your dispatch of the 6th. of July, arrived at this office: including the Narrative of Captn. Rodgers, the protest of Captn. Davidson, the copy of Mr. Pichons letter to Genl. Le Clerc & a copy of Mr. Lears commission. These documents afford abundant materials for an appeal to the justice of this government, for the reparation due both to the dignity of the United States and to the feelings of the individuals—and your letter indicates the best modes for the application of these materials. But, when I revert, *on the one hand*, to the series of facts which this government is well apprized of—shewing the amicable dispositions of the United States since the date of the convention (beyond which period of reconciliation, they have no right, in good faith, to seek for causes of complaint) And, when I review, *on the other hand* the settled an[d] systematic disposition displayed by the Minister of Exterior—after the great sacrifices made by the convention, still to narrow the ground of our claims, to oppose difficulties, rather than to obviate them, to the execution of those parts of the treaty which cannot reasonably be contested: When I see in his answer of the 10th. Thermidor—29 July—(which has been sent you)[2] to Mr. Livingstons reclamation of the 19 July in favor of Captns. Rodgers & Davidson, a pre-determination to suppose them guilty notwithstanding he saw the futility of Genl. Le Clercs accusations, and withal, the suspicion & reproach which shine through the varnish of his whole correspondence—I think it may not be

useful to press him with a repetition of complaints, until a more favorable juncture, on a case which he has already prejudged and which cannot be redressed without stigmatizing an Officer who has too much reason to rely on support *in every event* from this government. I shall therefore, I believe, leave it for the consideration of Mr. Livingston, unless he should be absent longer than he intended. I have thought it necessary, Sir, to be thus full on this point, to account to you for delaying to prosecute a subject which seems so justly to engage your solicitude—but which though a strong case makes only an item in the volume of complaint.

By a letter from Mr. Graham of the 15. August, we learn that it is understood at Madrid that the difinitive arrangements have been taken for the cession and evacuation of Louisiana before the French Ambassador St. Cyr left that place. He arrived a few days past in Paris. The french papers say he withdraws in search of health—Report says from disgust. I learn from a gentleman who passed out of Spain in his train, that the latter is most probable. But I presume it must be some personal, rather than National disgust. The stiffness and formality of the people & the laws of that Country, may bend too slowly and sullenly for the quickness & arrogance of the officers of this—but there is no reason to suppose that either of them will not bend, ultimately, as far as shall be required. It is thought there, Florida is not included in the cession: but whether Florida means what it did before the treaty of 63 or since I cannot ascertain. Whether this government really set a high value on this acquisition, or not—whether it is really intended as a point of annoyance to the United States & Spain or only as a *field of promise* to the army and to place hunters—I think it is too highly rated by many—both in France and in America. When we consider, *First* our own strength—*Secondly* The preponderance of England at sea—who from motives of self preservation, now more than ever, will keep the fleets of France and her allies pared down to a low standard—and can, at the first sound of War, destroy, if she cannot retain, all the investments made in their Colonies. *Thirdly* The insecurity, for various reasons of Collonial property, The want of Capital, credit, means, disposition and intelligence in this country to raise its commerce and manufactures to a successful competition with those of other nations.

It is not probable that the Capitalists here will adventure in the colonies, when money is so valuable at home, as to bring them 15. or 20. pr. Ct. & where *the government*[3] destitute of credit is always in the *market* at an enormous loss—for it is believed that notwithstanding the year 10, just expiring has been a year of peace, and they have *paid* none of *their debts* the *revenues* of the whole *year eleven* are already anticipated & they now are obliged to provide at a great sacrifice *fifty-five million* for the *current expenditure* of the ensuing *month*.

I say when we *consider* all these circumstances (without adverting to others of an exterior nature) I think in a very few years they will find Louisiana a burthen. In some of the Nos. of the Journal du Commerce, you will see some mention of appointments said to be made for Louisiana—which never appear in the Official paper. You will also find in them some notice of the transactions at Ratisbon. Doubtless the Emperor will not rilish the scheme of indemnities dictated by France & Russia—but when you remark that the Empire (in which many states favor the plan) is, since the treaty with the Turks of the 4th. June,[4] almost englobed by powers which will take their tone, at present, from this government, you will not doubt of his acquiescence for the time being. The troubles in Helvetia must also soon disappear.

By a late letter from Mr. Simpson dated at Tangier, to Mr. Skipwith, it appears he has succeeded in restoring peace with the Emperor of Morocco—he says nothing of the terms—or means. Enclosed is a letter from Obrien of the 16 August—one of the 22d. which is a duplicate of part of that of the 16. has come to hand[5]—he knew nothing then, of a report which circulated here some time ago, that Captn. McNiel had sunk two Tunisians & beaten a third nor does he seem to know any thing of a later report of the American squadron having landed, & lost some men, in the regency of Tripoli. Both are probably false. You will see by the last Nos. of the Moniteur that some new arrangement has taken place in the administration of this government. That the Grand Juge Regnier has added to his functions those of the Minister of justice and part of those of the Minister General of Police—which office is suppressed—it was the one which rendered its administrator more powerful than any other. The chief part of the business of it will now be done by the Prefet of Police. It is said that in a few days Mr Taleyrand will be transferred to the Ministry of the finances and that Joseph Bonaparte will be called to the department of Exterior Relations & Lucien to the department of War. It is impossible to say whether these reports are well founded or not—at any rate the difference will probably not be great to foreigners. I have lately been informed by a gentleman from London that Mr. Otto speaking of his mission to America was not decisive about it—and at all events, spoke of not going before the next spring. There have been some of the St. Domingo bills paid here, but the payments are made under a regulation which will, doubtless, exclude great part of them. All those not sold or negotiated by the original proprietors are paid but those which have been sold are not paid. And on this distinction being made those of the latter description have been selling at 25 pr. ct. loss. I have the honor to be, Sir, with true esteem & respect your Hbe. Sert.

THO. SUMTER JR.

RC (DNA: RG 59, DD, France, vol. 8). Partly in code (see n. 3). Docketed by Wagner as received 2 Jan.

1. See Livingston to JM, 19 Aug. 1802, and n.
2. See Livingston to JM, 30 July 1802, and n. 6.
3. The italicized words in this paragraph are those encoded by Sumter and decoded here by the editors; the RC has been decoded interlinearly by JM.
4. The treaty of peace between France and the Sublime Porte was signed in Paris on 25 June 1802 (de Clercq, *Recueil des traités de la France*, 1:588–89).
5. See O'Brien to JM, 16 Aug. 1802, with a 22 Aug. addendum, and n.

§ From William Willis. *19 September 1802, Barcelona.* Encloses a false register and Mediterranean pass taken from Capt. Thomas Lewis of the *Pomona.* "I am trying by All means in my power to find out to a Certainty the Author of this fabrication." Believes Lewis is involved; "I understand he has bought a vessel in Egypt & put her under American Colours, and Sold her in Malta, and what makes this Appear Stronger against Capn. Lewis, is his having Shewn Some American papers to Mr. Gautier of this place, previous to his departure." Gautier reported that William Baker, supercargo of the *Pomona,* accompanied Lewis at the time and that he had also seen "a Number of American Papers in Possession of Benjn. B. Mumford." Has no way of knowing how many counterfeit papers are in circulation. "[I] Am informed by a Person that Some of them were Sent to him Some time last winter, with one of the Plates of Engraving for the Pass. But he Assures me he does not know by whom they were Sent, as he found them in his Room at an inn. . . . He has Promised to deliver them to me, and I . . . Shall Send them to you. . . . I Shall demand from Capn. Lewis on Oath how he Came by these Papers which I have found in his possession, but Shall first Strive by moderate means to find out whether he has Any more Papers." Believes the fact that he is part owner of the *Pomona* may have led to "the insolent observations of Capn. George Lee" but declares that "there was no motive in me Even to Connive at a Vilaneous Act Like this, . . . Especially as neither me, nor my house . . . have ever had Any interest in Any other Ship than this one, and a tenth in her was too trifling for me to Sacrifice the interest of my Country, and violate my duty in So Essential a point."

RC (DNA: RG 59, CD, Barcelona, vol. 1). 3 pp.; marked "*Copy.*" In a clerk's hand, signed by Willis; docketed by Wagner. Enclosures not found.

To Albert Gallatin

Sir,   Department of State September 20th. 1802.

I have duly had the honor of receiving your Letter of the 8th. Inst.[1] It does not appear that the money, or any part of it, that you refer to, and which is held in trust by the Secretary of State, "for Jeremiah Condy & Co. and others," can with propriety, be applied towards the payment of a Debt from Jere: Condy or from Jere: Condy and Company to the United States—because Jeremiah Condy never had any separate Interest in the claim which produced the Trust, and Jeremiah Condy and Company, in

1797, assigned all their interest in that claim to Mr. Thomas Doughty of Charleston at whose instance the money has been transferred to the Bank of the United States: besides the amount of Jere: Condy and Co. or their assignees interest is still unsettled, as is that likewise of every other claimant, of whom there are many. Under these circumstances the Secretary of State is the Trustee of all the parties interested, for safe keeping the money, and finally paying it over in such proportions, as may be agreed upon, or be determined by a Judicial proceeding. I have the honor to be &ca.

JAMES MADISON.

Letterbook copy (DNA: RG 59, DL, vol. 14).

1. Letter not found.

From Benjamin Day

SIR   FREDERICKSG 20th Sepm 1802
    I beg Leave to inform you, the Barque Freedom Captn. Thomas Taylor, in the interest of Mr James Maury of Liverpool, is now lying at Tappahanock, where she is to load with Tobacco. She is consigned to me, and I take the Liberty of Soliciting your Assistance, with a consignment in her to his Address. Her freight is fifty Shillings ⅌ Hhd and 5 ⅌ Ct. primage—being a British Bottom her cargo is exempt from paiment of the countervailing Duty of 1/6 Sterling ⅌ 100 lb. Any commands you may favour me with shall be carefully Attended to. I am very respectfully Your Most Obedt.

BENJN: DAY[1]

SIR,
    Permit me to hand you a Copy of my circular Address to the Friends of Mr. Maury, and to hope it will be agreeable to you to countenance his Intention of an annual Ship in this River, by making him a Consignment in the Freedom. Requesting the Favour of your Answer, I am very respectfully sir, Your most obedt.

BENJN: DAY

RC (DLC). In a clerk's hand, except for Day's signature and postscript. Enclosure not found.

1. Benjamin Day (1753–1821) was a Fredericksburg merchant and onetime mayor of the city (*PJM*, 8:428 n. 2).

¶ From M. de Marentille. Letter not found. *20 September 1802, New Jersey.* Acknowledged in Daniel Brent to Marentille, 23 Sept. 1802 (DNA: RG 59, DL, vol. 14). Inquires whether aliens may acquire patents in the U.S. Brent assured him that "a law of Congress, of the 17th. April 1800. extends [the privilege] to aliens, who shall have resided two years in the United States."

From Bird, Savage, and Bird

SIR   LONDON Septemr. 21st. 1802

We have not had the honor to hear from you since our last respects of 21st July last pr Annawan & Copy pr Industry, but we have received from the Honble. Albert Gallatin, Secretary of the Treasury various remittances for £10560.13.5 & £3413.14.6 all of which being accepted will when received be carried to the Accounts in the Amounts directed by him.

Mr. Gallatin explains to us that the superintendance of our expenditures rests with you, and that our relation to his department is an accountability for the monies received from it.[1] We shall therefore account with him for the monies we receive & send him our Accounts and Vouchers. But we shall apply to you for what funds are wanted for the necessary disbursements, or in reimbursement of any advances the public Service may have called for from us, and shall attend to your Instructions in the distribution and expenditure of the Moneys, bearing in Mind that we are not to create subordinate Agencies, by payments in the Lump to any other person of Sums to be distributed & accounted for by them.

On this point we differed in opinion with Mr Erving your Consul who seemed to wish that we should transfer to his Account as Agent for prize Causes the monies remitted for the prosecution of Claims in prize Causes, for him to account with the Treasury for the disposal of them, but as Mr. King concurred with us that this would create the subordinate Agency we were specially instructed to avoid, and that our plan of making the actual payments on orders from Mr. Erving and sending over the Vouchers to the Treasury would be more in conformity with our Instructions we shall continue it, unless we receive other Instructions.

The late Remittances have put all the Accounts in Cash, and as the usual payments are going on you will be able to judge when it will be necessary to make fresh Remittances for the current Expences. We beg to call your Attention to what we have already written about a fund for contingent Expences at the disposal of your Minister, and also to the call for some farther Remittances for the expences of prosecuting Claims in prize Causes, there being Still large Arrears due the Proctors. We have the honor to be with respectful Esteem Sir Your most obedient & most humble Servants

BIRD SAVAGE & BIRD

RC (DNA: RG 59, Letters Received from Bankers).

1. Gallatin to Bird, Savage, and Bird, 6 July 1802 (extract in *Papers of Gallatin* [microfilm ed.], reel 7).

From Daniel Brent

DEAR SIR,   WASHINGTON Sepr 21. 1802.

Your favor of the 17th has been duly received.[1] I enclose the Duplicate of a letter, of the 25. May, from Consul Eaton (the original of which you have seen) on account of a Postcript, of the 4. June, which you have not seen.[2] I send you likewise a letter from Mr Olsen, with the paper to which it refers. His publication will supersede the necessity, I presume, of one on your part. I have acknowledged, in your absence, the receipt of this Communication.[3] The John Adams is still at the mouth of the Branch.

You will probably hear of the alarm which prevailed in Geo. Town on Sunday night, last, from the discovery of a supposed design on the part of the Negroes there to burn down the town, and of the very serious measures that were taken to prevent the execution of this design—in arming the Militia, and keeping them all night on guard. It gives me pleasure to inform you, after a full examination has been had into all the Circumstances of the supposed plot, that there appears now to have been no cause for serious alarm—tho' a few worthless fellows have been committed to prison under appearances of rather a suspicious cast, but not implicating such extensive, or any immediate, mischief, and Mr J. T. Mason has actually sold the reputed leader of the Party to some Georgia men, under the same appearances. The alarm, I believe, has entirely ceased.

Mr Taney, who was appd Commercial Agent some time ago for Dunkirk or Ostend, died last night in Geo: Town with the yellow fever. He had contracted the disease in Baltimore, whence he was but just come. I have the Honor to be, with great Respect and sincere esteem, Dear Sir, Your Obedt & very faithful servt.

DANL BRENT.

RC (DLC). Docketed by JM.

1. Letter not found.
2. For the 4 June postscript, see Eaton to JM, 25 May 1802, n. 1.
3. In a letter to Blicherolsen of 22 Sept. 1802, Brent acknowledged receipt of the Danish minister's 16 Sept. note to JM "with a copy, in English of the Ordinance to which it refers" (DNA: RG 59, DL, vol. 14).

§ From William Jarvis. *22 September 1802, Lisbon.* Has had no reply to his 9 Sept. letter to the Portuguese government about the prohibition on imported flour, a copy of which was enclosed in his 11 Sept. dispatch. "Notwithstanding I have every reason to suppose that what flour is on hand the 4th Jany. will be allowed to be consumed, but am afraid the importation after that time will not be suffered upon the old footing. A Gentleman whom I have convers'd with on the subject . . . conceives that the only chance remaining for an admission would be by holding out the idea of a duty being laid on our flour. . . . If the admission can be obtained even on these terms, It appears to me it will prove advantageous to us, inasmuch as our flour will always find a Considerable consumption, . . . provided they put no greater duty on our flour than the real expense of manufactureing wheat here; beside the advantage We shall always derive from our packages; barrels being transported into the Country with much more ease than can the imported wheat for manufactureing. . . . I do not know but that it would be best to have it admitted on almost any terms than to have it prohibited." Asks for JM's instructions on the subject before the prohibition takes effect, believing it will be proper to present another memorial at that time. "If this Sir should be your opinion, I submit to your judgment whether it would not be better for you Sir to write the Memorial."

Reports that Mr. Dunbar, who brought the commission from the United Insurance Company of New York, arrived on 20 Sept. "The Gentlemen named are Messrs. Dohrman, Bulkeley, & Herbert, but they are all [of] opinion that there would be an impropriety in even requesting his Excellency to be interrogated, & was the application made they were confident he would not comply." A similar application from Great Britain was refused by a former administration. "If we fail in obtaining His Excellency's evidence, I hope We shall succeed in a way that will answer all the purposes intended by the Commission. . . . The fact the Company want to substantiate Vizt. whether the Aurora was concerned in an illicit or prohibited Trade, can full as well be substantiated by an authenticated Copy of the proceedings against her in Para & by the Laws of this Country relative to the Colonial Trade."

Three ships from Philadelphia have been quarantined because of a report of yellow fever in that city by a captain from New York. One of them and a vessel from Baltimore and one from New York were cleared on Jarvis's application to the health officer. Ships from all other ports in the U.S. are admitted directly. Believes the captain of a twenty-two-gun Moroccan ship that arrived in port "some days ago" and stayed four or five days is the same one mentioned by Simpson and Gavino. Has had "no certain information" regarding General Lannes; "the report is that a Courier met him on his way to Paris with orders from Bonaparte for him to retire to an Estate he has 30 leagues from Paris." Mentions in a postscript that a dispatch from Willis and a copy of a circular from Gavino accompany his dispatch.

RC (DNA: RG 59, CD, Lisbon, vol. 1). 5 pp.; docketed by Wagner as received 22 Nov.

§ From Carlos Martínez de Yrujo. *23 September 1802, Mount Pleasant.* Announces the double marriage of the prince of Asturias to the princess of Naples and the Spanish infanta to the prince of Naples.

RC (DNA: RG 59, NFL, Spain, vol. 2). 1 p.; in Spanish; in a clerk's hand, except for Yrujo's complimentary close and signature.

From Stephen Girard

S<small>IR</small>   P<small>HILADA</small> 24. Septr. 1802.

Mr Joseph Curwen to whom you was so obliging as to give a Letter of Recommendation for Mr. Levingston Minister Plenipotentiary of the U. S. to the French Republic, writes me from Paris, that he wants fourteen Bills of Exchange drawn by the Administration of the French Colonies on the Treasurer of France or on the Minister of the Marine, also a delegation drawn by Mr. Sonthonax on Mr. Genet Minister Plenipotentiary of France to the U. S. of America.[1] As those Documents are inclosed in a Bundle containing sundry Vouchers relative to my claim against the French Government which I have deposited in the Secretary of State's Office in the Year 1795. I beg as a particular favour that you will be so good as to have said fourteen Bills of Exchange and Mr. Sonthonax's Delegation Selected and forwarded to me as soon as will be convenient. I am with Respect Your mot. obt. Servt

Letterbook copy (PPGi: Girard Papers).

1. On 29 Oct. 1802 Daniel Brent wrote Girard, enclosing nine of the bills of exchange "and the copies of the others, together with the original delagation" (DNA: RG 59, DL, vol. 14).

¶ From George Wilson. Letter not found. *24 September 1802*. Mentioned in Daniel Brent to Wilson, 18 Oct. 1802 (DNA: RG 59, DL, vol. 14), as a request for partial payment of the sum due for printing the laws of the last session of Congress. Brent conveyed JM's response that "as it does not consist with the practice of the Government to make partial advances in cases of such small interest, . . . he has declined the acceptance of your Bill, . . . especially, too, as it is to be presumed that the entire work will 'ere this, have been compleated and you may now be authorized to draw for the full amount of your claim, which is 94. dollars & 50 cents." Wilson was the publisher of the Jonesborough, Tennessee, *Newspaper and Washington Advertiser* (Brigham, *History and Bibliography of American Newspapers*, 2:1058).

From Louis-André Pichon

M<small>ONSIEUR</small>,   F<small>RANKFORT</small> P<small>ENSA</small>. le 25. 7bre. 1802.

Je vois par une correspondance qui a eu lieu dernierement entre Son Excellence le Gouverneur de la Caroline du Sud et l'agent commercial de la République française à charleston que les bruits qui ont circulé relativement aux prisonniers de couleur qui Sont Sur les fregates françaises de relâche à New York ont acquis assez de crédit pour exciter dans l'esprit du

Gouverneur de cet Etat des appréhensions qui lui ont paru assez Sérieuses pour être communiquée et pour exiger de Sa part des mesures de précaution. Mr. Le President des Etats Unis, J'en ai la confiance, ne partage point ces appréhensions et Je vous prie, Monsieur, de l'assurer qu'elles ne Sont point fondées.

Sachant que la présence des frégates pourait les faire naitre J'ai, dès leur arrivée, donné au commissaire de la République à New York des instructions propres à les prévenir et depuis Je me Suis rendu exprès dans cette ville pour hâter le départ de la division qui va mettre au premier moment à la voille pour france Sauf une frégate qui retourne à la Guadeloupe mais à laquelle on otera tous Ses prisonniers.

Afin de détruire plus efficacement toutes les impressions de cette nature J'ai l'honneur, Monsieur, de vous envoyer l'extrait des instructions que Je donne au commissaire de la Repe. française à New York.[1] Je vous prie, Monsieur, de vouloir bien les communiquer à Monsieur le Président des Etats Unis et d'agréer l'assurance de mon respect et de ma haute consideration.

L. A. Pichon

CONDENSED TRANSLATION

Sees by recent correspondence between the governor of South Carolina and the French commercial agent at Charleston that reports circulating about black prisoners on board the French frigates at New York have excited apprehensions in the governor and led him to express serious concern and to require precautionary measures. Feels confident the president does not share these apprehensions and assures JM they are unfounded. Knowing the frigates' presence could give birth to such concerns, gave instructions to the French commissary in New York to prevent them and then went to New York himself to hasten the squadron's departure. It will leave for France at the earliest opportunity, except for one frigate which will return to Guadeloupe with all prisoners removed. Sends JM an extract of the instructions he gave the French commissary in New York and asks JM to communicate it to the president.

RC and enclosure (DNA: RG 59, NFL, France).

1. Pichon enclosed an extract of his letter to Louis Arcambal, 25 Sept. 1802 (2 pp.; in French), requesting him to check ship manifests to see that all the West Indian prisoners who arrived in New York aboard the French frigates departed with them. Should any prisoners have escaped, he went on, Arcambal was to get descriptions of them so that Pichon might pass them on to the U.S. government.

§ From Elias Vander Horst. *25 September 1802, Bristol.* "On the other side is a Copy of my last respects of the 13t. Instt. . . . Our Harvest is now nearly closed and as the weather for gathering it has been very fine, there remains no doubt of its being excellent in quality as well as very abundant." Encloses newspapers and a London price current.

RC (DNA: RG 59, CD, Bristol, vol. 2). 1 p. Enclosures not found.

¶ From William Mumford. Letter not found. *25 September 1802, Virginia.* Mentioned in Daniel Brent to Mumford, 6 Oct. 1802 (DNA: RG 59, DL, vol. 14), as an inquiry about land patents. Brent replied in JM's absence that "the original or a certified copy of the will of Colo. Byrd should be sent hither, in order to [*sic*] his legal Representatives obtaining Patents for the land in question, and you will of course advise them of this circumstance."

§ From William Lee. *26 September 1802, Bordeaux.* Lists vessels with the number of seamen discharged from them since his 10 Aug. dispatch, "making sixty nine seamen to whom may be added forty six strollers whose names are registered in the office as coming from different ports of the Republic which together with the seventy three I had in charge at the date of my last amounts to one hundred and Eighty Eight men who have been thrown on my hands since the 26 July." Many are destitute, and there are so few direct opportunities to the U.S. that "it is impossible to provide for them as the law directs." However, this problem may soon be solved as France has "lately passed a law which has put a stop to the sale and Francisation of American and other foreign vessels." Encloses "a very singular law of the Consuls by virtue of which all blacks and men of Colour of whatever nation have been arrested here by the Commissary of marine and put into prison until reclaimed & sent off by the Agents of the Country from whence they came & if there is no agent to reclaim them they are sent off to the Colonies." Transmits a packet forwarded by Stephen Cathalan, files of the *Moniteur* and *Journal de Commerce*, and his consular bond.

RC (DNA: RG 59, CD, Bordeaux, vol. 1). 3 pp.; marked "duplicate." Docketed by Brent. Enclosures not found. On 30 Sept., Lee sent JM a nearly identical copy of this letter (ibid.).

From Vincent Gray

SIR,   HAVANA 27. Sepr. 1802

In the absence of Mr. Morton I have to acknowledge the receipt of your letter of the 11h. may last past on the subject of Captain Drew's Confinement at this city, and am sorry to have it in my power to say that he was not unjustly imprisoned.

The money taken from the chest of one of the late crew of the Sloop Sally of Bridgetown New-Jersey, was not taken by one of the owners as stated in his memorial, but as I am informed, actually taken by himself. And when given up or that part thereof not expended amounting to upwards of nine Hundred Dollars, he was liberated: after having suffered upwards of four months Imprisonment.

The Brigantine Hannah mentioned to have been purchased at Porto Rico by him, was not his property, but that of J. B Coursier of Philadelphia; and was while here, under the direction of J B. Rougier of this City Merchant, who received the amount of sales when condemned and sold; and also signed the Bill of sale. She was formerly the Schooner Hannah of Kennebunk, & not being entitled to a Register, it was arrested out of his hands, mutilated and transmitted to the proper Department.

After being liberated he departed from hence for the United States, in a vessel as I am informed bound to Charleston, South Carolina.

The evidence against him was in the first instance, so pointed and circumstantial, that no interference could with propriety be offered from this Department. I am Sir, Very respectfully, Your Mo: Ob. Servt.

VINCENT GRAY

P.S. I am informed that Captain Drew hath aged and respectable Parents residing in Massachusetts, therefore I hope that no part of the foregoing communication will reach them officially—so as to embitter the remainder of their days.

RC (DNA: RG 59, CD, Havana, vol. 1).

From Thomas Jefferson

DEAR SIR   MONTICELLO Sep. 27. 1802.

Unexpected delays in getting my carriage ready will render it impossible for me to leave this till Thursday or Friday, probably Friday: and as you will be gone or going by that time, and we shall meet so soon at Washington, I shall not have the pleasure of seeing you at your own house, but get on as far as the day will let me. Mr. Gallatin left N. York on the 21st. and expected to be at Washington before the 30th. My respects to the ladies & affectionate salutations to yourself.

TH: JEFFERSON

FC (DLC: Jefferson Papers).

§ From David Lenox. *27 September 1802, New York.* Informs JM that he has "caused to be Shipped on board the Sloop Olive Branch . . . bound for George Town, a Trunk containing all the Applications which were made to me during my Agency, together with the Answers returned from the Admiralty, which are all Alphabetically arranged in the Books N 1 & 2 which accompany them." Believes these books and papers should be deposited in JM's office, "where Government may be enabled to judge of the magnitude of the business in which I was engaged, as well as the satisfaction wh⟨ich⟩ I shall derive from a reference to cases where the parties may have supposed themselves neglected by me." Proposes to pay his respects "in the course of a few weeks." Mentions in a postscript that the trunk key and a bill of lading are enclosed.

RC (DNA: RG 59, CD, London, vol. 8). 3 pp.; docketed by Brent as received 30 Sept. Enclosures not found.

§ From James Maury. *28 September 1802, Liverpool.* Encloses a price current. "Since the peace the Application to me from distress'd American Seamen is greatly increased by the Numbers which have been discharged from the British Navy, and I have endeavoured to relieve the United States of the expences of their support by requesting the Masters of our vessels to take them, agreeably to the law of 14th April 1792,[1] but . . . these requests of mine are of late so frequently refused that I wish to be informed whether it would not be adviseable to have the refusing Captains represented to the proper Officer of the United States with the needful Vouchers for enabling him to issue process against them in the Courts there for the Fines they incur." If so, asks JM to inform him of "the Officer to whom I am to address myself & the kind of documents which will ⟨be⟩ admitted as proof."

RC and enclosure (DNA: RG 59, CD, Liverpool, vol. 2). RC 2 pp.; in a clerk's hand, signed by Maury. Enclosure is a printed price current, dated 28 Sept. 1802 (2 pp.).

1. For the "Act concerning Consuls and Vice-Consuls," see Gallatin to JM, 16 Aug. 1802, and n. 2.

§ From James Simpson. *28 September 1802, Tangier.* No. 51. Sent a duplicate of his no. 49 [3 Sept. 1802] with the *Boston* on 9 Sept. and a triplicate to Gavino on 10 Sept. Both were accompanied by a copy of his 1 Sept. letter to Moroccan minister Selawy. Encloses a translation of the minister's answer, the essence of which "amounts to a confession that they have not been able to offer any thing farther, in support of the claims they had attempted to set up." Observes that it is evident the purpose of the minister's letter of 6 Aug. was "to find out what we had to offer against their pretensions, and I fully hope they have met me so well prepared for them, that they will not readily come forward again with such." Believes it would be "highly proper" to transmit to the Moroccan government a copy of Mawlay Sulaiman's ratification of the treaty made with his father. "I shall likewise set [Selawy] to rights with respect to his Idea of no attentions having been paid the Emperor for eight years, whereas it is little more than half that time since I delivered him a Present." Such assertions prove "how little his Majestys present Ministers are acquainted with what passed during Ben Ottomans Administration." Selawy "pretends having rendered essential Service" and thus expects a gift; "to secure a continuance of his Friendship, it must be given." Reports that the emperor has ordered the two men at Taroudant to be sent to Mogador and permitted to embark there. The emperor's frigate, which sailed from Larache in August, has put into port at Tangier; it has taken no prizes. After seven months of "ineffectual applications in the Emperors name" for passports for the Tripolitan ship at Gibraltar, "a document under his Seal has at last been transmitted asserting the Vessel to be his, and demanding from all the Consuls here Passports for her as such." Encloses a translation of the paper sent to the consuls and a copy of "the Passport I have found myself under the necessity of granting." Has received word from Gavino about the approach of the frigate *New York* with the gun carriages. Notes that his no. 50 [14 Sept. 1802] "served only to advise my having taken the liberty of drawing a Bill on you."

RC and enclosures (DNA: RG 59, CD, Tangier, vol. 1). RC 4 pp.; docketed by Wagner. RC and enclosures printed in Knox, *Naval Documents, Barbary Wars*, 2:275, 280–81, 283, 284–86. The enclosures are a translation of Sidi Mohammed ben Absalom Selawy's letter to Simpson, 20 Sept. 1802 (3 pp.), expressing satisfaction that "Friendship and good harmony" between Morocco and the U.S. "have been continued" and pointing to his important role in mediating the dispute; an order of the emperor of Morocco, 17 Sept. 1802 (2 pp.), claiming the ship *Meshouda* and ordering "all the Consuls to dispatch her, and deliver their Passports"; and Simpson's passport for the *Meshouda*, dated 27 Sept. 1802 (1 p.).

From Robert Morris

SIR,   NEW BRUNSWICK 29. Septr. 1802

In consequence of a Certificate dated 6. Septr. 1802 from your office under the Signature of Stephen Pleasonton Clerk in your absence,[1] I have issued a Commission of Bankruptcy, among others, to Josiah Shinn & in consequence of a Notification thereof *Isaiah* Shinn has this day come forwarded [*sic*], & produces a Commission from the president appointing him a Commissioner of Bankruptcy, and says there is no such person, to his knowledge, as *Josiah* Shinn.

I therefore wish to be informed whether there is a mistake in the Certificate, or whether there is also a Commission to *Josiah* Shinn.[2] I am Sir with respect your very Huml Servt.

RM

Draft (NjR).

1. See Morris to JM, 3 Sept. 1802, and n.
2. On 2 Oct. 1802 Pleasonton wrote Morris to say that "Isaiah Shinn is the person appointed and not Josiah" (NjR).

§ From Louis-André Pichon. *29 September 1802, Georgetown.* The claim of French merchant Coulon, about which Pichon wrote JM on 7 Mar. 1802, having failed in

Congress, calls JM's attention to the manifest wrong that appears to have been done to Coulon.

Recounts the beginning of the affair. Two French prizes, the *Betty Cathcart* and the *Aaron*, the first of which was Coulon's, were taken into Wilmington, North Carolina, in July 1796. Disputes arose over what repairs could be made to the ships and what means of export would be allowed to the proprietors. The *Aaron* left on 7 July 1797 under suspicious circumstances and was subsequently seized and condemned in Portsmouth, New Hampshire, for importing sugar that had been declared as rice. But the *Betty Cathcart* never left port and was abandoned by Coulon on 1 June 1798. Under these circumstances, the comptroller of the treasury ordered the *Betty Cathcart* and its cargo sold on 29 June. The sale produced $57,432, of which $23,396 was assessed for costs and for duties on the cargoes of both ships, including $6,241 for the *Aaron*'s duties; the balance was paid to Coulon.

Summarizes the circumstances on which he bases the claim: (1) the *Aaron* and the *Betty Cathcart* could have left together by conforming to certain regulations that were the subject of the original dispute; (2) the *Aaron* left on 7 July 1797 and was subsequently seized and condemned for acts of contraband; (3) Coulon abandoned his property on 1 June 1798 because of circumstances at the time between the U.S. and France, hoping to obtain compensation during the peace that would follow; and (4) the instructions of 29 June 1798 ordering the sale authorized the collector to retain the amount of the duty owed on the *Aaron*'s cargo from the proceeds of the sale of Coulon's property, even though Coulon did not own the *Aaron*.

Points out that it was only the circumstance of Coulon's abandonment of his property in the U.S. that allowed the treasury to proceed against the *Betty Cathcart* for the alleged acts of the *Aaron*. After the Convention of 1800, Coulon's property should have been returned to him in good faith, deducting only the customary and legal charges. Instead, Coulon unexpectedly found an assessment levied against him that was in reality a confiscation of his property. In this action by the treasury a French citizen has been deprived of his property without any legal proceedings. Asks JM to bring these arguments to the president's attention.

RC (DNA: RG 59, NFL, France, vol. 1). 8 pp.; in French; in a clerk's hand, signed by Pichon. Docketed by Wagner.

§ From William Willis. *29 September 1802, Barcelona.* Transmits a copy of his 19 Sept. dispatch, since which nothing new has occurred. "I have not yet been able to get the Papers and Plate Promised me from the Person who has told me he has them, . . . but I am Confident he will make no bad use of them. As Soon as I get them, I Shall enclose a Set of them to you, and Shall Send the Plate. . . . The Name of the person who has these Papers, is James Mills, whose unfortunate Situation, and his being in Madrid much of his time precludes him even from Suspicion of having Any thing to do with the business of the fabrication or Circulation. . . . It Appears to me to have been a villanous plan in the Person who Sent them to Mills, to injure him if Possible, and Also to involve me in the injury, as I have advanced him a Large Sum to defend his Ship against the Spanish Government. . . . There is

now a Sweedish Frigate in the Road which will take under her Convoy two American Vessels which are here Ready to Sail."

RC (DNA: RG 59, CD, Barcelona, vol. 1). 2 pp. In a clerk's hand, signed by Willis.

§ From François de Navoni. *30 September 1802, Cagliari.* Asks to be named U.S.
agent and consul general in light of his long service as acting consul. Notes that he
entertained Captain Morris and his officers during their recent stay to their entire
satisfaction; by a letter of 27 Sept. Morris appointed him provisional U.S. commercial agent for the kingdom of Sardinia. Refers JM to his letter to the president which
accompanies this.

RC (DNA: RG 59, CD, Cagliari, vol. 1). 2 pp.; in French. Navoni's letter to Jefferson,
30 Sept. 1802 (ibid.) supported his claim in detail and enclosed a sample of Sardinian salt.

¶ From Gabriel Christie. Letter not found. *30 September 1802.* Mentioned in Daniel Brent to Christie, 1 Oct. 1802 (DNA: RG 59, DL, vol. 14), as an inquiry about
the appointment of Christie's son to consular office. Brent replied that "your son
has not been appointed to the place in question, and . . . that place is still vacant."
Brent also acknowledged the receipt "several days ago" of dispatches from Rufus
King carried by Christie.

¶ From Thomas Manning. Letter not found. *30 September 1802.* Mentioned in
Daniel Brent to Manning, 1 Oct. 1802 (DNA: RG 59, DL, vol. 14), as an inquiry
about documents submitted in support of Manning's claims against France. Brent
replied in JM's absence that he had made "a very full search for the papers alluded
to, but . . . without effect. . . . Under this circumstance, it is probable that these
original papers were sent to France, and have been since consumed in the fire of
which Mr. Skipwith speaks, in the letter herewith returned to you."

From Nathaniel Irwin

DEAR & HONOURED SIR   BUCKS COUNTY Octr. 1st. 1802
    I beg you will be the vehicle of a few sentiments to the Honble. Gideon
Granger, respecting the organiza[tion] of a post road in this vicinity—Viz
the old road from Philada to New-York. The objections to the projected
arrangements are that two post offices would be within less than 4 Miles of
each other—& no considerable Village at either place; & a Man would
receive an appointment as Deputy Post Master who is as destitute of principle & almost of Character as Lucifer himself. Besides the Post Master
intended for one of these places will not accept on these terms, nor will the
only Stage that passes the road carry the Mail under an obligation of stop-

ping so often. Some alterations in the proposed plan therefore will be inevitable. The plan I would propose & which I am sure will give the most general satisfaction I beg leave to detail as follows.

	Places	Distances	from Phila.	Names	Politics
1	Jenkin-Town	10¼ Miles	10¼	Willm. McCalla	Fedl. (but temperate)
2	Cross Roads	9¾	20	Wm. Hart	Fedl. Do.
3	Buckingham	7	27	Josiah Addis	Repubn.
4	New Hope	7	34	A good republican character may be

found in this place. I know severals but do not know whether they would accept. My local knowledge does not enable me to pursue the rout further. If the above arrangement is not adopted nothing will be gained in Republican Characters—another federalist (Elnathan Pettit) must be substituted for Wm. Hart & the change would be for the worse in every respect; & still two post Offices would approach within less than four Miles of each other & not the smallest Village at either place; or otherwise Josiah Addis, the most deserving character of the whole must be left out.

But if it is though[t] necessary to have a Post Office at Hatborough (alias Crooked Billet) Joseph Carr, a decided Republican & Inn keeper at the same place, should (in my humble opinion) receive the appointment instead of Samuel Coughlin.[1]

Pardon, my Dear Sir, the Marks of haste so obvious in this letter, written at a friends house on the public road & be assured that the ideas here submitted are dictated by no friendships or animosities, but by a desire of promoting the public weal & the reputation of our present Republican Administration. With pleasing recollections of former intimacies which no time can efface I remain Sir, your faithful friend & most humble servt

NATHL IRWIN

P. S. I make use of a separate leaf to mention in confidence that my son Henry remains unemployed:[2] that by a letter from the War office in June last I learn that the President was pleased to Nominate him to the Senate as a Candidate for an Ensignsy in the Army, but that the Senate did not decide on the nomination. Though the long delay & expectation has been injurious to him by preventing his engaging in other permanent business, yet I am persuaded, my dear friend, that I am much indebted to your friendship on this as well as on other occasions. Perhaps when the Senate Meets you can be further useful to your [. . .]

N. ⟨I.⟩

RC (DLC). Damaged by removal of seal. Docketed by Brent as received 6 Oct.

1. By 1816 the post road ran through Jenkintown, Buckingham, New Hope, and Hatborough, Pennsylvania, but of the candidates mentioned by Irwin, only William McCalla of Jenkintown was a postmaster (*ASP, Misc.*, 2:357, 367, 369, 376).

2. For Irwin's efforts on behalf of his son Henry, see his letter to JM, 7 Jan. 1802 (*PJM-SS*, 2:370–71 and n. 1).

§ From William Jarvis. *1 October 1802, Lisbon.* Forwards a duplicate of his last dispatch of 22 Sept. "Not haveing received a line from his Excellency in answer to my Communication of the 9th., I yesterday address'd a Note to him of which No 5 is a Copy, which I hope will produce something."

"Mr Dunbar preferred attempting to get the Papers relative to the Aurora & Four Sisters to take Copies of them before any application was made to Don João, for fear that the Govmt. suspecting that some National question might arise from it should refuse any sort of information; but as yet success has not attended the attempt; if it does not after three or four days . . . I shall write to the Minister on the subject."

Since the three American ships mentioned in his last dispatch were released from quarantine, three more have been released; "there are now under quarantine two Vessels from New York . . . & one from Philada. that arrived 4 days ago without any bill of Health whom I am apprehensive they will treat pretty rigorously."

"No 1 & 2 are Copies of several Copies of letters forwarded me by Mr Willis with a Copy of his letter accompanying them. No 3 is a Copy of an affidavit given before Mr Yznardie & of his letter. In the affidavit the Captn. has not mentioned where or when the Moor was seen, & those were the most essential circumstances to be known. . . . The description no ways answers to the Moroquin that was here. No. 4 is an Extract from the letter accompanying Mr Simpson's dispatch which is forwarded herewith."

Mentions in a postscript that he has just received an answer to his note of 30 Sept., "a Translation of which will be found on No 5." Adds in a postscript dated 2 Oct. that he is forwarding a packet just received from Willis and relates a report that a British brig without a passport was captured by "the Moroquin Ship that was in here."

RC and enclosures (DNA: RG 59, CD, Lisbon, vol. 1). RC 3 pp.; docketed by Wagner as received 21 Nov. Jarvis's numbered enclosures (8 pp.) are copies of (1) James Leander Cathcart to Stephen Cathalan, 28 Aug. 1802, including an extract of Andrew Morris's letter from Tripoli of 22 July, and another letter from Morris of 30 July, certified as a true copy by William Willis, 15 Sept. 1802 (see Willis to JM, 15 Sept. 1802, and n. 1); (2) Marianno Fontano y Vida to Willis, 7 Sept. 1802, reporting a ship combat involving a "Moorish Galliot," and Willis to Jarvis, 17 Sept. 1802, covering the former; (3) Josef Yznardy at Cadiz to Jarvis, 17 Sept. 1802, enclosing an affidavit of Capt. Mark Collins of the American ship *Fame*, attesting to a conversation with an English captain who described a "moorish Cruiser" of sixteen guns which was "cruising" for American vessels; (4) an "Extract of a letter from Jas. Simpson Esqr. dated Tangier 6 Sept. 1802," reporting the sailing from Larache of a twenty-two-gun frigate and asking for information "of her operations dureing her Cruise"; and (5) Jarvis to João de Almeida de Mello e Castro, 30 Sept. 1802, requesting a response to his letter of 9 Sept., with Almeida's 30 Sept. reply, stating that the answer "does not belong to his department [and] he has sollicited the necessary instruction for said purpose, which when he receives, he will send an answer with all dispatch."

§ From John Gavino. *3 October 1802, Gibraltar*. No. 99. Refers JM to his last dispatch, no. 98 [not found], enclosing dispatches from Simpson and O'Brien. Captain Campbell informed him on 25 Sept. that the *New York* "is coming out imediately" with gun carriages for the emperor of Morocco. "As this intelligence I deemd might be usefull to Consul Simpson in his Negociation with the Emperour I dispatchd him an advice Boat with the Account." Encloses abstract of Simpson's reply of 27 Sept.[1] On 2 Oct. orders came from Sir Richard Bickerton for the British squadron of five warships anchored at Gibraltar to "proceed aloft with all possible dispatch and to take with them full six months stores of all kinds." Supposes the movement arises from reports of France's intention to occupy islands in the Morea. In a postscript, mentions that the ship at Gibraltar, to be called the *Meshouda*, is ready for sea and only waits for passports and that the letter for Captain Campbell has been delivered.

RC and enclosure (DNA: RG 59, CD, Gibraltar, vol. 2). RC 2 pp.; docketed by Brent.

1. In the enclosed extract from his 27 Sept. 1802 letter to Gavino (2 pp.), Simpson expressed his satisfaction that the gun carriages were "so near at hand" and reported that in negotiations with Morocco "every matter is in the fairest train of perfect accomodation." Simpson also noted that the emperor's request to the consuls for a passport for the ship at Gibraltar was "granted by us all," and he enclosed a letter for Captain Campbell on the subject.

From Albert Gallatin

SIR.   TREASURY DEPARTMENT October 4th. 1802.

I have the honor to enclose the copy of a letter from the Collector of Norfolk, and of a correspondence which has taken place between him and the British Consul at that Place, on the subject of a seaman stated to have been a deserter from a British Frigate.[1] Whether it can be thought necessary to give any instruction, on that subject, to the collector, is a question which does not fall within the province of this Department. I have the honor to be, very respectfully, Sir, Your obedt. Servt.

ALBERT GALLATIN

RC and enclosures (DLC: Gallatin Papers). RC in a clerk's hand, signed by Gallatin. Docketed by Wagner, with his note, "Desertion from the Andromaché."

1. The copies enclosed by Gallatin (4 pp.) are William Davies to Gallatin, 26 Sept. 1802, covering the correspondence between Davies and the British consul at Norfolk, John Hamilton, which the collector transmitted "for such instructions" as the government might think necessary. Hamilton's letter to Davies, 25 Sept. 1802, contained an extract of a 24 Sept. 1802 letter received from Capt. Robert Laurie of the British ship *Andromache*, requesting the delivery of William Sawyer, a deserter from that ship "now on board the United States Revenue Vessel in Hampton Creek," and describing Sawyer; Davies to Hamilton, 25 Sept. 1802, as-

sured the latter he would write immediately to the commander of the revenue cutter; Davies to Captain Hamm of the revenue cutter *Patriot*, 25 Sept. 1802, recommended that Sawyer be discharged if found on board the *Patriot*; Hamilton to Davies, 27 Sept. 1802, inquired about the "obstacles to the giving up this Deserter" mentioned by Davies in conversation on 26 Sept. and observed that Captain Laurie "entertains the fullest expectation that he will be directly given up to him, agreeably to the practice which has prevailed in British Ports, with regard to the Deserters from the Ships of War of the United States"; and Davies to Hamilton, 27 Sept. 1802, explained that the obstacle was an act of the Virginia General Assembly of 21 Jan. 1801 but added that for "the discouragement of such irregularities I have directed that the man be forthwith discharged."

§ To Albert Gallatin. *4 October 1802, State Department.* Provides a "rough estimate, for a Remittance to the Bankers of the United States at London," listing $12,000 for diplomatic purposes, $13,000 for the British treaty, $5,000 for the relief of American seamen, including the agent's salary, and $26,000 for the prosecution of claims in prize cases, for a total of $56,000.

Letterbook copy (DNA: RG 59, DL, vol. 14). 1 p.

§ From Charles B. Cochran. *4 October 1802, Charleston.* Resigns his commission as marshal for the district of South Carolina because of "the injury which my agricultural concerns have received from my close and constant attendance on the duties of my office." Recommends his brother [Robert Elliott Cochran] to replace him.[1]

RC (DNA: RG 59, LAR, 1801–9, filed under "Cochran"). 2 pp.

1. An undated letter from Robert E. Cochran to JM, soliciting the appointment, was probably sent at about the same time (ibid.; 1 p.).

¶ From Oliver Farnsworth. Letter not found. *4 October 1802.* Mentioned in Daniel Brent to Farnsworth, 12 Oct. 1802 (DNA: RG 59, DL, vol. 14), as a request for payment for printing the laws of the last session of Congress. Brent conveyed JM's response that payment of $94.50 would be made "when the account shall have been liquidated at the Treasury Department." Farnsworth owned the Newport *Rhode-Island Republican*, 1801–5 (Brigham, *History and Bibliography of American Newspapers*, 2:1003).

§ From John M. Forbes. *5 October 1802, Hamburg.* Notes that he last wrote on 28 Aug. Reports that "another and, it is to be hoped, the last Revolution has taken place in Switzerland, 24,000 Men having entered Bonne, annulled all the existing authorities and reestablished the order of things as it existed prior to the dissolution of the Confederacy by the French invasion in 1798." Whether Napoleon will support this measure is uncertain, but "his protection has been formally Solicited." A rumor was circulated on 4 Oct. "of a still more important event having taken place in Russia—nothing less than that the Emperor Alexander had abdicated the throne and Committed his Government to two houses of Parliament"—a measure that would "probably be followed by a Change in the politics of Russia." The Austrian court may hope for just such an event to break the "all-powerful league between Russia, Prussia & France." France and Great Britain have not exchanged ambassadors, nor does it seem probable a commercial treaty will be signed between them. "It is still very doubtful whether Malta will be given up, the Emperor of Russia having refused to accede to the guarantee of it's independance stipulated by the treaty of Amiens." Relays for JM's decision "a proposition [that] has lately been made to me, to furnish me from an authentic official Source at Berlin all the most interesting particulars which may, from time to time, occur," at a cost of ten guineas per month. States that he considered it his duty to communicate to officials in Hamburg "the prevalence of the yellow fever at Philadelphia." Transmits a dispatch from the U.S. consul at Trieste. In a 7 Oct. postscript observes that the rumor from Russia has not been confirmed. "It appears, however, that a total Change of Ministry has taken place. . . . There is a degree of mystery still hanging over the business and many believe that something more serious has taken place." As to Switzerland, France disapproves of the reestablishment of the old government, and "two demibrigades are ordered there to propose a new Constitution."

RC (DNA: RG 59, CD, Hamburg, vol. 1). 3 pp.; docketed by Wagner as received 10 Jan.

§ From Josef Yznardy. *5 October 1802, Cadiz.* Encloses a copy of a circular received 4 Oct. from William Willis.[1] Forwards a packet from James Simpson and the register of the American brig *Glory*, Capt. John Waite, sold at Cadiz, and notifies JM of his endorsement of the register of the ship *Donaldson* of Norfolk, Capt. Duncan McFarlane, sold in New Orleans. Lists four American ships sold at Cadiz. Encloses a copy of a letter he wrote to Henry Hoit, supercargo of the ship *Jason*,[2] "which will inform you that nothing on my part is wanting to cumply with my Office; but the want of Literal Instructions deprives me of being able to oblige the Captains & Supercargos to give me notice of such Sales and deposit their Registers in the Consular Office."

RC and enclosures (DNA: RG 59, CD, Cadiz, vol. 1). RC 2 pp.; in a clerk's hand, signed by Yznardy. For enclosures, see nn.

1. Yznardy enclosed another copy of Cathcart's 28 Aug. letter to Cathalan reporting Andrew Morris's capture, certified as a true copy by Willis, 15 Sept. 1802 (2 pp.) (see Willis to JM, 15 Sept. 1802, and n. 1).
2. Yznardy's letter to Henry Hoit, 2 Oct. 1802 (2 pp.), complained of the fraudulent use of the *Jason*'s ship register and requested that it be returned to his office.

From Albert Gallatin

S<small>IR</small>,   T<small>REASURY</small> D<small>EPARTMENT</small> October 6th. 1802.

I had the honor to receive your letter of the 20th. ultimo, in answer to mine of the 8th. preceding.

As legal questions of some nicety may result from the right of priority secured by law, to the United States, from the interest of Jeremiah Condy in the co-partnership of Jeremiah Condy & Co., and from the nature of the trust vested in the Secretary of State, permit me to request you, not to pay any part of the money thus held in trust, without previously notifying the Comptroller of the Treasury, and to furnish this Department with a copy of the Deed of trust. I have the honor to be, very respectfully, Sir, Your obedt. Servant

ALBERT GALLATIN

RC (DLC: Gallatin Papers). In a clerk's hand, signed by Gallatin. Docketed by Brent.

From Christopher Gore

SIR,   LONDON Oct. 6. 1802.

I have the honour to acknowledge the receipt of your several Letters to Mr. King, under the following dates viz. 8 June. 20. 23. 23. & 26. of July, and 23. of August,[1] the latter by Mr. Brent; all of which came to hand since his absence from this place: that of June 8. covering Commission and Instructions to this Gentleman to adjust whatever remains to be decided in relation to the boundaries between the United States and the British Government, was received, and forwarded to him before he left Harwich.

According to his desire, and with a view to expedite the business, I requested an interview of Lord Hawkesbury, for the purpose of making to him such communications on this subject, as might enable him to enter on the negotiation, with effect, on the return of Mr. King. After having opened the business, at our first meeting, he requested it might lay over until Mr. Hammond, the Under Secretary of State, should come from the Sea-side where he then was for his health, to afford him an opportunity of confering with this Gentleman, who was much acquainted with the business to which the Communication referred. On Mr. Hammond's arrival I saw Lord Hawkesbury, and with the Map of the St. Croix, as reported by the Commissioners, under the 5th. Article of the Treaty of 1794. and Arrowsmith's Map of the United States,[2] endeavoured to trace out the Boundaries that were still requisite, to explain to him the views of the President, and to impress on his mind the reasonableness, and Justice thereof, in regard to the British Nation. He appeared disposed to accede to the propositions, so far as they relate to the boundary line through the Passamaquoddy, the mode suggested of adjusting that between the United States, and New Brunswick, and fixing the point intended in the Treaty of 1783. by the north-west Angle of Nova scotia, and establishing the boundary be-

611

tween such point, and the north-westermost head of Connecticut River. It is, however, to be understood, that the disposition manifested by his Lordship, was founded in the belief that on enquiry he should find the Islands in Passamaquoddy Bay to have been possessed by, and to belong to the respective Nations as the proposed line would place them, and that on further reflection no insurmountable objection should occur to the plan proposed for running the other Lines, and fixing the point referred to. On these Subjects he doubtless intends to consult with Colo. Barclay,[3] the British Commissioner for ascertaining the St. Croix, who is now in some part of Great Britain, and who is expected in London, early in the Winter. On that part of the Boundary which is to connect the north west point of the Lake of the Woods with the Mississippi, he observed that it was evidently the intention of the Treaty of Peace, that both Nations should have access to, and enjoy the free use of that river and he doubtless meant that this access should be to each Nation, through their own Territories. He remarked that Commissioners, which I had proposed for ascertaining the relation of the Lake of the Woods and the Mississippi, if any doubt remained on this head, and running the Line between these two Waters, according to your proposition, might establish such a boundary, as would secure to each Nation this object. To the remark I made no reply, other than by observing that the line suggested was what naturally seemed to be demanded by just interpretation where such a mistake had happened as was herein Supposed; but this I did, however, chiefly with a view of not assenting to his proposal, and in a manner rather declining than courting the discussion. It will probably be persisted in, and I much doubt if this Government will be inclined to adjust any boundary in this Quarter, that has not the right desired for its basis.[4]

I have considered it important to apprize you of the view entertained by the British Government in this respect, that the President may have an opportunity, if he should choose, to forward Mr. King any instructions relative to the boundary in question. The Papers marked A. herewith enclosed are copies of the Notes that passed from me to Lord Hawkesbury, and Minute⟨s⟩ of the proposals made him in conversation and traced out on the Maps before mentioned, and of his Note in reply.[5] These with the above detail of what passed in conversation, will communicate to you all that has been or probably will be done on this subject, before Mr King's return, which may be expected in November, and doubtless before Lord Hawkesbury will have an opportunity of consulting the persons alluded to, in his Note.

Your Letter of 20. July, with the inclosed copy of the Letter of the Secretary of the Treasury to the Comptroller, respecting the portages or carrying Places, and the exemption from Duty of small vessels trading between the Ports of the Northern, and North western Boundaries came to hand on the 10. September; and I lost no Time in stating their contents to Lord Hawkesbury in a Note, copy whereof is herewith inclosed,[6] in order to rebut any argument in favor of the pretensions of the British Traders, from a supposed acquiescence on the part of the Government of the United States, and to insist on such a construction of the Terms, portages and carrying places, as might comport with the Safety of the Revenue of the United States, and the interest of their Citizens. I afterwards had a Conference with him on this subject in which he acceded to the construction contained in my Note; and as to the Tonnage duty he said it certainly merited, and should receive all due consideration. Nothing has occurred here relative to the rencounter between the American armed ship Asia, and the British Ship Walker, as mentioned in one of Your Letters of 23 July. In conformity to the directions contained in your Letter 26 July, the sum of £12..16..10 has been paid to Mr. Elias Vanderhorst. I have the honour to be, with great Consideration and respect, Sir, Your most ob. & hum. Servt.

C. GORE

RC and enclosures (DNA: RG 59, DD, Great Britain, vol. 10); partial Tr (DLC: Monroe Papers). RC docketed by Wagner. RC and enclosures transmitted to the Senate by Jefferson, 24 Oct. 1803, and printed in *ASP, Foreign Relations*, 2:587–89. Partial Tr enclosed in JM to Monroe, 14 Feb. 1804 (DLC: Monroe Papers). For enclosures, see nn. 5 and 6.

1. For Daniel Brent's 23 Aug. letter to King, see King to JM, 10 June 1802, nn. 2 and 3.
2. Aaron Arrowsmith (1750–1823) was a British cartographer whose maps of North America, including those published in 1795 and 1796, were considered to be accurate and well executed.
3. Thomas Barclay (1753–1830) was born and educated in New York, fought as a Loyalist during the American Revolution, and moved to Nova Scotia at the end of the war. Among other government positions, he served as British consul in New York from 1799 to 1830.
4. Partial Tr ends here.
5. Gore enclosed copies of his letters to Hawkesbury, 24 Aug. 1802 (2 pp.), and 28 Sept. 1802 (2 pp.), enclosing minutes of their conversation (6 pp.); and Hawkesbury to Gore, 4 Oct. 1802, announcing his willingness to negotiate the points under consideration (2 pp.).
6. Gore to Hawkesbury, 22 Sept. 1802 (4 pp.).

§ From John Lamson. *6 October 1802, Trieste.* "Since my last of the 24th August, I have been informed by Mr Riggins that he has received a commission as consul for this port.[1] The reasons for my long abscence were explained to you in my letter of the 29th Decr. 1801[2] which however I conclude had not reached you, when this appointment was made. . . . I have been induced by this commission, to leave my Native country and friends to reside in this place, the voyage here has cost me much money; and as this circumstance affects not only my int[e]rest but my reputation in this City, I have thought my duty to address you this letter. Since my arrivall in Trieste I have neglected nothing in my power to procure every possible advantage for those of my fellow citizens who have visited this place. . . . Before I return to America shall wait your esteemed communications, and when I shall be informed that the Goverment have no further service for me abroad shall endeavour to act the part of a good citizen at home."

RC (DNA: RG 59, CD, Trieste, vol. 1). 2 pp.; docketed by Wagner.

1. For Lamson's replacement by William Riggin, see Joseph Covachich to JM, 16 Nov. 1801, *PJM-SS*, 2:246 and n. 1.
2. *PJM-SS*, 2:353.

§ From William Lee. *6 October 1802, Bordeaux.* Since his dispatch of 26 Sept., has received an arrêté of the consuls, which is enclosed. "I took the liberty to mention to you in my letter of July 22d. that notwithstanding the circular which the Secretary of the Treasury addressed in July 1801 to the Collectors and Naval Officers respecting bills of health many vessels left the United States without them and in consequence of this neglect were subject to a ruinous quarantine. It now appears as if some further Steps were necessary on the part of government to prevent our shipping from experiencing this inconvenience." Transmits a file of the *Moniteur* and *Journal de Commerce*.

RC (DNA: RG 59, CD, Bordeaux, vol. 1). 1 p. Enclosure not found.

§ From Samuel Nutting. *6 October 1802, Portsmouth.* "Enclosed you will receive my bill for publishing the Laws of the Union, in the Republican Ledger."

RC (DNA: RG 59, ML). 1 p. Enclosure not found. For Nutting, see Woodbury Langdon to JM, 6 Feb. 1802 (*PJM-SS*, 2:449 and n. 2).

§ From William Riggin. *6 October 1802, Trieste.* Acknowledges JM's letter of 18 Mar. [not found], enclosing his commission as U.S. consul at Trieste. "I accept with sentiments of real gratitude, this important trust. . . . I have exhibited my credentials to the Government of this place to be forwarded to the Court of Vienna and ratified accordingly. When I have notice of this being effected, I shall again do myself this Honor."

RC (DNA: RG 59, CD, Trieste, vol. 1). 1 p. Cover marked "Reced & forwarded by your Hble Servts Jas. Mackenzie & A Glennie London 22 Janry 1803"; postmarked Philadelphia, 28 Feb. Docketed by Brent.

Index

NOTE: Persons are identified on pages cited below in boldface type. Identifications in earlier volumes of this series are noted within parentheses. Page numbers followed only by n. (e.g., 185 n.) refer to the provenance portion of the annotation.

Aaron (French ship), 604

Aborn, Thomas, 347

Acadia (now Nova Scotia), 239

Adams, John: administration, 125, 138 n. 6, 185 n., 249, 350 n. 1, 365, 392; and appointments, 221 and n. 1, 448 and n. 1

Adams, John (American citizen in Barcelona), 582, 583 n., n. 2

Adams, John Quincy, 34–35, 334 n. 3

Adams, Samuel, 124

Adams (U.S. frigate), 319–20 n. 1, 342, 343, 399 and n., 516, 543; carries JM's dispatches, 135, 202, 431, 432, 507; at Gibraltar, 447, 472, 501, 545; in Mediterranean, 433, 452, 465

Addington; *see* Sidmouth, Henry Addington, Viscount

Addis, Josiah, 606

Addison, Lindsay, 168 n.

Addison, Thomas G., 463

Adet, Pierre-Auguste, 140, 265, 289, 348

Adriatic Sea, 46

Africa, 267 n. 1

Alabama River, 88 n. 4

Albania, 274

Albany, N.Y., 454

Albany Register, 213 n. 1, 568

Albemarle County, Va., 10, 124, 201; J. Monroe at home in, 566, 578, 581–82, 588

Alder, Charles, 52, 128

Alexander I (of Russia), 207, 231, 609–10

Alexander, Lawson, 341, 499 n.

Alexander, Sir William, 242 n. 13

Alexander (U.S. ship), 226

Alexandria, Egypt, 27, 559

Alexandria, Va., 257 n. 1, 284, 539; collector of customs, 356–57, 357; jail, 82

Algeciras, Spain, 342, 497

Algiers: captures Portuguese frigate, 224, 244, 270, 306; *Franklin* arrives at, 391 n. 2; French expedition to, 440, 471–72, 492, 558, 569 n.; navy, 188, 224, 225 n., 244, 270, 452 n. 3, 494, 495; relations with Denmark, 495, 496; relations with France, 383, 494–95, 545, 558, 569 n., 576; relations with Great Britain, 28, 30 n. 13, 328, 383, 495, 568; relations with Morocco, 141; relations with Netherlands, 472, 495; relations with Spain, 383, 388, 389 n. 1, 495; relations with Sweden, 495, 496; relations with Tripoli, 136, 159–60; relations with Tunis, 456, 495; relations with U.S., 306, 495, 496; treaty with U.S. (*1795*), 394, 431; U.S. annuities for, 161, 211 and nn., 414 and n. 1, 415, 430, 439, 442, 453, 505, 529, 584, 585, 586; U.S. consul at, 137, 138 n. 8, 202, 557; *see also* Jews, in Algiers

Alicante, Spain, 275, 392 and n. 1, 423, 424 n. 1, 563 n. 2; U.S. consul at, 392 and n. 1; *see also* Montgomery, John; Montgomery, Robert

Ali Pasha (of Janina), 274

Ali Pasha (of Tripoli); *see* Qaramanli, Ali Pasha

Allen, Ira, 375 n. 1

Allier, Chabot de l', 205, 206 n. 7

Almeida de Mello e Castro, João de, conde das Galveas, 217, 451, 452 n. 1, 508, 569 and n., 607 and n.

American Citizen and General Advertiser (N.Y.), 540, 541 n. 1

Ganteaume, Honoré-Joseph, 59, **60 n. 3**

Gantt, Thomas T., 539 and n. 3, 555 and n. 1

Garcia, Don Luis: owner of *Los Amigos*, 362, 363, 364 n. 1

Gardner, Gideon, 158 n. 3

Gardner, William Patterson: consul at Paramaribo, 589 and n., n. 1

Gascoyne, Isaac, 3, 4 n. 4

Gates, Horatio, 19–20

Gates, Mary Vallance (Mrs. Horatio), 19, 20

Gautier, Mr., 593

Gauvain, Mr.: acquaintance of Monroe's, 124, 221

Gauvain, Mrs., 124, 221

Gavino, John: consul at Gibraltar, 3, 57 n., 99 n. 6, 216, 398 n. 2, 452 n. 3, 483, 567–68 and n. 1, 584, 597, 602; accounts with Simpson, 141, 369, 517, 538; announces Morocco's declaration of war, 440, 441 n.; and case of *Rose*, 529; and Dale affair, 104, 105 n. 2; receives arms, 227; reports capture of *Franklin*, 417, 418 n. 1, 516 and n. 4, 580; letter from JM, 216; letters to JM, 187, 209, 270, 309, 328, 347–48, 349, 388–89, 446–47, 501, 545, 608

Gayoso de Lemos, Manuel, 73–74 n. 2, 261, 262 n. 1

Gazette of the United States (Philadelphia), 182 n. 1, 223, 224 n. 1, 422 and n. 1

Gelston, David: collector at N.Y., 30 n. 12, 349 n. 1; letter to JM, 123

General Greene (U.S. ship), 414–15; and annuity for dey, 430, 439, 442; and gun carriages for Morocco, 432, 439, 478

General Simcoe (British ship), 23, 152

General Washington (U.S. ship), 87

Genet, Edmund: French minister to U.S., 377, 380 nn. 10, 11, 598

Gennaro, Francisco: prince of Naples, 32 n. 4, 387, 417; *see also* Naples, kingdom of the Two Sicilies, double marriage

Genoa, 391, 559, 577

George III (of Great Britain), 120, 302

Georgetown, D.C.: blacks plan revolt at, 596

George Washington (U.S. frigate), 208 n. 2; carries annuities to Algiers, 211 and n., 584; commandeered by Algiers, 138 n. 5, 383, 384 n. 1; convoy duty of, 1, 39

Georgia: agreement with U.S., xxvii, 160–61 and nn., 171–72 and n. 1, 261, 321 and n., 352, 409–11, 425–27, 428 n. 1; and Bourbon County act, 409, 410, 411 and n. 3, 426, 427, 428 n. 4

Gérard de Rayneval, Joseph-Mathias, 348

Germany, 207 n. 1; reorganized by Napoleon, 367, 368 n. 7, 371 and n. 1

Gerry, Elbridge, 401 n. 1

Gerry, Samuel Russell, 401 and n. 1

Gibb, William, 463

Gibraltar: blockade of, 54, 55 n. 4, 105–6 n. 3, 151; British navy at, 608; ships from, quarantined, 573, 574 n. 1; as U.S. Navy port of call, 187, 412, 508, 585; U.S. trade with, 501; *see also* Gavino, John

Gibson, John: secretary of Ind. Territory, 382, 383 n. 1

Gibson, William, 355, 385, 387 and n. 1, 387, 396, 483–84, 486 n. 1, 528

Gillasspy and Strong: Philadelphia merchants, 211

Gilmor, Robert, 285 n. 2

Gilpin, George, **413 n.**

Gilpin, Joshua, **413 n.**; letter from JM, 433; letter to JM, 413

Girard, Stephen, 22 and n. 1, 25; letters to JM, 22, 598

Giraud, Marc-Antoine-Alexis, 164 n. 3

Glasgow, Scotland, 522

Glennie, Alexander, 7, 18, 436

Gloria (U.S. ship), 98, 99 nn. 1, 2, 5, 187 and n., 292, 294 n., 576, 577–78 n.

Gloria dal mar (Portuguese brig), 130, 131 and n. 4, 263–64, 310, 539

Glory (U.S. brig), 610

Gobs, Lewis G., 583

Goddard, Mr., 238

Godoy y Alvarez de Faria, Manuel de, 54, 80, 143; influence of, 30, 142, 146 n. 3; and Treaty of Amiens,

annuities for dey, 430; and pardons, 186, 225 and n., 225–26 nn.
1, 2, 248, 306 n. 1; portraits of, 56,
185–86 and n. 2; proclamation of
Talleyrand, 25, 28 n. 2; proposes
hospital at New Orleans, 159 n. 2;
purchases wine, 330; receives
anonymous letters, 223, 224 n. 1;
and relations with France, 68–69,
69 and n. 1; as secretary of state,
52, 377, 380 nn. 10, 11; sells tobacco, 525 and n. 4, 527–28; and
St. Clair's removal, 332; and T.
Coxe, 402 n. 6; takes issue with R.
Livingston, 578; travels to Monticello, 414; travels to Washington,
601; and U.S. claims against Spain,
548, 549; writes to emperor of
Morocco, 141, 415, 432, 442, 464,
507, 508, 509, 516 and n. 2, 517;
letters from JM, 83, 132, 138–39,
160, 194–95, 213, 322–23,
414–15, 441–42, 473, 478–79,
498, 501–2, 516, 524–25, 530,
537–38, 554–55, 568, 581–82;
letters to JM, 166, 185–86, 201,
223–24, 247–48, 401, 442, 460,
464–65, 476, 490–91, 497,
509–10, 522–23, 527–28, 541,
550–51, 566–67, 578, 588, 601
Jefferson (U.S. ship), 417 and n. 1
Jefferson College (Miss. Territory), 224
Jefferson County (Miss. Territory),
73–74 n. 2
Jenkins, Elisha: N.Y. state comptroller,
515
Jenkintown, Pa., 606 and n. 1
Jenner, Edward, 300 and n. 1
Jérémie, Saint-Domingue, 6
Jews: in Algiers, 294, 307, 456, 577,
584; in Tripoli, 1–2 n., 4–5 n.
John Adams (U.S. frigate), 431 n. 2,
551, 565, 588 and n. 3, 596; to fol-
low *New York*, 517, 527, 539
Johnson, Capt., 284
Johnston, Abel, 24
Johnston, William, 89 n. 2
Jones, Edward: commercial agent at
Guadeloupe, 441, 460; letter from
JM, 20; letters to JM, 210, 389
Jones, Edward: Treasury Department
clerk, 90, 92, 286

Jones, Evan, 87, 88 n. 5
Jones, John Paul, 587
Jones, Meriwether (*see* 1 : 316 n. 2), 340
Jones, Skelton, 340
Jones, Walter (*see* 2 : 100 n. 2), 340, 344
Jones, William (of Philadelphia), 25,
365 n. 2; letter to JM, 151
Jonesborough, Tenn., 483
Joseph II (of the Holy Roman Empire),
391
Joseph (U.S. brig), 583 n., n. 2
Jouett, John: purchase of sword for,
368 n. 4
Journal de Commerce (Paris), 592, 600,
614
Journal des Debats (Paris), 71, 72 n. 2
Joyce, John, 439 and n. 1
Joyes, Patrick, & Hijos: Madrid mer-
chants, 32
Judiciary Act of *1789*, 13, 16 n. 2
Judiciary Act of *1801*: repeal of, 16–17
n. 2, 169–70 n. 2, 294 n. 1, 312,
313 n. 8, 359–60 and n. 1

Kantzou, F. A.: Swedish consul general
at Lisbon, 398 n. 2
Keith, George Keith Elphinstone, Vis-
count, 328 and n. 3, 348
Kennebunk, Me., 239
Kent, Edward Augustus, duke of: gov-
ernor of Gibraltar, 348
Kentucky: land claims, 529–30 and nn.
Kentucky River, 183
Ker, David, 501, **501 n. 2**
Kerversau et Leborgne, Gerard de,
275–76 and nn. 2–4, 373
Kidder, John, 405–6 and n. 1
Kilham, Daniel, 432, 522
Kimball, Hazen, 47, 89 n. 2
King, Nicholas, 277–78, **278 n. 1**
King, Rufus: minister to Great Britain,
1, 4–5 n., 45, 52, 53 n. 1, 57, 302,
580; accounts with U.S., 47 n. 1,
407, 430; advances to Lafayette,
34–35; and annuities for dey, 165;
and boundary dispute, 148, 204;
and Cabot's appointment, 7–8 n.;
and claims against Great Britain,
336, 557; and claims commission
under article 7, 7, 8, 595; and convention of *1802*, 88 and n. 7; and
Convoy Act, 188 and n. 2; corre-